Teaching, Schools and Society

Teaching, Schools and Society

Edited by
Evelina Orteza y Miranda
and
Romulo F. Magsino

 The Falmer Press

(A member of the Taylor & Francis Group)
London · New York · Philadelphia

UK	The Falmer Press, Rankine Road, Basingstoke, Hampshire, RG24 0PR
USA	The Falmer Press, Taylor & Francis Inc., 1900 Frost Road, Suite 101, Bristol, PA 19007

First published 1990

British Library Cataloguing in Publication Data
Teaching, schools and society.
1. Schools. Social aspects
I. Orteza y Miranda, Evelina   II. Maggsino, Romulo F.
370.19

ISBN 1-85000-687-3
ISBN 1-85000-688-1 pbk

Library of Congress Cataloging in Publication Data
Teaching, schools, and society/edited by Evelina Orteza y
Miranda and Romulo F. Magsino.
    p. cm.
Includes index.
    ISBN 1-85000-687-3; — ISBN 1-85000-688-1
(pbk.);
1. Education — Aims and objectives.
2. Educational sociology   3. Teaching.   4. Classroom
environment.   5. Teachers — Training of. I. Orteza y Miranda,
Evelina.   II. Magsino, Romulo F.
LB41. T339   1990   90-41231
371.1'02 — dc20   CIP

Jacket design by Caroline Archer

Typeset in 10/12 Caledonia × 28 picas
by Graphicraft Typesetters Ltd. HK.

Printed in Great Britain by Burgess Science Press, Basingstoke
on paper which has a specified pH value on final paper
manufacture of not less than 7.5 and is therefore 'acid free'.

Contents

Contents

Acknowledgment

We are grateful to Mr Malcolm Clarkson, Falmer Press, for the encouragement that he provided us, especially at the initial stage of our conceptualizing and planning this text. We thank him for his patience and for understanding the difficulties in a collaborative effort involving writers and editors who have manifold academic and professional commitments.

We also wish to thank our contributors who readily expressed willingness to participate in this publication endeavour, unfailingly responded to our requests and accommodated our modest suggestions.

Needless to say, we acknowledge the varied and generous support which our respective departments and faculties extended to us.

Finally, we express our special recognition of the secretarial and technical assistance given to us at our institutions. Pat Draho, in particular, and Irene Block at the University of Manitoba typed and retyped materials to produce the manuscript in its final typewritten form. Martha Loeman and Joy Zimmerman at The University of Calgary also devoted much time and effort to a number of articles. If not for the unstinting and generous efforts of these wonderful secretaries, this text would not have reached the publisher. Remo Mamaril, Special Projects Officer in the Faculty of Education, The University of Manitoba, is extended our thanks for working magic on computers which occasionally resisted secretarial commands.

Preface

Expressed dissatisfaction with and current doubts about schooling raise the issue of responsibility on the part of both critics and educators involved in society's primary educational institution. On the one hand, educators in the field and prospective practitioners being prepared in teacher education institutions have the professional obligation to develop for themselves an adequate, coherent view of schooling. This view results from a solid understanding of its aims, its processes and the forces influencing it. Only with such understanding will present and future educators secure a sense of direction, implement effective school and classroom practices and eventually win or strengthen public confidence. On the other hand, educational critics, and even neutral observers, need to develop some understanding of similar things — school aims, processes and context — if they are to be fair at all in passing judgment on contemporary schooling.

How this understanding is to be achieved has been blurred by developments in the last few decades. The present generation is heir to the consequences of the challenges to authority, expertise and knowledge that justify the existence of societal institutions. Nonetheless, this volume reflects our commitment to the following view: More than ever, authoritative knowledge and expertise are needed if we desire to improve schooling at all. However, schooling can be improved only if we succeed in understanding it in light of the scholarly findings and insights provided by the different disciplinary studies serving as the foundations of education. We take it to be an inescapable conclusion that such disciplines as history, philosophy, psychology and sociology of education provide the lenses by which schooling can be examined clearly. We also believe that, with appropriate care and perceptiveness, educators can glean from them insights and generalizations that will not only deepen understanding but also promote effective practice.

Schooling is a complex institution with varied dimensions. Necessarily, any text examining it will have to be selective in the inclusion of topics to be covered. Moreover, because each of the topics cannot be addressed simultaneously by the various disciplinary perspectives, each chapter may not be expected to convey a comprehensive viewpoint. However within certain disciplinary limits, a number of articles in this volume have attempted to establish landscapes wide enough to view schooling holistically. Beyond this, we have attempted to focus on a theme which gives the volume a sense of coherence and unity, namely, 'Schooling — its tasks, processes, and context'. This theme is explored through a systematic and thorough examination of (i) the aims which may legitimately be expected of schooling as the primary formal institution charged with educating the young; (ii) the means, particularly the curriculum and the teaching-learning processes required to attain such aims; and (iii) the classroom, school and societal contexts which immeasurably affect the teaching-learning processes and, indeed, the whole of schooling itself. The chapters are clustered to facilitate extensive investigation of these three main concerns; consequently, the reader's cumulative understanding builds up meaningfully.

The first section of the text prepares the reader for an engaging, in-depth exploration by sketching a profile of schooling in contemporary society and by explaining its emergence and character through historical accounts. The text moves on to Section II, which addresses the central issue of school aims. It presents opportunities for reflection on the familiar yet thorny question, 'What are schools for?' by providing a number of alternative answers and elaborating on them. Section III addresses the curriculum as a tool for attaining school aims. The notion of the curriculum is precisely delineated; its dependence on knowledge is traced, and the pervasiveness of unconscious learnings, which in some ways reinforce and in other ways negate intended learnings, is examined. Section IV initially undertakes a conceptual mapping of the contours of teaching and its associated concept of learning. Subsequently, psychological findings are employed to highlight for practitioners and prospective teachers those considerations needing particular attention in their teaching. Then, an attempt is made to foster in them sensitivity not only to the contributions of the practicum and of the foundations studies, but also to the limitations and problems that their study in teacher education programmes presents. Section V examines not only the various stages in the growth of children's personality dimensions; it also analyzes the dynamics involved in the internalization of prejudice which still plagues modern, culturally diverse societies. The findings on student perspectives on a number of classroom phenomena are also discussed. The net effect is to make practitioners more watchful of, and ready to counteract, unintended and unconscious processes with harmful cumulative impacts. In Section VI, the internal workings of the school as sets of role players in different modes of interaction — specifically between the subordinate and the superordinate — are investigated. Further, the school's relationship to the wider society, particularly to its economic and political institutions, is untangled. In doing so, the need for practitioners to engage in critical reflection on their roles and practices is highlighted. Finally, Section VII focuses on teachers as professionals and as bearers of authority. Grounded on a realistic assessment of current developments, which challenge teachers' authority and place burdensome responsibility on them, policy re-commendations aimed at the restoration of respect for teacher authority are presented.

For educators, educational critics and, indeed, the interested layperson, the task is essentially the same: It is to understand what schooling is all about and how it can attain its legitimate aims. In developing this understanding, there is no substitute for rigorous, disciplined inquiry. Thus, the authors and editors hope that the readers will join them in a dialogue, by way of reflective analysis and evaluation, on the multifaceted aspects of schooling viewed through the lenses provided by the various foundational disciplines. To the extent that readers are stimulated to reflect on disciplinary perspectives which enlighten educational theory and practice, the main purpose of this text shall have been fulfilled.

1

Contemporary Schooling: Historical Context

INTRODUCTION

Bold speculation about the demise or radical transformation of schooling no longer reverberates in the conference halls, seminar rooms, or classrooms of schools of education. Short of an improbable educational revolution, schooling in its familiar form will almost certainly be with us in the decades to come. Retrospectively the death-of-schools or de-schooling scenarios of the sixties and seventies appear completely out of touch with reality.

Nonetheless, the scenarios were obviously symptomatic of the malaise that lingers among educational observers. The 1980s, in particular, witnessed a large number of reports and studies dissecting schools to diagnose their alleged illnesses and to prescribe corresponding cures. As may be expected in light not only of the complexity of modern societal and educational problems but also of their varying interests and expertise, educators have offered diverse assessments and prescriptions. In their chapter, Evelina Orteza y Miranda and Joyce Bellous briefly explore a few of the solutions recently offered by educators. The authors' main concern, however, is to investigate more deeply the main source of current educational difficulties. They are convinced that the proper and effective working of schools as an instrument of society cannot be attained unless the crucial educational issues arising from societal problems are addressed and resolved. The central issue for them is the question of aims and purposes of schooling. If schools systems are to operate intelligently, these aims have to be ascertained. Yet their identification has been frustrated by forces beyond the boundaries of school campuses and districts.

The identification of aims has been hampered by the apparent absence of core values — as well as their associated beliefs and predispositions — which are needed to give unequivocal direction to educational efforts. At least partly due to cultural diversity resulting in competing societal values, beliefs, and predispositions, the determination of school curricula, structures, and processes has been problematic. Unless these core values beliefs, and predispositions are identified and accepted, the schooling enterprise will continue its vacillation amidst competing forces.

Such vacillation was not much of a problem in the early history of the United States and Canada. Thus, as Schnell points out in his chapter, the largely non-formal and private provision for education in the United States was clearly targeted toward its corresponding clientele. Thus the Christian promoters of the education of the poor were unanimous in their concern for the glory of God and the inner spiritual satisfaction of the individual. For Thomas Jefferson, schooling was prominently to promote, among other aims, the republican citizen; Horace Mann's effort toward the development of mass public schooling not only went beyond Jefferson's aspirations but also aimed at universalizing 'true culture'. For a while, schools were perceived by consensus to be the agent for the political and social integration of the diverse population. However, the growth of schooling has been accompanied by lengthening lists of educational aims and increased responsibilities. Now that, as Schnell observes, the American schools' capacity to meet varied expectations has been questioned, groups with competing interests will be anxious to hold schools' preferred and undivided attention.

Similar developments characterize Canadian education. In his chapter, J. Donald Wilson notes that educational quiet existed in Canada as long as there was acceptance of the Judaeo-Christian moral code and understanding that non-denominationalism in schooling amounted to Protestant teachings and values. This harmony has been put to a test with the coming of non-Anglo-Celtic immigrants. So far the strategy of assimilation has proved ineffective. In his view, though educational systems have expanded and improvements in terms of such indices as participation rates, access, and material resources are evident, it is not clear that real progress has been achieved. A common system of beliefs and values, which will give coherence to different components of public education, is still lacking. Yet Canadians, no less than their American counterparts, demonstrate great expectations of their school systems. To what extent should schools attempt to meet these expectations?

1   The School in Contemporary Society

Evelina Orteza y Miranda and Joyce Bellous

Social Changes and Educational Responses

More than 2,000 years ago, Aristotle made an observation about education which strikingly applies to formal schooling in Canada and the United States today. In *Politics* (Book VIII, chapter 2), he said:

> As things are ... mankind are by no means agreed about the things to be taught, whether we look to virtue or the best life. Neither is it clear whether education is more concerned with intellectual or moral virtue. The existing practice is perplexing; no one knowing on what principle we should proceed — should the useful in life, or should virtue, or should the higher knowledge be the aim of our training; all three opinions have been entertained. Again, about the means there is no agreement; for different persons, starting with different ideas about the nature of virtue, naturally disagree with the practice of it.

However, disagreements seem to have become much more complicated and strident in contemporary times. Rapid changes have overtaken society. Political interests and ideologies compete for allegiance. Various conceptions of morality, encouraged by philosophical skepticism about the foundations of knowledge and human values and further abetted by developments in applied technology, confound laypersons and decision-makers alike. Individuals and groups clamor for the recognition and acceptance of their rights. How should schools conceive their tasks in light of this societal situation?

One recent popular response has been the advocacy of a return to the 'basics', a movement leaning toward the conservative orientation in education. Its stress on basic skills, particularly literacy and numeracy, has been an attractive one (Hirsch, 1987). However, unless the role of these skills in relation to other aspects of schooling and to societal demands is understood, the extent of its contribution to the educational process will remain unclear. Allan Bloom's (1987) *The Closing of the American Mind* could also be considered a conservative response at the level of tertiary education. It decries the loss of a center of thought in political, cultural, and intellectual matters. As he sees it, centrifugal, fragmenting forces have been at work in society; without such a center understood and endorsed at least by the majority, democracy will not work.

A second response, which has elicited enormous support largely because of its current availability and its practical, efficient application, involves the use of technology in education. Videos and computers are now permanent fixtures in educational institutions, from kindergarten to university. Beyond the use of technology for learning purposes, however, is the lure toward technology-oriented careers or occupation. Some cooperative programmes between business and schools may have this aim in mind. This second response emphasizes career education, a form of new vocationalism which advocates an academic preparation balanced with a heavy orientation toward vocational or career programmes. Career education aims to '... end the divisive, snobbish, destructive distinctions in learning that do no service to the cause of knowledge and do no honor to the name of American (education-al) enterprise' (Marland, 1971, p. 8). Its one important aim is to equip young-sters with the skills needed to live the lives of fulfilled human beings. In short, it promotes 'useful knowledge' (Marland, 1971, p. 6). Clearly, this advocacy raises an issue of paramount importance and resurrects Herbert Spencer's (1889) classic question: 'What knowledge is of most worth?' Because know-ledge is the concern of schools, the question begets our original question: 'What are schools for?'

The third response focuses on humanism and moral education. It ad-dresses the charge of oppressive and repressive school practices which allegedly border on indoctrinatory practices. This response aims at liberating students from fear through open classrooms and emphasis on the study of such topics as respect for learners as persons, student rights, freedom to question and to learn, critical thinking, responsibility, autonomy, and the like. These topics are examined based on the assumption that trust and caring should characterize the teacher-learner relationship. To attain its objectives, this response has enlisted values-clarification techniques which encourage students to say what they want to say without incurring the wrath or judg-mental reactions of others. Simulations, games and varied strategies have been devised to encourage self-respect among students and to have them 'get in touch with themselves' (Simon, Howe and Kirschenbaum, 1972). Kohl-berg's moral reasoning approach (Arbuthnot and Faust, 1981), based on his moral development theory, has also been employed. Indeed, the concern for moral development has spawned many other theories and approaches (Meyer, Burnhamn and Cholvat, 1975).

A more recent response stresses individual capacity to deal with the world through the development of critical thinking. Conferences and seminars on critical thinking have become part of the educational scenery. Educational systems have joined the movement. Thus, the California State Department of Education has created a Critical Thinking Network for educators; the Center for Critical Thinking and Moral Critique in Sonoma State University holds an annual conference on the subject. The movement's objective is to get away from rote memorization of facts and information and to develop capacities for independent and rational thinking.

Though clearly desirable, there remains some ambiguity within the movement because of the lack of unanimity about the notion of critical thinking. Richard Paul (1984) notes two senses of this term. The first is the 'weak sense ... (which) is a set of discrete micro-logical skills ultimately extrinsic to the character of the person, skills that can be tacked onto other learning'. In this sense, development in critical thinking involves cultivation of the processes, largely logical, required to arrive at justifiable and acceptable conclusions in different areas of intellectual endeavors. The second, strong sense requires 'a set of integrated macro-logical skills ultimately intrinsic to the character of the person and ... (requires) insights into one's own cognitive and affective processes' (Paul, 1984, p. 5). In the first sense, critical thinking is technical reason and is not different in emphasis from the higher-level cognitive capacities enumerated in Benjamin Bloom's (1964) taxonomy of educational objectives. The capacities suggested in Mortimer Adler's (1982) Paideia proposal could well count as critical thinking in the weak sense. For radical schools critics, however, these are not enough. For them, critical thinking in the strong sense is what is needed to respond to the alleged reprehensible character of school practices. Drawing from the works of Paolo Freire (1970) and Henry Giroux (1983), among others, these critics advocate the development of emancipatory reasoning which enables one not only to question taken-for-granted realities and to be conscious and in control of his or her own reality, but also to engage in and transform it. Which sense — the weak or the strong — should be promoted in schools remains an ideological problem.

Another popular response to the question about what schools are for centers on the culturally varied character of society and its classrooms. Canadian and American schools are no doubt attended by young people coming from a diversity of cultural or ethnic backgrounds. How to take into account minorities' interests and perspectives, especially when they seem to conflict with their dominant cultural counterparts, has been a persistent, nagging problem. Multicultural education or education for cultural pluralism remains a political problem in the two North American countries. However, its fate has been rather different in each country. For a while in the United States, the issue of cultural identity was thought not to be a serious one. It was assumed that the societal efforts to assimilate the ethnic minority groups into the mainstream dominant culture had been successful and that Americanization of immigrants had been accomplished. However, it is now clear that this is not the case (Fishman *et al.*, 1966; Glazer and Moynihan, 1970). The quest for cultural or ethnic identity resurfaced shortly after the end of World War II when the United States, with its educational exchange programs, permitted international students of various racial origins to stay on as landed immigrants. Continued entry of various nationalities through a somewhat relaxed immigration policy, social and racial tensions which finally erupted in the form of riots and demonstrations in the 1960s and 1970s, the influx of Spanish-speaking peoples, and the social dynamics generating the search for cultural roots — all these and other forces have produced calls for a serious and positive consideration of cultural pluralism in the country. As will be seen later, such calls have been heeded much less in the United States than in Canada.

Perhaps the most radical response to developments in society has taken the form of the deschooling movement. Spearheaded by Ivan Illich (1971), Everett Reimer (1972) and Carl Bereiter (1974), deschoolers have sought the dismantling of educational systems as we know them in favor of informal, freely chosen learning centers. For them schooling in a capitalistic society is inevitably manipulative and miseducative. No tinkering will make it otherwise; thus, it has to be eliminated. Yet, despited the vigor of their attack on current forms of schooling, the acceptability and practicability of their own proposals are difficult to envision in modern society. Rightly, as Dewey (1964) has suggested, the deliberate education of the young, requiring a more formal kind of structured experiences, is a necessity if a certain quality of social life is to continue. As he put it (p. 8):

> Without such formal education, it is not possible to transmit all the resources and achievements of a complex society. It also opens the way to a kind of experience which would not be accessible to the young if they were left to pick up their training in informal association with others, since books and symbols of knowledge are mastered.

The real problem seems to have been clear to Philip Jackson (1972) when he said that our schools 'are neither dead nor dying, but neither, unfortunately, are they marked by a degree of vitality and energy that befits the grandeur of their mission' (p. 22). This is not necessarily a negative comment on schools and schooling. Schools have a huge responsibility to society. But to have a certain grandeur of mission is not diminished if they share this mission with some other informal educational agencies in society. Schools, Lawrence Cremin (1961) advised, constitute only one formal educational agency; their role in society may in fact be more restricted than it was thought previously. The common perception that schooling is a panacea for individual and social ills should now give way to a more realistic and modest assessment of what schools ought to do as a formal educational agency of society. Yet, the problem posed by Aristotle at the beginning of this chapter is as real as ever. We still need to confront such questions as 'What are schools for?' 'What should they teach?' 'What is their relationship to society?'

Schooling in the Culturally Diverse Society

Education for cultural pluralism or multicultural education, advocated strongly in both Canada and the United States in the last two decades, constitutes a specific problem arising from 'too much democracy without a center understood and endorsed by a majority'. Though the transmission of core values is persistently put forward as the broad purpose of schooling (Mallea and Young, 1984, p. 96), the lack of agreement about a societal center debilitates attempts to describe the values which lie at its core.

Ironically, though Bloom (1987) decries the lack of cultural, political and intellectual center in the United States, it remains true that in that country there is still much more cultural focus than is found north of its border. Following the waves of immigration to the former in the last decade of the 1800s and the early decades of the 1900s, a nativistic reaction developed and became widespread enough to influence assimilationist efforts in society at large and in the schools in particular. This reaction was reinforced by a sense of nationalism during the war periods. This assimilationist orientation remained strong between the two wars despite the valiant efforts at providing an education suitable for such groups as the native American Indians, Africans and Mexicans. Since 1968, massive immigration from Latin America has brought major impact on the American social, economic and educational institutions. Calls for preservation of minority cultures have been loud. Yet, since the 1980s, a prominent move toward nationalism and cohesion has been apparent. As Magsino (1988, p. 9) points out, advocates of cultural retention have failed, in terms both of legislation and litigation, to institutionalize adequate provisions for bilingualism, biculturalism and multiculturalism in education. *Lau v. Nichols* (1974), together with other court decisions, and some legislation, such as the Bilingual Education Act (1968), excited cultural retentionists because of the prospects they promised during the 1960s and the first half of the 1970s. This short period has proved to be the happy heyday of American cultural retentionism on behalf of the minorities. From then on, both 'cultural pluralism and ethnic solidarity have been on the wane' (Magsino, 1988, p. 10).

Canada is a study in contrast. Whatever cultural consensus it might have enjoyed in the past, the disruptions in the 1960s and the assertive nationalist movement in Quebec doomed cultural consensus. The Official Languages Act (1969), which recognized and provided for the linguistically dual character of the country, was followed by the proclamation of former Prime Minister Pierre Trudeau's (1971) policy of multiculturalism within a bilingual framework. This policy, or a version close to it, became federal law under the Mulroney Government with the passage of the Multiculturalism Act (1988) in the Parliament of Canada. Officially adopted as law or as governmental policy in nearly all the provinces in the country, multiculturalism has become a significant factor in Canadian education.

At bottom, there are two competing ideological views related to cultural diversity. The first envisions the continued predominance of the majoritarian, founding cultures. In Canada, it is represented by the ideology of linguistic dualism based on the notion of the 'two founding nations', namely, the English and the French; in this view, other ethnic cultural contributions are, so to speak, simply grafted onto the main trunk (Rocher, 1984, p. 44). The second view, supporting the diversity inherent in multiculturalism, insists that the identities of the minorities must be appreciated, respected and retained. In Canada, this has been expressed in the view that the four components making up the country, namely, the French, the English, the natives and the ethnic communities (Parel, 1988), p. 175), should flourish in parity side by side within a national mosaic. These ideologies differ in their emphasis on two concerns: the 'need to preserve the languages and cultures of those who have been in Canada for many generations', and the 'need to preserve the languages and cultures of new immigrants while also integrating them into Canadian society' (Mallea and Young, 1984, p. 96).

Politically expedient sensitivity to pressure groups representing these opposed perspectives has made it characteristically 'Canadian' that gains made by the linguistic dualists stimulate challenges by the multiculturalists, and vice versa. The two 'founding' nations have traditionally dominated the political, social and economic structures; consequently, dualism has received support from powerful forces concerned that Canada and its institution will crumble without muscle-flexing on behalf of the founding peoples. Multi-culturalists, on the other hand, have drawn strength from minority interest groups motivated by the persistent fear that second class status stalks their silence. Evidently, the political pressure to comply with official linguistic dualism has generated resentful reaction from aggrieved minorities contesting for cultural and linguistic parity.

Core Values in Society and Schooling

Meaning-making is fundamental to being human in the normative sense; in other words, to be human at all, individuals must have not only the capacity to make sense of the world around them but also the predisposition to use such a capacity in life. Human beings *do* engage in meaning-making; it is ongoing for them and continues throughout individual, group, national or transnational experience. Newcomers to any given society continue to construct meaning in one of two ways: either by setting up old forms as barriers to what to them are new and strange cultural forms; or by voluntarily taking on (consciously or unconsciously) new cultural forms, which may sometimes wholly replace the old cultural forms from their original countries with an entirely new construction.

Cultural adjustment, however, is not true of the newcomers alone. Members of the host culture also engage in cultural meaning-making because the presence of newcomers requires a re-working of societal relationships and arrangements established for living in the same circumscribed territory. Anxiety arises because of the threat to the values and beliefs underpinning the existence of the host people.

The problem that needs to be resolved in culturally diverse societies relates to the need to reconcile cultural forms and thus to facilitate the adjustment and elimination of anxiety among the hosts and newcomers. Unfortunately our thinking, whether as theorists or as laypersons, is frequently clouded by certain tendencies. The three tendencies of *reification, ossification* and *relativization* (Burtonwood, 1986; Kallen, 1982; Lynch, 1986) serve to prevent change and to deny the integration of the cultural forms or elements from the cultures of the newcomers. In their various manifestations, whether moderate or extreme, they misrepresent cultural reality. To reify a culture is to perceive its bearers as passive recipients of implicit and explicit cultural forms or elements; these forms become imbedded concretely in people's minds and guide their behaviors and conduct. To ossify cultural boundaries is to presume a uniformity within a culture and to assume the illegitimacy of any cultural form which appears foreign or alien to the established one. Consequently, there develops an automatic rejection of change and a hardening of accepted cultural forms. To relativize cultural forms is to assign cultural forms as unique growths or creations of a given people or group. Thus, no cultural form or element is understandable outside of the way of life lived by any particular group.

The effect of reifying and ossifying cultures is two-fold. In the first place, they preclude change, innovation and development within and between cultures. Intercultural learning and exchange thereby become impossible. In the second place, these conceptual tendencies in viewing cultures can immediately be recognized as false because insiders within a given culture, except perhaps the very isolated ones, can easily experience and observe degrees of cultural diversity and cultural influx from other societies. Reification and ossification may not be difficult to falsify.

Cultural relativization may, however, not be easy to dispel. Cultural relativism is described as having two forms. Weak cultural relativism refers psychologically to empathy for the beliefs, values and predispositions exhibited by different cultural groups. Thus, there is no automatic concession that these cultural elements or forms are appropriate or acceptable. The strong sense of relativism refers to the idea that cultural forms cannot be understood apart from the culture which they comprise (Walkling, 1980). In this sense, therefore, each culture is valid on its own, and no one culture may presume to evaluate the cultural form of any other. One implication of this is apparently that societal fragmentation occurs when a given territory is occupied by groups carrying different cultures with them. Because each group brings with it its values, and because there is no way by which we may judge some values as superior to others, the notion of core values evaporates or becomes illegitimate (Bellous, 1989). Another implication is that we are precluded from employing organizing principles needed to guide the selection of educational purposes, content and methodologies which we could utilize to build inter-cultural understanding and respect. Ultimately, cultural relativization will so fragment society as to frustrate the development of a body politic.

To the extent that multicultural education or education for cultural pluralism has been conceived as a minority group interest, it can and has been identified as a threat to the nation's way of life (Joshee, 1978, p. 12). On the contrary, our view is that it is relativization, not interest in such education, which prevents our initial attempts to establish core values and promote an enriched way of life. This tendency erroneously calls into question the validity of making pedagogic decisions on the basis of overarching statements of purpose which historically have been derived, to some degree, from a consensus within the host culture. Though consensus has escaped us temporarily, we must still seek out grounds for its future restoration. What is required is the implementation of multicultural education or education for cultural pluralism as an approach founded on two things: common human forms of life; and social and political realities inherent in sharing a territorial boundary with an identifiable but changing history and cultural identity. Education of this sort would be committed to understanding one's cultural history so as to transform cultural identity into something connected with the past but dynamically wedded to the present and the future. Inevitably, the individual and national identity that schooling must begin to work on will have to be constructed through primary socialization.

Socialization and Core Values

In the process of becoming, an individual learns particularistic 'rules of the game'. The child secures a self-identity and develops a world-view through an emotionally charged, ongoing dialectic relationship with significant others. A cultural 'world' or sectors of it are mediated for the child who then constructs a subjective self that is 'massively real' and much more firmly entrenched in consciousness than the 'sub-worlds' internalized later. Primary socialization is fundamentally different and differently constructed in comparison with secondary socialization, such as schooling. The latter presupposes a preceding process, an already formed self, and an already internalized world. Essentially, secondary socialization, which schooling provides, is the acquisition of role-specific knowledge, the roles arising out of culture-specific division of labor (Berger and Luckman, 1967, pp. 149–66).

Because secondary socialization enables the internalization of cultural forms and institutions, schooling is a valuable instrument of the state. Schooling has the potential function of moving a child from home to national and perhaps even universal allegiances. But schooling involves contradictory roles. On the one hand, 'schooling is to make children fit the system; on the other it is to help children remake the system to fit them' (Wood, 1985, p. 92). Where there is a wide discrepancy between home and national values, conflict is unavoidable. The distance between the home and state is deeply felt in modern pluralistic nations such as Canada and the United States. For some, secondary socialization supplements primary experience; for others, the later socialization subtracts from the first, leaving the child empty of meaning.

The problem that primary socialization poses for secondary socialization, and vice versa, is multifaceted. In a pluralistic society, competing pictures of reality vie for attention as individuals continue to construct their reality through involvement in their private and public worlds (Wuthnot *et al.*, 1984).

The Pluralist State and Core Values

There are two traditions in the interpretation of what constitutes a pluralistic state. The older tradition, following de Tocqueville, conceives pluralism as a dispersion of power between two or more groups held together by common values or by an equilibrium of power. This implies that pluralism is an important condition for the stable operation of democracy. The more recent interpretation, following contemporary conflict theorists, associates pluralism with despotism and domination by a powerful group or minority. Contemporary writers are attempting to resolve the descriptive and normative contradictions between the equilibrium and conflicting schools of thought (van den Berghe, 1967).

The only way to sustain the equilibrium notion that pluralism is effectively at work in our democratic systems is to blindly ignore the lack of civil, political, social and economic equality between Blacks and Whites in the United States and between the Indians, Inuit, ethnic minorities and the dominant founding groups in Canada. This notion normatively has moral strength behind it in that we would want to see parity and harmonious balancing of different groups in society. In reality, however, it is doubtful that it has ever been fulfilled in these countries. On the other hand, though the notion of conflict may be closer to reality, it is hardly a desirable state of affairs to have powerful groups or minorities unilaterally determine the lives and ways of other minorities (or, even, of a weak majority). In any case, whatever is the social, economic and political reality, descriptive analysis of society will have to give way to a certain normative consensus on how such society should or ought to structure group and individual relationships. Indeed, the question of what to do with cultural diversity is central to the general issue of social relations in a plural society; that is, what rules about living together are, and how they should be applied. Schooling could play a vital and lively role in fostering harmonious relations of equality and mutual appreciation and in reducing (if not completely eliminating) conflicts among cultural groups.

Transmission, Transformation and Core Values

The confusing and contradictory roles that multicultural/pluralistic education may be expected to play include two basic orientations (Gibson, 1976; Magsino, 1985; Young, 1979). The expectation has to do either with the process of learning *about* diversity, or the process of assisting individual students *to be* 'multicultural/pluralistic people' by accommodating cultural diversity in some manner and to some degree. Whereas learning *about* involves intellectual gains, learning *to be* adds the development of certain tendencies which eventually may become established dispositions. Whereas the intention to learn about may be fitted into the pedagogy of any classroom in any state, the second intention moves the teacher into a contentious socio-political realm. The idea that students should become multicultural/pluralistic implies political ends.

Schooling as secondary socialization is a process by which pupils come to see and secure a place for themselves in society. Almost everywhere, schooling is essentially transmissionist. Its aim is generally to convey and reinforce the interests and beliefs which constitute the culture. The second orientation toward multicultural or pluralistic education is, by contrast, transformative in that it purports to move students beyond primary socialization. A commonly suggested pedagogic purpose of such education is to develop intercultural understanding, tolerance and respect for persons (Ghitter, 1984). This purpose implies that students should transcend the enculturated beliefs, values and predispositions which make up their identity as individuals and as part of their cultural group. Such an implication is antithetical to the transmissionist purpose. Transmissionist policies are necessarily frustrated by the fact of diversity because the latter, if valued, raises questions about the cultural elements, contents or forms to be passed on to children of either the dominant or the minority groups.

The problem for schools is to construct an explanatory framework for ways by which transformative and transmissionist purposes may be joined. It may be that the justifiable basis for *resocialization*, as suggested by Berger (1976), will have to be worked out so that this process may then be used to promote multiculturalism or pluralism in society and schools. Yet, even if multicultural or pluralistic education is seen as a partly transformative instrument aiming at preparing students to change society rather than just reproducing it, two important questions arise. The first is whether schooling by itself could accomplish that aim. For, on one hand, functionalist theorists would argue that schools can deal only with generally perceived social problems, not the underlying structural, societally basic ones (Gibson, 1976); on the other, critical theorists would argue that schools can change society (Livingstone, 1987). The second question has to do with the central role that personal and group identity plays in the formation of a national consciousness which might inform the eventual aims of education.

The Concept of Person as a Core Value

At present two extremes are possible with respect to the nature of one's identity. Either one is a national or one is not. Naturally, nationalistic zeal does not encourage the development of a universalized identity; rather, it confines identity within a given idealized conception. Where a pluralistic society, like the United States or Canada, fails to define precisely its national identity, the question, 'Who am I?' becomes a contentious one. Pluralism presents choice but also the possibility of confused identity for individuals.

The danger in this situation is the unexamined development of identity through unconscious internalization of external influences impinging on everyone. There is a need to ensure that development of self-identity, whatever it eventually may turn out to be, incorporates and is consistent with individual development as persons. But, here, we have to be careful. It is through primary socialization that one picks up an exclusivistic concept of a person. To be a person is to be like, for example, me. Within its framework, to share the world is to expect that everyone who is different will elect to join my vision of the world. To be unlike me is to be less than me and therefore neither entitled to, nor able to make appropriate use of, the rights and freedoms that I have. My nationalistic identity is based on convergence toward the dominant group's enculturated notion of personhood. Consequently, as part of the majoritarian society and an enculturated person within it, my sense of moral responsibility toward strange newcomers is weakened. To the degree that my national identity is unconsciously and uncritically shaped by my national identity, I as a moral person am reduced in my moral stature.

Thus, what is necessary in pedagogy is to come to see that enculturated or nationalistic definitions of personhood are inadequate. But what will a democratic society hold up as a model of personhood? How is this model to be constructed, accepted and promoted in socializing institutions? At present, bilingualism and biculturalism vie with multiculturalism or pluralism for a place at the core of national identities. Unfortunately, the United States and Canada can no longer assume a unicultural, unilingual character, or even a bicultural, bilingual one; in fact many other modern societies are pretty much in the same situation. Thus the challenge posed by pluralism in our attempts to conceptualize a non-ethnocentric notion of personhood remains a widespread and enormous one. Nonetheless, though the task looks insurmountable, at least recognition of the ethnocentric character of exclusivistic conceptions frequently imposed by majoritarians structures on weaker minorities and groups can be promoted in schools.

The change that is implied by multicultural or pluralistic education is transformative. This ultimate goal of schooling is consistent, in our view, with a society of citizens with freedom to determine their cultural allegiances and lifestyles. But there is no easy way toward this transformation if, politically, economically and socially, we proceed as if minority groups and their members *actually* have the same chance as members of the founding dominant groups for survival or success within the country without changes in established societal structures and institutions.

Diversity and Core Values

A further problem persists. At present, education in culturally diverse societies generally directs children toward recognition and appreciation of cultural diversity (see, for example, Alberta Teachers' Association, 1984). This support for cultural diversity is taken for granted, yet it remains problematic and raises an important question: 'On what grounds is diversity itself to be supported?' The reality of diversity is an empirical issue which can hardly be disputed. But the issue of what to do about it requires moral deliberation. The mere existence of diversity does not obligate a society to support its preservation; moral and legal considerations must first be addressed. Support for diversity is only one possible response among several to the presence of differences; others include indifference, acquiescence, tolerance and moral outrage, depending on the character of the divergent cultural element in question. Open-ended acceptance of cultural differences works against the consensus we need to build if this open-endedness welcomes fundamentally and morally objectionable elements which compromise the development of justifiable core values in society.

For the school, the problem of what to do with cultural diversity can be concretized as follows. Faced by having to promote understanding of various cultures in society, how do we treat cultural groups and their cultures equally, given that we, as educators charged with transmission, perceive some objectionable forms or elements in such cultures? Either we make judgments and, omitting the objectionable elements, identify or select acceptable ones which then we teach to our class; or, we identify or select those cultures which we are prepared to endorse and to which we may confine our discussion of diversity.

Unfortunately, we seem to run into trouble in either case. In resorting to the first strategy, we undermine the earlier and ongoing transmission process that children of minorities have gone through; we therefore work in opposition to the children's culturally derived sense of self. And, if we refuse to teach about what we perceive as objectionable elements in a given culture, we do not contribute to the idea of schooling as transformation of primary socialization. On the other hand, if we simply exclude cultures which, for us, contain serious problematic elements, we are not truly reflecting the diversity whose appreciation we are supposed to promote. In a democratic society, we presumably are committed to the value of human rights and thus feel compelled to extend these rights even to cultures that do not share the principle of equality with us. This, as Harris (1982) points out, is the paradox in multicultural or pluralistic societies.

Whatever the merits of the alleged paradox as Harris has conceived it, what we need to do is to be clear about where, precisely, the unequal treatment lies. It is, in important areas of life, usually difficult to establish a clear case of equal or unequal treatment. Undoubtedly, for one culture to be singled out for non-inclusion in teaching is, by that fact alone, a *prima facie* indication of unequal treatment. This could certainly give rise to the charge of cultural prejudice and discrimination. However, educators need not really be cornered into an either-or situation. They may, in principle, accept any culture for teaching as far as possible; they also may identify common cultural elements among various cultures for intelligent analysis and discussion in ways that will make them intelligible to young people. Even the view of cultural relativists, that cultural elements cannot be understood outside their over-all cultural contexts, may be used for educational as well as transmission-ist purposes. By explaining the origins and contexts of 'objectionable' cultural elements, their perceived irrational or malevolent character could vanish. How far this can be done successfully, however, still needs to be determined in practice. But that educators are required, in principle, to censor and unequally treat certain cultures in their teaching may be disputed.

Yet there is a real question of equality which Harris fails to address in his article. This vital equality issue relates to minority group members' equal enjoyment of opportunities and goods that a democratic, modern society has to offer. Even in well-meaning countries, like the United States and Canada, it may prove misleading, despite the flourish of rhetoric, to conclude that disadvantaged cultural minority groups are truly provided equality of oppor-tunity. Consider clear cases of unequal treatment in education: a Hutterite child who is being schooled in her own religious colony; a Native Indian child who is attending a school run by and for Natives; and a Vietnamese child who has been mainstreamed too soon and is submerged rather than immersed in an English language system.

The category of individual rights includes fundamental human rights and earned rights. Earned rights suggest a category which justifies unequal dis-tribution of rewards and status in society on the basis of merit. Yet each child in our example is excluded to some serious degree from earning her merit in a culture which measures such merit on grounds alien to her circumstances. She is distanced from the starting line because of group membership: either because of her community's choice to maintain ethnic or religious boundaries; or because of her inadequate cultural (linguistic) experience. Clearly, she cannot avail of a right to a job (earned right) because her human right to provisions (e.g., to an appropriate education) by which she can equally and meritoriously participate in the world of work is denied to her.

The dilemma that the equality rights issue presents is a continuation of the problem of knowing when to measure someone according to individual or group status. The earning of rights in a meritocracy is necessarily bound up with membership in the dominant group insofar as the criteria of merit have been devised by and applied traditionally to members of the dominant majority. Upbringing and environmental opportunities in the normal course of their lives enable children of majority groups to participate in the political, economic and social processes in society (that is, given acceptable levels of native capacity and individual effort). Thus, ordinarily, they can assume to climb the societal ladder merely on individual merit. But this is not ordinarily true of minority group members. They first require unequal or special treatment by way of affirmative or compensatory action to bring them up to the dominant group's starting line; only thus can they fairly compete in the meritocratic race. Without this provision for some catch-up process, all talk of equality is pointless.

Recent decades, it may be noted, have witnessed positive steps in the direction of affirmative action. In the United States, Title VI of the Civil Rights Act of 1964 provides for the protection of minority groups from discrimination by stating as follows (in Levin, 1983, p. 34):

> No person in the United States shall, on the ground of race, color, or national origin, be excluded from participation in, be denied the benefits of, or be subjected to discrimination under any program or activity receiving federal financial assistance.

The implication of this Title was clear for educational purposes. Pursuing the mandate, the US Department of Health, Education and Welfare issued a memorandum in 1970 requiring local school districts (receiving federal grant) to take affirmative steps to rectify English language deficiencies which resulted in the exclusion of minority children from educational programs (Andersson and Boyer, 1978).

In Canada, the framers of the Charter of Rights and Freedoms, which is part of the Constitution Act (1982), have seen it fit to state as follows:

> S.15 (1) Every individual is equal before and under the law and has the right to the equal protection and equal benefit of the law without discrimination and, in particular, without discrimination based on race, national or ethnic origin, colour, religion, sex, age or mental or physical disability.

In line with this section, federal and provincial governments have undertaken employment equity and English as a second language programs to promote equal opportunities for disadvantaged minority members.

The argument for admitting minority members into a relationship of parity with majority members is complex and needs to be addressed extensively. Suffice it to say that, legally and constitutionally, entitlement to political and economic opportunities (though not necessarily outcomes) is presumed to belong to all individuals. However, two obvious and serious inadequacies need to be pointed out. First, enabling legislation must be supplemented by legislation which actually designs and mandates programs to ensure that affirmative action is carried to fulfill the promise of equal enjoyment of rights. Whether it is the United States or Canada, it is doubtful that enough legislation has been passed to improve significantly the plight of disadvantaged minority groups. Second, where multiculturalism or pluralism is an accepted public policy, political and economic equality is not enough. Recognition of and provision for cultural equality of ethnic groups is a legitimate expectation. Unfortunately, nowhere is this true in the United States. Canada appears more generous in this regard. The Charter of Rights and Freedoms states:

> S.27. This Charter shall be interpreted in a manner consistent with the preservation and enhancement of the multicultural heritage of Canadians.

Moreover, the federal Multiculturalism Act (1988) has a decidedly cultural retentionist orientation. It is only fair to conclude that, with respect to preservation of minority cultures, Canada leads its North American counterpart. Despite all this, disparity between cultural groups is evident; full parity remains in the elusive future. Such parity will require elimination of the difficulties presented by relativization, the tension between primary and secondary socialization, the conflict between the transmissionist and transformationist orientations, the apparent incompatibility between cultural retention and equality of opportunity, and other contradictions.

Contemporary events in our society constitute a historic challenge to schooling. It is a challenge to be met with intellectual and moral vigor. But the prior task, as Bloom has suggested, is building a consensus to guide our societal and educational direction. Certainly, schools alone cannot attain it. However, they can share the grandeur of the mission to develop one.

Bibliography

ADLER, M. (1982) *The Paideia Proposal*, New York: Macmillan.

ALBERTA TEACHERS' ASSOCIATION MULTICULTURAL COUNCIL (1984) 'Statement of purposes', *Multicultural Education Journal*, 2, p. 46.

ARBUTHNOT, J.B. and FAUST, D. (1981) *Teaching Moral Reasoning: Theory and Practice*, New York: Harper and Row.

BELLOUS, J. (1989) A philosophy of multicultural education, Unpublished MA thesis, The University of Calgary, Calgary, Alberta.

BEREITER, C. (1974) *Must We Educate?* Englewood Cliffs, NJ: Prentice-Hall.

BERGER, P. and LUCKMAN, T. (1967) *The Social Construction of Reality*, Harmondsworth, England: Penguin.

BILINGUAL EDUCATION ACT OF 1968 (1978) in ANDERSSON, T. and BOYER, M. (Eds) *Bilingual Schooling in the United States*, Austin, TX: National Educational Laboratory Publishers, (pp. 223–8).

BLOOM, A. (1987) *The Closing of the American Mind*, New York: Simon and Shuster.

BLOOM, B. (1964) *A Taxonomy of Educational Objectives*, Condensed Taxonomy, London: Longmans, Green and Co.

BRETON, R. (1989) 'Multiculturalism and Canadian nation-building', in CAIRNS, A. and WILLIAMS, C. (Eds) *The Politics of Gender, Ethnicity and Language in Canada*, Toronto: University of Toronto Press, (pp. 27–66).

BURTONWOOD, N. (1986) *The Culture Concept in Education Studies*, Windsor, The NFER-Nelson Publishing.

CONSTITUTION ACT (1982), UK, c. 11.

CREMIN, L. (1961) *The Transformation of the School*, New York: A. Knopf.

DENCH, G. (1986) *Minorities in the Open Society: Prisoners of Ambivalence*, London: Routledge and Kegan Paul.

DEWEY, J. (1964) *Democracy and Education*, New York: Macmillan.

FISHMAN, J. *et al.* (1966) *Language Loyalty in the United States: The Maintenance and Perpetuation of non-English Mother Tongues by American Ethnic and Religious Groups*, The Hague: Mouton and Co.

FREIRE, P. (1970) *The Pedagogy of the Oppressed*, New York: Seabury.

FRYE, N. (1982) *Divisions on a Ground: Essays on Canadian Culture*, Toronto: House of Anansi Press.

FREY, N. (1988) *On Education*, Markham, Ontario: Fitzhenry and Whiteside.

GHITTER, R. (1984) *Final Report of the Committee on Tolerance and Understanding*, Edmonton, Alberta: Government of Alberta.

GIBBONS, R. (1985) *Conflict and Unity*, Toronto: Methuen.

GIBBONS, R. (1988) *Meech Lake and Canada: Perspectives from the West*, Edmonton: Academic Printing and Publishing.

GIBSON, M.A. (1976) 'Approaches to multicultural education in the United States: Some concepts and assumptions', *Anthropology and Education Quarterly*, 7, pp. 7–17.

GIROUX, H. (1983) *Theory and Resistance in Education*, South Hadley, MA: Bergin and Garvery.

GLAZER, N. and MOYNIHAN, D. (1970) *Beyond the Melting Pot: The Negroes, Puerto Ricans, Jews, Italians, and Irish of New York City*, Cambridge, MA: MIT Press.

HARRIS, J. (1982) 'A paradox of multicultural curriculum', *Journal of Philosophy of Education*, 16, p. 224.

HIRSCH, E.D. (1987) *Cultural Literacy*, New York: Houghton Mifflin.

ILLICH, I. (1971) *Deschooling Society*, New York: Harper Torchbooks.

JACKSON, P. (1972) 'Deschooling? No!' *Today's Education*, 8, pp. 18–22.

JOSHEE, R. (1987) 'The rights and responsibilities of multiculturalism', *Multicultural Education*, 3, p. 12.

KALLEN, E. (1982) *Ethnicity and Human Rights in Canada*, Toronto: Gage Educational Publishing.

KUPER, L. and SMITH, M.G. (Eds) (1969) *Pluralism in Africa*, Berkeley, CA: University of California Press.

LAU v. NICHOLS (1974) 414 US 563.

LEVIN, B. (1983) 'An analysis of the federal attempt to regulate bilingual education: Protecting civil rights or controlling curriculum?' *Journal of Law and Education*, 12, pp. 29–60.

LIVINGSTONE, D. (1987) *Critical Pedagogy and Cultural Power*, Toronto: Garamond Press.

MAGSINO, R.F. (1985) 'The right to multicultural education: A descriptive and normative analysis', *Multiculturalism*, IX, (1), pp. 5–11.

MAGSINO, R.F. (1988) Educational linguistic-cultural rights in three countries: Toward policy evaluation', *Canadian and International Education*, 17, pp. 2–26.

MALLEA, J. and YOUNG, J.C. (Eds) (1984) *Cultural Diversity and Canadian Education*, Ottawa: Carleton University Press.

MARCUSE, H. (1965) 'Repressive tolerance', in CONNERTON, P. (Ed.) *Critical Sociology*, Harmondsworth, England: Penguin, (pp. 301–29).

MARLAND, S. (1971) 'Career education', *The National Association of Secondary School Principals Bulletin*, 35, (5), pp. 1–9.

MEYER, J., BURNHAM, B. and CHOLVAT, J. (Eds) (1975) *Values Education*, Waterloo, Ontario: Wilfrid Laurier University Press.

MULTICULTURALISM ACT (1988) Ottawa: Minister of Supply and Services.

OFFICIAL LANGUAGES ACT (1969) Ottawa: Information Canada.

PALMER, H. (1975) *Immigration and the Rise of Multiculturalism*, Toronto: Copp Clark Pitman Publishing.

PAREL, A. (1988) 'The Meech Lake Accord and multiculturalism', in GIBBONS, R. (Ed.) *Meech Lake*, (pp. 171–9), Edmonton, Alberta: Academic Printing and Publishing.

PAUL, R. (1984) 'Critical thinking: Fundamental to education for a free society', *Educational Leadership*.

REIMER, E. (1972) *School is Dead: Alternatives in Education*, Garden City: Anchor Books.

REX, J. (1986) *Race and Ethnicity*, London: Open University Press.

RIZVI, F. (1985) *Multiculturalism as an Education Policy*, Victoria, Australia: Deakin University Press.

ROCHER, G. (1984) 'The ambiguities of a bilingual and multicultural Canada', in MALLEA, J. and YOUNG, J.C. (Eds) *Cultural Diversity and Canadian Education*, Ottawa: Carleton University Press.

SIMON, S., HOWE, L. and KIRSCHENBAUM, H. (1972) *Values Clarification: A Handbook of Practical Strategies for Teachers and Students*, New York: A. and W. Publishers.

SPENCER, H. (1889) *Education: Intellectual, Moral, and Physical*, New York: D. Appleton and Company.

STEWIN, L. and McCANN, S. (Eds) (1987) *Contemporary Educational Issues: A Canadian Mosaic*, Toronto: Copp Clark Pitman.

TRUDEAU, P.E. (1984) 'Statement of the Prime Minister in the House of Commons, 1971', in MALLEA, J. and YOUNG, J.C. (Eds) *Cultural Diversity and Canadian Education*, Ottawa: Carleton University Press.

University Affairs (1989) *30*, (8), p. 11.

VAN DEN BERGHE, P. (1967) *Race and Racism*, New York: John Wiley and Sons.

WALKLING, P. (1980) 'The idea of a multicultural curriculum', *Journal of Philosophy of Education*, *14*, pp. 87–95.

WOOD, G.H. (1985) 'Schooling in a democracy: Transformation or reproduction?' in RIZVI, F. (Ed.) *Multiculturalism as an Educational Policy*, Victoria, Australia: Deakin University Press.

WUTHNOT, R. *et al.* (1984) *Cultural Analysis*, London: Routledge and Kegan.

YOUNG, J.C. (1979) 'Education in a multicultural society: What sort of education? What sort of society?' *Canadian Journal of Education*, *14*, pp. 5–21.

2 The Evolving School: A Canadian Historical Perspective

J. Donald Wilson

Change and Variety of Historical Perspectives on the School

Michael Katz, an historian of education, has recently assessed critics' appraisal of the American public school system as follows (1987, p. 118):

> Their themes would be familiar to anyone today: schools had become too rigid; they did not lessen crime; they were unresponsive to the community; they taught reading and writing less effectively than had little country schools earlier in the century; they cost too much; they required too many administrators; educators had become martinets, unwilling to tolerate criticism and defensive of their systems.

This statement pertains to the American system not in the late 1980s, but rather in the 1870s, 'Plus ça change, plus c'est la même chose', one murmurs. 'History', the same scholar concludes, 'will not dictate new answers, but it can liberate us from old questions' (*ibid.*, p. 135).

The public school is one of the central institutions of the modern state. Since its creation in Canada almost 150 years ago, it has increasingly displaced the centrality of the family and the church in the education of children. While these educative agents still have a role to play in most children's lives, there is no denying that for most people the school has become synonymous with education. Consequently the school's role in Western society today may be considered to be similar in its centrality to that of the church in the Middle Ages.

Originally schools were products of single communities, set up by parents in accordance with their wishes for their children's education. Teachers were hired usually by three trustees elected to office by the parents and other ratepayers in the community. Other schools were private-venture operations. From the 1840s in British North America, however, schools became components of educational systems governed from the provincial capital. State-supported mass education was to guarantee universal literacy which, it was held, would promote popular enlightenment and rational behaviour on the part of the masses. In addition, education was to engender a 'proper appreciation (and acceptance) of one's place in society and to promote shared values and customs, thereby ensuring social stability' (Gaffield, 1985, p. 546). But the aims of school authorities and politicians were one thing and the motivation parents had for sending their children to school was often quite another. The official agenda always had a set of outcomes in mind designed to serve society's needs. But parental goals and the 'subjective experience of the educand', as Brian Simon says, often produced unintended consequences (Simon, 1984, p. 45). For example, that most native Indian leaders in Canada today are products of Indian residential schools is an ironic commentary on the popular social control hypothesis of educational history.

When it comes to a discussion of the history of education in Canada, the theme of this chapter, it is important to recognize that there is no one history, as C.E. Phillips (1957, pp. xi-xii) implied in his monumental *The Development of Public Education in Canada*, but rather many histories.[1] Thus, one feminist scholar has argued that the history of Canadian education is at the very least two histories — one history for males and a different one for females (Prentice, 1981). Aside from the obvious topics of sex-segregated schooling and male-dominated post-secondary education for over a century, one can point to the feminization of elementary teaching in the face of the evolution of patriarchal rule by principals, inspectors, superintendents and department of education bureaucrats. Patriarchal rule is, of course, equally evident in the history of Canadian higher education and remains true today. If we take another topic, the history of elementary and secondary education in Canada, we find that the story holds entirely different implications for the children of non-British/non-French ancestry than for the children of the dominant majority. For the former, school was and still is an agent of assimilation for immigrant children while immigrant children had their own goals and objectives. For other Canadian children, their schooling was entirely segregated from the mainstream public schools as in the case of native Indians and Blacks. In British Columbia, efforts, which proved unsuccessful, were made to segregate Chinese and Japanese children and/or limit the amount of schooling they could get. Other religio-ethnic groups, such as Mennonites, Hutterites and Doukhobors, sought to be left alone with varying degrees of success. Thus, it is clear that there are many histories of education in Canada.

In discussing the evolving school, this chapter charts briefly in the next section the evolution of schooling in Canada from the pre-public school era to the present and notes in passing the institutional changes and the shifting relationships between parents and teachers and between parents and the state. The following section focuses on the theme of progress. Though such themes as growth of educational bureaucracy, school as an agent of assimilation (or exclusion), feminization of teaching, and faith in public education are equally interesting, progress in education appears of greatest concern particularly because of declining faith in the school as a social panacea. The last section examines the sweeping reforms of the 1960s — reforms which initiated massive educational changes and to which, after about two decades, our era is still reacting.

From Private Schools to Public Schooling

Before the 1840s, in British North America, education was not universal, compulsory or, in most places, tax-supported. Being voluntary, education was a matter for the individual family to decide: what form it would take — whether formal or informal — and how much time, effort and money would be expended on a child's education. Such a situation was inherently unequal in terms of sex, race and class, but this was of no concern to the state at the time. Such formal education as existed took a variety of forms ranging from individual governesses and tutors hired by the wealthy to charity schools and Sunday schools used by the poor; from private venture and joint-stock schools by the 'middling classes' to industrial schools for native Indians. Language of instruction might be English, French, German, Gaelic or Algonkian. The school might or might not have a denominational base. The teacher most definitely would not be certificated and his or her qualifications might derive from being a clergyman, missionary, transient adventurer, or simple entrepreneur. Parental choice in the circumstances was uppermost in the determination of both type of schooling and preferred pedagogy which the child would receive. Many parents, in fact, saw no point to schooling at all and chose not to send their children to school. In such cases the child's socialization was effected by other more traditional means (Gidney, 1973, pp. 169–85; Wilson, 1970a, chapter 10).

All this changed when, for numerous reasons, school promoters succeeded mid-century in persuading colonial authorities and influential colonists alike that all children in British North America should be educated at school, that the schools should be relatively comparable in their structure and curricula, that the teachers should be trained and ultimately licensed, that all fees should be abolished to remove the disincentives to the poor of having to pay for their child's schooling, and that the costs inherent in such a school system should be borne, in most cases, by a common property tax supplemented by provincial grants (Wilson, 1970b, chapter 11). Thus, in the period of approximately three decades, schooling in British North America/Canada became free, universal and compulsory. This dramatic, indeed revolutionary, change of events, while containing many positive features, had the decided effect of infringing upon and ultimately seriously reducing parental choice. Not only did parents lose the right to determine whether or not their child would be schooled; they also lost the right to choose the child's teacher and most often to have a bearing on the curriculum and the pedagogy to which the child became subject. Now, to be qualified, teachers had to be trained in state institutions and be declared fit to teach by the state.

On the matter of religion and education, it became necessary for most provinces to devise, while accepting the inseparability of the two, a compromise because of the presence of numerous Christian denominations. A system of publicly supported denominational schools was considered too divisive, except in Newfoundland. Monopoly of public education by the 'state church', which many Anglicans favored, was violently opposed by other denominations. Non-sectarianism, the exclusion of any religious dogma or creed, was accepted only by British Columbia although the 1872 Act insisted that 'the highest morality shall be inculcated'.[2] The most common practice, therefore, was to declare the schools non-denominational. Religious instruction would be mandatory and often carried out by clergymen, but it would teach the common truths of Christianity and avoid proselytism. For most Protestant parents, this brand of religious instruction, favoring none but distinctly Protestant in tone, was satisfactory. After all, strictly denominational religious teaching could be dispensed in Sunday schools. With minor exceptions, only Roman Catholic parents objected to this state of affairs. Some provinces — Ontario, Manitoba (till 1890), Saskatchewan and Alberta — moved to counter these objections by establishing separate or dual confessional school systems. Quebec solved the issue by according separate public systems to Protestants and Catholics and, subsequently, in 1903, declaring Jews to be 'Protestants' for school purposes. Newfoundland adopted a true denominational system. Over the years, Prince Edward Island, Nova Scotia and New Brunswick, through administrative leeway, found ways of catering to substantial Roman Catholic minorities without making any formal legal alternatives to a single public school system. Only British Columbia (until 1977) made no provision whatsoever to meet Catholic objections to attending the so-called 'non-sectarian' public schools of that province. There, authorities justified their actions by invoking, as early as 1872, the doctrine of the separation of church and state, a doctrine which is probably un-constitutional in Canada. Reference to the following chart on the legal status of separate, confessional and denominational schools in Canada makes it clear that the extent of parental choice of public schooling based on religion is greater in Canada than in some countries like the United States, but is less than in others such as Holland (Beales, 1970).[3]

As compulsory attendance came to be enforced in the early years of the twentieth century, the effect was to reverse the presumption of parental control in education and to shift the locus of responsibility from the family to an institutionalized school operated by the various provincial governments. Now heterogeneous groups had to contend with each other over whose values, pedagogy and world view would be adopted by the local school or the provincial school system. Other developments intervened to shift attention away from religious issues to urbanization and industrialization, the building of the nation-state, the emergence of a consumer economy and eventually the welfare state. As long as there was a general consensus over what constituted a Canadian, an acceptance of the primacy of the Judaeo-Christian moral code,

Table 1   *Legal status of separate, confessional and denominational schools*

Non-denominational Public System	Administrative Leeway System	Separate School System	Dual Confessional System	(True) Denominational System
British Columbia	Nova Scotia New Brunswick Prince Edward Island Manitoba (from late 1960s)	Ontario Saskatchewan Alberta Northwest Territories Yukon Territory	Quebec Manitoba (until 1890)	Newfoundland

and an agreement, tacit or otherwise, that non-denominationalism meant Protestant teachings and values, then all was well. But, as Canada became more diverse both ethnically and religiously, the former consensus on these matters broke down. With the influx of tens of thousands of non-Anglo-Celtic immigrants into the cities and countryside, a bold challenge was thrown up to the preservation of Canadian identity. The public school was charged with the main responsibility of assimilating, if not the immigrant parents, then their children into the mainstream of Canadian life. This involved inculcating British values, attitudes and civic virtues with a view to 'imbuing the highest Anglo-Saxon ideals' toward the preparation for the 'pure gold of Canadian citizenship'. According to J.T.M. Anderson, the common school was well suited to the 'splendid work of racial unification'. The church, 'the only other great socializing agency', stood divided with deep denominational splits. The school, on the other hand, exerted 'its supreme influence over youthful minds at their most impressionable stage of development' (Anderson, 1918, pp. 7–9; pp. 95–104).

Serious efforts at assimilating the immigrants continued throughout the interwar years, and, as a new wave of immigrants hit Canada's shores in the wake of World War II, renewed measures were contemplated at assimilation. By this time Canada itself was changing. The war and its aftermath accelerated the loosening of ties with Britain. Economic and military ties with the United States became even closer and the US cultural impact on Canada intensified. Quebec nationalism reached a fever pitch in the 1960s and was not restrained by the findings and recommendations of the Bilingualism and Biculturalism Commission. The (so-called) Third Force, those Canadians of non-British, non-French origin by then representing close to one-fourth of the Canadian population, demanded their place in the sun as well. The first stirrings of disaffection among Canada's native population and the appearance of modern feminism added to the cultural upheaval. The public school was not and could not be unaffected by these pressures on the formerly quiescent Canadian cultural mosaic. For a brief interval in the late 1960s, Canada became defined as a bilingual-bicultural state, ostensibly marking the attainment of official dualism sought by Henri Bourassa and his ideological successor, Pierre Trudeau. But such was not to be, for in October 1971 Canada became officially known as a multicultural society in a bilingual state (Wilson, 1984, chapter 5).

In religious terms, Protestant teaching and values in the public school became much too narrow and specific for a nation composed more and more of non-Christians — Moslems, Buddhists, Hindus, Sikhs, and increasing numbers of atheists and agnostics — who resented the distinctly Christian and Protestant ambience of the public school classroom.

To meet these changes and the rising tide of materialism and secularism, the public school set aside its century-old Protestant ambience by first abolishing religious instruction and later condensing or omitting altogether religious exercises to begin the school day. The MacKay Committee reporting on religious education in Ontario's public schools in 1969 put a fine point on the matter of religious instruction which it termed a 'vehicle leading to religious commitment rather than to true education'. Declaring that 'the children of Ontario are exposed to Christian indoctrination', it recommended the discontinuance of the present course of study in religious education and the integration of 'information about world religions' into appropriate courses at all grades. In grades 11 and 12, an optional course on comparative religion was proposed (Ontario, Committee on Religious Education in the Public Schools of the Province of Ontario, 1969, pp. 21, 75). Similarly the Mackay Report urged that opening exercises should be 'inspirational and dedicational rather than confessional' and in secondary schools confined to student assemblies, graduation programs and other special occasions. Opening exercises, then, were not to be construed as a religious observance (*ibid.*, pp. 35f.). Similar patterns of reform occurred in other provinces as well in the 1970s ('Ritual disagreement', 1988, p. 51).

The public school, therefore, in keeping with societal changes, sought a neutral, value-free ground in terms of both ambience and moral instruction. In the 1970s, courses in values clarification and moral education replaced religious instruction. This development very much disturbed practising Christians, especially evangelical and fundamentalist Protestants who insisted upon their children being schooled in a 'godly' environment and railed against the 'godless' atmosphere of most public schools. To such critics, the public school did not display a neutral or value-free environment as claimed but operated in keeping with the very secular society in which the school functioned. The philosophy of the public school they characterized as secular humanism, by which they meant the sanctioning of moral relativism and secularism at the expense of traditional concepts of right and wrong, good and evil. They pointed to phenomena in society at large, such as the decline of respect for authority (the 'Death of Dad'),[4] the lapse of standards, the rejection of traditional value systems, sexual permissiveness and drug-taking, materialism and consumerism, and widespread hedonism. Then they linked these trends to similar ones they observed in the public schools: discipline problems in the classroom, declining educational standards, sex and drugs even in elementary schools, and incompetent, smug, and lazy teachers. Thus, these critics found their disillusionment with society reflected likewise in disillusionment with public education. This is the background to the noticeable increase in private school enrollment as well as public financial support of private schools in certain provinces. Once again, educational developments tend to mirror those of society generally, and so the rhetoric of private school supporters resembles that of contemporary North American neo-conservatism (Fisher, 1988, pp. 31–8; Fisher and Gilgoff, 1987, chapter 4). Privatization is a 'good thing', the public school 'monopoly' of formal education should be terminated, and parents should have the right to choose their children's education. Thus not only is the public system challenged but debate over the role of religion in education is reopened.

In summary, 'the zone of community consent' about public education, which had been quite large in earlier decades, has shrunk considerably in the 1980s as more diverse community interests question the place and role of public education in Canadian society. The 'great unwritten consensus'[5] about the purpose and value of schools of a century ago has been shattered.

Progress in Canadian Education

Progress in education might be measured in terms of material things, such as number and size of schools, textbooks, ventilation systems, indoor plumbing or school buses. Or it might be measured in terms of improved practices in implementing the educational process, such as pedagogical innovations, better trained teachers or curriculum changes. Of course, there is yet another way to view progress and that, too, may be applicable to Canadian education. That view holds that we get an impression of change, of things being 'new' and progressing, when in actual fact it is simply a deliberately calculated illusion to give us the impression of progress and change. The American social scientist Russell Jacoby (1975, p. xviii) has summed up this situation well in the following words:

> The evident acceleration of production and consumption in the economic sphere, and of hysteria and frenzy in life itself, does not preclude the possibility that a fixed society is simply spinning faster. If this is true, the application of planned obsolescence to thought itself has the same merit as its application to consumer goods; the new is not only shoddier than the old, it fuels an obsolete social system that staves off its replacement by manufacturing the illusion that it is perpetually new.

Let us leave aside for the time being any discussion of the notion of the illusion of change or progress.

Canadians, like Americans, have over the past century been wont to attribute societal progress, both social and economic, to the expanding public school system including more recently the post-secondary system. As early as 1842, a Maritime critic (George R. Young, quoted in Lawr and Gidney, 1973, p. 46) astutely observed the correlation between popular education and the attainment of economic progress.

> The improvement of the mind adds to the skill and manipulation of the hand, and thus enlarges its powers of production. The science and skill of the mechanic [skilled worker] are a part of his annual income ... and of course of the wealth of the state. If the hand of one man can be formed and trained to do the labour of ten, the food he consumes gives a ten-fold value to the products of its industry. The cultivation of the mind increases skill, multiplies inventions, and gives new power and facility to the mechanic. The intellect of a nation becomes thus its richest mine of Gold ... By making the system general, so as to embrace all, every mind and every talent is more likely to be developed, and the national powers of production to be of course increased.

It is remarkable how closely this line of argument resembles the rationale behind the highly-touted human capital theory as expounded by the Economic Council of Canada in the mid-1960s. This prestigious and highly respected body concluded that, once a high level of physical capital accumulation and advanced industrial organization had been achieved, further economic growth depended mainly on technical innovation. In turn, technical innovation depended on highly skilled and qualified 'brainpower'. Hence, more educated people with higher levels of formal education meant more productivity, and more productivity meant higher standards of living, something all Canadians presumably aspired to. Vast sums of public money were poured into all levels of Canadian public education in the mid-to-late 1960s precisely because of the confident assurances of success voiced by the Economic Council of Canada. In the period between 1960 and 1975, expenditures on all levels of public education including universities increased seven-fold. By 1969, Canada led the major industrial countries in the share of its Gross National Product devoted to public expenditures on education. Its figure of 7.6 per cent compared favorably with the Soviet Union at 7.3 per cent, bettered the United States at 6.3 per cent, and almost doubled the respective percentage figures for France, Japan and West Germany (Organization for Economic Cooperation and Development, 1976, pp. 28–9). The central role of the school in the economic and social development of the country was accepted by all industrialized and most third world countries.

Let us discuss progress in Canadian education in terms of technological, pedagogical and institutional elements. Examples of technological innovations having impact on public education are blackboards, indoor toilets, films and computers. Instances of pedagogical innovations are uniform texts, graded classrooms, child-centered education, team teaching and open-area classrooms.

Table 2   The spread of educational apparatus in Canada West 1850–66[6]

Year	Schools	with Bb	with G	with M
1850	3,059	1,649	168	1,813
1861	4,019	3,341	926	2,820
1866	4,303	3,964	1,136	3,265

Key: Bb = blackboard; G = globes or scientific apparatus; M = maps.
Source: Annual Reports of the Chief Superintendent of Education

Institutional innovations are exemplified by multi-grade/multi-roomed schools, rural school consolidation, technical and commercial schools, composite high schools and community colleges. All three types of innovation were often linked in any one reform period. To take but one example: the spread of blackboard use in Upper Canada in the mid-nineteenth century. This technological innovation, accompanied by the introduction of uniform textbooks, allowed for the shift of emphasis from individual, rote recitations based on the pupil's own book to the simultaneous method of teaching. The importance of this new method has recently been well described as follows (Prentice, 1984 Fall, p. 22):

> Simultaneous teaching was ... supposed to be more stimulating to children and, according to the reformed pedagogy, teachers were not only to instruct and control their pupils but to interest them ... [W]hole classes were now expected to rivet their attention on the teacher, or on the increasingly ubiquitous blackboards, and to work together.

The entire ecology of the classroom was fundamentally altered by the apparently simple innovation of a modest blackboard accommodated on an easel. By World War I, school suppliers advocated school room walls almost entirely covered with boards (Ibid., p. 26). Rote learning and the recitation method came to be replaced by a collective response and a new focus on the teacher. Attention came to be centred on the written rather than the spoken word as the blackboard necessitated greater silence and classroom control. All told, classroom relations among students and between students and teacher were fundamentally altered. The spread in the use of this technological/pedagogical innovation, as well as globes and maps, in the span of sixteen years is quite remarkable (See Table 2).

One is reminded of the almost reverse effects of a highly recommended American-inspired innovation of the late 1960s, namely the open-area classroom. In this innovation blackboard use was discouraged because, among other reasons, wall-space was at a premium. Instead of teacher-centered instruction, group work was stressed. Peer cooperation replaced individual student competitiveness; student-centered learning in groups meant by definition an absence of silence and little 'simultaneous' teaching for the whole class. And, finally, the open-area concept led to a breaking down of age/grade classification as older children were encouraged to assist younger ones (Cuban, 1984).

The theme of progress in Canadian educational history tends to imply that change and reform have been of a progressive nature. There is something reassuring about the word *progressive* as opposed to its most often applied counterpart, *traditional*. Perhaps that is why some political parties like to use such a term in their names. However, despite talk by both contemporaries and historians about the progressive nature of Canadian education, the fact is that it has remained essentially conservative. Fred Clarke, a noted foreign observer, referred to the 'prosaic sanity' of both Canadian society and education (Tomkins, 1986, p. 234). The most representative figures in Canadian educational history are not the root-and-branch reformers such as Charles Duncombe, Hubert Newland, Marshall McLuhan and Lloyd Dennis, but rather the conservative-minded Egerton Ryerson, Peter Sandiford, George Weir and Hilda Neatby. While the latter group favored change, the reforms they advocated were intended to preserve the 'prosaic sanity' of Canadian society or, as Vincent Massey once put it, to preserve 'the elements of human stability' which he contended were most 'highly developed' in the British Isles and northwestern Europe (Massey, 1948, pp. 29–30). The Ontario school inspector, in commenting on the progressive curriculum revisions of 1937, had much the same in mind when he said that the aim of the revision was 'to interest the child in his work, so that he wants to do what we want him to do' (Tomkins, 1986, p. 199). That sentiment would certainly have appealed to both Vincent Massey and Hilda Neatby, not to mention many critics of Canadian schools today. The report of the Massey Commission in 1951 and Neatby's best-seller *So Little For the Mind* in 1953 carried the same message. Canada was in grave danger of being Americanized and democratized and the greatest culprit was the sort of permissive, anti-intellectual, anti-cultural and amoral education advocated by the supporters of the American pragmatist John Dewey. If Canada was to be saved from the excesses of American life, the influence of American progressivism must be curbed and the British sense of order, stability and hierarchy restored.

Massey's and Heatby's criticisms of the materialism and anti-intellectualism of Canadian society in the 1950s and the educational system that fed into it had its counterpart at the turn of the century in George M. Grant, principal of Queen's University from 1877 to 1902. Speaking in 1901, Grant lamented: 'Judging by the tone of the public press, I for one am often saddened beyond the power of words to express . . .'. The problem was a 'vulgar and insolent materialism of thought and life' (Owram, 1986, p. 15). Grant's concerns seemed well founded if we can judge from the principles underlying the 'social efficiency' movement of the time. In 1915 an official Ontario teachers' manual expressed four purposes for this sort of education: an appreciation of liberty and the need to vote intelligently; the dissemination of knowledge for 'social progress and happiness'; the enhancement of the welfare of society which was much more important than enhancing 'the individual advantage of pupils'; and industrial efficiency to be promoted by means of practical subjects which would 'make each individual a productive social unit' (Ontario Normal School Manuals, 1915, chapter 17). A similar sentiment, indicative of the nation-wide acceptance of social efficiency, was a statement in 1930 by Langley B.C., high school principal, H.L. Mazer (quoted in Dunn, 1980, p. 23):

> A young life properly 'fitted into' the niche of industry to which it naturally belongs wears soon into an integral and smoothly functioning cog of industrial and social progress. It requires no adjusting, no oiling, no refining. Improperly 'fitted into,' as is often the case ... this young life becomes a slashing gear, a loose bolt, that soon must drop into the discard of unemployment. Or worse still, it threatens and impedes industrial and social progress, and thereby the peace of mind and well-being of the whole national life.

As the president of the Muncie, Indiana, school board said about the same time: 'For a long time all boys were trained to be President. Then for a while we trained them all to be professional men. Now we are training boys to get jobs' (quoted in Lazerson, 1987, p. 12).

The interwar period saw the extension of the school's responsibilities through the introduction of medical and dental services, school playgrounds, vocational guidance and psychological testing. More than ever the school was expected to help solve Canada's social problems deriving from high levels of immigration, economic depression and the onset of the consumer society (Strong-Boag, 1988, chapter 4). By the 1930s Canadian education had been thoroughly transformed from its nineteenth-century antecedents.

As noted above, despite much fanfare in the 1930s, fundamental reforms in Canadian education had to await the late 1960s. In the late 1940s and 1950s new school buildings and teacher supply became the first order of business. In the 1960s there was a widespread sentiment holding that education was an intrinsic good; everyone could benefit from having a good education. Similarly, at the societal level, public education was seen by many as the main instrument for bringing about a better society. Curious, inquisitive students prepared to challenge old-fashioned views would result, it was held, in a more innovative and egalitarian society, one prepared to meet the challenge of Soviet Communism as well as to elevate its standard of living to that found in the United States. Thus all political parties favored improved access to postsecondary education to allow for admission of more women, members of lower income groups, immigrants and native people.

By the mid-1970s, the above contentions were being seriously questioned by a restless public. Great sums of money had been spent, but the promised results in socio-economic advance had not been attained. Instead of stressing the liberating, individual advantages of schooling, the school was looked to in a more traditional, instrumental way as a panacea to solve immediate social and economic problems. Unemployment rates were high so schooling should be linked more closely to work. Rates of crime and public immorality were on the increase so the school should return to its nineteenth-century role as an expediter of moral reform. The school should take the lead in combatting thorny social problems, such as drug-taking and sexual permissiveness.

The parallels between mid-nineteenth century views of social reform and the last decade are quite startling. In that bygone era, the poor, ignorant, unemployed and criminal were lumped together as a degraded class. What we speak of today as the 'deprived' (in economic terms), they spoke of then as the 'depraved' (in moral terms). Back then, cities were thought to be threatened by a criminal class — the 'dangerous classes' — when in fact no such class existed. The likelihood of this class propagating a whole new class of criminals was held to be a very present danger. The social disease as represented by this class could best be cured, according to the reformers, by reliance on education, if not always for the depraved themselves then most certainly for their children. Fundamental political and economic change was proposed by some, such as the Chartists in England, but discounted or opposed by most. Universal schooling was the preferred solution.

In the 1980s not much has changed. Issues of crime, poverty and unemployment — all of which seem to be increasing — led to moral condemnation of the poor. Welfare benefits, it is held by some politicians, should go only to those 'want to work'. Even the solutions proposed are reminiscent of the mid-nineteenth century: Reimpose capital punishment; punish criminals, not the victims of crimes; and introduce school reforms. Suggested reforms include a crack-down on teachers, replacing permissiveness and choice with discipline, compulsory courses and external examinations; introduction of consumer, drug and sex education; reintroduction of some form of moral education with a view to character-building among students; gearing school, community college and even university education to job training so as to offset high unemployment; and allowing for an increase in public financial support of private schools as an alternative to public education. All this makes one wonder how much we have learned from the past about what exactly the school can be expected to accomplish. Clearly, despite all our good intentions, the school cannot reasonably be expected to act as a panacea for society's social and economic ills. As one American scholar notes, 'As educational purposes become all-embracing, the schools are left in the unenviable position of being criticized both for not doing enough and for doing too much' (Lazerson, 1987, p. 2).

This might be a good point to return to Russell Jacoby's quote about the illusion of change and progress, the sense people have that something new is unfolding when in actuality 'a fixed society', as Jacoby asserts, 'is simply spinning faster'. Recent studies by Neil Sutherland (1986, pp. 175–210), Robert Patterson (1986a and b), and George Tomkins (1986, chapters 10, 12) suggest, for example, that the much-touted progressive education of the

33

interwar years never in fact got implemented in the classroom.[7] Many curriculum changes and program revisions were announced in the 1930s right across Canada, but when you actually check out the classroom of the time you find that very little had changed from the previous decade, or even from the pre-World War I era for that matter. The formal discipline theory of studies which Putman and Weir (1925, pp. 118–21) condemned in British Columbia in their 1925 report continued, according to these findings, to predominate in Canadian schools of the late thirties and forties. Learning out of a book, similarly condemned as old-fashioned, persisted despite fanfare about the project method or the enterprise. Drills on the formal parts of grammar and arithmetic or the facts of history and geography remained, we are told, central to the pedagogy of those subjects, even though group-learning in a cooperative ambience has been advocated by the New Education proponents. *So Little For the Mind*, Hilda Neatby's diatribe against what she called the pervasiveness of progressive education in Canadian schools by the 1950s, was not wrong provided you accept that she was addressing the intentions of Canadian educators as reflected in their programs of study and policy statements. However, if you are to consider what actually got implemented, what got into the classroom, Neatby's book is profoundly wrong. Both Sutherland and Tomkins tell us that 'formalism', by which they mean those elements most hated by progressives, such as book-learning, drills and memorization, persisted throughout the second quarter of the twentieth century. By the same token selectivity in high school as a screening mechanism and an emphasis on the academic quality of education persisted in Canadian schools until the 1960s. For example, in Ontario the estimated retention rate between grades 9 and 11 from 1956 to 1958 was only 53 per cent. A decade later (1969 to 1971), because of efforts to turn the high school into a retaining institution, it had jumped to 84 per cent (Munroe, 1974, p. 215).

Sutherland's study of elementary schooling in the interwar period includes the following description (1986, pp. 182–3):

> Even those who enjoyed it [school] then, now recall a system that put its rigor into rote learning, the times tables, the spelling words, the 'Lady of the Lake', the capes and bays, 'the twelve adverbial modifiers (of place, of reason, of time ...)' and the Kings and Queens. It was a system based on teachers talking and pupils listening, a system that discouraged independent thought, a system that provided no opportunity to be creative, a system that blamed rather than praised, a system that made no direct or purposeful effort to build a sense of self-worth ...

All of this is far removed from democracy, anti-intellectualism and amorality which Neatby accused John Dewey of perpetrating on Canadian school children.

Further evidence of the immense gulf between declared intentions as reflected in curriculum guidelines and actual classroom practice can be found in Melinda McCracken's memoir of attending Churchill High School in Winnipeg in the mid-1950s (1975, p. 78):

> The lecture method of teaching, with the teacher standing at the front of the room and the class subserviently listening, didn't help. The teacher had control of the class; to ask a question, the student raised his hand and hoped the teacher would pick up on it. There was no encouragement or discussion. Kids were forbidden to talk to one another in class. You were supposed to sit there passively and have your little mind molded.

> The teacher took the textbook and went through it in the year. The teacher would set a page of problems for the day, or a chapter to read. You would take them home, do the problems, read the chapter and come back the next day, have members of the class read parts of the chapter, explain it a bit and then set another chapter and more problems. You weren't supposed to read beyond a specified page, or even so much as peek at the next page of problems, and so you didn't. The teacher took the responsibility for getting you through the book. If you did it yourself, you'd spoil it for yourself, because you'd only have to go through it all again at the pace of the whole class. It wasn't much of a challenge. You'd sit there listening to each tick of the minute hand on the big white clock overhead, as it inched towards the end of the period.

Once again McCracken's description of things reiterates the 'triumph of formalism', as Sutherland calls it, ironically at the very time that Neatby lamented the supposedly widespread use of progressive education in Canadian schools. The boring routine, regimentation and passive learning described above starkly resemble the very circumstances Dewey most deplored about American classrooms a half century earlier. Canadian-style democracy and British traditions were hardly under siege if we can accept McCracken's recollection as typical.

Educational Reform in the 1960s

The most long-lasting changes in the 1960s were probably structural and institutional, namely, the conversion of the secondary school from the screening institution it had been into a retaining institution. In all provinces retention rates for grades 9 to 11 shot up 50 to 100 per cent between the late 1950s and the early 1970s (Munroe, 1974, p. 215). Today most Canadian youth stay on till the end of grade 12 to acquire that basic credential for a good job (or any job), the high school diploma, which for many was the basic admission requirement to some post-secondary institution entailing another two to four years of schooling at a minimum. The other major structural change of the late

1960s was the democratization of post-secondary education, that is, vastly improved accessibility. This necessitated, on the one hand, the establishment of dozens of new universities and the expansion of the already existent 'old' universities. Student fees remained low relative to actual costs and student loans, and bursaries were widely available to qualified students. For non-university students there was the introduction in almost every province of a new system of community colleges, most of which provided both terminal diploma or university transfer programmes (Dennison and Gallagher, 1986). By virtue of these developments the formerly elite nature of Canadian post-secondary education, so cherished by Hilda Neatby, was smashed. Universities, mainly for the leadership training of the sons of the economically privileged, became a thing of the past. Young women benefited most, especially in the province of Quebec, but also much higher percentages of students from lower socio-economic groups gained access to higher education. Many of them were children of post-World War II immigrants. Universities and community colleges in fact became a tertiary level of public education, a development much deplored recently in Canada by the outraged authors of *The Great Brain Robbery* (Bercuson, Bothwell and Granatstein, 1984. Also Bloom, 1987).

As long as economic expansion continued, vast sums of provincial and federal money poured into public education. But the oil crisis in 1973 and subsequent recession were to change all this quite dramatically. The sweeping promises school reformers and administrators had made for education in the 1960s remained largely unfulfilled. More and better schools and keeping the young longer in school seemed not to be the answer for unemployment, underemployment and rising crime rates among youth. Parents and taxpayers became critical, contending they were not getting their money's worth despite the rising costs of public education. The situation was made worse by a decline in school enrollment figures, largely for demographic reasons (lower birth rates and immigration figures). Thus it became necessary for the first time in history actually to close schools in some cities for lack of students. Teacher militancy, sometimes leading to strike action, in the mid-1970s annoyed parents and taxpayers alike. Now school closings led to teacher layoffs and increased levels of unemployment among teachers. Criticism about the perceived decline in uniform standards of school achievement mounted[8] and blame was directed at lazy and incompetent teachers, the abolition of province-wide examinations, and vast student-choice provided by cafeteria-style curricula introduced in the late 1960s (Wilson, 1977, pp. 21–36).

By the mid-1980s a new trend was apparent, characterized by more provincial control and less local autonomy. There was also a noticeable shift in the predominant language of educational discourse. In the late 1960s and early 1970s stress was placed on attaining greater degrees of equity in education, if not in outcome then in educational opportunity, through, for example, ESL and race relations programs, and on more accessibility to post-secondary education. In the 1980s the language of educational reform stressed accountability, efficiency, individualism and private choice — what one report in British Columbia refers to as 'public expectations' (BC Ministry of Education, 1987, pp. 9–10).[9] Increasingly, individual and family rights are being juxtaposed against the state's traditional responsibility for overseeing the general public welfare. The new conservatism stresses the importance of individual rights and private choice, whereas traditional conservatism — that of John A Macdonald and John Diefenbaker — upheld the preservation of community ideals and the importance of shared values (Grant, 1965).

The direction these changes are likely to take is toward a more privatized system. This development is already apparent in the United Kingdom where a new Education Act in 1988 allows for individual schools to opt out of the control of the Local Education Authority (Aldrich, 1989). In British Columbia, the 1988 Sullivan Royal Commission on Education recommended that a certificate be awarded to all students after ten years of schooling together with an entitlement to two further years of education (BC Royal Commission on Education, 1988, pp. 91–102). Various modes of education are anticipated other than two further years of public high school. In practice, this might well emerge into a modified voucher system. Moreover, for some time, provincial education authorities have shown themselves favoring the increased use of home schooling. Presumably, for example, students could write their certificate examinations, which resemble closely the old matriculation examination, without having prepared for them in public school classrooms. In a B.C. Ministry of Education (1985) document appearing in 1985 and often linked directly to the Sullivan Report, the following claim is made:

> In British Columbia and elsewhere, it traditionally has been assumed that, in order to develop an informed citizenry and to prepare individuals for life in society, it is necessary to enforce school attendance. Today, however, this assumption is being examined — particularly by parents who wish to teach their children at home, and also by private firms who claim they can instruct the young in other settings as well as or better than schools can. As a result, a new notion of *attaining required levels of schooling* has emerged to challenge the traditional idea of *compulsory attendance*. This new notion is founded on pupils' achieving basic levels of skill and knowledge in schools, or elsewhere, irrespective of school schedules and in keeping with their own rates of progress and development (p. 11, emphasis in the original).

As one commentator (Stanley, 1988 Summer, p. 27) concludes, 'if the state is able to enforce attainment of "required levels of schooling", there is in principle no reason why it should require actual attendance at a public school. Private schools, tutors, or whatever arrangements an individual might wish to make, would do just as well, provided all students take the same examinations at the same times'. Substituting 'required levels of schooling' for compulsory school attendance presents a bold challenge to the values traditionally placed on public education and going back to at least the mid-nineteenth century.

However, for the moment, as we enter the 1990s, school participation rates are high; it would seem that both students and parents retain a strong faith in the value of formal education.[10] In 1985–86, 99–100 per cent of Canadian elementary school-age children were in elementary schools, 87 per cent of secondary school-age children were in secondary schools, and 23 per cent of university-age students were attending post-secondary institutions. Fifty-six per cent of this last group attended universities ('School systems', 1988, pp. 19–49). As we approached the end of the decade educational opportunities were certainly more equal than Canadians would have thought possible in 1945. The fact that less than 5 per cent of Canadian children attend private schools bespeaks a commitment to public education that Egerton Ryerson could only have dreamed of. Canadians may not have produced any new and original philosophy of education in over 150 years, but they do take pride in the material progress made in their systems of public education. Our commitment to common schooling remains strong. But so does public criticism, even disillusionment, with the schools.

Today, unlike the mid-nineteenth century and the turn-of-the century, Canadian society and consequently its schools are lacking in common belief systems. These common beliefs served in the past to make the various components of public education coherent. As Diane Ravitch (1985, p. 34) has commented in respect to American schools, 'a society that is confused and contentious cannot look to its schools to straighten things out, for the schools will reflect the same confusion and contention'. Yet we seem to be faced with a strange paradox as we approach 1990: Canadians demonstrate great expectations about what education can do and at the same time display diminishing confidence in what schools are actually achieving. It seems appropriate somehow to leave the last word to the famous (or infamous) Hall-Dennis Report which appeared just twenty years ago. In trying to resolve the inherent tensions between the social and individual aims of education, the report (Provincial Committee on Aims and Objectives in the Schools of Ontario, 1968, p. 55) concluded: 'How to provide learning experiences aiming at a thousand different destinies and at the same time to educate toward a common heritage and common citizenship is the basic challenge to our society'. To meet that challenge remains as urgent today as two decades ago. And the school, ever evolving, remains a central institution in attaining these goals.

Notes

1 For outstanding examples of the new history of education, see Gaffield (1985), Curtis (1988) and Houston and Prentice (1988).
2 The thinking underlying the separation of church and state in education was well expressed by British Columbia's Governor Seymour in 1867: 'It is vain to say that there are certain elementary matters in which all Christians, leaving out the Jews,

must agree. It is merely calling upon a man [teacher] picked at random, allured by a trifling salary, to do what the whole religious wisdom, feeling and affection of the world has not yet done' (Sissons, 1959, p. 378).

3 For an elaboration on this section, see Wilson and Lazerson (1982, pp. 1–22).

4 The expression is quoted by Silver (1980,) from Harry Ree who said, 'There's been a decrease in automatic, unthinking acceptance of authority. I've heard it called the Death of Dad'.

5 The terms are borrowed from the title of Fleming's work (in press).

6 The table was prepared by, and used with permission, from Curtis (1988, p. 280).

7 For a less negative assessment, see Stamp (1978, pp. 76–94).

8 For a sharp American critique of the decline of the traditional curriculum, see Hirsch (1987).

9 For a discussion of accountability and the new emphasis on excellence in education, see Savage (1988).

10 This seems to be true for the United States as well. See Tyack and Hansot (1982, Part III).

Bibliography

Aldrich, R. (1989) 'A common countenance: National curriculum and national testing', *Policy Explorations in England and Wales*, 4(1).

Anderson, J.T.M. (1918) *The Education of the New-Canadian*, Toronto: J.M. Dent.

Beales, A.C.F. (1970) 'Church and state in education: Public support for confessional schools in some English-speaking countries', in Nash, P. (Ed.) *History and Education*, New York: Random House, (pp. 256–79).

Bercuson, D.J., Bothwell, R. and Granatstein, J.L. (1984) *The Great Brain Robbery*, Toronto: McClelland and Stewart.

Bloom, A. (1987) *The Closing of the American Mind*, New York: Simon and Schuster.

British Columbia, Ministry of Education (1987) *Annual Report, 1986–1987*, Victoria: Ministry of Education.

British Columbia, Ministry of Education (1985) *Let's Talk about Schools: A Report to the Ministry of Education and the People of British Columbia*, (Five volumes) Victoria: Ministry of Education.

British Columbia, Royal Commission on Education (1988) *A Legacy for Learners: The Report of the Royal Commission on Education (1987–1988)*, Victoria: Ministry of Education.

Cuban, L. (1984) *How Teachers Taught: Constancy and Change in American Classroom, 1890–1980*, New York: Longmans.

Curtis, B. (1988) *Building the Educational State: Canada West, 1836–1871*, Lewes: The Falmer Press.

Dennison, J.D. and Gallagher, P. (1986) *Canada's Community Colleges: A Critical Analysis*, Vancouver: UBC Press.

Dunn, T.A. (1980) 'The rise of mass schooling in British Columbia, 1900–1919', in Wilson, J.D. and Jones, D.C. (Eds) *Schooling and Society in 20th Century British Columbia*, Calgary: Detselig.

Fisher, D. (1988 Summer) 'The future of public education: The Royal Commission and changes in the boundary between the public and private sectors', *Policy Explorations*, 3 (3), pp. 31–8.

Fisher, D. and Gilgoff, B. (1987) 'The crisis in B.C. public education: The state and the public interest', in Witherspoon, T. (Ed.) *The Political Economy of Canadian Schooling*, (chapter 4), Toronto: Methuen.

FLEMING, T. (in press) In the Imperial Age and After: Patterns of British Columbia school leadership and the institution of superintendency, 1849–1988. Typescript.

GAFFIELD, C. (1985) 'History of education', *The Canadian Encyclopedia*, Vol. 1 Edmonton: Hurtig Publications, (p. 546).

GAFFIELD, C. (1987) *Language, Schooling, and Cultural Conflict: The Origins of the French-language Controversy in Ontario*, Kingston, Ontario: McGill-Queen's University Press.

GIDNEY, R.D. (1973) 'Elementary education in Upper Canada: A reassessment', *Ontario History*, vol. IXV: pp. 169–85.

GRANT, G. (1965) *Lament for a Nation*, Toronto: McClelland and Stewart.

HIRSCH, E.D. JR. (1987) *Cultural Literacy: What Every American Needs to Know*, Boston: Houghton Mifflin.

HOUSTON, S.E. and PRENTICE, A. (1988) *Schooling and Scholars in Nineteenth-century Ontario*, Toronto: University of Toronto Press.

JACOBY, R. (1975) *Social Amnesia*, Boston: Beacon Press.

KATZ, M.B. (1987) *Reconstructing American Education*, Cambridge, MA: Harvard University Press.

LAWR, D.A. and GIDNEY, R.D. (Eds) (1973) *Educating Canadians: A Documentary History of Public Education*, Toronto: Van Nostrand Reinhold.

LAZERSON, M. (Ed.) (1987) *American Education in the Twentieth Century: A Documentary History*, New York: Columbia University Teachers College Press.

MASSEY, V. (1948) *On Being Canadian*, Toronto: J.M. Dent.

McCRACKEN, M.L. (1975) *Memories Are Made of This*, Toronto: James Lorimer.

MUNROE, D. (1974) *The Organization and Administration of Education in Canada*, Ottawa: Information Canada.

ONTARIO NORMAL SCHOOL MANUALS: HISTORY OF EDUCATION (1915) Toronto: William Briggs.

ONTARIO (1968) 'Provincial Committee on Aims and Objectives in the Schools of Onatrio', *Living and Learning*, Toronto: Ontario Department of Education.

ONTARIO (1969) Committee on Religious Education in the Public Schools of the Province of Ontario', *Religious Information and Moral Development*, Toronto: Ontario Department of Education.

ORGANIZATION FOR ECONOMIC COOPERATION AND DEVELOPMENT (1976) *Reviews of National Policies for Education: Canada*, Paris: Organization for Economic Cooperation and Development.

OWRAM, D. (1986) *The Government Generation: Canadian Intellectuals and the State, 1900–1945*, Toronto: University of Toronto Press.

PATTERSON, R.S. (1986a) 'The Canadian response to progressive education', in KACH, N., MAZUREK, K., PATTERSON, R.S. and DeFAVERI, I. (Eds) *Essays on Canadian Education*, (chapter 4), Calgary: Detselig.

PATTERSON, R.S. (1986b) 'The implementation of progressive education in Canada', in KACH, N., MAZUREK, K., PATTERSON, R.S. and DeFAVERI, I. (Eds) *Essays on Canadian Education*, (chapter 5), Calgary: Detselig.

PHILLIPS, C.E. (1957) *The Development of Education in Canada*, Toronto: W.J. Gage.

PRENTICE, A. (1984 Fall) 'From household to school house: The emergence of the teacher as the servant of the state', *Material History Bulletin*, no. 20: pp. 22, 26.

PRENTICE, A. (1981) 'Toward a feminist history of women and education', in JONES, D.C. *et al.* (Eds) *Approaches to Educational History*, Winnipeg: University of Manitoba.

PUTRAM, J.H. and WEIR, G.M. (1925) *Survey of the School System*, Victoria: King's Printer.

RAVITCH, D. (1985) *The Schools We Deserve*, New York: Basic Books.

'RITUAL DISAGREEMENT: THE EMOTIONAL ISSUE OF MANDATORY PRAYER', (1988, October 24), *Macleans*, p. 51.

SAVAGE, L. (1988 Summer) 'Equality and excellence in educational discourse: The case of British Columbia', *Policy Explorations*, 3 (3), pp. 9–18.

SCHOOL SYSTEMS (1988) *Canadian Encyclopedia*, Vol. III, p. 1949.

SILVER, H. (1980) *Education and the Social Condition*, London: Methuen.

SIMON, B. (1984) 'Can education change society?' in WILSON, J.D. (Ed.) *An Imperfect Past: Education and Society in Canadian History*, Vancouver: University of British Columbia Curriculum Centre.

SISSONS, C.B. (1959) *Church and State in Canadian Education*, Toronto: Ryerson.

STAMP, R.M. (1978) 'Canadian high schools in the 1920s and 1930s: The social challenge to the academic tradition', *Historical Papers*, Canadian Historical Association.

STANLEY, T. (1988 Summer) 'Schooling and the politics of public policy in British Columbia', *Policy Explorations*, 3 (3).

STRONG-BOAG, V. (1988) *The New Day Recalled: Lives of Girls and Women in English Canada, 1919–1939*, Toronto: Copp Clark Pitman.

SUTHERLAND, N. (1986, Spring/Summer) 'The triumph of "formalism". Elementary schooling in Vancouver from the 1920s to the 1960s', *B.C. Studies*, nos. 69/70, pp. 175–210.

TOMKINS, G.S. (1986) *A Common Countenance: Stability and Change in the Canadian Curriculum*, Toronto: Prentice Hall.

TYACK, D. and HANSOT, E. (1982) *Managers of Virtue: Public School Leadership in America, 1820–1980*, New York: Basic Books.

WILSON, J.D. (1970a) 'Education in Upper Canada: Sixty years of change', in WILSON, J.D. *et al. Canadian Education: A History*, (chapter 10), Toronto: Prentice-Hall.

WILSON, J.D. (1970b) 'The Ryerson years in Canada West', in WILSON, J.D. *et al. Canadian Education: A History*, (chapter 11), Toronto: Prentice Hall.

WILSON, J.D. (1977) 'From the swinging sixties to the sobering seventies,' in STEVENSON, H.A. and WILSON, J.D. (Eds) *Precepts, Policy, and Process: Perspectives on Contemporary Canadian Education*, (pp. 21–36), London, Ontario: Alexander Blake Associates.

WILSON, J.D. (1984) 'Multicultural programmes in Canadian education', in SAMUDA, R.J., BERRY, J.W. and LAFERRIERE, M. (Eds) *Multiculturalism in Canada*, (chapter 5), Toronto: Allyn and Bacon.

WILSON, J.D. and LAZERSON, M. (1982) 'Historical and constitutional perspectives on family choice in schooling: The Canadian case', in MANLEY-CASIMIR, M. (Ed.) *Family Choice in Schooling*, (pp. 1–22), Lexington, MA: Lexington Books.

3 The Evolving School: An American Historical Perspective

R.L. Schnell

Discourse of Education

Discourse and practice have left a heritage of live, decaying and fossil remains on the educational landscape. That landscape is, of course, part of a larger world constructed of social, political and economic events and ideas. Although educational discourse and practice seem to have an inner life of their own, they must nevertheless respond to the world in which they reside. That response is frequently seen to be slow and inadequate; however, no institution is free to pursue, without regard to external conditions, its own inner needs and interests.

In discussing formal education, we are faced with the problem that we have come to accept schooling as a universal experience and as the most significant institution in determining our future economic opportunities. Consequently we are incapable of appreciating a society where schools served a limited though crucial function (Bailyn, 1906). Moreover, the nineteenth-century school campaigns expropriated the discourse associated with the earlier traditions of education for citizens and rulers and applied it with great success in justifying the establishment of public systems of schools.

That rich tradition of educational discourse, an extended historical conversation on the purposes of education from the fifth century before the common era to the nineteenth century, had comprehensively probed the relationship between citizen and state, individual virtue and social controls, and rulers and the common good. From Plato and Aristotle, through the Renaissance humanists of the fifteenth and sixteenth centuries, to the leading thinkers of early modern Europe, e.g., Locke, Rousseau and Kant, the nature of the state, the attributes of citizenship and morality, and the relationship of education to all these concerns were extensively and compellingly argued even though no final answer could be provided (Bolgar, 1954; Marrou, 1956).

The discourse, except in a few remarkable cases, was limited by gender and class distinctions. In essence, the assumption was that all women and most men were born with saddles on their backs and that a small privileged minority were expected to ride them. Such limited views reflected accurately the social structures of most European societies. However, in the 1600s a new literature addressing the perceived needs of a growing unchurched urban poor began to appear.

The literature constituted a new discourse on two levels. First, on a vocational or technical stage, the discussion centered on the training for a new set of occupations. It dignified the preparation of the working classes and shopkeepers. The initial impetus to the discourse was religiously motivated and scarcely knew geographical or denominational boundaries. Three remarkable examples of religiously inspired effort are the Society for Promoting Christian Knowledge in England, the Brothers of the Christian Schools in France, and the Protestant schools of A. H. Francke of Halle, which represent Anglican, Catholic and Lutheran good works. The second level concerned not the education of princes and citizens but the socio-religious requirements associated with laborers and lower commercial classes, those lacking political and social power (Adamson, 1905; Jones, 1938; Laquer, 1976).

Briefly exploring historical antecedents and starting with colonial America, this chapter examines the interaction of educational discourse regarding educational objectives for an increasingly inclusive and expanding provision of formal education between 1800 and 1950. It also looks into some major demographic and intellectual changes in the United States during this period.

Historical Antecedents

The political and religious unrest of the seventeenth century contributed to the desire of upper and middle classes to insure social discipline among the poor. At its most limited level, religious instruction was advocated as the means of creating a God-fearing population and inoculating children of the poor against habits of sloth, debauchery and beggary. The impetus for the education of the poor and working poor was substantially religious but was clearly colored by fears of social and political unrest. Moreover, the promoters of the education of the poor were united by a common non-denominational perspective. As devout Christians more concerned with conduct than dogma, they sought to promote by an austere personal discipline the glory of God and the inner satisfaction of the individual. Their inner spiritual life was expressed in a simple and strict lifestyle and in a profound belief in their duty to succor the poor and the unfortunate. Accepting inequalities of wealth and poverty as the will of God, they proposed Christian charity and grateful acquiescence of the poor as the sure remedy for squalor, ignorance and vice. Education was deemed to be a particularly worthy form of charity in that it rendered its recipients more useful. Thus, schooling not merely fed and assisted temporarily. It was a charity that gave life-long benefits.

These early efforts to provide instruction grew from *no* conception of popular education, from *no* foundation of a common citizenship or from belief in the elimination of the ills of man or society. In contrast, promoters of education for the poor emphasized ignorance as a bar to virtue, instruction as social discipline, and its usefulness to religious belief and social stability.

Charity schooling also benefited from the growth of vernacular instruction in the seventeenth century, by which the circumscribed Latin training intended for choir boys was transformed into a basic core of knowledge and skills deemed essential for any trade or, indeed, for a decent life. The restricted training in subordination was intended to achieve its object by inculcating the right form of predisposition to accept authority. The importance of these early charity schools lay in the attempt to provide full-time education for the children of the poor not only in religious principles but in disciplines and skills which would enable the children to continue to behave according to those principles in later life.

The interest in the socio-religious education of the children of the poor indicated a significant shift in the understanding of the nature of education. The education of princes and citizens had long been dislodged from 'the automatic, instinctive workings of society and cast a matter of deliberation into the forefront of consciousness' (Bailyn, 1960, p. 21). But for the mass of people education had meant socialization, training and education in household, community, church and workplace. As Cappe put it in 1785, the purpose of charity schooling to the contrary was to effect a 'reformation of a class of persons, whom, taken as a body, we have long been accustomed to regard with suspicion' (quoted by Silver, 1965, p. 17). In brief, to prevent the presumed 'automatic, instinctive workings of society' from casting up new and ever larger generations of the unchurched and ill-disciplined, the promoters of charity schools called for radical intervention into the lives of the poor and laboring poor. Thus, they were required to justify their efforts both in terms of political philosophy and of practical pedagogy. The intent, restrictive in provision and outcome, was to shore up and render secure the religious, social and political order. Nonetheless, it was premised on the belief that education of the young would be proof against the most debilitating of social ills, and this certainly represented a new conception of the power of formal education.

We may, from the vantage point of the last two decades of the twentieth century, dismiss such optimism as naive. However, the advocates of formal education had some evidence from efforts to educate large populations, and they were heartened by new knowledge of the natural world. They hoped for new insight into the human and social world, as well, and enlisted the humanist tradition with its demands that the classics be read and studied to solve our daily problems of life. If the humanist tradition, which had not yet lost its power to transform, provided an example of the power of learning, then the belief that a restrictive form of education — a form with clear curricular limits, committed to the development of skills of literacy, and preaching a definite message of deference, obedience and responsibility — could shape character does not seem far fetched.

Though unsubstantiated by human experience, the belief in the power of formal education or schooling not simply to impart skills or knowledge but to mold human personality and control future conduct, while unsubstantiated by human experience, has died hard and very slowly. The original advocates of schooling as social control expected the process to be unambiguous. When their expectations were not met, the reaction was not to turn away from schooling but to propose new and more complex forms of education.[1]

Education in Colonial America

To give clarity to a discussion of the changing role and function of schooling in American life, the chapter will examine crucial points in the transformation of the school from the beginning of the nineteenth century to World War II. Educationists have been intrigued by the seemingly modern view of education held by seventeenth-century New England Puritans who enacted two remarkable pieces of colonial legislation in 1642 and 1647. The first law directed parents and masters to look to the education of their children and apprentices. This early public interest was nurtured by an intense biblicism, a commitment to literacy, a sense of community responsibility for the proper ordering of society, and a determination to preserve civilization in a wilderness (Ahlstrom, 1972).

The 1647 Act required towns of a certain size to maintain a school. It is not necessary to see the requirement as a sign of the failure of non-formal education agencies. Schools were essential parts of civilization and sociopolitical stability and were well imbedded in European life since the Middle Ages. Although the non-Puritan colonies lacked the same religious and communal energy and cohesion they, too, passed legislation encouraging private and community attention to education. However, the growing diversity of the eighteenth century and the sense of individualism worked against community responsibility for schooling, especially at a time when the function and results of schooling remained limited. By the end of the century, a belief in the liberating effects of agrarian life and free local political institutions combined with a faith in the indefinite perfectability of men to produce a confidence in the power of even limited schooling (Middlekauff, 1963).

Education for a Republican Citizenry

Perhaps the most striking statement of the supposed power of formal education was given by Thomas Jefferson in 1818. According to this author of the Declaration of Independence, the six objects of primary education were:

to give every citizen the information he needs for the transaction of his own business; to enable him to calculate for himself, and to express and preserve his ideas, his contracts and accounts, in writing; to improve, by reading, his morals and faculties; to understand his duties to his neighbors and country, and to discharge with competence the functions confided to him by either; to know his rights, to exercise with order and justice those he retains, to choose with discretion the fiduciary of those he delegates, and to notice their conduct with diligence, with candor, and judgment; and, in general, to observe with intelligence and faithfulness all the social relations under which he shall be placed. (Peterson, 1960, p. 239)

Jefferson's educational proposals for a politically active white male citizenry came near the end of a significant period of Americanization of the former subjects of the British Crown. In the half century, 1775–1825, the American identity was forged not only in a war of independence and the War of 1812 but in major population growth and internal development. Population grew from an estimated 2.2 million in 1770 to slightly over 11.2 million in 1825, an increase of nine million. Immigration during the same period probably did not exceed 400,000 (*The Statistical History of the United States from Colonial Times to the Present*, 1965).

Moreover the period was a time of political expansion and consolidation. The Northwest ordinance of 1787 set the conditions for the organization of territory outside the regional thirteen states and for admission of new states (eleven by 1821). The Louisiana and Florida purchases increased the territory of the United States from 889,000 to 1,788,000 square miles by 1819 (*Statistical History*; 1965 J1–12). The new Federal Constitution ratified in 1788 provided a more powerful and active central government while the first ten amendments, the Bill of Rights, declared in force in 1791, offered protection of basic rights nationally. New state constitutions and the movement towards a more inclusive franchise insured vigorous local and state politics. Limited immigration, political stability and territorial development, and separation from Great Britain fostered the self-absorption, even egocentrism, that dominates American life. By 1818, the children and the heirs of the American Revolution who were coming to political power had expectations of a great nation distinct from and superior to old world ones.

In retrospect, Jefferson's hopes for primary education seem grandiose, given the limited schooling proposed, and elitist, given his assumption that the best ought to govern. However, his expectations were at least consistent within his political and social ideas and defensible, given a particular view of individual and societal interaction. A believer in enlightenment and heir of the Renaissance, Jefferson saw education as a life-long enterprise, composed of many elements. Primary education was crucial, but certainly not sufficient, for the success of the enterprise. A whole range of activities was built on schooling: participation in democratic society, property holding and management, immersion in politics both immediate and through a free press, and reading aided by libraries. As a child of enlightenment, Jefferson prized intellect, talent and character and necessarily expected democratic leaders to be the most virtuous citizens. Perhaps Jefferson understood that not to recognize gradation in aptitude and virtue or a job well done meant that the best would be ruled by the less able.[2] Jefferson envisioned wide freedom of action for citizens and the ascendancy of a virtuous and talented leadership accountable to the citizenry. While political leaders should rise out of the best, Jefferson believed that the electors could definitely judge the actions of those in position of authority and render sound assessments.

Jefferson's view of education represented a rejection of the seventeenth-century new England Puritan assumption of the responsibility of government to intervene actively in controlling or even reshaping the social order. In brief, the state was not to control economic development and growth and not to lay too heavily on the citizens' private lives. While Jefferson clearly saw the scope and variety of educational experiences — mainly informal — his views were in harmony with the growing faith in the power of education to influence or shape human character and conduct. The school promoters who took up the campaigns for state systems of schools reasonably enough narrowed their focus to schools and largely eliminated the non-formal aspects so vital to Jefferson's conception.

Their more circumscribed view, however, did not mean that schooling would be less conceived of in political terms. Social and pedagogical concerns became more prominent as the relationship between schooling and public action was recognized as more problematic. Revolutionary political ideas dropped out of the discourse around schooling to be replaced by more limited ones. The common school promoters embarked on their campaigns in the 1830s at the time when the latent democratic bias and content in the American polity was rapidly realizing itself. In the process it drew upon the widespread diffusion of property — surely a leading theme in Jeffersonian thought — and upon a commitment to a natural rights philosophy derived mainly from John Locke. Besides fueling a tendency towards individualism and self-expression in economic, social and personal matters, the democratic bias realized itself in the gradual elimination of property tests for office holding and voting. Indeed, by 1860, universal white male suffrage was the rule in the United States (Williamson, 1960).

Promoting the Common School Ideal

Thus, to the natural inclination towards the democratic distribution or availability of social and economic opportunities was added the possibility of political participation for the entire white male population. The politicization of American life at the grassroots is made more clear by the lack of bureaucratic structures common in the Western nations that mitigated the direct expression of popular will. For good or ill, the American national and state governments were managed not by bureaucracies but by political parties and courts, which were close at hand, sensitive to voters and lacking in any real managerial competence.[3]

Consequently, the common school promoters saw the schools as effective means of ameliorating the excesses of individual interests and group antagonisms. However, their hopes were expansive, not restrictive, as with the charity school advocates. The intention was to foster internal controls that would guide free men in a political and socio-economic system that gave great scope for self-aggrandizement.

Because universal white manhood suffrage did not divide the American people as abolitionism or woman's rights did, its achievement was relatively smooth and its acceptance easy. Despite the hopes of some and the fears of others, the extension of the vote did not bring about revolutionary change. If, as Jefferson affirmed, the object of the American political enterprise was 'democracy made easy', then universal education was not only a social convenience but also a necessary political institution; not only to elevate the intellectual and moral faculties of the people but also to provide the practical understanding and competence to make the democratic socio-political machinery operate smoothly and effectively. Frequently, of course, the school promoters' rhetoric included dire warnings of the results of an electorate without moral or social controls.

Horace Mann (1796–1859) is frequently cited as the preeminent advocate of the indispensability of free school for the maintenance of a free and moral society. As Lawrence Cremin observed, Mann's 'quest was for a *public philosophy*, a sense of community which might be shared by Americans of every variety and persuasion ... to use education to fashion a new American character out of a maze of conflicting cultural traditions' (Cremin, 1957, p. 8). Even as early as 1837, when Mann embarked on his tenure as secretary of the newly-created Massachusetts State Board of Education, the possibilities of religious, ethnic and class conflict figured largely in the concerns about the viability of the republic. Increasingly after 1830, the generations who had come of age during the half century of intense social and political integration saw the growing stream of Roman Catholic or non-anglophone immigration as a threat to a developing national spirit and purpose. The rise of nativist organizations such as the American Republican Party who preached a gospel of anti-Catholicism and xenophobia was an impetus to rethinking the objectives of schooling in more conservative and socially integrative terms (Benson, 1964, pp. 114–22).

Mann's work represented more than a creative response to changed conditions; it also was an admission of the failure of non-formal and life-long education as means of political integration. The shift to schooling meant public support and public control to insure a non-sectarian religious and non-partisan political education and to expand the curriculum for the general education of all, that is, to democratize and universalize true culture.

In one sense Mann did not wish to give up entirely the belief current since John Locke that character and moral conduct were best, perhaps only, formed in the active world. He insisted that schools must foster 'self-government' and a 'voluntary compliance with the laws of reason and duty'. In brief, the school must be a self-governing community.

By 1848, when Mann resigned as secretary of the Massachusetts State Board of Education, the outlines of American common schooling were well drawn. Driven by political, social and religious imperatives, its advocates were laying the foundations of a non-sectarian, non-partisan and classless system. The pragmatic compromises worked out by the reformers were done against a significant shift in educational discourse. Increasingly the literature and ideas linking the education of the free man, the citizen and ruler, to the fundamental social and political questions radically transformed the discussion regarding the education of the poor and the working poor. The use of national states, the universal nature of citizenship, and the extension of suffrage practically destroyed the gap between subjects and citizens. The growing concern for social and political integration of diverse populations rendered the ideology and practice of charity schooling obsolete.

Interestingly, charity school promoters had assumed that the most promising means for breaking the cycle of dependency and pauperization were religious instruction and habit training of the children of dangerous and perishing classes. Nineteenth-century political conditions meant at least that the nature of the rescue had to be rethought. Eighteenth-century efforts were primarily to rescue children from pauperism, dependency and crime by means of instruction in religious principles, disciplines and skills that would enable them to behave according to those principles in later life. The insistence on responsibility and self-reliance would be a favorite theme throughout the nineteenth century as witnessed by the popular assumption that men would work only to prevent themselves and their families from starving. Thus, knowledge as to the consequences of idleness and improvidence was as essential as the inculcation of good social habits (Katz, 1983; Jones, 1971).

Popular education, even in its most restrictive form, offered more than fostering a predispositon to accept authority and responsibility for one's material survival. Education, now defined as schooling, became a debt owed to the state. An increasingly universal and compulsory citizenship was to be achieved by means of schooling. If popular education was frequently understood in political terms even in states without liberal or democratic parliamentary institutions, it also had a cultural and psychological dimension that reflected many of the tensions of early nineteenth-century thought. The basis for this dimension was a renewed historical conversation regarding human nature and its proper development. The discussion, much influenced by religious ideas and sentiment, can be dated from the writings of the Moravian educator and cleric John Amos Comenius (1592–1670) who proposed a theory of pansophic education that would teach all subjects to all men to foster our human qualities. Although Comenius' ideas were not widely accepted, they represented a growing psychological sensitivity to human development and the universal distribution of human potential throughout the population. John Locke (1632–1704) and Jean-Jacques Rousseau (1712–1776) popularized these notions in intellectually compelling and exciting treatises on education, human development and social interaction (Cassirer, 1963; Gay, 1964; Piaget, 1967).

In the nineteenth century, a new educational discourse was created by the Swiss Johann H. Pestalozzi (1746–1827) and the Germans Johann F. Herbart (1776–1841) and Friedrich Froebel (1782–1852). Inspired by the insights of Locke and Rousseau, romantic notions of human perfectability, and the desirability of human intervention in and control of the social world, these educators preached a gospel of moral and intellectual uplift. The first generation of common school promoters had naturally enough assumed both a simple cause and effect relationship between instruction and the production of good citizens and a generous estimation of the good that schooling could accomplish (Dunkel, 1969; Pollard, 1956; Silver, 1965).

By the last decades of the century, as with many other social schemes, instruction and a simple school organization failed to realize the dreams of the early school campaigners. The growing length of the school year, improved daily attendance, and longer stays at school raised problems of content and objectives. What had been suitable for limited attendance for children was not appropriate for adolescents. Longer scholastic life meant increased separation from the world of work; and older students raised questions surrounding the purposes of common schooling.

Changing Patterns of a Common Curriculum

American society changed remarkably during the nineteenth century. From a population of less than 4 million in 1790, the Republic reached 9.6 million in 1820, 31.5 million in 1860, and 76 million in 1900. Rural and urban settlement changed dramatically — from 5 per cent in 1790 to 7 per cent in 1820, 20 per cent in 1860, and 40 per cent in 1900. Despite the remarkable urban growth, rural settlement went from 3.7 million in 1790, 8.9 million in 1820, 25.2 million in 1960, and 45.8 million in 1900. It was not until 1920 that urban population exceeded rural population. After a period of relative calm between 1775 and 1820, immigration soared beginning in the 1840s. Between 1841 and 1900 over 18 million immigrants arrived and an additional 12 million during the period 1901–1914. Likewise, the workforce grew from 2.8 million in 1820 (when non-agricultural workers were only 812,000) to 10.5 million in 1860 (with 2.8 million non-agricultural workers), to 29 million in 1900, including 18.1 million in non-agricultural pursuits (*Statistical History*, 1965, A1–3, A228–229, C88–114, and D36–45).

Thus, the essentially agrarian society of Jefferson's memory rapidly disappeared under tidal waves of population growth, urbanization and industrial development, and immigration. Accompanying these remarkable changes was the gradual accelerating aging of the American people. The median age rose from 16.7 in 1820 to 19.4 in 1860 to 22.9 in 1900 and to 29 in 1940 (*Statistical History*, 1965, A86–94). In this teeming world of immigrants, rapid population and industrial growth, and personal opportunity, formal education played an essential, limited, but expanding role.

By the later decades of the nineteenth century, American schools had gradually evolved into three main strands serving youth beyond the rudiments. The most prestigious strand was the classical-humanistic tradition represented by the Latin Grammar School with its roots in the Renaissance scholarship of the fourteenth and fifteenth centuries. Its classical studies were the condition of admission to most colleges. In 1828 the Yale Faculty Report defended the singular importance of the classics by noting that 'the two great points to be gained in intellectual culture are the *discipline* and the *furniture* of the mind; expanding its powers, and storing it with knowledge'. Beyond this disciplinary view, the Report remarked that men of wealth 'should be of superior education, of large and liberal views, of those solid and elegant attainments ... which will enable them to adorn society by their learning, and to make such an application of their wealth, as will be most honorable to themselves, and most beneficial to their country' (Hofstadter and Smith, 1961, pp. 278–88).

The second strand incorporated the new practical subjects such as navigation and surveying as well as the modern studies of English, modern languages, geography and history. The institutional setting for these new subjects was a host of private academies. These diverse institutions, however, also provided a course of studies for college-bound students. Despite the problems associated with offering both a classical and a practical or modern curricula, the academies rapidly surpassed the Latin Grammer School as the principal means of formal education beyond the three Rs (Sizer, 1964).

The third strand, the growing system of common schooling, was the wave of the future. Starting as providers of the three Rs the common schools gradually expanded their curriculum as more children stayed for longer periods. The public high school emerged as an extension of the elementary schools in its offerings of English, mathematics, modern language, history, science, and of course, the ubiquitous Latin. With its origins in the common schools, the public high school was responsible for both preparing students for 'life' and collegiate studies (Krug, 1972).

By the 1890s the uncontrolled growth had created a sense of uneasiness among public school officials and of discontinuity between the high schools and the colleges which admitted their students. It also reflected major structural changes in late nineteenth-century America. A notable example was the growing professionalization of American life and the prominence of the expert whose competence and authority was based on training gained in the newly-emerging universities. These institutions, unlike the colonial and early republican colleges, stressed research and scientific knowledge over character. The largeness and discipline of mind lauded by the 1828 Yale Report was no longer adequate for a rapidly industrializing scientific and urban nation. The objective conditions giving rise to a seemingly endless procession of new careers were supported by Darwinism with its emphasis on disciplined inquiry and the use of scientific method to establish demonstrable facts. Once higher learning was linked to economic development and, ultimately, international power, the university with its commitment to research and technical training moved to the center of the American society. Once deemed essential for both personal success as career-making institutions and for national security as the source of technical experts and knowledge, the university in its relationship to the institutions that fed it became the subject of national concern beginning in the 1880s. The principal forums for the debate and resolution were the annual meetings of the National Education Association (NEA) and its National Council of Education (NCE). During the 1880s and 1990s, the problem occupied the attention of leading university presidents and professors as well as the chief spokesmen of the schools (Bledstein, 1976).

From Common School to Public High School

As Harvard University President Charles W. Eliot put it in an address at the 1890 conference of the National Educational Association, there was between the common schools and the colleges 'a very wide gap imperfectly bridged by a few public high schools, endowed academies, college preparatory departments and private schools, which conform to no common standards and are under no unifying control' (Eliot, 1909, p. 197). The crux of the problem and the most obvious sign of the gap lay in the issue of articulation, that is, the separation between what secondary institutions undertook in preparing students for admission to colleges and universities and what those institutions expected of their entering students. The issue of articulation had much exercised the representatives of secondary schools and colleges at the NEA during the 1880s. While the lack of a 'unifying control' might suggest that secondary schools were largely to blame for the chaos in the course of studies, such generally was not the case. If students wished to enter a particular college, they had to complete 'a specific course of study, which the schools were expected to supply. Consequently, depending on the often detailed requirements of the colleges, the school's course of studies was straitjacketed. Where colleges were strong and demanding, as for example with Northeastern private institutions and Midwestern universities, college entrance requirements affected secondary schools well beyond what one might have assumed, given the small numbers of students who were college bound. What was needed was a balance between the requirements of the colleges for adequately prepared matriculants and the freedom for the secondary schools — increasingly public — to develop courses of studies for the great majority of students who had no interest in post-secondary education.

Acting on a resolution of the National Council of Education in 1891, a group of college and secondary school representatives met at the 1892 NEA annual conference to consider the problem of uniform college entrance requirements (Sizer, 1964; NEA, 1963). On the urging of President Eliot, the meeting recommended the establishment of a representative committee to consult with experts in each subject and to make a formal report to the NCE. Chaired by Eliot, the Committee on Secondary School Studies (the Committee of Ten) held a series of conferences in December 1892. The final report was completed on December 4, 1893.

The Report, by starting with a circumscribed number of subjects to be considered at the conferences, limited the reorganized college preparatory curriculum to nine general areas: Latin; Greek; English; other modern languages; mathematics; physics, astronomy, and chemistry; natural history (biology, including botany, zoology and physiology); history, civil government and political economy; and geography (physical geography, geology, and meteorology).

Although the Report adhered to the tenets of mental discipline and accepted the dominance of classical studies and mathematics, it did offer a prominent and secure place for such modern studies as History, English, French, German and the natural sciences in the secondary schools. New methods of scientific inquiry in the form of laboratories and historical investigation of a restricted topic were advocated. Finally, the Report came down on the side of new subjects by accepting their power to achieve mental discipline (Kolesnik, 1958).

The Report, which gained widespread acceptance during the 1890s, was an effective response to the growing significance of secondary education as a common experience for American youth, replacing apprenticeship and other forms of child labor as preparation for the world of work. It also recognized the professionalization of American life, with the rise of the university-trained expert whose disciplined intelligence was essential for social as well as individual security. Moreover, by making the college-preparatory course in the public high schools more uniform, the Report closed the gap between them and the colleges and allowed for the development of other courses of study. It was the high tide of high school and college operation in setting curricular objectives.

By 1910, the National Education Association was the domain of public school administrators who were increasingly restive under what they perceived to be college control of the secondary school curriculum. Beginning in 1910, with the Committee on the Articulation of High School and College, secondary school administrators lobbied for a high school that would allow students to pursue diverse interests, that would prepare intelligent, progressive citizens, and that would provide specific training as well as general education. The assertion of independence was related to the growth of the public secondary sector in the quarter century following the Report of the Committee of Ten. In 1893, there were 59,000 high school graduates; in 1910,

156,000; and in 1920, 311,000. By 1920, high school graduates represented 16.8 per cent of the population of seventeen-year-olds. Now a mass system, secondary schools saw their reference group as other public schools and not the universities (*Statistical History*, 1965, H223–33).

The Commission on the Reorganization of Secondary Education, formed in 1913, represented a transformation from the conditions that had given birth to the Committee of Ten. Dominated by schoolmen and professors of Education, the Commission compressed the old nine curricular areas into six: Latin and Greek; English; other modern languages; mathematics; social sciences; and sciences. Another ten that the Committee considered were: the organization and administration of secondary education; agriculture; business education; household arts; industrial arts; music; physical education; vocational guidance; art education; and the articulation of high school and college. The committee members were, in the main, school administrators and educational specialists (Wesley, 1957, pp. 75–8, 198–299).

In *The Cardinal Principles of Secondary Education* (1918), the Commission asserted its main objectives to be: health; command of fundamental processes; worthy home-membership; vocation; citizenship; worthy use of leisure; and ethical character. The expansive purposes of secondary schooling met the objective conditions of the early twentieth century when adolescent school attendance became the norm. Activities and experiences that had originally been seen as part of life-long education and socialization were now included as part of the school's responsibility. Indeed, the term 'secondary education' reflected the understanding that the school had very broad socialization functions (NEA Report, 1918).

The expanded responsibility was and would be matched by a growing range of services and activities. The new responsibilities also moved pedagogy away from concern for moral and cognitive development and social integration to the problems of personal fulfillment and self-realization. Thus, secondary school and college were apparently moving away from each other; however, social and educational changes in the period 1920–1940 would reconnect them (Krug, 1972; Rudolph, 1962).

The interwar years witnessed a notable shift in immigration. After the passage of stringent quotas in the Immigration Act of 1924, the annual number of immigrants in the late 1920s averaged approximately 287,000, mainly because Canada and Latin American countries were not included in the quota system. During the entire 1930s slightly over half a million immigrants were admitted. The American population grew steadily during the two decades from 106 million in 1920 to 132 million in 1940. Rural population reached its maximum in 1940 at 57 million while urban population soared from 54 million in 1920 to 74 million in 1940. The growing gap between rural and urban population was highlighted by the changes in 'gainful workers'. Census statistics indicate that farm employment averaged around 11 million between 1900 and 1930 while non-farm employment rose from 18 million in 1900 to 38 million by 1930. By 1940, even with the disaster of the Depression.

non-farm employment had reached 42 million, with farm employment dropping to nine. Thus the 1930s showed only a 3.2 million growth in gainful workers that represented a gain of 4.7 million in non-farm workers and a loss of 1.5 in farm workers (*Statistical History*, 1965, C88–114, A1–3, A195–209, D36–45, D57–71).

Net loss from the farms averaged 700,000 annually in the 1920s and nearly 400,000 in the 1930s. Part of this substantial loss was made of Blacks who began leaving the South Atlantic and East South Central states in the 1880s and then the West South Central states in the 1890s for the Middle Atlantic and East North Central states and later for California. The massive movement of the black population after 1940 would radically transform American society and transfer many of the problems associated with racism, discrimination and rural poverty to the urban north (Statistical History, 1965, C74–9 and C25–73).

As suggested above, the early 1920s saw the appearance of virulent anti-semitism, anti-Catholicism, zenophobia, anti-radicalism, Anglo-Saxonism and the triumph of American nativism in the passage of the 1924 Immigration Act which shut the door to unrestricted immigration (Higham, 1963). It is not surprising that principal statements on education emphasized personal growth and adjustment, vocationalism and principles of inquiry. The political thrust of Jefferson's six objectives of primary education and the ideas of power and mastery were replaced by conflicting images that promised personal fulfillment and happy participation in family and community while promoting the processes of inquiry and the appeal to reason. In the face of hostile attitudes toward any dissent, the educators retreated to platitudes about personal growth and process in place of substance.

An interesting example of the narrowing of educational objectives is the statements issued by the Educational Policies Commission (EPC) beginning in 1938. The EPC was established jointly by the National Education Association and the American Association of School Administrators in 1935 'to prepare, publish, and disseminate, from time to time, statements of proposed policy regarding the conduct of educators in the United States, and the international relationships of American education'. The Commission had ten members and over a thousand consultants. Unlike the Committee of Ten which had emphasized the evolution of policies from discussion by elite members, the EPC was expected to make recommendations upon the basis of careful research and widespread survey of fact and opinion (Wesley, 1957; West, 1980, pp. 11–12).

In *The Purposes of Education in American Democracy* (1938), the Commission asserted that 'the general end of education in America at the present is the fullest possible development of the individual within the framework of our present industrialized democratic society'. Although it recognized that no definite statement of objectives was possible, the Commission believed that a general statement of educational objectives was desirable. The Commission subsequently proposed four groups of objectives dealing with 'a description of the educated *person*; of the educated *member of the family and community group*; of the educated *producer or consumer*; [and] of the educated *citizen'*; that is, objectives of self-realization, human relationship, economic efficiency and civic responsibility (Educational Policies Commission, 1938).

Mass High Schooling for a Democratic Vision

This new expanded list of objectives reflected both changes internal in schooling and external to it in the society. Formal education in the United States had undergone a major transformation during the interwar decades. First, when the Commission on the Reorganization of Secondary Education issued its 1918 report, secondary schooling had become a mass institution. In 1920, the 311,266 high school graduates were 16.8 per cent of the seventeen-year-old population. By 1938, 1,120,079 were 45.6 per cent. Even the Depression had failed to stop the growth. However, the growth in high school graduates did not merely mean that nearly half of the seventeen-year-olds were completing some kind of high school program. Indeed, one of the pressures that inspired the Committee of Ten was the need to balance the college entrance requirements with the fact that only a minority of students aspired to higher education. In 1918, the 440,000 students in colleges and universities represented 6 per cent of the 18- to 21-year-old population; in 1938, the 1,350,000 represented 13.96 per cent. Thus, higher education was rapidly becoming mass education during the 1930s. In 1918, 42,000 degrees were conferred; in 1938, 189,000 (*Statistical History*, 1965, H316–326 and H327–338).

The high school, the inheritor of the classical and modern programs, increasingly became an institution that combined college preparatory courses and increasingly diverse offerings that did not bar one from post-secondary education. In brief, high school was now the common experience of all youth, high school graduation soon to be the majority experience, and post-secondary study widely available. Corresponding changes were occurring in higher education with the growth of community colleges and the diversification of programs at degree-granting institutions. The estrangement of secondary school and college was softened not by a conscious effort at articulation but by the democratization of higher education.

The decades following World War II witnessed the completion of the diversification of the secondary school, with high school graduates representing 62.3 per cent of the population's seventeen-year-olds in 1956 (*Statistical History*, 1965, A223–33 and H327–38). At the same time, enrolment in institutions of higher education represented 30 per cent of the 18- to 21-year-old population. The United States seemed locked into an ever expanding educational enterprise with new opportunities at the secondary and post-secondary levels. A mature industrial power with a rising standard of living, and a world leader in science and technology, the nation seemed poised on a period of individual fulfillment and gratification. In spite of problems of the

Cold War and domestic racism, economic energy and human resources seemed adequate for continued growth, and the schools were still considered adequate means of meeting individual and national goals. A significant 1961 EPC report, *The Central Purpose of American Education*, attempted to establish 'a principle which will enable the school to identify its necessary and appropriate contributions to individual development and the needs of society'. Reaffirming the objectives set forth in *The Cardinal Principles of Secondary Education* in 1918 and in its *Purposes of Education in American Democracy* in 1938, the Educational Policies Commission asserted that, because the cultivated powers of the free mind were always basic in achieving freedom, the central purpose of the school was to develop the rational potentials of its students. Rational powers made all other human activities possible and effective (NEA *Journal*, 1961, pp. 13–16).

Another excellent example of the continuing assertion by public school officials of their ability to meet the diverse expectations of American society is found in the work of the NEA's Project on the Instructional Programs of Public Schools established in 1959. The National Committee was appointed at a time when the public schools, particularly secondary schools, were being criticized for their alleged failure to produce educated citizens and efficient and skilled contributors to national growth and the economy. Its 1963 report, *Education in a Changing Society*, proclaimed again the objectives of education commonplace since *The Cardinal Principles of Secondary Education*. In general, such values as respect for the worth and dignity of every individual, faith in everyone's ability to make rational decisions, shared responsibility for the common good, moral and spiritual values, emotional health, freedom to teach and excellence for all, represented goods that few would have rejected. The more detailed set of recommendations or 'decision areas', which followed upon consideration of what the National Committee believed to be major forces and trends transforming American society and inevitably the schools, were worded to elicit widespread acceptance. Recommendations calling for opportunities for developing individual potentiality; the provision for a common fund of knowledge, values and skills (an impressive list of competences to be acquired); attention to the problems of youth unemployment and juvenile delinquency; teaching about controversial issues and communism; and the provision for a comprehensive program of studies were generous and perhaps courageous pronouncements in 1963 (NEA, 1963).

The decision areas included consideration of organized content, which called for the organization of the curriculum to insure that students may progress, from early to later years, toward an increasingly mature utilization and organization of their knowledge and to help learners see that interrelationships and achievement of unity from the diversity of knowledge is basic to any organization of control (NEA, 1963). This was certainly in harmony with the basic views of those advocating the integration of separate disciplines by personal synthesis. The one area that the report directly avoided was the issue of race and racial separation. The many statements on individual needs and excellence for all can be read as advocating equal education for all without confronting the issue of overt discrimination.

It was in the final decision-area, organizing the school and the classroom, that the particular characteristic of major reports since 1918 was fully display-ed. The National Committee recommended that 'the vertical organization of the school should provide for the continuous, unbroken, upward progression of all learners, with due recognition of the wide variability among learners in every aspect of their development' (NEA, 1963). Many years ago, Max Ler-ner, the author of *America as a Civilization*, was asked to sum up the national and individual aspiration in a single word (Lerner, 1957). His response was 'access'. When access and individualism are joined in a world view, then the fate of American public schools makes sense. The genius of American life was the assumption of an apparently open-ended universe in which economic goods and their enjoyment were limited only by human effort. Related to this was a thorough going democratic sensibility that rejected deference and social class distinctions. Such an outlook was hardly congenial to distinctions on the bases of education, ascent and manners.

Limitations of Democracy

Schools were valued because they offered two services (Cremin, 1961). First, as all Americans came to value a middle class family life (that is, one in which the father's income enabled his wife and minor children to remain out of the workforce), extended schooling became a convenient and guarded place to care for adolescents. In the school, children and youth were supervised and educated by certificated teachers and other school personnel. The expanding list of educational objectives all testify to the enlarging scope of responsibility given the schools. As a universal experience, the high school was expected to provide a worthwhile educational experience that would not damage indi-vidual self-esteem. An image of secondary education as youth care made all the talk about the 'teaching of skills ... ways of creative and disciplined thinking ... fundamental understanding of the humanities and the arts, the social sciences, and mathematics ... appreciation of and discriminating taste in literature, music, and the visual arts' hollow rhetoric (NEA, 1963, p. 136).

The second consideration was the belief that education ought to be useful. As long as the mass of the populace received only a primary education, the utility of the three Rs and few other subjects hardly raised any problems. As long as higher education was not connected in any tight way with economic success and as long as energy and intelligence counted for more than creden-tials, the relationship between secondary schools, colleges and careers re-mained obscured. The rise of the university-trained expert moved American higher education to the center of the society and created a crisis in secondary-college relations by the 1880s. The work of the Committee of Ten helped to standardize university expectations of secondary school preparation and also enabled the schools to develop courses of studies for the vast majority of non-matriculating students. In brief, the high school then undertook college preparatory work in a form and content that was acceptable to most universities while developing more diversified programs, organizing more extracurricular activities, and offering more services to its students. Even for non-college preparatory students, the high school was a good place for their intellectual, social and emotional development. It provided a moratorium between childhood and the appropriate time for entering a career and marriage.

The transformation of higher education into mass education beginning in the 1930s created similar problems in the university (US President's Commission on Higher Education, 1948). The college since the late nineteenth century provided a general or liberal education for students whose life expectations made it socially or occupationally useful, trained others for specific professions, and prepared a small minority for graduate studies and scholarship. After World War II, colleges and universities increasingly offered an extended moratorium for young adults and, of course, promises of improved career changes.

Thus, the notion of what was useful could vary remarkably — from typing and auto mechanics to medicine — in terms of having knowledge and skills or of having a credential, e.g., a high school diploma, that would give one a chance at a job. Americans were never sure which kind of utility counted for more, and whether for most jobs a proxy in the form of a credential was just as adequate as the knowledge and skills it represented. It is arguable that American parents and students came to accept the proxy as the end of schooling.

Returning to Max Lerner, we can extend his characterization to include utility with all the definitional and social problems associated with its meaning in an educational context. Historians and educational critics have often liked American educational problems to its unremitting capitalism. While capitalism colored many American views of all their social institutions and their ways of life, that economic system functioned within a democratic polity celebrating individualism and ego-centricism as a political ideal. Consequently, the schools, and particularly those for youth, were expected to cater to all the interests of all students. As long as the realities of the international market and politics did not impinge on these values as expressed in the common school and its extensions, namely, the high school and mass post-secondary education, the institutions could develop according to the demands of a rapidly enlarging clientele.

The 1880s and the 1950s were two significant junctures when political and economic realities touched the schools. The 1880s crisis was much more easily handled. The technological and scientific advances were still limited to a few nations, and the required improvement in education and in the production of trained experts to compete in that arena were manageable. The 1950s and 1960s were years in which a new international economic, political and social order was being born and conventional beliefs about life and behavior were challenged at home (Coleman *et al.*, 1966; Jencks *et al.*, 1972).

The confident assertions in *Education in a Changing Society* were published on the edge of the political calamities of Vietnam, assassinations, urban race riots and widespread student unrest on college and university campuses. A new wave of educational critics moved from attacks on the content and method of public education to questions of the inherent value of schooling itself (Illich, 1971; Reimer, 1972; Bereiter, 1974). Although the public never accepted the idea of 'deschooling society', the old healthy confidence in schooling ability to solve social and economic problems received a blow from which it has not yet recovered. Perhaps it never will.

Notes

1   Paul Boyer (1978) has traced a series of reforms from tract societies and Sunday schools to the YMCA, Charity Organization Society and environmentalism. The failure or partial success of each effort set the stage for the next more ambitious reform.
2   For an able discussion of Plato's views on philosopher-ruler, see Natalie Harris Bluestone (1987).
3   As Stephen Skowronek (1982) succinctly put it: 'A highly developed democratic politics without a concentrated governing capacity made early America the great anomaly among Western states'.

Bibliography

AHLSTROM, S.E. (1972) *A Religious History of the American People*, New Haven: Yale University Press.

ADAMSON, J.W. (1905) *Pioneers of Modern Education in the Seventeenth Century*, Cambridge: Cambridge University Press.

BAILYN, B. (1960) *Education in the Forming of American Society*, Chapel Hill: University of North Carolina Press.

BENSON, L. (1964) *The Concept of Jacksonian Democracy: New York as a Test Case*, New York: Atheneum.

BEREITER, C. (1974) *Must We Educate?* Englewood Cliffs, NJ: Prentice Hall.

BLEDSTEIN, B.J. (1976) *The Culture of Professionalism: The Middle Class and the Development of Higher Education in America*, New York: Norton.

BLUESTONE, N.H. (1987) *Women and the Ideal Society: Plato's 'Republic' and Modern Myths of Gender*, Amherst: University of Massachusetts Press.

BOLGAR, R.R. (1954) *The Classical Heritage and its Beneficiaries*, Cambridge: Cambridge University Press.

BOYER, P. (1978) *Urban Masses and Moral Order in America, 1820–1920*, Cambridge, MA: Harvard University Press.

CASSIRER, E. (1963) *The Question of Jean Jacques Rousseau*, Bloomington: Indiana University Press.

CASSIRER, E. (1963) *Rousseau, Kant and Goethe*, New York: Harper and Torchbooks.

CREMIN, L. (Ed.) (1957) *The Republic and the School: Horace Mann on the Education of Free Men*, New York: Teachers College Press.

CREMIN, L. (1961) *The Transformation of the School: Progressivism in Education of Free Men*, New York: Teachers College Press.

CREMIN, L. (1961) *The Transformation of the School: Progressivism in American Education, 1876–1957*, New York: Knopf.

COLEMAN, J.S. et al. (1966) *Equality of Educational Opportunity*, Washington, DC: US Dept. of Health, Education and Welfare.

DUNKEL, H.B. (1969) *Herbart and Education*, New York: Random House.

ELIOT, C.W. (1909) *Educational Reform: Essays and Addresses*, New York: The Century.

GAY, P. (Ed.) (1964) *John Locke on Education*, New York: Teachers College Press.

GUTEK, G.L. (1968) *Pestalozzi and Education*, New York: Random House.

HIGHAM, J. (1963) *Strangers in the Land: Patterns of American Nativism*, New York: Atheneum.

HOFSTADTER, R. and SMITH, W. (Eds) (1961) *American Higher Education: A Documentary History. Vol. I.*, Chicago: University of Chicago Press.

ILLICH, I. (1971) *Deschooling Society*, New York: Harper Torchbooks.

JENCKS, C. et al. (1972) *Inequality: A Reassessment of the Effects of Family and Schooling in America*, New York: Basic Books.

JONES, G.S. (1971) *Outcast London: A Study in the Relationship Between Classes in Victorian Society*, Oxford: Oxford University Press.

JONES, M.G. (1938) *The Charity School Movement: A Study of Eighteenth Century Puritanism*, Cambridge: Cambridge University Press.

KATZ, M.B. (1983) *Poverty and Policy in American History*, New York: Academic Press.

KOLESNIK, W.B. (1958) *Mental Discipline in Modern Education*, Madison: University of Wisconsin Press.

KRUG, E.A. (1972) *The Shaping of the American High School, 1920–1941*, Madison: University of Wisconsin Press.

LAQUEUR, T. (1976) *Religion and Respectability: Sunday School and Working Class Culture, 1780–1850*, New Haven: Yale University Press.

LERNER, M. (1957) *America as a Civilization: Life and Thought in the United States Today*, (2 vols.), New York: Simon and Schuster.

MARROU, H.I. (1956) *A History of Education in Antiquity*, New York: Sheed and Ward.

MIDDLEKAUFF, R. (1963) *Ancients and Axioms: Secondary Education in Eighteenth Century New England*, New Haven: Yale University Press.

NATIONAL EDUCATION ASSOCIATION (USA) (1918) *The Cardinal Principles of Secondary Education*, Washington, DC: Government Printing Office.

NATIONAL EDUCATION ASSOCIATION (USA) (1938) *The Purposes of Education in American Democracy*, Washington, DC: National Education Association.

NATIONAL EDUCATION ASSOCIATION (USA) (1963) *Education in a Changing Society*, Washington, DC: National Education Society.

NEA *Journal* (1961) 'The central purpose of American education', pp. 13–16.

PETERSON, M.D. (1960) *The Jefferson Image in the American mind*, New York: Oxford University Press.

PIAGET, J. (Ed.) (1967) *John Amos Comenius on Education*, New York: Teachers College Press.

POLLARD, H.M. (1956) *Pioneers of Popular Education, 1760–1850*, London: John Murray.

REIMER, E. (1972) *School is Dead: Alternatives in Education*, Garden City: Anchor Books.

SILVER, H. (1965) *The Concept of Popular Education: A Study of Ideas and Social Movements in the Early Nineteeth Century*, London: MacGibbon and Kee.

SIZER, T.R. (Ed.) (1964) *The Age of the Academics*, New York: Teacher College Press.

SIZER, T.R. (1964) *Secondary Schools at the Turn of the Century*, New Haven: Yale University Press.

SKOWRONEK, S. (1982) *Building a New American State: The Expansion of National Administrative Capacities, 1877–1920*, Cambridge: Cambridge University Press.

THE STATISTICAL HISTORY OF THE UNITED STATES FROM COLONIAL TIMES TO THE PRESENT (1965) Stanford, CT: Fairfield Publishers. Series Z 1–19, A 1–3, and C 88–155 General Notes.

US PRESIDENT'S COMMISSION ON HIGHER EDUCATION (1948) *Higher Education for American Democracy: A Report*, (6 vols.), New York: Harper and Brothers.

WESLEY, E.B. (1957) *NEA: The First Hundred Years: The Building of the Teaching Profession*, New York: Harper and Brothers.

WEST, A.M. (1980) *The National Education Association: The Power Base for Education*, New York: Free Press.

II
The School and Its Tasks

INTRODUCTION

An institution deliberately established by society for its purposes, the school cannot avoid pressures to conform to societal expectations. Conformity to a particular expectation will certainly be required where consensus results in the formal adoption of an expected school aim by way of public law or policy. However, few expectations get institutionally adopted as aims in this way. More often, they get espoused by authoritative leaders or bodies and thus generate some degree of acceptability; somehow they influence professional and common thinking and affect school practices. In recent years, for good or for bad, expertise or leadership in various areas of endeavor, education included, has elicited skeptical reaction from the public; differences among lay groups and among experts themselves have deepened the uncertainty about societal expectations and thus about the aims that schools are meant to pursue. In light of the differences, the question arises: How are educators and school systems to arrive at aims which will provide unequivocal direction for the operation of schools and school systems?

Reacting against the current predisposition to defer unquestioningly to the public pulse, Romulo Magsino and John Long suggest that philosophical tradition remains a valuable discipline which offers reasoned strategies for determining the aims of schooling. In advocating the use of the synthetic philosophic approach, they start with the views of Aristotle and other philosophers who spoke of the intrinsic good, particularly happiness, as the controlling guide to human conduct and endeavors. They argue that schooling can contribute to the attainment of such good by promoting individual rationality. Every person needs this capacity to pursue varied specific goods in a way that would facilitate not only one's personal happiness but also that of society as a whole. Suggesting a notion of rationality broader than what is generally advocated and defended in philosophical and educational literature, they briefly trace the ramifications of their views for the curriculum, the issue of socialization, and the question of indoctrination in public and private religious schools.

Rationality, however, has usually been overshadowed by education as an aim of schooling. In educational as well as philosophical literature, it is generally assumed that schools are, first and foremost, an educational institution, that is, one which educates. A further automatic assumption made is that education is an intrinsic good, one which should be thought of not in terms of instrumental value or use but of enjoyment for its own sake. In his chapter, Harold Entwistle challenges this assumption. On the contrary, he argues, education is better conceived in terms of its instrumental value. To aim at education as primarily an intrinsic good is to divorce it from the ordinary affairs of living and thus to depreciate its value. Though he warns his readers about the dire consequences of unbridled, uncritical instrumentalism or utilitarian orientation, he nonetheless insists that the instrumental benefits of liberal education are real and that ways have to be found to make it relevant.

Though education and development of rationality are popularly advocated in both philosophic and educational literature, increasing focus on autonomy as an aim of schooling is evident. In her chapter, Evelina Orteza y Miranda argues the case for stressing autonomy. Locating it in the notion of the self, she delineates its relationship with other significant notions such as rationality, authenticity, freedom, and education. She recognizes their intricate relationships and the claims that these concepts have in schooling. Nevertheless, she argues that autonomy remains a crucial school concern not only because of pedagogical considerations but also because of the learners' moral claim: That they have the moral right to pursue their goals in life and to become what they want to become. In arguing thus, Orteza y Miranda highlights individual integrity in the midst of pressing demands from society.

Rationality, education, and autonomy are only some of the more compelling aims advocated in educational and common discourse. Whether they are mutually exclusive, whether they have common components for implementation in school practices, and whether they will prove satisfactory enough for the general public are questions which educators have to wrestle with inevitably.

4   Toward the Intrinsic Good: Happiness, Rationality and Schooling

Romulo F. Magsino and John C. Long

Taking Surveys with a Grain of Salt

Findings on public expectations of schools appear unequivocal. They show that schools are expected primarily to promote the preparation of young people for gainful occupation. Livingstone and Hart (1987) recount Canadian survey results showing consistently over the years that job preparation has ranked first among a number of identified school aims. In the United States, the findings are equally unambiguous. In their account of the 21st Annual Gallup Poll of public attitudes toward public schools, Elam and Gallup (1989) observed that: 'The pragmatic bent of the American mind is immediately apparent in their responses' (p. 48). In their view, this bent is evident in the respondents' answer to the following question: 'People have different reasons why they want their children to get an education. What are the chief reasons that come to your mind?' Thirty-three per cent (34 per cent in 1986) identified *job opportunities/better jobs* as a chief reason. Indeed, the next two reasons offered conveyed a markedly materialistic and individualistic orientation: preparation for life, better life (25 per cent); and financial security, economic stability (15 per cent). Further, many other reasons had the same character: to get better-paying jobs, for specialized training/profession, to become self-sufficient, for better/easier life than that of parents, and the like. The less materialistic, less individualistic reasons given are decidedly secondary. Offered as reasons by only small percentages of respondents were the following: more knowledge (9 per cent); teaches a person to think/learn/understand (6 per cent); to become better citizens (5 per cent); to contribute to society (4 per cent); to develop basic individual values (1 per cent); to develop an understanding and appreciation of culture (1 per cent); and to develop critical thinking skills (1 per cent).

Undoubtedly, the precision and clarity of these findings may be questioned. Close analysis of the itemized answers will reveal much overlapping among the reasons given. Nonetheless, for the empirically-minded, such analysis will sound no more than mischievous hair-splitting. After all, the weight of preference for certain aims of schooling is considerable. It would appear, if policy makers and administrators are to follow the wishes of the tax-paying public, that concerted and unequivocal efforts toward job preparation of young people should be undertaken by school systems.

Despite the decisiveness of survey findings, particularly on public expectations of the school, their implications for educational policy-making should be handled with caution. We need to understand the problems associated with basing societal policies and educational administrative arrangements on the public pulse exhibited in polling results. The first problem is intimated by this question: Should the direction of educational policies by shaped by the wishes of one-third of the respondents or, by extrapolation, one-third of the population represented by the respondents? The thrust of this question should be obvious. Public opinion, or the opinion of any given sector of society, is hardly ever unanimous. Even a homogeneous sector may not exhibit consensus on contentious issues within the society at large. Given the number of varied sectors interested in and affected by such issues, it is doubtful that anything close to consensus can be achieved.

However, though the socio-political problem of attaining consensus is real enough, it is resolvable through established mechanisms in a democratic society such as ours. Through elections, in which a contentious issue is dealt with as an element in party platforms; through referenda; or through legislative action based on a government's reading of both public sentiment and the public interest, resolution of festering questions may be reached. Yet, neither a favorable vote or referendum nor a survey of public opinion establishes the correctness or rightness of a policy decision. No matter how strongly held, a given public opinion, sentiment or standpoint may well be wrong. This point becomes evident when we realize that many atrocities and discriminatory practices and policies in different societies in the past, as well as the present, were derived from perceived or expressed public approval or desire. The second problem in basing policy decisions on survey results is that even decisive findings reflecting consensus may not provide the appropriate basis for determining what is right or wrong, good or bad, worthwhile or worthless. In the educational context, such findings may not serve as sound justification and grounding for policy making and administrative arrangements. How, then, do we arrive at the justification or grounding for educational policies and arrangements? Substantively, what aims should schools pursue?

The present chapter intends to demonstrate a traditional philosophical strategy which, frequently buried under the contemporary predominance of linguistic analysis and empiricistic thinking, may still prove its usefulness in ascertaining the aim(s) of schooling. In demonstrating this strategy, the chapter starts with a basic philosophical question: What ultimate value(s) should we humans aim at? Going against the tendency to seek answers by asking everyone or some representative respondents as if consensus (if possible at all) could provide the correct answer, this chapter will attempt to show that reflection on certain philosophical questions may lead to a defensible formulation of aims for schools. This reflection leads to the conclusion that determination of the primary responsibility of schools requires a consideration of basic intrinsic goods or values for individuals and society. The chapter will go on to demonstrate that attainment of such goods compels the school, as a societal instrument, to aim at rationality development on the part of the young. Finally, it traces the implications of its contentions for educational policies on a number of debatable issues such as the curriculum, indoctrination versus socialization, and religious orientation in schools.

Sovereignty of the Good as an Educational Imperative

Decades ago, a prominent philosopher, Jacques Maritain (1943), pointed to a number of unfortunate errors hampering educational efforts during his time. First among these was an apparent disregard of ends or goals in favor of educational means. He saw educational weaknesses exhibited, among others, by an attachment to the 'perfection of our modern educational means and methods and our failure to bend them toward the end' (p. 3). 'The child', he said, 'is so well tested and observed, his needs so well detailed, his psychology so clearly cut out, the methods for making it easy for him everywhere so perfected, that the end of all these commmendable improvements runs the risk of being forgotten or disregarded' (*ibid.*).

Whether the child and teaching methodology have been studied enough is, of course, debatable. Nonetheless, the thrust of Maritain's comments is unexceptionable. Insofar as schools and educational systems are a societal creation, their deliberate development and operation depend on human intents and purposes. The latter provide the rationale for or point to the educational institution — its organization, structures and processes at various levels. Consider the process of selecting a method or strategy of teaching. Clearly, researchers and practitioners have come up with a welter of methods and strategies, including those deriving from B.F. Skinner's operant conditioning. Admittedly, Skinnerian strategies can be very effective in promoting learning. Why then do we not extensively employ them? The answer is, at least partly, that we aim in democratic societies at encouraging the growth of thinking, self-determining humans rather than mindless, manipulable beings into which conditioning molds children. Without such an aim as this, not only do we lack guidelines for the selection of teaching methods; but also the 'art (of teaching or educating) loses its practicality' and 'its vital efficiency is replaced by a process of infinite multiplication' of discrete, even contradictory, means (Maritain, 1943, p. 3).

The perceived failure of educational systems have fortunately led to current re-examination of schooling and its aims (e.g., in the United States, by the National Commission on Excellence in Education, 1983; in Canada, by Radwanski, 1988 and the British Columbia Royal Commission on Education,

1988). Thus, in urging the government to undertake a complete overhaul of schools in the province of Ontario, Radwanski (1988) described the present system as one 'with no purpose' and 'running empty'. Very much like the Royal Commission in British Columbia, he called for a common high school curriculum based on liberal studies that would give everyone the skills to think independently and adapt to rapidly changing, technology-based society. Ironically, *Nation at Risk*, the report of the (US) National Commission on Excellence in Education, charted a different direction. It saw the mission of schools in terms of service to national interest: a rejuvenated economy for dominance in the international marketplace; a technological might for military security; and the social and political integration of immigrants for national harmony. Is there any way to determine which direction or goals are appropriate for schools and educational systems?

Traditional philosophy offers the possibility of resolving this question. Its branch, known as *axiology* — the study of value or the good — addresses the principles or criteria for determining the worthwhileness (or lack of it) of objects or states of affairs. It is expected that the worth or value of the object or state of affairs will serve as a guide for determining the rightness of human judgments and conduct associated with or affecting them. This expectation assumes that, in the nature of things, humans are purposive creatures pursuing goods or values of varying immediacy: Some are immediate, others are long-range. Humans also are thought to seek goods of varying importance. Some are called *intrinsic* goods, things or conditions that are desirable in themselves; others, known as *extrinsic* or *instrumental* goods, are desirable for the sake of some other goods to which they serve as means. In the hierarchy of goods, the intrinsic is regarded as superior to the extrinsic or instrumental. The logic of the hierarchy is illustrated in the case of Mary, an (any) adolescent wanting to make sense of someone's insistence that she should remain in school against her inclination. The strategy for an argument to persuade her to stay in school involves the following series of claims:

Remaining in school is good for Mary because it will give her knowledge and skills;

Having knowledge and skills is good for her because it will give her a job later;

A job is good for her because it will give her money;

Having money is good for her because it will enable her to buy whatever she wants;

Being able to buy what she wants is good for her because it will make her happy;

Being happy is good for her because . . . ?

In the series above, presuming for the sake of argument that each element is at least arguable, it is clear that only the last, being happy (contented, having fun, of feeling prestigious ...) may be categorized as intrinsically good. Being happy (contented, satisfied, and the like) is intrinsically good in the sense that it is desired in itself. Of course, this is not to say that it is the only condition that is intrinsically good. More will be said about this at a later point. For now, it is equally evident that the justification for each condition or thing is unidirectionally dependent on something else which points ultimately to some intrinsic good. It is in this sense that intrinsic goods control, determine or make meaningful our claimed instrumental goods.

Using the hierarchy of intrinsic and instrumental goods, we may evaluate more fully the public's expectation of schools as revealed in the Gallup Poll. The public view may reasonably be regarded as short-sighted in that the predominant number of respondents saw nothing beyond the merely instrumental, and that most of the reasons given for sending their children to school are largely in that category. In fairness to the public view, however, it must be noted that some volunteered expectations can be characterized as aiming at intrinsic goods. This is clearly so for about 1 per cent of the respondents who expected schools to promote happy (or happier) lives. This is not so clear with respect to about 25 per cent who saw schools as providing children with preparation for (better) life. In our materialistic society, this preparation for better life is usually associated with providing for jobs or financial security, so that this response may also be regarded as instrumentalist in character. Nonetheless, this response may in fact capture both the instrumental and intrinsic expectations of school: Preparation implies providing for the means toward a better (i.e., happier) life. Again, in fairness to the public view, we may attribute its apparent short-sightedness not to the respondents but to the question, which may be interpreted as asking for short-term or long-term aims.

In any case, reading the public mind need not preoccupy us. What needs to be noted is that, in defence of the public view, it can plausibly be argued that the respondents were simply being pragmatic or commonsensical (or perhaps philosophically sophisticated without knowing it!) in giving instrumentalist answers. In the first place, the notion of the good, or even of the happy life, is an exceedingly slippery one. Why give an answer that does not convey precise meaning? In the second place, why identify an expectation which schools are quite unlikely to achieve?

The problem of intrinsic goods and the place that happiness occupies amongst them pierces deep into the heart of the traditional study of values. A number of philosophers (e.g., Ackerman, 1980; Dworkin, 1985; Rawls, 1971) have deliberately eschewed any strong appeal to the notion of the good in formulating and justifying their ethical principles. But, as Galston (1980 and 1986) insists, insofar as principles are intended to guide human conduct, they must relate to intelligible motives for action. That is, they must 'invoke some conception of the good as the end of action — happiness, perfection, moral freedom, or the like' (1986, p. 92). Though he is disturbed by an apparent widespread belief that principles need not be founded on some view of the good, fortunately the traditional recognition of the inevitable linkage between goods, on one hand, and human principles of conduct, on the other hand, has not been dispelled. In particular, examination of happiness as an intrinsic human good abounds (Barrow, 1981; McGill, 1967; Telfer, 1980; Uyl and Machan, 1983).

As an undisputed intrinsic good, happiness has traditionally attracted philosophic attention. In their survey, Uyl and Machan admit that contemporary theorists are still struggling with much the same happiness-related issues which confronted their ancient counterparts (1983, p. 131). Nevertheless, the relevant considerations, issues and associated concepts have become certainly much sharper at this point.

Telfer (1980) and Barrow (1981) can be credited with pulling together important strands of thinking about the nature of happiness. They appear to agree that happiness has to do with the individual's attitudes, feelings or outlook on life. Thus, Telfer views it as 'a state of being pleased with one's life as a whole' (p. 9); Barrow states that 'the essence of happiness lies in having a favorable attitude toward whatever relationship one happens to have to one's circumstances' (p. 73). Put in a slightly different way, 'happiness would seem to be or to involve seeing the world as one would like it to be' (*ibid.*, p. 74). As he sees it, two logical implications appear to follow from this conception: (1) Happiness applies only to creatures with consciousness involving the 'capacity to stand outside of oneself, seeing oneself as an actor in a situation, and to envisage that things might have been otherwise' (*ibid.*, p. 72); and (2) it is incompatible with 'a wide range of concepts such as loneliness, agitation, depression, irritation, self-doubt, low self-esteem, guilt, remorse, and regret' (*ibid.*, p. 73). Broudy (1961) seems to have said as much earlier in observing that the happy or good life can hardly be predominated by pain, hardship, physical deprivation and emotional insecurity, and that it includes a sense of worth and achievement (pp. 26–37).

These authors agree that the element of subjectivity in the notion of happiness can be problematic. Indeed, people's attitudes of being pleased about their conditions in life will be largely shaped by subjective viewpoints. It is debatable that every individual's happiness is objectively a desirable one. After all, one's happiness may be based on ignorant understanding of one's conditions, on an underestimation of one's prospects and capacities, or even on delusions of grandeur! Telfer's strategy is to refer to a conception of happiness, namely, *eudaemonia*. Advocated by the ancient Greek philosopher, Aristotle, eudaemonistic happiness is interpreted by Telfer as living the life which is worth having for its own sake. Such happiness is constituted by a way of life; (hedonistic) satisfaction-oriented happiness, on the other hand, is a reaction to a way of life (1980, p. 39).

If our authors are correct, we are then bound to encounter something of a paradox. Though hedonistic happiness may, all things being equal, be generally regarded as desirable, it may be exhibited in less than admirable or enobling, or even reprehensible, actions or states of being. Arguably,

Hitler might have been a happy person before the tide of war turned against him. On the other hand, a life which we might objectively assess as worth living may not provide enough attitudes or feelings of satisfaction in given individuals. One rather suspects that many a man has deserted a life of virtue or intellectual pursuits in favor of wine and song. If such a life does not invariably produce attitudes or feelings of satisfaction, we could wonder how it could motivate or serve as an attractive human goal for everyone.

Aristotle may have given us the cue in solving this paradox. His discussion of happiness as the supreme good is not intended to show that all feelings of satisfaction count toward happiness for humans. In his search for a 'more precise definition', he suggests asking the question 'What is the function of man?' because, as he puts it, a person's good lies in the exercise of his or her function as a human being. As beings with a rational nature, a human being's function is to exercise reason. To paraphrase him, the good of the human being lies in the exercise of faculties in accordance with excellence or virtue as determined by human reason. By nature endowed with potential for rational and virtuous life, human beings have their function and happiness geared in that direction. In his words (in Singer and Ammerman, 1961, p. 242):

> While with most men there is a perpetual conflict between the several things in which they find pleasure ... those who love what is noble (virtuous) take pleasure in that which is pleasant. For the manifestations of excellence are naturally pleasant, so that they both are pleasant to them and pleasant in themselves. Their life, then, does not need pleasure to be added to it as an appendage, but contains pleasure in itself.

Analysis of happiness as pleasant feelings or attitudes arising from a life of virtue (i.e., consisting of virtuous activities exhibiting a human being's rational nature) eliminates the paradox. Happiness may now be desired for its own sake because of its pleasurable component and may also be regarded as desirable in the normative or valuative sense.

It is important to stress that, following Aristotle, the view of happiness espoused here is associated with a social-individual view of the human good. Taylor (1986) succinctly describes this view as holding that 'an essential constitutive condition of the search for it (human good) is bound up with being in society ... (A)n individual cannot even be a moral subject, and thus a candidate for the realization of the human good, outside of a community of language and mutual discourse about the good and bad, just and unjust ...' (p. 38). As a consequence, the realization of human happiness requires, at least as an essential element, the establishment of societal arrangements and mechanisms conducive to one's search for happiness. Further, it requires individual recognition of societal realities constraining subjective and objective conditions of happiness. In our perspective, we combine the subjective and the objective. Summarily, we may rest the solution of the paradox, in Broudy's (1961, p. 36) words, on:

the promise that if we order our conduct in accordance with certain principles, we shall not only win the approval of our fellow men, but we shall also experience pleasure, and this pleasure will be greater, more lasting, and more satisfactory than the pleasures that accompany action not so ordered.

In light of all this, another look at the Gallup Poll results on public expectations of schools highlights an indisputable point. Given the organic linkage between the individual and society, both the society-oriented and the individual-oriented expectations have certain legitimacy. For example, because the society-oriented expectation of effective citizenship contributes to satisfying societal membership and to harmonious political order, schools may be expected to contribute toward promotion of the effective citizen. Because the individual-oriented expectation of having a job is satisfying for the individual and is maximizing for the economic order in society, preparation for jobs is a defensible expectation of schools. Roughly the same may be said of many other perceived aims, whether in polls or in the academic literature (Brown, 1970). The task is basically the formulation of such an aim(s) that will be adequate yet realistic enough to provide for individual happiness and societal well-being. We believe that this aim is rationality.

Happiness, Rationality and Schooling

The predominant interpretation of the Aristotelian formula for happiness as the exercise of the virtuous — that is, the conduct of life activities with the use of distinctive human capacities, specifically rationality — may prove unduly restrictive, however, if rationality is viewed in a particular manner. In ordinary discourse and philosophical literature, there is a tendency to regard the rational as purely cognitive or contemplative. In this sense, rationality is exclusive and links narrowly with the abstract and the theoretical. It is regarded as having nothing to do with the course of ordinary human events or with the conduct of daily life. Thus, it is important to emphasize that engaging one's rational capacities is not to be confined, in our view, to a cognitive contemplation of nothing but the theoretical or the abstract. Following Aristotle, whose ethical theory concerns the use of reason in a person's life in society, our view of rationality is connected with life as lived by human beings in their social context. This is to say that rationality is applied in dealing with the vocational, interpersonal, social, aesthetic, religious, and other aspects of human living. Oakeshott (1962), whether his view of rationality coincides with ours or not, stated it in the way we find justifiable: 'Human conduct may be said to be 'rational' when it exhibits the sort of intelligence appropriate to the idiom of activity concerned' (p. 110).

Rationality may then be regarded as short-hand for the possession of varied understandings, attitudes and skills required to make sense of, to assess, and to deal with varied situations requiring judgment and action in life. Whether our notion of rationality is to be associated with the notion of education popularized (though subsequently rejected) by Peters (1966, 1977 and 1983) is a question that may be of interest at another time. For Peters, education involves the development of wide cognitive perspective bound with growth in knowledge and understandings attained through non-morally objectionable processes. We agree, as far as this goes. We argue, however, that knowledge, skills, attitudes and understandings cannot be confined to the various disciplines or forms of knowledge (popularized by educational writers such as Hirst, 1974) if we are to develop rational human beings. We would insist that young people be given knowledge, understanding, attitudes and skills as may be necessary in various *areas* of human endeavor — social, political, economic, vocational, medical, and the like. If the development of these rational human beings is what people would call *education*, then we will be prepared to argue that education is, or should be, the primary aim of schools.

But why should rationality, or education with our built-in notion of rationality, be the primary aim of schools? Why not job preparation, citizenship, moral development, financial security, self-sufficiency, and the like? The answer, though requiring extended argumentation in another context, may be stated briefly. Obviously, schools cannot provide for all these aims. Schools may opt for one or a limited number, but even attainment of such aims will not automatically ensure happiness. In fact, to concentrate on a limited number is to limit human options in life. It is effectively to narrow the arena in which human actors may act based on their choices. Thus, to concentrate on one or a limited number of the aims indicated above is to be unfair to human beings whose potential for varied happiness is enormous.

The last point is of crucial importance given what is assumed by our perspective. We believe that, in the nature of things, human satisfactions are varied. Satisfaction *is* satisfaction, and no one may say that another's satisfaction is not satisfaction at all. Each one has, in a very real sense, a privileged access to his or her satisfactions in life. By all accounts, it is desirable to expand individual satisfactions all across the board in the name of happiness as an ultimate value in life. But privileged access to one's feelings of satisfaction would necessarily require that individuals freely decide by themselves what things, conduct, state of affairs or lifestyles generate the most satisfactions. Clearly, the range of human satisfactions for individuals will be limited to the degree that rationality (in our sense) is not developed in them. Not having knowledge, understanding, attitudes and skills in varied aspects of human life, their choices will be dictated more by their circumstances rather than their free choice. This is precisely what is so objectionable about confining schooling to strongly expressed expectations related to job preparation. Gearing schooling efforts to such direction is bound to restrict the range of human goods that everyone is entitled at least to explore. Educationally, this has a distorting effect on the curriculum. Surely, historical study of the curriculum bears this out. As Kliebard (1984) has pointed out, the stress on the practical in American schools has crowded out liberal education courses intended to foster humanistic appreciations.

But, equally important, it is necessary that each individual develop the rationality needed for decision-making about ends and means in life. Such rational decision-making alone makes possible the formulation of individual desires which will do justice to legitimate societal demands and aspirations. Through rationality, we enlarge the overlap between subjective satisfactions and objective good, the valued and the valuable, the desired and the desirable. In brief, the development of rationality is an instrumental good vital to the attainment of the ultimate intrinsic good, happiness, in both its hedonistic and eudaemonistic senses.

It may further be argued that being rational or, perhaps more accurately, knowing that one is rational in the conduct of his or her life, is satisfying in itself. This is in part what Aristotle meant by alluding to a life of reason not needing pleasure to be added to it as an appendage; that it already contains pleasure in itself. Mill (1961) intended to convey this when he said that it is better to be a dissatisfied Socrates (insisting on the life of reason) than a satisfied or contented fool. In any case, to aim at rationality as a satisfying possession for everyone is to conceive it as an intrinsic good. If this line of thinking has any merit, it turns out that rationality is not simply an instrumental good; additionally, it has intrinsic value. Its claim as *the* primary aim of schools is reinforced.

Policy Implications

The Curriculum

If rationality is to be the primary aim of schooling, that is, if schooling is significantly to encourage and promote rationality as both an intrinsic and extrinsic value, what experiences ought children and youth to have in schools? And what features of schooling would be most consistent with the promotion of rationality as we have defined it?

The school curriculum must obviously catch our attention. In viewing it, the key question is, as Barrow and Woods (1988) suggest, 'What should the content be?' in light of our aims or ends. Based on the notion of rationality espoused here, exclusive focus on the forms of knowledge set out by Paul Hirst (1965 and 1974) will prove inadequate. Clearly, Hirst himself recognizes the role of other studies in the total curriculum though, if he is to remain consistent, he will regard their value simply in terms of promoting education defined as cognitive development. Unfortunately his view, we believe, is a rather constricted view not only of the basic subjects and other studies but also of schooling as a whole. Roughly the same observation may be made of RS Peters' (1966 and 1967) earlier views on education as the primary concern of schools. Additionally, Peters' formal criteria for being educated, especially the criterion of wide cognitive perspective, suggest that no one (or only a few, if at all) could ever claim to be educated. Barrow (1981) offers a more acceptable view in his observation that being educated is a matter of degree and that, though breadth of understanding might be considered a necessary condition, it might be achieved in different ways and need not be constituted in or carved from a particular range of forms or disciplines of knowledge.

So far, we have replied to the question of curriculum content in the negative. What, in a positive sense, would we favor? In short and, in general, the proposals of Barrow in *The Philosophy of Schooling* (1981) and of Adler in *The Paideia Proposal* (1982) are, in large part, illustrative of the curricular configurations consistent with the promotion of rationality broadly conceived.[1] These proposals do not hesitate to countenance a wide curricular framework which will promote a diversity of experiences and learnings conducive to the development of rationality suggested here and, eventually, to the good life in society. As well, each proposal is prepared to favor a core curriculum, that is, a curriculum for all, with a comprehensive character targeted toward preparation for various roles in life. *The Paideia Proposal* captures the essential commonalities we seek with respect to schooling objectives and the curricular program. As Adler (1982, p. 18) puts it:

> Here then are the three common callings to which all our children are destined: to earn a living in an intelligent and responsible fashion, to function as intelligent and responsible citizens, and to make both of these things serve the purpose of leading intelligent and responsible lives — to enjoy as fully as possible all the goods that make a human life as good as it can be.

> To achieve these goals, basic schooling must have for all a quality that can best be defined, *positively*, by saying that it must be general and liberal; and, *negatively*, by saying that it must be non-specialized and non-vocational.

Additionally, the Paideia Group, for whom Adler served as spokesperson, has specified the areas of subject matter critical to a basic schooling of twelve years. Adler has identified the three areas indispensable to basic schooling as language, literature and fine arts; mathematics and natural sciences; and history, geography and social studies. Why these three? He answers (1982, pp. 23–4):

> These comprise the most fundamental branches of learning. No one can claim to be educated who is not reasonably well acquainted with all three. They provide the learner with indispensable knowledge about nature and culture, the world in which we live, our social institutions, and ourselves.

Lest the Paideia group is thought narrowly academic, it has to be noted that the proposal speaks of auxiliary studies. These studies will fulfill the need of young people for health and for an outlet for their abundant energy. Instruction about health will therefore be provided together with physical education and participation in intramural sports and athletic exercises. Moreover, practical life skills are not neglected. Young people will be involved in 'a wide variety of manual activities, including typing, cooking, sewing, wood- and metalworking, crafts using other materials, automobile driving and repair, maintenance of electrical and other household equipment, and so on' (Adler, 1982, p. 33).

The Group does not forget the obligation of the school to promote the ability of young people to make rational choices about their careers later on in life. Again, Adler (*ibid.*) puts it succinctly:

> In the latter years, they (young people) should receive instruction to prepare them for choosing and finding a career. This is not to be done by requiring them to make a premature choice of a job and by giving them training for that particular job. Rather, the young person should be introduced to the wide range of human work — the kinds of occupation and careers, their significance and requirements, their rewards and opportunities.

What the Paideia Group has attempted to do is to provide a justification of a conception of schooling similar to Barrow's in *The Philosophy of Schooling* (1981, p. 111). His own analysis establishes, as 'vital elements', 'those things that are demanded by reference to the purposes of education, socializing, ensuring health and preparation for life and leisure'.

Altogether, Barrow and Adler tell us where to begin and how to end schooling, a process intended to promote the appreciation and enjoyment of the good life. Barrow says (1981, p. 111):

> At a basic level, reading, writing and numeracy are obviously vital skills both for our way of life and as a means to education. These must not be left to chance.

Sustain the general and liberal thrust for every child to the end of secondary schooling and ensure common learnings, says the Paideia Group (Adler, 1982, p. 21):

> Elective choices are appropriate only in a curriculum that is intended for different avenues of specialization or different forms of preparation for the professions or technical careers. Electives and specialization are entirely proper at the level of advanced schooling — in our colleges, universities, and technical schools. They are wholly inappropriate at the level of basic schooling.

One can see from Barrow's characterization of the 'vital elements' of schooling that education (as development of a wide cognitive perspective) is but one function of schooling though, for him and for us, a very important one. This suggests, of course, that schooling and education are not synonymous and implies that schooling might well encompass other functions.[2]

Socialization and Indoctrination

There is a sustained, and to us justifiable, consensus that socialization is one of the most important functions of schooling, whether viewed empirically or normatively. Socialization is clearly what the schools do (inevitably, some would say) and it is what they ought to do, many would add. For our purposes here, the key questions are these: Is socialization as a function of schooling inconsistent with the aim of rationality? Can socialization amount to indoctrination when certain distinctive environments in school systems (for example, religiously-oriented or denominational schools) are allowed, whether in the private or the public arena? Can the primary aim of rationality be preserved in these circumstances? Answers to these questions require clarification of the concepts of socialization and indoctrination and some discussion of what entitlements seem justifiable for any group of persons wishing to establish distinctive schooling environments for their children.

Generally, *socialization* is defined as the process of accustoming individuals to their culture or way of life and of influencing and habituating them so as to make them fully functioning members of a group. Barrow and Milburn (1986, p. 205) state their definition as follows:

> Socialization is the business of adjusting people to the way of life of the community, usually by way of initiation into its customs, beliefs, rituals, conventions, expectations, and demands, combined with instruction and the setting of examples.

It is easy to see from this definition why the school is strategically situated to carry out the socialization process. What is important at this point, however, relates to our claim that rationality, as a primary, over-arching aim of schooling, must set the framework for the socialization function. Otherwise, a serious disservice will be done to children and to the ambitions of their parents. Clearly, children must be comfortable and competent in their culture as a matter of survival and intelligent participation; parents, who are concerned with the well-being of their children, would certainly want their off-spring to become so.

Narrow intellectual preoccupation in schooling runs the risk of engendering an incapacity in individuals to consider the application and implications of their school-based learning for living rationally and well in the everyday world. This, of course, is not an argument to denigrate education as a school function. This is a reminder, however, that distinctively intellectual pursuits encased in formal disciplines are not necessarily the only way, much less the only effective way, to pursue rationality in living. There is also the additional important point that we would have to contemplate training in schools, if only as a necessary preliminary to both education (as cognitive development) and socialization. Children will have to be trained to read, write, speak and listen before either process can occur in any meaningful or intelligent sense (see Barrow and Milburn, 1986, pp. 227, 152–4, on *training* and *moral education*, respectively).

But what about the claim, notably by the de-schoolers[3] (e.g., Illich, 1973), that schooling is necessarily indoctrinative and that our effort at habituation to one's way of life or culture (socialization) cannot but be indoctrination? To the extent that schooled children are influenced to accept certain beliefs and values necessary for both personal security and social cohesion, is not education in the sense of critical awareness and understanding automatically overridden? Is not the pursuit of rationality, which is central to our position, jeopardized?

Following the publication of I.A. Snook's *Indoctrination and Education* (1972b), numerous works on the concept of indoctrination appeared; its alleged prevalent, insidious and dangerous presence in schools remains a target of criticism. How true this criticism is depends on how indoctrination is conceived. For all the analyses devoted to it, no standard usage seems to have decisively established itself. In philosophy, resolution of conceptual differences seems never to be reached in a 'knock-out' fashion. Frequently, like exhausted boxers, philosophical protagonists simply fade away from an arena where no referee exists. Often, as in the case of indoctrination, calls are subsequently made to set aside old assumptions underlying the dispute in favor of new ones to have the matter resolved. Thus, Neiman (1989) has suggested that discussion of indoctrination has been fruitless; it now should discard the essentialist assumption that there is an objective, ascertainable notion called indoctrination. This concept should now be viewed contextually, that is, within a context which includes a concern for ultimate aims of education and with a view of the 'excellences that educational practice is meant to transmit to students' (p. 58).

Without dealing with the assumptions behind Neiman's contextualist approach, we may note a valid point he raises. The question of what indoctrination is cannot be separated from what purposive agents in school systems are intending to achieve. In fact, our own approach, which starts from ultimate societal and educational goals and then suggests the kind of capacities schools may be legitimately expected to develop in the young, would seem to satisfy the contextualist strategy. Yet, we are still not spared of the task of communicating, with the use of concepts which others can understand, what processes and outcomes are incompatible with our goals and corresponding schooling practices. It may well be that the concept of indoctrination encompasses a set of practices and outcomes ruled out by our position emphasizing rationality as the primary aim of schooling. In this regard, the disputatious conceptual analyses of indoctrination in the last two decades may not have been entirely in vain. We may agree with Snooke's (1989) response to Neiman that 'we are as close about it as we could ever be', and that, at least, we now know that 'we have to *use* it in concrete instances to discuss ideas such as evidence, truth, and objectivity and see it as centrally involving a question about the legitimacy of certain kinds of influence on people's minds' (p. 64).

In light of previous analyses elsewhere[4] indoctrination may be at work where the imparting of information and ideas has, as its object or intent, the inculcation of unshakable commitment, belief or values; where adherence to them is sought in the absence of tests of truth or falsity publicly understood or practised by experts; and where the pedagogy of the teacher is insensitive to the requirement of giving reasons or the use of reasoning as a means of understanding a claim (even though it could not necessarily be proven true or false, as in the case of aesthetic, moral or religious claims).[5] It should be reasonably obvious that, from our perspective, these indoctrinative processes may be regarded as undesirable. They are incompatible with rational processes because the latter are primarily about the promotion of understanding which is subject to open evaluation and is antithetical not only to the use of non-rational schooling or teaching methods but also to the inculcation of unreasoned beliefs. But habituation, for example, to the demand of society that one drive on the correct side of the road (right or left, depending on the country in which one drives) is not a matter of unshakable belief and behavior. As an instance of socialization, it is simply a conventional expectation which may have to be revised in case, in some way, a decision is reached officially to require people to drive on the other side. So is the fact that one is taught that one lives in a free and democratic society, as long as this teaching is not conveyed as a truth which cannot be challenged or is regarded as certain and inviolate. In short, it does not seem reasonable to us to consider socialization, because it involves influencing others on matters of belief, values and predisposition, as necessarily indoctrinatory or to assert that socialization necessarily and unreasonably compromises the pursuit of rationality in schooling. But the possibility of socialization becoming indoctrination, of education being overridden, or of rationality being compromised must be considered. Thus, we still need to untangle socialization from indoctrination because of people's confusing one with the other in educational discourse.

We reject the claim that schooling, in general, and socialization, in particular, are necessarily indoctrinative. Naturally, the possibility of indoctrination going on in the name of socialization should be entertained. It may be more pervasive than we realize, even in our professedly open, democratic society. And setting down the demarcation line is not easy. Given the complexity of the conceptual mapping required, all we can do here is outline a basic, perhaps contentious position. We wish to claim, first of all, that socialization is, as a matter of fact, generally equated broadly with enculturation. Barrow and Milburn's 1986 definition, previously quoted in this chapter, can be easily used for the latter. In this broad sense socialization includes different types of processes. The following schema captures this point.

Figure 1   Socialization includes different types of processes

SOCIALIZATION (Broadly, Enculturation)

Education	Socialization (narrowly, integration)	Indoctrination
Process:	Process:	Process:
Critical, open evaluation of beliefs, values	habitual, informal accustoming and interaction	Deliberate attempt to inculcate unshakable beliefs, values and predispositions
Outcome:	Outcome:	Outcome:
Individual autonomy	Interpersonal relating and adjustment in society	Community cohesion and preservation

Conceived broadly, socialization encompasses education, integration and indoctrination. Each is no less a way of preparing individuals for life in society. Given this broad sense of the word *socialization*, it is easy to see why it may be regarded as indoctrinative; a critic obviously focuses attention on enculturation processes which have indoctrinative characteristics. But given this usage, it also encompasses education, although his latter process differs from socialization in the narrow sense and from indoctrination in its emphasis on individual autonomy and critical evaluation of reasons or bases underlying the content to be learned and accepted. Still, it remains a process of socialization: It involves being socialized into certain modes of thinking, valuing and behaving through activities (rituals!) associated with certain bodies of knowledge. To the degree that this claim is justified, our rejection of the alleged complete overlap between socialization and indoctrination is strengthened. If education and indoctrination mutually exclude each other, and if socialization includes education, then not all socialization is indoctrination as, indeed, the schema suggests.

We make a second claim: There is a narrow sense of socialization (see middle column of Figure 1) that emphasizes interpersonal relationships, whether they are found in the home, church, school or the community. As a process, socialization in this sense generally takes place at an informal, unconscious level; its function is the gradual integration of the young into their social contexts for their own well-being and for society's as well. In the home, parents engaged in this process generally do not consciously teach; the examples they set and the instruction they give their children are simply part of living. As part of living, rather than conscious learning, they are learned by children effectively. At some point in their interaction, parents may deliberately instruct children with respect to particular learnings. When they do, they may do so in educative or indoctrinative ways. But they may also do so in nothing more than pragmatic ways intended to insure that, because certain realities and expectations have to be confronted by their children, their young might as well learn those things needed to handle them. It would seem that these make for a large bulk of parent-children interaction. Though not educative in nature, they are not indoctrinative either. Where this socialization operates, any change in social realities and expectations will bring about a corresponding change in unconscious or deliberate parental instruction. Clearly, socialization in this sense goes on in various social contexts, including schools.

Socialization in Distinctive Environments

The risk of indoctrination might be most serious where a distinctive socialization environment, such as a denominational school, is favored. Where certain values and community or parental expectations are meant to surround and characterize the schooling enterprise and to orient individuals in particular ways, conscientious caution must be exercised. Barrow (1981, p. 54) sensitizes us to the problem:

> ... If the schooling system or individual teachers within the system (or parents) seek to induce unyielding commitment to various beliefs, that is to be deplored. Being actually anti-educational or a hindrance to it, it cannot be accepted as another legitimate function of the school. And let us not pretend that indoctrination as defined does not take place: it happens in an institutionalized way in Soviet Russia and China, it happens in some Muslim states and in some religious schools in Britain and North America, and no doubt in the Western World there are individual teachers in ordinary schools who are guilty of attempting to indoctrinate students.

The risks for rationality as a primary aim of schooling are real in denominational schools. For our position argued here, this may be especially prominent. The socialization process of accustoming the young to a minority cultural identity, religious persuasion or unique ethos, a religiously oriented school may anticipate and institutionalize the inculcation of unshakable beliefs, incontestable values and pervasive ethnocentrism. In the United States, this problem may not be serious in public schools because of their secular character backed up by a history of Supreme Court decisions upholding separation of church and state. Even there, however, earlier Supreme Court decisions such as *Pierce v. Society of Sisters* (1925) and *Yoder v. Wisconsin* (1972) have constitutionally established parental right to the religious education of the young. In Canada, the problem is more complicated because of the historical entanglement, still constitutionally preserved, between the church and state. The right to denominational schooling in publicly funded systems is imbedded in the Constitution Act, 1867 (formerly known as the British North America Act of 1867) and has recently been confirmed in Section 29 of the Canadian Charter of Rights and Freedoms.[6]

There are very important considerations requiring serious attention in relation to the extent of socialization (in the narrow sense) permitted of religious schools. In such schools, what obligations might be justified and what limits on the discretion of parents, teachers and school officials must be contemplated in the interest of preserving rationality as a primary aim, even as they are allowed to socialize their young into the unique or minority beliefs, values and behaviors accepted in their community?

The preceding discussion suggests that the right or privilege to establish religious schools for the education of one's children is not a *carte blanche* to practise indoctrination. If it is, the concept of religious education becomes bizarre because indoctrination is, by definition, the antithesis of education. The use of non-rational or irrational means to inculcate beliefs unshakably apparently offends rationality as an aim of schooling. Thus, it appears that the oppportunity for a distinctive socialization, including an appreciation and valuing of the parents' way of life and living, is permissible only as long as socialization does not rely exclusively upon non-rational processes. This means that we are prepared to accept religious upbringing as part and parcel of denominational or religious schooling. A serious acquaintance with the customs, beliefs, rituals, conventions and expectations of a religious (or cultural) group — socialization, in effect — is not necessarily the abandonment of rationality development as a school aim. Arguably, the promotion of rationality and the discovery of the good life does not preclude having opportunities to know and appreciate the perspectives of the engaged 'insider' any more than it would prohibit the criticism and skepticism of the disengaged 'outsider'. A skeptic of the possibility of preserving the virtues of the examined life in religious schooling, Callan (1988, p. 192) has expressed this very important point in this way:

> The problem seems to be that in order *seriously* to reject, much less accept, the life of faith one needs to examine it from a perspective other than the disengaged outsider's. One needs to enter, at least imaginatively, into a way of seeing the world where some central beliefs are sustained more by heroic (or foolhardy?) hope than by anything that could be properly be described as evidence and argument. Yet this experience presupposes an ability to set aside the rational-critical principle, to regard that, too, as just one possibility among others as one searches to discover the best way to life. If we educate our children in such a way that they never develop that ability, their rejection of religion may indeed be as unfree an act as the acceptance of faith by the indoctrinated zealot.

If this line of reasoning is, for our purposes, to be followed, then it requires a somewhat indulgent attitude toward the encouragement of religious faith by means of socialization as an aspect of the schooling process. However, such reasoning cannot authorize, with the same indulgence, 'business as usual in religious upbringing' (Callan, *ibid.*). Indeed, 'The essential tension between the examined life and faith must be made vividly apparent to children and adolescents as they grow in understanding, even if this obstructs parental efforts to elicit faith in many instances' (*ibid.*, pp. 192–3). This is a rigorous test of the denominational school's promotion of rationality and its commitment to educative purpose. For the advocates of religiously affiliated schooling, it may be very difficult to accept, especially in light of what a democratic pluralist ethos would seem to allow. For us who advocate rationality as the central aim in public schools, one significant implication seems inescapable: Religious faith will have to be construed 'as a matter of revisable commitment' (Callan, 1982, p. 184) in denominational schools.

Postscript: Back to the Good Life

Rationality as conceived in this chapter extends the notion of rationality that operates within the framework of individual forms or fields of knowledge. The rationality we advocate is captured by the phrase *rational conduct of life*, which implies individual capacity for intelligent reasoning and acting with respect to the demands of living in society. Schooling which aims at such rationality will be expected to provide student familiarization with and socialization or initiation into those areas that ordinarily individuals will encounter in life. Without these processes, the capacity for rational relating to one's social, economic and personal world becomes a hopeless enterprise. An unsocialized intellectual, for example, can hardly be expected to interact rationally with other human beings who do not see the world or live in it the way he does. The disciplines, forms or fields of knowledge should necessarily be provided for, but not so much to dislodge or crowd the components needed for life as humans have to live it, as to build on, to refine and, hopefully, to enrich them. Arguably, rationality requires, as a foundation, the rather mundane beliefs, understandings, values and practical skills that may be viewed more systematically and rigorously though organized knowledge at a late stage in the schooling of the child.

Clearly, this notion of rationality is informed by our idea that pursuit of the good life is what humans are all about. Given the diversity of human endeavors, lifestyles, abilities and inclinations, the instrumental value of rationality cannot be over-emphasized. It is through this means that one is enabled to determine the conduct of his or her life.

But what shall we say if a community of individuals — religious fundamentalists, for example — decide to school their children *indoctrinatively* into their religiously-oriented way of life? Does our position commit us to the rejection and prevention of such schooling?

Disturbing as it may sound to many, the logic of our argument does not compel rejection or proscription of such schooling. Initially it may be said that if individuals in their maturity decide to live a life of faith rather than rationality, determine that their young are to live likewise, and seek to establish a religious private school to indoctrinate their children, neither the state nor the majority has the legal or constitutional power to deprive them of the right to do so. Constitutional documents and court decisions ensure such right. But, morally, it may further be argued that the moral principle of respect for persons allows mature human beings to determine, from their perspective, how to live their lives and to discharge their responsibilities, short of palpable harm, toward the young who depend on them for protection, sustenance and upbringing. Between the principle of respect for persons and rationality (in the secularistic-scientific sense dear to the heart of many liberals) as principles in human life, the former would seem to weigh more predominantly. But how does the principle of respect for persons relate to our view of the good life and to the notion of rationality propounded here?

Our quick and short answer comes by way of another question: Why adopt the principle of respect for persons? In other words, what justifies it? Unable to argue fully for our view at this stage, something like the following may be presented. In the final analysis, underlying the principle of respect for persons — and most other moral principles, for that matter — is the bedrock of human reality: As human beings we are happiness-seeking creatures and, as such, continuously act to expand happiness-conducing experiences. Given this, moral principles may be regarded as the ultimate procedural principles human moral sense has devised both to guide human conduct in a way that will facilitate attainment of everyone's happiness and to prevent harm to others in every person's attempt to pursue his or her goal. If this thesis is correct or at least arguable, it makes sense to say that the question of indoctrinative schooling within a religious community must be answered in light of the principles to be employed to promote the happiness of the greatest number (meaning, the majority and the minority combined). Undoubtedly, the history of mankind is littered with evidence that suppression of one's most cherished beliefs, particularly the religious, has been the cause of strife in society. Clearly, denial of the right to religious schools — even particularly to indoctrinative schools — does not make sense in terms of attaining the human good if the consequence is prolonged and bitter resentment and conflict. In the first instance, it violates the moral principle of respect for persons which that good demands. This principle demands that, unless shown palpably incompetent to determine the course of their lives, individuals, and hence the communities they constitute, must be allowed self-determination. This is buttressed, additionally, if we go beyond the general to the particular — from the general idea of possession of religious rights by minority groups to the exercise of such a right by specific minority groups such as the Amish, the Mennonites and the Hutterites. Markedly these communities are characterized by peace, cooperation, caring for one another and absence of crime or violence. Assuming that members of these communities are happy in their own way, how can we justify offering as an alternative the (secularistic-scientific) conception of the rational life to live? Is there any strong justification at all for dangling before them a way of life which, in any case, exhibits internal seeds of discord arising from the principle of freedom, the built-in weaknesses in human nature, and the dislocations rampant in our secular-scientific society?

A concerned secularist may grudgingly grant self-determination to adult fundamentalist communities; he or she is unlikely to agree that these adult communities have the right to indoctrinate their young. Respect for persons, it may be insisted, applies to the young as well. Again, this is a complex issue that needs extended discussion. Suffice it to say, at this point, that children are not brought up in a vacuum; they grow and develop their beliefs, values, inclinations and skills impressed on them by their environment. Shall the secular state or the majoritarian community then take these children away from their parents and send them to the schools pervaded by the beliefs, values, inclinations and skills appropriate for the secular world? Unless the secularist is able to show that a completely neutral, non-predisposing school-ing is available to children of the religious, the proselytizing tendency to smuggle in the secular-scientific rationality and way of life may have to be dampened.

An important caveat needs to be introduced at this juncture. Broudy (1962, chapter 2) has perceptively suggested that, objectively as well as subjectively, the good life, whatever it may be, cannot be characterized by unnecessary and prolonged pain, physical deprivation and misery; by emo-tional insecurity; and by the absence of self-worth or sense of achievement. Philosophically, and legally with at least the first, fundamentalist religious communities are subject to these requirements. They are not at liberty to treat their children as they see fit in disregard of such requirements so long as they wish to maintain their self-determination on the basis of the argument advanced in this chapter.

Our sympathies should by now be clear. The character of life in our complex, industrialized, and modern society requires schooling which aims at the development of rationality. It should be, however, the rationality which equips people not only for intelligent but also for tolerant living. It is time to leave behind the narrow secularistic-scientific view of rationality. If rationality is to be a truly beneficial instrument for the human good, its enlarged conception must be accepted and promoted in schools.

Notes

1 The proposals by Radwanski (1988) in his study of the relevance of education and the issue of dropouts and by the British Columbia Royal Commission on Education also approximate some of our viewpoints in this chapter.
2 However, we do not mean to suggest that education is the function of schools alone.
3 *Deschooling* as a term was coined by Ivan Illich. Essentially, his invocation to deschool a society requires the disestablishment of the institution of formal educa-tion or state schooling on the ground that this exists to foster the cultural and

economic hegemony of certain groups of interests at the expense of learning which is valuable to individuals on their own terms and at the expense of education in its liberating or 'liberationist' possibilities (Illich, 1973).

4 A good collection of papers on indoctrination is Snook's (1972a) *Concepts of Indoctrination.*

5 For discussions on how the concept of indoctrination has been examined by scholars, see, for example, Barrow and Milburn (1986), pp. 109–12; and Barrow and Woods (1988), pp. 69–81. Notable in these discussions are the tests or criteria that one might use, singly or in combinations, to establish whether indoctrination is being practised, namely, the criteria of method, intention, content and consequence in the imparting of information and ideas.

6 The Constitution Act of 1982, passed by the Canadian Parliament, incorporated the original formulation of the right to denominational schooling in Article 93 of that Act. Additionally, the Charter of Rights and Freedoms, a formal part of the Constitution, contains this provision: 'Nothing in this Charter abrogates or derogates from any rights or privileges guaranteed by or under the Constitution of Canada in respect of denominational, separate, or dissentient schools'.

Bibliography

ACKERMAN, B. (1980) *Social Justice in the Liberal State*, New Haven, CT: Yale University Press.

ADLER, M. (1982) *The Paideia Proposal*, New York: Macmillan Publishing.

ARISTOTLE (1961) 'On the good', in SINCER, M. and AMMERMAN, R.R. (Eds) *Introductory Readings in Philosophy*, New York: Charles Scribner's Sons.

BARROW, R. (1980) *Happiness*, Oxford: Martin Robertson.

BARROW, R. (1981) *The Philosophy of Schooling*, New York: John Wiley and Sons.

BARROW, R. and MILBURN, G. (1986) *A Critical Dictionary of Educational Concepts*, Brighton, Sussex: Wheatsheaf Books.

BARROW, R. and WOODS, G. (1988) *An Introduction to Philosophy of Education* (Third edition), London: Routledge and Kegan Paul.

BRITISH COLUMBIA ROYAL COMMISSION ON EDUCATION (1988) *A Legacy for Learners*, Victoria, B.C.: Government Printing.

BROUDY, H.S. (1961) *Building a Philosophy of Education*, Englewood Cliffs, NJ: Prentice-Hall.

BROWN, L. (1970) *Aims of Education*, New York: Teachers College Press, Columbia University.

CALLAN, E. (1988) 'Faith, worship and reason in religious upbringing', *Journal of Philosophy of Education*, 22, pp. 183–93.

CONSTITUTION ACT (1982) Ottawa: Minister of Supply and Service.

DWORKIN, R. (1985) *A Matter of Principle*, Cambridge, MA: Harvard University Press.

ELAM, S. and GALLUP, A.M. (1989) 'The 21st Annual Gallup Poll of the public's attitudes toward the public schools', *Phi Delta Kappan*, 71, pp. 41–54.

GALSTON, W. (1980) *Justice and the Human Good*, Chicago: University of Chicago Press.

GALSTON, W. (1986) 'Equality of opportunity and liberal theory', in LUCASH, F. (Ed.) *Justice and Equality Here and Now*, Ithaca, NY: Cornell University Press, (pp. 89–107).

HIRST, P. (1965) 'Liberal education and the nature of knowledge', in ARCHAMBAULT,

R. (Ed.) *Philosophical Analysis and Education*, London: Routledge and Kegan Paul.

HIRST, P. (1974) *Knowledge and the Curriculum*, London: Routledge and Kegan Paul.

ILLICH, I. (1973) *Deschooling Society*, Harmondsworth, England: Penguin.

KLIEBARD, H. (1984) 'The decline of humanistic studies in the American school curriculum', in LADNER, B. (Ed.) *The Humanities in Pre-collegiate Education*, Eighty-third Yearbook of the National Society for the Study of Education, Part II, Chicago: National Society for the Study of Education, (pp. 7–30).

LIVINGSTONE, D. and HART, D.J. (1987) 'The people speak: Public attitudes toward schooling in Canada', in GHOSH, R. and RAY, D. (Eds) *Education and Social Change*, Toronto: Academic Press, (pp. 3–27).

MARITAIN, J. (1943) *Education at the Crossroads*, New Haven, CT: Yale University Press.

McGILL, J.V. (1967) *The Idea of Happiness*, New York: Frederick Praeger.

MILL, J.S. (1961) 'On utilitarianism', in LERNER, M. (Ed.) *Essential Works of John Stuart Mill*, New York: Bantam Books, (pp. 189–252).

NATIONAL COMMISSION ON EXCELLENCE IN EDUCATION (1983) *A Nation at Risk*. Washington, DC: US Government Printing Office.

NEIMAN, A.M. (1989) 'Introduction: A contextual approach', *Educational Philosophy and Theory*, 21, pp. 53–61.

OAKESHOTT, M. (1962) *Rationalism in Politics*, New York: Basic Books.

PETERS, R.S. (1966) *Ethics and Education*, London: George Allen and Unwin.

PETERS, R.S. (1967) 'What is an Educational Process?' in PETERS, R.S. (Ed.) *The Concept of Education*, London: Routledge and Kegan Paul.

PETERS, R.S. (1977) *Education and the Education of Teachers*, London: Routledge and Kegan Paul.

PETERS, R.S. (1983) 'Philosophy of education', in HIRST, P. (Ed.) *Educational Theory and its Foundation Disciplines*, London: Routledge and Kegan Paul, (pp. 30–61).

PETERS, R.S. (1988) 'Democratic values and educational aims', in HARE, W. and PORTELLI, J. (Eds) *Philosophy of Education: Introductory Readings* (pp. 339–57), London, Ontario: Wheatsheaf Books.

PIERCE V. SOCIETY OF SISTERS (1925) 268 US 510.

RADWANSKI, G. (1988) *Ontario Study of the Relevance of Education and the Issue of Dropouts*, Toronto: Government of Ontario.

RAWLS, J. (1971) *A Theory of Justice*, Cambridge, MA: Harvard University Press.

SNOOK, I. (Ed.) (1972a) *Concepts of Indoctrination*, London: Routledge and Kegan Paul.

SNOOK, I. (1972b) *Indoctrination and Education*, London: Routledge and Kegan Paul.

SNOOK, I. (1989) 'Contexts and essences: Indoctrination revisited', *Educational Philosophy and Theory*, 21, pp. 62–5.

TAYLOR, C. (1986) 'The nature and scope of distributive justice', in LUCASH, F. (Ed.) *Justice and Equality Here and Now*, Ithaca, NY: Cornell University Press, (pp. 34–67).

TELFER, E. (1980) *Happiness*, New York: St. Martin's Press.

UYL, D.D. and MACHAN, T. (1983) 'Recent works on the concept of happiness', *American Philosophical Quarterly*, 20, pp. 115–34.

YODER V. WISCONSIN (1972), 406 US 510.

5   Schooling and the Instrumentally Valuable

Harold Entwistle

The Function of Schools in a Complex Society

In modern society there are two differing and apparently irreconcilable conceptions of schooling. On the one hand, its purposes are considered instrumental: the preparation of individuals for specific social roles, especially as workers, thus, also contributing to the promise and political well-being of the state. The alternative view is that education is not primarily for satisfying extrinsic needs of either the individual or society; it should be valued only for its own sake.

To say that something is instrumentally valuable is to see it as a means to achieving some end outside itself; its value is not intrinsic, but lies in its capacity to contribute to the accomplishment of some extrinsic purpose or result. In this sense, consumers of educational services frequently want schooling to be instrumentally valuable. Parents, students, employers, politicians and taxpayers expect that students will emerge from full-time education with knowledge and skills which will relate to their future experiences in the business of everyday life, particularly in the workplace. Even some suppliers of educational services, especially teachers, take it for granted that preparing students for work is the major function of the school. Some subject matter is judged inappropriate for some children precisely because of the assumption that they will be uninterested in, or incapable of, anything but unskilled or semi-skilled work — they'll only be truck drivers, or waitresses, so what's the point of teaching them anything but the rudiments of the three Rs? Other students are enjoined to take subjects, especially at the more advanced levels, because the professional occupations to which they aspire require these as prerequisite to specialized college and university programmes. And although it is probably less common in families than it once was, there persists the view that since daughters will only get married as early as possible, advanced schooling for them is likely to be redundant. On this view, the most appropriate curriculum for girls would be a modern version of what Rousseau prescribed for Sophie, focusing instrumentally on the domestic arts and sciences.

The liberal view of education tends to be that these instrumental perspectives are short-sighted and misconceived, representing a 'hand to mouth' conception of education, inimical to equality of opportunity, and standing in the way of that complete, all-round development of the person which liberal educational rhetoric takes to be the point of schooling. This conception of education entails that learning which is educative should be undertaken for its own sake. Education requires that students should be initiated into worthwhile activities, knowledge and skills and they should be pursued not for their extrinsic ends, that is, instrumentally, as means to something else, but for their intrinsic value.

In this paper I want to assess the merits and shortcomings of both these points of view and to suggest that in whatever terminology we conceptualize education, it is insufficient to see it as the pursuit of learning for its own sake. In some sense, knowledge acquired in schools must make a difference to the way people live their lives. However, there are also several objections to the crude instrumentalism which frequently underpins discussions of public policy in education, and we begin with an examination of some of these.

Instrumentalism in Schooling: An Assessment

Foremost amongst objections to educational instrumentalism is the belief that schooling is inevitably impoverished by a tendency to exclude anything from the curriculum which fails to contribute to life in the marketplace. An instrumental view of curriculum tends ultimately towards justification of only that knowledge and skill which is socially or economically valued. From the point of view of the State which finances and legislates for public education, schooling seems primarily an investment, a contribution toward greater industrial productivity, eradicating budget deficits and balance of payments problems, getting ahead in space or winning the Cold War. Given this instrumental educational ideology, it is easy to dismiss claims for the inclusion of history, drama, music, literature, art and recreational activities in the curriculum. These are dismissed as 'frills' whilst, to the contrary, science, mathematics and computer technology seem easily justified as sound national investments. So the notion of education for its own sake is the justification for aesthetic education. Where an instrumental evaluation of schooling dominates, those aspects of the curriculum which nourish aesthetic sensibility — mainly the fine arts — are apt to be the first casualties. Much the same is true of an apparently 'useless' subject like history. From the point of view of the practical contingencies of life in the marketplace — trying to keep body and soul together, raising productivity, balancing the budget, governing states and defending their integrity — aesthetic experience and a study of the past inevitably wear the aspect of things at the fringes of life. They are for the idle, the rich, or average persons when they have nothing better to occupy their spare time. Hence, it is all too easy to dismiss aesthetic activities in schools to the periphery of the curriculum, to be indulged only when the serious business of learning to survive in the marketplace has been taken care of. Indeed, sometimes the language of education becomes indistinguishable from that of economics. Not only is education itself considered an 'investment', but also schools and colleges are 'plant'; graduates are 'products'; teachers' salaries become the subject of productivity agreements, and so on. Thus, criticism of an instrumental conception of education stems partly from a concern that schools should not be 'sold out' to politicians, economists, sociologists or the industrial-military complex.

More positively, the implications of insisting on learning for its own sake against an instrumental view of learning are that we thus acknowledge the importance of life activities which are the distinguishing mark of civilized communities. If education is to have relevance for life it must focus upon the best conceivable life, the life of 'civilized, rational man'. And one point about a great deal of civilized life is that it is a life of play. Play is non-serious, non-vital, not in the sense of being trivial or requiring little effort or commitment, but in being a non-instrumental activity, essentially unproductive of economic value (Huizinga, 1949). Many of our characteristically civilized activities have the non-instrumental character of play. This is not merely true of games like chess, golf, soccer or Bingo. Other pursuits which are highly esteemed in civilized societies — theatre and concert-going, poetry, making music and dance, painting, looking at pictures, for example — have the distinguishing features of play. Thus, whilst most people cannot avoid the biological and economic imperatives of the marketplace, in highly industrialized affluent societies marked by the growth of leisure, an increasing proportion of living is a life at play. But to say that an activity falls within the category of play is not to disparage it. Clearly, our civilized 'play' activities have little relevance to the problem of 'bringing home the bacon'. But they can be serious and important activities in the sense that they constitute much of what civilized living must be about. Arguably, therefore, it is this non-instrumental aspect of civilized life to which schooling should address itself.

Given the political, social and economic imperatives which are apt to fuel an instrumental view of schooling, the notion of education for its own sake is also necessary to safeguard the integrity of the individual learner. Conceived instrumentally, the curriculum frequently puts the interests of society before those of the individual. Personal interests and talents must often give way to what is socially or economically expedient. And, ironically, learners are often put in the position of denying their own interests and preferences in the willing acceptance of subject matter which has little intrinsic interest for them but which, they calculate, will benefit them vocationally. In much the same way, a curriculum conceived as instrumental to the national interest is a threat to educational equality. If the nation requires a large substructure of unskilled and semi-skilled labor, and if we assume (probably correctly) that the recipients of a good liberal education are unlikely to see themselves in such roles, then there will be considerable pressure to offer to the majority a curriculum which makes few demands upon their intellectual resources and which socializes them to accept their modest lot in life with resignation. In other words, a curriculum designed instrumentally to reproduce the hierarchically structured workforce of a modern industrial society must maintain, rather than attempt to diminish, inequality of achievement in schools.

A further problem posed by an instrumental conception of education lies in the very specificity of the goals and objectives which educational instrumentalism requires — objectives related to particular occupations, to the demands of the marketplace and of domestic life, for example. This specific nature of instrumental aims and objectives has two implications. First, it is inimical to the notion of life-long education. Logically, once a particular objective has been achieved, further learning is redundant. On an instrumental view of learning, education is arriving at a destination. Second, learning directed at specific objectives is especially prone to suffer from obsolescence. Schooling, which is a preparation for living in the breathlessly changing world of the late twentieth century and beyond, cannot be overly specific as to objectives if it really is to prepare young people for life in a post-industrial society. This point is most often made with reference to vocational and professional education, following the assumption that in future people will have to make several changes of occupation during a normal working lifetime. But it is also, and especially, true of the moral life. As any middle-aged person today knows, contemporary social, political, economic and moral problems are not those which confronted them as young people almost half a century ago. An obvious example of this are the changing sexual mores which accompany developments in technology affecting sexual behavior. A quarter century ago, the availability of the birth control pill seemed to liberate sexual behavior from age-old physical and moral constraints. But within a couple of decades, the spectre of AIDS has turned this technologically-based sexual liberation into a cruel joke. Anyone who believed he or she had solved problems of sexual behavior by employing a particular technique of birth control has a good deal of unlearning and relearning to do. Much the same problem is true of what has come to be known as chemical dependency. A quarter century ago, this was almost exclusively a problem of alcohol; now it is equally, if not more so, a problem of drugs.

But in fact, although having different manifestations at particular points in time, both sexual behavior and chemical dependency are only instances of enduring personal and social problems. The question is whether, given their changing manifestations during a single lifetime, we best address them head-on in schools as they currently present themselves or whether what is required is a liberal education which offers the young knowledge, skills and principles which transcend the immediate in place and time, and have enduring significance for the human condition. For example, both sex and chemical addiction involve moral questions which are not simply peculiar to either phenomenon at a particular moment in time. A notion of 'safe sex' ought to be concerned not merely with the techniques available in order to avoid unpleasant, even disastrous consequences of the sex act, but also, and especially, with the morality of respect for other persons, with self-respect, with care and reverence for one's own body and its functions. And these are 'eternal' considerations which confront the person, irrespective of the benefits, limitations and conveniences of a particular technology. Much the same could be argued of the knowledge required to understand and respond to the changing ways in which political, economic and cultural phenomena confront the modern citizen. A general understanding of the problems of ethics, which apply alike to sexual behavior, chemical dependency, race relations, poverty and aggressive nationalism is preferable in education to a focus only upon the local and immediate manifestations of these problems. We prepare for life in both its immediate and longer term perspectives by encouraging a disciplined consideration of moral principles, using as illustration whatever personal and social dilemmas that currently confront the young. These dilemmas will serve as concrete data to exemplify the perennial problems of personal discipline and social conscience — problems which confront human beings, largely irrespective of place and time. If education really ought to be instrumental towards assisting students in coping with the daily contingencies of life throughout their lifetime (including those problems which will immediately confront them as graduates), it ought to make them familiar with fundamental modes of thought and knowledge in relation to wide areas of human experience.

This familiarity is probably the best safeguard against the danger that, when acquired in pursuit of quite specific instrumental objectives, knowledge and skill learned in schools will become obsolete with rapid changes in technology and the challenges these pose to moral and political behavior. The problems, opportunities and dilemmas in life which face present and future citizens and workers are real and insistent. Of course schooling should provide us with resources to make sense of the fabric of our daily lives. Nevertheless, the popular assumption that we best prepare young people for life simply through a head-on confrontation with the concrete problems of contemporary life has to be resisted. We must teach the young to face the problems they will encounter on leaving school through a direct and exclusive focus on those problems. In a valid sense in which education should be a preparation for life, it must be preparation for 'life-long life', not merely for an immediately post-school life lived at a particular point in time. Indeed, education for life should include the distant prospect of life in retirement: People's ability to cope with life in retirement may depend on the quality of their formal schooling when young.

Limitations of Knowledge for Its Own Sake

No doubt there are excellent reasons for questioning an instrumental view of schooling and asserting the value of learning for its own sake. However, the insistence of liberal educationists that education is for its own sake has its own limitations and dangers. It can be used to justify preoccupation with those esoteric aspects of human knowledge which may interest the scholar, but which have little of the relevance for common experience which would justify their inclusion in a general education. Indeed, it is recourse to the doctrine of learning for its own sake used to justify obsolete or recondite knowledge which invites the stigma that some educational activities are merely repositories of 'inert ideas'. When we are in the realm of knowledge valued for its own sake, it is very much a matter of one person's meat being another's poison.

The criterion of intrinsic value is not sufficient to justify curriculum content, and may lead to learning which is barren without the correlate of 'for the learner's sake'. Perhaps learning should be disinterested. But to be disinterested is not to be uninterested. One must choose between a multitude of activities which are intrinsically valuable. And one chooses ultimately on the basis of what interests him or her. One cannot do everything worthwhile which might be done for its own sake, or learn everything that one might find interesting. Choice of an educational activity always has this subjective dimension. It reflects individual talent, dispositions, past experiences, and perceptions of future opportunities, as well as an estimate of one's limitations. Hence, what is learned matters to the learner. Dead knowledge or inert ideas are likely to be consequences of a stress on learning things for their own sakes, particularly when this learning is divorced from a concept of the learner as one having interests, concerns, purposes, talents dispositions and a point of view of one's own.

However, whilst the concepts of 'learning for its own sake' and 'for the learner's sake' are both necessary, they are together insufficient criteria for curriculum building. As well as being a justification for including obsolete or recondite knowledge having no power to quicken the imagination of the learner, they can also be justification for inclusion of curricular activities which are undemanding, trivial, even immoral. They must be applied subject to the condition that an activity is not mis-educational because it is unethical or anachronistic. Hence, a third correlative criterion is necessary: The curriculum must consist of activities which are culturally valuable. The learner does not exist in a cultural vacuum, and a curriculum which truly caters to his interests has to recognize the community in which the learner lives; not only its history but also the social and technological dynamics of the change to which it is subject.

It is this sense of the learner as one having purposes (shaped, in part, by the cultural imperatives of a particular society) which underpins the rhetoric of educational relevance and the related notion that schools should conceive their purposes instrumentally. The demands for relevance and instrumental learning are not merely the rhetoric of the philistine, the crassly materialistic, or the exploiters of other people. The notion dies hard that when schooling nears its conclusion, it should have equipped the student with knowledge and skills, especially vocational knowledge and skill, which are fruitful for life.

Further Arguments for Instrumentalism in Schooling

If educational instrumentalism has the limitations we have noted, how do we meet the legitimate demands of educational consumers for relevance in schooling?

The first possibility is to insist that liberal education itself has instrumental value. Though its modern apologists are apt to deny this possibility, some historians of education have stressed that the liberal arts curriculum has always been deemed to have instrumental value; sometimes as propaedeutic to the study of the liberal vocations, at other times as instrumental not only to the development of civic virtue but also as instrumental to the cultivation of wisdom (e.g., Bowen, 1972). The best known modern advocate of liberal education, R.S. Peters (in Peters and Hirst, 1970), initially disclaimed an instrumental implication in his concept of education, insisting that the undoubted useful, extrinsic outcomes of the kind of education he favored were merely an overspill or by-product of learning pursued for its own sake. There is no doubt, he conceded, that there can be 'cognitive overspill' into daily life from history, geography, mathematics, literature and the natural and social sciences, maybe even from philosophy. Knowledge of any of these may contribute to our understanding and appreciation of what we read in the newspapers or see and hear on radio, television and film. Such knowledge may also contribute to our ability to make more subtle political judgments, deal more effectively with bureaucracies, and be discerning and discriminating consumers of goods and services. In brief, 'academic' knowledge which is the stuff of the liberal curriculum may inform our leisure, improve our work, strengthen our citizenship, enrich our domestic lives, and contribute significantly to our life chances in all kinds of ways. But, Peters insisted, the possibility that demonstrable utilities will flow from it is not the primary reason for embarking upon the liberal education enterprise, especially since these utilities are fortuitous and unanticipated by the learner. This being the case, the motive for acquiring a liberal education can never be the expectation of particular benefits in the world outside the school. Implicitly, one's education promises no outcome beyond enjoyment of the activities into which one is being initiated — 'delighting in such things for their own sake'. This has drawn to Peters the criticism that his educated person would be most at home in that modern example of the Platonic symposium, the dinner party.

However, the reality of modern living is that an educated person spends far more time engaging in instrumental activities than in hedonistic leisure pursuits, such that the 'overspill' effects of one's education is considerable. They may even be, at least in quantative terms, its primary outcome. Therefore, it would be an odd conception of education for life whose contribution was only toward one's spare time preoccupations and not to those time consuming instrumental activities like earning a living and the various obligations which constitute one's domestic life and one's citizenship. All but the idle rich would be wise to reject an education which made no contribution to life except, marginally, to leisure. As Peters himself later concedes, 'Most of the actions we perform and activities in which we engage, arise from our "station and its duties"' (Peters, 1988).

In fact, in a different context, Peters acknowledges that the distinction between intrinsic and extrinsic ends, which had underpinned his earlier formulation of the concept of education, had become troubling:

> I began to feel an increasing dissatisfaction with the dichotomies in terms of which liberal education is usually interpreted. In particular I found difficulty with the dichotomy between 'for its own sake' and for the sake of some practical end ... It seems to apply hardly at all to a sphere of knowledge, sometimes referred to loosely as 'the humanities', which is of central importance in any attempt to determine the type of knowledge which should form the content of liberal education. (1977, chapter 4)

What prompted this unease was a recognition of those areas of human experience which are neither the detached, disinterested intellectual enjoyment of various forms of knowledge, nor those employing knowledge and skill for the achievement of particular practical tasks. Peters has in mind those experiences which draw upon that knowledge of the human condition which contributes to a person's sensitivity as a human being, 'a body of knowledge entertained with varying degrees of understanding, that is extremely significant or "relevant" to a person so far as it determines his general beliefs, attitudes and reactions to the general conditions of human life' (*ibid.*).

Earlier, employing the metaphor of life as a journey, Peters had intimated this sense in which a liberal education results not in arriving at a destination, but which contributes toward a person's travelling with a different point of view. Implicitly, one's knowledge becomes such a part of oneself that one's values, outlook, objectives and priorities have changed. Indeed, one has become a different person. However, given such a transformation of the person, the fact is that all life's various activities (those which are instrumental as well as those undertaken for their own sake) must come to be viewed differently: one's work, one's citizenship and one's family life, no less than one's spare time pleasures. One cannot travel with a different point of view to one's leisure, but not to work, or to the polling booth, or to market.

In this connection we may note the evidence that when employers demand education relevant to the workplace, what they usually want is an improvement in education somewhat along the lines conceptualized by Peters and other theorists of liberal education. In complaining that schools neglect the requirements of industry and commerce, employers are rarely asking for the teaching of specific technical or commercial skills, believing that this is best done by industry itself or by technical colleges. Their complaint is, rather, that young people leave school badly educated in a liberal sense; that they are insufficiently literate or numerate, or are lacking in the kind of knowledge usually associated with a good liberal education; or that they have not acquired the capacity to work independently and too often have to repeat a task which is badly done for want of appropriate work skills or a work ethic; or that they lack the capacity satisfactorily to adapt to the rapidly changing demands of technological innovation. Far from requiring a technically-oriented training in schools, it is arguable that these accomplishments — literacy, numeracy, general knowledge, adaptability in the face of change, the capacity to work independently, efficiently and responsibly — are amongst the fruits of a liberal education.

One implication of the view that liberal education contributes thus, instrumentally, to life's everyday activities, but only indirectly and in the fullness of time, is that when students ask of a curriculum, 'What use is this; what is the point of learning it?', there is no answer that can honestly be given and immediately satisfy the questioner. Peters' notion of education as initiation into worthwhile knowledge implies that, to the learner, this must appear something of mystery. Hence, there can be no satisfactory answer to a demand by students that what they learn must appear relevant, here and now, except that they must trust the teacher. It can only be hoped that, ultimately, they will come to recognize that something of value and relevance to life has indeed been learned. In fact, more appropriately, the teacher should suggest a different question: 'What might I become, as a person, if I learn the kinds of things which are in the liberal curriculum?' To anyone asking about the outcome of an education along the lines suggested by Peters, the answer is that he or she will discover different problems and opportunities in life, such that various kinds of knowledge and skill will become more relevant than have been originally imagined. Relevance is not a static perspective, given unalterably, once and for all time to a person. If it were, all that a relevant education would succeed in doing would be to confirm the individual in that station in life to which he or she belonged on first entering school. Anyone committed to extending opportunity through schooling, especially to socially disadvantaged children, has to employ a concept of relevance which is not tied to a given, static mode of life, but will effectively help to transform life.

Adults, especially those who are themselves the beneficiaries of a liberal education, no doubt appreciate its instrumental values. The correlations between improved life chances and the possession of a liberal education are as obvious to commonsense as they are to academic sociology. If parents are honest, their desire to give their children the best possible education is as much in recognition of its instrumental values as it is for the intrinsic pleasures it can also undoubtedly afford. But it is much more difficult to persuade young children that the often abstract knowledge which they are asked to acquire in school will ultimately be seen to have value in improving their daily lives, even their lives in the marketplace. Evidently, believing that the liberal curriculum can have instrumental value is an act of faith for the young. It requires a capacity for deferred gratification. And there is no doubt that, to some extent, this is a correlate of social calls. Insistence upon immediate gratification is taken to be a characteristic of working and lower class life — not, perhaps, surprisingly. The closer one is to the brute facts of subsistence, the more one's appetites (even one's hungers) need immediate gratification. Hence, with many children in schools, there is a chronic problem of motivation if a curriculum whose instrumental overspill lies in the distant future is to acquire relevance. But if, as we have argued, the instrumental benefits of a liberal education are real, the challenge to teachers is to make the connections between education and life explicit.

Toward Instrumentally Valuable Liberal Education

There are ways of meeting legitimate demands for relevance within the liberal curriculum itself. One of the ways by which liberal education becomes irrelevant occurs when the relationship between the concrete and the abstract is ignored. Occasionally, indeed, the claim is made that liberal education is about abstract knowledge. This is true in a sense which we have noted. That is, knowledge which is generalizable, not merely tied to particular phenomena at a particular place and time, is inevitably abstract knowledge. But if such knowledge is to be applicable, across time and place, it has to be clear how it relates to particular relevant instances in the world of human experience. Hence, effective schooling has to pay particular attention to the problem of the relationship between abstract and concrete, if abstract knowledge is not to remain inert knowledge. Concrete exemplification of abstract principles may be drawn from the past experience of persons and societies, or from imagined human experience in the future. Such principles can also have reference to the lives of students and their environment in the present. The principles of political, economic and moral life are present in the experience of children. Piaget has shown how principles of moral and political experience are exemplified in children's games (Piaget, 1934). And, as I have argued elsewhere, data from the world of work can be used as concrete exemplification in the learning and teaching of subjects from the liberal curriculum, especially language, mathematics, science, geography and history (Entwistle, 1970). Concrete exemplification of the liberal curriculum in order to point towards its instrumental value in daily life outside the classroom is an aspect of what Whitehead called the stage of romance in learning.

We observed earlier that history is often a casualty of schooling conceived in strictly instrumental terms. But mention of the concrete exemplification of knowledge and experience, which can be drawn from the past, suggests that the problem of relevance in education cannot be adequately addressed without taking the teaching of history seriously. I have already suggested that part of the problem of instrumentalism in education is the way in which perennial problems, predicaments and values become manifest in human life in different ways in particular times and places. And one of the contributions to coping with one's particular, present environment and the problems and opportunities it presents is the discovery that, albeit in a different guise, these are inevitable components of the human condition at all times and places. G.H. Bantock has written of 'the parochialism of the present', the illusion that one's own time is unique in the nature, volume and intensity of problems it experiences (Bantock, 1981). But the human race has a good deal of experience of much the same political, economic, social and cultural experiences that confront societies in the present day. Plagues and epidemics (not unlike AIDS), migrations of populations (such as those which exacerbate racial tensions today), natural and man-made disasters (such as those which create the refugee problem in the modern world), environmental pillage (like that which gave us the deserts and threaten the ozone layer today), aggressive nationalisms (which have been a major source of war throughout history down to the present day), as well as the positive contributions to civilization from individuals of great creativity, courage and prescience, seem to be, on the one hand, recurring scourges and, on the other, reassuring consolations of the human condition. To neglect history, as a narrowly conceived instrumental schooling often does, is not only to parochialize education; it is also to deny learners a kind of knowledge which, putting their own idiosyncratic dilemmas in perspective, is itself relevant to the understanding and handling of present experience.

For those not persuaded of the possibility that liberal education can have instrumental values, there remains the possibility of making room for instrumental knowledge and skill in schools by insisting upon a distinction between education and schooling. So far in this paper I have used the notions of school and education interchangeably. This is common enough in ordinary, everyday conversation, but perhaps more precision might be expected in an academic paper. Though there is considerable overlap between the two, schooling and education are not synonymous. Schools clearly have functions other than the singleminded education of children, and education often occurs outside the schools, in families, and in all manner of cultural institutions. Historically, schools have been concerned with all kinds of instrumentally valuable activities like health care, nutrition, road safety and driving instruction, charitable causes, as well as vocational training and religious indoctrination. At the present time they are urged to give instruction in form filling, getting a mortgage or signing an apartment lease, and so on through a range of market-relevant skills. But a curriculum devised from such a range of 'relevant' daily life skills would not add up to an education. Nor, as we have already argued, would it necessarily provide the best approach to enabling people to cope with the kinds of personal opportunities and dilemmas they will face throughout their lives. But, since 'he who pays the piper calls the tune', the State, which finances public education (as well as parents and religious bodies who finance private and parochial schools), can prescribe that its schools must provide whatever knowledge and skills are deemed necessary for its citizens. Some such prescriptions are not unreasonable; it seems perfectly appropriate that schools should devote time to instruction in road safety, or provide time for children to engage in charitable activities, like support for OXFAM or service to local senior citizens. These last may even contribute towards the school's distinctively educational function by exemplifying, concretely, the abstract moral principles which are the concern of moral education. But other non-educational activities imposed on the school, especially the many bureaucratic tasks required of teachers, can be an unreasonable intrusion on their work. The line between what is a legitimate instrumental task for schools to perform and what is not, is inevitably blurred. But whatever non-educational activities may seem reasonably required of schools, there is inevitably a danger that these will be in conflict with its educational role. As we have already seen, this is especially true of vocational training which, for many occupations, imposes strict limitations on the development of knowledge and skill. We have to ask how far meeting the State's need for a hierarchically structured labor force inevitably inhibits the school's educational function. Put simply, how far can the school deliberately limit an individual's development in the way required to socialize him or her for an unskilled or semi-skilled occupation, whilst at the same time attempting to cultivate the intelligence and moral and aesthetic sensibilities which education requires?

Bibliography

BAILEY, C. (1984) *Beyond the Present and the Particular: A Theory of Liberal Education*, London: Routledge and Kegan Paul.

BANTOCK, G.H. (1981) *The Parochialism of the Present*, London: Routledge and Kegan Paul.

BARROW, R. (1981) *The Philosophy of Schooling*, Brighton, Sussex: Wheatsheaf Books Ltd.

BOWEN, J. (1972) *A History of Western Education*, London: Methuen and Co.

COHEN, B. (1983) *Means and Ends in Education*, London: George Allen and Unwin.

CRITTENDEN, B. (1981) *Education for Rational Understanding*, Hawthorn, Victoria, Australia: The Australian Council for Educational Research.

ENTWISTLE, H. (1970) *Education, Work, and Leisure*, London: Routledge and Kegan Paul.

HIRST, P. (1974) *Knowledge and the Curriculum*, London: Routledge and Kegan Paul.

HUIZINGA, J. (1949) *Homo Ludens*, London: Routledge and Kegan Paul.

PETERS, R.S. (1977) *Education and the Education of Teachers*, London: Routledge and Kegan Paul.

PETERS, R.S. (1966) *Ethics and Education*, London: George Allen and Unwin.

PETERS, R.S. (1988) 'Democratic values and educational aims', in HARE, W. and PORTELLI, J.P. (Eds) *The Philosophy of Education*, Oxford: Oxford University Press.

PETERS, R.S. and HIRST, P. (1970) *The Logic of Education*, London: Routledge and Kegan Paul.

PETERS, R.S., WOODS, J. and DRAY, W.H. (1973) 'Aims of education — a conceptual inquiry', in PETERS, R.S. (Ed.) *The Philosophy of Education*, Oxford: Oxford University Press.

PIAGET, J. (1934) *The Moral Judgement of the Child*, London: Routledge and Kegan Paul.

WHITE, J. (1983) *The Aims of Education Restated*, London: Routledge and Kegan Paul.

WHITE, J. (1973) *Toward a Compulsory Curriculum*, London: Routledge and Kegan Paul.

6   Autonomy and Education

Evelina Orteza y Miranda

Introduction

In an open and pluralistic society like Canada or the United States, it is expected that individuals should be able and disposed to reach sound decisions for themselves at least in the more important areas of their lives. The expectation, however, is not easily achieved by everyone. Competing views on what constitutes public good, individual well-being, or good government abound and perplex individuals. As well, rapid changes taking place in society, in its moral, political, economic or technological aspects, make it necessary to understand vast amounts of data and information as a basis for considering these changes and assessing their impact on the quality of life. There must also be some guarantee that this kind of thinking can be done in a way that is as free as possible from the manipulation or influence of the mass media, the pressure of authority figures, and so on. It is, therefore, desirable and indeed necessary that schooling should have as one of its major goals the development of critical and independent thought and judgment, that is, the development of personal autonomy.

This chapter will first examine features of autonomy which may be judged central to, or constitutive of, its meaning. Arguing that autonomy need not be restricted to rationality, it will then examine and discuss the moral and epistemic autonomy of school subject matter and the autonomy of the learners.

Conditions of Autonomy

The word *autonomy*, which is made up of *auto* (one's own or my self) and *nomy* (a law), simply means one's own law. To exercise autonomy is to be

I express appreciation to Professor J. Douglas Stewart, The University of Regina, for his instructive and critical comments on a draft of this chapter.

subject to the self and its laws, thus to be self-ruling. An autonomous person is minimally an independent, self-governing individual.

While *one's own* or *one's self* may be a necessary condition of autonomy it is certainly not sufficient. If it were, person A who creates his or her rules, knowing them to conflict with acceptable societal moral rules or to be illogical or ill-informed, and acts on them, could then be considered autonomous. Yet acting on rules simply because they are one's own, with no regard for consequences, can hardly count as autonomy. If the instance of person A were to be universalized, a chaotic rather than an autonomous state would clearly be the result. To inquire into the concept further, it will be necessary to examine the relationships between self and rules and thus of the meaning of *one's own rules.*

Three Senses of Own

To say I own my rules is to say I am answerable to no one but myself for what I decide to do. No one else is to be blamed for consequences that arise because of what I do. *Own* means admit as in 'own up to one's wrong-doing'. It is to admit that one has freely adopted some rules which now are one's own. It could mean that the rules are adopted in the absence of external pressures, coercions or threats, and independently of what others say. Some of the concepts involved are independence, self-direction, responsibility and volition.

One's own could also be translated as *mine*, signifying ownership. To own something is to acquire something external to one's self. For example, acquiring knowledge of a second language is to acquire knowledge external to the one who is acquiring it. Similarly, *one's own rules* could refer to certain rules, laws, and the like, which are external to an individual and which one decides to acquire. In deciding to acquire something, one undertakes comparing, evaluating or ranking of things. Deliberation is necessarily present.

However, one may come to own or acquire something in such a way that it is not integrated into but is independent of a person's total frame of mind. In such a case, whether or not the owner possesses what she or he owns does not affect the owner. A piece of information acquired today and good only for tomorrow's examination, after which it vanishes from memory, leaves one no better or worse off. Either way it is not essential enough to determine one's ways of thinking.

A third sense of *one's own* implies that one is the originator or source of rules. It is not that a person acquires or chooses these rules from among those already existing but, rather, one *forms* his or her own rules. In a sense, these rules do not exist independently of one's self. *Own* in this sense, is akin to *own* in *my own children.* It means I am, in part, the source of their origin.

Is *one's own* (third sense) devoid of any public criteria? How could judgments be made between competing and conflicting rules if they are (privately) self-justified? Moreover, how does one know that one's rule is, indeed, one's own self-originated rule? How does self-origination, or what maybe called *internal ownership* come about? These questions will be dealt with in the sections that follow.

In contrast with external ownership, internal ownership requires active reflection. To choose to own something suggests alternatives. In reflecting upon which wants, opinions, objects, entities or rules to own, the chooser is not passive toward them. Whatever is chosen is not transported whole and intact to one's existing knowledge but is made to fit in with what one already has, becoming an intrinsic part of one's own self-concept. This deliberative process affects the person and, in turn, is affected as it relates and combines with all other qualities of one's self. The opinion, object or rule may, in the first instance, be identified objectively. But as it becomes part of one's total frame of mind, it may be difficult to isolate and identify objectively, for now some of its qualities are originated exclusively by that particular individual. It is now enmeshed with all that that person is. It becomes uniquely or truly his or her own. And the uniqueness is solely due to the particularity and singularity of one's self. No one else will have the object or the piece of knowledge acquired and manifested in action in exactly the same way as by that particular self. It is a *personal appropriation* of what is known, hence, appropriate, to the condition of the knower and fitting in with all of the knower's innermost convictions, feelings and emotions. The self generates or originates those qualities which are particular or singular to itself and which make for the uniqueness of what one owns. But this is not to say that it is self-originated out of nothing.

Adopting a rule as one's own is not simply to choose it from among already existing rules but rather *to form* one's own rule based on existing rules or facts which are judged relevant and particular to that formation, especially if they contribute some understanding on how this rule could function and fit in with the rest of one's knowledge. Discussion on its factuality and logic points to the public aspects of forming one's own rules. It is not completely subjective but it is centrally subjective due to the uniqueness, particularity and singularity of the self that makes something owned in the way it is owned. And the uniqueness of the self makes it one's own — no one else owning it in exactly the same way. Thus, it appears as though one's own rule, by virtue of its uniqueness, is of one's own making out of nothing because it may not resemble any other rule in its entirety. The formation, the form of the rule, and the rule itself seem to be wholly dependent on one's self, hence, self-originated.

The quality of uniqueness or particularity must be *grasped intuitively* as particulars of a person and cannot be subsumed under rules, generalizations and abstractions. In coming to own a rule and in owning it, one's self participates or enters fully in the making of some of its qualities. The unanalyzability of such qualities, or their being unnamed, is captured by such expressions as 'That is just the way she is' or 'You have to know him well to grasp his uniqueness'. To answer the question, 'How did you come to own your opinions and beliefs in that way?', one could provide some objective pieces of information and at the same time demur: 'I cannot express all there is to my experiences'. Words are not commensurate with them. One's self, in its fluctuations and incompleteness, necessarily participates in the making of one's rule or else it would not be indicative of autonomy even if public warrants are fulfilled.

The interest in self-origination is not in its 'purely naked ownership' (Peters, 1974a, p. 428) or in '. . . self-assertive ownership and power-seeking which is blind to all else' (Bonnett, 1986, p. 123). It is in promoting authenticity of one's self without necessarily disregarding rationality and in suggesting mutual relationship between public and private criteria, objectivity and subjectivity. In so doing, the staleness and boredom of subjecting others to second-hand knowledge and experience is avoided.

In summary, the preceding discussion showed that *own* in the sense of acquire, could mean that rules can be chosen and acquired independently of participation of one's self. Characterized by external ownership and doubtful presence of conscious self-reflection, this would indicate that autonomy may not be a characteristic of the above case. The second sense of *own*, to admit, involves the presence of one's self by identifying, to some extent, with rules acquired and owned. Admission of responsibility indicates participation of self. Minimally, the relationship could partake of autonomy. The third sense of *own*, as origination, secures the meaning of self-ruling. There is full participation and entry of one's self in formulating and arriving at the form that one's rules should take. This sense encompasses the formulation of a rule, an opinion, or the like, which is unique.

Autonomy necessarily presupposes a self that is the subject of freedom. But what is *self* and what could be an adequate conception of it?

Conceptions of Self

Arnold S. Kaufman (1973) qualifies *self* as *core self* and defines it generally as:

> . . . that constellation of relatively deeply rooted, important dispositions, knowledge of which helps us to anticipate and explain his actions over a relatively extended stretch of his total behavior. And when he acts in conflict with those dispositions they enable us to expect and to explain his discomfort . . . (p. 47)

Self is a basis for predicting and expecting someone to act or behave in certain ways under certain conditions. And when one's action is in conflict with one's important dispositions, it may be said that they are not deeply rooted or important dispositions. One may say, 'That's not his usual behaviour', or 'Something awful must have happened to make her act that way'. In rendering self a behavioral or observational matter, Kaufman manages to remove the complexities of self.

Alan Gewirth talks of the rational self which is '. . . that aspect of the total personality whereby one can ascertain and act according to what is logically and empirically justifiable' (1973, p. 43). An aspect of one's self and the criteria it observes are both specified without suggesting the presence of an unobservable entity guiding one's psyche. The total self, as a complex combination of various instinctual, emotional and conative elements, is guided and coordinated by the rational self. The self of autonomy is the rational self. 'Autonomy', Gewirth says, 'means that the rational self sets or accepts for itself the rational law' (1973, p. 41). To be autonomous, '. . . one acts as a rational person, in accordance with rationally justifiable norms whose rational justifiability one recognizes and accepts for oneself precisely because and insofar as one is rational' (*ibid.*). In short, the self is the rational self and autonomy is rationality. But why not the religious or emotional self? Emotion, says Gewirth, '. . . does not have the same kind of relative fixity and universality as is found in rational criteria' (*ibid.*, p. 43). In contrast, autonomy may be secured on public criteria of rationality, defined as '. . . the ability and disposition to take due account both of relevant empirical facts and of logically necessary connections' (*ibid.*, p. 42).

Rationality may be an aspect of self, but to say that it guides and coordinates other aspects of self is to suggest that rationality is more than an aspect of self. A part of a whole has been taken or mistaken to be the whole itself. Providing a normative definition of autonomy, Gewirth has arbitrarily restricted self, removing its complexities and liveliness.

Common to formulations of self is an assumption that self, whatever it is, is, more or less, permanent. To speak of the self as most deeply entrenched, deeply rooted, or last to be tampered with is to suggest that any change to one's ways, beliefs, and the like is peripheral to the self. For a self to be capable of explaining changes in one's behavior or beliefs, it must remain, more or less, fixed.

Such formulations also attempt to establish boundaries of self by positing certain logical and public characteristics. For if self is without limits, what could be the difference between autonomy and anarchy? (Gewirth, 1973, p. 41). But to set limits to self seems to lead to a paradoxical situation. If, for example, achievement of autonomy is by means of initiation into some forms of knowledge, this could mean that one first learns to become autonomous not by self-ruling over one's thinking, but by submitting and restricting one's self to some external criteria ruling over one's self, thus violating one's sense of ownership. How this could lead to autonomy appears problematic.

Self is also noted as an inner quality of a person. Its objective, public aspects, while informative of one's self, may not be altogether constitutive of one's self. Self could and does elude complete objectification.

If presence and freedom of self have to be argued as a necessary part of autonomy, perhaps self could be examined in such a way that it is not reduced to an objective matter or to rationality. We must acknowledge some of its own characteristics, for example, subjectivity, without necessarily allowing it to run away from intelligible discourse. A brief exposition of this view may now be attempted.

Self — a totality of one's past and future experiences. A self is a totality of one's experiences, past and future; it serves to differentiate one person from another, especially from the perception or judgment of others. In a significant way, self seems to be always in the past, constituted of all those past experiences which are reflected upon and figured out in order to fit them into one's sense of unity. It is also a source of information from which one could draw when making choices in the future or making the past. However, past experiences, when reflected upon, are described in objective terms, sometimes akin to a calculated language, as though the person talking about them were not a part of those experiences. The experiences, now an objective past, are abstracted and robbed of their dynamic qualities. Perhaps, this is necessary.

A living self needs to interconnect with other selves and this requires forms of communications that are rule-bound. This means that experience in reflection, couched in these forms, is not equivalent to the inner contents of one's lived experiences. Experience in reflection is necessary for a sense of community and interconnectedness in society, but it does not encompass all of experience or of self. A totality of one's experiences past and future, self cannot be fully expressed in forms of expression that are rule-governed.

Self cannot be objectified because it is partly in the future and involves some kind of self-making process. It is like an ideal of unity of all one's experiences, which one ascribes to one's self. At the same time, it is also '. . . present as the meaning and the ideal goal of each act . . .' (Barnes, 1967, p. 247), but self changes with each new act. Self, a becoming, is necessarily incomplete, indeterminate and not calculable in advance.

The ambivalence of self derives from its ambiguous need to establish for itself what may be called its finite, temporal space in a world shared by other selves. Self needs expression. Expression of one's self, however, could also become an accumulation of descriptions and explanations of one's self, constituting its limitation if not objectification. But a self that is totally and completely in isolation, speaking in one's private language, is not a self fully alive and could end up in a state of lunacy.

However, to be a self is to be in reality, to be an experiencing participant in one's immediate feelings. A live self is in flux, incomplete, with its self-originating potential (capacity, ability, power) to create infinite possibilities as it tries to resolve the tension that one transforms into some kind of unity. Whether the latter is achieved may not be the significant point but that the participating self in reality is characterized by freedom and acts freely, hence, autonomously, is significant. In this view, self is '. . . a power of choosing . . . at each moment the relation which we wish to establish with the world around us and with our own past and future experiences in that world' (Barnes, 1967,

p. 13). Self is essentially and constantly a choice, a free choice, hence not completely predictable.

On the one hand, self to be alive needs to interconnect with others, limiting one's freedom. On the other hand, a self alive is in flux and not always subject to advance calculation. An ambiguity in existence results in tension and in frustration. Self, its thoughts, convictions, and feelings that constitute its necessary uniqueness and particularity cannot be captured by generalizations and abstractions. But it is not completely unanalyzable and its facticity does not determine it. A familiar story could illustrate more vividly the concept of 'self' as a 'power of choosing'.

The story of Abraham: An illustration. This is the well-known story of Abraham commanded by God to sacrifice Isaac, his son: 'Take your son, your only son Isaac, whom you love, and go to the region of Moriah. Sacrifice him there as a burnt offering on one of the mountains I will tell you about' (Genesis: 22, v.2). There is something absurd about the command in that it goes against God's promise to Abraham that Sarah, his wife, who was past childbearing age, would bear him a son and that, through this son, God's covenant with Abraham would be fulfilled.

If Isaac was to be sacrificed, how could God fulfill His promise? Moreover, to kill Isaac goes against God's injunction of 'Thou shalt not kill'. What would guide Abraham in coming to an autonomous decision whether or not to sacrifice his son? Kaufman's view of self would say that Abraham would not likely obey this particular command. On three past occasions, he had disobeyed God. According to Gewirth, Abraham would have to go through a whole gamut of reasoning and deliberating to reach a rational decision characteristic of a rational self. On balance, it could be more reasonable or rational to disobey God and be within the boundaries of ethical communal norms. Abraham proceeded to act on God's instruction but, before he could slay his son, God intervened, saying, 'Do not lay your hand on the lad . . .' (Genesis: 22, v.12).

Abraham did not restrict himself to established communal ethical principles; he did not allow his reasons to control his decision. He showed that ethical rules of one's defined group and reason can be suspended, exceeded or transcended in making a decision. One could act completely and alone with one's innermost conviction that faith is higher than reason. Seemingly freed from an injunction of God, Abraham was self-sufficient, exercising his power to choose to believe on his own that God would fulfill His promise. His act was 'a leap of faith'.[2]

One cannot fully understand the motivations and the passion behind Abraham's actions by concentrating on the objectivity of the case. Instead, it is necessary to refer to the particularities of Abraham's life and take into account his self. One must try to suspend or transcend one's own ethical rules in order to understand Abraham, not as a determined member of a group, but as a self.

Self, however, does not do away with every externality or rule all the time. Autonomy suggests that not every decision one has to make is equally demanding of one's power to choose. Indeed, I could be grateful for some existing rules — traffic rules, for example — to which I willingly submit, eliminating the need to think about them daily. There could also be some problems on which I may not necessarily desire to exercise my autonomy because they do not figure in important areas in my life. If, however, for some reasons I decide to reflect and act on them, I would be free to do so and know how to go about them correctly.

Abraham's story points out that one's self can choose freely out of its own self-sufficiency. Because the self is indeterminate and open to infinite possibilities, it cannot be determined in advance. And its incompleteness provides the freedom to act. The self risks itself in its freedom to act in the presence of external norms, rules, and the like. One may initially submit to some rules or conventions and achieve autonomy but not solely and always by virtue of submitting to them. Rather, in submitting to them, one also learns to suspend them and comes to know when to abandon or transcend them and to be free to exercise the potential of self in creating its own infinite possibilities. Autonomy could be both a submission to certain external rules and at the same time a transcendence of such rules, a striving to reach out to one's self. In moments when this is achieved, as with Abraham, it may be said that 'one is a law unto one's self'. The paradox of restricting self in advance is overcome.

Autonomy: Necessary Conditions

Rationality

Presence of rationality is commonly considered a necessary condition of autonomy. For if autonomy has to do with self and its relationship to rules, in particular in assessing and weighing different specific ways of owning them, this implies the need to reason, '... to weigh the pros and cons of the alternatives ...' (Peters, 1974b, p. 340). To choose among them requires critical assessment and deliberation. Moreover, autonomy suggests self-ruling. This suggests that one's self is in control of one's reasons for whatever one is doing. One is free to choose when one chooses in accord with reason. Self-ruling means to be in control of one's rules over one's self, assuming rationality.

Consider these cases: (a) Suppose someone has reasons for choosing a particular candidate for a mayoralty election. Suppose further that one's reasons for choosing Miss X are identical with those of someone else. Could we conclude that the person did not exercise autonomy?; (b) Suppose that after a lengthy discussion about political dictatorship, your friend chooses to side with a dictator and obey all the decrees issued. You, on the other hand, disagree with your friend. Who could be said to display autonomy or presence of reason?

In the first case, we would be tempted to suspect that one copied or imitated the other's answer. In the second case, one would tend to side with the decision to disobey the dictator. After all, who could, in one's *right mind*, support dictatorship? But these are simplistic answers.

In the first case, it is possible that the two choices simply happen to coincide. Or it could be that after a thorough discussion, both come to the same decision. But identical decisions or conformity to decisions of others do not necessarily negate autonomy. It depends upon whether the decision was based on one's own reasoned judgment to concur and not on mindless habits. It is also possible that, after a discussion and debate, I could accept someone else's reasons to be mine, convinced that there is much sensibility to his or her reasons. On my own volition, I freely decide to accept one's reasons as mine and for good reasons. Even though the rationality employed in coming to a decision is based on second-hand reason, it is indicative of autonomy, nonetheless.

The second case may suggest that autonomy is necessarily connected with political morality. But this is not so. Good reasons could be given for dictatorships — for example, that a country needs a benevolent ruler to secure economic well-being and political stability. If these are subjected to critical assessments and if one accepts them on the basis of reasoned judgment, then one is acting autonomously. Whether it is morally right or wrong is irrelevant to autonomy. 'Great criminals are markedly autonomous men' (Dearden, 1971, p. 461). They could be completely rational and possess a resoluteness of will to act without moral scruples. Autonomy is not necessarily morality.

It may also be said that rationality is necessary to autonomy because, as long as one reasons in accord with some general principles, one could be free from other people's control and free to exercise independence of thought and action with regard to the conduct of life. One may be committed to a belief in God, but as long as one reasons, belief could remain open and subject to critical examination and even rejection. Holding beliefs does not necessarily restrict or negate autonomy. Rationality is a condition of freedom and autonomy. For the exercise of rationality to count as autonomous, however, it must involve one's own reasons. But what is one's own reason?

Authenticity

Earlier it was shown that one's own could mean that one is the undisputed origin of whatever is owned. There is no need to establish its validity by means of an external standard. To claim authenticity about something is to claim truth and genuineness about it, denying deceit, falsity and artificiality. *Authenticity* is, therefore, akin to one's own in the origination sense.

It is, however, also possible to claim something as one's own even if one were not its undisputed origin and, at the same time, claim authenticity. For it is in one's manner of holding and employing reasons which is said to be one's own. One may have learnt or picked up from someone else her reasons and now they are authentic of the person. They are now part of her total understanding and behavior. Reasons secured by memorization or mere repetition are not authentic reasons, however. They may be one's own but only in the external sense.

Autonomy, in its rationality and authenticity aspects, does not require that a person always operates only on the level of one's own akin to origination. I learn from others, accept pieces of information from respected authorities, obey the laws and even keep some revered traditions. To them all, I hold a rational attitude.

In summary, for a reasoning, which purportedly explains an action, to be authentic it must, according to Barrow (1975), meet these conditions: (1) It must genuinely be the explanation of the action. My reason may be empirically true but, if it is not a real reason, then it is not an authentic reason. My real reason for not translating a piece of literature from English to Spanish is that I cannot do it. This is the authentic reason. But I can also give a true reason saying I am too busy to do it. (2) The agent really believes in the reasons given. One does not only propound reasons for doing something but also cares about these reasons and strives to observe them. (3) The reasoning must relate to or fit other aspects of one's life. If authentic, my reasoning does not contradict my total set of beliefs but fits into or is consistent with it. Earlier, this was referred to as one's own in the origination sense or internal ownership.

Strength and Resoluteness of Will

Must one act autonomously all the time with regard to all things in order to be judged autonomous? First, it is clear that an autonomous person is able to think and act in a way explained by the activity of one's mind. One must have acted, say in the past, autonomously and is, therefore, so judged. Second, autonomy is a degree notion, hence, judgment is required to know which action is indicative of full, partial or minimal autonomy. To think for one's self and to hold firmly to one's views about life could be considered autonomous. But suppose that standards for thinking are not observed. How will this be judged? It might be easy to judge Abraham, Joan of Arc, the Virgin Mary or Martin Luther as fully autonomous at the most critical times in their lives. But not everyone can be expected, least of all required, to be autonomous in the same way and to the same degree. When to act autonomously and on what grounds depends upon the significance of the situation relative to the important areas of one's life. Third, an autonomous person would be expected to know what the more important areas of life are and be expected to exercise autonomy in them. However, there could be much disagreement over what the important areas of life are and, consequently, it may be difficult to recognize whether one is acting autonomously or not. When expected to act autonomously, and one does not, it may not be for lack of autonomy or of will but because the problem in question does not figure in an important area in one's life. Finally, it has to be admitted that even an autonomous person could be subject every now and then to weakness of will. The exercise of resolute will is a matter of degree in addition to being a contingent condition of autonomy.

The difficulty in mapping autonomy leads to difficulties in making conclusive statements about it. It is, however, safe to say that there are degrees of autonomy exercised with regard to most situations by a number of people. Banal and unexciting as this conclusion is, it is perhaps a close portrayal of what actually takes place in a variety of life's situations which require answers to practical questions.

Freedom and Independence

Autonomy usually implies freedom and independence. Freedom means complete absence of any kind of internal and external constraints. If autonomy implies freedom, it may not have a place in education, for education is a curtailment of one's freedom. Education, as the initiation into worthwhile cognitive and affective activities, is restrictive on epistemological and moral grounds. Matters of truth and treatment of learners as persons are obligatory. Education is not freed from every consideration; it is not free to do anything.

But certain relevant freedoms must be assumed as a prior condition of education for its procedures and goals, such as the development of learners' autonomy, to be achieved. The development of autonomy presupposes freedom to ask questions, to inquire and to expect to be taken seriously by the teachers. To be free to inquire into what one is studying in order to understand it is freedom relevant to one's learning. Freedom to engage in these activities presupposes freedom from fear, thought control, political oppression. These are some freedoms relevant to education.

To exercise one's autonomy, relevant freedom is necessary. If a student is prevented from expressing his views about something and from acting on them, his autonomy cannot be exercised. One may be free to think but prevented from acting. One, of course, could insist on exercising autonomy against all odds, aware of the dangers that may come about.

Relevant freedom is necessary to exercise autonomy but it is not a necessary condition for the development of autonomy (Dearden, 1975, pp. 3–18). An environment relatively free of rules or regulations does not necessarily lead to development of an autonomous character. A child brought up in a rigid atmosphere could develop into an autonomous character. The relationship between freedom and development of autonomy is, at best, a contingent one.

Independent-mindedness is associated with autonomy in the sense that an autonomous person is not easily convinced by every wind of doctrine. She tends to have a mind of her own and knows when to agree and to disagree. But autonomy is not independent-mindedness if this is taken to mean that she is steeled in her convictions, rendering them beyond examination and critical inquiry. This is closer to close-mindedness and stubbornness of will than to autonomy. An autonomous person is independent-minded in the sense that she tends to challenge conventional and traditional forms of thinking by disclosing their inadequacies. This means that her criticism is within the current and prevailing forms of inquiry. But if to challenge means to go beyond traditional forms of thought, how could they be recognized and on what grounds?

Autonomy is not independent-mindedness taken to mean complete independence. It is not an attribute of an individual, who is in complete isolation from everyone, but of one in the context of social relationships. Exercise of autonomy is not independence but an interdependence of individuals who in their lives are trying to figure out areas where they ought or ought not to exercise autonomy. Autonomy and its exercise are matters of degree and subject to one's judgment.

Features of a Moral Problem

Moral problems are occasioned by the fact that conflicts of interest could arise among individuals living in a group or society. To discourage such occasions or resolve conflicts, rules which function as regulatory principles binding on all are generated. Restrictions are intended to encourage a sense of shared living within a group and to increase areas of freedom judged meaningful and desirable in individual pursuit of intended ends. Rules and regulations which structure one's social life are attempts to deal with morals or moral behavior. At the heart of morality is the question: 'How ought I to live, considering that there are others like me, with similar feelings, pains, interests, hopes and dreams?'

Consider the following illustration: A student who is about to fail one of her subjects has resorted to cheating. She is successful, passes her subject and is not caught. She says that cheating is a matter of survival or knowing the tricks of the trade. Moreover, there is no harm done to others. Another student who is also failing does not believe that cheating in order to pass is morally right. What should this student do? Report the first student or do as she has done?

An obvious feature of a moral problem is the question whether an act is morally right or wrong. If cheating is morally right in this particular situation what are some reasons for it being so? The student says she did it for her own interest. No one is harmed. First, the student makes a moral judgment: One's act is morally right. Second, she gives reasons for her judgment and, finally, she appeals to some kind of a moral principle to justify her reasons. Are there grounds for agreeing with her that what she did is not morally wrong?

It may be agreed that to cheat could be one of many *creative* ways of surviving in a group. But, from this, it does not follow that any way of surviving, including cheating, is morally correct. What if one's acts could give rise to some consequences adverse to other people's self-interest? Indeed, the student says that, on grounds of consequence, her act is morally right: No one was harmed. Still, in her act, harm was done to the existing set of rules regarding societal or group standards of proper behavior. Suppose the student replies that her highest moral principle is her survival or promotion of her own self. Is this refutable or disputable?

It is difficult, if not impossible, to refute someone's overriding moral principles. If a person subscribes to a principle of justice and another to one of love and care, who is right? Disputation must simply go on to convince one or the other that one principle is to be preferred to the other on grounds of, say, comprehensiveness of principle, or societal stability.

In the example, the student may be shown that adhering to her moral principle is not without problems. Another person sharing the same principle could act in ways that, while promoting his interests, could be detrimental to her survival. If there is no other principle to appeal to in order to settle their disagreements, she may have to change her interests or submit to the other's interest. Moreover, if this principle were generalized, adverse effects on societal stability could be predicted. The student, however, could hold on to her moral principle even if she admits to some of its problems.

To a considerable extent, the difficulty in coming to an agreement on moral principles or specific forms of morality is that moral problems have to do with important areas of one's life, those that are closest to self-esteem or self-importance. The slave owner sees no moral problem with his treatment of slaves, justifying it on grounds of power or even economics. Slaves deserve what they get — the treatment is fair. Gangsters could violate certain rights of others when they go about killing and robbing victims. Their thinking and intentioned actions have to do with what they consider important to their lives. Whatever the differences, whether one is a believer in God, an atheist, or a Communist, she has her moral principles relative to some problems and actions. And sharing the same moral principle, as in the example of cheating, does not automatically lead to clearly defined *correct* solutions.

Second, there is no absolute certitude regarding the rightness of one's moral principles. Moral statements or judgments are neither analytic nor synthetic; they are neither absolutely true nor false. The judgment 'Stealing is wrong' is not true by definition. It is not an analytic sentence as evidenced by the fact that there is nothing illogical about the judgment 'Stealing is not wrong'. It is not a synthetic or an empirical statement. From the facts or act of stealing, no observations can confirm that it is wrong, bad or immoral to steal or that we ought not to steal. If 'stealing is wrong' were an empirical or factual statement, then the facts in themselves would be sufficient to establish the truth of the statement. But this is not so. The problem here is that the conclusion contains an 'ought' — one ought not to kill or steal — which is not contained in the factual premises or descriptions of the act of stealing. *What is* does not logically translate into *what ought* to be done. The question remains: 'How do we come *to know* what is morally right, wrong, good or bad?'

Even if one's moral judgment is acceptable in the sense that one observes matters of fact, relevant reasons, and appeals to a moral principle, this does not necessarily mean that one's moral judgment is automatically valid or morally acceptable. Conditions that have been proposed to deal with the validity and acceptability of moral judgments and principles include (i) universalizability, (ii) viewing human beings as ends in themselves, (iii) treating persons impartially, (iv) consequences, and (v) attention to relevant facts, logic and rules of reasoning. Based on these conditions, the student's cheating could be judged acceptable only if it can be argued that those in similar situations should also engage in cheating. What goes for one, goes for all others who are similarly placed. However, to universalize it could bring harm or do damage to existing rules of an educational system and adversely affect the running of schools. On the other hand, if the student says that no one else should engage in cheating, then she is claiming a special status. Impartiality regarding persons is thus not observed. When the student says that no one is harmed by her act, she is arguing that one's act is not right or wrong in itself but that its consequences could attest to its moral acceptability. This, however, separates one's intentions from the consequences of one's action. In sum, to make a moral judgment and a moral decision is to suggest that one is not making a decision for one's self alone but is also making a general (prescriptive) statement, saying that those in similar situations should do likewise. The student's moral decision to cheat is fraught with difficulties.

Clearly, decisions in the moral realm are intended to result in moral acts. Such acts are supposed to be autonomous. When one acts on a moral problem it must be the case that one's decision to act and one's action are one's own. Moral acts are the agent's and no one else's. Even if I act on the advice of others, still, in the end, my agency decides to take their piece of advice. Insistence on moral acts being one's own is tied to the idea of responsibility for one's action and the consequences arising out of it. Knowledge, understanding and intentionality are all necessary in a moral act. One's entire consciousness, heart-and-head together, is involved in coming to a moral decision to act in a certain way.

The discussion suggests that some acts giving rise to adverse consequences may not necessarily be in the moral realm and should not be subjected to moral judgments. Students who succumb to extreme pressures from their peers to do something morally wrong may show weakness of will but not necessarily neglect of responsibility for their actions. The teacher's task is to widen student understandings and autonomy so that they become more capable of genuine moral judgments and actions.

It is not mere autonomy, taken to mean freedom to do anything one might want to do, that is being argued in this chapter. Education is not interested in learners' becoming *merely free* but in enabling them to develop freely their thoughts and arguments regarding what they consider important, to plan their goals in life, and to generate their own moral principles, calling such conclusions their own. The importance of autonomy lies in its appropriate exercise in different areas of one's life.

Moral Autonomy and Education

Independence of thought and reasoned judgments are some of the expected outcomes of education. There is no disagreement on the value or desirability of autonomy for, to some extent, all human beings already exercise autonomy if it is taken simply to mean 'holding opinions and behaving as they see fit' (Barrow, 1975, p. 137). But the interest of education in autonomy is not merely to enable individuals to behave as they see fit but in acting to take account of matters of fact, logic and interests of others. 'Without morality', says Dearden, 'the more autonomous an agent is the worse he is likely to be' (Dearden, 1971, p. 461).

It will be instructive, at this point, to distinguish briefly between an educated person, an autonomous person and a morally autonomous person, and then to identify the common features they share.

An educated person is one who has a considerable breadth of knowledge and understanding. Her judgments are informed and her manner of acting toward things displays presence of reasons. These qualities of mind are considered individually and socially worthwhile, desirable and theoretically significant for understanding the natural and social worlds. To judge someone an educated person is not merely to account for one's training but to refer to one's frame of mind with regard to all things.

An educated person tends to be observant of the norms and logic˝of the various forms of knowledge and is dependent, in part, upon authoritative epistemic judgments. Presented with a problem, an educated person will deal with it according to established rules so as to arrive at a correct or reasonable answer. An impersonal standard is referred to. One could be cowardly, timid or inwardly unauthentic and be educated no less, so long as one's reasons and judgments meet public standards of facts and logic. An educated person tends to be knowledge-referring and conforming (Telfer, 1975, pp. 32–4).

Both the educated person and the autonomous person, share rationality. An autonomous person exhibits rationality in his thought and actions. He could also be regarding of standards of knowledge and truth. However, autonomy strongly suggests the necessary presence of self in one's deliberations. He necessarily refers his reasoned judgments to his self. He asks whether or not his judgments are authentic to himself. His motivation is not always and solely with an answer's being correct according to an external standard but whether his reasons fit in with his total set of beliefs. An autonomous person tends to be self-referring but may not be always conforming to matters of truth and morals (Telfer, 1975, pp. 33–4).

Autonomy is not exercised in isolation but in social relationships. It is, therefore, necessary that an autonomous person take account of truth and interests of others, or be morally autonomous. An educated person could be morally autonomous only in the limited sense that rationality is exercised. An autonomous person need not be morally autonomous. For both to be morally autonomous, taking account of interest of others must be an added condition.

A morally autonomous person is also like an educated person in that both tend to appeal to impersonal standards of correctness. The former appeals to principles which could be binding on all members of society. Likewise, an educated person appeals to universal standards of knowledge. An educated person, however, need not refer her appeal to her self whereas a morally autonomous person does to ensure that authenticity of self is accounted for.

In sum, an educated person may or may not be morally educated. That is, her adopted specific form of morality may not be necessarily informed of understanding and criticism of morals and ethics. She may not know how to go about reasoning about moral problems in ways appropriate to them. And it is still the case that a morally educated person may or may not be morally autonomous. And to enjoy moral autonomy does not mean that one could always exercise it. If moral autonomy is to be a long-term goal of moral education, it means that one's self must be taught to learn to subscribe to and observe rules, laws, etc., pertinent to moral matters. And these rules, as restrictions to self, could be some of the contents of moral education aimed at preventing objectification of self and securing moral autonomy.

The Learner and Autonomy

If the expression *autonomous learner* means that a learner is trying to learn something, then it must be the case that her freedom to think in any way she wants about anything is curtailed and restricted to that which is the object of her learning. To try to learn mathematics, for example, is to learn, among other things, its rules and manners of argumentations, and to do mathematics correctly. One is not autonomous, meaning, holding on to her own reasoned judgments about mathematics while learning mathematics. She may argue, on rationality grounds, that she should be allowed to say anything she wants to say and insist that it should be counted as mathematics because it is about it. For example, she may claim that mathematics is a difficult subject, that it should not be a required course in university, and the like. But these are not statements that one has to learn in order to learn mathematics. One's autonomy in a given subject is restricted by rationality which is further restricted by the rules of the subject. Rationality in poetry is quite different from rationality in sociology or philosophy, or in one's conduct at Safeway. In being restricted in her thoughts while learning something, one is being governed by something external to her. Autonomous learners, as clarified here, does not apply to one who is trying to learn something.

Beginners in a study are not autonomous with respect to the requirements of the study. On their own, they cannot raise questions of importance, for example, its logic or structure, because they would not know it at this point. Questions for further information, clarification and understanding could, of course, be raised but they could not question if this requires that they should be in clear command of the language of the field, its boundaries and critical methods. It is not to deny learners their right to question but, as beginners, they would not know how to assess the answers or judge which ones are reasonable, for they are not in possession of adequate knowledge on which to make critical judgments. To give in to their right to question, at this point, would be a futile exercise. It is more instructive and of greater benefit to the learners first to learn, understand and subscribe to the facts and theories of a subject and the rules governing its logic. With adequate knowledge, one could increasingly learn to question on an informed basis and, perhaps, develop some degree of autonomy (Candy, 1981, pp. 59–76).

It is sometimes suggested that epistemic autonomy, or autonomy in subject matter learning, could also mean refusal to accept prevailing standards of knowledge and inventing one's own. But how this is done such that one's thinking could be understandable even if it is based on something completely and entirely new to all is not clear. Frankena (1973), who suggests this possibility, could only say that it cannot be done if it does not initiate us into some of the forms of life and thinking we are already aware of. Similarly, Feinberg (1973) argues that rational reflection, in the manner of an autonomous person, assumes some settled principles or convictions from and within which to reason and test more tentative principles and proposals. Autonomy does not mean examining everything afresh in making a decision on something. This would paralyze thinking. Kaufman (1973) also suggests that to achieve autonomy is not outright to reject traditional thinking in a subject but to select from it questions, problems and thoughts that most effectively challenge prevailing modes of thinking, feeling, and judgment.

Clearly, the sense of autonomy regarding subject matters or epistemic authority is '... following rules that one has accepted for oneself' (Hirst and Peters, 1970, p. 32). Restricted within these rules, say those of science and philosophy, one exhibits ease and discernible freedom in manipulating the rules, testing them for necessity or adequacy, trying another rule, suspending the rules, and replacing them with some newly formed ones. One is not mastered or controlled by these rules; rather, one has mastered them sufficiently such that he can alter them in some significant ways and change their order to reach alternative or new conclusions. One works within these rules *as though* independent of them, hence, autonomous. All these attempts and variations, however, remain acceptable within the accepted framework of the rules. This is autonomy similar to Thomas Kuhn's (1970) concept of the normal phase of the development of science. One tries to understand an accepted paradigm and develop its implications as fully as possible without criticizing it. This sense of autonomy, presupposing some authority and expertise in a field, is achievable in varying degrees by most learners.

Even so, perhaps, students should be encouraged to try inventing ideas of their own and to replace current ways of thinking even if they are not in full command of the logic or discourse of the field. Attempts of this kind could encourage students to accept a characteristic of human knowledge, namely, that it is a human construct subject to continuous inquiry and examination. Participation of their own ideas in some fields of inquiry could result in new, insightful conclusions. Knowledge-making and inventing is not necessarily bound to pre-established rules.

If the notion of the autonomous learner does not always apply to objects of study, it could apply to the learner's manner of going about her learning tasks, described as self-directed or self-initiated. One judges what is acceptable to do independent of, and free from, external pressures and guidance from someone else. More and more responsibilities for one's learning, setting of goals, and programme management are accepted. Various learning strategies, for example, student-directed learning, independent study, one-to-one program, negotiated learning contract, and others, are encouragements of autonomy in learning.

Autonomy in learning, in the sense of self-directing and self-continuing, is a common expectation of society regarding graduates of schools and universities. Students, having learned to submit to certain rules on their own, and having become independent of experts and authorities, continue studying and learning long after they have left schools. It indicates a growing confidence in one's abilities to direct one's self and to judge the qualities of one's work. One may, of course, continue to accept authoritative statements when it is necessary to do so but, more importantly, one can now issue one's own reasons and judgments about something and judge them just as good as those of others. One need not always seek confirmation of one's judgments and actions from others; he may seek his own for authentication.

The justification for autonomy in learning is clear. On one hand the pedagogical justification could be that, when learners are consulted and allowed to participate meaningfully in coming to a decision regarding their studies, especially those aspects that mean much to them, they tend to learn more effectively and meaningfully. Their involvement releases them from some unnecessary psychological feelings of being dominated by external pressures or by an arbitrary will of someone who has no regard for what they have to say on their behalf. On the other hand, the moral justification for autonomy in learning is that relevant freedoms of learners are presupposed in education; for example, the freedom to be heard, to question, to be taken seriously in one's rejection of what is being taught, and the like. Indeed, autonomy in learning is a recognition of one's moral right to pursue one's goals in life and to become whatever one decides to become.

Development of Moral Autonomy

As an indeterminate entity, self needs to be mastered or controlled to exercise moral autonomy. To be mastered by moral rules is to suggest that when one is confronted with a moral problem one employs them without fail. When mastery of the rules over someone is complete, one may be said to be controlled by them. Nothing could prevent her from doing what she thinks is morally right to do (Baier, 1973, p. 106).

Acceptance of moral rules, to be autonomous, is based on one's reasoned judgment that there are good moral reasons for doing one thing and not something else. One is, therefore, actively involved in trying to master them. Moral rules are not merely dumped on the learners' lap.

To try to master something is to do something specific repeatedly; for example, mastering typing skills, producing a foreign language sound, and the like. It is close or similar to being trained to do something. When attempts at mastering something are successful, what one does appears to be done without effort or thought, but out of habit. Specific moral behavior, such as honesty or fair play, could appear to be habitual behavior when mastered.

Moral self-mastery teaching is also related to the teaching of virtue. Being virtuous '. . . is not simply a matter of doing things on isolated occasions, it is also a matter of the habitual exercise of the virtues. . . . (T)he acquisition of a virtue depends on the formation of a virtuous habit' (O'Hear, 1981, p. 124). Teaching moral virtues is a matter of teaching someone to do something. More importantly, it seeks to insure that what is taught becomes dispositional or habitual. It includes teaching how to behave and, more importantly, to behave. It must be the case that one who has moral self-mastery does not merely choose to decide, if one chooses to decide at all, but that one decides to be honest, to do that which one judges morally right to do, if one chooses to decide at all. Moral virtues incline people to act virtuously (Baier, 1973, p. 107).

Connecting the teaching of self-mastery with virtue, habit and training is not necessarily questionable. Peters (1974a) has convincingly shown that reason, intelligence and judgments could be involved in them, too. Moreover, it is easier for learners to understand and learn a specific rule or behavior rather than a generalization empty of specifications. Mastery of certain specific moral rules, or exhibiting specific moral behavior is, therefore, a condition of moral autonomy. To say that one is morally autonomous is to point out pieces of observable evidences that, indeed, one is so. The teaching of certain agreed upon moral virtues is, therefore, a content of moral education with moral autonomy as one of its aims.

Moral judgments are necessary in resolving moral problems. To render a moral judgment one has to have some qualifications relevant to it. If one disregards his own judgment and accepts another person's because of fear of contradicting this person, his moral judgments may be questioned. In contrast, knowing how little I know of certain moral matters, I could accept someone's moral judgments about war, earth pollution, and the like, reasoning that she knows more about them than I do. The point here is how to master making moral judgments. Baier (1973, p. 111) suggests four types of proposition involved in the process of reasoning that leads to sound moral judgments. (1) 'Answers to questions of whether or not it would be morally wrong for a given person to do a certain thing here and now.' (2) Answers to 'more general questions whether certain types of act, such as killing, are morally wrong for anyone or certain classes of people ... in some circumstances ...'. Type (2) propositions guide one in determining the rightness or wrongness or a specific act in (1). The Ten Commandments is an example of Type 2. (3) Statements of general moral principle, such as justice, the Golden Rule, and the like. These statements assess acceptability or validity of type (2) statements. (4) Statements about the nature, function and rationale of the institution of morality. They justify acceptance of general principles in (3). Understanding these propositions is vital in the development of autonomy. To master making moral judgments, it is necessary to make moral judgments. The latter is dependent upon one's mastery of the process of moral reasoning and judging. To the extent that one is in complete mastery of the process, one could be independent of others in making one's judgments. Indeed, mastery of moral judgments is basic to making independent judgments.

Central to moral autonomy is one's determination to act on one's decisions. It is not enough that one has habits and has mastered moral judgments. Additionally one must also have some moral self-determination. Discussed previously in connection with resoluteness of will, determination within the limits of morality could be an aim of moral education. To be morally autonomous does not mean that one must act regardless of all costs or always invite death and disaster. This could be discussed as an ideal moral behavior illustrative of heroes and martyrs. But it could also be argued that one's self-determination should be the basis for judging when a moral decision must be exercised at all costs. 'Better red than dead' is not necessarily a contradiction of one's self-determination to live up to moral principles. It could also secure one's original, morally intended ends. On the contrary, self-determination may not be conducive to autonomy if it means a stubbornness of will such that one's determination is beyond examination and inquiry. This could be fanaticism and not moral autonomy.

The teaching of moral autonomy, in sum, would constitute the teaching of specific moral virtues, followed by moral knowledge in the form of the propositions presented, and the teaching of moral self-determination. From habitual practice, to knowledge and on to moral judgments, learners could be initiated into the logic of moral autonomy.

It must also be noted that moral autonomy as discussed in this chapter is not to be equated with rational autonomy. Rationality is, of course, a necessary condition, but moral autonomy is not reducible to it. Some writers, such as John Wilson (1973), seem to suggest that not only is rationality central to moral autonomy but is also constitutive of it. Rationality, however, could lead one to treat other people's interests as logical items. An example of this is Adolf Eichmann who was extremely rational in thought and action but failed to exhibit moral autonomy. There is more to moral autonomy than rationality: the desire to do good, to care for others and to love.

In concentrating on rationality, Wilson (1973) is able to set up a scheme against which one could check out his actions 'to find out if he is morally autonomous'. For example, he could ask: 'Did I act for a reason?' 'Was I logically consistent?' An attitude of detached objectivity towards one's moral problem is encouraged to separate one's agency from one's action. Wilson is interested in generating rules, abstractions, and the like about cases of moral decisions. His interest is in the abstract and not in the involvement of the particularities of the self — with its feelings, anguish and elation — that is going through the trauma of making a moral decision. But uppermost in our moral concern are the personal lives that need self-governing, not whether any particular moral rule or principle is always universalizable. The particularities and singularities of their concrete experiences must be taken into account in order to portray their actual moral decision-making situations. More importantly, the unique elements of each experience must be noted; all these, rightly or wrongly, cannot be defined by an abstract formula.

In addition to the suggested components of moral autonomy, one more could be considered crucial to it. The central moral interest for teachers is the idea of *relationships with others*. It is not in rules, regulations or principles that our particular moralities lie but in how we meet or relate to others. Answers to such questions as 'How did I respond to her question?' 'How far did I listen to him and to what extent did I take account of his particularity?' would show whether one cares or cares to relate. In Noddings' (1984) words: '. . . The primary test (of my caring) lies in an examination of what I considered, how fully I received the other, and whether the free pursuit of her projects is partly a result of the completion of my caring for her' (p. 81). Affections and feelings are not denials of moral autonomy. They are recognized for what they are and incorporated as appropriate components of the experience of moral reasoning and judging. It is not in isolation but in our relationships with others that moral autonomy is exercised. A community or social structure (say, the classroom) which is characterized by a set of relationships (for example, caring), encourages its members to be committed to and for others and to respect everyone's individuality and particularity, and could engender resolution toward self-determination and promotion of the social good — in short, toward moral autonomy.

Moral or personal autonomy, the exercise of one's freedom to decide in what one judges to be important areas in life, suggests very clearly *some* knowledge of one's self. Without it claims to autonomy in learning or to moral autonomy, could be empty. But as the following story shows, it may not be easy to know one's self.

The Man of God, a play which Gabriel Marcel (1952) regards as one of his most important plays, centers on a Huguenot pastor in a Paris slum. Twenty-five years before, he was a minister in a mountain village. There, he had doubts about his own inner strengths and the genuineness of his calling, and went through a moral crisis. Moreover, his wife had confessed to him that she had committed adultery and that her daughter was not his child. Plunged into deep despair, he did not know what to do. But as gleams of light dawned on him, he felt he had to forgive his guilty wife and help her to regain her soul. His being able to forgive her, in turn, restored his confidence in himself and in his calling to the ministry. His reconciliation with his wife, his forgiveness of her, became in some sense the cornerstone of his new life. His role as a minister was somehow re-established by his act of pardon, satisfying to some extent his own need for being the man he wanted or aspired to be.

Twenty years passed. Suddenly, the wife's former lover, very ill and dying, comes back to their lives. Before he dies, he wants to see the girl whom he knows to be his daughter. The pastor feels that this is his legitimate right. Moreover, as a man of God, is he not expected to be compassionate and forgiving even to those who have betrayed him?

The pastor's wife, on the other hand, feels that if her husband has real love for her he should not welcome the man who had betrayed him. She reconsiders the whole past and concludes that her husband's forgiveness was a professional gesture, something to be expected of a pastor and from which he benefited as a professional. She inflicts her husband with her own doubts and he, in turn, loses his bearings. He does not know what to think about his act, about himself. Is it possible for a person like him to become his role so completely that he can neither hate nor love? In utter despair, Claude, the minister, cries out in anguish: 'Who am I? When I try to get hold of myself, I escape from my own clutches!' (Marcel, 1950, pp. 153–4). To this question, Marcel does not provide a neat, satisfying answer. The play concludes with a probing ending. So does this chapter.

Notes

1   I have benefited much from the various lectures of Professor Petra von Morstein on 'Self' delivered to the Apeiron Society for the Practice of Philosophy, Calgary, Alberta, Canada, 20 October, 1987, 17 November, 1987, and 29 March, 1988. I

have drawn freely from some of her ideas and incorporated some of them in this section of the chapter. I acknowledge my indebtedness to her.

2 The purpose of inserting Abraham's story is simply to illustrate vividly actions which could be characterized as 'a leap of human faith'. It is not intended to go into a more serious discussion of matters like Soren Kierkegaard's life 'stages', namely, the aesthetic, the ethical and the religious or into his discussion of the universal and the absolute. See Kierkegaard (1940 and 1941).

Bibliography

ATHERTON, J. (1988) 'Virtues in moral education: Objections and replies', *Educational Theory*, 38, pp. 299–310.

BAIER, K. (1973) 'Moral autonomy as an aim of moral education', in LANGFORD, G. and O'CONNOR, D.J. (Eds) *New Essays in the Philosophy of Education*, London: Routledge and Kegan Paul.

BARNES, H.E. (1967) *An Existentialist Ethics*, New York: Knopf.

BARRETT, R. (1981) 'Freedom, License and A.S. NEILL', *Oxford Review of Education*, 7, pp. 157–64.

BARROW, R. (1975) *Moral Philosophy for Education*, London: Allen and Unwin.

BONNETT, M. (1986) 'Personal authenticity and public standards: Towards the transcendence of a dualism', in COOPER, D.E. (Ed.) *Education, Values and Mind*, London: Routledge and Kegan Paul.

BOUD, D. (Ed.) (1981) *Developing Student Autonomy in Learning*, London: Kogan Page.

CANDY, P. (1981) 'On the attainment of subject-matter autonomy', in BOUD, D. (Ed.) *Developing Student Autonomy in Learning*, London: Kogan Page.

CARTER, R.E. (1984) *Dimensions of Moral Education*, Toronto: University of Toronto Press.

CHAZAN, B. (1985) *Contemporary Approaches to Moral Education*, New York: Teachers College, Columbia University Press.

COCHRANE, D.B., HAMM, C.M. and KAZEPIDES, A.C. (Eds) (1979) *The Domain of Moral Education*, New York: Paulist Press.

COCHRANE, D.B. and MANLEY-CASIMIR, M. (Eds) (1980) *Development of Moral Reasoning*, New York: Praeger Publishers.

COOMBS, J.R. (1980) 'Validating moral judgments by principle testing', in COCHRANE, D.B. and MANLEY-CASIMIR, M. (Eds) *Development of Moral Reasoning*, New York: Praeger Publishers.

CRITTENDEN, B. (1978) 'Autonomy as an aim of education', in STRIKE, K.A. and EGAN, K. (Eds) *Ethics and Educational Policy*, London: Routledge and Kegan Paul.

DEARDEN, R.F. (1971) 'Autonomy and education', in DEARDEN, R.F., HIRST, P.H. and PETERS, R.S. (Eds) *Education and the Development of Reason*, London: Routledge and Kegan Paul.

DEARDEN, R.F. (1975) 'Autonomy as an educational ideal: I', in BROWN, S.C. (Ed.) *Philosophers Discuss Education*, London: Macmillan.

DEARDEN, R.F. (1984) *Theory and Practice in Education*, London: Routledge and Kegan Paul.

DEVITIS, J.L. (Ed.) (1987) *Women, Culture, and Morality: Selected Essays*, New York: Peter Lang.

DOWNIE, R.S. and TELFER, E. (1969) *Respect for Persons*, London: Allen and Unwin.

DUNLOP, F. (1986) 'The education of the emotions and the promotion of autonomy: Are they really compatible?' *British Journal of Educational Studies*, 34, pp. 152–60.

FEINBERG, J. (1973) 'The idea of a free man', in DOYLE, J.F. (Ed.) *Educational Judgments*, London: Routledge and Kegan Paul.

FRANKENA, W.K. (1973) 'The concept of education today', in DOYLE, J.F. (Ed.) *Educational Judgments*, London: Routledge and Kegan Paul.

GEWIRTH, A. (1973) 'Morality and autonomy in education', in DOYLE, J.F. (Ed.) *Educational Judgments*, London: Routledge and Kegan Paul.

GILLIGAN, C. (1979) 'Woman's place in man's life cycle', *Harvard Educational Review*, 49.

GILLIGAN, C. (1982) *In a Different Voice*, Cambridge, MA: Harvard University Press.

HAMM, C.M. (1977) 'The content of moral education or in defense of the bag of virtues', *School Review*, 85, pp. 218–28.

HIRST, P.H. and PETERS, R.S. (1970) *The Logic of Education*, London: Routledge and Kegan Paul.

KAUFMAN, A.S. (1973) 'Comments on Frankena's "The Concept of Education Today"', in DOYLE, J.F. (Ed.) *Educational Judgments*, London: Routledge and Kegan Paul.

KAZEPIDES, T. (1979) 'The alleged paradox of moral education', in COCHRANE, D.B., HAMM, C.M. and KAZEPIDES, A.C. (Eds) *The Domain of Moral Education*, Toronto: OISE.

KLEINIG, J. (1982) *Philosophical Issues in Education*, London: Croom Helm.

KIERKEGAARD, S. (1940) *Stages on Life's Way*, Oxford: Oxford University Press, (Trans. W. Lowrie).

KIERKEGAARD, S. (1941) *Fear and Trembling*, Princeton, NJ: Princeton University Press. (Trans. W. Lowrie).

KOHLBERG, L. and TURIEL, P. (1971) 'Moral development and moral education', in LESSER, G. (Ed.) *Psychology and Educational Practice*, New York: Scott, Foresman.

LLOYD, I.D. (1988) 'Have you been autonomous lately?' in ORTEZA Y MIRANDA, E. and BELLOUS, J. (Eds) *Proceedings*, Far Western Philosophy of Education Society, Calgary: University of Calgary.

LYONS, N. (1983) 'Two perspectives on self, relationships, and morality', *Harvard Educational Review*, 53, pp. 135–46.

MARCEL, G. (1950) 'The man of God', in *The Mystery of Being, I: Reflection and Mystery*, Chicago: Henry Regnery.

MARCEL, G. (1952) *Three Plays*, London: Secker and Warburg.

MAYEROFF, M. (1971) *On Caring*, New York: Harper and Row.

MITCHELL, B. (1980) *Morality: Religious and Secular*, Oxford: Clarendon Press.

MODGIL, S. and MODGIL, C. (Eds) (1986) *Lawrence Kohlberg — Consensus and Controversy*, Lewes: The Falmer Press.

MULLETT, S. (1988) 'Shifting perspective: A new approach to ethics', in CODE, L., MULLETT, S. and OVERALL, C. (Eds) *Feminist Perspectives*, Toronto: University of Toronto Press.

NASH, R. (1988) 'Virtue in educational thinking', *Educational Theory*, 38, pp. 27–39.

NODDINGS, N. (1984) *Caring*, Berkeley: University of California Press.

O'HEAR, A. (1981) *Education, Society and Human Nature*, London: Routledge and Kegan Paul.

PETERS, R.S. (1970) *Ethics and Education*, London: Allen and Unwin.

PETERS, R.S. (1974a) 'Reason and habit: The paradox of moral education', in PETERS, R.S. (Ed.) *Psychology and Ethical Development*, London: Allen and Unwin.

PETERS, R.S. (1974b) 'Moral development: A plea for pluralism', in PETERS, R.S. (Ed.) *Psychology and Ethical Development*, London: Allen and Unwin.

PETERS, R.S. (1981) *Moral Development and Moral Education*, London: Allen and Unwin.

PHILLIPS, D.C. (1975) 'The anatomy of autonomy', *Educational Philosophy and Theory*, 7, pp. 1–12.

POJMAN, L.P. (1978) 'Kierkegaard's theory of subjectivity and education', in BERNARD, C. and MAYS, W. (Eds) *Phenomenology and Education*, London: Methuen.

POWER, C.F., HIGGINS, A. and KOHLBERG, L. (1989) *Lawrence Kohlberg's Approach to Moral Education*, New York: Columbia University Press.

RAZ, J. (1986) *The Morality of Freedom*, Oxford: Oxford University Press.

SHERWIN, S. (1988) 'Philosophical methodology and feminist methodology: Are they compatible?' in CODE, L., MULLETT, S. and OVERALL, C. (Eds) *Feminist Perspectives*, Toronto: University of Toronto Press.

SICHEL, B. (1988) *Moral Education: Character, Community, and Ideals*, Philadelphia: Temple University Press.

SIZER, N.F. and SIZER, T.R. (Eds) (1970) *Five Lectures on Moral Education*, Cambridge, MA: Harvard University Press.

SPENDER, D. (1981) *Male Studies Modified: The Impact of Feminism on the Academic Disciplines*, New York: Pergamon Press.

TELFER, E. (1975) 'Autonomy as an educational ideal: II', in BROWN, S.C. (Ed.) *Philosophers Discuss Education*, London: Macmillan.

VON MORSTEIN, P. (1982) 'Understanding works of art: Universality, unity, and uniqueness', *British Journal of Aesthetics*, 22, pp. 350–62.

VON MORSTEIN, P. (1988) 'A Message from Cassandra — Experience and knowledge: Dichotomy and unity', in CODE, L., MULLETT, S. and OVERALL C. (Eds) *Feminist Perspectives*, Toronto: University of Toronto Press.

WILSON, JOHN. (1973) *Moral Thinking*, London: Heinemann.

YOUNG, R. (1986) *Personal Autonomy: Beyond Positive and Negative Liberty*, London: Croom Helm.

III
Fulfilling School Tasks Through the Curriculum

INTRODUCTION

The variety of perceived and stated aims of schooling has complicated curriculum development and assessment. Where aims are unavailable, equivocal, or non-definitive, selection of curriculum components — not to speak of their evaluation — becomes susceptible to questionable forces including inertia or tradition, aggressive or dominant interest groups, and even whimsical decisions by educational authorities. Fortunately, despite the welter of aims representing various societal expectations, those who have thoughtfully reflected on schooling and its roles are perhaps not very far apart. Commission reports and other authoritative studies publicized during the previous decade have overlapping views on the aims that schools may be expected to pursue. Also, it may well be that apparent similarities, which can be found between stated aims in official documents and reports and the views of interested laypeople and experts, are enough to serve as common starting points for curriculum selection and implementation.

However aims are formulated, having them will set the proper stage for the process of curriculum selection. This process needs to start right, however; curriculum developers must possess an appropriate conception of curriculum. As LeRoi Daniels and Jerrold Coombs illustrate in their chapter, an improper conception of the curriculum could distort or mistakenly delimit curricular selection. This possibility may be avoided through conceptual analysis, which is an invaluable tool in clarifying concepts underlying our thinking and actions. After presenting what they regard as an appropriate conception of the curriculum, Daniels and Coombs emphasize the need for translating general aims into concrete objectives to guide the selection and organization of curricular content and instruction. Showing why the popular Skinnerian views on behavioral objectives should be rejected, they claim that translation is more suitably done by enlisting our capacity to conceptually analyze certain concepts marking desired objectives. Mindful that schooling involves persons and development of rationality, they insist that curriculum selection and assessment must respect the autonomy of the learners, the integrity of the disciplines of knowledge, and the demands of justice.

J. Douglas Stewart attempts the difficult task of outlining the substantive component of the formal curriculum. Similarly highlighting the need for direction provided by explicit aims, he advocates and justifies education as the most central goal of schooling. Without denying the need for basic learning, such as health education, in the over-all curriculum, he focuses on the crucial role of knowledge in the development of rationality and draws on the ideas of Paul Hirst who has popularized the forms of knowledge. Hirst's views have been, as Stewart admits, criticized on several grounds. He argues, however, that distinguishing logically separate forms of knowledge remains insightful and offers some lead in determining the content and organization of the curriculum. If rationality is, in important respects, tantamount to being initiated into and internalizing the forms of knowledge, the curriculum must include subjects representing them. If they are logically distinct, curriculum integration, whatever it might mean, should not compromise the study of each of the forms. And if they make for rationality which forms the central core of the educational product, then the forms of knowledge must form part of the core curriculum.

The formal curriculum comprises only a portion of students' cumulative school learnings, however. As Ishmael Baksh points out in his chapter, apart from the planned instructional activities, all other things learned in school are regarded as belonging to the hidden curriculum. The range of these 'other things' is wide, including sex role norms, expected student behaviors, values placed on knowledge, economic and political values, and student perceptions of their abilities. Baksh addresses their explanation and significance by elaborating on how they are viewed by varying sociological perspectives — particularly the functionalist, radical, and interactionist. Which theoretical perspective will prove to be the most perceptive remains to be seen. However, as Baksh states, understanding of schooling and the curriculum will be lacking as long as the workings and ramifications of the hidden curriculum are ignored.

7 The Concept of Curriculum

LeRoi B. Daniels and Jerrold R. Coombs

Analysis of Curriculum

Programmatic Definitions of Curriculum

Definitions given by curriculum theorists to delimit their area of concern tend
to distort the concept of curriculum — either by focusing on only one of the
several features of the concept or by misconstruing the basic category of
phenomena to which curricula belong. For example, people at various times
have mistakenly supposed that curricula belong to such categories as experiences of learners, sets of objectives and sets of materials. Although people
have experiences while following curricula, curricula are not experiences.
They are not sets of objectives or sets of materials, although, as we will see,
one must refer to objectives and content to produce a complete description of
a curriculum. Apart from such straightforward category mistakes, writers on
curriculum often produce programmatic accounts of the notion of curriculum.
Take the following as an example: 'A curriculum is all the experiences the
child has under the guidance of the school'. Clearly this definition has been
proposed because it implicitly supports a program of action which the author
favors, i.e., an expansion of the school's responsibilities well beyond what is
normally the case.

There is, of course, nothing wrong in principle with suggesting an expansion of the school's roles, but such a suggestion must be argued for and
justified. What is wrong with programmatic definitions is that they serve as
devices to avoid such justification. If we accept the idea that we ought to start
using the term *curriculum* to mean whatever happens to children, then,
because we implicitly recognize that curricula tell us what children and
teachers ought to do, we are inclined, without due and proper consideration,
to aggrandize the role and responsibilities of at least teachers beyond what
may be either justifiable or even possible.

Progress in delimiting the field of curriculum inquiry or curriculum
theory may well require development of a clear and defensible conception of

curriculum. Some of the features which must hold of any defensible curriculum, while present in the ordinary concept of curriculum, may need to be highlighted to encourage us not to overlook the ways in which curricula can justifiably play a role in the lives of people. Nonetheless, ordinary language must be our starting point for it contains the basic distinctions that our society has found useful in formulating some of its significant educational concerns.

The Concept of Curriculum in Ordinary Language

Perhaps the most important feature of a curriculum as it is ordinarily conceived is that it is, in a broad sense, an instrumental device; that is, it is devised, adopted and followed in order to achieve some purpose or goal. A curriculum is an instrument in the same way that a research strategy is an instrument.

The goal or purpose for which a curriculum is devised, adopted and followed is the promotion of learning. And this intention to bring about learning is always a certain kind of indirect intention. By *indirect* we simply mean that the object of the intention is someone else's action or some event or state of affairs produced by that someone else. In fact, it is typically twice removed. The curriculum maker or user believes that he or she can influence other persons (teachers) to, in turn, influence other people (students) to achieve certain objectives. People who make curricula intend instructors to facilitate the learning of something by a third party — such things as chemistry, the appreciation of good music, or the proper technique for broad jumping.

But not all instruments designed to promote learning count as curricula. This is necessary but is not a sufficient condition. There must be a certain assumption about the relationships among the teacher, the student and the curriculum. A curriculum is not an instrument that causes learning. Rather, it is designed to achieve its purpose by prescribing or regulating the intentional activities of persons — teachers and students. For a curriculum to achieve its purposes, it must have persons following it. Teachers follow it by presenting content in ways which they expect will encourage others to learn certain things. Students follow it by studying or by engaging in similar activities. It must be intended that studying (or something very like studying) will be involved rather frequently. We will return to this point below in our discussion of a particular conception of curriculum.

A curriculum is a set of rules or policies prescribing essentially, though not exclusively, activities to be pursued in order to learn. Although policies can be negative, telling us what not to do, curricula are always positive — telling someone what to do or what outcomes to seek. They are, in fact, conditional policies, telling us what to do or seek when certain kinds of problem or opportunity are believed to be present or imminent. So, for example, we might adopt the policy that whenever children reach the age of six they should study topic X; or, fearing the spread of AIDS, that we should introduce material about AIDS into the public school curriculum.

It is the perceived circumstances (problem or opportunity) which provide the source of the learning goals. Preventing the spread of AIDS provides the occasion to insert information about AIDS into the curriculum and leads to the establishment of teaching goals for that part of the curriculum. And introducing topic X to six-year-olds is done because we believe they can learn X and that it is good for them to learn X.

Curricula are features of institutions, such as schools. To have a context in which the notion of curriculum can sensibly be used, one must presuppose a fairly sophisticated type of social organization. Having a curriculum makes sense only in a society where such things as schools or at least apprenticeships exist.

Typically, curriculum guides and other relevant documents will contain directions, suggestions and so forth, about teaching methodology. However, they could not count as curriculum guides unless they also prescribe certain activities in a particular way — by specifying the content on which the activities are to focus. Curriculum, per se, does not concern itself with the way(s) in which topics are to be addressed. The latter are questions of method, not curriculum. It is no accident that the word *covered* occurs so often in talk about curricula. This term is completely neutral about the methods by which things are to be taught and learned. Consequently, it is ideal for focusing attention on the uniquely curricular concern — the content of the learning activities. We will return to this in a later section.

Finally, for a set of policies to count as a curriculum, they must recommend a reasonably coherent, ordered and relatively extensive set of content to be covered. Merely throwing together a list of things to be read or studied without any underlying pattern does not a curriculum make.

To summarize, in our ordinary language the term *curriculum* (a) is used to refer to an intentionally promulgated set of policies, the purpose of which is to promote learning in those who follow them; (b) these policies prescribe an ordered (or substantially ordered) and relatively extensive set of content to be covered with the intention of learning something; and (c) the policies only partially specify the activities to be pursued in that they indicate the content to be studied in the learning activities; they do not necessarily indicate how the content is to be studied or even what materials are to be used.

Curriculum and Instruction

The tendency to lump curriculum and instruction together as academic concerns is understandable, since they are complementary aspects of the conditions that promote learning achievements. Does this mean that we need a conception of curriculum encompassing all aspects of the conditions intended to promote learning? We think not. While it is difficult in some cases to separate curricular from instructional concerns, there are good reasons for keeping the two concepts distinct. A curriculum that specifies in precise terms what the teacher is to do is likely to be either unworkable or unsuccessful, for it cannot adequately take account of differences in the students or in the conditions under which the curriculum operates. Our ordinary concept of curriculum, being less restrictive, does not incur the same problems.

But there is a more important reason for keeping our conception of curriculum distinct from the concept of instruction. The content that is studied, we argue, should be neutral and common ground between teacher and student. It is, moreover, the focus of their interaction, a point of reference for their mutual activities. Because it establishes this common ground, the curriculum has moral significance. It helps us give operational meaning to our convictions that students are not in school to receive treatment, to be shaped by the teacher, or merely to experience positive personal interaction. They are there primarily to engage in purposeful activities from which they may have valuable learning attainments.

A social structure in which policies are made and followed is significantly different from one in which there are, say, only laws and commands. Policy makers depend upon symbolic pressure, not rank or punishments, to forward the enterprise. They assume that the people involved are persons who are capable of independent action and upon whom rationality can have some impact. The web of concepts in which curriculum is central seems to be based upon the same sorts of presuppositions.

The Curriculum as Neutral Ground

It is important to stress again what even the ordinary concept of curriculum rules out. An instrument that causes learning by regulating what happens to persons is not a curriculum. We would not, for example, say that Skinner's program for making pigeons play Ping-Pong is a curriculum. Nor does a program of brainwashing count as a curriculum. At least some of the intentional activities required by a curriculum must be those in which it is assumed that the intention to learn will be present. The activities may involve nothing more than submitting oneself to a certain sort of environment, for example, listening to a piece of music; however, such activities cannot be the whole of the curriculum. It must be intended that studying will be involved rather frequently. Certain experiences count as part of following a curriculum only when they are intended to promote learning. Both the experiences that students have and the activities they engage in that are unrelated to the intention to learn are extraneous to the curriculum they are following.

Making Sense of Curricular Aims

Our analysis of the meaning of the term *curriculum* suggests that a curriculum is an instrument that is followed by teachers and students to fulfill certain purposes. Thus, it is a necessary feature of following a curriculum that one have certain ends in view. Curricular goals vary along an indefinite continuum from the very abstract and general to the very concrete and specific. The more abstract goals generally include acquiring such things as knowledge and understanding, critical thinking, capacity for autonomous learning, good citizenship, self-discipline, creativity, good character and vocational competence. Very concrete objectives include such things as learning the structure of a hydrogen atom and learning the value of the rule of law.

From the point of view of curriculum, the primary function of general aims is to guide us in selecting more concrete curricular goals and to provide justification for our selections. If, for example, we have a general aim of promoting critical thinking, it serves to justify our choosing to pursue such goals as developing the ability to assess arguments, for doing a good job of assessing arguments is an aspect of critical thinking. This goal in turn justifies our adopting the still more concrete goal of promoting the ability to identify the conclusion of a deductive argument, since this is a necessary prerequisite to argument assessment. Typically, general aims do not tell us very much about the content that should be studied in order to achieve the aim. Rather it is our more concrete objectives that serve as ends in view to guide both the selection and organization of content and the mode of study.

One of the central concerns of both curriculum developers and teachers who use curricula is to translate the more general and abstract aims of the curriculum into more concrete objectives that can serve as ends in view. In recent years it has been popular to tell teachers that they must do this by specifying their goals in terms of behaviors students will exhibit as the result of their learning. This notion of behavioral objectives is one offshoot of a well-entrenched view of human learning known as behaviorism. Various ideas from behaviorist psychologists such as E.L. Thorndike and B.F. Skinner have become so popular among educators that they are accepted by many almost without question. However, as a theory of how human beings learn, behaviorism has serious flaws. It is important to recognize these flaws if one is to avoid such dangers as regarding students as 'things' to be conditioned to do what someone else has decided they should do or believing that all good teaching must be modelled on the methods used in conditioning experiments.

A thorough account of behaviorism is beyond the scope of the present chapter, but it is useful to consider some important features which are common to behaviorist positions and which have influenced educational theory and practice.

1 Behaviorism prescribes certain methods as being appropriate for

describing or explaining, as Skinner once labelled it, the 'behavior of organisms' (Skinner, 1938).

2   It also identifies certain kinds of terminology as appropriate for describing or explaining the behavior of organisms. The behavior of most (perhaps all) living creatures is to be described and explained without reference to the inner workings of the minds or non-physical aspects of any of these creatures. Therefore, in attempting to describe or explain human behavior, one must avoid all mentalistic terms such as purposes, ideas and beliefs, and use only terms which pick out behavior. 'Turning his head' might be acceptable behaviorist language, but 'trying to see his friend' would not.

3   In the application of these basic ideas, the behaviorist holds that learning must be understood in terms of the functional relationships among three concepts: response, stimulus and reinforcement, and that this set of concepts should also be used as the basic framework for conceptualizing teaching.

In Skinner's brand of behaviorism, one gradually gets the organism to respond as one wishes by providing appropriate reinforcement of successive approximations to the desired response. In educational applications of this form of technology, one is supposed to state very precisely what the outcomes are to be (precisely what response is desired to which stimulus) and then introduce an appropriate reinforcer when the appropriate response is made. Reinforcers are not to be conflated with rewards since the latter are mentalistic notions. What is to count as a reinforcer is established by experimental means — by finding out what will, in fact, change the organism's behavior when presented according to some appropriate schedule. On this account, a good curriculum is one which has precisely described goals (where *precise* means not only what it usually does, but also that only behavioral terms are used) and in which things are organized in such a way that approximations of the desired responses to stimuli are appropriately reinforced.

Although these ideas have had enormous influence on the ways people talk about and conduct educational enterprises, for reasons sketched below we believe they are philosophically unsound and educationally dangerous. Most of the explanatory concepts of ordinary language presuppose a purposive model of human activity — in exact contradiction to the chief ideas of behaviorism. The difference between these two models of human explanation is sometimes characterized as the difference between movement and action. Inanimate objects such as billiard balls and automobiles move, but they cannot act. Only creatures with purposes or intentions act. Although people sometimes do things unintentionally, most of the ordinary language terms we have for describing the doings of persons presuppose an actor — someone intentionally doing something; not merely an organism moving in response to a stimulus. Most of the central concepts used to talk about educational enterprises are also action concepts. One cannot give an account of what a curriculum is without presupposing that there are such things as persons who have goals; to try to reduce talk about curriculum to talk about responses to stimuli as a result of previous reinforcement is like trying to square a circle. Both teaching and studying are clearly and unmistakably intentional action concepts.

Trying, however unwittingly, to convert action concepts and action explanations into behaviorist concepts and explanations is a very morally hazardous enterprise for several reasons. (1) Behaviorism denies the existence of persons in the moral sense of this term, because persons are, by definition, creatures with purposes; (2) For the same reason, behaviorism cannot recognize that there are such things as moral issues and considerations. Morality makes sense only for creatures who have purposes; (3) To adopt a behaviorist view of curriculum is to accept a program in which some people (teachers, etc.) control others (students) by using means which do not respect their purposes or personhood. Not only does this run counter to the presuppositions of the concepts we normally use to discuss educational questions, it also runs counter, in our opinion, to a defensible conception of curriculum.

There is one final point to be made concerning the notion of behavioral objectives. One of the arguments used to support the use of so-called 'behavioral objectives' is that they are more precise than other kinds of objectives. Thus it is regarded as more precise to state goals in terms such as, 'Given a request to define the term *imperialism*, S will write a correct definition of the term', than to state them in terms such as 'S will come to understand what the term *imperialism* means'. Granted there is a need to spell out what, for certain purposes, we will count as evidence of understanding X (for example, we may be part of a team setting out standards for a state examination of students) we are not thereby being more precise about our goal. We are, for the purposes of testing, arbitrarily selecting, from the indefinite number of different ways to tell when someone understands something, one or two such bits of evidence. To equate such evidence with having the understanding is to distort seriously our understanding of what we are attempting to accomplish.

When we design curricula and try to educate people, we try to get them to study their world, acquire information, acquire new concepts, and so forth, and thereby come to see the world in new ways — and perhaps, as a result of these, to begin to act differently than they did before. It is wholly inadequate and, indeed, dangerous to conceive of such an enterprise from the narrow world view of behaviorism.

If it is a mistake to reduce our abstract aims to behaviors to be brought about on the part of students, how should teachers approach the task of translating general aims and goals into more concrete objectives? Basically this task is accomplished by analyzing the more abstract aim to determine what it implies in the way of constituent kinds of learning attainments. Perhaps the best way to clarify what is involved in such analysis is by example. Suppose we want to develop competence in critical thinking. We need first to answer the question, what is critical thinking? That is to say, we need to have a fairly clear understanding of what sorts of things the term *critical thinking* refers to or implies.

One way to approach the question is to ask what sorts of things people are doing in those situations in which we describe them as thinking critically. Now, if we look carefully at all of the various kinds of cases in which we regard persons as thinking critically, it is apparent that being a good critical thinker does not refer to doing any particular kind of thing. Critical thinkers do all sorts of different things. They do not all use the same procedures to approach problems; we can not suppose that the same mental processes are going on in their heads, for we do not know what is going on in their heads. What, then, leads us to call all of these diverse doings cases of critical thinking? Basically it is that in each case the thinker is self-consciously concerned with thinking in such a way as to conform to accepted standards of good thinking. A second thing we should notice from this analysis is that there are a large variety of different thinking tasks, each one having its own standards of adequate performance. Thus there is the task of determining whether or not to accept someone's deductive argument, the task of making a responsible moral decision, the task of judging the adequacy of research evidence bearing on some issue, the task of determining whether or not to accept the word of some presumed expert, the task of acquiring a clear understanding of what someone means by her statements, and the like. We say that a person thinks critically when she performs such tasks well or responsibly. Good performance of these tasks is performance which meets certain accepted standards. Consider, for example, the task of determining whether or not to accept a deductive argument. This task is done well when one accepts only those arguments that meet our established standards of sound argument. These standards say essentially that, to be sound, an argument must have premises or reasons that are true or warranted, and it must follow a form or pattern of argument that is valid. These tasks and their associated standards can be made still more concrete by analyzing them into constituent tasks and the standards for doing them well. Thus the answer to our question about what critical thinking refers to is that it refers to performing a large variety of thinking tasks in such a way as to fulfill the standards of good performance for each task. To find out what concrete objectives we should set for our curriculum, we must answer the further question, 'What enables and disposes persons to perform these thinking tasks adequately?' The answer to this question will describe what persons must know and what dispositions they must have if they are to apply the relevant standards in carrying out each of the various tasks. Such knowledge and dispositions can themselves be analyzed to determine what prerequisite concepts and values they depend upon. It is these fairly concrete kinds of concepts, knowledge and values that should guide us in formulating the curriculum. This same sort of analysis can be carried out for other abstract aims such as developing creativity and fostering good citizenship.

When the abstract aim we are trying to translate into more concrete objectives is the acquisition of some fairly large chunk of knowledge, we need to understand the relevant discipline if we are to arrive at appropriate concrete objectives. Suppose, for example, that our general aim is that students will come to understand Canadian history. We have to have a good grasp of Canadian history to be able to say what having an understanding of Canadian history implies in terms of more specific understandings. Indeed this analysis requires such expert judgment that we generally think it should be carried out by committees of experts in the discipline.

The general point we want to make is that translating our abstract aims into concrete objectives is not a mysterious process. It is primarily a matter of thinking very carefully and systematically about what our abstract statements of aims mean or imply.

General Criteria for Assessment of the Curriculum

How do we know when we have a good curriculum? The usual way of answering this question is to suggest that we simply test students who have followed the curriculum to determine the extent to which they have learned what the authors of the curriculum intended them to learn. While determining the consequences of following a curriculum is an important thing to do, our analysis of the concept of curriculum should make us skeptical of such a narrow approach to curriculum evaluation. While a curriculum is in a general sense an instrument, we have attempted to make clear that it is not an instrument for manipulating students by causing them to have various beliefs, habits, and the like. It seeks to bring about learning by promoting intentional learning activities. This means that students must be brought to accept the aims or goals of the curriculum as their own. A defensible curriculum must secure such acceptance while at the same time respecting the rational autonomy of students. That entails according them the right to make up their own minds about what they will believe and value on the basis of relevant reasons.

A curriculum that respects the rational autonomy of students has two features. First, the learning it intends to bring about is rationally defensible and, second, the studies that are prescribed focus on having students acquire good reasons for the beliefs and dispositions they learn. These two features are closely related. To explain what is required for a certain kind of learning to be rationally defensible it is necessary to say something about the kinds of traits that curricula are designed to promote in students. Generally speaking there are three broad categories of such traits: (1) propositional knowledge, that is, knowledge that something is the case; (2) ability, that is, knowing how to do something in the sense of being able to do it; (3) dispositional learning including values, attitudes, tendencies, habits and sensitivities. The traits on this list are not mutually exclusive. Rather, they overlap and interrelate in various ways. It is possible to give a much finer grained analysis of the kinds of learning promoted by a curriculum, but the following will do for present purposes.

Propositional knowledge is rationally defensible in so far as it is warranted by adequate, publicly accessible evidence. It is a necessary condition of a curriculum's being defensible that the beliefs it fosters are warranted by such evidence and that the studies it prescribes make this evidence available and intelligible to students. Abilities are also rendered rationally defensible by publicly accessible tests. A performance or activity counts as an ability to do X only if it demonstrably has certain results or meets certain standards. A curriculum is defensible only if the performances and ways of doing things it fosters meet the relevant public standards. It is not easy to give a brief account of what makes a value or disposition rationally defensible. Basically we want to argue that there are some values and dispositions, including many moral and prudential values, which are such that any person would have good reasons for adopting them. The good reasons consist in appreciating that these values are consistent or cohere with our most fundamental and firmly held convictions and thus in appreciating the contribution that their realization makes to living the sort of life we would rationally choose. To be defensible, a curriculum must attempt to foster only those values, attitudes and dispositions that are supported by such reasons.

There are several reasons for insisting that a curriculum which respects the rational autonomy of students must attempt to foster only rationally defensible traits in students. The primary reason is that this is the best way of protecting students from manipulation, that is, from being treated as a means to furthering the interests of other people. Dominant groups within society exert pressure on schools in various ways to develop within students beliefs and values they want students to have. Students cannot be treated merely as means to fostering the interests of dominant groups in society. However, if the traits fostered in them are ones they themselves would have good reasons for adopting were they mature and knowledgeable enough to appreciate such reasons, there are plausible grounds for their inclusion in curricula.

Obviously a person, or even a large group of people, may be wrong in thinking that there are good reasons for anyone to adopt a particular belief, value or attitude. Prejudices and superstitions are widespread. For this reason it is important that the studies prescribed by the curriculum attempt to foster learning by providing students with relevant reasons and by equipping students to appreciate the force of such reasons. If students have access to relevant reasons and some appreciation of what makes certain kinds of considerations good or bad reasons, they have at least some measure of protection against propaganda and indoctrination. A number of philosophers have argued that responsible teaching involves rational consideration of reasons (McClelland, 1976). We believe that responsible curricula must give pride of place to providing good reasons to students; providing good reasons does not necessarily mean simply giving students arguments. In some cases good reasons can be given to students by providing them with certain kinds of experiences together with the opportunity to reflect critically on them.

If this is to be possible a curriculum must be regarded as an arena for the open and uninhibited presentation, discussion and exploration of ideas. Many educational theorists are at least implicitly aware of the importance of conceiving of curriculum in this way. For example, in the literature on life-long learning or on global education it is not uncommon to find a reluctance to use the word *teacher* — particularly where the students are adults. This reluctance appears to be due to the assumption that teaching necessarily involves passing on 'truths' to passive students who are to accept them unquestioningly on the authority of the teacher. In any event, a defensible conception of curriculum will hold that curricula must be organized to maximize what, in another context, Paul Taylor calls the 'conditions for rational choice' (Taylor, 1961). A curriculum ought to help create the conditions for students to make free, impartial and enlightened decisions about what to believe and value. This is not, of course, simply a curricular matter — 'atmosphere' and methodology should also support creation of circumstances where giving and evaluating reasons is central.

To be defensible, a curriculum must not only respect the rational autonomy of students; it must also respect the integrity of the traditions of inquiry (the 'disciplines') through which knowledge is acquired, criticized and revised. Paul Hirst has argued that there are seven different forms of knowledge, each with its own unique concepts, logical structures and tests for truth (Hirst, 1974). Although there are good reasons to question the adequacy of the specific analysis of knowledge put forth by Hirst, it seems fairly clear that different traditions of inquiry produce different kinds of knowledge claims, and that these claims are warranted by different kinds of evidential argument. Mathematical claims, moral claims and claims of physics are not established, criticized and revised in the same way. Students will have little genuine knowledge or understanding and little ability to assess reasons responsibly if they do not understand how knowledge claims of the sort they are studying are established and revised. Thus a defensible curriculum must prescribe studies that provide an appreciation of the various modes of inquiry carried out in the pursuit of knowledge, and the standards of evidence and argument that regulate such inquiry.

Whatever else it may be, a defensible curriculum must be a just curriculum. It must not be biased in favor of or against any segment of its intended clientele. Typically this demand is expressed as the requirement that the curriculum treat students equitably. There is no space here to discuss all of the features a curriculum must have to be counted as equitable, but we do want to consider one aspect of a just curriculum, namely, gender equity. Curricular concerns associated with gender differences have undergone considerable evolution over the past fifteen years (Tetreault, 1986). When such concerns were first raised, it was assumed that gender differences should make no difference to the kind or amount of curricular resources given to persons. Now, although there is general agreement that gender differences sometimes justify differences in curricular provisions, there is considerable debate about how such differences should make a difference (Houston, 1985; Morgan, 1985). Differences in the treatment of males and females, which are prima facie inequitable, include differential access to courses and differential treatment with regard to teacher expectations and attention. That such inequities do permeate our educational institutions is a well documented fact (Spender, 1982). While progress has been made in removing some of the most obvious inequities of this sort, many of them have proved to be very persistent (Houston, 1985, p. 361).[1]

Differences in gender become relevant because the values which permeate the curriculum tend to be biased in favor of males. That is to say, ways of acting and interacting that are typically associated with males are more highly valued than those typically associated with females. Thus, if we treat gender differences as irrelevant in determining what is just curricular treatment, we run, as Houston puts it, 'a serious risk of encouraging an assimilation of women's identity, interests and values to men's' (p. 365). To put the matter another way, females are unable to profit from current curricular provisions to the same extent as males unless they adopt the values and ways of acting typically associated with males. Even when females succeed in taking on values typically associated with males, they do not profit as much as males from current curricular provisions, because the knowledge and abilities fostered by these programs are valued more highly when possessed by males than when possessed by females (Martin, 1981).

Since there are no grounds for preferring male values to female values within the educational context, such educational provisions are clearly unjust to females. They discriminate against females by unjustifiably making educational achievement and the acquisition of self-respect more difficult for them than for males. They also discriminate by providing resources for educational achievements that are more valuable for males than for females. None of these inequities is adequately addressed by treating gender differences as completely irrelevant to decisions about equitable access to education. Changing educational provisions such that females are treated in ways that are more appropriate to their values and ways of interacting with others addresses only part of the problem. Though such changes would enable females to have the same achievements as males, they would not enable females to have achievements of equal value. This latter problem can be solved only by changing the range of achievements, that is, kinds of knowledge, abilities, dispositions and appreciations that are fostered by our curricula. One option, of course, is to provide different curricula for males and females, each having its own uniquely appropriate goals and resources. A second option is to change our curricular goals in such a way as to foster a range of achievements for all students which are biased neither in favor of values typically associated with males nor in favor of those typically associated with females. There are, we believe, compelling reasons for preferring the second of these options. To accept the first is to permit our educational institutions to aid and abet the pandemic sex role stereotyping which limits the freedom of both men and women in our society. It is, moreover, to acquiesce to our society's current inequitable distribution of economic and social benefits and opportunities to women and men. Finally, we should note that many of the kinds of knowledge, abilities and dispositions which are typically thought valuable for women, such as those required for successfully raising children and nurturing families, are in fact equally valuable for men.[2]

Notes

1 Houston (1985, p. 361) reports that studies on teacher-student interactions indicate that, within coeducational classrooms, teachers, regardless of sex, interact more with boys, give boys more attention (both positive and negative), and that this pattern intensifies at the secondary and college levels. Girls get less teacher attention and wait longer for it. When they do get attention, it is more likely that the teacher will respond to them neutrally or negatively (though this depends somewhat on the girls' race and class). The reinforcement girls do get is likely to be for passivity and neatness, not for getting the right answer.
2 Martin (1981, pp. 97–109) identifies the competencies typically associated with females as those that are required to carry out the reproductive as opposed to the productive processes of society. Reproduction in this case is social reproduction, and it includes all of the things one does to maintain a family, for example, and make it a nurturing and supportive environment for a child to grow up in. Surely males as well as females bear responsibility for these reproductive processes.

Bibliography

BRENT, A. (1978) *Philosophical Foundations of the Curriculum*, London: Allen and Unwin.
DERR, R. (1977) 'Curriculum: A concept elucidation', *Curriculum Inquiry*, 7, pp. 145–55.
DIXON, K. (Ed.) (1972) *Philosophy of Education and the Curriculum*, Oxford, Pergamon Press.
EGAN, K. (1978) 'What is curriculum?' *Curriculum Inquiry*, 8, pp. 65–71.
HIRST, P. (1974) *Knowledge and the Curriculum*, London: Routledge and Kegan Paul.
HIRST, P. and PETERS, R.S. (1970) *The Logic of Education*, London: Routledge and Kegan Paul.
HOUSTON, B. (1985) 'Gender freedom and the subtleties of sexist education', *Educational Theory*, 35, pp. 359–69.
JOHNSON, M. (1967) 'Definitions and models in curriculum theory', *Educational Theory*, 17, pp. 127–40.
MARTIN, J.R. (1981) 'The ideal of the educated person', *Educational Theory*, 32, pp. 97–109.
MCCLELLAND, J. (1976) *Philosophy of Education*, Englewood Cliffs, NJ: Prentice-Hall.

MORGAN, K. (1985) 'Freeing the children: The abolition of gender', *Educational Theory*, 35, pp. 351–7.

MUSGROVE, F. (1968) 'Curriculum objectives', *Journal of Curriculum Studies*, 1, pp. 5–18.

SIEGEL, H. (1988) 'Critical thinking as an educational ideal', in WARE, W. and PORTELLI, J. (Eds) *Philosophy of Education*, Calgary: Detselig Enterprises, (pp. 107–22).

SKINNER, B.F. (1938) *The Behavior of Organisms*, New York: Appleton-Century-Crofts.

SPENDER, D. (1982) *Invisible Women: The Schooling Scandal*, London: Writers and Readers Publishing Cooperative Society.

TAYLOR, P. (1961) *Normative Discourse*, Englewood Cliffs, NJ: Prentice-Hall.

TETREAULT, M. (1986) 'The journey from male-defined to gender balanced education', *Theory into Practice*, 25, pp. 227–34.

WINCHESTER, I. (1977) 'Concept education and educational issues', *Curriculum Inquiry*, 7, pp. 331–42.

8   The Formal Curriculum and Knowledge

J. Douglas Stewart

Introduction

To anyone seriously concerned with education, it is unnecessary to point out the importance of curriculum. Most parents understand that what children learn in school follows an approved curriculum; instructors know that the curriculum is what they have responsibility to teach; and students of education soon learn that curriculum is an essential area of study in pre-service training. Yet these commonplaces fail to differentiate various conceptions of curriculum[1] or to make explicit the central issues such as purpose, content, structure, organization and justification of curriculum. Since the concept we are dealing with in this essay is that of formal curriculum of the public school (K-12), it will first be necessary to clarify and then briefly defend what schools are for. Without a broader understanding of what a curriculum is supposed to achieve it will simply not be possible to examine rationally the question of curriculum objectives and to develop some idea of the grounds on which the selection of objectives may be justified.

Goals of Schooling

I shall argue (briefly) that the primary and most central goal of the school is the general education of succeeding generations of young people. By education I shall mean the development of knowledge and understanding in virtue of which one makes sense of the world and deals intelligently with it (Peters, 1977 and 1981). To put it another way, education is the development of individual consciousness or mind through knowledge and understanding, or the achievement of personhood defined basically in terms of the breadth and scope of one's cognition. The more knowledge and understanding, the more mind or awareness one has and consequently the more fully a person one is. Why education should be the chief aim of schooling may be demonstrated roughly as follows: (1) central to the idea of education is a conception of human nature that puts mind or consciousness at the core of being a person; (2) to become persons more fully implies a development of mind, on which other significant aspects of human development such as the social, moral and emotional are necessarily dependent; (3) if school is to be concerned with the general development of persons then it must be concerned with the development of mind or consciousness and consequently with knowledge and understanding; (4) no societal institution other than school has taken on the task of systematically promoting the intellectual or cognitive growth of the vast majority of children, and this responsibility does not seem likely to change; (5) thus, for the sake of the general development of children, education must be the school's primary aim.

The school of course has other goals it must try to achieve, but, as we shall see, to an important extent they are dependent on knowledge and understanding and thus not as basic as the goal of education. They include the socialization of children, that is, helping them grow up as decent people and take their place constructively in society, and the promotion of their general physical health and well-being. Both goals are legitimate expectations society has of the school (Gallup and Clark, 1987) though they are by no means the responsibility of the school alone. Yet these expectations are a reminder that, in framing the goals, the wider socio-political context in which the school functions, as well as the more purely philosophical considerations about the nature of mind and knowledge, certainly needs to be taken into account. Socialization and the promotion of general health must not, however, be in competition nor incompatible with the school's primary aim of education.

Several objections can be raised against this account of the school's mission but only the more obvious ones can be dealt with here. First, libertarians have argued that it is wrong from a moral point of view for the education of children to be in the hands of the public or state school. This amounts, they say, to nothing short of the mass shaping and molding of children in accordance with the aims of those in power and therefore to an invasion of the most central area of individual freedom — the right to be the kind of person one is or wants to be (Mill, 1947; Bereiter, 1973). In a free society schools should stick to teaching 'facts and positive science exclusively' (Mill, *ibid.*, p. 109), to basic skills of reading, writing and calculation, and to providing child-care services (Beretier, *ibid.*, chapter 1), all of which, it is claimed, can be done without deliberately influencing the development of children as 'whole persons' (Bereiter, 1972, pp. 390–1). A second objection is that, in 'socializing' children, the school may be guilty of indoctrination or of conditioning the young to accept uncritically the socio-economic status quo and thus of killing the capacity and will for social judgment and action. A third argument holds that vocational training of the young is one of the most basic reasons for having schools and that any account of schooling, like this present one, which fails to identify such training as a goal is simply unacceptable.

With respect to the first criticism it needs to be pointed out that to teach facts, 'positive science', and basic skills as the libertarians would have it just is (in part) to be educating a person under the knowledge component of the concept (see pp. 159–64). Unless facts and skills are taught without any organizing principle or framework whatsoever, which is unlikely even in the libertarian classroom, neither can be taken as neutral or without influence on a person's beliefs and actions. The fact that the road from Regina to Saskatoon is icy may convince me to take the bus instead of driving or not to make the journey at all. In teaching facts, some influence on the development of children as persons is inescapable. Moreover, why should the libertarian view of education as the mass shaping of children be accepted? In fact an argument for schools providing a general education through knowledge and understanding is the greater rationality and independence of judgment it yields. The main target of the libertarian critique seems not to be the school's goal of education at all but the quality and content of teaching, whether there is allegiance in teaching to norms of truth-telling, and whether school procedures are just and fair so that impressionable minds are not taken advantage of. These are certainly legitimate concerns, and they demand our utmost attention especially with the power and influence teachers have. But they are concerns about the *means* of schooling, not its *ends*. That the means used by an institution like school may be flawed on moral or epistemological grounds need not invalidate the goals the institution has. The libertarian objection to education as the basic purpose of public schooling fails by and large.

So also do criticisms of the school as an agency of socialization. There are two points to make. One is that not all forms of socialization are indoctrination and that not all indoctrination is necessarily undesirable (Thiessen, 1985). The reality is that certain basic moral and social attitudes and habits are a necessary condition of any civilized community and cannot, therefore, simply be a matter of individual choosing. These attitudes and habits (e.g., honesty, kindness, caring, fairmindedness) need to be developed early in life and often before reasons can be grasped. For this purpose, methods that are essentially non-rational may be required, including adult example, reminding children of basic rules of good conduct and consistently enforcing such rules, reading them stories with moral-social themes, and penalizing children when they choose to do what is wrong. Such procedures may well be a form of 'soft' indoctrination but, insofar as they do not degenerate into mindless forms of drill, subterfuge or acts of adult tyranny that thwart the development of reason and judgment, they are justifiable procedures of early moral socialization. The second point is that school socialization needs to be based on a firm knowledge and understanding of social facts and on what is involved in democratic forms of life. It should therefore be done within a framework of basic moral principles of justice, concern for others, and respect for truth that apply equally to students, staff and administration, At the very least this means that, as students move through school, they ought to be encouraged to develop and express informed opinions on matters of school and societal governance and on social issues such as the treatment of minorities, the elderly or the unemployed. It also means that students need opportunities in school to participate in genuine decision-making.

As far as the question of vocational training is concerned, recent contributions (Hamilton, 1986; Malpas, 1986; Weisberg, 1983; Wilms, 1984) have concluded that it would be unwise for schools to incorporate such training as a goal. Since the workplace is better equipped than school to keep abreast of rapid technological changes affecting vocational training, an increasing number of employers want to train new people in relevant work skills on the job rather than have them trained at school. What the workplace *would* like to have from schools are young people with a good basic command of language, a general knowledge and understanding, a willingness to learn, and moral qualities of honesty, considerateness, and the like. It can also be argued that a general education enables a person to adjust more realistically to varying conditions in the workplace than does a schooling that focuses on vocational training. The latter does not provide the same kind of resources to fall back on when a person's training becomes outdated or when one becomes under or unemployed. It seems that if the school were to stick to its chief end of education and its other goals it would *implicitly* be attending to a general kind of vocational preparation of its students. It would then be unnecessary to single out vocational training as a further goal; to do so would take valuable time away from the school's main task.[2]

Epistemological Considerations Underlying Curriculum

Now that a rationale for public schooling has been sketched, our discussion of the formal curriculum (K-12) and the considerations on which it is based can start to take more shape. Since a curriculum is a means to an end rather than an end in itself, a good curriculum would be one which specifies the areas of content and types of experience necessary for the achievement of (i) a general knowledge and understanding of the world [the meaning of which is yet to be clarified], (ii) an initiation of the young into society, and (iii) sound health habits and attitudes. Three questions arise. What are the more specific objectives a K-12 curriculum will need to incorporate? What is the nature and scope of learning required for those objectives? How might the curriculum be organized for best results in learning? To the extent that philosophical thought can shed light on these questions they shall be addressed in the last two sections of this essay. In the meantime we need to explore more thoroughly what knowledge is and what status knowledge claims and performances purport to have since it should be fairly clear by now that the most basic objectives of curriculum must be cognitive in kind. This does not of course imply that a formal curriculum can do without objectives that are non-cognitive. Reference has already been made to attitudes, habits and dispositions in connection with goals, and there is what Mary Warnock (1986) and others call the *education of the emotions*. But even these entities have necessary cognitive underpinnings. To develop any moral-social habit or disposition presupposes that a child has some concept of others and self, of public and private; and it is hard to conceive of how an emotion could be felt or experienced in the absence of certain cognitive appraisals or readings of situations.

Knowing How and Knowing That

According to Ryle (1949), a basic distinction in knowledge is that between knowing how and knowing that. We speak of knowing *how* to shoot a puck, bake a cake, or operate a word processor; and of knowing *that* 1988 is a leap year, that Mackenzie King was Prime Minister of Canada during World War II, and that under standard conditions water boils at 100 degrees Celsius. In the stock use of the term, *knowing how* implies being able to do something up to an agreed standard of performance.[3] Yet it can be easily misconstrued. Mortimer Adler (1982, pp. 26–7) plays havoc with the concept by making it appear that *knowing how* is simply a matter of a skill perfected by practice and to be sharply contrasted with *knowledge of facts and formulas*. This may be close to the truth for low-level performances such as knowing how to dog-paddle but for most cases and certainly those of educational relevance like Adler's own list of intellectual skills — knowing how to calculate, estimate and exercise critical judgment (p. 23) — the matter is more complex. As Charles Bailey (1984, pp. 56–7) points out, 'We must be careful not to conclude that because we normally ask for proof (of knowing how) by performance there is no difference between the knowing and the performing'. Knowing how to vote implies a good deal more than simply being able to make an X on a ballot. It presupposes a concept of voting, some knowledge and assessment of issues and candidates, and a disposition to vote, none of which reduces to an overt skill at ballot-marking. In sum, the knowing involved in *knowing how* normally requires a wider framework of knowledge, judgment and disposition (Malikail and Stewart, 1987). To equate the concept merely to its behavioristic component of skill or performance is a misleading and potentially dangerous thing to do.

Knowing that, on the other hand, is propositional knowledge embedded in statements using symbols with publicly agreed or shared meanings. Since a proposition is whatever may be asserted or denied (Flew, 1975) and is in principle either true or false, then to have propositional knowledge is to know that something is or is not the case. If we know that the Vikings were the first Europeans to reach North America it must be true and there must be good evidence in support of the claim. Considerations of truth, of the grounds or evidence for belief, and objectivity are thus central to knowing that. Scheffler (1965) usefully distinguished between *weak* and *strong* senses of propositional knowing. The former simply involves having bare facts or correct information as in knowing that 2 plus 3 is 5 or that *Superior* is the name of the largest Great Lake. This is a matter of true belief. The latter or strong sense implies having good reasons for what is the case. It is to have justified true belief or an understanding that goes beyond the facts themselves. Although knowing facts (weak sense) is necessary to understanding, it is not sufficient. This reference to understanding, which is the relating of facts to wider conceptual or theoretical frameworks and thus to making greater sense of human experience, needs to be examined more thoroughly.

Forms of Knowledge and Understanding

Some of the most influential philosophical work in knowledge and the curriculum is that of P.H. Hirst (1974), Philip Phenix (1964), L.A. Reid (1986) and, to a more limited extent, Michael Oakeshott (1972). Despite points of disagreement in the positions, to some of which we shall return, there are areas of concurrence most important for a basic understanding of the nature of knowledge and its significance for the curriculum. (1) It is agreed that human knowledge, or more generally the accumulated intellectual and cultural experience of mankind, is not unified or all of a piece but differentiated into a number of distinct domains. These are variously referred to as forms of knowledge and understanding, traditions or forms of thought, ways of knowing, ways of responding to the world, and realms of human meaning. (2) They each stand for an objective body of meaning and truth and in sum are said to constitute the basic ways in which the world can be known or experienced and understood: The mathematical, the scientific (natural or physical), the interpersonal (knowing other persons), the aesthetic, the moral, the philosophical and the religious. (3) Forms of knowledge are basic in that there are no underlying or more fundamental levels of knowing on which these forms are somehow dependent, but that they are themselves the foundations on which other less fundamental levels of knowledge rest. The latter are sometimes called fields, examples of which are medicine, engineering and environmental studies. (4) Forms are logically distinct and autonomous. Knowledge of other persons, for example, is said to differ in *kind* from a knowledge of numbers. Knowledge of the natural world differs in turn from each of these and is reducible to neither. Moral knowledge is claimed to be logically independent of knowledge and understanding in religion. Literature and the fine arts seems to be a further form in its own right. (5) Despite these claims for uniqueness and independence, forms are nonetheless logically connected or interrelated. Science necessarily draws on mathematics. Moral understanding and judgment in turn requires factual knowledge from science and also draws upon knowledge of other persons, while some socio-historical claims demand moral understanding. There are necessary mathematical aspects to understanding music; some religious claims require elements of historical or philosophical understanding; and morality is integrated into religion. That

these cross-linkages do not negate the claims for logical autonomy or independence of the forms (Phenix, 1964; Hirst, 1974) is explained as follows:

> That experience or knowledge in one domain is *necessary* to that of
> another in no way implies that it is *sufficient*. Of itself no amount of
> mathematical knowledge is sufficient for solving a scientific problem,
> nor is science alone able to provide moral understanding. What we
> must recognize is that the development of knowledge and experience
> in one domain may be impossible without the use of elements of
> understanding and awareness from some other. But even when in-
> corporated into another domain these elements retain their own
> unique character and validity ... It thus seems that the form of
> interrelationship between the independent domains of knowledge
> and experience can only be properly understood by recognizing first
> the basic differences between them, and by seeing how they are
> interlocked when one domain employs elements of another without
> any loss to the independent character of each. (Hirst and Peters,
> 1970, pp. 65–6)

(6) Forms of knowledge enjoy equal epistemological status even though some,
like the scientific, have made enormous strides both theoretically and practically. Such consequences, however, do not make one domain any more valid
or legitimate a way of knowing than another.

Let us for the moment accept these basic claims of the forms thesis, as
we might call it, and see where they lead. On what grounds can the basic
divisions in knowledge be made, and can they be sustained? Is it the type of
reasoning involved that differentiates one form from another, the type of
evidence employed, or the relationship of evidence to conclusion? Is it
perhaps the nature of the objects which the forms of knowledge take (e.g., the
natural world, works of art, numbers, interpersonal relationships, etc.) that
justifies the divisions?

According to Hirst (1974, p. 85) who has dealt with this question more
fully, since a form of knowledge is centrally the domain of true propositions,
forms are necessarily differentiated by (i) their central concepts or leading
ideas; (ii) their distinct logical structure; and (iii) truth criteria by which each
basic type of proposition is tested. Now there certainly seems to be something
to this claim. As far as mathematical knowledge and experience is concerned,
it does appear to be marked out by a family of distinct concepts or ideas
including those of number, integer, ratio, variable, function, equation, point,
line, triangle, graph and so on. Moreover any statement that expresses
numerical or geometrical relationships, with the exception of axiomatic truths,
are testable for their truth value by means of logical deduction. Understanding the natural world on the other hand seems to demand a quite different
family of concepts including those of space, time, mass, energy, and other
derivative notions such as molecule, oxidation, force, velocity, momentum,
erosion, photosynthesis, planet and so on. The test for truth of empirical

claims such as 'water is a conductor of electricity' or 'plants require light for their food production' is observations by the senses and/or experimentation, not logical deduction. Knowing other persons draws upon concepts for states of mind — intending, desiring, believing, hoping, thinking, feeling — and a host of derivative social ideas like immigration, land claims, slavery, nation, feudal system, trade union, market economy, inflation, national debt, war and revolution. Historical statements about the intentions, purposes, or beliefs of individuals or groups ('The Puritans fled England for America in search of greater tolerance and freedom') are good examples of interpersonal knowledge claims; and they are logically distinct from such claims as 'The speed of light is 186,000 miles per second' or 'The square on the hypotenuse equals the sum of the squares on the other two sides'. Equally, both the aesthetic way of knowing and moral knowledge and understanding are marked off by other different conceptual networks. A moral judgment, which is concerned with what *ought* to be rather than with what *is*, must be distinct from other types of judgment such as the empirical and aesthetic. Basic to philosophical knowing are notions of dialectic, law of thought, definition and concept; whereas ideas central to experience of a religious kind include those of ultimate being, transcendence, heaven, incarnation, prayer and worship.

The gist of logical structure, a second feature of a form of knowledge, is that the concepts involved in a way of knowing are governed by particular rules of usage, and that the rules of usage for one domain of knowing do not govern the concepts in any other domain. In other words, what determines meaningfulness in a given form of knowledge is its particular logical structure. Making sense in mathematics is a function of what the rules that govern *mathematical* concepts permit and not what the rules permit that govern moral, scientific or religious concepts. That propositions like '2 plus 3 is 5' and 'water is composed of hydrogen and oxygen molecules' make sense whereas those like '2 plus 3 is sinful' and 'water is blessed with a fine sense of humor' do not, is evidence of two distinct logical structures at work. Thus what counts as meaningful within forms of knowledge is not something that can be a matter of individual choosing. These seemingly unremarkable observations might be unnecessary were it not that serious category mistakes have been made. What impeded the development of scientific knowledge and understanding in the fifteenth-sixteenth centuries was precisely a belief that the natural world in the larger scheme of things could be satisfactorily explained and understood in terms of the concepts and structures of philosophy and religion rather than in terms of the concepts and structure of science itself.

Taking Stock of the Forms Thesis

It might be wondered what happened to the third feature, the criteria of truth, since beyond those stated for the domains of mathematics and science no further mention of truth conditions has been made. Perhaps only mathematics and science can be justified as forms of knowledge after all and that the so-called remaining forms either collapse into one or other of these two or they are simply bogus as the logical positivists have held (Ayer, 1936 and 1971). This conclusion, however, is too quick. That there are apparently missing criteria of truth is not in itself a sufficient reason to abandon the present thesis. In the moral realm, for instance, objective truth criteria for many judgments are available provided such judgments are read as conclusions derived from irreducible moral principles and relevant factual and definitional premises. Even though a teacher may say that whether it is right or not for her to humiliate her students is a matter of individual opinion, this does not entail that the judgment 'one ought not to humiliate one's students' has no determinate truth value or that it cannot be derived objectively from basic moral principles and facts. As for the religious way of knowing, the lack of agreed truth criteria for its claims has not rendered experience of a religious kind unintelligible or uniquely private. When members of a faith community worship they are taken to be engaging in a form of activity that has public features that draw upon shared language and concepts structured to deal with the world in a distinctly meaningful way. Such experience has a legitimate claim as a form of understanding. It seems also to be the case that even though the truth criteria for the interpersonal realm are difficult to articulate, at least sometimes we can speak of having objective knowledge of other persons or minds and of sometimes knowing better than they do themselves what they are feeling.

A number of difficulties remain nonetheless (not that the foregoing observations are all nicely settled); only some of the more problematic for curriculum can be taken up here.[4] First of all, it is odd that in Hirst's (1974) statement of the forms thesis no reference to human action is made, particularly in connection with the moral domain. If we consider R.M. Hare's analysis of the prescriptive force of moral concepts like ought and right (1952, 1979 and 1981), there is a close connection between moral judgment *and* action. Moral judgments are action-guiding. They are what we are supposed to do. If a person sincerely says he ought to respond more kindly to members of minority groups then this is what he does, other things being equal (i.e., he is not physically or psychologically incapacitated to so act). Without actions consistent with them, moral judgments are necessarily incomplete. They are less than full judgments. Therefore any account of moral knowing that, like Hirst's, is cashed out in terms of valid judgments of moral right and wrong must surely have to include moral action as an integral component of that knowing. Yet moral action, and the elements of moral dispositions, attitudes and emotions related to such action are precisely what Hirst's account seems to overlook.

A further serious matter is that no reference is made to human affect in the other ways of knowing, and no recognition is given to performative knowledge identified earlier as knowing how. Yet elements of an affective and a performative kind are nonetheless features of forms of knowledge even where they might be least expected. Mathematical knowing and understanding can hardly be characterized without reference to a commitment to standards of accuracy, precision and clarity; or scientific knowing without a love or respect for standards of empirical evidence and truth. And how can there be a knowledge of other persons or of what others feel or think without the engagement of empathy (Gribble and Oliver, 1973)?

But it is the aesthetic realm that seems to be dealt with least satisfactorily by the forms thesis. According to Hirst, though not to Phenix or to Reid, it would be sufficient for knowing in the fine arts that a person first discerns what propositions or statements particular works of art make (e.g., what is Rodin's *The Thinker* saying?] and then assess whether the works state something that is true, using appropriate aesthetic truth criteria whatever these may be. It would of course be completely irrational to deny that paintings, sculptings, poems or performances of music and drama have meaning or make statements of some kind. But to what extent there is objective meaning and truth in the arts, and whether works of art as statements can be tested in any significant sense are moot points. To view works of art primarily or essentially as true propositions may simply be overlooking the central points and creating a too narrow or rigid view of aesthetic meaning and experience (notwithstanding claims like Iris Murdoch's, 1970, for example, that the arts and the selfless attention we can give them are enormously valuable in discerning the Good). But in the distinctively expressive realms of art, music or drama, where *responses to* works of art as such may be more germane to aesthetic knowing than the *statements* they may be making, are criteria of truth necessarily all that relevant? Might not criteria of beauty, elegance or serenity, and the like, matter here instead of those of truth? Reid (1986, p. 38) is surely correct to insist that 'a most important thing about art *is* the enjoyment, the direct experience of it as ongoing experience'. He continues:

> We are not primarily concerned with a work of art as a vehicle to carry a message, but in the thing itself as it is presented to perception. This is contrary to the fundamental nature of language. In linguistic communication the vehicle is transparent, we see 'through' to the message it carries ... But when we take up an aesthetic attitude, the vehicle becomes *opaque.*
>
> This is true even in the literary arts whose very substance is language. We are not interested in the poem simply as a vehicle communicating a message of the poet. We are interested in the whole complex structure of meanings inherent in it including the rhythm and the music of the language, and the penumbra of secondary meanings which words can carry. (pp. 47–8)

Within justifiably wider and more comprehensive views of the aesthetic domain, the activities of making, creating and performing, far from being outcasts in the fine arts way of knowing as they seem to be on Hirst's account (though again not for Phenix and Reid), are themselves important dimensions to this realm although how to make or perform a work of art is not a necessary condition of aesthetic understanding. Yet to have children engage in aesthetic making and performing in school does help them to develop some idea of what is possible in fine arts, how it is possible, and, perhaps most important of all, a greater awareness of the expressive dimensions of human experience.

Summing Up

What our taking stock of the forms seems to show is this: That the thesis that knowledge is differentiated into a number of logically distinct realms is powerful and insightful. As we shall see, it has important implications for the selection of curriculum objectives and content. But the thesis, or Hirst's particular version of it, suffers from an interpretation of ways of knowing that is too heavily restricted to propositional knowledge. It is a thesis, therefore, that needs to be embellished at crucial points. Some indications of where and how this embellishment needs to be done have been given. Clearly not all the ways of knowing are as fully propositional as the mathematical and the scientific. Arguably, components of *knowledge that* are necessarily present in all the forms including significantly the moral and the fine arts; this is one of the crucial points in the thesis. However, for some of the forms to be more fully conceptualized, it is necessary to go beyond strictly propositional knowing to include the further dimensions of actions, doings, makings, performings, as well as the affective components of feelings or emotions, attitudes and dispositions. We shall give the last word here to Jonas Soltis (1981, p. 103):

> The human capacity to do, to invent, to create, to make, to develop skills, arts, crafts, and dispositions in the service of 'humanness' is part and parcel of human knowledge ... knowledge is not just what is contained in heads and books but also in hands and actions as we take part in social living. Knowledge viewed singularly as truth about the world is too narrow a view ... Knowing how to do something and how things are done is every bit as important as forms of knowledge as is knowing something is true or false ... our concept of knowledge has been broadened beyond what can be stated in words so as to include such legitimate categories as proper action and human skill.

Objectives in Formal Curriculum

It is well to recall the following points: That, under the goals of schooling, cognitive objectives are logically the most fundamental kind; and that human sense-making and consequently our knowledge and understanding of the world is constituted by several distinct forms of cognition, modified along the lines suggested. A formal curriculum (K-12) will therefore need to feature the following major objectives — scientific understanding, mathematical under-standing, knowing other persons, knowing in the fine arts, moral understand-ing, religious understanding and philosophical knowledge (to include at least the defining and clarifying of concepts, logical reasoning, detecting and avoid-ing fallacies). These broadly stated objectives will of course have to be cashed out in more specific, lower-level targets which at the same time are not beyond the reach of children and adolescents.

Before proceeding, a comment on religion in the curriculum is in order. Unless the distinction between teaching for commitment to a particular faith and teaching for religious understanding is carefully maintained, the inclusion of religion can be easily misunderstood. To foster and nurture religious faith in the public school is not justified by the goals of schooling. The educational value of such an objective is marginal, and it is by no means a requirement of socialization. A person can be a good citizen without being religious. Yet religion is a distinctive way humans have sought to make sense of experience and so to learn about the nature of religion and to develop an understanding of it as a form of life does have educational value. The meaning and signi-ficance of different types of religious faith and the historical events that influenced their development as well as the role played by religion in the formation of culture should all be explored. For Canadian schools, the most relevant instance of the relationship between religion and culture is the influence of Christianity and Judaism on Western Civilization and it is to these faith systems that the greater attention should be paid. The significance of various religious practices, rituals and symbols are important to understand, too, since they constitute a part of contemporary social reality. Such know-ledge would also seem to be helpful and perhaps necessary in the develop-ment of religious tolerance. These matters cannot be developed further here; however, eloquent cases for religious education in the state school have recently been advanced along similar lines by Mary Warnock (1988) and John Haldane (1988).

In cashing out some of the other broadly-stated objectives, let us take scientific understanding first. What more specific objectives would a general understanding of the natural world entail? In light of our earlier work, it would seem to require a basic knowledge of the language and concepts science uses, without which a scientific way of thinking and responding to the world would simply not be available. It would entail a knowledge of many basic facts about the natural world in its different aspects — its more common phenomena such as the water cycle and life cycle, the forces of nature (gravitational, centrifugal, electro-magnetic, etc.), the processes of nature (freezing, melting, decaying, rusting, regeneration, fertilization, etc.), energy, motion, light, and so on. Experience with the method science uses to explore the natural world and an understanding of the role and relationship of hypoth-eses and empirical data to the conclusions that scientific investigations reach must be central objectives as well. There is, too, the distinction between empirical data and matters of opinion that needs to be grasped, as well as some understanding of the nature and place of causal laws of generalizations in scientific explanations and how in general such explanations differ from mathematical, socio-historical or moral explanations.

While this abbreviated treatment does not consider the question of logical and psychological sequencing of objectives (Hamlyn, 1967 and 1978) for the achievement of scientific understanding, perhaps it is sufficient to indicate the flavor of what is involved. It would need to be duplicated for the other broad forms of understanding. Here again the languages and concepts for mathematics, the fine arts, morals, and socio-historical knowing, along with many basic facts about numbers and their relationships, human groups, events, and actions must be among the most fundamental objectives. So must the procedures employed respectively in measuring and calculating, framing historical conclusions, making moral judgments and creating objects in fine arts. The curriculum also needs to specify objectives that differentiate human actions and their justification from natural occurrences and their causal explanations; critical thinking in mathematics from that in science, the arts, morals and history (McPeck, 1981); and moral emotions from feelings associated with the arts.

Table 1 is a synopsis of objectives that are distinctive of different curriculum areas and is an indication of the levels of generality/specificity at which such objectives operate. By breaking down even further the lower-level objectives (found in lower-case print) it can be imagined how finite lesson targets can be derived. Not all forms of understanding are represented in the table nor do the columns begin to provide complete lists of objectives necessary for each. It should also be stressed that the lists are by no means of exclusively educational value. Topics associated with the human body (column 1) such as smoking or drugs may be justified under the health purpose of schooling, while the respiratory system, nutrition and contagious diseases may be justified on both general educational and health grounds. Democratic government, settlement patterns and social customs (column 3) may be justified for reasons of socialization and general education.

The most fundamental objectives of all, the *serving competencies*, as Bailey (1984) has called them, are of course those of reading, writing, speaking and listening; arithmetical operations; moral-social habits and dispositions; and physical fitness. They are indispensable preliminaries to education and socialization. It is hardly necessary to deal with these any further here other than to note that the considerable time in elementary schooling needed for their development underscores not only their importance but also the fact that achievement in these basic areas is not as good as it should be.

Curriculum Organization

With these objectives of formal curriculum (K-12) in mind, it can now be asked on what principles or criteria the organization of curriculum ought to

Table 1 *Curriculum Objectives for General Education* (Illustrative Only)

Understanding the natural world	Understanding numerical, geometric ideas and relations	Understanding the world of persons	Aesthetic understanding	Moral understanding
Scientific Explanation Experimental Method	Mathematic Reasoning, Deduction, Proof	Socio-Historical Explanation	Aesthetic Expression, Appreciation	Moral Judgment, Justification, Behavior
— plant and animal life	— basic operations	— eras of the human past	— reading, writing, speaking	— habits, dispositions
— natural phenomena	— measuring	— where we live and why	— stories, literature	— moral ideals
— mass, energy, motion	— geometric properties	— adapting to the environs	— painting, sculpting, movement, drama, musical performance	— moral rules
— air, water, light	— equations	— social customs and mores	— arts and environment	— moral actions
— land formation, climates	— graphs	— nations, government	— artistic eras	— moral emotions
— solar system	— functions	— institutions	— aesthetic feeling	— moral reasoning, principles, social knowledge
— human body	— series	— community	— art appreciation	
— simple machines	— ratios	— group behavior		
— everyday technology	— probabilities	— social control		
	— interest rates, bonds, interest rates, bonds,	— empathy		
	etc.			

proceed. Does the nature of knowledge itself determine the organization or is it to be settled primarily by psychological considerations about human learning and motivation or by some combination of principles?

School Subjects: The Clones of Forms?

Historically, the school subject has been the basic unit of curriculum organization. Geography, for example, organizes knowledge of land formations and climates within a particular conceptual framework that develops understanding of these features and of how they influence human habitation and customs. It employs scientific ways of thinking but also deals with knowing other minds. Geometry provides a concrete demonstration of logical deduction from premises to conclusion using geometric ideas and relationships as its subject matter. It epitomizes the idea of proving a proposition. Biology is a selection of ordered facts and concepts necessary in understanding living things in their natural environments. History develops a sense of time and place and a knowledge of other persons. It uses historical analysis and empathy to discern what people in the past have endured, sacrificed, suffered and accomplished, and to explain why. Health informs us about our bodies, nutrition and prominent contagious diseases, and of values and attitudes necessary in sound personal relationships.

It may seem that a subject-centred curriculum is more or less a replica of forms of knowledge. As well, the critics (see below) are convinced that such a curriculum not only reproduces but reinforces knowledge fragmentation that disrupts childrens' learning. We need therefore to examine more carefully whether subjects and forms are related in any way and, if so, what the relationship might be.[5]

There cannot of course be a one-to-one correspondence between forms and subjects, or a direct derivation of subjects from forms. For this to be the case, it would have been necessary for the articulation of the forms of knowledge to have preceded in time the formation of school subjects, that is, without a prior awareness of forms, no subjects. Yet this is obviously quite wrong. The existence of subjects, or indeed the framing of them, has neither awaited nor been dependent on the forms of knowledge. Literature was a subject in its own right well before aesthetics was cashed out as a distinct way of knowing; history as a subject existed long before knowledge of others. Second, even if a direct derivation of subjects from forms were possible, the structure of subjects would have to reflect the divisions and structure of knowledge much more faithfully and rigorously than they do (mathematics subjects being an obvious exception perhaps). Third, school subjects can change radically both in number (there may now be several hundred) and in scope (social studies has been stretched well beyond history and geography to encompass psychology, economics and sociology), whereas the basic forms of understanding have not altered significantly in their limited number and even less so in structure. It is therefore misleading to think of subjects as copies of forms of knowledge or as directly corresponding to them, and to say that subjects are a necessary deduction from forms. Is there some other relationship?

With the differentiated map of knowlege that the forms thesis provides, there is first of all a much better understanding of the ways of knowing that different subjects like literature, history, geography, health, art or biology actually explore. In going beyond a conception of subject as simply bodies of information to a conception of subjects as also embodying theoretical frameworks necessary to understanding and dealing with aspects of the world intelligently, forms of knowledge have brought the educational value of subjects much more to the fore. They have helped clarify the key ideas or concepts different subjects deal with, and they have made us more conscious of the types of evidence and truth tests which subjects draw upon, the different patterns of reasoning involved, and the types of judgments that subjects make. Moreover, forms have helped set the record straight about the necessary cognitive underpinnings of subjects and why it is a confusion to think of subjects as being neatly divided between affective and cognitive domains. At the same time forms increase our awareness of the types and range of emotions appropriate to different subject matter. In terms of curriculum planning and the teaching of subjects, such benefits can hardly be inconsequential.

To Integrate or Not: Is That the Question?

To the critics, nonetheless, school subjects are a mischief. They arbitrarily and artificially compartmentalize school knowledge into isolated bodies of learning. Remote from and irrelevant to the experiences of children, these bodies of learning (it is claimed) have little, if any, meaning for them. An adherence to traditional (i.e., 'outmoded') methods of teaching has also been blamed on school subjects, and they have even been held responsible for creating rigid institutional structures (Martin, 1982)! But before we decide whether the abolition of subjects and the integration of the curriculum might be justified, it is first necessary to clarify some terms.

The basic idea behind *integration* is that, by making the content of a curriculum *experience-friendly*, children will relate more readily to school learning and thus be able to make greater sense of the world in which they live. For this to be achieved, it is necessary to restructure the content around the interests children have, or at least around what is familiar to them from everyday life, rather than to segregate it into discrete and formal subjects. Their learning, it is said, will then be continuous or flowing and more natural since it will be in greater tune with their outside world. Dewey's (1915 and 1933) problem-centred curriculum is an example of integration in which children used the unifying method of experimental inquiry to explore various kinds of problems that fell within the scope of their interests and experiences. Such an organization, he believed, was instrumental in developing their awareness of various human conditions and an ability to deal constructively with them. A more recent version of integration is the *theme-based* approach (Pring, 1976). Themes such as *community, transportation, power, peace* and *sea* bring together elements from several domains of knowledge relevant to a particular center of interest. Transportation merges what would otherwise be separate or piecemeal areas of learning in science (combustion, transformation of energy), in art (design elements of transportation systems) and social studies (transportation as related to human needs and desires).

Where it is necessary for understanding — as with mathematics in physics or chemistry and with empirical knowledge of the properties and limitations of physical materials in art — relating content across different subjects of the curriculum is of course unexceptionable. But does this justify an all-out integration of the curriculum? Subjects and their boundaries are, on one hand, certainly not arbitrary constructions. There are good epistemological and educational reasons for the ways subjects are structured. What does seem to strike one as artificial, on the other hand, is the kind of enforced unity of subject matter often found, for example, in a curriculum of integrated themes. Yet, for the achievement of multidisciplinary themes, a basic knowledge of the different relevant disciplines is presupposed, for which a subject-centered organization is surely the more effective at least so far as clarity of objectives and a coherent organization of content are concerned (Evans and Davies, 1985).

But can a curriculum of subjects satisfactorily meet some of the other criticisms levelled against it? Let us see. First, to think that a subject-centered curriculum should be blamed for what is often considered an undesirable talk and chalk method used for teaching it is to confuse curriculum with instruction. Logically, the organization of a curriculum does not dictate what the methodology must be. It is conceivable (and a matter for empirical research to show) that the use of narratives, group discussions, dramatizations, independent library study, films and field trips may be as well or better suited to a subject organization than any traditional method. Second, since most subjects involve some integrated material, it follows that they cannot be as alien to the idea of integration as might be thought. We have seen that subjects frequently draw upon each other and many are capable of pursuing objectives in several domains of knowing. Although moral understanding is not the central objective of literature, through its use of moral language, its vivid examples of good and evil and moral struggle, and its insights into human character, literature can nonetheless open the mind to greater moral awareness. Social studies develops understanding of scientific, interpersonal and moral kinds; and so does health. Moreover, teachers of disciplines can themselves be effective agents of integration. The teacher who draws connections between literary works and the socio-historical contexts in which they are set or written makes literature both more insightful and enjoyable. A science instructor who relates the laws of nature to environmental concerns of pollution, the greenhouse effect or forest destruction, and these in turn to human desires or intentions, opens up new dimensions of understanding all within a subject context.

It might finally be objected, however, that an integrated curriculum for at least the elementary grades is justified on the grounds that children experience the world in a relatively undifferentiated or holistic way. Even if this is true, a curriculum that tries to mesh with the seamlessness of those experiences places severe limits on longer-term educational growth and development. Undifferentiated is not the same as integrated, so thinking that the experiences of children are just naturally of a certain formless kind is not itself a good reason for an integrated curriculum. In order to have children begin to grasp 'the extraordinary range of options for living and thinking' it is necessary for the curriculum actually to make 'breaks' with their everyday experiences (Flodden, Buchmann and Schwille, 1987, p. 484) and to initiate them into what are strange or unfamiliar disciplinary concepts that empowers them to see and 'describe the world in reliable, often surprising ways' (*ibid.*). Kieran Egan (1983 and 1986) has also argued that in exposing children by means of stories and fables to the imaginary worlds of monsters, witches, fairy princesses, giants, aliens and the like, the abstract moral concepts of love and hate, good and evil, courage and cowardice are learned 'most profoundly' (1983, p. 361), and new dimensions of understanding are opened up to young minds. The psychological point seems to be that introducing children to what is unfamiliar or out of the ordinary is not something that they necessarily find opaque or that dulls and deadens their interests in learning; rather it intrigues them and engages their learning. The logical point is that unless these breaks with ordinary experience are achieved and the familiar is made strange, the intellectual and other dimensions of children's development simply cannot get off the ground.[6] Unfortunately, with the idea of integration and the romantic but misguided notions that go along with it, there is every likelihood that an integrated curriculum will end up pandering to relatively unstructured experiences and ones that are of primarily a local and limiting variety. Untutored by the theoretical or disciplinary concepts and the forms of understanding in which they are embedded, the education of the young will necessarily be at risk.

Must a Curriculum Have a Core?

It may seem fitting that a core curriculum, which implies that certain areas of learning have been identified as essential for the general education of everyone, and therefore compulsory for all,[7] just goes with the territory of subject-centeredness. This does not follow; however, it is not true that an integrated curriculum must be core-less, or that a curriculum must have a core at all, as the 'cafeteria' version illustrates.

Several challenges to the core can be made: That agreement on its content is impossible and that any selection is therefore arbitrary; that its compulsory feature is morally unjustified; and that core is a patently elitist notion.[8] On the first point, it is not clear that reasonable agreement is beyond reach. Most people seem ready to accept that certain areas of learning are essential to a general education although it is by rational argument that this content has to be justified and not by consensus.[9] In this context, justification entails first a rationalization of the goals of public schooling and analysis of the nature of knowledge, followed by areas of learning required to achieve the goals. These matters have already been dealt with, and so in effect an outline of a basic argument for a core and its content has been sketched. The list that follows identifies areas in the core for public education:

literacy (including keyboard skills)
numeracy (basic computations) and mathematics
natural sciences
literature
history and geography (national and world)
fine arts
technology and culture
health and physical education
moral and social education
religious education
practical arts (technical/commercial/home)

With allowance for the qualifications mentioned below, a core should be limited to grades 1–10 rather than extended to K-12 as seems to be more commonly advocated. It is premature for kindergarten. On the other hand, by grade 10 most students have reached the school-leaving age and, for many, this is their last exposure to a systematic general education. Not all areas listed in the 1–10 core should be required in each of those years. There is neither time nor necessity for extended exposure to practical arts or keyboard skills. Religious education should be centered primarily in the middle years where a greater curiosity about the phenomena of religion, its meanings and relationships to social life is found. Topics in technology and culture may be dealt with in this period as well. Since it is not possible for all subjects in each of the required areas to be taken in the core, only those that are basic or paradigm to an area should be given core status. Other further courses in an area may be left optional, depending on individual interests. Notwithstanding a core for grades 1–10, it is imperative that subjects in language and literature, in either mathematics or science, and in history or social studies be required through grade 12. Student achievement in language arts needs constant emphasis and attention; and a modified extended core, as suggested, will discourage premature specialization and provide a more balanced growth of knowledge and understanding to the end of secondary school. Although not a formal area of teaching, moral and social education should also be stressed throughout.

The justification of a compulsory core turns on the claim that children are not, generally speaking, in the best position to know what their educational needs are and that the intrusion on freedom demanded by a core is more than offset by the greater long-term freedom achieved through increased general awareness, independence of thought and judgment and moral-social development. Complex questions remain to be dealt with here but these go well beyond the scope of this chapter.

Notes

1 For a fairly comprehensive examination of different conceptions of curriculum and their degrees of adequacy see Tanner and Tanner (1975).
2 However, secondary schools should certainly provide accurate information on the kinds of work there are and advise students on how to go about locating work and preparing themselves for interviews. There is also a case for technical, industrial or commercial arts classes in middle and/or secondary schools (see section on 'A Core Curriculum') provided they are not taught as a form of narrow job training but as a general introduction to what is possible with human skills and with making things out of raw materials. Such perspectives can provide a sense of personal pride and satisfaction as well as give some insight into the nature of the world of work.
3 Other uses of knowing how do not necessarily imply being able to do something. For example, a person may know how a car is driven, that is, knows what one must do in order to drive a car, without actually being able (or knowing how) to drive. In this case the former type of knowing how is propositional and, unlike the latter type, has no performance component.
4 Numerous criticisms of the forms thesis have been made. Most, however, are on points of detail rather than challenges to the basic idea that knowledge is of several fundamental kinds. See for example Barrow (1984); Brent (1978); Griffiths (1986); Hindess (1972); Phillips (1971); and Pring (1976). A radical Marxist critique, on the other hand, claims that all knowledge is socially relative and that school knowledge is, consequently, a matter of negotiation between student and teacher, see Harris (1978); Sarup (1978); Young (1971). Despite the popular appeal of the relativity of knowledge, the position is logically flawed (Trigg, 1973) and practically very limiting.
5 For the discussion of this question I am grateful to my colleague, J. S. Malikail. Any flaws that remain are mine.
6 In an excellent chapter on 'Learning and Experience' in his book *The Philosophy of Primary Education* (1968), Robert Dearden argued for a curriculum that necessarily makes school learning discontinuous with children's everyday experiences. He differentiated perceptual and practical concepts, namely those of colours, shapes, textures, and of socially functional objects such as chair and telephone, respectively — all of which children learn informally early in life and which bring order to everyday experience — from theoretical concepts such as lunar eclipse, fossil, manor house and migration that organize in 'highly systematic ways our ordinary "common sense" experience and in so doing greatly increase our intellectual understanding of it' (p. 116). It is the latter category of theoretical concepts that may seem strange to children but into which the curriculum must formally initiate them.

7 There are several recent examples of provincial and national core curricula. Saskatchewan (1987) is implementing a K-12 core; a British Columbia Royal Commission (1988) has recommended a new core for grades 1–10; an Ontario government-commissioned study (Radwanski, 1988) has called for a core curriculum; and in England and Wales a new national curriculum with an extended core has recently been approved (Department of Education and Science, 1987).

8 Radical objections to core curriculum by sociologists of knowledge have been made on grounds of social injustice among others. See Alan Harris (1977) and D.H. Tripp and A.J. Watt (1984). A response must be the subject of another paper.

9 During the lengthy curriculum review period in Saskatchewan, essentially no public disagreement emerged over the subject areas proposed for the K-12 compulsory core. What did come under attack, however, was an incredibly weak justification the Department of Education mounted for the core (Stewart, 1987), and the devious manner in which the goals of education for the province were determined and then presented to the public (Cochrane, 1987).

Bibliography

ADLER, J.J. (1982) *The Paideia Proposal: An Educational Manifesto*, New York: Macmillan.

AYER, A.J. (1936) *Language, Truth and Logic*, Harmondsworth: Penguin Books.

AYER, A.J. (1971) 'Conversation with A.J. Ayer', in MAGEE, B. *Modern British Philosophy*, New York: St. Martin's Press. (pp. 48–65).

BAILEY, C. (1984) *Beyond the Present and Particular: A Theory of Liberal Education*, London: Routledge and Kegan Paul.

BARROW, R. (1984) *Giving Teaching Back to Teachers: A Critical Introduction to Curriculum Theory*, Sussex: Wheatsheaf Books.

BEREITER, C. (1972) 'Schools without education', *Harvard Educational Review*, 42 (3).

BEREITER, C. (1973) *Must We Educate?* Englewood Cliffs, NJ: Prentice-Hall.

BRENT, A. (1978) *Philosophical Foundations for the Curriculum*, London: George Allen and Unwin.

COCHRANE, D. (1987) 'Taking our directions from Washington', in COCHRANE, D. (Ed.) *So Much for the Mind: A Case Study in Provincial Curriculum Development*, Toronto: Kagan and Woo Limited. (pp. 37–61).

CORE CURRICULUM ADVISORY COMMITTEE (1986) *Program Policy Proposals*, Regina: Saskatchewan Department of Education.

DEARDEN, R. (1968) *The Philosophy of Primary Education: An Introduction*, London: Routledge and Kegan Paul.

DEWEY, J. (1915) *The Child and the Curriculum: The School and Society*, Chicago: University of Chicago Press.

DEWEY, J. (1929) *The Quest for Certainty: A Study of the Relation of Knowledge and Action*, 1929 Gifford Lecture. New York: E.P. Putnam's Sons.

DEWEY, J. (1933) *How We Think*, Chicago: Henry Regnery Company.

EGAN, K. (1983) 'Children's path to reality from fantasy: Contrary thoughts about curriculum foundations', *Journal of Curriculum Studies*, 15, pp. 357–71.

EGAN, K. (1986) *Individual Development and the Curriculum*, London: Hutchinson.

ELKIND, D. (1986) 'Formal education and early childhood education: An essential difference', *Phi Delta Kappan*, 67, pp. 631–6.

EVANS, J. and DAVIES, B. (1985) 'Problems of change, teaching and control in mixed ability curricula: A case study of integrated studies', in CLUFF, E.C. and PAYNE, G.C.F. (Eds) *Crisis in the Curriculum* (pp. 106–17), London: Croom Helm.

FLEW, A. (1975) *Thinking about Thinking*, Glasgow: Fontana/Collins.

FLODDEN, R., BUCHMANN, M. and SCHWILLE, J. (1987) 'Breaking with everyday experience', *Teachers College Record*, 88, pp. 485–506.

GALLUP, A.M. and CLARK, D.L. (1987) 'The 19th Annual Gallup Poll of the public schools', *Phi Delta Kappan*, 69, pp. 17–30.

GOODLAD, J. (1986–87) 'A new look at an old idea: Core curriculum', *Educational Leadership*, 44, pp. 8–16.

GRIBBLE, J. and OLIVER, G. (1973) 'Empathy and Education', *Studies in Philosophy and Education*, VIII, pp. 3–29.

GRIFFITHS, M. (1986) 'Hirst's forms of knowledge and Korner's categorical frameworks', *Oxford Review of Education*, 12, pp. 17–30.

HALDANE, J. (1988) 'Religion in education', *Oxford Review of Education*, 14, pp. 227–37.

HAMILTON, S. (1986) 'Excellence and transition from work to school', *Phi Delta Kappan*, 86.

HAMLYN, D.W. (1967) 'The logical and psychological aspects of learning', in PETERS, R.S. (Ed.) *The Concept of Education* (pp. 24–43), London: Routledge and Kegan Paul.

HAMLYN, D.W. (1978) *Experience and the Growth of Understanding*, London: Routledge and Kegan Paul.

HARE, R.M. (1952) *The Language of Morals*, New York: Oxford University Press.

HARE, R.M. (1979) 'Language and moral education', in COCHRANE, D.B., HAMM, C.M. and KAZEPIDES, A.C. (Eds) *The Domain of Moral Education* (pp. 89–106). New York: Paulist Press.

HARRIS, A. (1977) 'The impossibility of a core curriculum', *Oxford Review of Education*, 3, pp. 171–84.

HARRIS, K. (1978) *Education and Knowledge: The Structured Misrepresentation of Reality*, London: Routledge and Kegan Paul.

HINDESS, E. (1972) *Forms of Knowledge: Proceedings of the Philosophy of Education Society of Great Britain*, Supplementary Issue, VI (2).

HIRST, P.H. (1974) *Knowledge and the Curriculum: A Collection of Philosophical Papers*, London: Routledge and Kegan Paul.

HIRST, P.H. and PETERS, R.S. (1970) *The Logic of Education*, London: Routledge and Kegan Paul.

MALIKAIL, J.S. and STEWART, J.D. (1987) *Personal and Social Values and Skills*, A study completed for the Saskatchewan Department of Education Core Curriculum Investigation Project (Contract No. 09–85–0190). Regina: Saskatchewan Education.

MALPAS, R. (1986) 'Education and industry: A working partnership', *Royal Society of Arts Journal*, CXXXIV.

MARTIN, J.R. (1982) 'Two dogmas of curriculum', *Synthese: An International Journal of Epistemology, Methodology and Philosophy of Science*, 51, pp. 5–20.

McPECK, J. (1981) *Critical Thinking and Education*, Oxford: Martin Robertson.

MILL, J.S. (1947) *On Liberty*, New York: Appleton-Century-Crofts Inc.

MURDOCH, I. (1970) *The Sovereignty of Good*, London: Routledge and Kegan Paul.

OAKESHOTT, M. (1933) *Experience and its Modes*, Cambridge: Cambridge University Press.

OAKESHOTT, M. (1972) 'Education: The engagement and its frustration', in DEARDEN, R.F., HIRST, P.H. and PETERS, R.S. (Eds) *Education and the Development of Reason*, London: Routledge and Kegan Paul, (pp. 19–49).

OSBORNE, H. (1984) 'The language metaphor in art', *Journal of Aesthetic Education*, 18.

PETERS, R.S. (1977) *Education and the Education of Teachers*, London: Routledge and Kegan Paul.

PHENIX, P. (1964) *Realms of Meaning*, New York: McGraw-Hill Book Company.

PHILLIPS, D.C. (1971) 'The distinguishing features of forms of knowledge', *Educational Philosophy and Theory*, 3, pp. 27–35.

PRING, R. (1976) *Curriculum Organization*, London: The Open University Press.

PRING, R. (1976) *Knowledge and Schooling*, London: Open Books.

RADWANSKI, G. (1988) *Study on the Relevance of Education and the Issue of Dropouts*, Toronto: Ontario Department of Education.

REID, L.A. (1986) *Ways of Understanding and Education*, London: Heinemann Educational Books Ltd.

ROYAL COMMISSION ON EDUCATION (1988) *A Legacy for Learners*, Victoria: Department of Education.

RYLE, G. (1949) *The Concept of Mind*, New York: Barnes and Noble.

SARUP, M. (1978) *Marxism and Education*, London: Routledge and Kegan Paul.

SASKATCHEWAN, DEPARTMENT OF EDUCATION (1987) *Core Curriculum Plans for Implementation*, Regina: Department of Education.

SMART, N. (1986) *Concept and Empathy: Essays in the Study of Religion*, New York: New York University Press.

SOLTIS, J. (1981) 'Education and the concept of knowledge', in SOLTIS, J. (Ed.) *Philosophy and Education. Eightieth Yearbook of the National Society for the Study of Education*, part 1, Chicago: University of Chicago Press, (pp. 95–113).

STEWART, D. (1987) 'Cutting to the core: Curriculum mishaps in Saskatchewan', in COCHRANE, D. (Ed.) *So Much for the Mind: A Case Study in Provincial Curriculum Development* (pp. 124–35), Toronto: Kagan and Woo Limited.

TANNER, D. and TANNER, L.N. (Eds) (1975) *Curriculum Development: Theory into Practice*, New York: Macmillan Publishing Company.

THIESSEN, E.J. (1985) 'Initiation, indoctrination and education', *Canadian Journal of Education*, 10, pp. 229–49.

TRIGG, R. (1973) *Reason and Commitment*, Cambridge: Cambridge University Press.

WARNOCK, M. (1986). The education of the emotions', in COOPER, D.E. (Ed.) *Education, Values and Mind: Essays for R.S. Peters*, London: Routledge and Kegan Paul, (pp. 172–87).

WARNOCK, M. (1988) *A Common Policy for Education*, Oxford: Oxford University Press.

WEISBERG, A. (1983) 'What research has to say about vocational education and the high schools', *Phi Delta Kappan*, 64.

WHITE, P. (1980) 'Political education and moral education or bringing up children to be decent members of society', *Journal of Moral Education*, 9, pp. 147–55.

WILMS, W.W. (1984) 'Vocational education and job success in the employer's view', *Phi Delta Kappan*, 65.

YOUNG, M. (Ed.) (1971) *Knowledge and Control*, London: Macmillan.

9   The Hidden Curriculum

Ishmael J. Baksh

Introduction

Scholars often distinguish between the 'formal' or 'official' curriculum and the 'hidden' curriculum. The former is concerned essentially with the presentation of knowledge and typically entails a division of subject matter into the various disciplines or fields in which the school undertakes to give instruction. Each field is usually outlined in a syllabus, and the teaching more often than not leads to some form of test or examination. The formal or official curriculum consists basically of the planned instructional activities of the school. The hidden curriculum, on the other hand, has been described as 'all the other things learned during schooling' apart from the official curriculum (Meighan, 1981, p. 52). These 'other things', studies suggest, take an immense variety of forms. They may include learning how to satisfy the teacher's requirements, grasping how to survive in the school setting, or knowing when cheating is tacitly approved (Eggleston, 1977, p. 15). They may embrace all the 'norms and values that are implicitly, but effectively, taught in schools and that are not usually talked about in teachers' statements of end or goals' (Apple, 1979, p. 84). Many discussions relevant to the hidden curriculum succeed mainly in identifying elements of that curriculum and exploring how they are generated or sustained. Others examine the hidden curriculum within frameworks provided by sociological theory. As a result, any overview of the hidden curriculum must draw upon analyses — often conducted from differing sociological perspectives — of numerous aspects of schools and schooling. This chapter will provide such an overview and then conclude with a brief discussion of the effects and implications of the hidden curriculum.

Some Aspects of the Hidden Curriculum

Ideas relating to sex role, student behaviors and characteristics, knowledge, economic and political values, and students' abilities all form part of the hidden curriculum. In all such areas research has produced substantial information about the nature of the hidden curriculum and the ways in which this curriculum manifests itself. A brief description of selected aspects of the hidden curriculum is given below, the aim being mainly to reveal something of the nature and breadth of this unofficial curriculum.

Sex Role Norms

Schools tend to communicate indirectly a variety of notions relating to sex role differentiation. Through curricular materials, student-teacher interaction, staffing patterns and other features of school life, they induct students into the status, behaviors, personality characteristics and educational or occupational choices customarily regarded as typical of one sex or the other, though such results are not among the objectives the official curriculum is intended to achieve.

Curricular materials, for example, have long fostered distinctions between the sexes. Children's books or stories about males have vastly outnumbered those about females, communicating the idea that males are worthier of attention and are superior in importance and status to females (Sadker, 1975, pp. 319–20). Females often appear in school materials simply as background figures. They are even rarer in secondary school and college textbooks, and when they are included their contributions to society are underplayed. Their role in such developments as the women's suffrage movement and women's trades unionism is either ignored or dismissed in a few words (Kelly and Nihlen, 1982, pp. 170–1). Females are consequently denied a part in public life or in the shaping of history, which is again suggestive of a secondary status. Furthermore, persistent use of such 'sexist' terms as *man, mankind* and *he* to refer to both sexes helps to underline the inferior status accorded women in society.

Curriculum materials have also presented mainly conventional models for the sexes (Martin and Macdonell, 1982, p. 251; Pyke, 1977, pp. 429–30). In children's books, males are likely to be depicted in activities outside the home and females as wives and mothers immersed in domestic pursuits. Males engage in a greater variety of occupations, the more interesting ones usually regarded as male domains. Again, the images of scientists available to students are largely males, which suggests that science is primarily a male subject (Kelly, 1985, pp. 135–6). When females are presented outside the home, it is likely to be in such roles as nurses, teachers and secretaries. In short, curricular materials often inform students that particular kinds of educational or occupational choices are appropriate for one sex rather than the other.

Such materials may also echo traditional beliefs about the behavior and personality characteristics suitable for each sex. Much of the reading matter implies that 'feminine' behaviors are 'domestic, passive and centered indoors' while 'masculine' ones include dominance, high activity levels and a marked ability to succeed at chosen tasks (Delamont, 1980, pp. 17–18). Males on the whole appear to demonstrate much greater aggression, physical exertion, problem-solving skill and productive or constructive behavior, while females seem to exhibit more conformity, the carrying out of orders, verbal activity and indulgence in fantasy (Stockard, 1980, p. 24). In recent years, of course, there has been as improvement in the depiction of the sexes in textbooks. Females are represented much more frequently than in the past and are shown active in a variety of careers. However, sex differences in behaviors and interests have by no means disappeared from curricular materials (Powell and Garcia, 1985).

Sex variations in the quality and quantity of teacher-student interaction may also indicate to students that differing status, ambitions, behaviors and characteristics are appropriate for males and females. Boys tend to receive more attention than girls in terms of approval, disapproval, instruction and being listened to. Their participation in class is sought out more often by teachers than that of girls: They are asked more questions and more of their ideas are accepted by teachers (Russell, 1980; Stanworth, 1983; Acker, 1983). When girls venture to comment during discussions their remarks are often greeted with derision by males, who quickly change the direction of the discussion to one in which they dictate the terms and in which their experience is drawn upon while that of girls is excluded. Consequently, the power differences of the sexes are perpetuated, and the female experience is deemed of little value, which helps preserve the widespread perception that females have a lower status than males. The lesser exposure to teacher attention may also suggest to girls that education is not as important for them as it is for boys (Kelly and Nihlen, 1982, pp. 172–4).

In student-teacher interaction, girls are reinforced less often than boys, but when they receive such reinforcement it is more often than not for being passive, docile, obedient and neat (Serbin, 1983, p. 22). The types of questions addressed to the sexes also intimate that specific kinds of interests and activities are suitable for each sex. For example, teachers make more observations concerning clothes and physical appearance to girls than to boys and give boys priority in the use of certain masculine types of classroom materials (Delamont, 1980, p. 30). Teachers' tolerance of male dominance in laboratories, where boys frequently hog apparatus and confidently participate in the proceedings, may also serve to strengthen the notion that science is a masculine interest (Whyte, 1984). Indeed, the failure of schools to confront students with less conventional sex role models (for example, women as engineers or scientists) typically lessens the chance of students' contemplating unorthodox subject interests (Smith and Erb, 1986). Not surprisingly, girls learn greater helplessness than boys in mathematics and science (Ryckham and Peckham, 1987).

Staffing patterns in schools may also be a source of sex role messages (Pyke, 1977, p. 431). Females constitute a relatively small proportion of school principals even at the primary/elementary level, which emphasizes the notion that it is normal for males to have greater status and power than females. The preponderance of males at all levels of administration in the educational system lends support to the belief that the desire for achievement is a masculine tendency (Delamont, 1980, p. 87). The numerical strength of female teachers in the primary/elementary school confirms the view that women are suited essentially for nurturant roles, while the clearly evident sex differences in teaching specializations at the high school and to some degree the post-secondary levels (e.g., males in mathematics and science, females in literature and languages) 'may well tell students that particular subject matter is legitimate knowledge for one sex rather than both sexes' (Kelly and Nihlen, 1980, pp. 169–70) and might thus incline the sexes toward differing pursuits and interests.

Student Behaviors and Characteristics

Another group of messages forming part of the hidden curriculum concerns the behaviors and characteristics the school deems appropriate for students in general. Students are taught in subtle ways that conformity and passivity are desirable attributes. The physical arrangement of the conventional classroom itself — with the large teacher's desk at the front and the smaller students' desks facing it — stresses the teacher's position as an authority figure and the students' role as largely one of doing as they are directed (Meighan, 1981, pp. 18–19). The process of timetabling, too, is not without significance. Students, particularly in the primary/elementary school, usually have little or no say in determining the subject offerings and their scheduling and must accept that they are to be passive recipients of what others consider important (*ibid.*, p. 81). On the whole, the hierarchical organization of the typical school informs students that people in the higher reaches of the structure have a right to command while those below are to do as they are told without question (*ibid.*, p. 116).

It has been argued, indeed, that through their 'unofficial' three Rs schools often suggest to students that they must yield to the requirements of the organization (Jackson, 1968). These three Rs, which students must learn if they are to survive comfortably in the classroom, are the various Rules, Routines and Regulations enforced by the school and the teachers. For example, students may have to line up for particular purposes, wait for a certain time to be admitted into the classroom, or refrain from talking to one another during lessons. As a result, they must learn to put up with considerable delay (e.g., when waiting for other students to catch up with the work), denial of desires (e.g., when talking is not allowed) and interruptions (e.g., when seatwork is stopped for the teacher to answer one student's questions). Students must have patience; they need high degrees of tolerance for the demands of the organization.

The idea that students must learn to be passive and listen to those in authority is often implicit in teacher-student interaction. Studies of this dimension of classroom life imply that schools have not changed much over time. Research conducted over two decades ago showed that teachers typically did most of the talking and limited their students mainly to responding to them, so that the classroom tended to be teacher-dominated, fact-centered and talk-oriented. Instruction involved an enormous amount of seatwork and the textbook was the major teaching tool. Students were expected to be in their seats and to remain quiet unless called upon by the teacher (Orlosky, 1982, pp. 144–50). A more recent example of American research along similar lines provides evidence that such classroom features persist. Data gathered from over one thousand elementary and high school classrooms show among other things that most class time is spent with teachers lecturing to the group or with students working on written assignments as directed by the teachers, that teachers out-talk students by a ratio of nearly three to one and that most student-teacher interaction takes the form of students simply responding to the teacher, who asks mostly direct, factual questions (Sirotnik, 1983, pp. 16–22). Schools and teachers would apparently often have students believe that being passive and subordinating themselves to the teacher are normal aspects of the student role.

Views of Knowledge

Another important part of the hidden curriculum consists of the views of knowledge subtly transmitted by the typical school. In this connection, the timetable may be a rich source of messages. For example, the division of the curriculum into subject areas and the subsequent assignment of these fields to slots in the timetable may well suggest to students that knowledge is best thought of as compartmentalized. The allocation of specialists to teach such subjects at the high school and beyond is likely to reinforce such an impression. An alternative view, that of knowledge as interrelated, is therefore substantially ignored. Again, the exclusion of some subjects from the timetable might imply that those fields of study are less important or useful than the ones scheduled. When certain practical subjects are omitted, for instance, the reasons given by school boards might emphasize a shortage of funds but this in itself is an admission that particular subjects cannot compete with others for funding and the they are of lesser status and importance. Such phenomena, along with the allocation of differing amounts of time to various subjects, may easily be seen by students as indicating the diverse status and importance accorded both the school subjects and the teachers who are involved in them (Meighan, 1981, p. 83).

The official curriculum itself often presents particular views of knowledge. The type of material included in school syllabuses, for example, reveals what the school is prepared to admit as worthwhile knowledge. Thus, in music there may be no serious treatment of folk or popular music, which implies that these are of lower status and are not really art in the same way as classical music. Similarly, there may be dialects and local cultures in the communities served by the school but education often ignores these and indeed stresses acquisition of a mainstream language or culture, which is tantamount to saying that the local ones are inferior and relatively unimportant. A further implication may well be that the people characterized by such language and culture are inferior. In colonial societies, indeed, school systems often served to teach the language and culture of the imperial society and essentially to ignore those of the colonized groups, certainly a vital means of informing them not only of the lower status assigned their language and culture but, consequently, also of their own social inferiority.

Through their handling of the official curriculum, schools are also inclined to teach that among the subjects they offer some are of greater worth than others. In many school systems, certain subjects are deemed compulsory. For graduation with a high school certificate, for example, passes in such areas as mathematics, language and science may be among the requirements. This differentiation of subjects into compulsory and elective has a bearing on their status. At the same time, a variety of other phenomena may reinforce prevailing views of the rank of specific subjects. Resources are not always allocated equally among subjects: If attention is given more to providing good science laboratories than to developing the physical education facilities, students might justifiably conclude that science enjoys greater regard than physical education. Again, the common practice of reserving specific subject concentrations for superior students while steering others into somewhat different areas tells students something of the status of various fields of study. Distinctions are also likely to occur *within* broad fields: British literature may have more prestige than Canadian literature while the pure sciences tend to be granted a higher standing than an applied science such as home economics (Meighan, 1981, p. 97).

Schools often lead students, also, to think of knowledge not as something evolving but as one of the givens in the school, consisting of facts or bits of information that must be learned. Even science is often taught this way, with teachers 'portraying their subjects as ready-reckoner systems of true answers, rather than principles of thinking through problems and constantly reviewing answers always held as probabilities, rather than certainties' (Meighan, 1981, p. 98). Generally, schools are inclined to pass on to students the received perspective on knowledge and the curriculum: Both knowledge and the curriculum are seen as natural, legitimate entities, existing in their own right. The alternative view — the reflexive perspective, which sees the curriculum as an artefact, as something merely constructed by teachers and others who are guided by their own perceptions of what is important for students — does not have wide currency in schools (Eggleston, 1977, p. 52).

Ishmael J. Baksh

Economic and Political Values

In addition to communication notions regarding sex roles, behavior and personality characteristics and knowledge, schools may influence students' thinking in other areas. The organization of the conventional classroom into rows of single desks, for instance, stresses the desirability of individual work and effort, a marked feature of economic life in North American and similar societies. There may also be unadvertised instruction of a political nature. The material culture in schools — the flag, the pictures, the decorations and the exhibits — frequently link the classroom to the nation as a whole and help sustain a sense of nationhood (Johnson, 1980). In glorifying the values and achievements of a particular society, textbooks in such fields as social studies and literature may reinforce nationalistic sentiments (Reynolds, 1980, pp. 37–9). While the regular school curriculum has little or no impact on students' political attitudes unless special teaching methods are employed, certain school and classroom practices may encourage a less authoritarian disposition in the young. Thus, the schools with an open classroom climate — that is, schools in which students may engage freely in making suggestions about the conduct of the classroom and in which they have opportunities to discuss all sides of a controversial issue — appear more likely than others to encourage less dogmatic views in students. Also, student participation in school governance through student councils, extra-curricular activities and the like seems to produce similar effects. Apparently, patterns of school governance may give students clues about acceptable forms of political behavior (Ehman, 1980, pp. 108–12).

Students' Perceptions of their Abilities

The hidden curriculum may also affect students' perceptions of their own abilities. Substantial evidence exists that when teachers expect some students to perform better than others they might actually induce the students to produce such results (Hurn, 1978, p. 159). How far teachers generate such effects by giving students appropriate signals is a matter for more thorough study. Research certainly suggests that when teachers have higher expectations for particular students they are likely to interact differently with them. They may, in comparison with the other students, allow them more time to answer questions, provide them with more clues about the correct answer, give them more praise for correct answers, and treat them more warmly (Hurn, 1978, pp. 152–7; Braun, Neilsen and Dykstra, 1975). Such teacher behaviors no doubt create conditions conducive to pupil learning. They may also function as signals informing pupils of the teachers' high regard for them and therefore influencing how they view their own abilities.

It appears, too, that grouping practices may play a role in telling pupils what their school thinks of their competence. There is some disagreement as to whether placing students into separate groups/programmes according to their ability or mixing them in the same classrooms regardless of ability makes any difference to their academic success and general classroom adjustment (Gregory, 1984, p. 223; Slavin, 1987; Vanfossen, Jones and Spade 1987, pp. 104–5). Nevertheless, research evidence exists that separating students by ability affects their self-concepts. It is widely accepted that students in low-ability groups tend to have lower self-esteem than those in high-ability groups (Abadzi, 1985, p. 36). A potent factor at work here, it seems, is the stigma of being assigned to an inferior group (*ibid.*), but a consciousness of having a lower rank may be developed in other ways as well. For instance, weaker students may be kept out of specific subjects or may be assigned special textbooks or other materials. As early as the first year of school, pupils become aware of variations among groups in terms of reading materials, in progress through class work and in academic performance, and they begin assigning ranks to the various groups, regarding themselves as either superior or inferior to members of other groups (Eder, 1983, pp. 153–5). It seems, then, that grouping practices may furnish students with clues which they use to assess their own ability.

The above is by no means a complete picture of the hidden curriculum; it merely indicates how far and wide that curriculum ranges. No doubt, schools transmit other messages relating to sex role, behaviors and personality characteristics in general and passivity in particular, views of knowledge, attitudes, norms, values and student ability. Sufficient evidence has been presented, however, to suggest that the hidden curriculum is a highly pervasive element in schooling.

Sociological Perspectives and the Hidden Curriculum

A number of writers bring to bear on the discussion of the hidden curriculum specific theories about human society or about processes that occur in human society and in so doing shed additional light on the function of that curriculum. They do not necessarily employ the term *hidden curriculum* but their theories provide them with frameworks within which to analyze notions allegedly implicit in schooling and communicated to the young, though without being acknowledged in the formal curriculum. The following sections outline three theories and show how the hidden curriculum is viewed within the framework provided by each of these perspectives. The three theories are designated here as the functionalist, the radical and the interactionist.

The Functionalist Perspective

One theory that has been drawn upon with considerable frequency is functionalism. Now there have been many variants of functionalism (Timasheff,

1967, pp. 216–18), but a widely accepted theme in writings informed by this perspective is that a society contains many components each of which contributes to its functioning and survival. Thus, the political system is concerned with how power is obtained, distributed and used in the society, while the social class system is a means of ensuring that people in differing positions receive a fair reward and that the most talented people are encouraged by the promise of greater rewards found in the more prestigious pursuits in the society. In its ideal state, then, society works very smoothly, with all the parts functioning harmoniously to perform the tasks necessary for the survival of the society. This is, of course, a highly simplified account of functionalism but it does permit some insight regarding how the hidden curriculum appears from such a perspective. The educational system is a major component in society and one of its vital functions is to foster a common set of values, norms and beliefs, that is, to socialize the young. If members do not possess such a fairly uniform set of values, norms and beliefs, there is likely to be a great deal of confusion — and perhaps even conflict — over how people should live in society, and no education is complete without substantial attention to this problem (Morrish, 1972, pp. 53–4). It is in this process of socializing members to fit effectively into the society that the hidden curriculum plays a role.

In establishing social groups of various kinds, for example, schools offer pupils the opportunity to develop social skills relevant to adult life. Involvement in student councils and other such extra-curricular groups permits an introduction to many elements of the political process, 'from the power of the vote (and the voter) to the frequent frustrations inherent in a democratic system' (Goslin, 1965, p. 66). Again, schools are the sites of many informal social groups and, through participating in these, the child may master the skills necessary for getting along and interacting with others in adult life. In the peer group, the child can try out different ways of behaving without fear of serious repercussions on the part of peers, unless she or he ignores milder warnings or signs of disapproval for unacceptable acts. Games and other informal activities are the arena for such experimentation. In addition, peer groups and their activities are usually guided by unwritten rules or expectations, and learning to conform to rules is a valuable outcome of sharing in these (Goslin, 1965, pp. 66–9).

It must be noted as well that school personnel, particularly teachers, tend to serve as models exhibiting the attributes, norms and values that make them worthy of emulation, though the influence of any specific teacher is likely to be less than that of individuals in more lasting and intimate contact with children. Furthermore, the inclination of teachers to stress the middle-class standards of behavior, taste and interest that lie at the heart of mainstream culture helps to develop a common set of norms and values and in this way to keep the society stable. Schools also resort to a variety of rewards and punishments in order to encourage the behaviors they deem acceptable. The rewards may include prizes, extra privileges, special mention by teachers or principals, praise or other such devices. Punishment may take the form of detention, scolding, loss of privilege or other penalties. The main goal is to get students to accept both formal and informal rules and regulations, and helping students learn to abide by rules and regulations is one major way in which the school prepares the young for adult life (Goslin, 1965, pp. 69–71).

The Radical Perspective

The view of society as a smoothly functioning entity, with all components contributing to the well-being of the whole and thus helping to generate an overall harmony, is challenged by other theorists, who tend to regard society as an arena in which particular groups seek to preserve or increase their privileges. In other words, it is only certain groups that benefit substantially from the way the society functions. There is the ever present possibility — and sometimes the actual occurrence — of tension or even open conflict between the privileged and the less favored segments of the society. Various institutions, it is claimed, serve the interests of the dominant groups by perpetuating or reproducing the society in its existing form and by legitimizing that form, that is, by leading people to believe that it deserves acceptance. This radical perspective, not surprisingly, sees schools in capitalist societies such as Canada and the United States 'as serving the interests of elites, as reinforcing existing inequalities, and as producing attitudes that foster acceptance of this status quo' (Hurn, 1978, p. 44).

There are, of course, differing versions of and emphases within radical theory. One of its important themes, however, is that schools tend to provide different groups in society with varying levels of knowledge and skill that fit them into specific places in the labor force, with class, race and sex strongly influencing people's chances of success. Thus, women have been kept an underprivileged and even exploited group. In the United States, for instance, schools help through both the formal and the hidden curriculum to maintain gender inequalities, though family responsibilities and discrimination in the workplace also lead to less opportunity for females to achieve success (Kelly and Nihlen, 1982, pp. 163–6). Again, in Canada, the steering of the young into different vocations through schooling has been part of a broader social process 'through which the positions of power and privilege in twentieth-century capitalism has been reserved for men' (Jackson and Gaskell, 1987, p. 196).

Much of the radical writing, however, deals with the perpetuation of social-class inequalities in capitalist societies. It is argued that schools are an integral part of the capitalist system, channelling lower-class students into jobs at the bottom of the occupational hierarchy for the most part and generally facilitating access by middle- and upper-class students to positions at the top of that hierarchy (Kantor and Lowe, 1987, p. 68). Through tests and a curriculum that favor middle-class students, for example, the school leads students of humbler origins in relatively large proportions to failure and to the less prestigious programs of study. At the same time, it teaches a variety of notions and attitudes that serve the interests of elites in the society.

Students, some writers claim, learn that particular bodies of knowledge, forms of language and even physical attributes are of higher status than others. The more theoretical or cultural subjects (e.g., mathematics, physics and literature) are superior to the more practical ones (e.g., industrial arts and home economics); standard English is better than regional, working-class speech, and a lowered voice and neutral tone are more desirable than an emotional one. Such preferred elements of schooling are associated with high-ability students but they in fact tend to be parts of the culture of the higher classes. In thus giving prominence to higher-class culture, schools are in reality saying to students that the people in the higher classes are superior to others and deserve their high status in the society (Giroux, 1983, pp. 268–9). In other words, schools legitimize the culture and status of those who belong to the higher social classes.

In addition, students are taught the norms and values of a capitalist society. Indeed, such norms and values are so embedded in the assumptions, practices and materials found in schools that participants may not even be conscious of them and do not easily see the world as capable of taking any other form (Apple, 1979, p. 5). The world in its existing form appears perfectly natural and inevitable. The norm of competition, for example, is an important part of the culture of capitalist societies: It is thought that people are by nature competitive and that an open competitive society — such as a capitalist one — is the most appropriate for human beings. School practices reflect and reinforce such beliefs: Students are generally expected to compete for marks and other awards. Such behavior is perceived as normal, and cooperative activities seldom occur. Individualism, also, is characteristic of capitalist societies: People are expected to concern themselves primarily with achieving their own personal success rather than that of a larger group or community. In schools, individualism is reflected in the insistence that students work independently and in the arrangement of classrooms, with their rows of single desks, to promote individual effort. In the course of their processing of students, schools in capitalist societies also communicate notions central to the dominant ideology. For example, they inform the young through their examination system that students participate in a contest or competition open to everyone and that success comes to those who have talent, work hard and fully exploit their opportunities. An important by-product of such instruction, some radical writers believe, is that students learn to blame themselves rather than the society for whatever failure they experience in life. If, as they are taught, life is an open contest, with success gained by hard-working people of talent, and if by the examination process they are led to believe they are inferior in ability, the only option open to them in explaining their failure is to blame it on their own inferiority and not on a society they have been induced to regard as fair and open.

In societies such as Canada and the United States, curricular materials, too, are likely to stress capitalist norms and values. A study of seventeen widely used American high school history textbooks, for instance, reports that the historical accounts distort reality and on the whole favor capitalists and the capitalist ideology. The textbooks tend to ignore such unpleasant aspects of industrialists' activities as low wages and poor working conditions or, if they mention them, to exonerate the industrialists. Thus, low wages are on occasion attributed to a willingness of immigrants to work cheaply — rather than to capitalists' eagerness to use immigrant workers to keep wages down — and poor working conditions to the growing size of organizations which allegedly made it difficult for owners to watch personally over their workers' well-being. The textbooks also refer to the success of individuals who, like Andrew Carnegie, supposedly worked hard, saved their money, invested wisely and made fortunes. They unobtrusively underscore the capitalist notions that society is open and that success comes to any talented person who works hard and makes full use of his or her opportunities. In reality, most industrialists had access to funds which enabled them to become heavily involved in money-making ventures (Anyon, 1979).

Also relevant to the hidden curriculum is the theme in some radical writing that 'through its classroom relations schooling functions to inculcate students with the attitudes and dispositions' necessary for participation in the capitalist hierarchy (Giroux, 1983, p. 262). In this connection Bowles and Gintis (1976) and Carnoy and Levin (1976) argue that the social relations of the school correspond to those of the workplace and that schools are therefore able to teach the norms and values of hierarchical work organizations. According to Bowles and Gintis (1976), for example, schools serve the capitalist order in part by developing differing norms and values in people destined to occupy positions at differing levels of the workforce. Students who complete their formal education at the high school level — and they are usually lower-class individuals fated to enter the lower-status occupations — are in general exposed to classroom practices which require conformity to rules, provide little flexibility in choice of tasks or of the way tasks are to be accomplished, and stress closer supervision. Students are taught such values and behavioral norms as following orders reliably, punctuality and respect for authority, all appropriate for lower-status occupations. Students proceeding into post-secondary education, on the other hand, enjoy greater latitude and consequently superior opportunity to develop initiative, flexibility and other traits vital in higher-status positions. In spite of such general trends, however, the character of schools and classrooms might vary within any particular level of the educational system according to the students' social-class background and their likely occupational destinations. In other words, high school students pursuing a highly academic university-oriented curriculum might well have classroom experiences differing from those following a vocational program. Similarly, schools serving middle-class neighbourhoods might well treat their students differently from those catering for lower-class communities.

The notion that children of varying social backgrounds might have school experiences that fit them for differing levels of the workforce has been explored by other scholars. Thus, Wilcox and Moriarty (1976) report on teacher-pupil interaction in two elementary schools, one serving a lower-class and the other a middle-class neighbourhood. They compare the two schools in terms of teachers' use of internal and/or external control. Classified as fostering *internal* control are classroom interactions in which the teacher treats the child as a self-directed person capable of managing a process of activity in an independent way on the basis of internalized standards and goals. Designated as encouraging *external* control are interactions in which children follow rules, directions or procedures specified by the teacher on the basis of her formal authority. The study finds that, while children at both schools are exposed to external behavioral standards set by the teacher, it is only in the middle-class school that the children experience internal control, in being taught for instance that they are personally responsible for maintaining the quality of their school work or for making sensible use of class time. Instead of being dictatorial, the teacher asks the latter students to consider whether they had used their time wisely. Wilcox and Moriarty (1976) conclude that the middle-class students are being socialized for pursuits at the higher levels of the workforce where, typically, greater self-direction is necessary, while lower-class pupils are being prepared for jobs requiring rule-following and conformity to the demands of authority figures.

Anyon (1980) arrives at similar conclusions following observation of classroom interaction in five elementary schools serving neighbourhoods that differ from one another in terms of parental education and income levels. In the working-class schools, work is mechanical and involves little decision making or choice by students, who are required to adhere to steps laid down by the teacher and often memorized as notes. In mathematics and language arts, for example, specific steps to be followed in working out a problem or in writing are imposed upon the students. Generally, there is little discussion, student contribution or initiative, or use of supplementary material, and students spend much of the time copying notes from the board. In examining classroom interaction in the schools serving neighborhoods progressively more privileged in economic and educational respects, however, Anyon observes increasing teacher encouragement of student activity, initiative, independent work, discussion, creativity and self-direction. Oakes (1982), also, finds evidence of differential student-teacher interaction in groups varying in socio-economic status and consequently claims to have found support for the Bowles-Gintis thesis. However, the generalizability of such findings has been questioned by Ramsay (1983), whose own study discloses greater diversity among and within schools serving particular types of neighborhoods than the foregoing research suggests.

The Interactionist Perspective

A third theoretical perspective that sheds valuable light on at least some elements of the hidden curriculum is the interactionist. This approach emphasizes the meanings or interpretations people bring to bear on the conduct of their daily lives. Human beings, it claims, tend to act toward *objects* (i.e., persons, places, situations or things) on the basis of the meanings such objects have for them. Students, for example, may regard as a good teacher one who is not too weak or too strong but has found the middle way in maintaining authority in the classroom, who has a sense of humor, who makes classes interesting, and who is understanding (Gannaway, 1984). A good teacher never fails to respect the students as a person, always teaches effectively, shows no weakness of will, does not insult students and is fair to all (Rosser and Harre, 1984). Students tend to respond to their teachers according to how far the latter meet such criteria. Generally, then, people develop perspectives or frameworks which they employ to understand the world (Woods, 1983, p. 7). Having arrived at their own interpretations, they are likely to decide upon appropriate strategies, plans of action that will in their judgment enable them to achieve their goals.

While students may bring particular perspectives or frameworks to their dealings with schools, however, they encounter teachers, principals and others with their own perspectives on schooling. Students may have certain ideas regarding what makes a good teacher, or they may distinguish between adult culture (i.e., the things stressed by the school) and *their* interests (i.e., social activity, play and fun) and may define a good school as one that permits a fair opportunity to engage in the latter (Davies, 1982; Pollard, 1982, p. 32). Teachers, on the other hand, may have their own views about the nature of a good classroom. Typically, they seek to maintain their authority and control pupil activity (Woods, 1983, p. 105); they abhor noise (Denscombe, 1980); they are clear about what students should know and what answers students should give to their questions (Woods, 1983, pp. 105-6); and they hold specific views about how students should perform to be regarded as intelligent (Hammersley, 1974).

It is inevitable, therefore, that pupils must come to grips with many complexities that are not formally acknowledged in the school curriculum. For the pupil coming to a class for the first time, 'the learning of the hidden curriculum becomes an urgent necessity, preceding any hope of effective participation in the official curriculum' (Eggleston, 1977, pp. 113–14). Students must ascertain, for example, where they might sit, what delicate balance of attention and indifference they might exhibit in class, with what vocabulary and intonation they might interact with the teacher, and what the teacher's expectations are with respect to talking in class and the performance of written work (*ibid.*, p. 114). They must learn that to be regarded as intelligent by teachers they must participate in class, demonstrate appropriate attitudes and produce acceptable answers. When teachers ask questions they tend to have certain answers in mind as the correct ones and students must learn to find the answers teachers want, but they must also recognize that teachers claim the right to determine who will answer as well as which answers are acceptable (Hammersley, 1974).

Students must acquaint themselves, also, with the behaviors teachers might believe appropriate for different parts of a lesson. Though there are variations among teachers, the typical lesson contains five phases: (1) The entry phase, (2) the settling down or preparatory phase, (3) the lesson proper phase, (4) the clearing up phase, and (5) the exit phase (Hargreaves, Hestor and Mellor, 1984). Teachers are inclined to have fairly specific ideas regarding how pupils should act in each phase. In the settling down or preparatory phase, for instance, pupils are expected to sit on — or remain in close proximity to — their assigned seats; they may talk with one another but without shouting, and they must cooperate in any distribution of equipment or materials. In the lesson proper phase, a sequence of sub-phases is evident, though one or more of these may be omitted or combined with others. In the first part of this phase the teacher is highly active — usually talking — and the pupils are relatively passive, being expected to watch and listen to the teacher. They are not to engage in talk and movement or to interrupt the teacher with superfluous or irrelevant comments and questions, unless the matter is urgent. In succeeding parts of the lesson proper phase students are more active, though there are unwritten rules they must learn and follow.

In general, students need to determine what the teacher's behavioral expectations are, what the teacher's limits for social and fun activities in the classroom might be, and what the teacher's requirements are for passing the course or at least meeting minimum standards of performance. It is perhaps not surprising, then, that pupils often employ humor to test out new teachers (Woods, 1983, p. 120), that they take time to probe the ground rules preferred by each teacher (Davies, 1982), or that they greet their new teachers with a wait-and-see period and also employ various strategies to type-cast them (Beynon, 1984). The occurrence of such strategies constitutes evidence that students are attempting to come to grips with the hidden curriculum which is so 'vast, detailed and complex' (Eggleston, 1977, p. 114).

The Hidden Curriculum: Effects and Implications

The impact of the hidden curriculum is likely to vary from one student to another. For one thing, as some radical scholars suggest, students may well resist the messages they receive from the school. Girls, for example, are not necessarily passive subjects on whom institutions might readily leave their stamp. They do not always become quite what schools apparently seek to make them: They may resist or filter messages concerning sex roles and often emerge unaffected by the forces contributing to sex role differentiation (Kelly and Nihlen, 1982, pp. 171–6). Students in general might often resist the official labels, meanings, demands and impositions of the school; they may, for example, tune out of classroom instruction, bug the teacher, slow down the pace of work by injecting humor, and circumvent classroom rules or requirements in a variety of ways (Everhart, 1983). Alternatively, as some interactionist writers note, students may attempt to negotiate with the teacher regarding such matters as school rules and procedures, quantity of classroom work and standards of performance, and seek to bring about a classroom environment that is a compromise between what they desire and what teachers wish to impose upon them (Pollard, 1982; Ball, 1984). Successful resistance and negotiation will certainly tend to lessen the impact of the hidden curriculum on at least some students.

In a sense, the hidden curriculum may even facilitate achievement of some of the objectives pursued by schools. If, for instance, students have learned to act as teachers expect them to or have negotiated with their teachers a set of classroom rules with which they feel fairly comfortable they are perhaps more likely to attend to the instruction the school wishes to impart. On the other hand, the hidden curriculum has the potential to undermine many educational goals. For example, schools commonly assert that they seek the full development of each student's intellectual potential. Yet, through teacher expectations, grouping, sex role messages and other phenomena they may actually discourage the full intellectual development of particular groups of students. Radical writers often contend, indeed, that schools are *not* designed to secure the maximum development of all students. Again, a formally accepted goal of many educational systems is the fostering of critical thinking in students. In reality, however, schools apparently tend to teach docility and passivity and in subtle ways to encourage an uncritical acceptance of nationalism, sexism and other bigotries. As well, instead of promoting social development, schools may actually encourage anti-social tendencies, for instance by producing divisions among students supposedly based on differences in intellectual ability. In these and other ways, the hidden curriculum is often likely to work against the official goals of the school. In addition, the hidden curriculum may alienate many students from the school. For example, the stock of knowledge students bring from their own backgrounds and experiences may well be neglected in favor of the teachers' stocks of knowledge or whatever schools regard as legitimate or desirable knowledge, with the result that school work may be less meaningful to students than it might be. The requirement that they learn to be passive and docile, too, may make many students antagonistic toward schools (Baksh and Martin, 1986, pp. 117–21).

Clearly, an analysis of the school curriculum is incomplete if it ignores the hidden curriculum. Yet, the reaction of scholars to the hidden curriculum has been quite varied: Many curriculum theorists ignore it or fail to recognize it; other writers argue for the abandonment of the conventional school because of its allegedly undesirable effects, while still others feel that the most negative aspects of the hidden curriculum can be controlled or that alternative ways of organizing and conducting schools may be adopted so as to eliminate the hidden curriculum (Meighan, 1981, p. 62). The least that educators and teachers might do, it seems, is to become aware of the hidden curriculum. As Marland (1983) argues, 'as much as possible should come out of the hidden into the ostensible curriculum so that it can be critically and professionally scrutinized and related to wider aims' (p. 149). Such an analysis will enable educators and teachers to determine what corrective actions they might take.

This chapter presents simply an overview of the hidden curriculum and of relevant theoretical and practical considerations. Eggleston (1977) and Meighan (1981) offer more thorough discussions of the theoretical and practical issues arising once the existence of such a curriculum is recognized. Parsons (1968), Dreeben (1968) and Inkeles (1972) elaborate in a fairly sophisticated fashion on the role of the school from a functionalist perspective. Giroux (1983) provides a succinct but highly readable survey of the major and recent radical schools of thought, most of which either implicitly or openly accept that a hidden curriculum is found in schools. Apple (1979, 1982 and 1987), Bowles and Gintis (1976), Carnoy and Levin (1976 and 1985), and Cole (1988) present analyses of the hidden curriculum from a radical perspective while Woods (1983) does so from an interactionist viewpoint. Hurn (1978), Hargreaves (1982), Angus (1986), Apple and Weis (1986), Kantor and Lowe (1987) and Cole (1988) advance interesting critiques of specific theoretical perspectives employed in examinations of the hidden curriculum. The reader wishing to pursue this topic in greater depth will find such writings highly rewarding.

Bibliography

ABADZI, H. (1985) 'Ability grouping effects on academic achievement and self-esteem: Who performs in the long run as expected', *Journal of Educational Research*, 79, pp. 36–40.

ACKER, S. (1983) 'No-woman's land: British sociology of education 1960–1979', in COSIN, B. and HALES, M. (Eds) *Education, Policy and Society: Theoretical Perspectives* (pp. 106–28), London: Routledge and Kegan Paul.

ANGUS, L. (1986) 'Developments in ethnographic research in education: From interpretive to critical ethnography', *Journal of Research and Development in Education*, 20, pp. 59–67.

ANYON, J. (1979) 'Ideology and United States history textbooks', *Harvard Educational Review*, 49, pp. 361–86.

ANYON, J. (1980) 'Social class and the hidden curriculum of work', *Journal of Education (Boston)*, 162, 67–92.

APPLE, M.W. (1979) *Ideology and Curriculum*, London: Routledge and Kegan Paul.

APPLE, M.W. (Ed.) (1982) *Cultural and Economic Reproduction in Education*, London: Routledge and Kegan Paul.

APPLE, M.W. (1987) *Teachers and Texts: A Political Economy of Class and Gender Relations in Education*, New York: Routledge, Chapman and Hall Inc.

APPLE, M.W. and WEIS, L. (1986) 'Seeing education relationally: The stratification of culture and people in the sociology of school knowledge', *Journal of Education (Boston)*, 168, pp. 7–33.

BALL, S. (1984) 'Initial encounters in the classroom and the process of establishment', in HAMMERSLEY, M. and WOODS, P. (Eds) *Life in School: The Sociology of Pupil Culture*, London: Open University Press. (pp. 108–20)

BAKSH, I.J. and MARTIN, W.B.W. (1986) *Teaching Strategies: The Student Perspective*, St. John's: Faculty of Education, Memorial University of Newfoundland.

BEYNON, J. (1984) '"Sussing Out" teachers: Pupils as data gatherers', in HAMMERSLEY, M. and WOODS, P. (Eds) *Life in School: The Sociology of Pupil Culture*, London: Open University Press, (pp. 121–44).

BOWLES, S. and GINTIS, H. (1976) *Schooling in Capitalist America*, New York: Basic Books.

BRAUN, C., NEILSEN, A.R. and DYKSTRA, R. (1975) 'Teacher's expectations: Prime mover or inhibitor?' *The Elementary School Journal*, 76, pp. 181–8.

CARNOY, M. and LEVIN, H.M. (1976) *The Limits of Educational Reform*, New York: McKay.

CARNOY, M. and LEVIN, H.M. (1985) *Schooling and Work in the Democratic State*, Stanford: Stanford University Press.

COLE, M. (Ed.) (1988) *Bowles and Gintis Revisited: Correspondence and Contradiction in Educational Theory*, Philadelphia: The Falmer Press.

DAVIES, B. (1982) *Life in the Classroom and Playground*, London: Routledge and Kegan Paul.

DELAMONT, S. (1980) *Sex Roles and the School*, London: Methuen and Co. Ltd.

DENSCOMBE, M. (1980) 'Keeping 'Em Quiet: The significance of noise for the practical activity of teaching', in WOODS, P. (Ed.) *Teacher Strategies*, London: Croom Helm. (pp. 61–80).

DREEBEN, R. (1968) *On What is Learned in School* Reading, MA: Addison-Wesley Publishing Company.

EDER, D. (1983) 'Ability grouping and students' academic self-concepts: A case study', *The Elementary School Journal*, 84, pp. 149–61.

EGGLESTON, J. (1977) *The Sociology of the School Curriculum*, London: Routledge and Kegan Paul.

EHMAN, L.H. (1980) 'The American school in the political socialization process', *Review of Educational Research*, 50, pp. 99–119.

EVERHART, R.B. (1983) *Reading, Writing and Resistance: Adolescence and Labour in a Junior High School*, London: Routledge and Kegan Paul.

GANNAWAY, H. (1984) 'Making sense of school', in HAMMERSLEY, M. and WOODS, P. (Eds) *Life in School: The Sociology of Pupil Culture*, London: Open University Press, (pp. 193–203).

GIROUX, H.A. (1983) 'Theories of reproduction and resistance in the new sociology of education: A critical analysis', *Harvard Educational Review*, 55, pp. 257–93.

GOSLIN, D.A. (1965) *The School in Contemporary Society*, Glenview, IL: Scott, Foresman and Company.

GREGORY, R.P. (1984) 'Streaming, setting and mixed ability grouping in primary and secondary schools: Some research findings', *Educational Studies*, 10, pp. 209–26.

HAMMERSLEY, M. (1974) 'The organization of pupil participation', *The Sociological Review*, 22, pp. 355–68.

HARGREAVES, A. (1982) 'Resistance and relative autonomy theories: Problems of distortion and incoherence in recent Marxist analyses of education', *British Journal of Sociology of Education*, 3, pp. 107–26.

HARGREAVES, D.H., HESTOR, S.K. and MELLOR, F.J. (1984) 'Rules in play', in HARGREAVES, A. and WOODS, P. (Eds) *Classrooms and Staffrooms*, London: Open University Press (pp. 25–35).

HURN, C.J. (1978) *The Limits and Possibilities of Schooling*, Boston: Allyn and Bacon, Inc.

INKELES, A. (1972) 'A model of modern man', in HAMMOND, N. (Ed.) *Social Science*

and the New Societies: Problems in Cross-cultural Research and Theory Building
East Lansing: Social Science Research Bureau, Michigan State University
(pp. 59–94).

JACKSON, P.W. (1968) *Life in Classrooms*, New York: Holt, Rinehart and Winston.

JACKSON, N.S. and GASKELL, J.S. (1987) 'White collar vocationalism: The rise of
commercial education in Ontario and British Columbia, 1870–1920', *Curriculum
Inquiry*, 17, pp. 176–201.

JOHNSON, N.B. (1980) 'The material culture of public school classrooms: The symbolic
integration of local schools and national culture', *Anthropology and Education
Quarterly*, XI, pp. 173–90.

KANTOR, H. and LOWE, R. (1987) 'Empty promises', *Harvard Educational Review*, 57,
pp. 68–76.

KELLY, A. (1985) 'The construction of masculine science', *British Journal of Sociology
of Education*, 6, pp. 133–54.

KELLY, G.P. and NIHLEN, A.S. (1982) 'Schooling and the reproduction of patriarchy:
Unequal workloads, unequal rewards', in APPLE, M.W. (Ed.) *Culture and Econo-
mic Reproduction in Education* (pp. 162–80), London: Routledge and Kegan
Paul.

LISTON, D.P. (1988) 'Faith and evidence: Examining Marxist explanations of schools',
American Journal of Education, 96, pp. 323–50.

MARLAND, M. (1983) 'Curriculum matters', in MARLAND, M. (Ed.) *Sex Differentiation
and Schooling*, London: Heinemann, (pp. 141–62).

MARTIN, W.B.W. and MACDONELL, A.J. (1982) *Canadian Education: A Sociological
Analysis*, Scarborough, Ontario: Prentice-Hall Canada Inc.

MEASOR, L. and WOODS, P. (1984) 'Cultivating the middle ground: Teachers and
school ethos', *Research in Education*, No. 31, pp. 25–40.

MEIGHAN, R. (1981) *A Sociology of Educating*, London: Holt, Rinehart and Winston.

MORRISH, I. (1972) *The Sociology of Education: An Introduction*, London: George
Allen and Unwin Ltd.

OAKES, J. (1982) 'Classroom social relationships: Exploring the Bowles and Gintis
hypothesis', *Sociology of Education*, 55, pp. 197–212.

ORLOSKY, D.E. (1982) *Introduction to Education*, Columbus, OH: Charles E. Merrill
Publishing Company.

PARSONS, T. (1968) 'The school class as a social system', *Socialization and Schools*,
Cambridge, MA: Harvard Educational Review. (pp. 69–90).

POLLARD, A. (1982) 'A model of classroom coping strategies', *British Journal of
Sociology of Education*, 3, pp. 19–37.

POWELL, R.R. and GARCIA, J. (1985) 'The portrayal of minorities and women in
selected elementary science series', *Journal of Research in Science Teaching*, 22,
pp. 519–33.

PYKE, S.W. (1977) 'Sex role socialization in the school system', in CARLTON, R.A.,
COLLEY, L.A. and MACKINNON, N.J. (Eds) *Education, Change, and Society: A
Sociology of Canadian Education*, Toronto: Gage Educational Publishing Ltd.
(pp. 426–38).

RAMSAY, P.D.K. (1983) 'Fresh perspectives on the school transformation-reproduction
debate: A response to Anyon from the antipodes', *Curriculum Inquiry*, 13, pp.
295–320.

REYNOLDS, J.C. (1980) 'Textbooks: Guardians of nationalism', *Education*, 102, pp.
37–42.

ROSSER, E. and HARRE, R. (1984) 'The meaning of trouble', in HAMMERSLEY, M. and
WOODS, P. (Eds) *Life in School: The Sociology of Pupil Culture*, London: Open
University Press, (pp. 204–10).

RUSSELL, S. (1980) 'Learning sex role in high school', *Interchange*, 10, pp. 58–66.

RYCKHAM, D.B. and PECKHAM, P. (1987) 'Gender differences in attributions for success and failure situations across subject areas', *Journal of Educational Research*, *81*, pp. 120–5.

SADKER, M. (1975) 'Sexism in schools', *Journal of Teacher Education*, *XXXI*, pp. 317–22.

SERBIN, L.A. (1983) 'The hidden curriculum: Academic consequences of teacher expectations', in MARLAND, M. (Ed.) *Sex Differentiation and Schooling*, London: Heinemann. (pp. 18–41).

SIROTNIK, K.A. (1983) 'What you see is what you get — consistency, persistency, and mediocrity in classrooms', *Harvard Educational Review*, *53*, pp. 16–31.

STANWORTH, M. (1983) *Gender and Schooling*, London: Hutchinson.

SLAVIN, R.E. (1987) 'Ability grouping and student achievement in elementary schools: A best-evidence synthesis', *Review of Educational Research*, *57*, pp. 293–336.

SMITH, W.S. and ERB, T.D. (1986) 'Effect of women science career role models on early adolescents' attitudes toward scientists and women in science', *Journal of Research in Science Teaching*, *23*, pp. 667–76.

STOCKARD, J. (1980) *Sex Equity in Education*, New York: Academic Press.

TIMASHEFF, N.S. (1967) *Sociological Theory: Its Nature and Growth*, New York: Random Press.

VANFOSSEN, B.E., JONES, J.D. and SPADE, J.Z. (1987) 'Curriculum tracking and status maintenance', *Sociology of Education*, *60*, pp. 104–22.

WHYTE, J. (1984) 'Observing sex stereotypes and interactions in the school lab and workshop', *Educational Review*, *36*, pp. 75–86.

WILCOX, K. and MORIARITY, P. (1976) 'Schooling and work: Social constraints on equal educational opportunity', *Social Problems*, *24*, pp. 204–13.

WOODS, P. (1983) *Sociology and the School: An Interactionist Viewpoint*, London: Routledge and Kegan Paul.

IV
Fulfilling School Tasks Through Teaching and Learning

INTRODUCTION

No matter how solidly conceptualized, selected, and organized, the curriculum does not have much value unless it is experienced by students in meaningful and effective ways. Once the curriculum has been selected and organized in accordance with valid and justifiable aims, the worth of the schooling process hinges on the quality of transaction between the teacher and students. Clearly, as the main initiator of student learning, the teacher is naturally expected to have the skills to elicit such learning. Consequently, it is popularly held that teacher preparation institutions should emphasize teaching methods and strategies, particularly those whose effectiveness has been demonstrated by research and practice.

William Hare recognizes the need for teachers' possession of practical skills. However, he takes issue with the popular practical orientation in teacher preparation. In his view, a teacher requires much more than the capacity to use practical skills. The teacher's understanding of the concept of teaching itself is indispensable for intelligent teaching. Such understanding establishes the framework of constraints and opportunities surrounding his or her role. Equally important, the teacher should be able to analyze and ask probing questions about the conclusions and prescriptions on teaching methodology coming out of research and practice. This capacity to understand, analyze, and evaluate is deeply rooted more in philosophy than other disciplines; thus, the philosophical contribution to the preparation of teachers should not be underestimated: Indeed, Hare's article shows the philosopher of education at work in untangling and relating the concepts of teaching and learning and in assessing the claims that have been made on behalf of research findings on certain teaching strategies.

The link between teaching and learning, briefly explored by Hare, is the central focus of Paul O'Leary's chapter. His views are initially contentious: That learning something cannot be true unless it is the result of self-determination, that learning x cannot be true unless x is true or exhibits standard behaviors, and that all learning is teacher-dependent do not sound intuitively right. Through analysis, however, O'Leary seeks to convince. Indeed, a case can be made for the view that, as he implies, one cannot really be regarded as learning actively unless she — including her consciousness, desires, and voluntary participation — is involved. It can equally be argued that *having learned x* makes sense only where the learner can exhibit the standard behaviors, or meaningfully express the propositions, which comprise x. And, finally, it can be argued that, insofar as x consists of behaviors or propositions, having in fact learned it requires a standard against which the learner's behaviors or statements are to be measured; this has to be communicated to the learner in one form or another by the standard-bearer for the learner to know that she has learned. If correct, O'Leary's views have important and negative consequences for the increasingly popular advocacy of self-learning.

Indispensable as the capacity for analysis may be, it is not likely to be sufficient for sustaining a teacher in the classroom. Teaching is at least partly a craft and thus requires getting things done. Surely a large number of teaching activities can be uniformly undertaken; also, pupils have enough similarities to justify following generalized procedures even as teachers remain alert to cases requiring individual attention. Whether in relation to group or to individual learning, however, psychology offers insights and generalizations which contribute toward intelligent practice. Philip Winne and John Walsh elaborate on what is known as instructional psychology and how its findings can contribute to classroom practice. Drawing from psychological research, they show how teachers can profit from familiarity with the conditions under which classroom tasks are accomplished by students, the cognitive plans they use to complete their tasks, and the way students perceive the products of learning. They also demonstrate how research findings on motivation can be enlisted for instructional purposes. In doing so, they hope to show that transforming a novice teacher into an expert requires a large measure of knowledge from instructional psychology.

Propositional knowledge is generally and rightfully held inadequate, however, for the art or craft of teaching. Such knowledge will have to work in practice. Teacher education programs, therefore, are regarded as woefully incomplete without the practicum, that is, that component of teacher education which provides actual classroom and teaching experiences for prospective teachers. The practicum, which takes a variety of forms, will ensure familiarity with the real world of teaching and develop practical skills which are merely viewed theoretically in coursework at the university. In her chapter, Norma Mickelson emphasizes the value of the practicum. She readily admits, however, that numerous factors conspire to negate its value. Some factors are generic to educational studies, such as the lack of integration of theory and practice and the lack of rigor in the selection of students entering faculties of education. Others are specific to the practicum; as Mickelson puts it, there is frequently a lack of suitable conceptualization and willingness to undertake changes needed to make the practicum a truly effective element of teacher preparation. It is time, she says, to seriously consider a new model which stresses active inquiry and participation in decision making on the part of student teachers.

The assumed ideal product of teacher preparation is the professional teacher. Recent developments painfully remind us that that ideal is not being realized in a substantial number of teachers in the field. In his article, Romulo Magsino cautions us, nonetheless, that a general condemnation may not be fair to teaching as a professional undertaking. Though some critics believe that professionalization of teaching is virtually impossible, he insists to the contrary. His strategy involves getting at the core notion of a profession as an occupation whose practice depends on theoretical knowledge and showing that teaching can indispensably profit from foundational studies — history, philosophy, psychology, and sociology of education. These studies facilitate perspectival understandings enabling teachers to engage in meaningful reflection and decision making in their classroom practice. Findings and insights from such studies are already available and should be provided to prospective teachers, together with proven practical skills which research and field practice have confidently identified. Combined with other components in teacher education and with the development of a moral commitment required by a voluntary decision to engage in teaching, professionalization may not be an impossibility.

10   Teaching: Nature, Norm and Numbers

William Hare

The Conceptual Analysis of Teaching

Faced with the imminent prospect of having to teach a class for the first time, student teachers predictably favor the acquisition of basic survival skills over the exploration of philosophical questions, even when these are related to the teaching context. Nevertheless, there are reasons why student teachers need to reflect philosophically on the enterprise of teaching, on what teaching is and ought to be, and on what research on teaching has to offer. These reasons can have a bearing on one's ultimate survival as a teacher. Chief among these is simply the fact that the way in which we think of teaching has an influence on the way in which we teach. Constraints and opportunities emerge from our theoretical framework. To remove the constraint is at once to create an opportunity. Philosophy has an important role to play in permitting such opportunities to present themselves.

Obviously enough, teaching will suffer if teachers lack certain practical skills. The relevance of methods classes is widely acknowledged. It is not so readily appreciated that teaching can be adversely affected in other ways also. We can, for example, slip into a rather narrow view of teaching and arbitrarily limit what we see as possible, with the result that certain methods or objectives do not arise for us as live options. Another pitfall is to accept uncritically what passes for good teaching without asking what teaching, at its finest, might be like and whether there are certain ideals which should guide teaching. Finally, we can allow ourselves to be influenced by research findings without pausing to ask searching questions about the interpretation and application of these findings.

Philosophy has a contribution to make in each of these areas. There is such an enormous literature, however, that there can be no attempt here to summarize the field or to explore the complexities which have arisen in any detail. Our task must be more illustrative, inspired, of course, by important suggestions in the literature, as we try to substantiate the claims made on behalf of philosophy. Any attempt to do this, however, is likely to encounter a certain initial skepticism based on general considerations which need to be addressed directly.

The first kind of doubt is raised by Robin Barrow (1983, p. 194) who suggests that certain concepts, including teaching, are relatively unproblematic. We know well enough what teaching is, and we do not need the kind of sustained, conceptual inquiry into teaching which might be needed with other concepts. Barrow is not dogmatic about this and concedes that there will be room for disagreement about which concepts are unproblematic. Others have certainly agreed with him in this connection, notably Jacques Barzun (1946, p. 4) who turned with great dispatch from the endless controversy about education to the more manageable topic of teaching. It is not easy, however, to declare that a concept just is inherently unproblematic. Those which, we may think, ought to be can be made problematic as they become enmeshed in theories and slogans. When, elsewhere, Barrow (1979, p. 202) argues that the teacher cannot be both non-directive and teaching, this is because he believes that others have become confused about the nature of teaching. Perhaps we have only raised a dust where otherwise we might see clearly, but now conceptual clarification is needed if only to recall us to commonsense.

A very different objection arises from those who believe that conceptual inquiry is ultimately futile. Far from being unproblematic, the concepts prove unamenable to analysis. In the words of a recent and fair-minded critic, counter examples arise to defeat any analysis (Hendley, 1986, p. 5). Here the objection is not that the approach taken by philosophers of education in the recent past was too linguistic or too arbitrary. These are faults of conceptual inquiry as practised, not as such. Talk of stagnation and futility, however, suggests that the whole enterprise is in vain. On this point, however, it is worth recalling the remark of Etienne Gilson (1957, p. 24)[1] that, even where definitions are not possible, it can be profitable to attempt them. Perhaps more was promised in the heyday of analytical philosophy of education than was, or could have been, delivered. But now we need to ask what was learned along the way.

Although there was a tremendous burst of conceptual inquiry concerning teaching in the twenty-year period from 1955 to 1975, it would be a mistake to think that earlier philosophers of education had not addressed these issues. Certainly, some recent analytical philosophers of education managed to give the impression that earlier contributions had been almost entirely wrong-headed. The proper task of philosophy, the careful demarcation of concepts, had degenerated, we were told, into the formulation of high-level directives (Peters, 1967, p. 15), presumably more airy than lofty. This was a hopeless caricature, of course, but Dewey, Russell and others were effectively written off. Enthusiasm for conceptual analysis has now waned considerably, and former devotees are anxious to dissociate themselves from the errors of misguided youth (White, 1982, p. 5). Conceptual clarification is dismissed as so much idle chatter. It is a kind of sport, diverting at times, but pointless and often boring. No doubt there is an element of poetic justice in this sudden reversal of fortune, but we are perilously close to concluding that if conceptual inquiry is not all important, it is not important at all. Such an about-face will not serve to recover the tradition of philosophy of education and might lead us to throw out the achievements of the analytic period along with the dregs.

The Polymorphous Nature of Teaching

Even if we are inclined to think that the notion of teaching is straightforward, we soon encounter comments and questions about teaching which force us to reflect on our everyday assumptions. In particular, we encounter the sugges-tion that something or other cannot be taught, and it is clear that the claim is not based on experience, nor is it one which is to be tested in an experimental way. An answer can only be found, if at all, by thinking about the idea of teaching. Socrates (Plato's *Meno*, in Hamilton and Cairns, 1961) took the view that virtue could not be taught, partly because it was not knowledge and partly because those who professed to be teachers of virtue were themselves confused about the matter. Kant (1781)[2] held that while rules could be taught, judgment could not. Judgment is something which comes with practice but no one can teach another person a sense of judgment. Jacques Barzun (1946, p. 32) cited tolerance, democracy and citizenship as improper objects of teaching. These cannot be taught because they are attitudes, not subject matter. And a recent textbook for high school politics courses asserts that no one can be taught to think. At best, a few suggestions can be offered to the learner (Tinder, 1986, p. 2).

These claims run counter to widely held views. If we judge by the enormous efforts which have been made in recent years to develop education-al programmes in moral education and critical thinking, one would have to conclude that there is a strong belief that such matters can be taught and are among the most important items on any list of educational aims. Of course, those who deny that teaching is possible with respect to these objectives do not mean to suggest that virtue, judgment and the ability to think are not worthwhile, only that they must be acquired in some other way. Favorite answers would include practice, experience, personal discovery and example.

Before exploring this issue and the questions it raises about teaching, we need to ask if anything really hinges on this disagreement. After all, everyone agrees that the achievements in question are desirable, and even those who exclude the possibility of teaching are often prepared to say that the teacher as a person is instrumental in their emergence. Barzun, for example, con-cedes that such achievements occur as by-products of good teaching. They come from a teacher, not from a course (1946, p. 9). It begins to sound suspiciously like a verbal dispute, and a trivial issue. It may be, however, that matters of consequence lurk behind such a seemingly superficial dispute. If teachers define their work primarily as teaching, then what they attempt will be related to what they view as possible given their understanding of this concept.

If we ask what is basic to our idea of teaching, it seems clear that we cannot begin to explain it without introducing the idea of learning. We know that people can learn things without the benefit of teaching, and so there is a clear sense in which learning does not require teaching. This is not always clear in practice, however, where we can slip into the view that learning only goes on in the context of teaching and this risk is increased if we define the learners as pupils. If this mistake is avoided, there remains the related one of thinking that the only worthwhile learning is that which results from teaching. One serious practical consequence of this is a failure to utilize in our teaching what the student has learned independently.

Teaching, however, does require learning in the sense that learning of some sort is the objective at which teaching aims. Certainly, the central case for teachers, leaving aside team teaching, is that in which one person sets out to act in such a way that what is to be learned can be learned by others from what he or she does. Many different kinds of learning may be intended, from carpentry to calculus, but that some intended learning outcome is necessary can be seen from the nonsense which results otherwise. Think, for example, of teaching in an otherwise empty classroom or in a language foreign to, and beyond the comprehension of, the students. In a different case, what sense could we make of setting out to teach someone what that person already understands and, therefore, cannot learn?

Of course, all of these examples can be made intelligible, but in each case this is done by smuggling in the objective of learning.[3] For example, the room might be empty because the teacher is recording a lesson for educational television. The use of a foreign language might be designed to foster appreciation of the situation of a newly arrived immigrant who must grapple with a new language. Again, we may aim at a deeper understanding of what a student in some way already grasps, or at pursuing further implications of ideas already covered. These cases, however, can now be understood as teaching precisely because we have found a way to reintroduce learning as an objective. Our central case involves teaching others, so the notion of teaching oneself falls outside it and should, I suggest, be considered a derivative form of teaching though one which is important in its own way. It is not our primary example of teaching because it derives its status as a kind of teaching by analogy with the case where one person teaches someone else. When we teach ourselves, we are in effect learning on our own without the benefit of teaching. But we set about the task in ways which resemble to some extent the situation in which we have someone else as a teacher. Perhaps we have a teach-yourself book, where another person is in the background as teacher. Or we set ourselves drills and tasks as a teacher might. Our learning does not just happen, as it often does when we learn on our own, so there is some further resemblance to the standard case. But there are important differences too. We cannot very well explain something to ourselves, yet explanation is a common form that teaching takes. So teaching oneself is a kind of halfway house, a notion important enough if it serves to remind us of the need for learners to start to assume greater responsibility for their own learning and to leave their teachers behind (Jackson, 1986, p. 104; Fenstermacher, 1986, p. 40).

Analogies are also at work in many of the cases which suggest that teaching can be unintentional. There is, for example, a view, found in Wordsworth and others, that portrays nature as teaching moral virtue more effectively than the philosophers. This is a dramatic way of marking the occasion of one's learning and of identifying the experiences which elicited it. It is as if we had learned from a teacher, but this is a metaphorical extension of literal meaning. We understand the point, and it is effective, because we draw on the case of one person teaching another. In other cases, however, we are, at most, just a step away from our central case of teaching. We sometimes hold that someone is teaching others, perhaps her children, just by the way in which she behaves, with no reference to any intentions (Siegler, 1963). In such a case, we find example, repetition, authority and other common features of teaching situations which make a sharp division or boundary seem somewhat arbitrary here. Teaching is, to some extent, a vague notion, and one can only make it more precise than it really is through stipulaiton. What is more important than deciding where to draw the line, however, is recognizing that in teaching one thing many other kinds of learning may be going on. John Dewey (1963, p. 48) made the point very effectively when he exposed what he called the greatest of all pedagogical fallacies, namely, the belief that the person is learning only the particular thing being studies at the time. We set out, let us say, to teach history or physics and we may or may not have much success. But perhaps students are learning that these subjects are boring, or that we ourselves are unenthusiastic because we are out of our depth. There are many possible results in the form of attitudes, interests, traits and inferences which may not have been intended, but which can be attributed in some way to our work as teachers. The hidden curriculum is often concealed from teachers also, and Dewey's warning may serve to prompt us to examine our teaching more critically. The concept of unintentional teaching may prepare us to find in the results of our efforts more than we had bargained for.[4]

These possible results also serve to remind us how extensive the notion of learning is. We may think immediately of knowledge, as it seems Socrates did, when we ask what can be learned, but clearly learning can go beyond knowledge even if this is understood to include both skills and information. Students can learn to appreciate something, to take an interest, to become more open-minded or critical, to look for problems, to tolerate criticism, and so on; but none of these is the same as acquiring knowledge. To be open-minded, for example, is not to possess a certain type of knowledge, but to acquire an attitude with respect to knowledge. To have learned to look for problems is to have developed a certain habit and also perhaps to have realized that something is worth doing. A limited notion of what can be learned breeds a limited notion of teaching, one which helps to explain Passmore's (1967, p. 202) law that all subjects tend towards an instructional state. We forget what can be learned from them, and thereby undermine our own efforts to teach them well. There is a tendency, however, to insist that such things as attitudes can only be caught or picked up. They cannot be taught (Peters, 1967, pp. 11–12). What lies behind this idea, I believe, is an unreasonably narrow view of the forms which teaching can take. The objection fails to recognize that teaching activities are polymorphous. When it is said that only suggestions can be offered, it is clear that the contrast is with a rule, formula or theory which can be given in instruction so that what is to be learned is explicit and complete. Surely, however, a good suggestion, at the right time, may be the very thing which will help us to learn. The teacher will need judgment to know when the time is right, and judgment may well grow out of practice. But we can be set to practice in relevant ways by others with experience who know how and when to offer useful comments. If successful learning here is less predictable than in direct instruction, this only confirms Spinoza's view that all excellent things are as difficult as they are rare.[5]

Sometimes it is objected that we cannot properly speak of learning or teaching in these cases because the outcomes basically happen to people. They are not achievements on the part of the learner (Peters, 1967, p. 12). Of course, it is admitted that they do not just happen, at least normally; they are only likely to occur in certain circumstances. Nevertheless, they are a kind of contagion. Against this view, we need to remember that we cannot sensibly deny that a person has learned something even though he or she was not trying to learn that thing, and perhaps could not have tried to learn it. When we notice or realize something, a mistake perhaps, or an implication, there is no doubt that we have learned something although we did not set out to learn it. We can be struck by an idea, but it would be very odd to claim that we were trying to be struck by it (White, 1967, pp. 66–73). When we learn a lesson the hard way, perhaps by having our unlocked car stolen, we could hardly set out to learn this without somehow having learned the lesson already. So learning can happen, but it is learning nonetheless and may be immensely important.

If the learner cannot claim an achievement because he or she is overtaken in this way, perhaps some other person can! What was to be learned, the attitude, interest, habit or ability was learned because someone else behaved in a certain way. An example was set, an attitude displayed, enthusiasm was evident, with the result that learning was fostered. These cases are not open to the sort of objection brought against B.O. Smith's analysis of teaching as a system of actions intended to induce learning (1968, p. 13). Philip Jackson, (1968, p. 90; also Scheffler, 1960, pp. 57–8) points out that this is broad enough to cover giving medicine to a hyperactive child so that be or she might benefit from instruction. But here, of course the learning which follows is only made possible by what is done. The child does not learn from what is done. We can look further than Jackson does for a generic account of teaching as I have indicated. Jackson wonders why we should bother. The answer is that such an account can serve to undermine a restricted view of teaching.

Teaching aims at learning but does not always succeed. The fact that it is not always causally efficacious, however, is not a reason to conclude that there is not a causal relationship here. Gary Fenstermacher (1986, p. 39)[6] warns us against being easily lulled into thinking that one causes the other just because there is a conceptual relationship between teaching and learning. He concludes that learning is not an effect that follows from teaching as a cause. Certainly we need to recognize that teaching can fail to produce the desired learning; but often it is successful, and the student's learning results because teaching is effective. No doubt other factors are also necessary, but the teaching is a causal factor, either as a further necessary condition or a sufficient condition given the other factors present.

Fenstermacher is anxious to revise our general account of teaching from one which assumes a causal connection between teaching and learning to one which views teaching as that which enables others to study successfully. One central task of teaching, he insists, is to enable the student to perform the tasks of learning. He links this with teaching the student to learn how to learn. Now, this suggestion fits in well with the view that learning is a more extensive notion than we sometimes think. We can overlook the possibility of learning that which will enable one to go on learning on one's own. Learning is a task as well as an achievement, and teaching can enable us to pursue the task. This is conceptually accurate and worth pointing out.

It does not follow from this, however, that the causal view is mistaken or that the generic account needs to be revised. We might believe that the most important kind of teaching is that which leads to learning how to learn, but that would take us out of the conceptual into the normative realm, and Fenstermacher makes it clear that his claim is conceptual. The problem is that he does not restrict himself to the claim that one central task of teaching is to enable what he terms 'studenting' to occur.[7] He also claims that this is the task of teaching. As we have seen, however, teaching can also aim at producing the sort of learning which happens when a student is struck by an idea. Here the notion of a prior task eventuating in an achievement for the student does not properly apply. In this case, learning happens and it is attributed to teaching.

Even in those cases where learning results as a genuine achievement, it may be proper to speak of learning being imparted. When an explanation is offered by a teacher, the student may be willing to pay attention and to follow the account. The teaching, however, need not set out to enable these tasks to occur; it may presuppose them in certain cases. An explanation is given, but it is not implied that the learner does nothing. When a student understands an explanation, learning as an achievement results and it is produced by teaching. Explaining after all is one of the forms which teaching takes.

Furthermore, in those cases where the aim of teaching is to enable the student to pursue certain tasks, becoming able to pursue them is also something which has to be learned. We are able to undertake certain tasks when we have learned to do so. The achievement is to be in a position, and perhaps to be willing, to undertake the task. Learning as an achievement has not been eliminated, but is to be seen at the same time as a step toward further achievements rather than a final end. So even with a recognition of studenting as a central aim of teaching, we still retain that generic sense of teaching as acting in such a way that what is to be learned can be learned from what is done. The only difference concerns what is to be learned. If these results can be attributed to teaching, then a causal account still applies.

A Normative Perspective on Teaching

The intense preoccupation with conceptual analysis which characterized philosophy of education in the recent past meant that attempts to set out, in normative terms, ideals which teaching ought to satisfy were dismissed as 'high-level directives'. Traditional 'philosophical' reflection on teaching was thought to have missed the mark. Instead of inquiring into the meaning of teaching, where argument could be brought to bear, it became embroiled in endless and unprofitable controversy about values on which philosophers had no special competence to pronounce.[8] This extreme view is now in retreat and perhaps even old-fashioned. But it remains important to see how philosophy is relevant to the normative debate.

The first contribution arises in response to the fashionable view that idealized conceptions of teaching, while splendid no doubt, are certainly mythical. The concept of the hidden curriculum reaches beyond the claim that in teaching one lesson you may also be teaching another, to the claim that the very activity of teaching itself inescapably contains certain lessons whatever is being taught. Sometimes this appears as the claim that the pupil learns that only what is taught is valuable (Illich, 1973); elsewhere as the claim, a paradox of sorts, that before teaching takes place at all, we are taught what teaching means (Sharp, 1980). The inevitable lesson is that some are authorized to speak and others forced to listen. If these claims were true, ideals such as freedom, open-mindedness and independence, would be spurious, and any normative recommendation would flounder. Ought, after all, implies can.

The initial role of philosophy here is to show that the alleged inevitability is itself spurious. It is one thing to claim that it is always possible that a student will learn that the only worthwhile learning is that which one's teachers provide, and quite another to assert that this is inevitable. First, it is not the only conceivable inference, hence it is not logically inevitable. Second, taken as a causal claim, it is open to challenge on empirical grounds and capable of being offset by other factors. For example, the danger can be openly discussed to ensure that it does not occur by default. As teachers, we can actually employ the hidden curriculum to advantage by showing, in our behavior. that we do value the knowledge the student has which we have not taught.

The inequality involved in the teacher/student relationship, which the earlier discussion of self-teaching and its limits shows to be necessary, is supposed to generate the paradoxical conclusion that, before we can begin to promote open-mindedness and critical thinking in our teaching, our normative aspirations are scuttled at the outset by the authoritarian relationship implicit in any teaching. If this were only intended to promote consciousness-raising by alerting us to the possibility of our best efforts being undermined, it would be unexceptionable. But as a would-be logical barrier, it crumbles on critical examination. First, even if it were true that teaching presupposed an authoritarian framework, there is no reason in principle why teaching could not prepare the ground for an assault on that framework. Experience might, and in fact does, I believe, show that certain approaches to teaching are more conducive than others to the emergence of autonomous thought. Second, moreover, while the teaching relationship does imply that the teacher is in some sense an authority with respect to the relevant subject matter, this is not at all the same as reading authoritarianism and deference into every situation. This is conceptual sleight of hand. Of course, if the student is studying at all with a teacher, he or she is necessarily attending in some way to what the teacher says or does. This need not however, be slavish and uncritical, and if it were the teacher could discourage it.

Teaching does attempt to construct a certain framework of beliefs, assumptions, attitudes and expectations, but it is not the existence of a framework per se which threatens normative ideals such as creativity, autonomy or critical reflection. A framework-free education, in any case, makes no sense. The crucial question, however, is whether or not teaching sets out to encourage students to demand evidence for claims and to accept the possibility that longstanding beliefs may have to be abandoned. In this way, long-term objectives need to be taken into account in the assessment of teaching before the charge of indoctrination can be levelled.[9]

If a non-authoritarian conception of teaching makes sense, as it surely does, what is to be said in favor of such a view? Here we come to the second task of philosophy in the normative area, that of setting out and defending certain ideals which teaching must pursue. The fact that these are ideals is no reason to conclude that they have no bearing on the practical business of teaching. If they cannot be completely realized, teachers can look for ways in which they are more closely approximated.

When Bertrand Russell (1916), for example, suggested that teaching requires humility, he was attempting to characterize an attitude which philosophers of education since Socrates have judged to be central. Russell recognized the need for philosophical comment here because the suggestion is somewhat paradoxical, as can be seen from the preceding discussion of authoritarianism. He captured the puzzle by speaking of 'an unaccountable humility — a humility not easily defensible on any rational ground, and yet somehow nearer to wisdom than the easy self-confidence of many parents and teachers' (p. 147). The teacher knows so much more than the child. Why then the need for humility? Part of the answer, as Russell saw, lies in the Socratic reminder that the teacher is capable of inflicting great damage on his or her students. Socrates pointed out that knowledge cannot be carried away in a parcel: 'When you have paid for it you must receive it into the soul: You go away having learned it and are benefited or harmed accordingly' (Plato, *Protagoras*, in Hamilton and Cairns, 1961). The skills of the teacher, like other skills, can be put to good or bad use. And, as we have seen, the actions of any teacher can have unintended consequences. The teacher needs to be conscious of the position of trust he or she occupies, and seek to teach in such a way that students become able to make their own informed and impartial choices.

The concept of trust brings to mind the sorry Keegstra episode (Bercuson and Wertheimer, 1985), where humility was noticeably absent and swaggering self-confidence the defiant note. This fatal sense of one's own infallible judgment underscores the importance of humility. Socrates was the first to challenge the smugness of teachers concerning their own mastery of the subject they professed to teach. His target, of course, was the sophists who needed to take the first step in the direction of wisdom by recognizing their own limited knowledge. It is the conceit of wisdom which leads Protagoras, for example, to believe that he is better than anyone else at helping others to acquire a good and noble character (Plato, *Protagoras*). The fundamental problem with this attitude, as Socrates makes clear elsewhere (Plato, *Laches*, in Hamilton and Cairns, 1961), is that we cannot advise someone how to attain virtue if we ourselves do not understand what it is.

The general point being made here applies in any subject area. All views are capable of being revised, and even if our teachers have a sound academic preparation (as Keegstra did not), there would still be a need to recognize that one's beliefs are vulnerable. In this way, humility is part of the attitude of open-mindedness (Hare, 1985, p. 8). Certainly, as Dewey (1985) was quick to point out, the teacher is the member of the group with larger experience and riper wisdom, but the 'learned man should also still be a learner' (Dewey, 1916, p. 184). This will involve not only adding to one's store of knowledge, but also coming to realize that certain of one's beliefs have to be abandoned. The kind of humility which amounts to open-mindedness involves healthy self-criticism and is not at all the same as neurotic doubt.

The teacher who recognizes the rights of the student and the fallibility of claims to knowledge is presumably someone prepared to teach in a critical manner (Siegel, 1986, p. 40). The student is encouraged to ask for reasons and the teacher is prepared to respond to them. All this implies that the teacher's ideas are not beyond criticism. Dewey deplored the situation in which 'children are hushed up when they ask questions; their exploring and investigating activities are inconvenient and hence they are treated like nuisances' (1933, p. 56). It is a nuisance if we adopt the view that teaching is nothing more than the efficient transmission of information from teacher to student. A critical approach, however, demands that we 'respect the student's intellectual integrity and capacity for independent judgement' (Scheffler, 1973, p. 67).[10]

The character of this attitude can be seen if we take note of the ambiguity in Quintilian's remark in the *Institutio Oratorio* (1921, Book 2), that the teacher must be ready to answer questions. A teacher might be prepared to answer questions seeking information, but unwilling to entertain questions which raise objections with respect to the ideas being advanced in the lesson. The critical manner requires a willingness to accept the second kind of question also, and such an attitude amounts to respecting the student as an independent source of ideas. Russell (1916, p. 152)[11] spoke of reverence in this connection and viewed education as enabling students to choose intelligently. All too often, in practice, students are viewed as the potter views the clay, and their questions meet with dogma or stony silence.

The concept of respect is completely misunderstood when it is thought to imply a teaching situation in which any and every student response calls for acceptance by the teacher (Sadker and Sadker, 1985). There is some evidence apparently that this is the most frequent teacher response, one that implies that the student's comment is correct or appropriate, but which stops short of praise. Many teachers, it seems, never indicate that an answer is incorrect or inappropriate. Textbooks for teachers sometimes explicitly recommend the acceptance response, especially with respect to divergent questions (Orlich *et al.*, 1985, p. 171). In fact, in the literature on questioning as a teaching strategy, one of the most neglected areas is what we might call the challenge question where the student is required to support what he or she has just said.[12] The uncritical acceptance of student responses fails to show respect precisely because it does not take the responses seriously. If the responses are treated as equally useful and interesting, they are not being evaluated and considered. Any response will receive the same treatment.

This example actually illustrates a more general mistake which one encounters, namely, that normative ideals are interpreted as directly implying procedural rules which can be read off in a straightforward way. When it is said, to take another example, that a classroom should manifest a spirit of discussion, this is to state a normative ideal about the importance of teachers and students being willing to listen seriously to the ideas of others and being prepared to reconsider their own views. We move too quickly, however, if this normative ideal is translated into a procedural recommendation in favor of discussion methods where the latter are interpreted as eschewing formal instruction. The fact is that a great many teaching strategies can display a spirit of discussion.

The result is that we fail to do justice to the ideal in practice because we impose arbitrary constraints on their expression. We recognize, for example, the importance of teaching in an open-minded manner, but we make the mistake of concluding that certain actions necessarily violate this norm. It has been maintained recently that the use of the word *prove* in the science classroom demonstrates a lack of open-mindedness (Moore, 1982, p. 479). What has happened here is a failure to understand the nature of the normative ideal in question. Our ideals are bound to suffer if we do not pause to think critically about the concepts which give them expression. In this case, it is a failure to recognize that it is not the words we use but the way in which we use them which is decisive. It is the attitude which lies behind the word which determines whether or not this ideal is met.

The Numbers Game

To talk sense, said Whitehead (1949, p. 19), is to talk in quantities. And generations of educational researchers have shown that they have taken this remark to heart. A massive amount of quantitative research has been undertaken in an attempt to determine what makes an effective teacher. Depressingly, however, many believe that we are no nearer to being able to offer firm evidence in support of preferred approaches (Barrow 1984a, p. 145).[13] Disenchantment has set in concerning quasi-experimental research modelled on the natural sciences, and interest has centered of late on qualitative research with its emphasis on description, interpretation, case studies, fieldwork and particular circumstances. John Dewey, however, ought to have made all of us nervous about either/or choices. Quantitative research findings continue to appear and require an intelligent response from the teacher.

For example, it has been held since at least the time of Socrates that asking questions can be an effective teaching strategy. Yet it is also apparent to many teachers that their efforts in this direction are frustrated. Often few answers are forthcoming and the Socratic model degenerates into one in which the teacher answers his or her own questions. Some years ago, Mary Budd Rowe (1978) examined this problem and discovered that, after asking a question, the teacher would wait one second or less for a student to answer. Moreover, once the student had responded, the teacher would wait less than one second before commenting on the response. Rowe conducted an experiment to see what would happen if the teacher extended the wait time after asking a question and after the student had responded.

The results were impressive. The length of student responses increased as did the number of unsolicited student responses. There was evidence of more speculative and confident responses, and slow learners made a greater contribution as teachers discovered that they had been giving these students less time to respond. All of this is carefully measured and dramatically represented in graphs showing the speech pattern in the classroom before and after wait time is extended. These results, however, do not translate into a rule-like formula which can be mechanically applied in the classroom. We can agree with Rowe that one second is hardly enough, but teachers will need to exercise their own judgment in deciding how long to wait. What the research does is create awareness of a phenomenon and demonstrate how it can be altered. It puts the teacher in a better position to make an intelligent judgment.

A philosophical perspective can complement the teacher's efforts in this regard. Increasing confidence on the part of the students was measured in Rowe's experiment by fewer voice inflections. But when does confidence shift into complacency, and speculation into idle digression? Here we need more than a simplistic behavioral criterion to guide us. An overall sense of one's educational objectives is necessary if good judgments are to be made. Rowe noticed that verbal rewards from the teacher tended to offset the benefits of wait time and promote the inflected voice response. She recommended 'near neutral verbal rewards' (p. 212). The problem here, of course, is that we are not just teaching the subject matter involved in the question but also attitudes. There will surely be times when the teacher will want to burst in enthusiastically, given a certain response without observing the requisite pause or the nearly neutral tone. The teacher needs to remember also that techniques can backfire if their use is all too obviously calculating, and can pall as they become commonplace. Dewey (1895) warned against the blind observance of rule and routine, and noted that 'the machine teacher ... makes his school a mere machine shop' (p. 201).

Recent empirical research has severely challenged the tradition we have inherited from Socrates with respect to questions as a teaching strategy and has claimed that a question is more limiting than a statement (Dillon, 1979). This claim to some extent reflects an alleged conceptual difference between a question and a statement, but the main purpose is to make an empirical claim buttressed with solid evidence. Dillon (1985) has made a detailed study of classroom interaction, comparing and contrasting the use of questions posed by the teacher with the use of alternative strategies such as declarative statements. With precise results set out in charts and tables, Dillon concludes that teacher questions prevent discussion. Students respond twice as long to non-question alternatives and, in addition, raise their own questions and speculate beyond the reading. Contrary to Rowe, he claims that the pace of the questions makes no difference.

Dillon suggests that further studies be conducted to see if his results can be falsified. The question, however, is whether or not any empirical research can show that questions are more effective than statements. Dillon's own conclusions have become more definite over the years: from his tentative view in 1979 that non-question alternatives might be useful now and then, to his 1985 view that questions simply foil discussion and non-question alternatives foster it. The former view presents the teacher with a suggestion, whereas the latter makes a law-like generalization. To make the comparison, however, one would have to judge that the tone of the questions and alternatives is similar, that the teachers are equally keen to make their strategies work, and are equally talented at posing appropriate questions or framing alternatives at the right moment. These factors cannot be read off from class transcripts in the same objective way as length of response. Moreover, if it is true that questions have been over-emphasized, then alternatives presently have the advantage of novelty.

We may be tempted to regard the results as decisive because simplistic, conceptual reasons suggest that we really should not be surprised. A question is thought to tell one what kind of answer to give, whereas a statement is supposed to leave the response open. But if questions can limit, statements can lead. Everything depends upon the kind of question or statement, the context in which it occurs, and the way in which it is put. Contrary to Dillon, statements are not intrinsically more surprising than questions. In the hands of a good teacher, a question need not say 'Supply this bit of information and stop.' It may be made clear that the presuppositions of a question are themselves open to challenge in just the same way as the positive assertions in a statement. We also need to resist the notion that attitudes can be determined in a purely formal way by identifying the kind of comment a teacher makes, for example, an indirect question rather than a direct one. An indirect question, such as 'I'd like to hear more about that', might be encouraging and supportive (though it might also be threatening); but 'I'd like to see you prove that' might convey a very different message.

Despite the reservations which empirical researchers themselves often express, the search continues for evidence that some particular strategy is more effective than others. In recent years, one approach to teaching which caught the imagination of teachers in Britain and North America arose in the context of dealing with controversial material. The Humanities Curriculum Project began in England in 1967 and adopted a teaching strategy designed to protect the student from the teacher's own biases. This strategy came to be known as procedural neutrality which meant essentially that the teacher was to be neutral in the classroom with respect to the substantive issue being discussed, but committed to standards of argumentation and respect for evidence. The teacher, in effect, was to serve as a neutral chairperson as the students discussed the controversial topic (Stenhouse, 1970).

It would be a great mistake to believe that the debate over the Humanities Curriculum Project was side-tracked by a verbal dispute. Lawrence Stenhouse suggested at one point that impartiality or objectivity would have been a better choice of word than neutrality. These other concepts, it must be noted, do not necessarily imply that the teacher is constrained from presenting to the class his or her own sincerely held point of view. This constraint, however, was built into the strategy adopted by the Project (Stenhouse, 1970, p. 106). Indeed, it is by contrast with such a possibility that the distinctive strategy of the Project stands out. Those philosophers who defended the possibility of the teacher sharing his or her views with the students also accepted the values of impartiality and objectivity.

Philosophers who raised such points were strongly condemned for ignoring the 'empirical reality in the classroom'. They had, as one caustic comment put it, not allowed their minds to be clouded by looking at the available evidence (Stenhouse, 1975b, p. 130). It was allowed that, from a philosophical point of view, the idea of a teacher giving his or her view and being seen to remain open to criticism was impeccable. But it was claimed that observation shows that it does not seem possible to satisfy this in practice (Stenhouse, 1975a, p. 118). Experience shows, we were told, that it is 'almost insuperably difficult' (Stenhouse, 1970, p. 106). But how could research show this in any generalizable way? The Humanities Curriculum Project conceded that situational verifiability is necessary. In other words, teachers need to examine what is possible in their own situation. If many teachers have been seen unsuccessful in demonstrating commitment combined with impartiality, there is no implication that another teacher must fail.

What would be involved in seeing that such attempts are unsuccessful? This is a complex matter calling for interpretation and judgment. If the students adopt the teacher's point of view, this may be simply the result of his or her position of authority. Equally, however, it may be because the arguments presented by the teacher were judged by the students to be convincing; or because their own reflection on the evidence and arguments led in the same direction. If the force of authority were at work, how lasting is this effect? Is it, perhaps, in time a stimulus to the student's own critical reflection on the issue in question? Clearly, there are difficult judgments involved here, such that confident pronouncements based on appeal to 'research'[14] are quite misleading.

To what extent do we know that the teachers observed are those who, in general, manage to communicate to their students that they take their ideas seriously? Identifying these would be no easy task, of course, but it would surely be a prelude to forming a representative sample. We might hypothesize that such teachers could state their own views and be seen as remaining open to criticism. I am not aware, however, that any serious attempts have been made to gauge the effectiveness of such teachers, nor to assess the performance of teachers who have become sensitive to their position of authority and who attempt to offset this influence.

It is hard to avoid the impression, despite appeals to what research is supposed to show (Klohr, 1971), that philosophical assumptions encouraged the view that empirical confirmation was not required since we were really dealing with necessary truths. For example, non-neutrality was simply equated with promoting or propagating one's own view on the basis of authority. Being neutral was identified as being open-minded (Stenhouse, 1969). Such assumptions are not likely to incline anyone to ask how far a teacher who reveals his or her commitments is being open-minded, or to help anyone to recognize open-minded teaching in practice.

The Humanities Curriculum Project tested its claims concerning procedural neutrality in the context of the controversial topic of racism. Earlier research (Miller, 1969) had indicated that attempts to promote racial tolerance through teaching might actually be counterproductive. A study in 1971, however, based on six schools employing the strategy of procedural neutrality, reported that 'there was no general tendency towards intolerance after a seven to eight week teaching programme' (Verma and Macdonald, 1971, p. 199). Stenhouse (1975b) expressed the view that there was reason to believe that 'modest positive effects might accrue from six weeks to one term's teaching to adolescents in the area of race relations' (p. 309).

There are several points to note, however, before we accept even these very tentative research findings. First, it is admitted that the groups compared in the 1969 and 1971 studies were very different. The former group consisted of older students who were generally judged to be highly prejudiced. The latter group were younger, generally better educated and holding less prejudiced attitudes. We cannot assume that the strategy of procedural neutrality would have been effective with the former group. Second, later studies which compared procedural neutrality with a non-neutral approach failed to find significant differences between them (Verma and Bagley, 1979). Both produced favorable attitudinal changes. Of course, there are many doubts about the reliability of such tests, but at least we have no basis in research for concluding that procedural neutrality is more effective than other strategies. The Humanities Curriculum Project is an example of research into teaching where the numbers were never really there at all, but the impression was created that one had only to open one's eyes to discover the empirical confirmation. The confident, one might say arrogant, dismissal of objections was out of all proportion to the available evidence. This is not to say that the impressions gained in what was essentially qualitative research are of no value. No doubt the authority status of teachers is more dominant than we had imagined. Perhaps it is very much more difficult than anyone had realized for a teacher to reveal his or her views and succeed in fostering independent-mindedness among the students. These impressions ought to make the teacher pause. But it is a pause during which the teacher's intelligent judgment needs to be exercised, not surrendered to the fallible judgment of others.

Conclusion

What emerges from the preceding discussion is the indispensable element of critical judgment in teaching. First, teachers need to think seriously about the nature of their enterprise if they are to avoid impoverished accounts which only limit their view of what is possible. The ability to seize such possibilities, however, is not something which can be reduced to a formula. Second, it is necessary to escape the trap of ideological argument which attempts to portray ideals as spurious if the importance of principles such as respect, humility and integrity is to be appreciated. The interpretation and translation of such ideals, however, demands intelligent reflection. Third, it is crucial that teachers become aware of certain phenomena and practices which can interfere with their ideals. Here research drawing on classroom observation is central. But such findings do not lend themselves to rule-like remedies. Conceptual, normative and empirical awareness is necessary, but it needs to be transformed by critical judgment into something meaningful and relevant. In this connection, philosophical reflection is invaluable.

Notes

1 For a similar point, see Black (1983, p. 76).
2 A similar point occurs in Hume (1751).
3 Many such claims are discussed in Cochrane (1982).
4 The possibility of such consequences also shows the important connection between sincerity of purpose and assessment in teaching. See Hare (1970, p. 42).
5 This is the famous, final remark in his *Ethics* (Spinoza, 1889, Originally written in 1677).
6 His claim here does not depend on, or relate to, the dispute in philosophy as to whether reasons can be causes.
7 Fenstermacher falls into error when he claims that without teachers we would not have the concept of student. This confuses an institutional sense with a general sense. His claim is true with respect to the notion of pupil, but not with respect to that of student. We can study on our own. See Hare (1978).
8 Educational philosophers tended to accept the sort of view set out in Nowell-Smith (1954, chapter 1).
9 On this point, see Siegel (1986, p. 48). Also Hare (1985, chapter 5).
10 Scheffler states in *The Language of Education* (1960, p. 60) that his concern is essentially to provide a descriptive definition of teaching, an account of the accepted meaning. I have myself argued that some examples seem to bear out his claim (1979, p. 83), yet others fail to satisfy the criteria which Scheffler states. It seems clear that a normative element has been introduced.
11 I have discussed Russell's views at length in Hare (1987).
12 Meredith Gall (1970) comes closer than most with respect to this.
13 Barrow (1984a) has developed the most significant philosophical critique of research on teacher effectiveness.
14 Sometimes touted by others as 'hard-nosed field experiments'. See Klohr (1971).

Bibliography

BLACK, M. (1983) *The Prevalence of Humbug*, Ithaca, NY: Cornell University Press.
BARROW, R. (1979) 'Back to basics', in BERNBAUM, G. (Ed.) *Schooling in Decline*, London: Macmillan Press.
BARROW, R. (1983) 'Does the question "What is education" make sence?' *Educational Theory*, 33, pp. 3–4.
BARROW, R. (1984a) *Giving Teaching Back to Teachers*, Brighton, Sussex: Wheatsheaf.
BARROW, R. (1984b) 'Teacher judgement and teacher effectiveness', *Journal of Educational Thought*, 18, pp. 76–83.
BARZUN, J. (1946) *Teacher in America*, Boston: Little Brown and Company.
BERCUSON, D. and WERTHEIMER, D. (1985) *A Trust Betrayed: The Keegstra Affair*, Toronto: Doubleday.
COCHRANE, D. (1982) 'Why it is in your interest to have a clear concept of teaching', in

William Hare

Cochrane, D. and Schiralli, M. (Eds) *Philosophy of Education: Canadian Perspectives*, Don Mills, Ontario: Collier Macmillan.

Dewey, J. (1964. Originally published 1897) 'My pedagogic creed', in Archambault, R. (Ed.) *John Dewey on Education*, New York: Random House.

Dewey, J. (1964. Originally published in 1895) 'What psychology can do for the teacher', in Archambault, R. (Ed.) *John Dewey on Education*, New York: Random House.

Dewey, J. (1933) *How We Think*, Boston: D.C. Heath.

Dewey, J. (1966. Originally published 1916) *Democracy and Education*, New York: The Free Press.

Dewey, J. (1963. Originally published 1938) *Experience and Education*, New York: Collier Books.

Dillon, J.T. (1979) 'Alternatives to questioning', *High School Journal*, 62, pp. 217–22.

Dillon, J.T. (1985) 'Using questions to foil discussion', *Teaching and Teacher Education*, 1, pp. 109–21.

Fenstermacher, G.D. (1986) 'Philosophy of research on teaching', in Wittrock, M.C. (Ed.) *Handbook of Research on Teaching* (3rd Edn.), New York: Macmillan.

Gall, M. (1970) 'The use of questions in teaching', *Review of Educational Research*, 40, pp. 707–21.

Gilson, E. (1957. Originally published 1927) 'The ethics of higher studies', in Pegis, A.C. (Ed.) *A Gilson Reader*, New York: Image Books.

Hare, W. (1970) 'The roles of teacher and critic', *Journal of General Education*, 22, pp. 41–9.

Hare, W. (1978) 'The concept of study', *Saskatchewan Journal of Educational Research and Development*, 8, pp. 40–6.

Hare, W. (1985) *In Defence of Open-mindedness*, Montreal: McGill-Queen's University Press.

Hare, W. (1987) 'Russell's contribution to philosophy of education', *Russell: The Journal of the Bertrand Russell Archives*, 7, pp. 25–41.

Hendley, B. (1986) *Dewey, Russell, Whitehead: Philosophers as Educators*, Carbondale, IL: Southern Illinois University Press.

Hume, D. (1957. Originally published 1751) 'An inquiry concerning the principles of morals', in MacIntyre, A. (Ed.) *Hume's Ethical Writings*, (Section IV), London: Collier-Macmillan.

Illich, I. (1973) *Deschooling Society*, Harmondsworth: Penguin Books.

Jackson, P.W. (1968) *The Practice of Teaching*, New York: Teachers College Press.

Kant, I. (1964. Originally published 1781) *Critique of Pure Reason*, Book 2, (trans. N. Kemp Smith) London: Macmillan.

Klohr, P.R. (1971) 'A regeneration of the humanities', *Theory into Practice*, 10, pp. 147–8.

Miller, H.J. (1969) 'The effectiveness of teaching techniques for reducing colour prejudice', *Liberal Education*, 16, pp. 25–31.

Moore, R.W. (1982) 'Open-mindedness and proof', *School Science and Mathematics*, 82, pp. 478–80.

Nowell-Smith, P.H. (1954) *Ethics*, Harmondsworth: Penguin Books.

Orlich, D.C. et al. (1985) *Teaching Strategies: A Guide to Better Instruction* (2nd Edn), Lexington, MA: D.C. Heath.

Passmore, J. (1967) 'On teaching to be critical', in Peters, R.S. (Ed.) *The Concept of Education*, London: Routledge and Kegan Paul.

Peters, R.S. (1967) 'What is an educational process?' in Peters, R.S. (Ed.) *The Concept of Education*, London: Routledge and Kegan Paul.

Plato (1961) 'Laches', in Hamilton, A. and Cairns, H. (Eds) *The Collected Dialogues of Plato*, Princeton: Princeton University Press.

PLATO (1961) 'Meno', in HAMILTON, E. and CAIRNS, H. (Eds) *The Collected Dialogues of Plato*, Princeton: Princeton University Press.

PLATO (1961) 'Protagoras', in HAMILTON, E. and CAIRNS, H. (Eds) *The Collected Dialogues of Plato*, Princeton: Princeton University Press.

QUINTILIAN (1921. Originally written ca. 90. A.D.) *Institutio Oratoria*, (trans. H.E. Butler), London: Heinemann.

ROWE, M.B. (1978) 'Wait, wait, wait . . .' *School Science and Mathematics*, 78, pp. 207–16.

RUSSELL, B. (1916) *Principles of Social Reconstruction*, London: Allen and Unwin.

SADKER, D. and SADKER, M. (1985, January) 'Is the O.K. classroom O.K.?' *Phi Delta Kappan*, pp. 358–61.

SCHEFFLER, I. (1960) *The Language of Education*, Springfield: Charles C. Thomas.

SCHEFFLER, I. (1973) *Reason and Teaching*, Indianapolis: Bobbs-Merrill.

SHARP, R. (1980) *Knowledge, Ideology and the Politics of Schooling: Toward a Marxist Analysis of Education*, London: Routledge and Kegan Paul.

SIEGEL, H. (1986) 'Critical thinking as an educational right', in MOSHMAN, D. (Ed.) *Children's Intellectual Rights*, San Francisco: Jossey-Bass.

SIEGLER, F.A. (1963) 'Comments', in WALTON, J. and KUETHE, J. (Eds) *The Discipline of Education*, Madison: University of Wisconsin Press.

SMITH, B.O. (1968) 'A concept of teaching', in MACMILLAN, C.J.B. and NELSON, T. (Eds) *Concepts of Teaching: Philosophical Essays*, Chicago: Rand McNally.

SPINOZA, B. (1889. Originally published 1677) in *The Chief Works of Benedict De Spinoza*, (trans. R.H.M. Elwes), London: George Bell and Sons.

STENHOUSE, L. (1969, July 24) 'Open-minded teaching', *New Society*.

STENHOUSE, L. (1970) 'Controversial value issues in the classroom', in CARR, W.G. (Ed.) *Values and the Curriculum*, Washington, DC: NEA Publications.

STENHOUSE, L. (1975a) *An Introduction to Curriculum Research and Development*, London: Heineman.

STENHOUSE, L. (1975b) 'Neutrality as a criterion in teaching: The work of the Humanities Curriculum Project', in TAYLOR, M. (Ed.) *Progress and Problems in Moral Education*, Windsor: NFER.

TINDER, G. (1986) *Political Thinking: The Perennial Questions*, (4th Edn), Boston: Little, Brown and Company.

VERMA, G.K. and MACDONALD, B. (1971) 'Teaching race in schools: Some effects on the attitudinal and sociometric patterns of adolescent', *Race*, 13, pp. 187–202.

VERMA, G.K. and BAGLEY, C. (1979) 'Measured changes in racial attitudes following the use of three different teaching methods', in VERMA, G.K. and BAGLEY, C. (Eds) *Race, Education and Identity*, New York: St. Martin's Press.

WARNOCK, M. (1975) 'The neutral teacher', in BROWN, S.C. (Ed.) *Philosophers Discuss Education*, London: Macmillan.

WHITE, A. (1967) *The Philosophy of Mind*, New York: Random House.

WHITE, J. (1982) *The Aims of Education Restated*, London: Routledge and Kegan Paul.

WHITEHEAD, A.N. (1949. Originally published 1916) *The Aims of Education*, New York: Mentor Books.

11   The Concept of Learning

Paul O'Leary

Introduction

In examining the concept of learning, the first two sections of this chapter will be putting forth two claims about the conditions under which S *learned* X is true. The first is that S *learned* X cannot be true unless X is the result of self-determination. This hardly uncontroversial contention means that having learned something is a result of the learner's own voluntary efforts. Because of this feature we have good reason to distinguish between learning and conditioning. The second claim says that S *learned* X cannot be true unless the learner has successfully complied with certain standards of correctness. What correctness consists of varies according to whether what is learned is an ability, a disposition or knowledge.

All this however, is a prelude to the main question of the chapter: To what extent is learning teacher-dependent? In suggesting that *all* learning is teacher-dependent, I shall have to defend this claim against certain obvious objections. Moreover, I shall need to show how *believing another*, which is the core of being teacher-dependent, is also compatible with regarding all learning as the result of self-determination.

I hope this chapter shows that a correct conceptualization of human learning is pretty nearly an indispensable condition for understanding the significance of teaching to learning. Such a conceptualization requires us to draw upon the resources of philosophy as they are utilized in our understanding of human action and human knowledge. I am far from thinking that the matters raised here will finally be settled in the course of this chapter. However, I certainly do hope that my remarks will provide at least some insight into the complex network of issues surrounding human learning.

Learning and Conditioning

Consider three cases in which S has learned something:

(a) S learned that Henry VIII had the gout;
(b) S learned to speak French;
(c) S learned to be tactful.

In (a) we have a case of *learning that* where the object of learning is some knowledge. In (b) and (c) we have examples of *learning to*. They differ in that in (b) the object of learning is an ability whereas in (c) the object is a particular disposition. If each of these claims (i.e., that learning has taken place) is true, then it is also true of each case that S has undergone a change. In (a) S has changed from not knowing something to knowing it; in (b) the change is from not having an ability to having it; in (c) S changes from not having a particular disposition to having it. In short, whenever anyone *learns that* or *learns to*, he or she acquires some knowledge, ability or disposition. No one can learn what one already knows or learn to do what one is already able to do, or learn to be what one already is.

In saying all this, we are not thereby committed to the view that the human mind is some sort of *tabula rasa* passively waiting to be written on by the environment. Indeed, some have taken the view that, unless human beings had been equipped with certain unlearned capacities, then the knowledge, abilities and dispositions they do in fact acquire would have been very unlikely achievements. But suppose we allow that humans do indeed have some unlearned capacities which set predetermined limits to what it is possible for humans to acquire in the way of knowledge, abilities and dispositions. Does this mean that, in consequence, we are required to view the human mind as some sort of *tabula inscriptiva* whose content gradually unfolds right down to the very last detail? Not necessarily. Preprogramming does not everywhere exclude some degree of variation in result. If we assume, for example, that we could not learn any language unless we had an unlearned capacity for language acquisition, this would not determine whether one learned French, English, German, and so on. Which particular language a person learned would presumably be a function of which linguistic community he or she grew up in. Although learning requires beings who are capable of acquiring knowledge, abilities and dispositions, important questions obviously remain about the manner in which these things are acquired. Is any manner of acquiring knowledge, abilities and dispositions to be regarded as learning? Or does learning require special conditions to apply before it takes place?

Suppose we call a person's knowledge, abilities and dispositions, his or her competencies. Can we define *S learned X* as *S acquired a certain competence*? Certainly we can. But to do so overlooks important issues connected with different explanatory presumptions behind our understanding of how human beings acquire certain of their competencies. If, for example, we identify learning with conditioning, we appeal to a different set of presumptions than if we distinguish, as I wish to do, between conditioning and learning. To bring out these different explanatory presumptions, let us examine, first of all, just what is involved in conditioning.

To begin with, consider a case in which someone has acquired the ability to contract the pupil of one eye by issuing a self-command. An explanation of how this ability has been acquired might go as follows. In the first stage of training, a bell is rung just before a light is flashed in one of the subject's eyes. After several trials, the sound of the bell alone suffices to get the pupils to contract. At the next stage, the subject is instructed to close and open the circuit connected to the bell and the light by closing and opening his or her hand at the verbal command of the experimenter. This allows the verbal command to be connected, by way of hand movement and the sound of the bell, to the pupillary contraction. The next step eliminates both hand movements and the bell, leaving only the experimenter's vocal instructions as the conditioned stimulus through which the subject's pupil contracts. In the final stage, the experimenter has the subject repeat the verbal instructions, aloud at first, then in a whisper and finally subvocally. Each of these stimuli could suffice to induce the pupil to contract. At the end of the experiment the subject is able to command his or her own pupillary reflex.[1]

This case is an example of what has become known as *classical conditioning*. In such cases the explanation of an acquired ability is put in terms of the gradual replacement of an unconditioned stimulus (e.g., the light flashing in the eye) by a conditioned stimulus (e.g., a subvocal command), where the latter elicits the same response (e.g., the pupillary contraction) as did the unconditioned stimulus. But what happens in cases when a new kind of response is acquired? Classical conditioning only covers cases in which the same response (or nearly the same) is elicited, thanks to stimulus substitution, by new stimuli. But we often acquire new patterns of response whose shaping and maintenance cannot be explained in terms of stimulus substitution. It is at this point that the notion of *operant conditioning* can be introduced. In this kind of conditioning the basic explanatory notion is reinforcement. That is, certain consequences of a particular response increase the probability of that kind of response occurring again in similar sorts of circumstances. Accordingly, a child's acquisition of the disposition to behave politely is the result of certain consequences of his or her polite behavior in the past (e.g., being praised, being given candy, etc.) having 'selected' that kind of behavior while also reducing the probability of impolite responses.

What sort of explanatory presumption lies behind both classical and operant conditioning? Often views about conditioning are allied with psychological behaviorism — that is, allied with the view that our understanding of human beings can be achieved without utilizing concepts which refer to *states of mind*, such as belief, desire, understanding, etc. Indeed, it is sometimes taken to be a requirement of scientific explanation that such *mentalistic* concepts be eliminated. It seems to me, however, that anti-mentalism is a less fundamental explanatory presumption of conditioning than the presumption that the explanatory paradigm for human behavior, as well as everything else, consists in its having a deterministic structure. That is, conditioning presupposes that any explanation of how humans acquire particular competencies requires relating a certain set of conditions in a law-like fashion to the emergence of that competence, so that if these conditions obtain then the competence will emerge. Accordingly, the general form of those laws which govern classical conditioning will be as follows:[2]

> For all uS, uR, cS and cR, if uS uR, and uS is paired with cS, then (after a time) cS cR, where uR and cR are very similar responses, and where probability (cR, given cS) 0, but varies depending on the strength of the initial link, the number of times cS has been presented without uS, and so on.

For operant conditioning, its laws will have the following general form:[3]

> For any response R, and for any reinforcing stimulus rS, if R is emitted, and R is followed by Rs, then probability (R) increases.

To identify learning with conditioning requires us to claim that all explanations of how human beings acquire their competencies follow one or the other of these two patterns. Rejecting this identification could be achieved by showing either that some explanations of how humans acquire their competencies, although deterministic in structure, nevertheless do not fall into either of the conditioning patterns, or by showing that some explanations can be non-deterministic in structure. Suppose we examine the latter alternative.

Consider the following. A young girl notices her older sister skipping rope and admires the latter's skill. She also tries her hand at it and fails. Consequently she asks her sister for some help. The older girl faces her sister, holds her hands and, together, they do the jump and rebound movements. As a result the younger girl picks up the jump and rebound movements. Next however, come the arm and wrist movements which need to be coordinated with the jumping and rebound movements. Finally, the older girl gives the skipping rope to her younger sister and, *voila*, the younger girl has acquired the knack and succeeds.[4]

One of the things that holds such a series of incidents together is the younger girl's obvious desire to learn how to skip rope. If the explanation of how she acquired her ability had a deterministic structure we would have to say that this desire (along with much else such as noticing, admiring, trying, etc.) came about because of certain antecedent conditions which, in law-like fashion, necessitate, or make highly probable, the occurrence of such a desire. But although certain of our desires do indeed arise in this fashion (e.g., the desire for food because of hunger) this is not true of all human desires. The young girl's desire to skip rope, for example, arises because she finds skipping an admirable skill. But *because* in this case does not link antecedent conditions to the desire in law-like fashion but rather links reasons to it and reasons generate desires in a non-deterministic fashion. Thus a person could have what he or she takes to be good and sufficient reasons to desire something, yet he or she remains indifferent to it. If reasons were connected to desires in a deterministic fashion this could not happen. Yet it does.[5]

The objection against regarding all cases of acquiring competencies as cases of conditioning is based upon viewing some of the elements which fit into many explanations (e.g., desiring, noticing, trying, believing, understanding, etc.) as not necessarily susceptible to being treated as events which come about through law-like attachment to antecedent conditions. As we have just seen, in some cases, such as desire, the elements can be generated non-deterministically by virtue of an agent's reasons. In others, such as noticing, the very existence of such a state in an agent is due not to law-like antecedent conditions which cause the state to come about but rather to certain voluntary actions by the agent, which serve as logical ingredients of the state being the sort of thing it is. For example, an agent cannot notice things unless he or she is attending to them. Attending, however, is not part of a cause which is independently describable and external to the act of noticing. Rather, attending is a logically necessary part of what it is to notice anything — that is, noticing *is* successful attentive seeing.

Because of considerations such as these we have good reasons to believe that not all acquired competencies need to be accounted for by way of a deterministic explanatory structure. A brief way of characterizing non-deterministic explanations of how humans acquire certain of their competencies is to say that such explanations try to show how such competencies are an agent's achievements. Such explanations try to reveal an acquired competence as the successful upshot of an agent's self-determination — that is, the explanation tries to show how the agent makes himself or herself to be the sort of person who has a certain competence by virtue of his or her voluntary actions.

The difference between viewing competence as the end result of a law-like causal sequence and viewing it as an agent's own achievement is deep and important enough to warrant a verbal distinction to be made between them. It is to mark this difference that I have distinguished between *S has been conditioned to X* and *S has learned X*. Moreover, identifying having learned something with agent achievement reflects more accurately the 'folk' psychological assumptions made by both teachers and students. For students and teachers often address one another and themselves in a vocabulary and in a manner which accepts voluntaristic presumptions. Thus, teachers may urge students to be more attentive and try harder, while students may complain that they don't know what the teacher wants and cannot understand what is going on.

Learning and Standards

Suppose we now turn our attention to the second condition under which *S learned X* is true. Consider for a moment a point of contrast between the man acquiring the ability to initiate his own pupillary reflex and the young girl becoming competent at skipping rope. Although both cases are success stories in that the acquired abilities are the successful upshots of certain antecedent incidents, it is only in the girl's case that the success is the agent's own achievement. Each case differs from the other in the type of description to be offered of the relation between antecedents and upshot. In the man's case this relation can be put in terms of a law-like series of stimulus substitutions. But in the girl's case the relation between incidents and upshot can be viewed in the same way as we view the relation between tasks and achievements.[6]

When a doctor treats a patient, she has succeeded when the patient has been cure. Curing the patient is the successful upshot of treating him. Similarly, winning a foot race is the successful upshot of running in it, while finding my wallet is the successful upshot of my looking for it. Of course a doctor may treat a patient, a runner race, and I look, without success. But notice one thing that is characteristic of those task verbs which are used to describe what an agent is doing. We can substitute for them other descriptions which indicate what the agent is trying to do. Thus treating the patient is the same as trying to cure him, running the race is identical to trying to win, while looking for my wallet is the same thing as trying to find it. When we say that an agent is undertaking a task relative to a certain achievement what we are saying is that agent's actions can be viewed as cases of trying to bring about a certain upshot. In the example of the young girl, her actions, such as practising the jump and rebound movements and practising coordinating wrist and arm movements, have a task-achievement structure in that these movements can be redescribed in terms of the girl trying to get these movements right. She may fail in this just as the doctor may fail to cure his patient. But having learned how to do something ranks as an achievement of the learner's task. Just as doctors try to cure their patients, what learners try to do when learning how to do something is to get things right — that is, they try to comply with the standards that constitute doing that thing correctly. When they succeed, they have learned.[7]

When X is an ability, successful compliance with certain standards of correctness is a necessary condition of the truth of S *learned* X. But of course, abilities are not the only sort of competence which a human being can learn. He or she can also learn to be a person with a certain sort of disposition, as well as having *learned that*. Does learning in the case of dispositions and in the case of *learning that* also require successful compliance with standards of correctness?

Suppose we first consider dispositions. Although every learned disposition has been acquired, not every acquired disposition has been learned. For there are among those dispositions which have been acquired some which have not been learned since they have been conditioned. A learned disposition, but not a conditioned one, arises by virtue of an agent's voluntary actions. But being the upshot of voluntary actions does not suffice to mark a disposition as having been learned. Consider the difference between saying of someone that he has become lazy and saying that he had to learn to be lazy. In the first case, the person's laziness may be regarded as the result of his knowingly and willingly neglecting doing things and, in general, letting things slide — a case of a disposition resulting from voluntary actions. But in the second case, there is the (paradoxical) suggestion that the person had to work at becoming lazy — perhaps because deliberately letting things go is strongly counter to the agent's inclinations. There is then a difference between voluntarily acquired dispositions and learned dispositions. For while the latter are indeed the upshot of voluntary actions, these actions are marked by a special effort on the part of the agent.

Is the effort involved in learning to be a person with a certain sort of disposition a matter of trying to comply with standards of correctness? Before directly considering this question something needs to be said, however briefly, about the phrase *standards of correctness*. Since the sort of dispositions which one can learn may include vices as well as virtues, it should be obvious that the standards of correctness one complies with need not be the ones which make a particular disposition a good or correct one to have. What are these standards then? They are the sort of considerations we need appeal to when correctly claiming that a particular person has a certain disposition. When, for example, we correctly describe someone as cruel this is done when we believe, also correctly, that he or she is deliberately doing such things as injuring, embarrassing or humiliating others. Thus the distinctive manifestations of particular dispositions serve as standards of correctness.

Distinctive manifestations of particular dispositions function as standards of judgment always, but not only, in the context of correct judgments which are made in the third person (e.g., 'He is cruel because he deliberately humiliates others, etc.'; 'She is generous because she often offers help to others, etc.'). However, from the perspective of the agent (i.e., from a first person perspective) these distinctive manifestations serve as his or her standards only in cases where the agent is *cultivating* that disposition. An infant may be ill-tempered because he scowls, throws tantrums, fusses a great deal, and so on, but he does not have this disposition because he has tried to cultivate the arts of scowling, throwing tantrums and fussing. However we may eventually explain his ill-temper, it has not been learned. Even in cases where the particular disposition clearly results from the agent's voluntary actions, we need not assume that these actions were undertaken to develop that disposition. Indeed, the distinction between simply becoming lazy and learning to be lazy rests primarily not on the latter but on the former involving an agent's attempts at acting in conformity to that disposition's typical manifestations. In short, when a disposition is learned, an agent has successfully complied with the standards of correctness for that disposition.

We can now turn to cases of learning that. When someone has *learned that P*, has he or she successfully complied with standards of correctness? If so, what sort of correctness are these the standards of? The most direct route to take here is to see what marks one of the differences between *coming to believe that P* and *having learned that P*. In cases of believing something, what is believed can be either true or false. Consequently, a person can come to believe what is false. But when a student has learned, for example, that Ottawa is the capital of Canada, not only has he or she come to believe it, but has also come to believe what is true. It seems, then, that successful compliance with standards of truth is a necessary condition of the truth of S *learned that P*.

There is one very important objection to this claim that having learned that P requires compliance with standards of truth. Suppose for example, a child claims to have learned that whales are fish and that squirrels hibernate. Although, in both cases, what is believed by the child is false, we are not logically required to claim that he or she did not learn these things. It seems, then, that S *learned that P* can be true even when P is false. Does this mean that successful compliance with standards of truth is not a necessary condition for having learned that P?

When something functions as a standard of truth, it does so by determining the sort of considerations that constitute good reasons for believing something. But having good reasons for believing something does not guarantee that, in this particular instance, what is believed is true. So it is possible that one may have good reasons for believing something which turns out to be false. This possibility need not undermine our confidence in regarding our standards as indeed standards of truth. Usually rejection of certain current standards as standards of truth occurs when it is found that their correct use produces anomalous results. If we cannot find out in a particular case why our standards have led to what is false suspicion may indeed begin to dawn although rejection is not inevitable. Applying this to cases of learning, having learned that P, where P is false, presumably no more requires a denial that standards of truth are complied with in having learned, than does coming to believe what is false on the basis of good reasons, require us to reject these reasons as good ones.

Cases in which a student has learned what is false are cases in which learning is teacher-dependent. They are teacher-dependent in that learning what is false can be explicated in terms of believing another that P. So, for example, if a child has learned that squirrels hibernate, what we mean is that she has believed a teacher when the latter has told her that squirrels hibernate. But if this is a genuine instance of learning that, then presumably one needs to comply with a standard of truth. The only thing that can serve as such a standard in cases of learning what is false, is the teacher's testimony. The student complies with such a standard when he or she believes the teacher. But how can a teacher's testimony be a good reason for believing something when it leads to believing what is false? Furthermore, how do such cases comply with the first condition of having learned something, namely, that it is the result of self-determination? For if an agent has come to believe that P *because* of his or her own efforts, how can he or she come to believe it *because* of a teacher?

One way of resolving these two problems is to treat cases of having learned that P, when P is false, as satisfying different criteria than do cases of having learned that *P*, when *P* is true. The effect of this, however, is to allow that only having learned that *P*, when *P* is false, is teacher-dependent. Not only do I think this to be false but, contrariwise, believe that a case can be made for viewing *all* learning as teacher-dependent — that believing another that *P*, permeates *all* learning.[8]

Learning and Teaching

If a case is to be made for viewing *all* learning as teacher-dependent, not only do we need to resolve the two problems raised above, but we also need to rebut at least two objections to it. The first objection is to the scope of the claim. It says that not all learning is teacher-dependent since at least some learning is dependent upon experience. Of course, the term *experience* is exceptionally wide-ranging, covering as it does matters as diverse as observation, imitation and trial-and-error. But the force of this first objection does not rest upon careful differentiations being made between various types of experience. It only maintains that at least some experiences are sources of learning, which are logically independent of believing others. Consider, for example, a student learning to play chess. As in all cases of learning, the student will have learned to play chess only when he or she has successfully complied with certain standards. The objection to the teacher-dependence thesis maintains that, in such a case, although the student may receive help from others, this sort of intervention is not logically necessary to his or her coming to comply with the standards involved in chess. It is quite otherwise, however, with something like trial-and-error. For without this, it would be (logically) impossible to learn how to play chess. Thus it is (or so it seems) that humans are able to learn in a way which is logically independent of others.

How sound is this objection? Its point is that one cannot successfully comply with the standards of an acquired ability without trial-and-error, or, more generally speaking, practice. While this is no doubt true, it does not dislodge the teacher-dependent thesis. For the latter does not maintain that experience is unnecessary to learning. Rather, part of its claim is that even a learner's experience is not independent of others. For although something like trial-and error is logically indispensible to attaining compliance with the standards involved in an acquired ability or disposition, coming to recognize what these standards are is also logically indispensible to such an achievement. But how can a learner come to recognize *Y* as the standard to be complied with in learning *X* except through others revealing it as the standard? All other means of finding out seem unavailable to an absolute beginner.[9]

Rebutting the first objection in this way only establishes one half of the thesis that all learning is teacher-dependent. For it only establishes (a) that all learning requires the recognition, by the learner, of *Y* as the standard to be complied with in learning *X*, and (b) that this recognition cannot be achieved without others revealing it. What we have not yet shown is that a learner's recognition of what others reveal as standards necessarily involves believing another that Y is the standard to be complied with in learning X. It is at this point that we can begin considering the second objection to the claim that all learning is teacher-dependent.

When a learner recognizes that Y is the standard to be complied with in learning X, he or she (a) comes to believe that Y is the standard, and (b) Y *is the standard of correctness for X* is true.[10] Although the second objection to regarding all learning as teacher-dependent allows that a learner comes to believe that Y is the standard for X because of others revealing it, it rejects the view that coming to such a belief is necessarily through believing another. Suppose we consider a case in which it appears that coming to a belief that Y is the standard of X occurs without believing another. Such an example might be provided by altering the earlier case of the young girl learning to skip rope. This time, suppose that no one offers to help her and she has to learn on her own. Presumably she could do so by observing others skipping rope and then imitating the movements until she got them right. In such a case although we could say that the girl, because of what others revealed by means of their actions, achieved a true belief as to what constitutes the standards for skipping rope, we could not say that she did so by believing these others. Believing another requires that what is revealed by another be done by way of an intentional communication. In the earlier unaltered version of the girl learning to skip rope, she recognized the standards that are to be complied with through her sister's help. In that example, her coming to believe that what her sister is showing her are indeed the standards is due to her believing her sister. This is a genuine instance of believing another since the sister is engaged in such intentional acts of communication as telling, commanding and demonstrating. Such, however, is not the case in the altered version. Thus it is, so the objection concludes, that although all learning requires recognition of the standards to be complied with through others revealing them, in some cases at least, this can occur without the learner believing others. Thus not all learning is teacher-dependent.

Central to this second objection is the view that believing another can take place only in cases of intentional communication. For something to function as an act of communication, the only things necessary are a sender, a receiver and a message. The message, however, need not be intentionally sent in order to have an act of communication take place between the sender and receiver. Thus, a slip of the tongue, a gesture or a facial expression may communicate a message to the receiver from the sender, although the latter does not intend to send that message. In trying to rebut the second objection, the main question is whether receiving an unintended message requires believing the sender.[11]

Suppose I am talking with a colleague. As our conversation wears on, I notice that his face is taking on an expression which I interpret as indicating his growing exasperation with me. When I ask him if indeed he is becoming exasperated with me, he denies it. Now, according to the second objection to viewing all learning as teacher-dependent, whether to believe or disbelieve my colleague can only be asked, in this case, of his denial. It cannot be raised over his facial expressions. But, as any consummate actor (or court-room lawyer) knows, facial expressions as well as gesture can be faked so as to make an audience believe things about the actor which, literally speaking, are not true (e.g., now he is indignant, now angry, now exasperated, etc.). So too with a consummate liar — he or she can also use facial expressions and gestures to send a message which the sender knows is not true. If, in the case of my colleague, I disbelieve his denial while taking his facial expressions to be a genuine indication of his feelings, this is because I assume he is not playing some kind of fantastic game with me in which he fakes his expressions while telling the truth. When anyone takes something like a facial expression or a gesture as conveying an unintended message, there is a presumption to the effect that the sender is not faking them. In short, the receiver believes the sender.

Now return to the example of the young girl learning to skip rope by observing and imitating others. In imitating what she observes others doing, she tacitly presumes (safely enough) that these others are not part of some giant conspiracy formed to fool her about what is involved in skipping rope. Imitation in this example is not only a sincere form of flattery, but it also requires believing others. Thus the view that all learning is teacher-dependent can fend off the second objection.

It is clear, by now, that viewing *all* learning as teacher-dependent does not carry with it the assumption that no individual learn anything on his or her own. But when an individual learns this or that on one's own, this is made possible because she, through her efforts, has successfully complied with the standards of correctness for the domain in which he or she has learned this or that. Individuals do not discover (learn) on their own by having a blank mind upon which the world writes clear messages. What is noticed and what is ignored in the process of learning new things reflects what has been accepted as the standards of inquiry. Regarding *all* learning as teacher-dependent means that acceptance of these standards requires each of us to believe others as to what these standards are. Without believing others as to standards, we cannot learn new things on our own. These standards may, of course, change over a period of time. But, however much they may change, standards reflect not so much individual discovery as the agreements reached by, to use a phrase of C.S. Peirce, 'the community of inquirers'. Without any such agreements by a particular community, no individual can learn. [12]

Viewing standards as agreements reached by a community has a bearing on one of the two questions raised at the end of the last section. How, it was asked, can a teacher's testimony be a good reason for believing something especially when such testimony sometimes results in a student coming to learn what is false? This question becomes especially important in the light of the claim that all learning is teacher-dependent; that is, all learning requires a learner's acceptance of a teacher's testimony as to what the standards are for learning X. Can a teacher's testimony be a good reason for believing that Y is a standard of X, even if it turns out that Y is not the standard of X?

There are important similarities between the testimony of a witness as to what he saw, heard or did, and that of a teacher about the standards of correctness for X. To the extent that a witness or a teacher is believed to be out to deceive others, we have good reason not to accept her testimony. Accepting the testimony of another presupposes that we view the other as truthful. But being truthful is not the same as being unmistaken. And as far as testimony is concerned, not only can a witness or a teacher be mistaken as to what each is testifying to, but the auditors can likewise be mistaken about what is being communicated. So accepting the testimony of another also presupposes that we take ourselves and the other as not being mistaken about the content of the testimony being given. But, in view of the fact that both witnesses and teachers can sometimes be less than truthful, while they as well as their auditors can be mistaken, is their testimony that P, still a good reason for believing that P?

The need for testimony occurs precisely in those cases in which we have no other means of finding out what is the case. Whether a particular witness or teacher is both truthful and unmistaken as to her testimony cannot be verified by means which are non-testimonial. If it were, then we could know what we need to know without testimony. This does not leave us helpless, however, since there are some means available which, though they do not directly test the testimony itself, do so indirectly by creating suspicions about the witness. Thus, if it is known that a particular witness is not exactly the most truthful of humans, or that he has a special interest to protect, or is easily confused, then we have reason to treat his testimony with a certain degree of circumspection. So too with a teacher. If it turns out that a particular teacher is careless in the way she communicates standards to students, or has a special axe to grind, or is badly trained, then we have some reason to be wary of her testimony as to the standards involved in learning X. So, although testimony can result in false beliefs, this does not require us to reject it as a standard of truth since often enough special explanations can be given as to why things go awry. In this respect, testimony is like any other standard of truth. In operating with testimony, we presume, until there is reason to believe otherwise, that others are truthful and, along with ourselves, competent at understanding messages.

So far we have treated witnesses and teachers as alike. There is, however, one important difference between the two. When giving testimony, a witness can be regarded as the original source of the beliefs of those who believe him. He is a *source* since it is by believing the witness that others come to believe as they do; a witness is 'original' because he is testifying to what he himself has seen, heard or done.[13] In communicating standards, a teacher is also a source of a learner's beliefs as to what these standards are. However, a teacher is not the original source of these standards since the origins of these are to be found in the agreements of a particular community.

Thus, whether believing a teacher about standards is a good reason for believing rests not only upon a teacher's truthfulness and competence but also upon the legitimacy of a particular community as an origin of these standards. Lack of confidence in such a community can, as can lack of confidence in a teacher, make learning impossible.

What grants such legitimacy to a particular community is an important question whose exploration would carry us well beyond the bounds of a single chapter. Nevertheless, enough has been said, I think, to allay at least certain initial doubts as to how a teacher's testimony can serve as a standard of truth even though a student may, because of a teacher, come to learn what is false. It is now time to conclude this chapter by considering the second question raised at the end of the last section: How can standards be learned?

Why is this a problem? Recall that one of the conditions of having learned X is that it is a result of self-determination. In addition, having learned requires that one come to believe that Y is the standard to be complied with in learning X. But if all learning is teacher-dependent in the sense I have tried to describe, the belief that Y is the standard of X can only be acquired by an individual because of the testimony of the teacher. Yet if such a belief is not the result of conditioning but due to a student's voluntary efforts, how can it also be due to the teacher? In short, how can standards be learned?

When a student comes to believe that Y is the standard of X because of a teacher's testimony, the latter serves as the *grounds* of the student's belief. The *because* is the because of rational connection. But believing something is also a state of mind whose occurrence may be because of such things as conditioning, hypnotism, drugs, etc. In these cases the *because* is the because of causal connection. This distinction between rational and causal connections allows us to view the learning of standards in a way which appears to be free of internal incoherence. For such learning is rationally connected to a teacher's testimony, while causally connected to an agent's own voluntary efforts. We have already seen how testimony can provide good grounds for belief. But, in what way can an agent cause himself to believe something?

In cases where a person's beliefs are due to conditioning, hypnotism, drugs, etc., there is no necessary concern on the part of the causal agent about the truth of the belief being inculcated. Whether or not the conditioner or hypnotist believes what she is inculcating in another is not relevant to her success. But from the perspective of the one who believes, believing that P, and believing that P is true amount to the same thing. If, then, an agent's own beliefs are the successful upshot of her own voluntary efforts, the latter must be the sort of actions in which the agent necessarily shows a concern for the truth of the matter. But what sort of effort, when successful, has as its upshot, if not true belief, at least the belief that something is true?[14]

When one comes to believe that P for the reason Q, we can describe this as a case in which the agent concludes P because Q, where the *because* involves a causal connection. The agent causes herself to believe P by an act of concluding from believing *Q*. This act of inferring one thing from another does not presuppose for its occurrence that what functions as a premise and what as a conclusion *do in fact* have a rational connection with one another.

Its occurrence does presuppose, however, that the agent regards inference as a truth-preserving act and is thus disposed to make inferences on the basis of what he or she takes to be standards of truth. Putting this together with what has already been said about testimony, a student learns that *Y* is the standard of *X* when (a) a teacher's testimony is a standard of truth, (b) the student is disposed to believe the teacher, (c) the teacher communicates that *Y* is the standard of *X*, and (d) the student understands the teacher and believes that *Y* is the standard of *X*.

One final question. If all learning is teacher-dependent, what about the student's disposition to believe the teacher? Is this also learned? Where the *teacher* refers to a specific teacher of a particular competence, a student does indeed learn to believe him, rather than someone else, about the standards involved in that particular competence. One learns, for example, that the history teacher can be relied upon to convey the standards of historical inquiry but not, say, those of mathematics. This is the sort of thing which the schools communicate to students. But where the *teacher* is used in a less specific sense to refer to any other person from whom one learns, then the disposition to believe the teacher seems to be unlearned. The claim that all learning is teacher-dependent presumes that all humans start off with the presumption that others are trustworthy and informed. Unfortunately, the one thing that is learned is that the latter is not true of everyone. However, the thesis that all learning is teacher-dependent does not require for its truth that everyone be trustworthy and informed — only that some be so. Where the *teacher* is used in its more specific sense, the elements of subject-matter, trustworthiness and competence become especially important. For lack of it may eventually serve to undermine confidence in the very community of inquirers that these teachers represent, thus making learning in these domains an unlikely achievement. And if this occurs, there is not very much point in having schools.

Teaching and the Ethics of Belief

How does viewing all learning as teacher-dependent influence our conception of what is distinctive about the relationship between teachers and students? Since learning and conditioning differ from each other, the distinctive features of the teacher-student relationship, centering as it does on learning, differ from those features which mark the relationship between the conditioner and the subject who is to be conditioned. Although both types of relationship are cases in which there is a dependence of one person upon the other, since learning always requires believing another, whereas being conditioned does not, the relation between teachers and students is characteristically marked by what may be called an ethics of belief. For in believing another, a student trusts that a teacher is being truthful — two notions which are clearly ethical. But trust and truthfulness are not uniquely normative for the relationship between teachers and students. However, what is distinctive here is that a student's trust in the teacher's word is legitimatized by an ethics of belief which claims that one should believe certain things on the basis of another's epistemic authority. Such a claim runs strongly counter to what I take to be the prevailing view, namely, that each person should believe solely on the basis of available evidence and that authority, no matter how legitimate, does not function as evidence. If the argument of this chapter is at all correct, such rugged epistemic individualism is misplaced.

Notes

1   This example has been taken from G. Vesey (1967, pp. 62–3).
2   uS = unconditioned stimulus
    uR = unconditioned response
    cS = conditioned stimulus
    cR = conditioned response
3   These two formulations can be found in Owen Flanagan (1984, pp. 105–6, 108).
4   This is a slightly modified version of an example found in Vesey, *op cit.*, p. 62.
5   There are many complex issues surrounding the reasons-versus-causes issue when it connects with deterministic-versus-non-deterministic explanations. Obviously we have only touched the surface of these issues. Later on in this chapter, I will be distinguishing between rational and causal connections where the latter is still non-deterministic.
6   For the task-achievement distinction, see Ryle (1949, pp. 149–52). See also R.S. Peters (1967, pp. 12–14) for the application of tasks and achievements to the differences between conditioning and learning.
7   I have oversimplified this example a bit. For in learning how to skip rope there may be more than one sort of task and achievement involved. In order to learn how to skip rope, the girl not only has successfully to practise the correct movements, but, given the earlier scenario, she also has to succeed in understanding her sister's instructions, imitate her movements, etc. There are important questions that can be raised as to whether, for example, *understanding* is an achievement of some task and, if so, what sort of task it is. But at this point these questions need not detain us.
8   In identifying *believing another* with *believing a teacher*, I do not mean to exclude cases in which the *other* may be a book, map, and so on. But believing a book, map, etc., is not what is primarily believed in such cases. What we primarily believe is the author, map maker, and so on. Nor am I using the term *teacher* to refer only to school teachers. Rather it refers to any person through whom learning takes place.
9   Of course standards can be invented by an individual without the aid of others. But this is not so much learning standards as inventing them.
10   The use of the singular expression *the standard* is only a matter of convenience. It should not be taken as claiming that abilities and dispositions have only one standard that has to be complied with. Indeed, they may be plural.
11   Since we are concerned with human learning, in what follows I will be assuming

that both sender and receiver are human. Of course this need not be the case since the sender could be a book, a map, a blueprint, and so on. Such cases could, however, be construed as secondary acts of communication, but still acts of communication since the primary sender is an author, cartographer, engineer and others. The primary receiver is a reader. Complications ensue, however, when messages are conveyed from one machine to another. Are these still acts of communication when the message stored by the receiving machine does not get sent to a human (or at least intelligent) receiver? Could such interaction between machines, if they are indeed genuine acts of communication, still be cases of teaching and learning?

12 There is ample room for controversy here. Does regarding standards as the result of some kind of agreement, mean that they are arbitrary? Is this an open invitation to some kind of relativism? Can standards reached this way also be standards of truth in cases of *learning that*? I shall only be concerned with this latter question in what follows.

13 The idea of an original source is an adaptation of an idea found in G.E.M. Anscombe (1979, pp. 146–7).

14 From a first person point of view, is the formation of belief necessarily truth-centered? Could not a person believe something simply because it is comforting to so believe? If the comfort provided by a belief is thought by the agent to be a reason for believing it, we still have a truth-centered motive. In such a case, truth-centered motives could be dispensed with only if it were possible for an agent to claim that he or she cared only for the comfort and not a whit for its truth. He or she might then seek the help of a hypnotist, for example, to ensure the fixity of such a belief. But then one would no longer believe for reasons and thus would not be *learning that*. For problems connected with such possibilities see B. Williams (1973, pp. 136–51).

Bibliography

ANSCOMBE, G.E.M. (1979) 'What is it to believe someone?' in DELANEY C.F. (Ed.) *Rationality and Religious Belief*, South Bend, IN: The University of Notre Dame Press.

BROWN, S. (1972) 'Learning', *Proceedings of the Aristotelian Society*, (Supplementary), 46, pp. 19–39.

COOPER, D. (1987) 'Assertion phenomenology and essence', *Proceedings of the Aristotelian Society* (Supplementary), 61, pp. 85–106.

DAVIS, A. (1986) 'Learning and Belief', *Journal of Philosophy of Education*, 20, pp. 7–20.

DEARDEN, R.F. (1979) 'The assessment of learning', *British Journal of Educational Studies*, 27, pp. 111–24.

DEARDEN, R.F. (1974) 'Education and the ethics of belief', *British Journal of Educational Studies*, 22, pp. 5–17.

FLANAGAN, O. (1984) *The Science of the Mind*, Cambridge: Massachusetts Institute of Technology Press.

FRICKER, E. (1974) 'The epistemology of testimony', *Proceedings of the Aristotelian Society* (Supplementary), 61, pp. 57–83.

HAMLYN, D. (1973) 'Human learning', in PETERS, R.S. (Ed.) *The Philosophy of Education*, Oxford: Oxford University Press.

HARDING, J. (1985) 'Epistemic dependence', *Journal of Philosophy*, 82, pp. 335–49.

LEWIS, C.I. (1955) *The Ground and Nature of the Right*, New York: Columbia University Press.

PETERS, R.S. (1967) 'What is an educational process?', in PETERS, R.S. (Ed.) *The Concept of Education*, London: Routledge and Kegan Paul.

QUINTON, A. (1987) 'On the ethics of belief', in HAYDON, G. (Ed.) *Education and Values*, London: Institute of Education.

RHEES, R. (1969) *Without Answers*, London: Routledge and Kegan Paul.

RYLE, G. (1949) *The Concept of Mind*, London: Hutchinson.

SIEGEL, H. (1988) 'Rationality and epistemic dependence', *Educational Philosophy and Theory*, 20, pp. 1–6.

SKINNER, B.F. (1968) *The Technology of Teaching*, New York: Appleton-Century Crofts.

VESEY, G. (1967) 'Conditioning and learning', in PETERS, R.S. (Ed.) *The Concept of Education*, London: Routledge and Kegan Paul.

WHITE, J.P. (1972) 'Learning', *Proceedings of the Aristotelian Society*, 46, pp. 41–58.

WILLIAMS, B. (1973) *Problems of the Self*, Cambridge: Cambridge University Press.

12 Instructional Psychology and Teaching

Philip H. Winne and John Walsh

What is Instructional Psychology?

Everyone teaches. Parents teach their children how to work the TV and what to say to be polite. Teenagers teach friends about the opposite sex and how to do algebra. Children teach their playmates rules for the games they invent and what new words mean. Sometimes, you teach yourself a better golf swing or how to cope with someone refusing a date. Of course, teachers instruct students of many ages in all sorts of subjects.

What is common among all these cases? What is unique to each? If you were the 'instructor' in one of these situations, how would you teach? What would you have to know to be a good teacher? What would you need to do so that what you know about teaching could be put into practice? How would you know if your 'student' was learning what you were teaching? If you wanted to talk about the way that you teach with someone else, how would you describe it so that it makes sense? Answers to these and similar questions can be found in part, in the field of instructional psychology.

One way to introduce the field of instructional psychology is to separate it into two components, instruction and psychology. In this section we first present important features about the psychological component of instructional psychology. Thereafter, we sketch major aspects of the instructional component of the term.

Psychology is Studying Behavior Scientifically

Behavior is what people do, what they say, how they act, what they feel, and how they think. To study what an instructor and students do during instruction, an instructional psychologist observes them. Sometimes, observations are made without changing the way instruction unfolds naturally. The instructional psychologist just watches, taking notes and often audiotaping or videotaping what the participants do. At other times, an instructional psychologist observes people participating in instruction by creating special tasks for them to perform. Tasks can be as simple as answering a question about the spelling of cat or as complex as designing a system of transportation to service a rapidly expanding metropolitan area.

As a scientific discipline, instructional psychology has three key features. First, every specialized field, whether it be music or auto mechanics, uses *specialized terms* which *describe* the people, objects and events that are important in that field. Instructional psychologists choose their terms to highlight critical differences between ideas that our everyday language might muddle. Most of us would be content to describe a reading assignment as 'hard'. An instructional psychologist might refer instead to a particular index that compares how difficult it is to comprehend a chapter's main idea for a reader who has average ability in a particular grade.

Second, central questions in instructional psychologists' study of instruction are *why* and *how*. To know why is knowing what causes instruction to unfold as it does and being able to identify features of that instruction which affect how students learn from it. When an instructional psychologist knows why, teaching at least can be explained. When it is possible for a teacher to manipulate causes, such as the phrasing and timing of feedback about a student's work, instruction can be designed to promote specific outcomes such as mastery of material and interest in a subject.

Third, instructional psychologists have agreed on rules that prescribe how to gather data, how to judge its qualities and how to combine different types of information to form general principles about instruction. As a group, these rules are called the *scientific method*. Following these rules decreases the likelihood that an instructional psychologist will misinterpret observations. One important rule, for example, is borrowed from surveying and is called triangulation. It says that an observer can be much more sure about the accuracy of an interpretation if it is supported by three (or several) different types of observation. The interpretation that a student is interested in making maps is made much more certain if the student says so, can be seen to spend most of her free time in the library copying maps of her neighborhood, and tries to create maps that show how ideas in her biology homework relate to one another.

Instruction is Deliberately Changing What a Student Knows and Can Do

There are two important parts to the description of instruction as deliberately changing what a student knows and can do. First, a deliberate act is one that has an objective, a goal. Occasionally, the objective of instruction may not be apparent to a student. If what a teacher does qualifies as instruction, however, the teacher must be clear about the objective. Otherwise, what happens is just happenstance, not instruction.

Second, instruction is defined not only by what a teacher does while trying to instruct, but also by what a student does in trying to learn (Winne, 1985). Instruction must be accompanied by learning, that is, by a relatively permanent change in a student's behavior — what the student says and feels, and how the student acts and thinks. To know all about instruction, then, one needs three different kinds of observations. Some observations provide selected information about a student's behavior before instruction. Other observations characterize aspects of the teacher's and the student's behavior during instruction. The third type of observations records information about differences in the student's behavior after instruction as compared with behavior before instruction. Only with all three sets of observations can you justifiably claim that instruction changed a student's behavior.

To summarize, instructional psychology is a hybrid discipline. From the parent discipline of psychology, it adopts special methods and terms to help describe and explain instruction. Questions regarding how and why features of instruction affect student learning are central to instructional psychology. By providing answers to these questions, instructional psychologists aim to improve the ways teachers teach and students learn.

In the remainder of this chapter, we turn our attention to a few of the many areas of active research in instructional psychology. Specifically, we overview research bearing on two topics: How students think as they try to learn from classroom work, and how motivation influences students' participation in instruction. Since the chapter is far too short to inform you thoroughly about all areas of instructional psychology, our aim is to whet your appetite for discovering more about this field. To this end, we encourage a trip to your library to browse introductory textbooks about educational psychology or a visit with a professor of educational psychology in your institution.

Students' Thinking during Instruction

Classroom Tasks

If you were to ask students what they did in school today, your question would be greeted by many different answers. A typical elementary student might reply that she completed worksheets at her desk, read aloud in a reading group and listened to the teacher talk about Jacques Cartier's early exploration of Canada. A junior-high student might tell you that he completed a biology lab on the digestive system of an earthworm, solved some algebra problems in math class and watched a British production of *King Lear* during English period. At the university level, a student might indicate that she listened to an interesting lecture on the poetry of Sylvia Plath, then studied for her calculus midterm in the library for the remainder of the day.

Although each of these students had vastly different experiences at school, there is one important element that they all shared. They all completed activities or tasks that were designed either to teach new information or to practise newly acquired skills (Marx and Walsh, 1988). Each task was deliberately set to achieve an instructional goal. Notice as well that students were active while they completed these tasks. They listened, read, wrote, perceived, remembered, understood and, generally, thought deeply about how to do their work. Moreover, these students probably used knowledge about similar tasks that they had accomplished in the past to guide their current thinking. In this way, they used knowledge about themselves as learners to tackle new work.

An appropriate starting point for discussing students' thinking then is with classroom tasks, since tasks are the focus of so much of students' cognitive efforts. In the following, we describe facets of classroom tasks which influence how students think, bringing out some of the complexities as well as the richness of students' mental life in classrooms. Along the way, we illustrate how research and theory in instructional psychology might be used to improve the thinking that students use to accomplish everyday work in schools.

To begin, we need a working definition of classroom tasks. Classroom tasks are cognitive demands that are placed upon students to change what they know and feel and how they think when doing succeeding tasks. We have used the phrase *cognitive demands* to emphasize a number of differences between classroom tasks and other sorts of tasks that regularly confront us in everyday life. The word *cognitive* highlights the fact that classroom work is of a mental nature. This is in contrast to other tasks we might face such as jogging on a track, washing test tubes or returning a library book. These tasks require little mental effort. We describe tasks as demanding because we wish to underscore that they pose goals that must be met. This is to say, tasks require students to seek solutions. Last, and perhaps most importantly, we note in the definition that classroom tasks aim to change students in a cognitive way. Tasks, at least in a general sense, must improve the minds of learners. If they do not, they are obviously of little value in schools.

We have said that classroom tasks are set to achieve particular instructional aims. In a perfect and much simpler world, teachers would merely give the class work to do, and all the students would perform each task in the assignment using the same thinking and would obtain the same results. We know, however, that this is not the case. Students often respond very differently to the same task. They do not always get the right or appropriate answer, and they may not even be working on the same task despite the fact that they appear to be doing so. In short, students' cognitive activities during instructional tasks as well as their achievements may vary greatly.

The observation that students' achievements on a given task often differs is neither new nor surprising. What is more challenging, however, is to understand elements of classroom tasks which may be responsible for such differences. From the vantage point of instructional psychology, the nature of tasks is described by three interrelated factors: (1) the conditions under which classroom tasks are accomplished by students; (2) the cognitive plans students use to complete tasks; and (3) the products or solutions students produce when tasks are completed.

Task conditions

Tasks are established in the classroom under certain conditions that characterize the circumstances, rules and constraints within which students behave. Some classroom work, such as examinations, are highly constrained; students' access to information and the range of acceptable responses are restricted. Other classroom tasks, such as creative writing and group projects, contain few directions and permit students considerable latitude in how they work and what they produce.

One important condition of any task is the amount of control teachers exert over the ways tasks are to be completed. Some teachers maintain rigid control over work. They set all tasks, do not permit much interaction between students and generally value individual efforts and achievement. Other teachers encourage group efforts and design instructional tasks to be done in a cooperative way.

We do not want to suggest that one of these approaches is always better. Which is better depends greatly on the goals of instruction. What we do want to examine, however, is how the amount of teacher control can influence the ways students think about tasks and, ultimately, the knowledge and motivations they learn from doing these tasks.

Research on students completing tasks in groups shows that they can approach these tasks in vastly different ways (Corno and Mandinach, 1983). Some students, who have been called self-regulated learners, set intermediate goals for complicated tasks and transform the information they are provided to integrate it with what they already know. Others adopt a role in group activities of being task managers. They do not integrate much information on their own. Rather, they tend to gather resources for others to complete the group project, then apply relatively simple types of thinking, such as plain rehearsal, to learn the information that others developed. Still other students take their cue for cognitive efforts from other students in the group. These recipient learners acquire and transform information by listening to others rather than doing their own exploring in the new territory of knowledge. In doing so, they circumvent some of the major cognitive requirements of classroom work.

As you read the previous description of self-regulated learners, resource managers and recipient learners, you may well have recognized some of the students with whom you have worked on group projects. What you may not have recognized is that each of these different types of students actually is working on a different task. The resource manager, for example is directing mental effort toward gathering resource materials but doesn't have skills for linking these bits of new information. This student, however, is not working on the task intended by the teacher, although he or she may appear to be doing so. Similarly, the recipient learner's task is to try to learn the content of the project by copying others' efforts. The information that this student acquires does not include that important skill of knowing how to recognize when new information is important to completing a task.

While each of these students is working on a different task, it is important to note that each might appear to achieve the same product if asked to answer an essay question on what they found out. They also would likely be seen as contributing to the group effort. Yet, the cognitive benefits which each student reaps are very different.

There are many other task conditions that influence how students think. An abbreviated list would include the type of media used to present tasks, whether there are secondary tasks such as questions embedded in the main task, and the time allocated for completing tasks. These and a number of other conditions shape how students go about learning from classroom work and, thus, what they learn.

Students' cognitive plans

Any discussion of classroom work would be incomplete without describing the cognitive plans that students use to solve tasks. A cognitive plan is a series of steps in thinking that students use to complete a part of a task or an entire task. Although there are many kinds of plans that students use, we focus on three main types that are especially common and useful — memory, procedural and comprehension plans (see Weinstein and Mayer, 1986).

Many tasks in school require students to memorize bits of knowledge. Knowing the capital cities of the provinces, remembering the names of prime ministers, and learning foreign language vocabulary all require students to memorize. When students approach this kind of task, they can select a plan to think and learn efficiently. For example, students may use mnemonic devices, such as ROY G BIV to remember the colors of the visible spectrum of light (red, orange, yellow, green, blue, indigo and violet). Students learning another language often find that using images helps to memorize vocabulary (Levin, McCormick, Miller, Berry and Pressley, 1982). For instance, a student trying to remember the Spanish word for letter (*carta*) might imagine a letter inside a large shopping cart. In this example, the foreign word is made more meaningful by linking it to an image of something that sounds like the new word (cart, carta). Upon hearing or reading *carta*, the student recalls the image and 'sees' that it contains a letter.

Of course not all school tasks are accomplished only by memorizing and, therefore, not all plans are memory plans. A second important kind of plan concerns the procedural knowledge that is required when completing a task. Procedural plans are used when tasks can be solved by applying a predictable formula or rule for processing information, that is, an algorithm. Much of elementary school mathematics requires this type of plan. For example, if you were asked to divide two fractions, you would apply a procedural plan to invert the divisor, then multiply the two fractions. Notice that you do not need to understand why this algorithm works to accomplish the task. All that is required is correctly applying the rule.

Research on procedural plans that students use in classroom work has been a particularly strong area of study in instructional psychology in the last decade. One interesting finding from this work is that students can apply the wrong procedural plan but sometimes still obtain the correct answer (Brown and Burton, 1979). It therefore is very important that teachers detect these buggy plans by analyzing students' errors. Consider these subtraction questions completed by an elementary student: $88 - 3 = 85$; $83 - 4 = 84$; $93 - 6 = 93$. This student used the same procedural plan for both questions, but only the first is correct. Can you identify the buggy plan that causes the mistake?

The third type of cognitive plan students often use is a comprehension or understanding plan. These plans are employed when learners draw inferences about information, apply previously learned procedures to new situations, and paraphrase and transform academic content.

In general, comprehension plans help students learn by enriching new information with the information that they have already learned. For example, when a student takes notes in a lecture, she is using a comprehension plan if she translates the main points of the lecturer into her own and then creates her own example of each main point. This translation and elaboration personalizes the information so that it is more meaningful, producing comprehension that goes beyond merely memorizing the main points.

You have likely experienced the effects of personalizing information by applying a comprehension plan when you borrowed a friend's lecture notes. As you read the notes, you were probably baffled by some of the content. What your friend meaningfully translated can appear incomprehensible to you. The comprehension plan your friend used resulted in information that was transformed idiosyncratically because it rested on his prior knowledge, not yours.

More will be said about students' cognitive plans later. What is important to note now is that the demands of classroom tasks are met by students when they use organized ways of thinking about these tasks, that is, when they apply cognitive plans (Winne, 1985). Plans will differ depending on a task's requirements, that is, whether the task requires the student to use a procedure, comprehend new material or memorize information. From the perspective of instructional psychology, a large part of schooling is devoted to teaching students' plans and when to use them with certain tasks. Indeed, the notion of teaching students' cognitive plans resembles very closely a major aim of schools — to teach students how to learn.

Task products
The last major element in classroom tasks is the products that students create. Products are the results of students' cognitive plans that have been carried out under the conditions set for a task. In this section, we discuss the clarity with

which the product is specified by the teacher. This is one of the many features of task products that influence students' thinking.

You may have had the unpleasant experience of receiving a graded assignment and learned that you misunderstood what the professor wanted in the question. As you looked through the assignment you probably said, 'If the assignment had been clearer, I would have received a much better mark'. You likely said a few other things as well!

Specifying clear and agreed-upon goals which communicate what products are to be sought in tasks is a major problem for both teachers and students. Researchers have found that considerable discrepancies can exist between teachers' representations of task goals and those of students (Winne and Marx, 1982). In some cases, this results from teachers not being very sure about the products they want students to create. Obviously, teachers ought to be precise in planning for and communicating classroom tasks.

Confusion about the products for tasks can occur for other reasons. Students can fail to comprehend the kind of product required for a task because teachers do not make their intentions known. For example, one teacher interviewed in a recent study started a language arts lesson by reading the beginning of a story to the class. The teacher's intended goal was to focus students' attention on characteristics of stories that require readers to make inferences. Students interviewed in the class following the lesson perceived that they were to remember the details of the specific story rather than its general characteristics. They reasoned that this was the product that usually was expected when stories were read to them. Here, the students had used their knowledge of a predictable classroom routine to infer the goal of the task. Students failed at the teachers' intended task because the teacher did not clearly signal its intended product.

Not all products of tasks can be specified with the same degree of clarity. Products for tasks that require students to use memory plans, for example, are easy to specify. Other tasks, such as essays, which require mixtures of several procedural and comprehension plans, can be difficult to specify clearly. This is because the task itself requires learners to shape the conditions of subtasks within their own essays and define parts of the overall product to some degree. Adding too much information to an essay assignment would impede one purpose of this assignment, namely, having students demonstrate their use of comprehension plans.

In summary, the clarity of descriptions for tasks will influence the cognitive plans and general thinking used by students. Teachers can help ensure that students use appropriate cognitive plans by being clear about the products in setting tasks. Further, teachers need to communicate their intended goals clearly to students. Although these two measures will help students produce high quality task products, tasks which require some kinds of cognitive plans will necessarily be rather ill-defined.

Although much more could be said about classroom tasks as a topic of research and theory in instructional psychology, the preceding at least gives a flavor of the richness of this aspect of classroom life. We now turn to another major topic in instructional psychology, student motivation.

Motivation and Students' Participation in Instruction

We began the last major section on students' thinking during instruction by imagining that you had asked students what they did in school today. Although that survey covered much ground about students' cognitive processing and tasks, it is still fundamentally incomplete. There is a second basic question that you must ask these students to gain a full measure of understanding about their participation in instruction. It is: Why did you do what you did today? This question is about motivation, but as we will see, it is not a question only about motivation. This is to say that answers to questions about motivation involve much more than students' wants, interests or feelings. Keep this important point in mind as we explore the topic of students' motivation and its relation to their participation in instruction.

What is Motivation?

Motivation is a slippery idea. For instructional theorists, motivation accounts for three interlocked aspects of behavior (Winne and Marx, 1989). First, motivation influences which tasks students select to do. Second, motivation shapes qualities of students' temperament and involvement with a task. Temperamental qualities of behaving include how much effort students put into their work and the degree of interest they show about a task. Third, motivation affects how persistent students are, including how long they work at a task and how quickly they return to work if interrupted. To decide whether a student is motivated, observe (1) what they select to do, (2) what temperament they show when they do it, and (3) how persistent they are in what they do. These are the observations that provide information about whether a student is or is not motivated.

How do teachers motivate students?

Most people unschooled about motivation answer this question with replies such as, 'Teachers choose topics that students will find interesting' or 'Teachers implore students to consider how important learning is'. These kinds of answers are true, but they are not precise. A more precise answer is that a teacher tries to motivate students by *prompting* them *to think* in particular ways *about specific information*. To understand a teacher's attempts to motivate students thus requires a consideration of these three features.

To illustrate each of these three features, suppose that last Friday a teacher taught students a step-by-step method for writing clear descriptive paragraphs. Today, Wednesday, in assigning them the task of writing a descriptive essay about free trade, she urges students to 'Think carefully!' This phrase is a prompt because it suggests (quite strongly) that students do something. The something that the teacher intends students to do is to remember one of the cognitive plans we described earlier. Finally, the specific information that students are to remember is the method they were taught for writing clear descriptive paragraphs.

Does 'Think carefully!' also qualify as a teacher's attempt to motivate? Comparing this prompt to each part of the definition of motivation discussed earlier, we see that the teacher clearly intends that students will select one plan as the approach to writing the essay rather than some other method. Second, the prompt's meaning — be careful — and the teacher's vocal emphasis (which we show with the exclamation mark) implies that the teacher expects students to apply the plan diligently. This is a temperamental quality of work by which students take care to check each part of their work against the plan. Third, although it isn't apparent at first, the teacher also is trying to affect students' persistence. By definition, all plans have a goal. If students follow the plan, they will persist until they reach the goal of having produced a well-formed descriptive paragraph. When students have achieved the goal of a plan, they have not only finished the task, but they also will have written a better essay because they followed the plan. Presumably, this accomplishment might entice them to write more descriptive essays and, when they do so, to apply the plan they have practised to their writing. In other words, they will persist at writing in the way that they were taught. So, this prompt is an attempt to motivate. Notice that 'to motivate' is a verb. It is what a teacher tries to do. Do students have motivation, the noun, when their teacher tries to motivate?

Motivation has two parts
As the preceding example reveals, the teacher never directly controls students' behaviors or feelings (Winne, 1987). Rather, teachers typically try to motivate students by prompting students to recall and use knowledge. Some of this knowledge is connected to motivation, such as what happens if a plan is put to use in a task, or whether the accomplishments of the plan have value. These are chunks of knowledge that students learn in and outside school.

Students do not learn feelings of satisfaction or happiness. But they do learn motivation when they create connections between the knowledge they have about tasks and their feelings. Students decide what to do (like selecting to follow a task plan), to do it (temperamental qualities of how they apply the plan), and how to be persistent (whether writing a good essay is worth being late for a favorite TV program). Students base these decisions on the specific connections they have learned between each of these features of their behaviour and the feelings they already possess. In the next section, we will identify five types of these connections that account for students' expressions of motivation in the ways they perform tasks.

To summarize these points, a teacher intends to motivate students by prompting knowledge that students have learned. Some of the knowledge teachers prompt is about the curriculum and task-plans for writing — call this *task knowledge*. Some other knowledge concerns the connections students have learned between task knowledge and feelings. Call this *motivational knowledge*. Students' motivation thus has two parts: task knowledge and motivational knowledge. Both types of knowledge jointly determine a student's motivation.

Is there always something to be motivated about? Yes. If you think a moment, this is utterly logical. Saying that someone is motivated always means they are motivated about something in particular, that is, a task. As you know, a student's motivation does not always match what the teacher intends in her prompts to motivate. After the next section about motivational knowledge, we examine why a teacher's attempts to motivate students might not match students' motivations.

What Types of Connections Make up Motivational Knowledge?

Let us return to the first major section to elaborate a few of the students' answers to the question, 'What did you do in school today?' The elementary student might say, 'I read aloud because I like reading'. The junior-high student might reply: 'I completed my biology lab on the earthworm because I need the extra credit to stay eligible for basketball. I did the algebra problems in class so I could get close to Patti by getting help from her'. The university student might say, 'I studied for my calculus midterm in the library because I had to avoid distractions'.

All these answers reflect a connection between the student's task knowledge and what we have called motivational knowledge. The elementary student knows she is a good reader and enjoys using the skills that comprise reading just because it is enjoyable for her. She has an intrinsic *incentive* to read aloud. The junior-high student understands there is extra credit to be gained by performing a task, and he knows what work is needed to earn it. In other words, he knows what *outcome to expect* for his work. As well, he judges that working on his biology lab has more *utility* than trying some other way to stay eligible for sports. In algebra, he expects some difficulty solving the word problems on his own. That is, his *expectation of efficacy* is low if he has to do the problems alone. The university student knows that her success at studying depends on putting maximum effort into it. In other words, she *attributes* her success at studying to effort. Here is a memory plan for remembering the five connections that make up motivational knowledge. Put the names of the connections in this form: attributions, efficacy expectations, incentives, outcome expectations and utility. Then, use just the first letter of each part of motivational knowledge to stand for the whole connection, and make the letters into a mnemonic: AEIOU (Winnie, 1985). Motivational knowledge about a task is the complete set of AEIOUs plus the feelings that students have learned to attach to each of these five types of knowledge.

The AEIOUs are one part of overall motivational knowledge that these students have learned. Each A, E, I, O or U is connected to a constellation of feelings that a student remembers when thinking about one of the AEIOUs. Thus, to understand students' motivation thoroughly, teachers must understand much more than just a student's feelings. Teachers also must know what knowledge the student has about self and about tasks, as well as the connections between these types of knowledge and basic feelings such as satisfaction or boredom. Moreover, because motivational knowledge is learned, complete instruction means teaching students motivational knowledge just as much as it means teaching them task knowledge about history, reading and all the other parts of the school's curriculum.

Why Teachers' Prompts to Motivate can Fail

We have said that teachers prompt students to recall and use motivational knowledge and that motivational knowledge pertains to a task. Earlier, we gave an example of a teacher urging students to 'Think carefully!' We chose to label this a prompt because it is not guaranteed that students will have motivation to do what the teacher intends, namely, use the step-by-step method for writing clear paragraphs. What makes the guarantee less than certain? Here are four answers and some examples of each (Winne, 1982).

Students may not attend to the prompt
If Mark is busy trying to find his notes on Egypt, the topic he will write about, when the teacher says, 'Think carefully!', he may miss the prompt entirely. If so, the odds that he will select the intended method for writing good paragraphs may be small. In the teacher's view, Mark will not appear motivated if he does not use the method.

Students may misperceive the prompt
'Think carefully!' is quite a general injunction. Megan might perceive that the teacher wants her to spend a lot of effort thinking, but may be unclear about how she is to think. If Megan does not connect her teacher's prompt with the special method for writing paragraphs, she might select the wrong plan to use for this task. The teacher may conclude from this that Megan is not motivated.

Students may be incapable of carrying out what is prompted
Paul was absent for the last three days. He has not learned the method for writing that the teacher is prompting students to use. Kerry has not really mastered the method. Both of these students will not be able to use the method, and the teacher may interpret these students' behavior as low motivation.

Students may not be motivated to follow the prompt

Remembering the AEIOUs, there are at least five possible ways that the teacher's prompt can fail for those students who attended to it, correctly perceived that the prompt meant to use the method, and were capable of using the method to produce a clear essay. Let us briefly examine each connection in turn.

Viv participated in the practice session on using the writing method which the teacher scheduled for last Friday's English period. She applied the method so successfully that the teacher chose Viv's essay to read to the class. Unfortunately, Viv attributes her spectacular success to luck rather than to her ability. Rather than chance failure after such a glowing success, she elects to spend her time gathering facts so that her essay is 'just started' by the end of today's period.

Frank also has mastered the method, but he does not really believe he has done so. He was at the dentist during the period when the class practised using the method, so he did not have the opportunity to receive feedback about his competence. As he has a very low efficacy expectation, he decides to doodle instead of writing.

Lorne does not value writing. He has never found satisfaction in the process itself, and he feels that all the work he has applied to earn high marks just isn't worth it. Lorne's incentive is very low, so he has decided just to do something else.

Lorraine wonders about the purpose of this assignment. When the class practised using the method last Friday, Lorraine followed the method exactly, but the teacher did not say much about her essay. She is not sure what will happen if she tries to do today's assignment the same way. Lorraine has a weak outcome expectation.

Dawn has mastered the method, but she values her teacher's attention more than writing a good essay. The utility of writing a good essay is not as high as feigning a bit of incompetence and getting some extra attention. She selects a different task, one which involves manipulating her teacher.

Summary of teachers' failures to motivate

The first three ways that teachers' prompts to motivate students fail to relate directly to students' task knowledge. When students do not attend to prompts, they are not attuned to the general conditions of the task. When students misperceive a prompt, the teacher has not made the conditions of the task clear enough. If students are incapable of doing what is prompted, there are two possibilities: Either the conditions for students to perform the task are not conducive to carrying out task plans, or the students are not able to perform the task plans because these plans have not been acquired or mastered. Finally, each of the AEIOUs can explain why students are not motivated to do the task as the teacher intends. In these cases, students may not select to do the task which the teacher poses, may not carry out the task with a temperament that the teacher would view as 'good' temperament, or may not persist at the task.

Students can Motivate Themselves

One of the main goals of education is to enable students to *transfer* or to use what they know in new situations. For example, students who learned how to write clear paragraphs in English hopefully will transfer this skill to writing their biology lab reports and, if necessary, to recounting the events they observed about a car accident. Since the AEIOUs of motivational knowledge are types of information that students learn and connect to basic feelings, it follows that motivation also should transfer.

Teachers almost always hope that students will develop interest in the subject matter. How does interest develop? How can a teacher instruct so that students transfer interest they express in the classroom to other settings? These are a few of the central questions in a newly developing area of instructional psychology called self-regulation.

What is interest?
If a student teacher, let us call her Joan, is interested in instructional psychology (or Canadian history or learning French or gymnastics), what might this mean? Let us use the various elements of motivation — selection, temperament and persistence and the AEIOUs as a checklist for analyzing the notion of interest.

First, people interested in instructional psychology select to read about it and discuss it with friends. Second, such people do these things with a certain temperament. That is, they speak with excitement about topics in instructional psychology and even seem devoted to looking for opportunities to use instructional psychology as a way to talk about and examine teaching. Third, if they are really interested, they are persistent in these first two types of behavior (sometimes to the point of boring you with their persistence!). Notice what this part of the analysis has done. The mysterious thing called interest has been redefined in terms of what you can observe about Joan rather than leaving the notion of interest as a vague something that Joan just has or does not have.

How might Joan have learned to be interested in instructional psychology? The AEIOUs are the keys to this puzzle. Joan attributes her progress in using instructional psychology to what she knows and how much effort she applies in using her knowledge. She rarely says that luck or unusual help from other people explains how well she transfers her knowledge about instructional psychology to analyzing a lesson. Joan also has positive efficacy expectations. It may take a lot of effort to succeed at using instructional psychology to analyze a lesson but, in the end, she expects to do well at the task. Joan has incentive to transfer her knowledge about instructional psychology. It is simply enjoyable to understand why a lesson works or falters. She also knows, from past experience, the degree of understanding she will achieve for different levels of effort; she has clear outcome expectations. Finally, understanding a lesson in terms of principles of instructional psychology (e.g., realizing that students did not use a valuable memory plan because the student teacher she is observing prompted a plan that students had not practised well enough) is much more useful to her in planning her own lessons than simply seeing' that the lesson did not work. In each of these ways, except for incentive, Joan is regulating her approach to learning about teaching. What can be inferred from Joan's behavior is that she is really interested in trying to apply instructional psychology in her student teaching.

How might students develop interest?

Since Joan learned to be interested in applying instructional psychology, the obvious answer to this question is to teach her the right kinds of connections, described by the AEIOUs, that make up interest. For instance, how might you teach Joan attributions? Here is how one researcher (Morgan, 1985) taught students to be aware of their attributions.

Students taking a university course were taught a method for setting objectives for studying. An objective specified: (a) their task for a single session of studying, (b) study conditions (e.g., in a quiet setting like the library), (c) the plans they would apply (e.g., a procedural plan for reading the chapter assigned, then writing out an outline), and (d) the specific products they would create (e.g., capturing the main ideas and their structure). Then, the students were given a simple job. Every time they studied, they were to state just a few objectives, pick their own criterion that indicated when their objectives were met, and write down in a notebook how many of their objectives were actually met in each study session.

Students who regulated their studying according to this plan had a good opportunity to learn that the effort they put into studying contributed importantly to whether they met their objectives. Compared with students who studied using whatever methods they had developed through previous experience, students who regulated their studying found the course material more interesting. Equally as important, the students who regulated their studying learned more content than other students who used their usual studying methods. According to our previous analysis of interest, these two outcomes go hand in hand in prompting interest in the course topic.

If Joan had been a member of this class, she would have learned to attribute her successes to effort at using a plan and she would have had the knowledge needed to apply in observing her partner in student teaching. Both are indispensable parts of Joan's developing interest in instructional psychology. She would be in a good position to transfer the behaviors we would recognize as *having interest* to her while student teaching.

Expert Teaching is Good Instructional Psychology

We began this chapter by stating that practically everyone teaches. Parents teach their children, you teach your friends and you frequently teach yourself. To be sure, you have some notion of what to do when you are called upon to teach, but for the most part you would likely consider yourself a novice. In this closing section, we show how developing from a novice teacher into an expert teacher requires a large measure of knowledge about instructional psychology.

Whatever else might characterize an expert, it is certain that experts possess knowledge that novices do not. Experts are able to describe the subject matter of their expertise in finely grained ways. Finely grained descriptions allow experts to make distinctions that would not be apparent to the novice. Such descriptions almost always make use of a technical vocabulary because ordinary language often lacks the precision necessary for details and subtle distinctions.

Expert teachers are able to distinguish aspects of instruction that novices fail to notice. Even from our limited discussion of classroom tasks and student motivation, you have been introduced to new vocabulary and have seen complexities which may have gone unnoticed before. Classroom tasks, we hope, are no longer simply things that students do. They are, as we have noted, composed of a complex set of conditions, which are linked to students' cognitive plans and products. In a similar vein, student motivation is not simply a matter of students wanting to work hard or to be liked. As we have discussed, students are motivated by teachers' use of prompts and by the motivational knowledge they have about themselves as learners. In short, you have begun to make some fine distinctions using a technical vocabulary and you have enhanced your expertise.

Experts not only make subtle distinctions, but they also are able to explain why phenomena are as they are. An expert teacher knows how to instruct and why instruction is or is not successful. In our brief description of classroom tasks and student motivation, we have shown that effective instruction depends on a better knowledge of how classroom tasks and student motivation operate to influence student learning. We have seen why some classroom tasks are instructionally successful and why others fail to change students' thinking. Further, we have noted why some attempts to motivate students fail and why other attempts work. In all of this, you have begun to learn the how and the why of instruction.

In summary, an expert teacher knows about factors that influence how an instructional lesson develops and how each of these factors can affect student behavior. Such a teacher gathers observations about what each student brings to instruction and uses this information to match instruction to students. An expert teacher also possesses a well-developed technical vocabulary. This is not just a command of fancy words; rather, this vocabulary encodes deep knowledge that allows the teacher to characterize precisely what a student knows, thinks and feels, as well as the kinds of instruction that might help students achieve important objectives. In short, our parting message is a simple one: An expert teacher requires a sound grounding in the psychology of instruction.

Bibliography

BERLINER, D. and ROSENSHINE, B. (1987) *Talks to Teachers: A Festschrift for N.L. Gage*, New York, NY: Random House.

BROWN, J.S. and BURTON, R.R. (1979) 'Diagnostic models for procedural bugs in basic mathematical skills', *Cognitive Science, 2*, pp. 155–92.

CORNO, L. and MANDINACH, E.B. (1983) 'The role of cognitive engagement in classroom learning and motivation', *Educational Psychologist, 18*, pp. 88–108.

GAGNE, E.D. (1985) *The Cognitive Psychology of School Learning*, Boston, MA: Little-Brown.

GAGNE, R.M. (1985) *The Conditions of Learning*, (4th Edn), New York: NY: Holt, Rinehart and Winston.

LEVIN, J.R., McCORMICK, C.B., MILLER, G.E., BERRY, J.K. and PRESSLEY, M. (1982) 'Mnemonic versus nonmnemonic vocabulary-learning strategies for children', *American Educational Research Journal, 19*, pp. 121–36.

MARX, R.W. and WALSH, J. (1988) 'Learning from academic tasks', *Elementary School Journal, 88*, pp. 207–19.

MAYER, R.E. (1987) *Educational Psychology*, Boston, MA: Little-Brown.

MORGAN, M. (1985) 'Self-monitoring of attained subgoals in private study', *Journal of Educational Psychology, 77*, pp. 623–30.

NICKERSON, R.S., PERKINS, D.N. and SMITH, E.E. (Eds) *The Teaching of Thinking*, Hillsdale, NJ: Erlbaum.

NOVAK, J.D. and GOWIN, D.B. (1984) *Learning How to Learn*, New York, NY: Cambridge University Press.

STIPEK, D.J. (1988) *Motivation to Learn: From Theory to Practice*, Englewood Cliffs, NJ: Prentice-Hall.

WEINSTEIN, and MAYER, R.E. (1986) in WITTROCK, M. (Ed.) *Handbook of Research on Teaching*, (3rd Edn, pp. 315–27), New York, NY: Macmillan.

WINNE, P.H. (1982) 'Minimizing the black box problem to enhance the validity of theories about instructional effects', *Instructional Science , 11*, pp. 13–28.

WINNE, P.H (1985) 'Steps toward promoting cognitive achievements', *Elementary School Journal, 85*, pp. 673–93.

WINNE, P.H. (1987) 'Why process-product research cannot explain process-product findings and a proposed remedy: The cognitive mediational paradigm', *Teaching and Teacher Education, 3*, pp. 333–56.

WINNE, P.H. and MARX, R.W. (1982) 'Students' and teachers' views of thinking processes for classroom learning', *Elementary School Journal, 82*, pp. 493–518.

WINNE, P.H. and MARX, R.W. (1989) 'A cognitive processing analysis of motivation within classroom tasks', in AMES, R. and AMES, C. (Eds) *Research on Motivation in Education: Volume 3, Classroom Tasks and Student Thinking*, Orlando, FL: Academic Press.

13 The Role of the Practicum in the Preparation of Teachers

Norma I. Mickelson

Teacher Education as an Area of Concern

Teacher education has been an area of concern for decades — never more so than at the present time when the nature and efficacy of public education is being questioned both by the general public and by the teaching profession itself. In his well researched book, *A Place Called School*, Goodlad (1984) states not only that 'teacher education programs are disturbingly alike and almost uniformly inadequate', but also that 'the conventions to be broken and the traditions to be overcome ... are monumental' (p. 315).

Assuming this to be a valid observation, whether or not faculties of education are able to respond to legitimate criticisms is a matter of considerable speculation. Clifton (1985), for example, argues that because the overall ethos of teacher education programs is mythological and ritualistic rather than scholarly, most faculties of education are unable, even unwilling, to alter their habitual ways of doing things.

Certainly, from an historical perspective, teacher education has seemed remarkably impervious to change over the past several decades. In spite of this, however, continuous, though sporadic and frequently unsuccessful, attempts have been made to improve teacher preparation programs. Tyler (1987) believes that the overall effectiveness of education can be improved and that public calls for reform can be the stimuli for that improvement. Given that the will to reform teacher education is present, it is possible, if not probable, that a similar dynamism holds true for teacher education.

Among the conventions and traditions, which appear to be in need of major change, two stand out as being highly significant: first, the pervasive belief that teacher education programs lack intellectual substance and, second, the inadequacy of field experiences in the education of teachers.

The concern about the intellectual rigor of teacher education programs is widespread. Generally, education programs are thought to consist of methodology courses to the exclusion of substantive content. In fact, the phrase *mickey-mouse* has often been used to denote the lack of rigor in teacher education. Whether or not this is entirely justified, many scholars have noted this problem. According to Lanier and Little (1986) for example:

> the de-intellectualization of teacher education feeds on itself; the capable are discouraged from entering teacher education by what they see there ... Low status keeps the power to organize change out of the hands of those closest to the field. Teachers ... themselves assign teacher education a low priority. (p. 565)

Furthermore, according to Lanier and Little (1986) there appears to be a growing body of research indicating that the typical experience of teachers in schools is 'non-educative at best and mis-educative at worst' (p. 565). This is evident in practicum situations which can exemplify exactly the opposite of what the student is being taught at university. One such example would be where, in a language arts course, students are exposed to recent research in language acquisition while at the same time are observing in a classroom a typical phonics lesson and round-robin reading, both of which run contrary to recent research in literacy acquisition. School-experience programs, having been designed in various patterns to provide 'real-life experiences' at the pre-service level may well, in fact, simply reify the status quo. Also present practicum experiences often place student-teachers in situations of conflict — on the one hand in their university classes they are exposed to emerging research and theory insofar as pedagogy is concerned, while on the other hand they are expected to 'handle' classrooms where precisely the opposite of what they have been led to believe appropriate is happening.

Given a choice, however, student-teachers believe that their school experiences are more valuable to them in preparing to be teachers than are university courses. In a recent study at the University of Victoria (Mickelson, 1987) 86 per cent of the respondents at the elementary and secondary levels believed that in preparing to become teachers, school experiences were more helpful than was their university course work. When the data were stratified into elementary and secondary levels, results were remarkably similar. In both cases, over 85 per cent of the students placed more value on their practicum experiences than on their university course work.

It is not difficult, then, to see why educational practice in the public schools remains substantially unchanged over time. Student teachers appear to believe that what they see and experience in schools during their practicum is essentially what education should be. Thus, when they themselves become teachers in charge of their own classrooms, they simply recreate the status quo. Thus, the role of the practicum in the preparation of teachers becomes a highly significant factor for it is the practicum which appears to be the determining factor in establishing the *modus operandi* of neophyte teachers.

Unfortunately, theory and practice are rarely integrated in teacher education programs. Unless ways are found to integrate clinical experiences with academic course work, little if any real change in faculties of education is likely to occur. In considering the important influence of the practicum in determining the belief system of the student teacher, then, care must be taken to place the field experiences into the total context of teacher education. Changes made only to the practicum — to its length or placement in the school year, for example — will be cosmetic at best.

Much has been written about the practicum experience in teacher education and there is extensive documentation to suggest that it has been a recurring concern over the past several years. One wonders if anything new can be added.

What follows is an attempt to outline some of the major concerns relative to teacher education in general and the practicum in particular, and to suggest courses of action which might be followed if any real change is to occur. The viewpoints expressed are based on long experience working with the pre-service and in-service education of teachers.

General Issues in Teacher Education

One of the first issues to be addressed has to do with the calibre of students entering teacher-education programs. In short, it needs to be of the highest possible standard. It is a cliche to suggest that in order to facilitate students' higher order thinking, the facilitators themselves must be able to think conceptually about important issues. Much has been said about literacy and teachers. Popham and Kilby (1987), for example, note that in every subject matter area it seems justifiable to expect competence beyond a basic skills level. There can be no question that in order to teach writing, teachers themselves need to be able to write; in order to teach mathematics, teachers need to understand the essential nature of the discipline; and in order to teach science, teachers must understand the scientific method and model it in their daily classroom practice. A superficial understanding of a discipline can only result in a superficial approach to the education of children. This again underscores the need for prospective teachers to be competent in those areas in which they intend to work.

It does not require a social revolution in order to ensure that only the best possible candidates enter the teaching profession. What is required is simply determination on the part of faculties of education to admit only those students who have demonstrated a high level of achievement. What constitutes academic excellence, of course, is a matter for each institution to decide. However, a combination of a high grade point average (A or B, perhaps) and recommendations from previous teachers as to the leadership potential of applicants should ensure that only top-level candidates are admitted. Academic excellence and leadership potential are not end products in teacher education — they are only initial requirement.

Insofar as standards of excellence are concerned, a second aspect of teacher-education programs must be addressed, and this has to do with sponsor teachers. Students in education faculties who are preparing to be teachers need to be exposed to those who themselves are master teachers. Far too often, no careful selection of sponsor teachers is made and students find themselves in classrooms where neither competent management nor appropriate teaching occurs. This is not a new problem. As long ago as the early 1970s, Goodlad (1970) was arguing for cooperation between schools and teacher-preparation institutions in identifying master teachers and designating appropriate schools as *key* or *demonstration* schools. While it might be argued that it is difficult to identify master teachers in the absence of universally accepted criteria, principals can identify those members of their staffs who are able actively to engage their students, who demonstrate through their evaluations that their pupils are making progress, who are enthusiastic, and who are current in their knowledge of the disciplines in which they are working.

The interaction of top-calibre students with master teachers would make possible practicum situations in which the negotiation of appropriate learning experiences could occur. All too often, however, student teachers feel that they must imitate exactly the management style and pedagogical practices of their sponsor teachers. When asked what they considered to be the most serious limitation of their practicum experiences, professional year students[1] replied along the following lines:

'having to teach in the established manner'

'not enough freedom to set up my own behavior management systems'

'inability to organize the daily schedule to my liking'

'no choice of what to teach'

'it's like being a teenager. You are always told what to do.'

Faculties of education very often feed this prototypic approach to clinical experiences by insisting that sponsor teachers outline for their students with careful precision exactly what is to be taught and then requiring them to plan each lesson in detailed, pre-ordained form before they ever go near a classroom. Very little opportunity is provided for student teachers to interact with sponsor teachers on the basis of having been participant-observers in the classroom. What seems to be missing is a questioning perspective — one characteristic of an ethnographer, for example. In fact, as Wood (1985) notes, such a perspective has the potential for building bridges between practice, theory and research, inducing, as it does, observation and reflectiveness. On this basis, then, student teachers and their sponsors might consider their shared experiences in negotiating a suitable practicum grounded in the actual context of a specific classroom situation. In the typical practicum, however, the focus is on 'teaching' with little or no attention paid to how learning occurs, either on the part of the student-teachers themselves, the sponsor teachers, or the pupils in the classroom.

If it were ever to be the case that faculties of education were prepared to accept only the highest quality applicants and master teachers to serve as sponsors, an interesting question arises as to the role of the university supervisor. All too often the university faculty member is seen to be simply an observer. Students are 'taught' methods courses in isolation from the classrooms in which they will be teaching and faculty supervisors drop in occasionally to see how the students are doing.

University faculty members presumably are competent in their disciplines. They attempt to transmit essential concepts about teaching and learning to student teachers who, as student teachers, are expected to translate theory into educational practice at the same time as meeting the expectations of their sponsor teachers. Unfortunately, however, very often these sponsor teachers, faced with the day-to-day running of their classes, are unaware of what is being taught at the university or, indeed, of the fact that student teachers should be encouraged to think for themselves in translating current theory into educational practice. What is important to the classroom teachers is maintaining their normal, curricular momentum without too much interruption. Thus the student teachers are faced with a dilemma — a dichotomous set of expectations which is almost impossible to meet.

Clearly, an entirely different model of supervision needs to be developed. One possibility would be to have the faculty member, the school sponsor and the student teacher work as a team for purposes of developing appropriate practicum and evaluation activities. All three would participate in the teaching and learning activities and would negotiate meaningful practicum experiences. Through open discussions based on observations about the nature of the class, the strategies currently in use by the teacher and recent methodological and pedagogical developments, an approach would be rationalized which would prove to be a learning experience for all three members of the team. In a very real sense, a small educational community could develop. Scott Peck (1987) argues that rarely do individuals develop any real sense of community in their professional lives. This seems particularly true of teachers. In a peculiar kind of way, teachers, although constantly involved with people, find their profession a lonely one. Rarely, once certified, do they ever see what others do. Rarely do they share their concerns, their insecurities, or even their successes in professional interaction. In the teaching profession homogeneity, not heterogeneity, is valued. And yet, as Scott Peck argues, even in a group in which individuality is encouraged and in which individual differences flourish, consensus can evolve. What is being considered here is a process of consultation, of collaboration and of negotiation within a practicum experience. Boundaries between teacher, student teacher and faculty member blur: Each becomes a member of a team, a teacher, and a learner.

It is doubtful if such a model has ever really been attempted in teacher education. Rather, in a linear fashion, student teachers are exposed to methods courses, to pre-planning lessons, to executing them and finally to being evaluated on their performances. Unless this sequential approach to teacher education is significantly altered, very little, if any, degree of change can be anticipated in educational practice. The practicum experience offers one of the few real opportunities for significantly improving teacher education and, subsequently, education itself.

One of the most significant problems which student teachers face is exhaustion. In a recent interview, one student teacher stated: 'I am always pressed to perform. There is never time to be reflective or contemplative'. According to Brown (1987), in fact, it is not uncommon for students today to be criticized for this very lack of contemplation and thoughtfulness. Thoughtfulness, he argues, is characterized by careful, reasoned thinking; yet many schools provide too few incentives for reflection and problem solving and at the same time provide too many incentives for just getting by. Undoubtedly, this is a common experience in teacher education. When asked the question, 'What did you find to be the most difficult aspect of your practica?', students invariably included a concern about time. 'Lack of time', 'inadequate time', 'overload', and 'time management' were commonly stated problems.

Dealing with the myriad of tasks involved with educational management is also a problem of significance for students in a practicum experience. It is not only demanding of time but also exacts a high energy toll. Friemier (1987), suggests that

Getting the best and brightest teachers into the teaching profession is not enough. We must stop undercutting teachers by creating conditions of work that blunt their enthusiasm and stifle their creativity. (p. 9)

He goes on to say that empowering teachers is the key; by *empowerment* he meant giving teachers opportunities to make professional decisions and implement curricular practices which lead toward the realization of established goals. Teachers are professionals and they must be treated as such if the profession itself is to achieve a stature in society which recognizes education as one of the keystones of progress. Where teachers are empowered, they are able to serve as models for neophytes with whom they are working. If this is true of the mature professional, it is even more applicable to the student teacher. Practicum experiences need to be devised which do not totally deplete the energy and drain the creative potential of student teachers. Working cooperatively in pairs might be one way to accomplish this as would the provision of time in the day for reflection and discussion. Daily planning time might also be provided so that student teachers would not be faced with late-night planning sessions. Furthermore, a careful analysis needs to be made as to the efficacy of having student teachers write out in explicit detail what it is they intend to do in the classroom. To suggest, as many professionals do, that in the practicum experience the student should 'sink or swim' or should 'cope fully with the real world' is to deny the growth process. It seems equally as spurious to suggest, when a student is not placed with a master teacher but rather with one less than competent, that the practicum experience will be a lesson in how not to teach.

One of the hallmarks of a professional is an attitude of informed inquiry. This is particularly significant for teachers who have the responsibility of evaluating not only student performance but also program effectiveness and their own growth as professionals. Burdened as they are with both pedagogical and management demands and with conflicting expectations of performance in their practicum, it is highly unlikely that student teachers will display either the will or the capacity for systematic and scholarly problem solving, for evaluating their own performance, or for considering program evaluation. Indeed many, if not most, student teachers will rarely experience situations where teachers and/or faculty members approach their tasks as participant observers or researchers. Characteristically many teachers look to curriculum guides, work-shop leaders, textbooks or university methods instructors for 'how to' ideas. Frank Smith (1986) argues strongly for the return of professionalism to the teaching force. He notes that good teachers

> do not allow themselves or their 'apprentices' to engage in pointless, ritualistic activities. Instead, . . . (they) manifest attitudes and behaviors that learners become interested in manifesting themselves . . . . (p. 171).

Smith goes on to decry the absence of good models of teaching and inquiry for student teachers. He states that

> Some of the most rigid and unimaginative teaching practices I have seen have been in the daily routine of teacher preparation in colleges of education. There is a vicious circle here. Teachers are taught to perpetuate in grade schools the way they usually are. The teachers are taught so effectively that many never learn that there is an alternative — and the college professor's justification is that they are preparing teachers for the schools that already exist. (p. 202)

The models of clinical experiences or practica currently in use in most teacher education programs hardly encourage active inquiry. One of the significant questions in preparation programs, then, must be 'how to overcome the record of intellectual dependency' when 'the ethos of the occupation is tilted against engagement in pedagogical inquiry' (Lortie, 1975, p. 550). Unless faculties and colleges of education are prepared to model and encourage active inquiry in their programs, particularly in their clinical experiences, it is hardly likely that significant change will occur or indeed that teaching will ever fully develop the degree of professionalism necessary to effect change in the system. Providing time for student reactions and suggestions might go a long way towards helping faculties realize the problems encountered by students in their practica. Whether or not faculties of education are sincerely interested in listening, however, is an open question.

Not only should student teachers themselves become active questioners in their clinical experiences but they should also be encouraged to focus on the current (and expanding) research base available with respect to teaching and learning. As Othanel Smith notes (1985), 'principles should be taught in such a way as to enable practitioners to place a given practice in context and to understand why it is effective' (p. 689).

The issue of exploring the research base for educational practice becomes critically important both in pre-service practicum experiences and in the in-service education of teachers. It simply is not good enough, once having qualified for an education degree or a teaching certificate, to expect a permanent sinecure. An attitude of continuous, life-long learning needs to be generated and fostered during professional pre-service programs and practicum experiences and carried into an individual's active, professional career. During the past decade, for example, so great have been the new insights into the nature of human learning, particularly with respect to literacy acquisition, for example, that teachers trained even as recently as ten years ago are seriously outdated and handicapped in their ability to generate learning in their students. Wittrock (1980) and his colleagues at the University of California among others, have underscored the importance of active involvement in learning. They use the term *generative learning* to denote the importance of individuals being able to generate or activate their own learning strategies. Goodman (1986), Bruner (1986) and Wigginton (1985) have similarly detailed the importance of active or generative learning in the educative process.

While exceptions do occur, unless the genesis of active inquiry is firmly established in pre-service programs and clinical experiences, it is highly unlikely that generative learning will develop later. And yet, the essence of professionalism rests with precisely this attribute. Pre-service education should, of course, translate into in-service enquiry and life-long learning. When teachers do not feel challenged and personally rewarded in their occupational activities, they might as well leave the profession, particularly if they find it undervalued and lacking in professional rewards. A longitudinal study of North Carolina teachers, for example, revealed 'among other findings that the most academically proficient teachers are also the most likely to leave teaching. The result: a steadily deteriorating talent pool' (Schlechty and Vance, 1981, p. 106).

In the face of considerable evidence that those who choose to major in teacher education are, as a group, less academically able than most other college majors (Weaver, 1979, p. 30), it hardly seems defensible that even among this group, the most talented may well be leaving the profession. Until and unless significant changes occur in the ways in which we attract and educate students in our teacher-education programs, Goodlad's (1984) concerns about implementing programs of teacher education of such length, depth and quality that they will be effectively separated from most of the conventional ways of teaching may well be prophetic. Unfortunately:

> Studies of the context of teacher education ... convey one over-
> riding impression: Institutional policies, structures and resources that
> might be expected to foster the quality of teaching and teacher
> education appear to do the opposite. (Lanier and Little, 1986, p. 565)

Those responsible for teacher education and, in particular, for the practicum, have tended to focus not on substantive issues but on delivery systems
and the form and duration of clinical experiences. Perhaps, we would agree
with Shakespeare that 'The fault, dear Brutus, is not in our stars but in
ourselves that we are underlings'.[2]

The Practicum as a Focus of Teacher Preparation

Imbedded as they are in university degree programs, practica take various
forms. Many teachers preparation programs are generic in nature — that is,
they are housed in faculties of education and carry with them an education
degree (a Bachelor of Education degree, for example). In these programs,
clinical experiences often begin in the first or second year of the program and
these are largely observational in nature. The actual practicum — in which
students practise-teach — usually occurs in the final or next to final year of
the degree program.

Other teacher-qualification programs are diploma-type programs and
generally build on an already earned Bachelor's degree in a faculty other than
education (often Arts, Fine Arts or Science). These programs are normally
either one or two years in duration and the practicum occurs in the final
phases of the diploma year(s).

Practicum sequences, either in degree or diploma programs, take various
forms. Traditionally students participate in two or three practica of fairly short
duration (two or three weeks in length). Often the first practicum will occur in
the fall term of the school year, the second one in the spring term and the
final practicum will be held close to the end of the school year. The obvious
rationale underlying this traditional pattern has been to alternate clinical
experiences with on-campus work, to enable students to experience different
age-grade levels and alternative teaching styles, and to allow them time to
internalize their experiences and reflect upon what they have learned as
student teachers. Unfortunately for many, this approach is perceived as being
disjointed and piecemeal. Finding themselves in three different classes and
often having to adjust to three changing teaching styles and organizational
patterns, students often became overwhelmed. Furthermore, the major
emphasis of their practica is one of organization and management, not educational leadership or the development of a personal approach to teaching.

In an attempt to avoid this problem, while at the same time providing
alternating clinical and academic experiences, many schools of education

maintained the three-practicum pattern but had the students return to the same class for all three practica. While this avoided the piecemeal aspect of the practicum and involved only one sponsor teacher, it had the disadvantage of exposing the student to only management system and a single teaching style. Where the mentor was both competent and imaginative, students appeared to flourish. On the other hand, those placed in less than optimal situations floundered.

A third common practicum pattern is sequential in nature. In this model, students undertake their academic work in large blocks of time (usually half a year) either before or after an extended practicum. The rationale underlying this approach is that students will have a long period of time in the classroom and, if the practicum occurs first, will be able to consolidate their experiences as a foundation for their academic work. On the other hand, if the clinical experiences follow the academic term, students are expected to be able to apply the theory they have been studying to their pedagogical and management strategies.

Several problems emerge in this model, however. In the first place, it is controversial as to whether the practicum should precede or follow the academic work. Some faculty members believe that, having experienced a term in a classroom, student-teachers will be better able to assimilate academic work because they have had a broad experiential base on which to build. Simon Fraser University in British Columbia adopts this stance and places students in classrooms for an extended block of time before they attend University classes. On the other hand, two other provincial institutions, the University of Victoria and the University of British Columbia choose to have their students attend classes on campus before they undertake a practicum. It is of interest to note that there appears to be little, if any, difference in the success and/or failure rate of student teachers trained in these two types of programs. What does appear to be significant is the students' perceptions across programs that large blocks of time should be devoted to the practicum experience. Others, however, feel that a practicum before the academic work places students in jeopardy insofar as they have no theoretical rationale for what they are doing.

Another approach to the practicum is one often called *internship*. In this type of program, students spend their entire professional year in the school setting taking their academic work concurrently with their clinical experiences. In some internship programs, students complete some of their course work before the school year begins (during a summer-session, for example) and some of it at the conclusion of the school year. This is a demanding approach to teacher preparation and students appear to have mixed feelings regarding it. They appear to believe that there are obvious advantages but they also enunciate several concerns. In answer to the question, 'What did you find to be the most valuable aspect of your practicum?', intern students responded:

'working with experienced teachers'

'gradual progression into the system'

'taking full responsibility for the classroom'

'beginning on the first day of school'

'long-term planning'

'working up to 100 per cent teaching time'

'having full involvement in all aspects of the school'

'the length of the practicum'

'realizing one's own capabilities'

'feedback from the sponsor teacher'.

On the other hand, they stated, for example, that they were concerned about:

'operating in another teacher's environment for so long'

'adapting to the assigned teaching'

'maintaining my energy level'

'remaining calm and organized'

'attending classes at the same time'

'handling the overwhelming responsibilities'

'overload'.

When asked how they would change their practicum program if they had the opportunity to do so, students in internship typically responded in the following way:

'complete course work before the practicum'

'be certain that supervisors are in agreement about expectations'

'refurbish and better develop the methods courses'

'provide more contact with the other interns'

'shorten university classes during the practicum'

'observe more teachers'

'allow me more freedom in the classroom'

'create methods courses that are applicable to the practicum'.

One of the major concerns about internship programs has to do with the obvious entrenchment of the status quo. Clearly, after having been in one class for such a long period of time, much of what the classroom teacher does will have become consolidated as 'the-way-to-go' for the student teacher. Organizational patterns and management strategies will have transferred themselves from the teacher to the student. Given the present concerns about North American education, one cannot help but wonder if teacher cloning through longer practicum is appropriate. Certainly, *more* is not necessarily *better*, in spite of the pervasive belief that longer practicum periods will result in better teacher education. At issue is the quality, not the quantity or duration, of the experience. Unless students are exposed to experiences which exemplify the implementation of current theory to practice, they are not likely to consider their university education relevant to their practicum experiences. In fact, quite the opposite will occur.

A final approach to practicum experiences that will be discussed is imbedded in competency or performance-based education. Although it would be comforting to believe that a set of definable competencies for teaching could be developed and handled sequentially by all candidates for entry to the profession, the probability of its accomplishment has not been borne out in experience. In 1974, David Maxwell argued that the teacher-student relationship is one characterized by heterogeneity, not homogeneity. He noted that:

> An approach borrowed from the natural sciences has been transferred to a far more complex setting in which the assumptions so readily met in the natural sciences ... are inseparable barriers. To think that we can stipulate the 'specific behaviors' of the competent teacher ... is not to think. To believe that 'research' will provide us these specific behaviors and the means to measure them reveals ignorance of the research methodology upon which the model rests. (p. 311)

Micro-teaching as a solution to many of the problems associated with the practicum experience in many programs arose out of the notion of performance-based teacher education. The idea was that students would work with small groups of other students (usually, in fact, peers) to demonstrate competencies related to the teaching act. This model presupposed that teaching sequences could be defined, mastered and transferred from the university campus to the classroom at some later date. Unfortunately, much of the early promise of micro-teaching was not borne out in fact. Success in micro-teaching, conducted in university classrooms or laboratories and isolated from the reality of large classes and complex pedagogical expectations, did not, in fact, transfer to actual classrooms.

Many of the attempts at reform in teacher education have focused only on structural change involving the practicum — where to place it in the program and how long to make it, for example. Rarely have the qualitative aspects of the practicum experiences or the dynamics of clinical, cooperative learning involving all participants — sponsor teachers, student teachers, pupils and faculty members — been addressed. If the role of the practicum in the preparation of teachers is to reach its potential, significant changes in its conceptualization and implementation appear to be necessary. Perhaps the first and most important task to be undertaken is a critical appraisal of precisely those changes which appear to be required, of the 'conventions to be broken and the traditions to be overcome' (Goodlad, 1984, p. 315).

Summary

That students believe the practicum experience to be the most valuable part of their teacher preparation programs is not a novel idea. It is, however, an important one. Indeed, it may well be that student perceptions about the importance of the practicum to their growth as professionals are valid. For better or worse, entry to the teaching profession is gained by way of the practicum. The model of teaching and learning that is internalized through the practicum experience may well be the pedagogical determiner for the teacher for years to come. Therefore its importance can hardly be over-stressed.

In order to improve both teacher education and, indeed, the quality of education itself, a critical re-assessment of present teacher preparation programs appears essential. Such re-assessment will neither be easy nor will it be comfortable. Certain conditions appear to be necessary. To begin with, faculties of education must accept only students of the highest academic caliber. Monitoring and continuous evaluation of these students throughout the program need to occur to ensure that the high entrance standards are maintained. In addition, the candidate's professional suitability for working with children must be continuously evaluated. The practicum is probably the only forum where this can occur with any real validity.

Only master teachers should be chosen as practicum sponsors. The practicum itself needs to be a negotiated experience involving the student, the sponsor teacher and the university faculty member acting as a minute community of scholars dedicated to supporting each other's growth and development as true professionals. All are learners and all are teachers.

The conditions under which student teachers work in their practicum need to be modified to insure time for discussion, for thoughtful reflection about what is going on, and for contemplation which allows for creativity to surface. Professional empowerment does not arise out of exhaustion; it develops as a function of feeling in charge of one's experiences. Furthermore, an attitude of active inquiry needs to be fostered during clinical experiences. Students should be encouraged to ask 'why' and to question the pedagogical practices to which they are exposed and for which they ultimately become responsible. Unless practising teachers accept and encourage their student teachers in an active, vital inquiry orientation, many of the most competent among them may well leave the profession.

Any serious attempt at reform will require not only a program of planned change but also a significant period of time to develop. Tyler (1987) believes, for example, that 'it takes six or seven years to get a reform really working as intended' (p. 279).

Finally, faculties of education, charged with the responsibility of teacher preparation, will need to demonstrate not only the will to examine their current practices but also the ability to bring about change.

Notes

1 In this study, 175 elementary and secondary student-teachers completed a survey questionnaire. The questionnaire explored student-teacher perceptions about their practicum experiences. Questions were either (1) forced choice, such as: Rank in order (1 being the best) who was most helpful to you in completing your practicum successfully: Methods Teachers _____, Seminar Leader _____, Supervising Classroom Teacher _____, Fellow Students _____, Faculty Supervisor _____; or open ended, such as: 'What did you find to be the most difficult part of your practicum?' Data from this study are used throughout this chapter.

2 Quote from Julius Caesar, Act 1, Scene 2, Line 134.

Bibliography

BROWN, R. (1987) 'Who is accountable for thoughtfulness?' *Phi Delta Kappan*, 1987, pp. 49–52.

BRUNER, J. (1986) *Actual Minds, Possible Worlds*, Cambridge, MA: Harvard Educative Press.

CLIFTON, R.A. (1985) Knowledge and Mythology in Teacher Education. Paper presented at the Annual Meeting of the Canadian Society for the Study of Education, May, 1985.

FRIEMIER, J. (1987) 'Bureaucracy and the neutering of teachers', *Phi Delta Kappan*, 1987, pp. 9–14.

GOODLAD, J. (1984) *A Place Called School*, New York: McGraw Hill.

GOODLAD, J. (1970) 'The reconstruction of teacher education', *Teachers College Record*, 1970, pp. 61–72.

GOODMAN, K. (1986) *What's Whole in Whole Language*, Toronto: Scholastic.

LANIER, J. and LITTLE, J. (1986) in WITTROCK, M. (Ed.) *Handbook of Research on Teaching*, New York: Macmillan.

LORTIE, D. (1975) *School Teacher*, Chicago: University of Chicago Press.

MAXWELL, W.D. (1974) 'PBTE: A case of the emperor's new clothes', *Phi Delta Kappan*, 1974, pp. 306–11.

MICKELSON, N.I. (1987) *Unpublished* paper presented at Westcast Conference, 1987.

PECK, M.S. (1987) *The Different Drum. Community Making and Peace*, New York: Simon and Schuster.

POPHAM, J.W. and KILBY, W.N. (1987) 'Recertification tests for teachers: A defensible safeguard for society', *Phi Delta Kappan*, 1987, pp. 45–9.

SCHLECHTY, P.C. and VANCE, V. (1981) 'Do academically able teachers leave education? The North Carolina case', *Phi Delta Kappan*, October, 1981, pp. 106–12.

SMITH, F. (1986) *Insult to Intelligence*, New York: Arbor House.

SMITH, O.B. (1985) 'Research bases for teacher education', *Phi Delta Kappan*, 1985, pp. 685–91.

TYLER, R.W. (1987) 'Education reforms', *Phi Delta Kappan*, 1987, pp. 277–80.

WEAVER, T.W. (1979) 'In search for quality: The need for talent in teaching', *Phi Delta Kappan*, 1979, p. 29.

WIGGINTON, E. (1985) *Sometimes a Shining Moment*, New York: Doubleday.

WITTROCK, M. (Ed.) (1980) *The Brain and Psychology*, Toronto: Academic Press.

WOOD, P. (1985) 'Sociology ethnography and teacher practice', *Teaching and Teacher Education*, 1, (1).

14 Professionalization and Foundational Studies in Teacher Education

Romulo F. Magsino

The Pressure to Professionalize Teaching

The last decade has seen some vicious and sensationalistic media assault on the teaching profession.[1] Cover or article titles, such as 'Help! Teachers Can't Teach!' (1980), 'Why Teachers Fail' (1984), 'Why Our Teachers Can't Teach' (1984) and 'Can the School Be Saved?' (1983), grabbed public attention and subjected teachers to unfair and demeaning generalizations. Superficial and selective, the articles highlighted alleged cases of teacher illiteracy and other incompetences as if they were true of all those in the teaching profession. Their authors also gave the impression that public disenchantment or dissatisfaction with teachers predominantly characterized the mood of the time.

In reality, however, these articles were less than convincing. Thus, in the United States, only 2 per cent of all American public school parents surveyed by the 21st Annual Gallup Poll of attitudes toward public schools gave such schools a rating of *fail*. On the other hand, 57 per cent of the parents rated these schools *A* or *B* (Elam and Gallup, 1989). This should reflect favorably on public school teachers. In Canada, the 1984 survey of the Canadian Education Association showed that 46 per cent of all respondents gave the rating of *A* or *B* to the quality of teaching in Canadian schools (Livingstone and Hart, 1987, p. 7). In the Canadian province of Ontario, only 6 per cent of responding parents surveyed by Goldfarb Consultants were not satisfied with teachers at all; 20 per cent were very satisfied, 57 per cent somewhat satisfied and 18 per cent a little satisfied, this despite the article's title, 'Teacher Rated as only 'Fair,' *Star* Survey Says' (Schiller, 1987, p. 10). With the exception of Quebec, where schools were assessed rather badly, 55 per cent of all respondents in the rest of the Canadian provinces believed that the quality of schooling today is better than that of their own in the past (Livingstone and Hart, *ibid.*, p. 8). These statistical reports do not seem to indicate massive public alarm over the quality of schools or teaching at all.

Yet respected reports appear to agree that 'teachers and, by implication,

teacher training programs, are responsible' for the perceived crisis in education (Weis, 1989, p. 2). Such reports as *A Nation at Risk* (National Commission on Excellence in Education, 1983)[2] and *Making the Grade* (Twentieth
Century Fund Task Force on Federal Elementary and Secondary Education
Policy, 1983) in the United States, and the 'Report Card on [Ontario] Schools'
(1987) in Canada all appear to place substantial blame on teachers and teacher
education. This penchant for criticism of teachers and teacher education has
been exhibited recently in Ontario where a report by Fullan and Connelly
(1987) has concluded that students are being short-changed by the current
teacher education system which fills schools with young teachers who are not
ready to assume full responsibility in their classrooms.

Unfortunately, the implications drawn against teachers and teacher
education may prove unfair. For example, after analysis of the qualifications of
education students and the conditions of teaching in school systems, Kerr
(1983, p. 131) suddenly and unabashedly concluded that the American
'teaching corps is unacceptably incompetent'. Yet, as Weis (1989) and Cornbleth (1989) pointed out, the reports or studies on which such a judgment is
based have undertaken no sustained investigation of the extent to which (if at
all) the quality of teaching has declined over the years, or of the degree to
which teachers (and teacher educators) are responsible for the alleged failures
of pupils and the public schools. As is now known, teachers very often have
no control over many societal and pupil-related factors affecting the processes
and outcomes of instruction. Inescapably we may accept that our teaching
cadre harbors some incompetent teachers. How many they are and what
causes directly account for their incompetence, we still do not know. The
task, however, is not to point fingers at any one factor related to their
performance until satisfactory analysis of all relevant considerations has been
undertaken. It may be that Kerr (1983) was more to the point when she
asserted as follows: 'There is a disturbing duplicity in a society that itself fails
to create conditions that would foster teaching competence and then complain
of incompetent teachers' (p. 131).

Every sector interested in and affected by education has obligations to
contribute to the quality of teaching. Faculties of education have a primary
duty to determine the kind of teacher education required to promote teaching
competence from day one of the teacher's involvement in the field. Aspiring
education students, on the other hand, have the obligation to participate
actively in the preparation process not only by learning the teacher education
curriculum but also by developing foundational understandings underlying
teaching activities. Without these understandings and, perhaps, without their
appreciation, teaching practice will prove unintelligent and meaningless. In
more cryptic terms, teachers might just as well discard their aspirations for
the status of professionals.

In the subsequent sections of this chapter, it will be shown that the
development of competent professional teachers is an eminently reasonable
aspiration for faculties of education. It will be argued that professionalization

of teaching requires viewing the preparation of teachers not so much in terms of standardized teaching competencies as in terms of interpretive and critical understanding promoted by foundational studies. In pursuit of this argument, this chapter will discuss the notion of a profession and then examine whether teaching may be regarded as such. It will then explore the role of foundational studies in teacher preparation in faculties of education.

The Notion of a Profession

The status of teaching among various pursuits in society has been contentious. Corwin (1965), Lieberman (1958) and Ornstein (1976) have denied full professional status to teaching. They, however, view it as a semi-profession inching its way toward achieving full professional status. Other writers, no less skeptical of the status of teaching, further doubt the desirability of teachers' aspiration for professionalization. Not only is teaching lacking in arcane knowledge that marks the true, traditional professional; professionalization could also open up the floodgates preventing, until now, the inundating flow of malpractice lawsuits against teachers (Covert, 1975 and 1988).

A plausible way toward the resolution of this issue requires determination of the criteria built into the notion of a profession and then an assessment of the extent to which teaching satisfies these criteria. The task is far from easy: Writers on the topic disagree among themselves in their characterization of the notion of profession. Becker (1962) surveyed various authorities on the topic and found them holding as follows:

Abraham Flexner — a profession
1 involves intellectual activities
2 requires these activities to be learned
3 involves practical, not simply theoretic or academic activities
4 involves organized activities
5 involves the use of techniques
6 is motivated by altruism;

Carl Saunders — a profession
1 involves the application of intellectual techniques to the ordinary business of life
2 involves techniques acquired as a result of prolonged and specialized training

Ralph Tyler — a profession
1 has a generally recognized code of ethics
2 has a technical organization based on general principles rather than on rules of thumb;

Lloyd Blausch — a profession
1 involves specialized skills based on long study and training
2 measures success in terms of quality of service

  3 has a professional association for maintaining and improving service and for enforcing a code of conduct.

Other authors have examined the notion of a profession and come up with their own formulation. Thus, Cogan (1953) has concluded that a profession has the following elements:

  1 Practice is founded on relevant abilities and on understanding of the theoretical structure of some department of learning or science
  2 The abilities and understanding are applied to vital practical affairs of human beings
  3 Practices are modified by knowledge of a generalized nature and by accumulated wisdom and experience
  4 Its first ethical imperative is the altruistic service to the client.

Hall (1972), on the other hand, has offered the following:

  1 use of a professional organization
  2 belief in public service
  3 sense of calling
  4 belief in self-regulation
  5 autonomy.

The sampling of formulations provided by writers will show the lack of unanimity in their thinking with respect to what criteria determine the professional status of a given calling or occupation. Though certain elements or criteria appear with some degree of frequency, no one set appears to be the same as another. In fact, Becker (1962) found that, using any given set, it is questionable whether any profession actually and fully satisfies all relevant criteria. Thus, in the case of the medical profession, substantial numbers of practitioners are under the employ of governmental institutions and consequently to some degree are impeded in the exercise of their autonomy. Yet there is no questioning of their professional status.

Becker's strategy in attempting to slide over the difficulties was to sidetrack the question of what a profession *is* and to argue that the term *profession* is an honorific, normative one. In other words, the designation of *profession* is a sign that practitioners falling under the designation are willing to see themselves as bound by a 'set of interconnected characteristics which symbolize a morally praiseworthy kind of occupational organization' (p. 34). In a sense, for him, the designation is an ideal to be lived up to; a group of practitioners may be regarded as professionals to the degree that they satisfy the ideals of their practice. Using his strategy, Becker analyzed the various criteria available in the literature and came up with certain criteria or characteristics on which substantial agreement was obtained (pp. 33–40):

  1 possession of monopoly on some esoteric and difficult body of knowledge

2 knowledge is considered necessary for the continued functioning of society
3 practitioners have altruistic motivation and responsibilities are enforced through a code of conduct
4 practitioners occupy esteemed position in society.

For purposes of this discussion, we may assume that Becker was precise in his analysis and survey of various existing formulations. Nevertheless, it may be observed that he has failed to identify the basic, distinguishing and necessary normative standards for determining whether an occupation of calling is a profession. An examination of the ideal criteria or standards he has enumerated will reveal that they are not equally on all fours. A full argumentation on behalf of what will subsequently be presented as necessary criteria cannot be undertaken on this occasion. Nevertheless, there are good grounds for agreeing with Blackington (1968) that, among the criteria surveyed so far, possession of complex knowledge and understanding guiding occupational practice may count as the necessary and distinguishing mark of a profession. Blackington also suggests that public service is a basic, distinguishing criterion. However, it will not do. It may be necessary but it certainly is not a distinguishing criterion. Just about any legitimate occupation may fulfill an admirable and important societal service. Farming and fishing, generally not regarded as profession, are certainly indispensable services to society. Prestige, autonomy, code of ethics, professional organization, long training and selective entry will not do either. Autonomy may be regarded as a feature of a profession because its practitioners possess requisite knowledge and understanding which justify their claim to expertise and therefore freedom from interference in their practice. Long training becomes an added feature in determining membership because the mastery of complex knowledge, understanding and skills makes necessary some extended initiation and immersion into the profession's body of knowledge and know-how. A code of ethics is developed insofar as the exercise of knowledge and understandings generates power on individuals who may have to be regulated to avoid abuse and indiscretion. A professional organization is formed and selective entry is instituted to insure that only those with actual expertise are legitimated for practice and to enforce internal rules among the possessors of professional status. Finally prestige, if not wealth, could very well accrue to a professional practitioner who has successfully met the requirements of selective membership. All these, however, depend on practitioners' possession of expert knowledge and understanding generally not available to laypeople. In light of the above, the following may reasonably be offered as a definition: A profession is an occupation whose effective practice depends on possession of complex knowledge and understanding by its practitioners and on subsequent arrangements intended to insure appropriate public service. This definition, together with the various suggested criteria mentioned, may be captured by the following schema which categorizes such criteria as *societal*, *means*, *preparation* and *practice* criteria.

Figure 1   Criteria of a profession

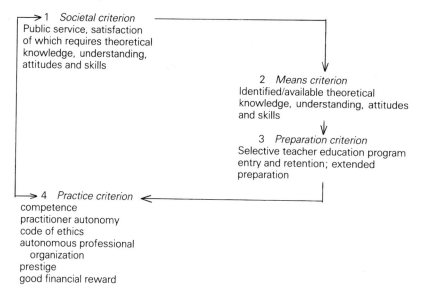

1   *Societal criterion*
Public service, satisfaction
of which requires theoretical
knowledge, understanding,
attitudes and skills

2   *Means criterion*
Identified/available theoretical
knowledge, understanding, attitudes
and skills

3   *Preparation criterion*
Selective teacher education program
entry and retention; extended
preparation

4   *Practice criterion*
competence
practitioner autonomy
code of ethics
autonomous professional
    organization
prestige
good financial reward

Teaching as a Profession

Is teaching a non-profession, a semi-profession or a full-fledged profession? This question has been a belabored one and it is doubtful that consensus on an answer will be forthcoming soon. Educational history shows that one reason for the failure of teaching to command the status of a profession is that, for a long time, it was believed that the subject matter to be taught was simple, that just about everyone who knew that subject matter could teach, and that no lengthy or rigorous teacher preparation was required for teaching. This is a public image with which teaching has been associated and has had great difficulty shedding.

Whatever may have been true historically, teaching in contemporary times has become much more complicated. The store of knowledge to be transmitted has not only expanded considerably but also has become esoteric. The need to develop young minds in non-authoritarian ways while simultaneously in competition with varied societal influences and distractions has necessitated sophisticated understanding, knowledge and skills, mastery of which would take lengthened teacher preparation and selective entry. It is thus no accident that recommendations in various reports (Holmes Group, 1989; Fullan and Connelly, 1987; Task Force on Teaching as a Profession, 1986) have called for extended teacher education. Truncated, half-hearted and incoherent preparation is simply no longer acceptable. Systematized, rigorous and effective programs are now an imperative. This is true for elementary teaching no less than secondary teaching. Holding the attention of the very young for the learning of some abstract subject matter is no mean task; teaching a simplified subject matter is not as simple as it may sound. If there is any lesson learned from the structure of the disciplines movement in the 1960s, it is that learning a body of knowledge requires effective, meaningful grasp of key concepts serving as foundation for spiralling, expanding ideas later on. Any teacher without solid mastery of a body of knowledge being taught is likely to impede rather than facilitate subsequent learning by the young.

Contemporary teaching satisfies the societal criterion indicated above. Clearly, teaching fulfills vital public service requiring theoretical knowledge, understanding, attitudes and skills. It measures up to the means criterion in that it already has a growing, identifiable body of subject matter for use by professionals. The trend has been, in teacher preparation institutions, to establish selective entry into extended teacher preparation programs; this increasingly fulfills the preparation criterion. To a significant degree, it conforms to some requirements of the practice criterion. Teachers already have fully formed professional organizations, implement codes of ethics and, at least in some Canadian jurisdictions, have progressed in terms of satisfactory financial rewards and prestige.

For teacher education institutions and teacher educators, the center of debate remains the means criterion. Are there bodies of theoretical knowledge and understandings as well as associated skills and attitudes or predispositions underlying the practice of teaching? Are they of such nature that will require systematic and lengthy teacher preparation comparable to that of law and medicine? Despite reservations on the part of dissenting academics, most studies on teacher education assume that bodies of knowledge underlying teacher education exist and that lengthy preparation is justified. The (Carnegie) Task Force on Teaching as a Profession (1986) has recommended the abolition of the undergraduate degree in education and the initiation of professional teaching education at the graduate level. This graduate level work will build on a base of sound undergraduate education in the arts and sciences. The Holmes Group (1986), an organization of American deans of education who are committed to educational reform, is similarly in favor of phasing out the undergraduate education major in member institutions and replacing it with graduate professional programs in teacher education. Fullan and Connelly (1987) in their report, *Education in Ontario*, have recommended that a four-year BA or BSc degree and a lengthened one-year pre-service program be made prerequisites for teacher certification — prerequisites which, in fact, are long established and implemented as one route to certification in many jurisdictions in Canada.

The length and character of teacher preparation depend, however, on the the extent and complexity of subject matter knowledge and professional knowledge to be mastered. There is no doubt that the former (subject matter knowledge) is extensive and complex; thus prescribing a basic arts or science degree as a prerequisite for entry to a teacher education program and for certification makes sense. To sharpen our grasp of the problem involved, it is useful to examine the typical or standard configuration of most pre-service teacher education programs. Regardless of how they are combined, components of such programs are generally as follows:[3]

1 liberal education component — studies in arts and sciences to broaden understanding and perspectives of prospective teachers;
2 disciplinary foundations component — studies of disciplines such as history, philosophy, sociology and psychology which would prepare students for studies in the foundations of education;
3 teachable subjects component — studies in one or more disciplines or fields of knowledge as major studies or concentrations representing teachable subjects in school systems, e.g., mathematics, social studies;
4 foundations of education component — studies in disciplines whose concepts and theories promote development of perspectives on educational processes and contexts, e.g., history of education, philosophy of education, psychology of education, sociology of education;
5 methodology component — studies in generic methodology dealing with teaching principles or rules which cut across subject matter and age levels, as well as specific teaching methods for particular teachable subjects;
6 practical component — studies involving classroom observation, student teaching, micro-teaching, internship; component involves the application of professional knowledge to practise at different levels of sophistication.

Though these components constitute much of the total configuration of a typical teacher education program, their comparative weights or emphases differ in different teacher education institutions and jurisdictions. How long they are studied and the route taken to complete all of them vary. Conjoint degree programs (requiring a basic arts or science degree for entry to shortened education degree studies) and integrated programs (combining arts, sciences and education courses for a Bachelor of education degree) are two of the most popular. In any case, it is undisputed that the first three components are fully available and would require extensive study in the university. The availability of the knowledge base for the latter three has been the target of skepticism.

The reason for skepticism is not difficult to find. Schon (1987, p. 12) highlights it pointedly when he asked the question: 'Can the prevailing concepts of professional education ever yield a curriculum adequate to the complex, unstable, uncertain and conflictual worlds of practice?' By implication, critics of teacher education programs allege that teaching practice involves large areas of indeterminate, rule-defying situations and creative judgment-making for which generalizations formulated by educational research are inadequate.

This criticism does not lend to any easy answer. In one sense, it is difficult to dispel. Insofar as such criticism assumes the need in teaching for theories, laws or principles similar to their applicational counterparts in the physical sciences, educational research does not have much by way of response. Sometime ago, Broudy (1972, pp. 54–6) observed that applicational theory — exemplified by the chemical theory used to guide the manufacture of synthetic fabrics or the theory of mechanics for guiding the work of engineers — as found in education was 'pitifully small'. Nearly two decades of scientifically oriented research may have brought some change in that picture. Gage (1985) and Berliner (1987) confidently defend the current research base of the art of teaching. Noting that knowledge is power, and that it commands respect in our technologically oriented society, Berliner (p. 31) proudly asserts that 'Educational research is fully prepared to bring that kind of power to the teaching profession'. As he sees it (*ibid.*), 'The educational research community is providing practitioners with more and more findings, concepts, and technologies that are closely related to their performance as teachers in the classroom'.

Yet the skeptical thrust of the question is not dispelled easily. Theories, laws and generalizations in the physical sciences are regarded as such to the degree that they uniformly apply over a given range of phenomena. It has been argued that in principle no similar ones can be discovered or formulated to cover human actions or behaviors unless they are intended to apply to physiologically controlled or non-rational, non-conscious human activities. Thus, Doyal and Harris (1986) demonstrate the falsity of the assumption 'that physical events and human actions are essentially the same sorts of things and that nomological explanatory principles are therefore applicable to such actions' (p. 52). Tom (1984) and Barrow (1984) have examined this assumption in the context of education and have found it wanting. Tom, in particular, has assessed the widely held belief that teaching is a natural phenomenon and thus can be regarded as a technical endeavor whose strategies can be theoretically ascertained and whose teaching problems can each be eliminated theoretically with one-best scientific solution. In response, it has been argued, by Braybrooke (1987) for example, that the social and the behavioral sciences are truly scientific and are capable of developing full-fledged theories and laws. Yet even these defenders hedge their case with qualification. As Braybooke himself puts it (p. 129):

> ... People are shifting, in response perhaps to changes in technology, to new social rules, or because people are following reasons of their own idiosyncratic rules rather than social ones. We have in such cases prospects of explanations from both naturalistic and interpretive

social science running to the bottom of the phenomena. To the extent that the unsettling and shifting is at bottom to be attibuted to intentions, and with them choices that cannot be made intelligible by reasons, the chances for social science of explaining the changes at issue are diminished.

We can infer from this that social and behavioral sciences can come up only with theories, laws or generalizations having limited explanatory and predictive, and hence applicational, power. This being the case, the criticism that a truly scientific base for the application of theory to the practice of teaching (in the way scientific theory is applied to engineering) is unattainable cannot but be decisive.[4] Even the staunch advocate of a scientific base for the art of teaching, Berliner (1987), acknowledges this much (p. 27):

> We have a number of problems in interpreting educational research. These problems limit the generalizability of our findings in a way that does not occur in other professions. Classrooms are complex, dynamic environments ... Our classrooms are constantly changing: the time of year, current events, special needs of our students — these and other factors sometimes all plot to throw up barriers to implementing educational research in ways that will prove its usefulness.

For all this, however, the knowledge base in the practice of teaching may yet turn out to be substantial if we view existing social and behavioral bodies of knowledge in another way. In Broudy's (1972) terminology, we may view such knowledge as *interpretive* rather than *applicational*. As he suggested, much of what we find in the social and behavioral sciences consists of theories, laws or generalizations which provide basis for the interpretation of the teaching phenomena. Through them, classroom processes and schooling contexts are understood, interpreted and evaluated in such a way that practitioners are enabled to deal with them intelligently, effectively and creatively. These theories, in most teacher education institutions, are offered through studies in history, philosophy, psychology and sociology of education — studies that are generally referred to as foundations of education. For an appreciation of these studies, a closer examination of their nature needs to be undertaken.

The Foundations of Education: Nature and Role

At the height of the popularity of the competency or performance-based teacher education (C/PBTE) in the United States, there was fear that the impending demise of the foundations of education was merely a matter of time. The practical, non-theoretical orientation of the C/PBTE presumably would make unnecessary any systematic or serious study of theoretical matters underlying educational practice. Competence or performance as exhibited in specific teacher behavior targeted toward specific pupil behavior was all that mattered. Theory, though perhaps valuable for those who specialized in the identification or formulation of competencies and specific teaching techniques, was not expected of the practitioner who needed only to apply the concrete, determinable performances in teaching situations.

The apprehension was fueled by the fact that the foundations of education field was in disarray or state of crisis (Shea, Sola and Jones, 1987). Its identity was in a schizophrenic state and the name *foundations of education* was used to designate a wide variety of courses apart from the usually associated studies in the history, philosophy, psychology and sociology of education. Introduction to education, curriculum theory, comparative issues and trends in education, school law, multicultural or cross-cultural education, school organization and management, and other course titles have been regarded by faculties of education as foundation studies.

Though still a formidable force, C/PBTE is not likely any longer to make further inroads against foundation studies. The big push in legislative bodies, by the public, and in faculties of education appears to have tapered off, and recognition of the need for professionalization through theoretical studies rather than merely technical know-how is once again evident. Still, a clear picture of the foundation studies and their role needs to be provided.

Tozer and McAninch (1986) convey valuable insights about what foundation studies have been all about. From the beginning, around the 1890s, those who worked at incorporating foundation courses to broaden the training of teachers recognized that the predominant feature of the teacher education programmes proposed at the time promoted 'adaptation and adjustment to the emerging industrial and social order' (Tozer and McAninch, 1986, p. 7). However, even then, progressive educators such as John Dewey, William Heard Kilpatrick and Boyd Bode were already 'making contributions toward a more creative and critical approach to the education of teachers' (*ibid.*). Through their efforts, there developed the conception of teachers 'not as technicians who were simply to pass on knowledge to the next generation, but as potentially critical and independent thinkers who could induct their pupils into the process of "scientific" and democratic problem solving themselves' (p. 8). By the 1940s, a conception of the foundation studies which emerged had a number of characteristics. They were (1) grounded in a rigorous study of society; (2) cross-disciplinary and required integrated courses of study; (3) critical, initiating students into coherently argued critiques of social and educational processes, institutions and contexts; and (4) intended to help students build their own individual points of view (p. 10). Further developments have not eliminated these characteristics. By 1986, Tozer and McAninch felt justified in offering the following description of the foundation studies: 'Social foundations of education instruction examines social institutions, processes and ideals in a cross-disciplinary course of study that is critical in orientation, and that helps students develop informed, normative points of view regarding society, schooling and education' (pp. 23–4).

Historically, the examination of issues and problems related to education and society typically enlisted insights from various disciplines studied though the contributions of single or collaborating authors from a given discipline. The interdisciplinary approach was exemplified by Smith, Stanley, Benne and Anderson's 1956 volume described by Tozer and McAninch as follows (p. 19):

> *Social Foundations of Education* is a collection of key readings by important scholars in a variety of education-related disciplines ... Contradictory selections are often posed against one another so that the student, with the help from ample editorial material, can examine arguments from conflicting sides of an issue. The student is exposed to coherently argued critiques and defences of American social and economic arrangements and the philosophies that support them.

Unfortunately, this text suffered from the 'relative scarcity of historical perspective' (p. 22), a perspective which figured prominently in earlier materials designed for use in foundations courses.

The cross-disciplinary character of foundational studies within one course, the historical model of such studies, has not been uniformly adhered to. Varied approaches have been used. A popular one is by the study of a foundational cluster of separate discipline-based courses, particularly history, philosophy, psychology and sociology of education. It remains an open question whether this alternative approach destroys the character and intent of foundation studies. In favor of the separate disciplines approach it can be argued that solid, critical and perceptive understanding of society, schools and educational processes cannot really be achieved without deep immersion into each of the parent disciplines supporting foundation studies. It may also be claimed that the usefulness of foundation studies cannot be maximized without sufficient familiarity with the concepts and theories of the parent disciplines. The contrary argument, in favor of the cross-disciplinary approach, is that separate study of the disciplines divert learners away from the distinctively cross-disciplinary insights that integrated studies provide. Teaching and learning situations, no less than the wider issues surrounding schooling, are cross-disciplinary rather than disciplinary matters. Clearly, either approach can be argued. Without attempting to settle the matter, we may note that the either-or approach to the matter may be an inappropriate one. Ideally, it may be that solid studies in the foundations should begin with the study of a limited number of disciplinary foundation courses and then proceed with synthesizing cross-disciplinary studies.

Rightly, the Council of Learned Societies (1986) is not disturbed by the proliferation of approaches or courses labelled *foundations of education*. Its support for diversity is based on the 'belief that an over-riding and profoundly important academic and professional purpose' unifies all who are engaged in the foundations of education. This purpose is 'the development of interpretive, normative, and critical perspectives in education' (pp. 3–4). The Council elaborates on this three-point purpose as follows (pp. 4–5):[6]

1   The *interpretive* perspectives, using theories and resources developed within the humanities and the social and behavioral sciences, assist students in examining and explaining education within differing contexts. Foundational studies promote analyses of the meaning, intent and effects of educational institutions, including schools. Educational thought and practice inevitably reflect particular contexts and beliefs. They can be perceived differently from various historical, philosophical, cultural and social class perspectives. Education, whether in the form of schooling or some other arrangement, thus cannot be understood merely in terms of its present and immediately visible characteristics. Understanding follows from attempts to interpret educational thought and practice within their special contexts and to translate them from one perspective to another. This deeper level of understanding is required of scholars who expect to increase knowledge about education and of practitioners committed to the delivery or improvement of educational services. The effectiveness of both kinds of professionals depends fundamentally on their intelligent comprehension of educational thought and practice. A major task of foundational studies is to provide the resources, incentives and skills students require in performing the interpretive functions.

2   The *normative* perspectives assist students in examining and explaining education in light of value orientations. Foundational studies promote understanding of normative and ethical behavior in educational development and recognition of the inevitable presence of normative influences in educational thought and practice. Foundational studies probe the nature of assumptions about education and schooling. They examine the relation of policy analysis to values and the extent to which educational policymaking reflects values. Finally, they encourage students to develop their own value positions regarding education on the basis of critical study and their own reflections.

3   The *critical* perspectives assist students in examining and explaining education in light of its origins, major influences and consequences. Foundational studies promote critical understanding of educational thought and practice, and of the decisions and events which have shaped them, in their various contexts. These multi-dimensional modes of analysis encourage students to develop inquiry skills, question educational assumptions and arrangements, and subject them to critical review. In particular, the critical perspectives provided through foundational studies enable students to examine equality and inequality in the distribution of educational opportunity and outcome. They promote understanding of past and present patterns of exclusion in education, the causes of exclusion and inequality, and the educational needs and aspiration of excluded minorities. Finally, foundational studies encourage the development of policymaking perspec-

tives and skills in searching for resolutions to educational problems and issues.

So convinced is the Council (1986, p. 8) of the importance of attaining the common purpose of foundation studies that it recommended devoting at least one-sixth of the professional preparation program leading to initial teacher certification to humanistic and social foundation studies aside from additional studies in the behavioral foundations of education. At this time, when calls for reform in teacher education are in abundance, the recommendations from the Council should be given the serious consideration which it deserves.

Concluding Comments: Professionalization as a Moral Imperative

More than a decade ago, an American court heard a case against a school board charged with malpractice (Peter W. v. Unified School District of San Francisco, 1976). Peter and his parents had sued for damages allegedly because he graduated from high school, complete with a diploma, but with literacy skills at the grade 8 level. The parents had diligently consulted with the homeroom teacher every year to find out how Peter was doing academically. They were told that he was performing as well as most other members of his class. It appeared that the parents had a strong case. Yet the school board was exonerated. The court's decision, though welcomed by the board, was thought negatively to reflect against the teaching profession. The court reasoned, in part, that in the absence of identifiable standard of care and performance in the field of teaching, it was not possible for the court to determine if, and to what degree, the teachers in the school board failed to discharge their teaching obligations. Courts ordinarily do not resort to such reasoning in the case of malpractice lawsuits against medical doctors, lawyers and engineeers whose professions have established standards of competent practice. To some, the exoneration of Peter's teachers and school board amounted to professional insult. Of course, cynically, one may swallow professional pride and simultaneously ask: Why attempt to establish standards of competence and professionalize at the cost of losing malpractice lawsuits?

To ask whether teaching should professionalize and thus make it open for the public to subject teachers to malpractice lawsuits presumes that litigation against a teacher will succeed only where standardized competencies are identified and formulated as expectations of practitioners. This presumption is subject to debate (Covert, 1987 and 1988; Foster, 1987 and 1988) which we need not join in this article. The question is intriguing, however, because of its cynicism. It unfairly represents teachers and educators in general as unwilling to assume the responsibilities associated with their positions. Such misrepresentation does injustice to most teachers who see their teaching not simply as gainful employment and source of livelihood but also as satisfying engagement in public service, particularly to the young.

Naturally there may be sectors within the field whose concern for the former overshadows the latter. If true, the conclusions drawn by Radecki and Evans (1982) should prove disturbing. These researchers found, in their extensive study of the Sudbury (Ontario) teachers' strike, that strikers were no longer motivated by concern for their pupils. In their words (p. 169), 'the 1979 negotiations and the 1980 strike showed that they see themselves as worker, concerned first and foremost with their conditions of work and job security.... We must conclude that the Sudbury strike had little considera-tion for the welfare of the students and the quality of education'.

If this conclusion reflects the reality in some quarters at least sometimes, it would not harm future and present-day practitioners to re-examine their commitment to the enterprise of teaching. If such commitment is simply to what are generally contained in teacher contracts or to what the courts of law may regard as legally acceptable expectations of teachers, the notion of teaching as a profession has no promise whatsoever. As we found earlier, at the heart of a profession is a body of knowledge and theories required by a given practice or occupation in pursuit of some public service. Unfortunately, the requirements for the public service of teaching cannot be fully captured in contractual legal agreements or judicial decisions following court litigation. One reason for this is already obvious. Despite notable strides in the last two decades, the theories, generalizations and findings in education (forming what we may call educational studies); their technical application to educational practice (including classroom teaching and management); and their satisfactory formulation in a way that would lend to a systematic inclusion in teacher education curricula leave much to be desired. Consequently, confidence in an adequate specification of standard teaching practices and competencies is not warranted. Even if an unlikely consensus on basic learning outcomes were achieved, any satisfactory formulation of teacher competencies and practices expected to elicit such outcomes would remain elusive.

The problem is perceived by Wilson and Cowell (1989) in a different way. In their view, the problem is not that educational studies are in their infancy. It is, rather, that they 'have been corrupted by false perceptions of themselves' and assimilated by false models (p. 22). Though largely unexcep-tionable, it may be unwise to prejudge (Wilson stipulates caveats on the matter) how much educational studies and research will yield in terms of theories and findings with applicational impact. As we have earlier discov-ered, if researchers are correct, research is already generating methodology or practice-oriented generalizations for use in classrooms. Arguably, the possi-bility of applicational theory becoming substantially significant in guiding practice cannot be underestimated. We cannot a priori assume the absence of some common conditions and circumstances, or of some similar abilities, backgrounds and dispositions which allow the use of common practices. Yet we have also found inherent limitations in theories, laws and generalizations that educational studies will produce. Thus, though as a practical matter we should not assume that educational studies have nothing to contribute toward applicational theories and findings, nonetheless we need to re-orient our thinking with respect to what educational studies can contribute to the professionalization of teaching.[5] Broudy's (1972) recommendation that such studies be viewed not only as applicational but also as interpretive — as bodies of knowledge and understanding which promote our interpretation, analysis, evaluation, criticism and innovation in teaching situations — makes a lot of sense. Professional teaching may be seen as intelligent practice based on the combination of interpretive and applicational theories and findings that hold the promise of efficacious and judicious attainment of school aims. Whatever is available at this time should be sufficient basis for professional practice. Undoubtedly, theories and findings in such disciplines as history, philosophy, psychology and sociology of education are available and can contribute to intelligent practice.

The motivation for teachers to professionalize through available applicational and interpretive theories and findings need not come from legalized requirements. Teachers, prospective or practising, are moral agents and, as such, are morally accountable for taking agreements seriously. Though specific, standardized competencies remain unformulated or unavailable, teachers are nevertheless obligated morally to do what needs responsibly to be done to attain the aims of the institution that they have decided freely to join. As voluntary members of an institution committed to the promotion of learning, teachers have the moral obligation to equip themselves with and intelligently use whatever resources are available from educational studies to facilitate learning on the part of the young. This moral obligation is that of one who has developed expectation on the part of others around him or her simply by joining an institution with some professed purpose. That obligation is to the school authorities with whom mutual agreement is formally reached; to parents who are compelled (or delegate responsibility to educators) to send their children to school; and to the wider society which has the right to expect that the personnel of its deliberately organized institution will seriously endeavor to promote institutional objectives. But, most of all, this moral obligation is owed to the pupils. Children have the right to goods and processes which promote not only their well-being but also their development as autonomous, rational human beings capable of intelligent life in a complex society (Magsino, 1986). Professional teachers, among others, have the responsibility to provide for this right.

A profession is a committed response to a need for public service by way of practices based on or enlightened by theoretical knowledge and understanding. If teaching is not as yet regarded as a full profession, it is probably, at least in part, because we have not succeeded in getting prospective and practising teachers to make use of available disciplinary resources in appropriate ways and because we and outside observers have imposed on ourselves 'false models'.

A more promising model sees professional teaching as intelligent judgment-making and activities, based on interpretive and applicational

Romulo F. Magsino

theories and knowledge, in the teachers' discharge of their responsibilities. The moral imperative for intelligent practice is unquestionable; disciplinary resources are already available and increasing. Full professionalization of teaching is not an impossible dream.

Notes

1 For an interesting general account of the criticisms and possible reasons for them, see Mazurek (1986).
2 The starkly pessimistic assessment of American schools by the National Commission on Excellence in Education report, *A Nation at Risk* (1982), may be compared side by side with a more optimistic assessment by Boyer (1983) who was commissioned by the Carnegie Foundation for the Advancement of Teaching.
3 These components have been highlighted by such writers as Broudy (1972) and Smith (1987).
4 Entwistle (1988) offers an alternative way of viewing the limitations of the theoretical base for the practice of teaching. For him, what we have in education are generalizations, each of which has incorporated common features of individuals, things or situations within a given category. As a generalization, each is theoretically sound; applied, however, it may not be able to account for or deal with the unique or idiosyncratic features of a given situation.
5 For a position close to what is argued here, see Carr (1983).
6 The author wishes to thank Dr Allan Jones for permission to quote from the Council extensively.

Bibliography

BARROW, R. (1984) *Giving Teaching Back to Teachers*, London, Ontario: Althouse Press.
BECKER, E. (1962) 'The nature of a profession', in National Society for the Study of Education, *Education for the Profession*, Part II, Chicago: National Society for the Study of Education, (pp. 22–46).
BERLINER, D. (1987) 'Knowledge is power', in BERLINER, D. and ROSENSHINE, B. (Eds) *Talks to Teachers*, New York: Random House, (pp. 3–33).
BLACKINGTON, F.H. (1968) 'The profession as an idea', in BLACKINGTON, F.H. and PATTERSON, R.S. (Eds) *School, Society and the Professional Education*, New York: Holt, Rinehart and Winston, Inc, (pp.16–29).
BOYER, E. (1983) *High School. A Report on Secondary Education in America*, New York: Harper and Row, Publishers.
BRAYBROOKE, D. (1987) *Philosophy of Social Science*, Englewood-Cliffs, NJ: Prentice-Hall.
BROUDY H.S. (1972) *The Real World of the Public Schools*, New York: Harcourt Brace Jovanovich.
'Can the schools be saved?' (1983, May 9) *Newsweek*, pp. 50–8.
CARR, W. (1983) 'Can educational research be scientific?' *Journal of Philosophy of Education*, *17*, pp. 35–43.
COGAN, M. (1953) 'Toward a definition of profession', *Harvard Educational Review*, XXIII; pp. 33–50.
CORNBLETH, C. (1989) 'Cries of crisis, calls for reform, and challenges of change', in

WEIS, L., ALTBACH, P., KELLY, G., PETRIE, H. and SLAUGHTER, S. (Eds) *Crisis in Teaching*, Albany, NY: State University of New York Press, (pp. 9–30)

CORWIN, R. (1965) *Sociology of Education*, New York: Appleton-Century-Crofts.

COUNCIL OF LEARNED SOCIETIES IN EDUCATION (1986) *Standard for Academic and Professional Instruction in Foundations of Education, Educational Studies, and Educational Policy Studies*, Ann Arbor, MI: Prakken Publications, Inc.

COVERT, J. (1975, January) 'Second thoughts about the professionalization of teachers', *The Educational Forum*, pp. 149–54.

COVERT, J. (1987) 'The profession of teaching. A reply to Professor Foster', *Canadian Journal of Education*, 12, pp. 214–17.

COVERT, J. (1988) 'Educational malpractice and the future of teaching', *Education Law Journal*, 1, pp. 183–97.

DOYAL, L. and HARRIS, R. (1986) *Empiricism, Explanation, and Rationality*, London: Routledge and Kegan Paul.

ELAM, S. and GALLUP, A.M. (1989) 'The 21st Annual Gallup Poll of the public's attitudes toward the public schools', *Phi Delta Kappan*, 71, (1), pp. 41–54.

ENTWISTLE, H. (1988) 'The relationship between theory and practice in education', in HARE, W. and PORTELLI, J. (Eds) *Philosophy of Education. Introduction Readings*, Calgary, Alberta: Detselig Enterprises, (pp. 23–32).

FOSTER, W. (1987) 'Educational malpractice: Educate or Litigate', *Canadian Journal of Education*, 11, pp. 122–51.

FOSTER, W. (1988) 'Educational malpractice: A rejoinder', *Canadian Journal of Education*, 12, pp. 218–28.

FULLAN, M. and CONNELLY, F.M. (1987) *Teacher Education in Ontario: Current Practice and Options for the Future*, Toronto, Ontario: Ontario Ministry of Education.

GAGE, N.L. (1985) *Hard Gains in the Soft Sciences*, Bloomington, IN: Phi Delta Kappan.

HALL, R. (1972) 'Professionalization and bureaucratization', in HALL, R. (Ed.) *The Formal Organization*, New York: Basic Books.

'Help! Teachers can't teach!' (1980, June 16) *Time*, pp. 52–60.

HIRST, P. (1983) 'Educational theory', in HIRST, P. (Ed.) *Educational Theory and its Foundation Disciplines*, London: Routledge and Kegan Paul, (pp. 3–29).

HOLMES GROUP (1989) *Tomorrow's Teachers*, East Lansing, MI: The Holmes Group.

KERR, D. (1983) 'Teaching competence and teacher education in the United States', in SHULMAN, L.S. and SYKES, G. (Eds) *Handbook of Teaching and Policy*, New York: Longman, (pp. 126–49).

LIEBERMAN, M. (1958) *Education as a Profession*, Englewood Cliffs, NJ: Prentice-Hall.

LIVINGSTONE, D.W. and HART, D.J. (1987) 'The people speak: Public attitudes toward schooling in Canada', in GHOSH, R. and RAY, D. (Eds) *Social Change and Education*, Toronto, Ontario: Academic Press, (pp. 3–27).

MAGSINO, R. (1986) Professionalism in Education and Children's Rights to Education. Paper presented at the conference of the Canadian Society for the Study of Education, Guelph, Ontario.

MAZUREK, K. (1986) 'Crisis in confidence: Speculations on the assault on the teaching profession', in KACH, N., MAZUREK, K., PATTERSON, R. and DeFAVERI, I. (Eds) *Essays on Canadian Education*, Calgary, Alberta: Detselig Enterprises, (pp. 227–44).

MOORE, T.W. (1974) *Educational Theory: An Introduction*, London: Routledge and Kegan Paul.

NATIONAL COMMISSION ON EXCELLENCE IN EDUCATION (1983) *A Nation at Risk*, Washington, DC: US Government Printing Office.

ORNSTEIN, A. (1976) *Teaching in a New Era*, Champaign, IL: Stipes Publishing Co.

ORNSTEIN, A. (1981, November) 'The trend toward increased professionalism of teachers', *Phi Delta Kappan*, pp. 196–8.

PETER W. V. San Francisco Unified School District (1976), 60 Cal. App. 3d 814, 131 Cal. Reptr. 854.

RADECKI, H. and Evans, S. (1982) *The Teachers' Strike Study*, Toronto, Ontario: The Minister of Education.

'REPORT CARD ON OUR SCHOOLS', A special report, *The Star*, (Toronto), Issues for April 25, April 26, May 2, May 3, May 9, & May 10, 1987.

SCHILLER, B. (1987, May 2) 'Teachers rated as only "fair", *Star* survey says. Report card on our schools series', *The Saturday Star*, pp. 1, 10–11.

SCHON, D. (1987) *Educating the Reflective Practitioner*, San Francisco, CA: Jossey-Bass, Publishers.

SHEA, C., SOLA, P. and JONES, A. (1987, Spring) 'Examining the crisis in the social foundations of education', *Educational Foundations*, Number 2, pp. 47–57.

SHULMAN, L.S. (1987) 'Knowledge and teaching', *Harvard Educational Review*, 57; pp. 1–22.

SMITH, D. (1987) 'Redesigning the curriculum in teacher education', in MAGRATH, C.P., EGBERT, R. and Associates (Eds) *Strengthening Teacher Education* (pp. 87–96), San Francisco, CA: Jossey-Bass Publishers.

TASK FORCE ON TEACHING AS A PROFESSION (1986) *A Nation Prepared: Teachers for the 21st Century*, Washington, DC: Carnegie Forum on Education and the Economy.

TIBBLE, J.W. (1966) *The Study of Education*, London: Routledge and Kegan Paul.

TIBBLE, J.W. (1971) *An Introduction to the Study of Education*, London: Routledge and Kegan Paul.

TOM, A. (1984) *Teaching as a Moral Craft*, New York: Longman.

TOZER, S. and MCANINCH, S. (1986, Fall) 'Social foundations of education in historical perspective', *Educational Studies*, Number 1: pp. 5–32.

Twentieth Century Fund Task Force on Federal Elementary and Secondary Education Policy (1983) *Making the Grade*, New York: Twentieth Century Fund.

WEIS, L. (1989) 'Introduction', in WEIS, L., ALTBACH, P., KELLY, G., PETRIE, H. and SLAUGHTER, S. (Eds) *Crisis in Teaching*, Albany, NY: State University of New York Press, (pp. 1–7).

'WHY OUR TEACHERS CAN'T TEACH', (1984, September) *Quest*, pp. 35–40.

'WHY TEACHERS FAIL', (1984, September) *Newsweek*, pp. 50–8.

WILSON, J. and COWELL, B. (1989) *Taking Education Seriously*, London, Ontario: The Althouse Press.

WITTROCK, M. (1986) *Handbook of Research on Teaching* (3rd Edn), New York: Macmillan and Company.

V

The Classroom: Locus of Encounter Between Individual and Society

INTRODUCTION

Professional teachers, who are competent in autonomously determining which teaching strategies should be employed in specific teaching situations, do so in the context of personal and social relationships with individuals and groups in the classroom. Thus, mere mastery of subject matter and teaching methods is insufficient; with whom and under what circumstances certain things are to be done requires understanding and perspectives which foundational studies supply. Daniel McDougall demonstrates the contributions of psychology, one of the foundational studies, in helping teachers promote students' psycho-social development by addressing prejudice, an endemic, disturbing problem in any society where cultural differences exist. He shows that, like psycho-social and moral development, the development of prejudice involves several stages and is affected by a number of important factors in society. Conceptually linked with categorizing individuals on the basis of race or other related criteria, racial prejudice springs from the ethnocentric view that one's in-group possesses the attitudes, values, and behavior which are superior to those of other groups. Through the processes of socialization, such as identification and modeling, and the influences of the media and reading materials in school, prejudice becomes part of the thought processes and behaviors of the young. Fortunately, development of prejudice may be prevented. Through an understanding of the psycho-social processes involved and the use of certain teaching methods discovered or verified by research, classroom teachers can contribute significantly to the reduction of prejudice in society.

The problem of prejudice in society and its reduction through teacher efforts in the classroom highlights the close connection between society and schooling. It suggests that coping with our tasks as educators requires an understanding of society, an understanding which makes our perspectives on schooling meaningful and realistic. This does not make undesirable or impossible, however, any attempt to examine the school as a unit all by itself and apart from its social context. As Wilfred Martin points out, the school has its own cultural identity; as such, it has its own identifiable cultural elements and processes, the understanding of which will promote effective classroom practice.

Martin explicitly states his assumptions in discussing classroom culture. Sympathetic to the interactionist perspective in sociological theory, he assumes that social objects or situations do not have meanings in themselves; that these objects and situations are invested their meanings subjectively by people or individuals who encounter them; and that these meanings are modified and re-modified through the process of interaction. He observes that, more than likely, students' understanding or perceptions of school objects and situations are different from those which educators hold and which they would want their students to internalize insofar as these are consistent with the intent of schooling. It is also arguable that student perceptions are worthy of consideration by educators. Taking them into account will enable the teacher to interact with students more respectfully and effectively. Thus Martin elaborates on the results of his comprehensive study of student perceptions related to school rules, teachers' pets and class victims, and student embarrassment.

15 Psychological and Educational Perspectives on the Development and Reduction of Prejudice Among Children and Adolescents

Daniel McDougall

Introduction

Development in childhood and adolescence is uneven and convoluted. The road to maturity, while relatively smooth for some people, is not without its hazards. For example, many young people are plagued by prejudice although it is a problem which occurs throughout the life cycle. During the course of psycho-social development, several forces combine to produce prejudice. The struggle for identity is one such force. Adolescents, partially in response to the crisis of identity, may form in groups which exclude visible minority idividuals. The unequal treatment of minority group members violates the respect-for-others principle of morality. Moral development, then, is related to prejudice. Concept formation and socialization are two additional forces which may spread prejudice among youngsters. Since they often learn, moreover, by observing the behavior of others, observational learning may explain the effects of television and literature on young people's interpersonal behavior. While education is not a panacea, there are instructional innovations which reduce some of the problems of youth such as prejudice.

Psycho-social Development

Eric Erikson (1963) extended Freud's concept of the rational process of the personality, the ego, by postulating psychosocial stages of ego development. These stages are reflected in individuals' understanding of who they are and their relation to the social environment. Without denying that psycho-sexual development proceeded much as Freud suggested in his well known stage theory, Erikson assumed that there are eight psycho-social stages, with positive and negative aspects, covering the entire life span. This is in contrast to Freud's view which emphasized childhood and early adolescence.

During the first year of life, Erikson's *stage of trust versus mistrust,* the child whose needs are well satisfied will trust the social environment. Children learn trust when their hunger is satisfied, when their thirst is quenched, when their bodily discomforts are eased, and when all this is done within a reasonable timeframe and consistently by a loving caregiver who holds, touches and communicates with them in supportive, nurturing ways. Distrust develops when the caregiving is inconsistent, harsh and unsatisfactory. This distrust of people will influence later social-emotional development. Moreover, trust versus mistrust may become a concern at later stages of development. The trusting child, for example, may learn distrust through unhappy school experiences.

The *stage of autonomy versus doubt* occurs among two-and-three year olds. Driving children toward autonomy are their blossoming psychomotor skills: walking, running, climbing, grasping, pushing, pulling, etc. Whatever it is, they wish to do everything for themselves. To the extent that parents permit children to do everything on their own at a comfortable rate, to that extent will they experience autonomy. Should the parents be too restrictive, impatient or overly protective, then the children will be doubtful of their own ability to control the environment. This doubt may carry forward into adolescence and even adulthood. Later more positive experiences may overcome earlier insecurity, just as later negative, social interactions may undermine the sense of autonomy.

Erikson sees four- or five-year-old children, now at the stage of *initiative versus guilt,* confronting the problems of initiative and guilt. With increasing command of psychomotor skills such as language, children initiate more and more activities which affect other people. Depending on how significant others such as parents react to these self-initiated behaviors, children will either feel comfortable as initiators or they will begin to feel guilty. Disapproval feeds this guilt whereas support builds the sense of being an originator of action.

This *stage of industry versus inferiority* is Erikson's version of what the six- to eleven-year-old may experience in psychosocial ego development. The child's central interest is in the workings of the immediate physical world: How does this thing work? What does that thing do? — these questions consume the child's attention. With encouragement of undertakings such as building a fort or baking cookies, the child learns diligence. Since children at this stage are at school, teachers as well as parents influence development. Discouragement through inappropriate criticism in either environment may be offset by praise and reward in the other.

According to the psychoanalytic view, at about eleven years of age youngsters enter the puberty stage. Children's physiological changes, coupled with psychosexual development, begin to arouse interest in resolving the earlier rivalry with the same sex parent through attachment to members of their own age group. Erikson's *identity versus role confusion stage* extended this view of development to include other problems faced by the young adolescent, such as those associated with a developing intellect. Adolescents begin to see their world differently. There is a need in the adolescent for faith in ideals, some person, or philosophy worthy of trust. Fearing that they may be misled, adolescents may express the need for ideals by cynically mistrusting authority figures. They wish to serve others, but only if it is freely chosen. If there is a hint of influence from teachers or especially parent, they will rush to avoid their elders' influence rather than be demeaned in the light of their own perspective or that of their peers. Adolescents aspire to an identity beyond what they possess and, to this end, will trust those who allow them to expand toward desired goals. Any attempt by others to limit seeming unrealistic ambitions will be vociferously rebuked.

Not all adolescents will have a terribly difficult time adjusting to societal demands. Erikson (1968) observes that those who are fortunate enough to become involved in activities — technological, economic or ideological — which provide an outlet for young people's idealism will fare reasonably well. Should this expression be thwarted, however, the young person's reactions may be very strong indeed.

Erikson goes on to say that establishing an identity associated with a job is probably one of the central problems facing adolescents. While clarifying occupational identity and attempting to achieve temporary stability, young people may cling fanatically to peer-group standards, thereby seeming to lose independent thought and action. Exclusivity abounds and those who are visibly different from the ingroup, say in skin color or accent, may feel the sting of discrimination. But Erikson feels that this intolerance is necessary to offset the feeling of identity loss. Teachers may reduce its effects by introducing common, superordinate goals which bring greater acceptance of outgroup members and increased interethnic group-helping among classmates. Cooperative learning (described later in the chapter) is a teaching technique which promotes cohesiveness. Effective teachers take a proactive approach to helping youngsters overcome discomfort.

The task for adolescents is to achieve ego identity: determining who they are, where they are going, and where they have been so that there is a sense of continuity. Significant others such as parents and teachers will have promoted the adolescents' achievement of identity by helping them enter adolescence with confidence — trusting, autonomous and able to initiate actions and pursue goals diligently. In addition, larger societal factors influence the ease with which self-identity is realized. Minority group status will, for example, make it more difficult for some adolescents to determine who they are and where they are headed. Some will not achieve ego identity. Minority group status may produce a negative identity based on antagonism toward a more powerful majority group. This development would be unfortunate because the adolescent who is a member of a minority could create an identity founded on the positive aspects of that minority's culture (Santrock, 1981).

Lack of achievement of a positive self-identity during adolescence, while problematical, does not mean that it cannot be attained at a later stage. Indeed, even individuals who find themselves uncertain about their identity during adolescence may be challenged at later stages to assess again their personal identity.

Upon entering young adulthood, the *stage of intimacy versus isolation*, the developmental task is to attain intimacy with another person. Erikson sees achievement of an intimate interpersonal relationship as a significant goal. It means not only physical intimacy but also sharing life's struggle and caring for another person while maintaining integrity of the self. Without a sense of intimate friendship with others, isolation develops and the individual feels alone.

With middle age, *the stage of generativity versus self-absorption*, individuals often become concerned with passing on skills and knowledge to the rising, younger generation. The person becomes involved with the wider environment, both social and physical. What will be left for those who follow? Failure to gain a sense of concern for future generations will likely produce stagnation and boredom, coupled with concomitant, excessive attention to satisfying personal needs and over-indulgence in the self.

Should individuals at an advanced age, the *stage of integrity versus despair*, perceive their lives as flawed with many goals left unreached and perhaps unreachable, there will be despair. Having missed capitalizing on various opportunities in life, the person will be regretful and malcontent. For example, the elderly, retired teacher who, as an adolescent, desired to be a doctor may be miserable about this failure. However, those who perceive their lives as productive and useful will experience a wholeness and integrity sustaining them in old age.

Erikson, then, characterized development throughout the entire life cycle as being a progression of stages each of which has its own unique problems. Elkind (1972) notes that Erikson gave due regard to societal influences on the development of an identity as well as individual responsibility for resolving conflicts. That failure at one stage may be overcome at a later period is a positive feature of Erikson's construction. Confusion during adolescence, for instance, does not condemn one to a life of identity conflict.

Moral Development

There are, according to Kohlberg (1969), three broad levels of moral development: preconventional, conventional and postconventional morality. Within each of these levels individuals move through two stages. In response to criticism and research evidence, Kohlberg and his coworkers (e.g., Kohlberg, Levine and Herver, 1983) have adjusted the stage theory, but the essential elements remain.

Those persons who think at the preconventional level are mostly young children, but some adolescents and maladjusted adults operate at this level.

Stage 1 (*punishment-obedience orientation*) individuals follow rules because they fear punishment; they are self-centered and are unable to take the perspective of others. Stage 2 (*instrumental-hedonistic orientation*) persons see justice as the result of situations where there is an equal exchange. They remain egocentric but will cooperate as long as their own needs are met.

Societal standards of conduct are generally accepted by those who operate at the conventional level. Stage 3 (*orientation to pleasing others*) individuals conform to rules and regulations to please others, especially authority figures. Doing one's duty is high on their list of priorities. Stage 4 (*maintenance of the social order*) persons conform to standards because the proper functioning of society requires adherence to rules and regulations.

Postconventional morality is characterized by abstract thinking and an interrelated set of concepts and principles. A more flexible approach to the application of the rules is assumed. Laws are followed as long as they meet the needs of people, but when laws become disfunctional they must be changed. According to stage 5 (*contractual-legalistic orientation*) persons, changes would take place within the bounds of the procedures agreed upon by the larger society. Few individuals attain stage 6, *universal-ethical orientation*. But those who achieve this advanced level have an independent moral structure which includes abstract understanding of natural justice, human-heartedness and a sense of human dignity which transcends conventional statement of laws.

Elementary school children as well as some secondary school adolescents mostly operate at a conventional level of morality which places them in stages 3 or 4. They have incorporated rules of conduct in a more or less unthinking fashion. A problem for these individuals is to move away from parental control and to apply the rules in an independent and thoughtful way. In so doing they demonstrate that the rules have been internalized (Ausubel and Sullivan, 1970). Those who do not internalize will be able to verbalize the rules, but they will not be self-directing.

Gradations in moral thinking exist, and teachers, through values clarification exercises, advance the moral thinking of students. Such advance is needed particularly in relation to prejudice. According to Daniels, Douglas, Oliver and Wright (1978), prejudice is a moral issue. When people (prejudicially) treat others unequally for irrational reasons they violate the respect-for-persons principle of morality. Values clarification allows students to see prejudice as irrational and immoral. This clarification involves students in learning the following skills: distinguishing value judgments from other evaluations, reasoning about values, and identifying different sorts of value assessments. The values clarification approach helps pupils use these skills in altering their already formed beliefs and attitudes as well as those which are still emerging (Simon, Howe and Kirschenbaum, 1978).

Davidson (1977) showed that tolerance is significantly related to the higher stages. Fewer ethnically prejudiced remarks are made by high-stage children. This finding suggests that tolerance is promoted by stressing the development of the fundamental values of moral maturity. Students at one stage of moral development are most readily moved to higher levels by problem solving with students who are at the next higher level (Kohlberg and Davidson, 1977). By confronting moral problems such as the relationship of immigration to employment, students shift to higher stages of moral development. Education to Kohlberg and Mayer (1972) is the achievement of high stages of moral and cognitive development.

Grusec and Lytton (1988) summarized criticisms of Kohlberg's theory of moral development. They note that, given more familiar moral dilemmas than those presented by Kohlberg, children may reveal more sophisticated moral thinking. Furthermore, the theory may be biased against women, although Grusec and Lytton cite studies which show that sex differences do not exist in the attainment of advanced moral reasoning. The relationship between cognitive development and moral development is contentious, with Kohlberg claiming priority for logical analysis whereas some of his critics opt for social interaction as the basis of moral thinking. A related criticism is that exposure to particular kinds of models may affect children's moral sophistication. For example, the predominance in young people's lives of models who threaten punishment for misdemeanors may explain children's propensity for authority-oriented, lower-level moral reasoning.

The Development of Prejudice

The acquisition of prejudiced attitudes proceeds through eight age-related stages of development. Katz (1976) created this scheme after considering the available evidence. (Other schemes exist: for example, the three stage system postulated by Goodman, 1964.) As development progresses, children begin using the categories available in their culture. Categorical thinking helps in the resolution of problems, but it can also produce prejudice. In this section, prejudice and discrimination are defined, the stages of development are outlined, and the difficulties arising from the categorization of experiences are discussed.

Prejudice and Discrimination

According to Harding, Proshansky, Kutner and Chein (1969), a set of ideal norms — rationality, justice and human-heartedness — helps define prejudice. The norm of rationality includes processes of thinking that one uses in determining one's conclusions and actions, that is, seeking correct information, being cautious in drawing conclusions, making qualified inferences, and so on. Stereotypic thinking, an example of prejudice, violates the processes of such thinking. The norm of justice evokes the standard of equal treatment for all. The female student who finds that it is her sex rather than her ability which is preventing her from obtaining a leadership role in the classroom is receiving unequal treatment. The norm of human-heartedness is the acceptance of all individuals as essentially human regardless of their differences. Persons who are intolerant of others because they are different are deviating from the norm of human-heartedness. Prejudice is a failure to meet the standard of conduct implied by one or more of these ideal norms.

Discrimination is the outward manifestation of inner prejudice; in a sense, it is the conative aspect of prejudice. But as Simpson and Yinger (1985) caution, the relation between prejudice and discrimination is complex. Rather than prejudice always resulting in discrimination, it may be that discrimination at times results in prejudice. For instance, prejudice may be a means of rationalizing away the upset created when one has treated an individual inequitably. There is, then, an interactive relationship between prejudice and discrimination.

Stages in the Development of Prejudice

Katz (1973a, 1973b and 1976) has attempted to identify stages in the development of prejudice. The first stage of prejudice development is called the *early observation of racial cues*. Depending upon the child's maturation, observation of cues related to an outgroup may or may not have an effect upon the child. Delay of racial cue observation results if the child does not have the opportunity to encounter such cues as in the case when outgroup members are not part of the child's environment. Little is known empirically about the particular schedule of development in this stage, but it generally occurs before the child reaches three years of age. *Formation of rudimentary concepts* is the second stage wherein the child can differentiate among stimuli such as ingroup and outgroup members and a label is provided by those close to the child. For instance, a parent may say, 'He is a half-breed'. An evaluative element may be added so that the child begins avoiding the Metis playmate. The evaluative statement may give the impression that there is something wrong with the outgroup member. This second stage begins developing before age three and is usually consolidated by the time the child is four. *Conceptual differentiation* is the third stage through which the child passes. Given a label for the outgroup, further observation of positive and negative examples from outgroup members will allow children to receive evaluative feedback for their responses. Attributes are probably learned through the verbal responses to the children such as, 'He is an Indian even though he dresses like you'. Additional evaluative comments such as, 'And stay away from him', promote concept formation through cue redundancy. Campbell (1973) describes an incident from her life which illustrates how children learn as well from directly observing the behavior of their parents:

> The school was built in Spring River when I was nine. It was three miles away, and on opening all the parents had to bring their children

for registration. Because it was a mixed school, whites and half-breeds were gathered together officially for the first time, but the whites sat down on one side of the room while the half-breeds sat on the other. (p. 45)

The next stage, *recognition of irrevocability of cues*, lacks evidence for the typical age at which it develops. This fourth stage is characterized by the child realizing that certain cues about people change while others do not. For example, cues related to age change. Obviously, children normally grow into adults. However, racial membership usually does not change over time. An accurate concept of a group is dependent upon the child learning to label and identify correctly both those who are, and those who are not, members of the group. As well, he must learn that group membership is generally unchanging as far as race is concerned. When these difficult achievements have been made, the child has reached the stage of *consolidation of group membership* which usually begins by about age five and continues for an unspecified time. The sixth stage is known as *perceptual elaboration* and is dependent upon the child learning to differentiate between *us* and *them*. During this stage perceived differences among groups are emphasized, especially for children subjected to much evaluative feedback. Moreover, the within-group differences of the outgroup are reduced. Perceptual elaboration begins before the child enters grade 1 and continues throughout the elementary school years. The next stage called *cognitive elaboration* refers to the process by which the child's early, rather ill-formed attitudes, which are referred to by Katz as *concept attitudes*, become true racial attitudes. It is assumed that concept attitudes lay the foundation for racial attitudes, but the relationship between them is not well understood. It is probable that children's experience with minorities as well as the behavior of parents, peers and other significant people in their social milieu affect development of prejudice most markedly during the elementary school years. Toward the end of this period, the stage of *attitude crystallization* is reached.

A study by Kirby and Gardner (1973) confirms the trend toward greater consolidation of intergroup views with increasing age. They found that older English Canadian children showed the most consensus in their views about Natives while the youngest members showed the least consensus. The child eventually forms rather stable attitudes which remain unchanged unless drastic alterations in the social environment occur.

According to Katz, then, there are eight states of acquisition of intergroup attitudes. The stages do not have rigid boundaries so that one stage may shade gradually into the next and they may actually overlap. The age relationships are not fixed and unchanging; they are only approximations.

Categorization and Prejudice

Katz suggests that there are parallels between the thought processes of the prejudiced adult as described by Allport (1958) and the preoperational thought processes of the young child (3–4 years of age) as described by Piaget. At this stage the child has difficultly seeing that similar members of a given class are separate and different individuals. Because two individuals are highly similar in one attribute, for example, skin color, the child concludes that they must be alike in other characteristics. Developmentally, there is a stage in the child's life when the apparently distorted reasoning of the pre-judiced person is normal. Adults, however, who revert to this simplistic form of thinking, may be defending themselves against a threat through the de-fence mechanism of regression. For them simplistic, categorical thinking is usually maladaptive.

The tendency towards categorization and the way reasoning develops may lead naturally to prejudice. As a means of ordering the mass of stimuli from the environment, humans tend to categorize experiences. Categories obscure individual differences and they tend toward oversimplification so that prejudiced thinking may result. In general, humans have a great capacity to learn from experience. Concepts are the result of attempts to categorize experience. De Cecco and Crawford (1974) define a concept as 'a class of stimuli which have common characteristics. These stimuli are objects, events or persons' (p. 288). Concepts are classes of stimuli and we know these classes by their names: We may group people by geographic region of origin, for example, John is a Euro-Canadian whereas Tony is a South Asian-Canadian. John, born in England and now living in Canada, is an instance of the concept named *Euro-Canadian* which includes many other Canadians of European ancestry. The concept excludes those who are not of this ancestry, for exam-ple, Tony. Concepts are classes of stimuli, not particular stimuli. When effective concept learning occurs, individuals correctly identify a person as a member of a particular ethnic group. They may then react to the person as a member of a group rather than as an individual; discrimination occurs.

When we classify the confusion of stimuli which are received from the environment, then, individual differences are obscured. If race is the basis for the classification of two persons, other non-essential characteristics may be ignored and oversimplification occurs. The characteristics which are ignored may be equally important from another perspective (or way of classification), but, for the purposes of racial classification, they are neglected.

Cultures vary in the importance they give to race as a social classification. In the United States, for instance, there is a heavy emphasis on racial classification (Williams and Morland, 1976). In Canada, it is increasing in importance. Through emphasis, the young child realizes the significance of race and is sensitized to messages about race. Williams and Morland provide the example of the teacher who, having been asked to record the number of Euro- and Afro-Americans in a class, tells all the Blacks to stand and be counted and then after they are seated asks all the Whites to stand. Confronted by this sort of experience, children are bound to assume that there are two types of students in the room and that the social classification is important. Add to this example a variety of other experiences and the child will probably begin to use race as a main way of categorizing people.

Thinking in categories is necessary as a means of effectively dealing with others, and it is a device for predicting the outcome of our efforts at solving problems. In task-oriented problem solving, as described by Coleman and Hammen (1974), the individual appraises the situation by categorizing the problem as similar or dissimilar to previous experiences. This is useful because if the situation is similar to previous encounters, the person may apply solutions which have worked in the past. This simplifies the problem but the danger is that oversimplification may occur as in the case where a stereotype might be used to react to, say, socialists, Jews or South Asians.

Whereas Brigham (1970) points to the ambiguities of the meaning of stereotype, Secord and Backman (1974) suggest that individuals do three things when they stereotype: They recognize a category of people (e.g., South Asians); agree on the attributes of the members of the category (e.g., hardworking); and assume that any member of the group has all the attributes of the category (e.g., Tony is a South Asian; therefore he must be hardworking). The danger is that an adequate account will not be taken of individual differences such that we may brand all South Asians, for instance, as liars on the basis of an experience with one who lied. Tajfel (1973) states that as much stereotyped simplification is achieved as possible. Even when the facts run against our categories, there is a tendency to preserve the categories. Illustrative of this preservation is Allport's (1958) reference to the device of admitting exceptions: 'Some of my best friends are Jews, but ...' (p. 23). Categorical treatment of individuals, such that mere membership produces the assumption that the person has all the characteristics of the category, is basic to stereotyping. Categorization is useful, but it may ensnare us in prejudice and many people are trapped.

Socialization in a Bigoted Society

While Canadian discrimination has tended to be concealed rather than highly visible, and to be a matter of custom rather than of official policy (Hughes and Kallen, 1974), oppression of Canadians of Japanese descent during World War II is an exception. This blight on the record of relations among ethnic groups in Canada is vividly described by Adachi (1976). Briefly, people became fearful that Canadians of Japanese descent and more recent Japanese immigrants might aid a Japanese invasion of Canada. As a result, all individuals of that ethnic group (nearly 21,000 people, three-quarters of whom where Canadian citizens) were evacuated from the west coast and placed in internment camps in the interior of British Columbia and elsewhere, where living conditions were somewhat less than ideal. There was much financial loss and the possible psychological damage is illustrated by the many moving interviews recorded by Barry Broadfoot (1977) in *Years of Sorrow, Years of Shame: The Story of the Japanese Canadians in World War II*. One interviewee, a teacher who taught at one of the camps, recalls a Japanese-Canadian high school student whose average achievement dropped by more than 35 per cent after moving to a camp (p. 247).

Hughes and Kallen make that point that racism rather than wartime security may have been mostly responsible for the ill treatment of the Japanese in Canada. They base their argument on the fact that some deportations to Japan took place after the War and that with the exception of the highly visible Hutterites, Canadians of German descent did not receive similarly harsh treatment. Supporting Hughes and Kallen are the observations by Adachi (1976) that as late as 1948 Japanese Canadians could not enter the protected zone on the west coast without a permit from the RCMP and that at least one person was sentenced to a year of hard labor for breaking this regulation. Long after Japan had been defeated, Canadians of Japanese descent were still being persecuted.

Ethnocentrism

Underlying the use of prejudice as a means of securing wealth and power is the phenomenon of ethnocentrism which is the view that the attitudes, values and behavior of the ingroup are singular and correct. Prejudice is partially the result of competition between or among groups. People in groups cooperate but there is also competition and conflict for society's advantages. For example, Montero (1977) quotes this observation:

> There is a certain bigotry here, a bias that seems to be dormant . . .
> At the beginning of the second world war, there were factories in
> Toronto that posted notices offering employment stating: Englishmen
> need not apply. (p. 186)

In order to maintain preferred status, people will even invent beliefs which are biased in their favor. Ethnocentrism results from socialization where the ingroup is seen as right and having a natural claim to favored status. Hence, it functions as a way of justifying wealth and power.

There are particular beliefs which support prejudice. For example, the majority may accept the belief of predestination such that minorities are seen as innately inferior and, as a consequence, discrimination seems valid. Discrimination is sometimes rationalized under colonial rule by viewing the indigenous population as lacking the skills necessary for self-governance and for modern technology. The Canadian government, for instance, practises paternalism in controlling Native lands and many apparently legitimate land claims remain unsettled (Hughes and Kallen, 1974). In addition, Indians on and off the reserves are badly housed. Hughes and Kallen report that in 1967 about

57 per cent of Natives on reserves, as compared with 11 per cent for the national average, lived in substandard housing. Inuit in the North also have problems of housing supply and overcrowding. The indigenous people of Canada are further economically disadvantaged by the lack of relevant education which creates high dropout rates from schools resulting in restricted job opportunities. Complications arise from the lack of jobs on reserves and from other influences such as discriminatory hiring practices in the cities. Unemployment among Natives is at a much higher level as compared with that among non-Natives. Thus, by failing to create non-discriminatory hiring practices, to offer effective education, to supply adequate housing, and to give Natives control of their own resources, the majority retains its privileged position.

The expression of ethnocentrism varies with the situation. Simpson and Yinger (1985) point out that ethnicity may be emphasized in attacking a group during times of economic depression: Excessive competition for jobs may create demands for reduced immigration and for selective employment. However, economic factors can also be expressed during times of economic stability. That is to say, hopes of gain predominate rather than fears of loss.

French-speaking persons in the province of Quebec have historically held a disadvantaged economic position relative to English-speaking persons. While the situation is changing, because of factors such as the official government policy of bilingualism, many English-speaking youngsters are still receiving the message that French Canadians are somehow inferior because they do not generally speak unaccented, fluent English. Hughes and Kallen observe that there is a consensus which tends to preserve the place of each minority group within Canadian society. These authors outline factors, including economic ones within French Canadian society in Quebec, which have preserved the status quo. Historically, the Quebec French Canadian's society was highly conservative, agricultural and tied closely to the Catholic Church. Within this frame of reference, the French Canadian farmers were to value large, cohesive families and to shun materialism.

Inheritance customs, where one son received the family farm, and the inability of most families to send their remaining sons to institutions of higher learning created a situation conducive to the rural-urban shift of young males. Before the advent of industrialization of Quebec in the twentieth century, many sought jobs in other provinces and in the United States. The loss of these young males served to aid in the preservation of a relatively stable and traditional French Canadian society. As the twentieth century progressed, Quebec became a manufacturing center due to investment by British Canadians and Americans. Increasingly, French Canadians were able to obtain industrial jobs in Quebec. However, they were kept from occupying the upper echelon management positions. These were reserved for the English-speaking majority group members. The basis for this discrimination was largely language in that the French worker was allowed to rise, say, to a foremanship in order to deal with other French workers but not beyond.

Their language made identification easy and their lack of facility in the language of business (English) allowed others to keep them in their place. Eventually the French Canadians' frustration with a minority position produced changes in the structure of society which are continuing today.

Socialization

The process of socialization has been implicated in the development and maintenance of prejudice. Brophy (1977) notes that the socialization process results in the development of certain characteristics rather than others. In the early stages of childhood, the child's experiences are controlled by the parents. During adolescence, older siblings, friends, teachers and the mass media will supplement the influence of the parents. However, much of the young people's learning, according to Milner (1975), is through imitation of unintended examples given by the parents. Parents encourage a particular social atmosphere for their children by restricting the choice of clothes, reading material and how youngsters spend their time. It might be concluded that parents directly teach social attitudes to their children. The evidence for this comes from intuition that this should happen, for most of us can recall receiving directions from our parents about such matters as playmates. Intuition is supported by research. For example, Kirby and Gardner (1973) showed that older English Canadian children's attitudes towards French Canadians were more similar to their parents' views than to those of younger children. Thus, where the agents of socialization are bigoted, children will tend toward bigotry. There are exceptions, however, as the following situation illustrates:

> His parents threatened him with everything if he married a black girl ... But after a couple of months, my parents asked them over. My own parents were not too happy about our plans either ... When Jim's parents had arrived and we were all sitting there together in the living room very uncomfortable and still and very formal, my mother in a quiet voice said, 'If you'll excuse me, I'm going to turn out the light. I think that what we all need to talk about is best discussed if we are not sidetracked by color'. You know, after that, everyone started slowly to really talk about the problem. And how they felt. But really honestly. Nobody pretended any more. And after about three hours of sitting there in the dark bringing out all their fears, everyone seemed to feel okay. (Montero, 1977, p. 190)

Early Learning

Williams and Morland (1976) outline a theory of prejudice which is based upon the early learning experiences of the child with light and darkness.

These authors assume that most children have early experiences which lead them to prefer light rather than darkness. In the light the child is visually oriented to his environment while darkness produces disorientation. This preference for light is strengthened by need satisfaction being primarily met during the day time. Fear of darkness appears between the ages of two and four. Children at this age have developed a visual orientation to their environment, learned that some things are frightening, and developed an active imagination. Suppose that, while alone in a darkened room, the child dreams that there is a beast in the closet and cries for help. The parents rush into the room, turn on the light, comfort the child and search for the beast. Reassurance is given that a beast is not there. The child has associated darkness with fear and light with fear reduction. These associations may be strengthened by other experiences with darkness. During thunderstorms when the sky darkens, thunderclaps may frighten the child. More than this, at night, the child is generally cut off from the many pleasant interactions experienced with the family. In these ways, a strong preference for light over darkness if acquired.

There are two basic consequences of this preference for light. First, there is a tendency for dark colors and darkness universally to represent the negative aspects of life and for light and light colors to represent the positive. Second, young people are predisposed to evaluate light objects as good and dark objects as bad. The apparent prejudice of the pre-schooler is not necessarily racial in origin. While Williams and Morland see the roots of prejudice in the child's early experiences with light and darkness, they do not underestimate other cultural influences.

It may be that reinforcement is the basic process for learning prejudice. Siblings or parents may differentially reinforce behavior such as reactions to light and darkness. Katz (1976) suggests that the affective elements of intergroup attitudes may well be learned through differential reinforcement. Katz, however, has reservations about the view that all aspects of prejudice are explained by reinforcement; attitudes subsume rather complex responses which are not usually rewarded consistently. Parents may be ambivalent in their expression of prejudice with the result that their child receives ambiguous messages about how to act, for example, toward a friend from a minority group. Katz concludes that the relationship between youngsters' attitudes and those of their parents is not yet clearly understood and that resolution must await longitudinal investigation.

Identification

Prejudice is a cultural element which is perpetuated by the socialization process. Identification is a basic mechanism of socialization through which young people may adopt the prejudice of significant others (e.g., parents, siblings, peers, teachers) in their environment. Identification, a psychoanalytic construct, refers to the subtle process whereby a person unconsciously adopts the characteristics of the model (Mussen, Conger and Kagan, 1974). The model is often the same sex parent. The characteristics of the parent, may be adopted; if the parent is bigoted, the child may become bigoted whereas if the parent is tolerant, the child may become tolerant. Behavior acquired by identification tends to be emitted spontaneously without direct rewards being applied, and to be relatively stable. Identification, then, is a process which partially explains how young people adopt the prejudices of others.

Mussen, Conger and Kagan explain that identification originates with the awareness of physical or psychological similarities with the model. Identification will be strengthened or weakened by the degree of attractiveness of the model. Warm, accepting, rewarding adults are more likely to be identified with than cold, rejecting, punishing ones (Bandura and Walters, 1963). Seeing the model as attractive and assuming that being more like the model might lead to possession of the model's desirable traits and resources, youngsters adopt many of the model's characteristics and thereby increase identification. A person can begin to feel similar to a model in three main ways: Actual similarities in appearance and/or in personality may be seen; behavior similar to the model may be displayed; and others may describe similarities between the adolescent and the parent. People become more or less identified with models; it is a continuum which may range from very slight to very great. Identification shows how socialization may produce prejudice. Once prejudice has been established in a culture, the process by which culture is transmitted (socialization) becomes the most important determining variable.

Modeling

Within the identification process, young people are probably doing a lot of observation learning or modeling. Modeling is the type of learning where 'from observing others one forms an idea of how new behaviors are performed, and on later occasions this coded information serves as a guide to action' (Bandura, 1977, p. 22). Bandura and Walters (1963) state that individuals can learn deviant behavior as well as conforming behavior through modeling.

It is obvious that many behaviors are acquired through the observation of real-life models, but symbolic models are becoming increasingly important. Symbolic models may be created pictorially and through the use of oral or written instructions. Combinations of these modes of expression are of course possible. Parents are apt to be less influential as models because of the great amount of time children spend watching television. Bandura and Walters state that rate and level of learning varies with the way the model is presented; for example, parental verbal instructions may be less effective than audio-visual presentations from television. Bandura and his colleagues during the 1960s conducted a number of studies which showed that aggression by symbolic and real-life models is imitated by youngsters.

Daniel McDougall

The Influence of the Media

Studies of the influence of media violence on viewers have largely confirmed modeling effects. For example, Donnerstein and Donnerstein (1976) showed that a film depicting white aggression against Blacks resulted in white observers imitating this behavior even when they viewed retaliation by the Blacks. La Marsh, Beaulieu and Young (1977), after surveying the effects of TV in Canada, concluded that a relationship exists between TV violence and aggression. In a major review of studies of the effects of mass media, Liebert and Schwartzberg (1977) summarized the correlational studies included in the US Surgeon General's report which showed an association between seeing violence on TV and aggressiveness. Observation of aggression in cartoons taken from the typical Sunday morning presentation significantly increased aggressive behavior by pre-school and elementary school viewers. Interestingly, Liebert and Schwartzberg described studies showing that, after viewing an aggressive act performed by a television villain, children of elementary school age are more aggressive when the villain has some redeeming characteristics than when the villain is uniformly bad. What is of interest here is that Archie Bunker of the formerly popular TV series *All in the Family* was a lovable character who was bigoted. His lovable nature may have contributed to some viewers becoming more prejudiced than they would if Archie had uniformly 'bad' motives (Vidmar and Rokeach, 1974).

The Effects of Literature

Books have high status in our society and they are one of the main sources of information in the school. Several studies have shown that Canadian school books place minority groups in an unfavorable light. McDiarmid and Pratt (1971) studied statements made about Christians, Jews, Moslems, Negroes, Indians and immigrants in authorized social studies texts in Ontario for grades 1 to 13. A total of 143 texts were examined, some of which were eliminated due to insufficient references. Of the six groups, Christians and Jews were treated most favorably while Negroes and Indians were treated least favorably. Considering the term most frequently applied to each group, Pratt and McDiarmid state: 'We are most likely to encounter in textbooks devoted Christians, great Jews, hardworking immigrants, infidel Moslems, primitive Negroes and savage Indians' (p. 45). History texts contained more stereotyped descriptions than geography texts did. Moreover, McDiarmid and Pratt cite several studies such as Sevigny (1966) and Hodgetts (1968) which have shown that Canadian history texts are often biased presentations of either French or English Canadian history.

Lupul (1976) completed a study of the portrayal of Canada's other peoples in senior high school history and social studies textbooks in Alberta from 1905 to the present. 'Other peoples' include indigenous peoples, Metis,

Orientals and European continental immigrants, especially southeastern Europeans. Other peoples constituted about 27 per cent of the Canadian population in 1971. Lupul divides the period under study into three sections, the last of which is post-1960 with an emphasis on 1970 to 1976. Among the references studied in this period, a history by J.S. Moir and D.M.L. Farr entitled *The Canadian Experience* largely ignores Canada's other peoples with the exception of the Metis. Lupul cogently remarks: 'But how does one explain the failure to notice the fortunes of the Icelanders in Gimli, the Mennonites in the Red River Valley, the Orientals on the west coast, the Blacks in Nova Scotia and Ontario, the Doukhobors in Saskatchewan and British Columbia and the Hutterites in the prairie provinces? The book's title is thus a misnomer, for what can "the Canadian experience" be where practically a quarter of Canada's population is ignored'? (p. 20) Lupul deals with another core reference *Challenge of Confrontation: Canada 70*, a series of six paperbacks by the Toronto Telegram's editorial team on the Canadian predicament. In this series Canada's other peoples are dealt with extensively in two volumes: *The Prairie Provinces: Alienation and Anger* and *Ontario, The Linchpin*. Despite increased attention to the diversity of the Canadian cultural mosaic, Lupul criticized these volumes for being essentially assimilationist. He also criticized the reference, *The Official Languages*, a report of the Royal Commission on Bilingualism and Biculturalism, for stressing cultural dualism as represented by French and English Canadians at the expense of the other contributors to our culture. Another text found lacking was *Canada: Unity in Diversity*, written by J. Hamelin, F. Ouellet, M. Trudel and P.G. Cornell. It contains lengthy accounts of the Indians and Eskimos but it does not do justice to other peoples' contributions, especially in the area of language. In general, the portrayal of the other peoples in Alberta high schools' history and social studies textbooks has been most superficial, with only a few groups receiving adequate treatment. The books used in recent years have failed to accommodate the stated goal of multiculturalism to the linguistic and cultural goals of Canada's other peoples.

Jones (1974) summarized the findings of a survey which examined social studies textbooks (history) used in Saskatchewan schools in grades 1 to 12. References to racial, ethnic and religious groups as well as the kind of treatment accorded women were examined. A sample of 60 of 200 authorized textbooks were selected on the basis of teacher completed questionnaires about which texts they used and these were subjected to a McDiarmid and Pratt (1971) content analysis. There was in fact a marked differential treatment of the various minority groups. For example, Christians were dealt with most favorably and they were described as great, devoted and loving. Native North Americans received more unfavorable references and they were labeled as hostile and warlike savages. (Sluman, 1967, found biased treatment of the native Indians as well.) Jones discovered other groups which were described stereotypically: Jews, Negroes, Eskimos and Moslems. Women were generally shown in a positive light but they were stereotyped as being helpful, hardworking and pretty while their active role in history was largely overlooked.

Jones also reported the findings of a survey of Saskatchewan's elementary school readers for the possible existence of sex bias. A random selection of one reader from each series in each grade from 1 to 5 was made. Findings revealed that male characters dominated numerically and they were more favorably presented than females. A high degree of sex-role stereotyping existed for both sexes. The author concluded that the effects of this stereotyping on those children whose behavior differed from that which was presented must be especially damaging. Babin (1976) reported the results of a survey of Ontario school textbooks for biases against the aged, labor unionists and political minorities. Seventy-eight were found to have 104 biased references. Biased statements against the aged appeared principally in English primary stories where the aged were viewed condescendingly. In general, the texts contained little history of the labor union movement and little information about the benefits Canadian society has received because of the movement. Regarding political minorities, the bias was of emphasis and omission rather than direct prejudiced statements.

Canadian school books have obviously been biased. While books are not the only source of prejudice in our society, as important transmitters of culture in the schools, they supplement other sources.

Revision of factual textbooks is possible, because as long as the prose remains clear and interesting and the information accurate, bias can be removed without censorship becoming an issue. Revision, not censorship, is advocated. That is, authors revise their texts because legitimate, objective criticism has revealed weaknesses. Rather than limiting the expression of knowledge which some segments of society might label unconventional, controversial or unacceptable, revision would correct thoughtless omissions and delete unjustly derogatory statements about minorities. To facilitate revision, guidelines such as those developed by McGraw-Hill for the equal treatment of the sexes help avoid negative or discriminatory rendering of minorities (Gross, 1979).

The situation is different for works of fiction. Books such as the Dr Dolittle books certain prejudiced statements which reflect the uninformed views of earlier times (Milner, 1975). How can we deal with these books? Opposing solutions have been advocated. On the one hand, Phillips (1973) recommends keeping books containing prejudice as valuable teaching tools to show that this sort of thing occurs. On the other hand, Milner feels that many children may be harmed because, in ethnically homogeneous areas where a sense of urgency is lacking, prejudiced literature may pass without notice and the ideas may be uncritically absorbed. Nevertheless, even young children recognize distortion, and with the help of their teachers the effects of bias will be reduced.

Innovations to Instruction

Specific teaching methods have been developed to reduce prejudice. For example, Katz and Zalk (1978) tested the effectiveness of four short-term procedures for altering white students' racial attitudes. There were (a) reinforcement of black as a color, (b) white children's vicarious contacts with Blacks, (c) white students' increased positive, equal-status contact with Blacks, and (d) perceptual training in the differentiation of minority group faces. Results showed that when time is limited vicarious contact and perceptual differentiation are the most effective in reducing prejudice, and these two methods are now considered in greater detail.

Vicarious Contact and Perceptual Differentiation

Vicarious contact was produced by presenting a tape-recorded story which depicted a child who, upon arriving home from school, secures medical aid for his/her sick grandmother. While the story was being told, the students watched slides of black participants. This technique supports the findings of Litcher and Johnson (1969) that multi-ethnic readers are effective in reducing prejudice.

Perceptual differentiation is an important approach to creating more positive racial attitudes, especially when direct contact is difficult. This conclusion is based on the observation that faces of other races appear more similar than those of the ingroup (Katz, 1973a). This may lead to the generalization of negative attitudes to all members of a visible minority group. However, young people can learn to perceive facial differences among outgroup members. Katz (1973b) and Katz and Zalk (1978) helped children become more familiar with the faces of Blacks by reinforcing correct naming of pictures of Blacks and by practice in distinguishing between sets of two black faces. Perceptual differentiation of minority groups facilitates tolerance of individual differences (Cantor, 1972). This conclusion implies not only that there be investigation of other cultures but there also should be familiarization of the model representatives of a group such that accurate identification of their pictures from a mixed array of photographs is assured. The development of perceptual processes is another way to increase tolerance (Katz, 1976).

Promoting Success

Frustration, aggression and failure
Because certain frustrating learning conditions, such as scapegoating, lead to aggression, teachers should design instruction so that students succeed more

often than they fail. That is, students should have their correct answers confirmed and their errors identified, but the dominant experience should be success rather than failure. Excessive failure to achieve goals produces frustration which may set the stage for discrimination amongst students.

Aggression may follow from frustration. The purpose of the aggression is to destroy a block to need gratification. But because this may entail a high risk of retaliation (e.g., a feared authority figure may be the obstacle), the person may direct aggression toward individuals who are relatively lacking in power, such as members of minority groups. A scapegoat is found and the aggressive person rationalizes hostility by seeing the true or imagined flaws of the minority.

As empirical evidence accumulates, however, it becomes obvious that frustration does not always produce aggression and that the characteristics of the social situation are important in determining what behavior might flow from frustration. A basic condition for aggression seems to be the arbitrary interruption of a sequence leading to a goal. When inhibitions to aggression are strong or when non-aggressive responses to a frustrating event have been learned, aggression may not occur. But when a situation lowers inhibitions against aggression, hostile acts happen more frequently. Frustration is not a necessary condition for aggression. Aggression may be learned directly, as in the case of any behavior — through modeling or suitable contingencies of reinforcement (Secord and Backman, 1974). Nevertheless, where particular circumstances exist, frustration may produce aggressive, discriminatory acts.

Sears, Maccoby and Levin (1975) identify punishment as a condition which allows frustration to give rise to aggression. Academic failure is a particularly insidious form of punishment. While progressive promotion policies have reduced the number of students failing whole grades, there are still many who are made to repeat a year, and pupils continue to experience too much failure in their daily work (Hamacheck, 1978; Hathaway and Rhodes, 1979). Being both frustrating and punishing, failure may produce aggression. Moreover, excessive failure lowers self-esteem and the latter condition is also associated with aggression (Rosenbaum and Staners, 1961; Coopersmith, 1967). When failure predominates, aggression against minority group members is one possible outlet for the resultant frustration.

Competition and evaluation
North American schooling is highly competitive. Unfortunately competitiveness contributes greatly to pupils' frustrations. Youngsters soon become aware of competition (Johnson and Johnson, 1976) and strive to out-perform their classmates. As students progress through school, competitiveness increases (Johnson and Johnson, 1975). This does not always have to be the case because cooperation can be learned. Due to their more advanced cognitive development, moreover, adolescents learn cooperation more readily than younger children. North American students are not irrational competitors;

given appropriate instruction they cooperate with each other (Sagotsky, Wood-Schneider and Konop, 1981).

At the root of competition in the schools is the norm-referenced or relative marking system which predominates. Where students' performances are assessed in relation to well defined groups such as classmates or agemates, norm-referenced grading and reporting exists. The five-category, letter-grade system of the high school (A, B, C, D, E) and the three-category system of the elementary school (above grade, at grade, below grade and its many variations) are interpreted in relation to the average achievement of the class. That is, the letter grade of B may mean above average performance. A major problem with normative reporting is that teachers may erroneously make favorable or unfavorable evaluations. The average child who is placed among brilliant classmates, for instance, may receive inappropriate low grades. In norm-referenced systems, some students succeed while others fail, possibly producing for the losers lowered self-esteem. Moreover, competition may actually produce interference in the efforts of some students by others and overall group achievement and cohesiveness may suffer.

Through the use of criterion-referenced grading and marking, achievement is stressed without emphasizing inter-individual competition. A criterion-referenced grading and reporting system lowers competition for scarce, high grades. The student's actual performance within a subject is assessed and the report card usually contains a list of specific skills and knowledge rather than broad subject matter categories. Criterion-referenced approaches are adopted because they more readily permit a different emphasis. Typically the teacher stresses not only mastery of the important skills and knowledge but also improvement relative to the individual's past performance rather than in comparison to peers. Consistent adherence to these procedures will diminish competitiveness among students and lessen feelings of failure.

Cooperative learning

Another method of reducing competition is to stress cooperation whenever possible in achieving the goals of instruction. Cooperation exists when two or more individuals work together for their mutual benefit to reach the same end. According to Johnson and Johnson (1978), students should learn in a manner which is best suited for the particular activity. Some tasks, such as writing a poem, are best accomplished independently; other activities, such as team sports, are enhanced by friendly competition; still others, such as researching local environmental concerns, are most productively undertaken by groups of students working interdependently. For the most part, the teacher determines what method suits a specific task. How the teacher structures the learning situation greatly affects the nature of the pupil interactions, that is, whether they are independent, competitive or cooperative. Moreover, whether or not the task is cooperatively accomplished influences the affective and cognitive instructional products. Through cooperation, students learn that it is unnecessary for some to lose so that they can succeed, and that it is possible to support their peers in achieving objectives. The by-products are increased self-esteem, greater liking for others and improved relations among members of groups.

The jigsaw technique illustrates effective cooperative learning (Aronson, Blaney, Stephan, Sikes and Snapp, 1978). In this method, a class is divided into groups of five or six pupils and each member receives a limited amount of information about a topic. In order to fit the segments of the topic together into a unified whole, the students are dependent upon each other; inter-dependency is thereby created. After receiving their topic segment and studying them independently, the pupils join other classmates who have the same segment and help each other learn the topic. Their counterparts, who have the same elements of the subject, may act as sounding boards in checking individual comprehension and presentation. Next the pupils return to their original groups to instruct each other within a specified time limit. Students are dependent upon each other for full understanding of the topic: Each student contributes to the knowledge of others and individual perform-ance is dependent upon the assistance of all members. Besides setting broad limits on the curriculum, the teacher facilitates group interaction and pro-motes positive group living. The teacher is not the sole source of information as may be the case in a more teacher-oriented classroom (Aronson, Bridgeman and Geffner, 1978). The research on the jigsaw technique has generally been most encouraging. The technique enhances student self-esteem, lowers com-petitiveness and produces more positive feelings among group members. Cooperative learning improves student perception of ethnically different classmates. It produces increased friendships and interactions among students from different ethnic backgrounds (DeVries, Edwards and Slavin, 1978; Slavin and Madden, 1979). A cooperative learning environment promotes ego-enhancing, prosocial explanations of successes and failures both for individuals and their classmates; whereas competitive situations are conducive to ego-deflating explanations of the other person's successes and failures (Aronson *et al.*, 1978).

Social role taking was identified by Aronson, Bridgeman and Geffner (1978) as the fundamental process underlying the effects of cooperative learn-ing on prosocial behavior. In general, role taking (empathy) is the ability to guess what another person is thinking, feeling or seeing. It develops as the child matures (Flavell, 1973), but even young children exhibit some ability to see the perspective of another person (Hetherington and McIntyre, 1975; Zahn-Waxler, Radke-Yarrow and Brady-Shaw, 1977). It is a learned skill which improves with training (Chandler, 1973; Hohn, 1973; Weiner and Wright, 1973). Young people who learn cooperatively show greater ability to take another person's perspective than those who learn in a competitive situation (Aronson *et al.*, 1978). Johnson (1975) found that there is a positive relationship between cooperativeness and role taking ability. Understanding

and tolerance of others who are different from oneself are fostered by cooperative learning.

Summary

Although not all individuals while growing up are unduly troubled, the
developmental process as characterized by Erikson poses challenges which
demand adjustments. Successful adaptations occasion greater psychosocial
maturity, but unsuccessful attempts at resolving developmental tasks may
retard advancement and create problems for future attainments. During
childhood and adolescence, various social and psychological factors combine
to produce prejudice. According to Kohlberg and his colleagues, prejudice is
a moral problem and as such can be ameliorated by moving youngsters to
higher levels of moral reasoning.

Prejudice may follow a developmental sequence. While the processes of
concept formation and ethnocentrism contribute to the development of prejudice, conditioning and identification in early learning may also kindle prejudice in people. Modeling or observation learning, whether through real-life
or the symbolic models of the media, books and materials at school, affects the
development of prejudice.

Social scientists are slowly building techniques to curtail prejudice. Instructional innovations such as vicarious contact, perceptual differentiation,
criterion-referenced evaluation and cooperative learning foster tolerance and
understanding.

Bibliography

ADACHI, K. (1976) *The Enemy that Never Was: A History of the Japanese Canadians*,
Toronto: McClelland and Stewart.
ALLPORT, G.W. (1958) *The Nature of Prejudice* (Anchor Books Edn) Garden City, New
York: Doubleday.
ARONSON, E., BLANEY, N., STEPHEN, D., SIKES, J. and SNAPP, M. (1978) *The Jigsaw
Classroom*, Beverley Hills: Sage.
ARONSON, E., BRIDGEMAN, D.L. and GEFFNER, R. (1978) 'Interdependent interac-
tions and prosocial behavior', *Journal of Research and Development in Education*,
12, pp. 16–27.
AUSUBEL, D. and SULLIVAN, E. (1970) *Theory and Problems of Child Development*,
(2nd Edn), New York: Grune and Stratton.
BABIN, P. (1976) 'Biased texts discovered, removed from approved lists', *Ontario
Education Dimensions*, *10* (2), p. 6.
BANDURA, A. (1977) *Social Learning Theory*, Englewood Cliffs, NJ: Prentice-Hall.
BANDURA, A. and WALTERS, R.H. (1963) *Social Learning and Personality Develop-
ment*, Toronto: Holt, Rinehart and Winston.
BRIGHAM, J.C. (1970) 'Ethnic stereotypes', *Psychological Bulletin*, 76, pp. 15–38.

BROADFOOT, B. (1977) *Years of Sorrow, Years of Shame: The Story of the Japanese Canadians in World War II*, Toronto: Doubleday.

BROPHY, J.E. (1977) *Child Development and Socialization*, Toronto: Science Research Associates.

CAMPBELL, M. (1973) *Halfbreed*, Toronto: McClelland and Stewart.

CANTOR, G.N. (1972) 'Effects of familiarization on children's ratings of pictures of whites and blacks', *Child Development*, 43, pp. 1219–29.

CHANDLER, M.J. (1973) 'Egocentrism and antisocial behavior: The assessment and training of social perspective-taking skills', *Development Psychology*, 9, pp. 326–32.

COLEMAN, J.C. and HAMMEN, C.L. (1974) *Contemporary Psychology and Effective Behavior*, Glenview, IL; Scott, Foresman.

COOPERSMITH, S. (1967) *The Antecedents of Self-esteem*, San Francisco: Freeman.

DANIELS, L., DOUGLAS, L., OLIVER, C. and WRIGHT, I. (Eds) (1978) *Prejudice: Teacher's Manual*, Toronto: Ontario Institute for Studies in Education.

DAVIDSON, F.B.H. (1977) 'Respect for persons and ethnic prejudice in childhood: A cognitive-developmental description', in TUMIN, M.M. and PLOTCH, W. (Eds) *Pluralism in a Democratic Society*, New York: Praeger.

DE CECCO, J.P. and CRAWFORD, W.R. (1974) *The Psychology of Learning and Instruction: Educational Psychology*, (2nd Edn). Englewood Cliffs, NJ: Prentice Hall.

DEVRIES, D.L., EDWARDS, K.J. and SLAVIN, R.E. (1978) 'Biracial learning teams and race relations in the classrooms. Four field experiments using Teams-Games-Tournament', *Journal of Educational Psychology*, 70, pp. 356–62.

DONNERSTEIN, M. and DONNERSTEIN, E. (1976) 'Variables in interracial aggression: Exposure to aggressive interracial interactions', *Journal of Social Psychology*, 100, pp. 111–21.

ELKIND, D. (1972) *Erik Erikson's Eight Stages of Man*, in BIEHLER, R.F. (Ed.) *Psychology Applied to Teaching: Selected Readings* (pp. 120–37), Boston: Houghton Mifflin.

ERIKSON, E.H. (1968) *Identity: Youth and Crisis*, New York: Norton.

ERIKSON, E.H. (1963) *Childhood and Society* (2nd Edn), New York: Norton.

FLAVELL, J.H. (1973) 'The development of inference about others', in MISCHEL, T. (Ed.) *Understanding Other Persons* (pp. 66–116), London: Blackwell.

GOODMAN, M. (1964) *Race Awareness in Young Children* (2nd Edn). New York: Crowell-Collier.

GROSS, B. (1979) *Teaching Under Pressure*, Santa Monica, California: Goodyear.

GRUSEC, J.E. and LYTTON, H. (1988) *Social Development: History, Theory, and Research*, New York: Springer-Verlag.

HAMACHEK, D.E. (1978) *Encounters with the Self* (2nd Edn), New York: Holt, Rinehart and Winston.

HARDING, J., PROSHANSKY, H., KUTNER, B. and CHEIN, I. (1969) 'Prejudice and ethnic relations', in LINDZEY, G. and ARONSON, E. (Eds) *The Handbook of Social Psychology* (2nd Edn, Vol. 5), Don Mills, Ontario: Addison-Wesley.

HATHAWAY, W.E. and RHODES, H.C. (1979) *Disadvantaged Learners: The Nature of the Problem and Some Potential Solutions*, Edmonton: Alberta Education.

HETHERINGTON, E. and McINTYRE, C. (1975) 'Developmental psychology', *Annual Review of Psychology*, 26, pp. 97–136.

HODGETTS, A.B. (1968) *What Culture? What Heritage?* Toronto: Ontario Institute for Studies in Education.

HOHN, R.L. (1973) 'Perceptual training and its effects on racial preferences of kindergarten children', *Psychological Reports*, 32, pp. 435–41.

HUGHES, D.R. and KALLEN, E. (1974) *The Anatomy of Racism: Canadian Dimensions*, Montreal: Harvest House.

JOHNSON, D.W. (1975) 'Affective perspective taking and cooperative predisposition', *Developmental Psychology, 11,* pp. 869–70.

JOHNSON, D.W. and JOHNSON, R. (1975) *Learning Together and Alone: Cooperation, Competition, and Individualization,* Englewood Cliffs, NJ: Prentice-Hall.

JOHNSON, D.W. and JOHNSON, R. (1976) 'Student perceptions of and preferences for cooperative and competitive learning experiences', *Perceptual and Motor Skills, 42,* pp. 989–90.

JOHNSON, D.W. and JOHNSON, R.J. (1978) 'Cooperative, competitive, and individualistic learning', *Journal of Research and Development in Education, 12,* pp. 2–15.

JONES, L. (1974) 'Sex and race stereotyping in textbooks', *Query, 5,* (3), pp. 19–21.

KATZ, P.A. (1973a) 'Perception of racial cues in preschool children, a new look', *Developmental Psychology, 8,* pp. 295–9.

KATZ, P.A. (1973b) 'Stimulus predifferentiation and modification of children's racial attitudes', *Child Development, 44,* pp. 232–7.

KATZ, P.A. (1976) 'The acquisition of racial attitudes in children', in KATZ, P.A. (Ed.) *Toward the Elimination of Racism,* Toronto: Pergamon Press.

KATZ, P.A. and ZALK, S.R. (1978) 'Modification of children's racial attitudes', *Developmental Psychology, 14,* pp. 447–61.

KIRBY, D.M. and GARDNER, R.C. (1973) 'Ethnic Stereotypes: Determinants in children and their parents', *Canadian Journal of Psychology, 27,* 127–43.

KOHLBERG, L. (1969)

KOHLBERG, L. and DAVIDSON, F.B.H. (1977) 'Appendix B: The need for moral education to make ethnic pluralism work', in TUMIN, M.M. and PLOTCH W. (Eds) *Pluralism and a Democratic Society,* New York: Praeger.

KOHLBERG, L. and MAYER, R. (1972) 'Moral development as the aim of education', *Harvard Educational Review, 42,* pp. 449–96.

KOHLBERG, L., LEVINE, C. and HERVER, A. (1983) *Moral Stages: A Current Formulation and a Response to Critics,* New York: Kruger.

LA MARSH, J.A., BEAULIEU, L.A. and YOUNG, S.A. (1977) *The Royal Commission on Violence in the Communications Industry: Approaches, Conclusions and Recommendations* (Vol. 1), Toronto: Queen's Printer of Ontario.

LIEBERT, R.M. and SCHWARTZBERG, N.S. (1977) 'Effects of mass media', in ROSENZWEIG, M.R. and PORTER, L.M. (Eds) *Annual Review of Psychology* (Vol. 28), Palo Alto, Calif: Annual Reviews.

LITCHER, J.H. and JOHNSON, D.W. (1969) 'Changes in attitudes toward Negroes of white elementary school students after use of multiethnic readers', *Journal of Educational Psychology, 60,* pp. 148–52.

LUPUL, M.R. (1976) 'The portrayal of Canada's 'other' peoples in senior high school history and social studies textbooks in Alberta, 1905 to the present', *Alberta Journal of Educational Research, 22,* pp. 1–33.

McDIARMID, G. and PRATT, D. (1971) *Teaching Prejudice: A Content Analysis of Social Studies Textbooks Authorized for Use in Ontario,* Toronto: The Ontario Institute for Studies in Education.

MILNER, D. (1975) *Children and Race,* Harmondsworth, Middlesex, England: Penguin Books.

MONTERO, G. (1977) *The Immigrants,* Toronto: Lorimer.

MUSSEN, P.H., CONGER, J.J. and KAGAN, J. (1974) *Child Development and Personality* (4th Edn), New York: Harper and Row.

PHILLIPS, M. (1973) 'The acceptable face of racism', *Race Today, 5,* pp. 306–7.

ROSENBAUM, M.E. and STANERS, R.F. (1961) 'Self-esteem, manifest hostility, and expression of hostility', *Journal of Abnormal Social Psychology, 63,* pp. 646–9.

SAGOTSKY, G., WOOD-SCHNEIDER, M. and KONOP, M. (1981) 'Learning to cooperate: Effects of modeling and direct instruction', *Child Development, 52,* pp. 1037–42.

SANTROCK, J.W. (1981) *Adolescence: An Introduction,* Dubuque, IA: Brown.

SEARS, R.R., MACCOBY, E.E. and LEVIN, H. (1975) *Patterns of Child Rearing*, Evanston, IL: Row, Peterson.

SECORD, P.F. and BACKMAN, C.W. (1974) *Social Psychology* (2nd Edn), New York: McGraw-Hill.

SEVIGNY, R. (1966) *Analyse de Contenu de Manuels D'histore du Canada*, Maitrise non publiée, Université Laval, Quebec.

SIMON, S.B., HOWE, L.W. and KIRSCHENBAUM, H. (1978) *Values Clarification: A Handbook of Practical Strategies for Teachers and Students* (rev. Edn), New York: Hart.

SLAVIN, R.E. and MADDEN, N.A. (1979) 'School practices that improve race relations', *American Educational Research Journal*, 16, pp. 169–80.

SLUMAN, N. (1967) 'The textbook Indian', *Toronto Education Quarterly*, 5, (3), pp. 11–12.

TAJFEL, H. (1973) 'The roots of prejudice: Cognitive aspects', in WATSON, P. (Ed.) *Psychology and Race*, Chicago: Aldine.

VIDMAR, N. and ROKEACH, M. (1974) 'Archie Bunker's Bigotry: A study in selective perception and exposure', *Journal of Communication*, 24, pp. 35–47.

WEINER, M.J. and WRIGHT, F.E. (1973) 'Effects of undergoing arbitrary discrimination upon subsequent attitudes toward a minority group', *Journal of Applied Social Psychology*, 3, pp. 94–102.

WILLIAMS, J.E. and MORLAND, J.K. (1976) *Race, Color and the Young Child*, Chapel Hill: University of North Carolina Press.

ZAHN-WAXLER, C., RADKE-YARROW, M. and BRADY-SMITH, J. (1977) 'Perspective-taking and prosocial behavior', *Developmental Psychology*, 13, pp. 87–8.

16   The Culture of the School

Wilfred B.W. Martin

Introduction

Until recently, the school was not generally studied as an independent entity. Instead it was often considered in relation to its social environment and studied as a unit in terms of political, religious, economic and other societal processes. In the last couple of decades there has been significant interest in, and a growing body of research on, the school as a social unit which has developed traditions within itself. Drawing on concepts developed in areas other than education, Besag and Nelson (1984) suggest different approaches to understanding the process of schooling, with each approach highlighting particular features of this process. For example, from a political orientation, the school is perceived as an alienating process. It may also be viewed as an administrative institution representing a variant of the bureaucratic model. Certain features of the school are highlighted when it is analyzed in relation to the characteristics of total institutions as identified by Goffman (1961). Relatedly, the school can be regarded as a labeler when labeling theory is used to analyze its social structure and the interaction process therein. Besag and Nelson (1984) apply Edward Hall's (1959) matrix for cultural analysis to the school and thereby identify some of the primary message systems in this setting. To pursue the idea that the school is a cultural identity and to isolate features of the culture of the school the present discussion (1) points to a definition of school culture, (2) outlines the elements of school culture which have been identified by researchers, and (3) draws on an ongoing research project in Canadian schools, which addresses issues relating to the way students experience the culture of the school.

Appreciation is hereby expressed to Ishmael J. Baksh for comments on an earlier draft of this paper.

311

Wilfred B.W. Martin

Toward a Definition of School Culture

One definition of *culture* is that it consists of everything we think, do and have in society. In other words, it is the attitudes, values, norms, knowledge, behavior and material objects of society. Some scholars prefer to give a somewhat narrow definition of culture by referring only to the values, norms, knowledge and plans of action (the blueprint) which constitute the societal or group ethos. The presence of a culture means that a tradition has developed and that group features are passed from one generation to another. Group members have distinctive beliefs about social objects (persons, places, things, orientations). They have common interests and shared values which give rise to social norms. Actions which comply with these norms tend to become ritualistic. Hence, rituals and ceremonies are integral parts of the culture of the group. Culture is made by people and learned through interaction. It is the common property of the group, cumulative, but constantly changing. While providing individuals with plans of action, a blueprint for action, it also motivates them to want to act in certain ways. In effect, the culture of the group may be seen as an integrating force in the group while allowing for, even creating the conditions for, change. Culture is a group phenomenon, but it is transmitted through individuals, and individuals may affect the culture imparted to them in the process of transmitting it to others.

In offering a definition of organizational culture, Schein (1985, pp. 6–7) argues that organizational culture is 'the deeper level of *basic assumptions* and *beliefs* that are shared by members of an organization, ... and that define in a basic 'taken-for-granted' fashion an organization's view of itself and its environment'. To add to this view of organizational culture and to focus specifically on the school, the suggestion here is that school culture may be seen to be a multiplicity of overlapping, converging, but sometimes separate and divergent, beliefs, values, norms, rituals and ceremonies. These parts of the school culture are associated with three all-encompassing, intricately intertwined, arenas within the school: *organizational, curriculum* and *action* arenas.

The organizational arena is the formal organization of the school including the authority structure between teachers and students, the written and unwritten rules in the school, and the schedule of classes and activities. These dimensions have varying degrees of visibility in the organizational arena as well as variation in their effectiveness for achieving the normative overall expectations held for schooling by different audiences, such as students, teachers, administrations, parents and others.

While the principles which guide the development of school curriculum establish the cultural milieu in which the curriculum dimension of the school is to function, the formal packages of curriculum and the multitude of meanings and messages, which become part of the implementing processes, combine to make up the curriculum arena in the culture of the school. In fact, the implementation processes form part of the action dimension of school culture in that the action arena includes teacher and student strategies as they negotiate a social order in the school. In addition to being centrally a medium for teaching and learning the formal curriculum, teacher-student interaction is a learning experience unto itself. During those interactions the subtleties of the hidden curriculum emerge to become part of the culture of the school.

In addition to viewing the culture of the school as the totality of organizational, curriculum and action arenas in this setting, there are the occupational culture of teachers and the student culture as revealed in peer processes. In some ways these features of teacher and student lives may appear separate from the organizational, curriculum and action arenas within the school, but they are interwoven into the fabric of school culture.

Research on Elements of School Culture

Early analyses of the school as a cultural entity include Waller's (1932) classical work on *The Sociology of Teaching* and Gordon's (1957) investigation of the social system of a high school. Waller argued that youth have a special culture which is apart from the adult world. The culture of youth manifests itself in the school in the form of unorganized play and games, and through athletics, debating, school clubs and other activities like school paper. Also as identified by Waller (1965, pp. 120–33), ceremony is a major feature of the culture of the school, especially at secondary and post-secondary levels. These ceremonies include opening exercises, assemblies, commitment ceremonies, pep meeting, organized cheering, school songs, recruiting, morale ceremonies, martyrdom ceremonies, scholastic ceremonies, unanimity ceremonies, purification ceremonies, commencement season ceremonies and school spirit ceremonies. Gordon (1957) highlighted, among other things, the importance of informal and semi-formal dimensions of school life to student prestige. Later works of Corrigan (1979), Everhart (1983) and Willis (1981) point to the informal group relationship as the core reason for the development of a counter-school culture. In fact, these relationships often develop as students' resistance to the authority structure of the school and to the formal curriculum. Moreover, research on the strategies which students use in their interactions with teachers suggest that students have considerable influence on the student-teacher interaction process (e.g., Ball, 1980; Denscombe, 1980; McLure and French, 1980). Sarason (1971) addresses the problem of change within the school by focusing on the programmatic and behavioral features of school culture. The programmatic dimension of the school is seen to include school programs and the schedules developed to deliver these programs. The behavioral regularities include overt behavior such as laughing, crying, fighting, talking, concentrating, working, writing, question-asking, question-answering, test behavior and performance, stealing, cheating and unattending (Sarason, 1971, p. 71). Using ethnographic methods in a case study of twelve non-academic boys in one British school and in five comparative studies of groups of boys in other schools in the same British town, Willis

(1981, pp. 11–50), identifies the elements of school culture to include (1) students' opposition to authority and their rejection of those who conform, (2) the informal group, that is, the counter-school culture, (3) *dossing, blagging* and *wagging*, (4) *having a laff*, (5) boredom, (6) *excitement* that is, breaking the law, and (7) sexism and racism, that is, boys' sense of superiority over girls and the majority's over ethnic minority groups.

In his review, Woods (1983, pp. 78–89), discovered three main themes which have dominated the study of student culture: (1) The degree to which student cultures are influenced by the organization of the school; (2) the extent to which student cultures are derived from social class; and (3) how gender differences give rise to differential treatment. Thus, after studying ability grouping as an organizational strategy in one comprehensive school, Ball (1981, p. 252) noted that mixed ability classes weaken anti-school culture. In such arrangements, those who would join in anti-school activities are spread over different classes. Effects of social class have also been explored. One view is that an anti-school culture develops as a reaction to the middle-class values that generally operate in the school. Another view is that an anti-school culture is more a product of a lower class culture of the students than it is a reaction to the middle-class values of the school. Willis (1977), for example, argues that working-class students create their own counter-culture. A similar observation is made by Nelsen (1985). Drawing on Crespo's (1974) study of the career of those who skip school, Nelsen suggests that when students new to lower tracks are placed in groups with a high proportion of students who have already skipped school, their interaction patterns develop around 'a consciousness of a kind'. Finally, the majority of the research on school culture suggests that student cultures are mainly male dominated. The impression gained from this research is that girls adjust to the cultures set by the boys. However, it has been suggested that female culture is very much a part of student culture. Because research on student cultures has been dominated by males, the female aspect of those cultures have not been identified (McRobbie, 1980).

Experiencing the Culture of the School

Within the sociological tradition, there are two opposing approaches to the study of culture. One is to focus on the objective dimensions of culture, that is, its characteristics, the blueprints for behavior, and the patterns of behavior. Another is to focus on the subjective realities, that is, the experiences of people, singly or collectively, in the culture. At the core of experiencing the culture of one's group is the idea of *meanings*, more specifically, the meanings which people give to the elements of their culture. By making certain assumptions about meanings one is led to a greater understanding of how culture becomes a part of an individual's experiences, how the culture of the group constrains people, and how individuals contribute to the developing culture of their group. A study of the way students experience schooling, for example, could lead to an appreciation of the constraints and freedoms in the school environment and an awareness of the extent to which students participate in the developing culture of the school.

Working with assumptions concerning meaning as presented in symbolic interactionism, the present writer studied the schooling experiences of high school students in Atlantic Canada. Before presenting findings from this study, it is appropriate to outline interactionist assumptions and to illustrate them in terms of students and schooling. First, there is the assumption that people act toward things (including persons, places, material objects, values systems, norms and behaviors) on the basis of the meanings which those things have for them. High school students, for example, act toward their peers, their teachers, the formal curriculum in general and specific courses in particular, school rules, extra-curricular activities, class periods, the actions of others in the school, and all other aspects of schooling on the basis of the meanings which those social objects have for them.

Second, there is the assumption, as presented by Blumer (1969, p. 2), that there is nothing inherent in an object that determines its meaning. Put differently, objects do not have meanings in themselves, and, in everyday life, there is a continuous process of contributing meanings to them. To illustrate in the school setting, the argument is that there is nothing inherent in the formal curriculum in general or in specific subjects like biology or history which give them their meanings. Similarly, extra-curricular activities such as sports or drama and music festivals do not have inherent meanings in themselves which come across to all people in society, not even all those within the same school or within the same classroom. Curriculum content is person-made and culture-bound. In other words, it is based on a set of ideas, beliefs and values. Even though there may be almost universal agreement within the context of a culture or subculture on the importance of certain subject areas or courses, which in fact may be the reason why they were included in the curriculum of the school in the first place, students do not necessarily give a subject area or course within that subject similar meanings. Not only are there different interpretations for subjects and courses, but there are different meanings given to class schedules, to school rules, to teachers, to one's peers and to other social objects in the school. Student actions such as teasing, joking, kicking up a fuss, asking questions, answering questions, working and tuning out are of interest because the meanings they have for students may be different from those which teachers have for them. In fact, students do not necessarily agree on the meanings of such actions. Given that there are cultural meanings for all social objects in the school, that culture is a group phenomenon — that is, it exists apart from individual members — and that individuals must operate within a cultural environment, it is apparent that the individual mind is not an independent variable in giving definitions to situations. In the case of students in the school, for example, the organizational and curriculum structures are extremely important, if for no other reason than the restrictions which they place on students. The parameters of student course selection and of their participation in extra-curricular activities are well defined. Indeed, indications are that these structures are often seen, at least from the student perspective of schooling, to be a culprit in their negatively oriented experiences in the school.

A third assumption is that meanings which people have for social objects are developed, modified and remodified through the process of interaction. This assumption emphasizes the view that meanings are person-made. That is to say, for example, that culturally held definitions for such things as formal education, schools and school curriculum have been person-made, developed through time and passed, with certain modifications, from one generation to another. Turning to more specific social objects in the school such as teachers, teaching strategies, school rules, academic subjects, particular classes and extra-curricular pursuits, the assumption is that the overall meanings given to these and related social objects are passed from one generation of students to another. They are passed from high school students in one level or class to the incumbent students. To emphasize the idea of cultural definitions, it should be noted that meanings which students give to any of the social objects generally fall within a range of more or less acceptable meanings. However, while falling within such a range, the meanings which students attach to each other, to their teachers and to all aspects of school life come through their interactions with one another.

Underneath these assumptions regarding meanings is the idea that, while students' definitions of situations and actions may generally fall within an acceptable range, they represent a multitude of interpretations and meanings. Rather than working from a stimulus-response model, which suggests that individual and joint actions are automatic and habitual, or from a model based on the belief that structural features of the situation are the ultimate determinants of student actions, the present focus on the student perspective of schooling assumes that in developing plans of action, students give meanings to the social, physical and temporal features of the situation at hand (Stebbins, 1971). The immediate social environment of students includes their peers, teacher strategies, the curriculum, extra-curricular activities, school rules and the dominant belief system of the school. The physical environment of the school is usually demarcated by clearly defined boundaries. The availability of teaching and learning aids within these boundaries obviously varies from one school to another, and the meanings given to the importance of these facilities may also differ from one school to another as well as among teachers and students within any one school. The temporal dimension of the school is usually clearly defined in terms of beginning, ending, periods, sessions, days, weeks and terms. Even though there are exact times for entering and leaving schools and well-defined schedules to be followed, the meaning of time often arises from the attitudes, actions and social interactions in the setting. For any one class period of forty-five minutes, some students might be having a good time, while others are having a bad time. For some, time is dragging while for others it might be flying. Relatedly, some may try to kill time, while others attempt to make up for lost time.

To elaborate further on the idea that culture of the school is a group phenomenon, with student meanings given to school life occurring within this context, it can be noted that, even though there is often a preponderance of cultural definitions providing the framework for interactions in the school, students' actions are often somewhat problematic. They are especially problematic at the beginning of the school year when teachers and students are new to each other (Ball, 1980). Even though shared meanings arise and collective definitions develop over time, negotiations and related processes of social exchange continue to be important in maintaining social order in the school (Martin, 1976; Woods, 1978). Students are not only influenced by the culture of the school, with their individual and collective meanings for different dimensions of school life, they also influence this culture. However, given the teacher-student authority structure of the school, it may be argued that students have very little influence on the social organization of the school as reflected in the formal organization and curriculum arenas of schooling. Whether or not this is actually the case as measured by some objective criterion is an interesting question. Aside from, yet a dimension of, this question is the issue of meanings which students give to different aspects of schooling. Findings from an ongoing study of the schooling experiences of high school students in Atlantic Canada as described by Martin (1984, 1985 and 1987), are presented here to illustrate the meanings which students have for school rules, and for teacher attitudes and actions as they give rise to pets-victims phenomena and student embarrassment.[1]

Meanings of Rules

Varying degrees of saturation have been discovered in students' comments on fifteen categories of rules. In other words, many students from different schools and representing each grade level have expressed similar ideas about each of the following categories of rules: (1) dress requirement; (2) talk and noise in the classroom; (3) student movement in the school; (4) bathroom rules; (5) smoking; (6) school dances; (7) chewing gum; (8) areas where food cannot be consumed; (9) required subjects; (10) workload; (11) physical education and sports; (12) boy-girl relationship; (13) punctuality; (14) locked out of school; and (15) leaving the school grounds. The meanings which students have for school rules are seen by staying close to the data, in their perceptions of the need for rules, in the terms they use to describe rules, and in their ideas relating to fairness in the school.

One dimension of the meanings of rules comes from students who observed that 'rules are necessary' to achieve the aims of schooling. As reasoned by students, it is necessary for schools to have rules 'because otherwise students might try to take over the school'. Concerning the possibility of problems from students if appropriate rules are not enforced in the school, many students seem to agree with the observation 'that some rules have to be put down for some students who are always damaging school property'. While claiming that rules 'are not always easy to abide by', different students admitted that 'school activities and the way the school is run' have strong influences on students' attitudes. The need for rules for keeping students in check while giving them a degree of freedom was echoed by students from all parts of Atlantic Canada. Rather than being 'a hindrance as some students may think', school rules are often perceived to be 'necessary for a smooth-running school'. In other words, school rules are often seen to be designed 'to help' students 'get their education'.

Many students made reference to a need for flexibility in rules but often noted that strict enforcement of rules 'on such things as having your homework done' and 'passing assignments in on time' is 'for the good of the student'. The necessity of enforcing some of the 'not so serious rules' was noted in the claim that they are 'for the benefit of the school'. The need for rules was indicated by a girl who asked: 'What good is it for a person to go to school if there aren't any rules for him to go by?' This respondent suggested that all students 'should obey the laws and rules at school the same as' they 'would obey the laws or rules of the land'. She challenges us to 'imagine what it would be like if everybody went around doing just what they wanted to do'. The seriousness of rules was also alluded to by other students who observed that 'some of the rules should be carried out with great thought'. One boy suggested that rules exist mainly 'to please the teachers' who 'use them for their own benefits'.

According to some respondents, all school rules are acceptable and they see no reason why students should not follow them. It is not surprising, however, that other students do not share this view of school rules. It has been observed, for example, that 'some rules are alright for some students', but they are not appropriate for others. A number of students from different schools also expressed their understanding of, and agreement with, certain rules while questioning the need for other rules in the school.

Students use a variety of terms to describe the rules in their schools. These terms are of interest because they sensitize us to the attitudes, actions and reactions of students as they develop their individual identities, and as they contribute to the interactive roles of students and teachers in the unfolding of the social order of the school. The negatively oriented terms which students have used in their reference to rules include *childish, stupid, dumb, ridiculous, outrageous, disgusting, foolish, crazy, silly, weird, the pits, a pain, a bore, sad, junk, bull, baloney, nonsense* and *lousy*. As illustrated by the definitions which students give to rules, there are almost as many students who have positive orientations toward school rules in the present study as there are students who have negative orientations to these rules. The positively oriented terms they use to describe school rules include *alright, good, excellent, important, reasonable, make sense, great, not too bad, interesting, respectable, proper, fair, acceptable* and *understandable*.

The idea of fairness seems to permeate all facets of student life, especially those involving teacher-student interaction and/or teacher expectations for students. These facets include the expectations teachers have for student behavior, the selection of students for activities in the school, the attention students receive from their teachers, and the assessment of student behavior and academic performance. A focus on the student-perceived fairness in the school as it relates to rules shows that students have notions of fair teachers, fair principals, fair rules and fair schools as separate entities, and that these entities are nevertheless interwoven with one another. While teachers and principals are the people who implement rules (rules which are seen to come from the school organization or to be developed by teachers and principals), students, in their thinking on fairness in schooling, have different concepts of school and the roles of these people. One of these concepts of school seems to place teacher and/or principal at the core of the school. Hence, these personnel are judged by their fairness in implementing rules. Some students have judged their teachers to be totally fair, while other students have defined teacher actions as *unfair*, at least sometimes. According to the comments of other students, certain teachers are fair while other teachers are not.

A second concept of school as revealed in the present data seems to have rules rather than teachers as the core of the schooling process. Students who view the school in this way focused mainly on the fairness of the rules, rather than on the fairness of their teachers as such. Students who, in their observations on fairness, made simultaneous reference to teachers and rules as separate, yet interrelated, entities exhibit a third concept of school in that they to some degree point to the complex interconnection among these entities in the process of schooling. In commenting on the notion of fairness, other students may be seen to be giving a fourth concept of school in their emphasis on teachers and schools. A few respondents in the present study displayed another perspective on the idea of schooling by focusing on schools and rules as if they were separate entities, but the fact that they were referred to simultaneously by these students suggests that they may be viewed as interrelated.

Teachers' Pets and Class Victims

On the surface, the classroom may appear to be a relatively simple structure involving two well-defined social roles: teacher and student. Teachers, however, must play roles such as judge, mediator, resource person, helper, friend and confidante, referee, detective, ego-supporter and group leader. Similarly, the myth of the singularity of the student role is soon dispelled when one attempts to isolate the variety of categories which teachers have for students of varying age, sex, intelligence and personality. Some of these categories (or social identities) are defined by the formal organization of the school, while others are created, developed and changed, and are continually evolving in the classroom. For example, while certain students become defined as teachers' pets, they and others may be seen as victims of classroom life. Two important aspects of the identities of pets and victims as related to high school students must be noted here. One is the fact that, even though the categories of pets and victims may be a relatively stable part of classroom culture, the students in these categories may vary from time to time. The fact that certain students are categorized, that is, given one social identity in one way, and other students are categorized in another, is partly a result of the interaction strategies employed by each of the combatants in this setting. Another aspect of the classroom pets-victims phenomena centers on who defines a student as a pet, a victim or both.

A brief look at each of four themes which have been identified in student observations relating to teachers' pets and class victims illustrates how students experience this aspect of school life. These themes are (1) teachers' attitudes toward students, (2) teachers' criteria for student categorization, (3) the nature of favors and mistreatment in the classroom, and (4) consequences of favoring and mistreating strategies.

Concerning teachers' attitudes toward students, the answer to the question, 'Do teachers have pets?' may well depend on whether the respondents are teachers or students, and perhaps, which teachers and which students. Even without asking this question of the students participating in the present study, many of them clearly presented the view that teacher's pets constitute an important part of the classroom culture.

Teachers' pets are students who are seen, or see themselves, to be at the favoring end of a favoring-mistreating continuum in teacher-student interactions. On the other hand, class victims may be defined as students who, from the student perspective, are either mistreated or neglected by the teacher (relative to the treatment and attention given to other students) to the extent that they (or others) see themselves as experiencing mistreatment or neglect. Many students felt that 'some teachers are always picking on certain students', even when those students are not doing 'anything wrong'. It was also felt that particular students got more help with their academic work than others.

While the teacher perspective on student pets and class victims is an important dimension of these phenomena, the present research focuses on the student perspective of classroom life. It is argued that if students believe that teachers have pets and victims, this belief is important in students' definitions of teachers, of teachers' actions, and of their own plans of action in interacting with teachers and other students. In other words, regardless of whether teachers' pets and class victims exist from the teacher perspective, and whether students misinterpret the actions of teachers toward specific students, the subjective reality of teachers' pets and class victims for students is extremely important in their definition of classroom situations and in their developing plans of action.

Comments from students representing different schools indicate their belief that most teachers would deny having pets and mistreating or neglecting some students. However, students are convinced that teachers favor certain students over others and that some students are victimized because of this. The present study indicates that many students perceive teachers to have sharply contrasting attitudes toward different categories of students, and that they develop equally contrasting plans of action toward them. More specifically, teachers were seen to favor teachers' pets and to mistreat or neglect those seemingly destined to become class victims. Students reveal well established views regarding the criteria which teachers are seen to use in categorizing them as pets or not. For example, the process of selecting students as pets is often seen to be related to teachers' liking for students. Conversely, students perceived as being 'picked on' are generally those that teachers are believed not to like. Many of the students in the present study, who referred to teachers' pets and class victims in their outlines of school experiences which concern them, pointed out that some teachers select students they like best for their pets while those they dislike become class victims. Generally, however, they did not specify what they thought were teachers' reasons for liking some students and disliking others.

Indications are that the selection of a student as a pet may be tied with the amount of information the teacher has on that student. It has been claimed that the teachers who 'know too much about the students' personal lives tend to show favoritism toward certain students'. Teachers' prejudice toward students has sometimes been attributed to the fact that those teachers had been in the same school 'too long' and consequently knew the students 'too well'. However, it has also been pointed out that other teachers who have been in the same schools for an equally 'long while' do not show such prejudice.

The development of the class victim is, from the student viewpoint, often tied with the mood of the teacher, with student participation in sports or lack thereof, and with age of students. In commenting on the criteria which some teachers are perceived to be using in selecting their pets, students generally referred to the reasons other students do not become pets, and in some cases why particular categories of students are mistreated and even neglected. The present data reveal that six variables are thought to be relatively important in the teacher selection of pets and class victims. They are (1) academic performance, (2) student behavior, (3) family background, (4) geographical location, (5) gender, and (6) teacher disliking students. In addition, many students claimed that teachers categorize them, especially as it relates to their being 'picked on' by teachers, without the students' identifying the reason for this classification.

Another dimension to teachers' pets/class victims phenomenon in the school is the nature of favors and mistreatment which students perceive to be a part of teacher-student interactions. Specifically, favors and mistreatment have been isolated as they occur in (1) teachers' expectations concerning student behavior, (2) teachers' selections of students for specific activities, (3) amount of attention students receive during regular teaching-learning endeavor, and (4) assessment of student performance.

While studying the ways students experience pets-victims phenomena, this researcher isolated the student-perceived consequences of the favoring mistreating strategies employed by teachers. To elaborate, some of the students in the present study saw themselves as teachers' pets and thought that their classmates also saw them in this way. Without delving into the intricacies of the classroom, we might assume that a teacher's pet would have considerable prestige in their interaction with other students. However, the present data indicated that this is not necessarily so; students who were defined as teachers' pets frequently found it difficult to gain classmate acceptance. Apparently, they were often on the receiving end of jokes amongst their peers. Some of those who saw themselves as pets felt guilty concerning favors received from teachers. And while teachers generally seemed to favor pets, they were also sometimes perceived to hold greater expectations of them than of other students. In so doing, teachers placed certain pressures on their pets. Interestingly enough, students who perceived themselves as pets, like those who perceived themselves as victims, offered several negative comments concerning classroom pets. For certain students it seemed that being a teacher's pet meant that one was also victimized, although obviously in a different manner from those who were mistreated or neglected. It may also be that pets were victimized by peers; students who attempted to garner favor from their teachers were usually disliked.

The consequences of mistreatment or neglect for non-pets and class victims, as perceived by high school students, were manifested in student feelings of 'being left out' of the teacher-initiated interactions, in the way teachers evaluated their academic work, and in the disciplining process in the school. Pets-victims phenomena also resulted in students' developing a dislike for certain teachers whereas antipathy and empathy were nurtured amongst the students themselves.

Student Embarrassment

To embarrass means 'to confuse; perplex; also, to disconcert'. It 'implies some influence that impedes thought, speech or action, and may be used with reference not only to persons but to the things they plan or desire to do' (*Webster's New Collegiate Dictionary*, 1967, p. 267). Embarrassment is a complex feeling experienced in the presence of others. It is in line with the feeling of mortification, that is, a painful sense of humiliation, in that it may be brought on by one's own, or another's, fault or failure. Embarrassment generally develops unintentionally in that it is spontaneous, arising in the flow of interaction. It is caused by a loss of poise, as in the case of a student who trips over a desk. A student may also lose poise when he or she does not measure up to the demands of the situation. Teacher expectations of a student as expressed through frequent or difficult questions asked of him or her, or through evaluation of student work, may bring a student's credibility into account, thereby resulting in student embarrassment.

In contrast to the unintentional variety of embarrassment, there are situations where plans are made to discredit individuals. The resulting embarrassment, which may be seen as deliberate embarrassment, is evident in practical jokes, teasing, deflating false fronts and public degradation. Practical jokes and teasing are undoubtedly parts of the evolving social structure of most groups of high school students. Looking at teacher-student interactions from the student perspective, certain teachers are often perceived to be intentionally embarrassing their students 'in front of the class'. Whether the embarrassment which students experience is intentional or unintentional, the interactions in the social setting affected are interrupted and the role performances are impeded or inhibited, at least temporarily.

Given the authority structure of the classroom and the power processes in teacher-student interactions, it is not surprising that embarrassment is a common phenomenon in this setting. Students are on the lower rung of the legitimate authority ladder in the classroom, and there is a widespread belief among them that their attempts at vying for power positions in this setting are often nullified by teachers' use of their legitimate authority position. These features of teacher-student interactions have conditioned many to accept the somewhat negative orientation of students to teaching-learning processes as natural for this environment. Underneath these apparently 'normal' expectations of student domination of authority figures in academic institutions, and arising from their experience of problems associated with the intrusion by teachers in their private affairs, students ascribe the real causes of their embarrassment to certain teacher orientations. These causes revolve around (1) the extent to which teachers fail to show understanding and patience, (2) the extent to which teachers lack care and respect for their students, (3) the teachers' being rude and ignorant, (4) the teachers' giving favors and holding grudges and (5) the teachers' holding the you-are-still a-kid orientation toward many students.

From a pedagogical viewpoint, there is one overriding question about the consequences of student embarrassment: What are the consequences of student embarrassment for the teaching-learning endeavor? There are certain social-psychological consequences of embarrassing experiences which are significant in themselves as well as for any bearing they might have on student learning in the classroom. These social-psychological consequences include student dislike for teachers, their becoming mad at teachers, their fear of teacher actions, and their development of negative self-concepts. For the most part, the implication is that student learning is negatively affected by each of these consequences of embarrassment. One positive effect of embarrassment on student learning was noted by a small number of students. Their argument was that when students experience embarrassment because of not studying or because of failing to complete written homework on time, they become 'afraid not to be prepared', that is, they become afraid of teachers' reactions which could cause embarrassment. Hence they are motivated to study in order to avoid such negative experiences in the classroom. It has been observed that 'if teachers are too slack', not 'forcing' students, not 'yelling at' them, not 'getting on' their 'backs', students may not experience embarrassment, and 'nothing gets accomplished because there is too much freedom in class'. It is generally felt, however, that embarrassment has negative consequences for student learning. In fact, indications are that embarrassment and related processes of insults, humiliations, sarcasms and jokes are contributing factors to students' desires to quit school.

Conclusion

The culture of the school has become the focus of considerable research in recent years. Particular attention has been given to the influence to student culture on the social organization of schooling and to the development of counter-cultures among students. A definition of school culture is presented in this paper and the elements of school culture as identified in earlier research are reviewed. After outlining certain assumptions concerning meanings and illustrating the relevance of such an approach in attempting to get at ways students experience schooling, this article draws from an ongoing study of the schooling experiences of high school students in Atlantic Canada to focus on the meanings which students give to school rules, to pets-victims phenomena and to student embarrassment. The suggestion is that this approach in the study of school culture can lead to a further understanding of the complexities of teacher-student interactions and to an appreciation of the consequences of student experiences on their social-emotional well-being and on their overall performances in the school.

Notes

1   This study has used a survey questionnaire, structured and unstructured interviews, and observational techniques as it explores the social construction of reality among high school students in New Brunswick, Newfoundland and Labrador, Nova Scotia and Prince Edward Island.

Bibliography

BALL, S.J. (1980) 'Initial encounters in the classroom and the process of establishment', in WOODS, P. (Ed.) *Pupil Strategies: Explorations in the Sociology of the School*, London: Croom Helm, (pp. 143–61).
BALL, S.J. (1981) *Beachside Comprehensive*, Cambridge: Cambridge University Press.
BESAG, F.P. and NELSON, J.L. (1984) *Foundations of Education: Stasis and Change*, New York: Random House.

BLUMER, H. (1969) *Symbolic Interactionism: Perspective and Method*, Englewood Cliffs, NJ: Prentice-Hall.

CORRIGAN, P. (1979) *Schooling the Smash Kids*, London: Macmillan.

CRESPO, M. (1974) 'The career of the school skipper', in HAAS, J. and SHAFFIR, B. (Eds) *Decency and Deviance: Studies in Deviant Behaviour*, Toronto: McClelland and Stewart, (pp. 129–45).

DENSCOMBE, M. (1980) 'Pupil strategies and the open classroom', in WOODS, P. (Ed.) *Pupil Strategies: Explorations in the Sociology of the School*, London: Croom Helm, (pp. 50–73).

EVERHART, R.B. (1983) *Reading, Writing and Resistance: Adolescence and Labour in a Junior High School*. Boston: Routledge and Kegan Paul.

GOFFMAN, E. (1961) *Asylums*, Garden City, NY: Anchor Books.

GORDON, C.W. (1957) *The Social System of the High School*, Glencoe IL: The Free Press.

HALL, E.T. (1959) *The Silent Language*, Greenwick, CT: Fawcett Publications, Inc.

MACLURE, M. and FRENCH, P. (1980) 'Routes to right answers: On pupils' strategies for answering teachers' questions', in WOODS, P. (Ed.) *Pupil Strategies: Explorations in the Sociology of the School*, London: Croom Helm, (pp. 74–93).

MARTIN, W.B.W. (1976) *The Negotiated Order of the School*, Toronto: Macmillan of Canada.

MARTIN, W.B.W. (1984) 'Student perception of teachers' pets and class victims', *Canadian Journal of Education*, 9, pp. 89–89.

MARTIN, W.B.W. (1985) *Voices from the Classroom*, St. John's: Creative Publishers.

MARTIN, W.B.W. (1987) 'Students' perceptions of causes and consequences of embarrassment in the school', *Canadian Journal of Education*, 12, pp. 277–93.

McROBBIE, A. (1980) 'Setting accounts with sub-cultures: A feminist critique', *Screen Education*, 34.

NELSEN, R.W. (1985) *Sociology and the School: An Interactionist Perspective*, London: Routledge and Kegan Paul.

SARASON, S. (1971) *The Culture of the School and the Problem of Change*, Boston: Allyn and Bacon.

SCHEIN, E.H. (1985) *Organizational Culture and Leadership*, San Francisco: Jossey-Bass Publishers.

STEBBINS, R. (1971) 'The meaning of disorderly behavior: Teacher definition of a classroom situation', *Sociology of Education*, 44, pp. 217–36.

WALLER, W. (1965) *The Sociology of Teaching*, New York: John Wiley and Sons, Inc. (1st published in 1932).

WEBSTER'S NEW COLLEGIATE DICTIONARY (1961) Springfield, MA.: G. and C. Merrian Co. Publishers.

WILLIS, PAUL (1981) *Learning to Labor: How Working Class Kids Get Working Class Jobs*, New York: Columbia University Press.

WOODS, PETER. (1978) 'Negotiating the demands of schoolwork', *Journal of Curriculum Studies*, 3.

WOODS, P. (1983) *Sociology and the School: An Interactionist Perspective*, London: Routledge and Kegan Paul.

VI

The Intersection Between School and Society

INTRODUCTION

That society as a creator, sustainer, and context of schooling may legitimately influence it in various ways is rightly taken for granted. Creation and maintenance of this institution would be pointless were it to dissociate itself from the intents and workings of society. Yet it is doubtful that society as a whole exercises a unitary, consensually derived direction for schooling. Society, long regarded as a conglomeration of individuals, groups, and institutions working towards a common good, frequently does not live up to its definition. Pursuing different goods, its various components collide, work at cross purposes, or impose their will covertly or overtly on one another.

Early in his first article, Samuel Mitchell shows the lack of coordination and harmonious linkages among educational participants, which hinders the attainment of common societal goals through effective schooling. The resulting failure has led to different movements and programs intended to improve schooling. Thus, the currently popular excellence movement has been given a big boost by a number of panel, commission, and foundation reports seeking consensus on schooling. Mitchell warns us, however. Such consensus could work, consistently with the intents of dominant vested groups in society, to strengthen their dominance and correspondingly depress the conditions of disadvantaged groups. Thus he suggests an alternative strategy, namely, increasing the meaningful participation of groups that have interests at stake in education — for example, parents, the general public, and working class groups. Cautioning about the involvement of business executives and even university experts acting on behalf of corporate interests, Mitchell advocates giving voice to subordinated individuals and groups in society. In particular, he argues the empowerment of teachers and suggests innovative strategies which could enable them to challenge the dominance of big business and big government.

Whatever the efficacy of Mitchell's proposals, they are not likely to succeed unless their implementation is based on adequate understanding of school systems. Such understanding is certainly not easy to attain. It is complicated enough by the differing perspectives of educational participants and critics. Further complications are introduced by the fact that educational systems are segmented, with each segment operating with some degree of independence from the others. In his second article, Mitchell attempts to demonstrate the segmentation between the different components of educational systems. He observes that walls of autonomy exist between educational professionals. Moreover, walls between students, on one hand, and teachers and administrators, on the other, exist. One problem is therefore how to break down the walls without adversely affecting professional autonomy which centralized authority in closely linked, structured systems could jeopardize.

The solution appears to be the introduction of creative innovations. However, as Mitchell points out, some suggested innovations are nothing more than creation myths which do not truly provide meaningful participation and real advantages for those that schooling is supposed to benefit. New schemes allow creative thinking only in spite of the system; efforts to promote student participation generally end up with few students being involved. Status barriers and role expectations attached to being teachers and principals frustrate truly creative innovations. Recent promises are made by way of new developments such as the effective schools movement and the advocacy of loosely linked systems. Whatever solution holds sway in the future, Mitchell believes that schooling needs teachers who have earned their autonomy to determine their own teaching.

17 The Powers of Society and the Promises of Education

Samuel Mitchell

Introduction

The practitioner's immediate concern with day-to-day school events can prevent the development of a sense of social continuity between work, family life and the schools. Broader social effects can be grasped by seeing the relationships between economic, political and cultural influences not as abstractions but as interconnected parts of one whole process. A broader perspective will show that the entire social fabric is involved in stratifying the positions that individuals occupy as a result of their education and in categorizing the relative importance that education has in comparison to other institutions.

To move beyond showing the simultaneous stratification of the educational institution and the education of individuals, this writer examines different dimensions. Individuals are shown to develop class consciousness after both political and symbolic understandings are obtained. Thus, the increasing importance of political position and symbolic role is examined. Organized groups in society, acting to bring about social change, are revealed as first developing economic concerns and later focusing on political and cultural goals as well. The opposite directions for individual and group development are then shown to create a separation of public and private spheres.

Public and private domains can be brought together through social movements. Thus, the development of individuals within a social movement is explored as a way to transform school influences into an alternative to existing practices within schools. The study of social dynamics is intended to create an awareness of critical possibilities for schools. Sociology can be more than a support for existing practices within schools. A knowledge of society can serve merely as a scapegoat for educators who want to avoid any action. However, when the competitive structures of society is exposed, then the possibilities for alternative actions by teachers and administrators are increased. Dominant, competitive forces from society can be criticized and challenged by more compassionate educators who want changes in both schools and society.

Perspectives and Change

Individuals in schools have a very limited view of education. For students, education appears to be the responsibility of individual teachers (Everhart, 1983). Teachers limit many of their views and actions in their own classrooms (Lortie, 1975). Administrators see themselves as evaluating the entire school system without usually thinking of how permeable the boundaries of the system are (House, 1974). Few of the players in school are aware of the more impersonal influences that affect their work and aims (Sarason, 1982). Crises, such as budget cuts in government grants or drug problems among students, bring about an awareness of the background against which these performers act (Johnson, 1983). However, once the crises disappear, schools go about their tasks in isolation from society unless a new pattern of interaction and mutual dependency develops. Such isolation appears to be the norm even in communist countries whose claims to a larger vision fade when revolutionary movements lose the vitality of their songs and slogans.

The very distance between society and school life is like a fog that makes an understanding of the relationship difficult. However, social influences can be shown to include economic, political and cultural aspects. Economic aspects involve the allocation of resources, politics involves the engineering of consent, and culture involves the cognitive map upon which resources are transmitted by such inventions as markets and forms of legitimate authority. The economic effects on schooling can be demonstrated rather easily through quantified considerations which can, in turn, be shown to relate to political and cultural functions of schools. It is from the political and cultural relationships that new purposes for schooling can be developed when the pace of social change accelerates. With an understanding of common purposes, alternatives to present practices can be suggested.

The attempt to bring about changes in schools first develops from cultural and political activities. Economic influences do not easily generate links between local groups and schools because of the separation of societal institutions and the consciousness of those involved in each type of organization (Hall and Carlton, 1977). In contrast, cultural programs, French immersion or oral history, for example, can be seen as links between the perspectives of those in schools and the activities of those outside of schools. New programs for the governance of schools, such as school councils, are less frequently developed than are curriculum programs. However, government programs that involve the citizens' giving legitimacy to existing structures have emerged at the policy level in most countries in the last two decades (Beattie, 1985). Top down government programs for targeted groups, such as in special education, are, however, often impossible to relate to individual classrooms. Economic relationships between education and work groups are seldom developed with a classroom focus by teachers. Vocational education programs have been influenced much more in their evolution by administrators than they have been by teachers (House, 1974; Daft and Becker, 1978,

p. 109). Career education in its various forms is removed from classroom practices. Teachers, as the core of education, are isolated from transportation and marketing changes; they might, just as well, prefer to be teaching Latin (Waller, 1967). The inconsistencies between economic policies and school practices can result from schools being expected to achieve goals that are more easily realized in the workplace.

The Pocketbook and Education

The difficulty of individuals perceiving the relevance of economic phenomena is shown by a series of conflicts. Teachers in high schools within industrial areas seldom think of the high unemployment rate as affecting classroom discipline problems even if job shortages are shown to mean that students stay in school because of lack of opportunities and that their forced attendance produces considerable resistance (Mitchell, 1967). Farming cycles are better understood in rural areas in terms of such effects. Students who have well paid labor jobs do not particularly see the relevancy of vocational education programs for job placement (Stinchcombe, 1964). For students, academic programs are a mirage in relation to their future careers. Teachers, similarly, do not see their own performance as influenced by the salary increases they may receive (Lortie, 1975, p. 182). Teachers do see themselves as being cheated as compared with the rewards that businessmen receive. Though administrators have more developed relationships with businessmen than do many teachers, the administrators have struggled to develop even simple sharing of meeting facilities as a form of barter with industry. Businessmen who occasionally become teachers have undergone cultural shock as they deal with undisciplined students in vocational education (Ryan, Newman, Mager, Applegate, Lasley, Flora and Johnston, 1980, pp. 186–8).

Cooperation between businessmen, teachers and students has been shown to be difficult and the distance between their three roles is substantial. The relation is beyond impersonally providing for qualifications for the labor force. A life style can be developed from the efforts of a grade 1 teacher and can have continuing effects on students' careers (Pederson, Fauchner and Eaton, 1978). Schooling can develop ways of living, as Europeans have long recognized. In America, cooperative education has revealed that industry and education find it difficult to work together because of the differences between the two institutions (Feldman, 1985). Programs from the excellence movement, which have developed in both education and business, are, as later discussed, having very different effects in the two institutions. Educators have found it difficult to believe that economic effects should be primary, and businessmen have believed that they are always primary. Businessmen, who have complained loudly about the low standards in education, have seldom had direct contact with local schools or even had the experience of hiring many graduates of their local system (Hall and Carlton, 1977, p. 69).

The separation between business and schools should not lead anyone to ignore some obvious relationships between them. Students are increasingly employed in part-time jobs. Such jobs are a source of immediate income to meet growing adolescent needs, but the jobs have little long-term significance. The part-time jobs mean that students can work long hours, neglect their school work and opt out of extra-curricular activities. When students seek predigested courses and school social life disappears, the meaning of education can be transformed by these jobs. School, then, becomes 'unpaid work' (Hall and Carlton, 1977, p. 69).

Social Stratification

An instrumental view of education in terms of its immediate benefits is certainly consistent with the calculation of economic rationality. However, the immediate view of education in terms of consumption for adolescent needs is not consistent with the benefits that accrue to the winners for the longer term in either business or education. The experts who are to become the planners in a society need a far better articulated education. The future experts may, for example, be the minority such as those who become the analysts for computers as opposed to mere programmers (Olson, 1987). The losers who see that education is not going to provide them with economic benefits become the delinquent problem of schools. The losers who, in an English study, despise the 'earholes' seek tough masculine jobs and ignore the writing tasks that schools expect of them (Willis, 1978).

Students who believe that education will not improve their chance for tough jobs and students who are on their way to being experts are both affected by changes in labor markets. Teachers and lawyers are two professional groups that have seen their market situations change dramatically. Occupations, such as engineering, which are closer to business, regularly rise and fall in terms of unemployment (Gerstl and Jacobs, 1976). The distance between the professions and the educational system makes planning about goals quite difficult. The pull of unskilled work for alienated students makes it likely that these students will drift with economic changes. Certainly, many students have found that liberal reforms for either a new start or higher education have led to the frustration of unemployment (Harvey, 1974).

Neither the unskilled work nor the professions deal with the personal meaning that school or work can involve. The development of children into creative individuals seems to happen in spite of the economic and social systems (Mitchell, 1971, p. 311). The contribution of children, such as their art work, is often unrecognized due to their subordination to adults (Speier, 1976, p. 152). Like higher social classes, some ethnic groups preserve an accent on cultural learning beyond education's contribution to ethnic survival (Lind, 1974, p. 26). But childhood, social class and ethnic differences have not become the basis for greater individualization in education.

The most direct carrier of social differentiation is the families from which students come. The families have repeatedly been shown to account for more of educational achievements than does schooling (Marjoribanks, 1979). However, differences among individual families in comparison to schools are *not* harnessed for the development of changes within schools. For educators, parent involvement is often seen as a mechanism to involve parents in schools' plans and to obtain parents' support for school programs. When seen at all by school personnel, parents tend to be viewed as problems; this is particularly the case with single or working parents who are believed to have 'latch key' children (House and Lapan, 1978, p. 119; Kratzman, Byrne and Worth, 1980). The deficit view of families is, strangely enough, stressed by educators. In contrast, the achievement of particular groups, such as the new Asian children, is given grudging recognition rather unlike the focus on difficulties for lower-achieving immigrants (Butterfield, 1986). Similarly, teachers have been shown secretly to resent upper-class parents while they much more openly resent working-class parents. It is with only the middle-class parents that teachers, on the basis of shared values, avoid a deficit label (McPherson, 1972). Teachers and administrators plan and evaluate their programs on the basis of rather standardized and idealized conceptions of students and families (Becker, 1952). The clients are expected to fit the educational pyramid like uniform stones.

The Government and the Grass Roots

Awareness of differences is developed when some groups, who do not fit the school's formula, are visualized. Special programs are developed for these clients on the basis of such relative differences. Special education has been subject to attempts to cover up comparative social influences with professional labels. Broader and more ambiguous labels tend to replace more limited ones; the *learning disabilities* rubric replaces the *mentally retarded* category (Gartner and Lipsky, 1987). The subordination of current ethnic and racial groups continues a pattern of defining cultures as problems, a pattern which began with the Irish immigrants (Sarason and Doris, 1979). Special programs progressively find larger and larger numbers of students who, along with their parents, do not fit the regular classes (Sarason and Doris, 1979; Lind, 1974). However, specific subordinate groups may resist their exclusion from the main program.

Just as it is true for special education of deviant children, parent education is largely built upon communications and involvement with those who might attempt to alter the status quo. Parent involvement programs do, however, show that teachers who follow the procedures for relating to parents find unexpected virtues in dual working parents, single mothers and lower-class families. The achievements of children with single parents are seen to be greater than those who have two parents when the single parents are taught to provide support and reading practice in the home (Epstein, 1985, p. 211). Similarly, when using an entire program of home schooling, single parents have been reported to be successful in teaching their own children mathematics even when their own education has been deficient in this area (Holt, 1981).

Teachers who practise parent involvement report the same support received from both working-class and middle-class parents (Epstein, 1985). Teachers who do not practise the coordination of teaching with parents continue to see the working-class parents as unsupportive. Similarly, many teachers believe that working mothers are a problem for education even when they, themselves, are working mothers. Perhaps we need to get such teachers to talk to themselves about the potential of parent roles for education!

Aside from the understanding of dual roles for the individuals involved, the significance of parental involvement in transforming education has been realized in the last twenty years. Some programs, such as French immersion, are the direct result of efforts by concerned parents; for the first year of the program in a Montreal suburb, parents, rather than the school board, paid the teachers involved (Canadian Education Association, 1983). These programs usually focus on middle-class parents. But regardless of class membership, the contribution of any parent is constantly underestimated and undermined by the bureaucracy in control. Schools often drastically underestimate the contribution of parents.

Even for ongoing programs, the contribution of active parents can be enormous. In one large-scale survey, 4 per cent of parents spend twenty-five hours or more helping teachers each month, but three times as many parents were prepared to spend this much time and had never been asked by the schools (Epstein, 1986, p. 281). Among the active parents, large numbers have increasingly been trained as teachers and some function as educational experts (Gold and Miles, 1981). But some administrators claim that parents who are certified as teachers could not function as teachers because they are not employees of the school board. Teachers are also less than willing to seek the help of such trained parents. Schools have hardly begun to seek the parents who have either specialized knowledge or social skills to assist with educational tasks.

Though parent involvement has been contained and limited by schools, recent changes in education have repeatedly brought about parent activities in unexpected ways. Parent involvement is indirectly implicated in almost all of the major political battles in education. Since the challenges of the student movements beginning in the 1960s, a variety of industrialized countries have sought the support of parents in maintaining the system. Some parents in England and North America have also been involved in grassroot activities that promote innovations in education (Beattie, 1985). In North America the earlier end of racial segregation and the activities of the civil rights movement were a large and dramatic challenge to the status quo in education. In this regard, parents led significant strikes against schools. Interestingly, the experts and administrators have often been unable to solve the desegregation problem; homemakers on task forces assembled for the crises have been somewhat more successful (Johnson, 1983). However, programs for socio-economic groups which required membership and involvement of parents or community members have led to an increasing sense of federal governmental interference in the two past decades, particularly in the US where local control has had a long history (Sarason, 1982, p. 72).

Governmental programs have led, in turn, to a change in the agenda for education. The translation of political programs from plans or laws to the local level of schools is a constant problem. For women's programs, as is the case with many other innovations, supportive administrators and colleagues are necessary for the programs to become meaningful for the teachers who are involved (Weiler, 1988). For innovative programs to succeed with students, the commitment of school personnel appears to be crucial (Smith, Klein, Prunty and Dwyer, 1986). When special educators act as advocates for programs they are much more successful (Grant and Sleeter, 1986); for example, those for handicapped people or cultural groups. Without the commitment of advocates, school personnel can destroy innovative programs. In one high school, an expert on integration of the handicapped was met by the resistance of teachers to his talk; the teachers were betting on how long the specialist would speak (Cusick, 1983, p. 117).

The detailed specification of American legislation for integrating the handicapped has led to a declining number of integrated students, and some of the integrated cases are, in actuality, segregated classes within integrated schools (Gartner and Lipsky, 1987, p. 377). Exceptional teachers with an understanding of the school culture are required (Sarason, 1982, p. 257). Special education coordinators who can work with school principals and with existing authority structures are necessary for the continuation of these tasks and for success in them. The initial support and interest of parents have often been undermined by professionals taking over the programs (Singer and Butler, 1987, p. 142). The result is that most programs of mainstreaming do not meet complex conditions and amount to no more than 'relatively sincere tokenism' (Sarason and Doris, 1979, p. 380).

The Rhetoric of Standards

A new set of programs, which has hardly attempted to discover the supporting conditions for success, is associated with the excellence movement (Tomlinson and Walberg, 1986). In a large number of reports supporting the excellence aims, economic and political influences are being marshalled to demonstrate the failure of American education (Priessen, 1985). The report, *A Nation at Risk*, features a melodramatic play of words:

> . . . the educational foundations of our society are presently being eroded by a rising tide of mediocrity that threatens our very future as

a Nation and a people. What was unimaginable a generation ago has begun to occur — others are matching and surpassing our educational attainments. If an unfriendly foreign power had attempted to impose on America the mediocre educational performance that exists today, we might well have viewed it as an act of war. We have even squandered the gains in student achievement made in the wake of Sputnik challenge. (National Commission on Excellence in Education, 1983).

A Nation at Risk has been the most widely publicized of a series of reports. However, other more academic reports use unusual devices such as an imaginary character to dramatize the need for reforms. The Carnegie Foundation report was 'larger than a book — including film, television and newspaper interviews, and Carnegie School Grants' (McDonald, 1987, p. 30). Each of these devices probably obscures both the present situation and the limits of the proposed reforms. Rhetoric tends, at best, to hide the relevancy of research studies as the effort to reform education becomes more frantic. In the background papers for *A Nation at Risk*, research on effective schools is said to be not decisive and significant, but when junior high schools are considered the research on effective schools is considered critical for the review of these schools (Tomlinson and Walberg, 1986, pp. 14, 129). It may well be that the unstructured quality of the middle schools makes effective school research more important for them than for other sectors of the system. However, no such reconciliation between research and policy is made by the various writers in the publication.

Just as a separation between research and education is reinforced by the current mammoth reform effort, so is the divergence between the world of teachers and experts. The conflict within the reform movement is that it wants more professional teachers and at the same time it wants to control them more than ever (DeYoung, 1986). A preoccupation with student achievement and productivity is matched by teacher exams and career stages. Thus, the heavy hand of the Texas program for both teachers and students led to this program being called the Texas chainsaw massacre (Timar and Kirp, 1988, pp. 65–80). Evaluation of teachers' improvement in a Virginia program was based on very explicit expectations as follows:

> ... Instructors are directed not to offer their own unique, in some cases highly idiosyncratic, views of effective teaching, however successful these views might be. Instead, they are encouraged to transmit sensitively a standardized curriculum that reflects public knowledge of the competencies. (McNergey, Medley and Caldwell, 1989, p. 70)

Teachers of the world may soon have only their chains to lose!

The excellence movement is probably the first movement in education that is based upon international educational standards. The Sputnik crisis in the 1960s was developed from an attempt to equal Russian achievements in technology. The concern now is to match Japanese educational standards (Tomlinson and Walberg, 1986, p. 301). The Japanese are in the process of reconsidering their own standards, at least in official reports (Shimahara, 1988). Significantly, important business leaders, such as the founder of Sony, Masaru Ibuka, have advised the government on reforming Japanese education. Though reform in Japan is trying to move towards decentralization, its academic standards reinforced by the involvement of the corporate culture is still a model for the Americans.

Other countries are as eager as the Americans to equal the Japanese economic achievement, which is assumed to be related to their educational attainment. However, in Canada, Great Britain and Australia, more standardized academic achievement is combined with an emphasis upon social adjustment (Stewart, 1987, p. 125; Cunningham, 1988). In Alberta, for example, a course in career and life management must be wedged into an academic program. In a few schools the adjustment course is, interestingly, combined with a word processing course and both courses replace electives. The message seems to be that adjustment and technology can be combined to develop more productive students.

Consistent with the excellence movement, productivity of students and teachers rather than the complexity of individuals is emphasized. In their reform movement, however, the Japanese seem to be questioning the conformity of individuals to their system just as others are attempting to emulate it (Shimahara, 1988). Surprisingly, in education far more than in industry, the reform movement is separated from the creative development of individuals (Peters and Watermen, 1982, p. 322). Just as was the case with efficiency efforts in the past, the more external aspects of the new efforts towards quality movement have been more readily accepted by school administrators; school executives have been less willing to develop people by subtle changes in the organization's culture (Berman, 1986, p. 107). Thus, the excellence movement can become an umbrella for including more adjustment for gifted students as with the Gates program (Fetterman, 1988). Some of the dynamics within the excellence effort are similar to those generated by Sputnik crisis when guidance counselors were introduced, supposedly to find mathematical and scientific talent (Miles, 1964). Yet the goal of increased efforts by students and teachers does not carry any clear avenues for individual development of the people most involved. The lack of such alternatives may be as much a result of the single dimensional thinking built into the schools as it is from the excellence movement.

In both schools and business, there has been an attempt by the myth makers of quality control to develop a singular and common culture. Private schools have been seen as having such a singular sense of direction (Cusick, 1983). The curricular direction of private schools has augmented their strong and consistent set of disciplinary standards. From this value position, public schools provide students with what the educators think the students need, not what they ought to have. When the perception by one teacher is unrelated to what another teacher thinks students need, then you have fragmentation of standards in public schools. The disintegration of standards in public schools is believed to be so substantial that public school teachers send their own children to private schools (*ibid.*, p. 123). If the choice for private education is made on the basis of the standards they display, then value choices are being made explicitly and rationally.

In education, however, choices are not usually made clear and not in such an organized fashion. It is often denied that equality in education is being surrendered in anyway as a result of emphasis on quality (Tomlinson and Walberg, 1986, p. 49). Often the rhetoric of the excellence movement is so grand that the only choice appears to be between quality reforms and continuing chaos. Neither chaos nor equality is made to appear as an important alternative by those supporting the excellence movement. As was true of the relationship to research studies, the rhetoric of reforms simplifies the complex problem of varied goals that can only be partially set in some order of priority.

One fringe of the reform movement supports individual schools in developing unique programs; this is certainly a different value emphasis. However, the more organized the reform movement is in its links with both business and government, the more uniform are the programs that are developed. The emphasis on private schools or unique public ones has led to a portrait analysis of schools and the expectation that such schools have a mission to follow (Lightfoot, 1983). In areas where there is the least industry and fewest blue ribbon panels, such as South Carolina, state support has meant local development of excellence programs (Timar and Kirp, 1988). However, in other more typical situations, such as in Canada, this has not occurred (Kilpatrick, 1988). Local school improvements may require some direct link with a major movement even though the most creative changes occur at the fringes rather than at the movement's center.

The Dominant Consensus Position

The panels, commissions and foundations are a way of subordinating schools to experts while stressing a corporate culture within education. The creation of an individual school culture requires schools to obtain status and power so that they can resist this uniform mold. However, social stratification limits the cultural variety among schools. Supposedly with a unique culture, Indian schools in the western plains, for example, have often been shown strikingly similar to slum schools in eastern cities (Wax, Wax and Dumon, 1964). When businesses and power groups hold very uniform expectations of the school system, then the very concept of culture is transformed. Intended to represent the different and often equal contributions that all groups can make, the original relative concept of culture becomes changed.

Schools are already affected by the power of individuals within schools.

Additionally, schools are affected by groups in society that have more power than they do, for example, in matters of access to schools. Individual schools are further affected by the groups' power position. Since these groups determine standards of success in the social and occupational realm, middle-class schools inevitably breed competition and possessive individualism to insure students' future success. In contrast, because their students have little motivation and chance of success, working-class schools are limited to controlling and coping with the resistance by students and their parents (Lind, 1974; Carnoy and Levin, 1985). Working-class schools are similar to the colonies, and middle-class schools are like the home empires. The excellence movement will reinforce this difference unless it can develop some recognition of alternative aims.

The alliance between government, business and academics can reinforce a hegemony or dominance by the current governing group. When cultural groups are reinforced rather than subordinated, variety and complexity of unusual quality appears in education. When Montreal went beyond bilingual schools to trilingual schools, opportunities for the development of cultural alternatives, language proficiency, and the relationship between language and thought were opened (Genesee, 1983). Originally, the trilingual schools were confined to those that taught the curriculum in French, English and Hebrew, but, increasingly, other languages, such as Greek, have become the alternative to Hebrew. However, the trilingual programs meant that an ethnic or cultural group has attained a great deal of acceptance within society. The difference in the treatment of language between bilingual programs and English as a Second Language course is enormous. In English as a Second Language, usually the teacher speaks little, if any, of the student's original language. In bilingual programs in Canada, usually two teachers representing the two different languages are involved in the school program. Though trilingual curriculum does not further expand the number of teachers involved, the recognition of language and culture groups is achieved by the added competencies of the teaching staff.

From the cultural group's position, great changes have also occurred; the trilingual groups are no longer concerned with survival or acceptance by the original dominant culture. The limited concerns of many lowly new immigrants have yielded to growing political, cultural and educational aims for their descendants. In wanting to maintain a common and singular culture, the American excellence movement is said to be an attempt by English, white and male groups to maintain control; singular school standards are being honored as a result (Shor, 1986, p. 158). If a subordinated group can be kept from moving beyond an economic concern and prevented from competing for legitimate power within society, then control by the predominant group can be maintained. It is the lack of power that has particularly reduced Indian tribes to a poverty level. Subordinate groups must contest power. However, power will probably corrupt if pursued alone and absolutely. Thus, individuals in the groups must move towards cultural and personal goals.

Alternatives for Education

The excellence movement certainly represents a continuation of long-standing business values within schools and among educational researchers. Teachers, who were well organized or 'all business' as shown in sociological research by the 1930s, were successful; such values than that the goal of doing is more important than the aims of personal development in education (Waller, 1967). Along with the efficiency movement of the 1920s, the search for one set of effective teachers has for a long time been based on similar business values within educational research (Purkey and Smith, 1983). For whom is effectiveness and efficiency important, teachers or businessmen? The more interesting secrets of teachers have often died with them as separate classroom walls kept teachers apart (Lieberman and Miller, 1984). Values of sociability and development are very different from the practical and private emphasis that has guided educational practice and research! Understanding how to develop variety, sociability and idealism is related to a different set of standards for running any organization (Mitchell, 1971). There may be more to education than individual accountability for common standards as currently sought by those who would return to business fundamentals!

Variety and creativity may be obtained when educational research and practice become more diversified. The women's movement has represented not only one of the most direct challenges to the position of male experts but also the promise of new research directions. Intellectuals have increasingly argued that research should include greater subjectivity and more continuous evolution from private experience to public positions to speak in the language experiences of women (Weiler, 1988). Beginning to be asked are questions about what the immersion programs mean for females who are more successful than males in immersion classes. A few attempts to show that, in French immersion programs, students must pay closer attention do not push the issue very far (Morrison, Pawley, Bonyn and Unitt, 1986). For middle-class groups, such as those involved in the Canadian Parents for French, questions are being raised about leaving the curriculum to experts.

For working-class groups, establishing any sense of ownership over the school curriculum is a major achievement. In one poor black community, parents became so involved that even the parents, who were paid as volunteers, worked more than twice as much as they were paid to do (Comer, 1980). In another similar community, ownership of the program developed in a series of six steps:

> The mothers reported that many behavioral and learning problems
> in school seemed to disappear when 1) their child experienced an
> alliance between mother and teacher; 2) they were able to help
> teachers become more perceptive and responsive to the needs of
> their children; 3) their participation in classroom life helped to reduce
> the workload of teachers; 4) they were able to directly perceive and

fully comprehend the complexities and burdensome nature of the teaching role; 5) they could teach some of the teachers, who were not parents, something about nurturance and mothering; 6) they began to perceive the school as belonging to them. (Lightfoot, 1978, pp. 173–4)

The emerging sense of ownership in education by such a subordinated group is very precarious. Parent groups of paid volunteers can become cynical about the schools or uninvolved with the program (Sussman, 1977, pp. 118–42). The involvement of parent groups inevitably runs counter to some professional group's claim to expertise. In the poor working class, it is one thing for parents to help teachers with their art work, but it is an entirely different matter for parents to intrude on the sphere of the psychologist who was doing the study (Comer, 1980, p. 178). The dominance of psychologists over teachers and parents continues, just as laypersons are still omitted from the development of new programs similar to the French immersion. Parents from social levels higher than the teachers' can intimidate the latter because of their status and influence in the school (Sussman, 1977, p. 156). Professionals often become humble enough to talk to common folk when their innovations don't work; when innovations are effective the experts' claims to planning are asserted. The effectiveness of bilingual schools, just like the successes of effective schools, still leads to a belief that schools should be controlled by experts (Leithwood and Montgomery, 1987, p. 7).

Aside from their own successes, educational experts do not seem to be aware of the growing power of corporate interests in education. Corporate power has been increasingly brought into education by joint programs with industry (Berman, 1986, p. 106). Some of these programs have focused upon the problems of inner cities such as Adopt-a-School Program, the Boston Compact, and the Academy of Finance. Programs for exchanging personnel have been practised in Canada and the United States and are known as the Ryerson Plan (Apple, 1982). Cooperative programs for schools between industry and universities have also developed (Feldman, 1985). The Xerox Corporation set up the Institute for Research on Learning which it runs together with the University of California's Graduate School of Education (Kearns, 1989). Industrial leaders like the president of Xerox can, on the one hand, speak of the programs that they run with schools and, on the other hand, advise schools on how they ought to be like 'the smartest high tech companies' (Kearns, 1989, p. 7).

The involvement of business executives with government or policy commissions further augments direct corporate power. The foundations or the non-profit corporations give more support to those in business positions and suggest more of a consensus than any direct expression of self-interest by business people would ever provide (Berman, 1984). Head Start programs which were once so challenged are now a part of the consensus of efforts to promote excellence and to get the poor into the race for success (Kearns,

1989). However, more importantly, through paternalistic programs, the dependency of the poor is enhanced. The chances of subordinate groups developing their own culture and education programs are diminished.

Intellectuals who help maintain the dominance of centralist programs are themselves caught in the corporate web. Communications, education and culture, more generally, have long been recognized as one variety of imperialism that can include even the most selfless scientist (House, 1974). However, the scholars who prepare background papers for business and government reports, such as *A Nation At Risk*, are particularly subject to cooptation. What they think and write is caught in publicity and reward systems governed by interests other than their own (Tomlinson and Walberg, 1986). Academic experts can provide a further cloak for hegemonic consensus that corporate interests have so recently contrived in relation to schooling. Neither academic values nor the values of subordinate groups are promoted by their expedient practice.

The Political Evolution of Marginal People

The problem with corporate hegemony is that its enhanced influence can make the development of grassroots positions more difficult for subordinated individuals. In the women's literature, it is argued that acquiring a voice, initially expressed as rejection of experts' positions, is a very significant step (Weiler, 1988). Similarly, teachers have acquired a voice; the voice is often a rejection of experts because, like women's groups, they have been subjected to abuse by the experts. A kindergarten teacher, for example, says of the excellence movement:

> There is a real danger that in the current educational atmosphere, primary classrooms are being reduced in spirit and scope, with rigid curricula and 'teacher proof' materials turning teachers into technicians and children into products. (Martin, 1987)

Differences among teachers and parents make it difficult for them to contest for power. Groups of teachers, particularly at high schools, are showing signs of greater resiliency against the corporate culture than kindergarten teachers have (McDonald, 1987). In the past, parents have questioned experts but, more often, parents have been attracted to the experts' positions, particularly where experts have focused on a widely publicized issue. On an issue, parents have reacted to challenge the school's programs. Thus, parents are likely to be tempted to seize upon one of the issues in the excellence bundle, such as requiring more homework. Still, the hegemony of corporate culture may make an alliance between parents and teachers more difficult even if it can not prevent a resistance movement from being formed.

However, since internationally-based standards are seen as increasingly being set for school achievement by a corporate culture, it is important to see how far teachers have gone in organizing and developing their own positions. Parent groups, particularly working-class ones, are less likely to challenge dominant positions. Only when spokespersons for both parents and teachers emerge will organic ties develop between the two groups.

Today, even articulate teachers are held in check by the manipulative approaches of school administration. Current staff training practices reinforce teachers' working under the hegemony of administrators. Cooperative programs developed by administrators working with teachers have used the literature on teachers' level of concern (Anderson, 1981). Administrators work with teachers' personal concerns about how an innovation will affect their day, long before discussing the innovation's philosophy. The mechanics of the innovation are then developed between personal needs and program philosophy. The programs interestingly assume that there is a hierarchy of concerns, even if most teachers never get beyond the middle level of the hierarchy. Such hierarchy parallels the limited achievements of teachers, for in this literature teachers are often seen as confined to the use of innovations at a mechanical level (Anderson, 1981). School improvements based upon the concerns literature have led to teacher evaluation efforts; evaluation by educational authorities enables them to reassert their control over teachers dumbfounded by the pace of innovations.

The activity of a local teachers' group shows that teachers can handle theoretical matters and that they can do so when they challenge the powers that be (McDonald, 1987). As is true of most teacher groups, the group that evolved a theoretical position and sought power started with a purely social function. A meeting over pizza, which started with their barking about student aggravation, became, in this notable case, a discussion group because the teacher members wanted to be less 'insular and self-absorbed' (*ibid.*, p. 27). Initially a discussion group, the teachers prepared a written criticism of one of the excellence reports. The group took an increasingly political position by ignoring the advice of their school superintendent to take a more moderate stance (*ibid.*, p. 30). As a result of the teachers' publicized activities, an expert who was writing a new report came to talk with them before his new position paper was finished. He noted that 'the teacher's voice can contribute to school policy essential knowledge that is available from no other source' (*ibid.*, p. 31).

Aside from influencing the experts, this particular teacher group reached the power centers with their ideas. The teachers wanted the school district policy makers to listen to them for a change. The teachers' views were based upon particular situations and could be stated, initially, as a story or parable. However, they later brought together anecdotes and theories so as to 'use anecdotes to illuminate the insufficiency of anecdote just as the group was later to use theory to illuminate the insufficiency of theory' (*ibid.*, p. 34). Together with experts, they presented papers on policy matters to the public at large. From a discussion group, these high school teachers developed into and became a source of power.

Unexpected Innovations

The merging of teachers with experts could be a model for teachers to become organized as a social movement. The acquisition of power can enhance the importance of a position. On most issues, there is neither a dialogue nor any form of collaboration evident between researchers or between researchers and teachers (Noddings, 1987, p. 394). With little initial commitment by those involved, the most significant effect of innovation has often been the formation of school leagues initiated to discuss and implement research findings (Lieberman and Miller, 1984, pp. 129–34). Describing the evolution of the most famous network, the League of Co-operating Schools, a key participant says, 'The "experts" learned the limits of their expertise. All of us were experts from one time or another' (*ibid.*, p. 131). In this case, informal sharing evolved from a stage at which experts gave authoritative formal luncheon talks to another stage of information sharing and social support in sessions to which everyone came with bag lunches.

Other research networks make clear that experts are involved so as to encourage the exchange of ideas and the emergence of a common identity. Like the League of Co-operating Schools, these other efforts show that expert and laypersons maintain less of a front with each other. For example, the first large scale study of innovations by Paul Mort led to the formation of a school council in New York, New Jersey and Connecticut. Increasingly, a common cause was sought in a writing consortium and a new computer group. The association initiated by Mort has since led to a combination of practice and research beneficial to both teachers and researchers (*ibid.*, p. 133).

The unanticipated result of innovation research leading to activity among experts and teachers is in contrast to the usual lack of dialogue between researchers and subjects. The lack of such collaboration is one reason why educational research has been argued to be so 'uneducational' (Noddings, 1987, p. 394). It is, however, striking that concern for commitment among teachers and reactions against the excellence movement with its mechanistic assumptions have not led to a teacher movement displaying many of the characteristics of the high school teachers' group discussed earlier. Involvement with the social forces challenging power in society does not immediately bring about the merger of individual, professional and social concerns resulting in the formation of collaborating groups of teachers. In fact, in talking about the transforming quality of a social movement, writers on education, such as Maxine Green, are led to citing the resistance movement in France, for example, rather than progressive movements within education (Lieberman and Miller, 1979, p. 34).

Educational research on innovations refers to the social effects of involvement, but the effect upon individuals alone has been most accentuated. One of the more detailed studies of innovation, the Network Study, has pointed out that for both teachers and students the most striking effect of innovations is the sense of being 'set apart' from other schools (Huberman and Miles,

1982, p. 394). A sense of 'a part together' can, further, lead students to identify with teachers who are particularly innovative. However, this social effect seems to separate schools and individual classes rather than expand them.

Classroom practices include either more self-directed individual activity or more structured approaches where the teacher was more accountable (*ibid.*, p. 252). For people in schools, innovations are an individual stripping process slowly joined with concerns for social relationships and professional functions (Chart 1). When teachers see their actual classroom practices change, they often feel naked. They then expand their personal repertoire of teaching approaches. If they have been more traditional in using structured, whole class teaching, they become more progressive and use less tailored group activities.

Compared with individuals in such movements as Poland's Solidarity, there is no evidence that groups of teachers develop different conceptions of society

Figure 1   User Change During Implementation

Type/Items
1 *Changes in everyday classroom practices*:
(Daily organization, routines)
More individualization, more sustained individual contact
Pupils more 'in charge', self-directed, self-paced
Less time for other activities; other subjects driven out
More accountable to outsiders, more policed
Less structure, less prearrangement
More structure; regimentation
Multiple materials, no longer one text, manual, set of workbooks
No longer able to monitor whole class
Changes in scheduling
2 *Repertoire expansion*:
Ability to individualize, differentiate
More 'meat' in curriculum, more approaches to call on
Greater skill in diagnostic/testing procedures
3 *Relational changes*:
Closer to pupils, more concern for pupils
Closer to other teachers (in team)
More egalitarian relationships with pupils
4 *Better understanding, comprehension, of*:
Actual ability/skill levels of pupils
Emotional problems of pupils
How the school system operates, who has power/influence
Principles and procedures for mastery learning
5 *Self-efficacy*:
More resourceful, effective
More self-confident
Less energy, low investment, burnout
6 *Transfer*:
More organized in general, better at planning
Using skills, procedures in other subject matters
7 *Changes in attitudes*:
Able to trust pupils, less need for control
8 *Changes in professional self-image*:
Myself as a teacher

(Touraine, Dubet, Wieviorka and Strzelecki, 1980). However, the fragmented and isolated pattern of teachers' lives makes broader conceptions very unlikely (Sarason, 1982). Yet teachers develop closer and more equalitarian social relationships with students and other teachers as they experience innovations (Chart 1). The relational changes are, at times, negative: One teacher told a student objecting to a new career education program, 'The hell with what you want, I'm 32, you're 17' (Huberman and Miles, 1982, p. 256). Interestingly, teachers' understanding of how learning occurs includes knowledge of how power is exercised; for them, understanding learning means knowing how things actually work.

With practical understanding, an awareness of social relationships and an expanded skill range, teachers assume control of innovations rather than succumb to them (*ibid.*, p. 252). Teachers' self-efficacy improves their ability to transfer skills between innovations and their attitudes toward their pupils become more positive. Consequently, teachers' professional image is transformed. However, studies show that most teachers working with innovations never get beyond the matter of social relationships, the third step (See Figure 1).

Social Movements

When teachers follow the example of social movements and evolve their own movement, teaching will perhaps develop a new alternative position to help set policy for education. Such a movement will highlight the concern for fidelity in student and collegial relationships and cast doubt on the excellence movement (Noddings, 1987). It will share Simone Weil's insightful ideas about social movements. For her, Solidarity and Catholic radicalism are a relevant source of understanding of how to live with conflict and when not to place faith in rational procedures in teaching. The desire to live with people in creative conflict would thus replace the desire for an absolutist world built from abstract ideas (Mitchell, 1966).

In classrooms, as well as in society, teachers would exercise influence over people first of all by being able to feel like the person whom they want to influence. If teachers know that they are in an Anglophone area with Anglophone students who are studying French, a relevancy and meaningfulness in their study must be established. Thus, in Calgary, where one community celebrates Bastille day and another has a French church and a French bookstore, signs of past struggles could be related to French teaching in the community. Available resources include French Canadians, groups and companies that have remained in the city, even if forced into subordination. For meaningful learning, other resources can be enlisted further; education has recently rediscovered the significance, for example, of stories and parables (Egan, 1987). Such stories and parables can be a basis for exploration of change in education. They are a way of avoiding being so realistic that one's imagination is lost by adjusting to the status quo.

Past struggles and new alternatives are part of a current, living message. The current message will include the commitment of persons trying to bring about change. Nothing can influence others more than knowing that commitment is shared by both speaker and listener, and expert and layperson (Mitchell, 1966). Within a social movement there is, to be more correct, no sharp line between the expert and layperson. Following through with our example, bilingual teachers should not be alienated from their students, and English parents should be involved in learning French and improving the program for their children. Relationships between students and teachers, and teachers, and researchers, should be far closer.

Conclusions

From each of their perspectives, the groups involved in schools see the shadows of power in society. Economic pressures are most directly seen by administrators through the budget, by teachers through their evaluation and their salaries, and by students experiencing the need for part-time jobs Parents, in ways we have not begun to examine, may be influenced by the educational programs. However, it is only within the innovations of the past two decades that choices for these stakeholders have begun to be clear. Innovations involve either more equality or higher standards in education. Programs stressing greater equality of education and accessibility to government have included mainstreaming special education students, women's studies and parental involvement with schools.

The excellence movement in the last decade has come to combine greater accountability of schools through academic productivity, greater direct corporate control over education, and repeated, though unrecognized cooptation of researchers and planners to the movement. Thus far, criticisms of the excellence efforts are as numerous as they are uncoordinated. Yet, small groups of teachers and social movements in other contexts reveal the transformation that can result when groups resisting dominant power become organized and when intellectuals pursue more enlightened goals. Educators. together with their allies, can mount significant challenges to the hegemony of big business and big government. People can be more developed intellectually and socially within schools by their strong personal experiences in this new resistance movement.

Bibliography

ANDERSON, B. (1981) The relationship between training and the adoption of an innovation. Unpublished Master's thesis, The University of Calgary, Alberta.

APPLE, M. (1982) *Education and Power*, Boston: Routledge and Kegan Paul.

BEATTIE, N. (1985) *Professional Parents*, London: The Falmer Press.

BECKER, H.J. and EPSTEIN, J.L. (1982) 'Parent involvement; A survey of teacher practices', *Elementary School Journal*, 83, pp. 85–102.

BECKER, H.S. (1952) 'Social class variations in the teacher-pupil relationship', *Journal of Educational Sociology*, 25, pp. 451–65.

BERMAN, E. (1984) 'State hegemony and the schooling process', *Journal of Education*, 166, pp. 239–53.

BERMAN, E. (1986) 'The improbability of meaningful education reform', *Issues in Education*, 3, pp. 99–112.

BUTTERFIELD, F. (1986, August 3) 'Why Asians are going to the head of the class', *The New York Times, Education Life*, pp. 18–23.

CANADIAN EDUCATION ASSOCIATION (1983) *French Immersion and School Boards: Issues and Effects*, Toronto: Canadian Education Association.,

CARNOY, M. and LEVIN, H. (1985) *Schooling and Work in the Democratic State*, Stanford: Stanford University Press.

COMER, J. (1980) *School Power*, New York: Free Press.

CUSICK, P. (1983) *The Equalitarian Ideal and the American High School*, New York: Longman.

CUNNINGHAM, P. (1988) *Curriculum Change in the Primary School Since 1945*, London: The Falmer Press.

DAFT, R. and BECKER, S. (1978) *The Innovative Organization*, New York: Elsevier.

DEYOUNG, A. (1986) 'Educational "excellence" versus teacher "professionalism": Towards some conceptual clarity', *The Urban Review*, 18, pp. 71–84.

EGAN, K. (1987) 'Literacy and the oral foundations of education', *Harvard Education Review*, 5, pp. 445–72.

EPSTEIN, J.L. (1985) 'Home and school connections in schools of the future: Implications of research on parent involvement', *Peabody Journal of Education*, 62, pp. 18–41.

EPSTEIN, J.L. (1986) 'Parents reactions to teacher practices of parent involvement', *Elementary School Journal*, 86, pp. 277–94.

EVERHART, R.B. (1983) *Reading, Writing and Resistance*, London: Routledge and Kegan Paul.

FELDMAN, M. (1985) 'The workplace as educator', in FANTINI, M. and SINCLAIR, R. (Eds) *Education in School and Nonschool Settings*, Chicago: National Society to the Study of Education.

FETTERMAN, D. (1988) *Excellence and Equality*, Albany, NY: Albany State University of New York.

GARTNER, A. and LIPSKY, D.K. (1987) 'Beyond special education: Toward a quality system for all students', *Harvard Education Review*, 57, pp. 367–95.

GENESEE, F. (1983) 'Bilingual education of majority language children: The immersion experiments in review', *Applied Psycholinguistics*, 4, pp. 1–46.

GERSTL, J. and JACOBS, G. (Eds) (1976) *Professions for the People*, New York: John Wiley.

GOLD, B. and MILES, M. (1981) *Whose School is it, Anyway?*, New York: Praeger.

GRACEY, H.L. (1972) *Curriculum or Craftsmanship*, Chicago: The University of Chicago.

GRANT, C.A. and SLEETER, C.E. (1986) *After the School Bell Rings*, London: The Falmer Press.

HALL, O. and CARLTON, R. (1977) *Basic Skills at School and Work*, Toronto: Ontario Economic Council.

HARVEY, E. (1974) *Educational Systems and the Labour Market*, Don Mills, ON: Longmans.

HOLT, J. (1981) *Teach Your Own*, New York: Delcorte Press.

HOUSE, E. (1974) *The Politics of Educational Innovation*, Berkeley: McCutchan.

HOUSE, E. and LAPAN, S. (1978) *Survival in the Classroom*, Boston: Allyn and Bacon.

HUBERMAN, A.M. and MILES, M.B. (1982) *Innovation Up Close*, Andover, Mass.: The Network.

JOHNSON, S.M. (1983) 'Performance-based staff layoffs in the public schools: Implementation and the outcomes', in BALDRIDGE, J.V. and DEAL, T. (Eds) *The Dynamics of Organizational Change in Education*, Berkeley: McCutchan.

KEARNS, D. (1989) 'An education recovery plan for America', in SCHULTZ, F. (Ed.) *Education 89–90*, Guildford, CT: Dushkin.

KILPATRICK, I.F. (1988) An analysis of educational change in Alberta from The Worth Commission 1972 to the Secondary Education Review 1987. Unpublished Master's Thesis, The University of Calgary, Alberta.

KRATZMAN, A., BYRNE, T. and WORTH, W. (1980) *A System in Conflict*, Edmonton: Alberta Labour.

LEITHWOOD, K.A. and MONTGOMERY, D.J. (1987) *Improving School Practice using Innovation Profiles*, Toronto: The Ontario Institute for Studies in Education.

LIEBERMAN, A. and MILLER, L. (Eds) (1979) *Staff Development*, New York: Teachers College, Columbia University Press.

LIEBERMAN, A. and MILLER, L. (1984) *Teachers, Their World, Their Work*, Alexandria, Virginia: Association for Supervision and Curriculum Development.

LIGHTFOOT, S.L. (1973) *The Good High School*, New York: Basic Books.

LIGHTFOOT, S.L. (1978) *Worlds Apart*, New York: Basic Books.

LIND, L.J. (1974) *The Learning Machine*, Toronto: Anansi Press.

LORTIE, D. (1975) *School Teacher*, Chicago: The University of Chicago Press.

MARJORIEBANKS, K. (1979) *Families and their Learning Environments*, London: Routledge and Kegan Paul.

MARTIN, A. (1987) 'Back to kindergarten basics', in OKAZOWA-REY, M., ANDERSON, J. and TRAVERS, R. (Eds) *Teaching, Teachers and Teacher Education*, Cambridge: Harvard University Press.

McDONALD, J. (1987) 'Raising the teacher's voice and the ironic role of theory', in OKAZOWAK-REY, M., ANDERSON, J. and TRAVERS, R. (Eds) *Teaching, Teachers and Teacher Education*, Cambridge: Harvard University Press.

McNERGNEY, R.F., MEDLEY, D.M. and CALDWELL, M.S. (1989) 'Making and implementing policy on teacher licensure', in SCHULTZ, F. (Ed.) *Education 89–90*, Guildford: Connecticut, Dushkin.

McPHERSON, G. (1972) *Small Town Teacher*, Cambridge: Harvard University Press.

MILES, M.B. (Ed.) (1964) *Innovation and Education*, New York: Teachers College, Columbia University Press.

MITCHELL, S. (1966) The people shall judge. Unpublished paper. Provincial Convention for Alberta Federation of Home and School Associations.

MITCHELL, S. (1967) The quest of beginning teachers: Discovery of competence. Unpublished paper for Teacher Education and Certification Conference, The Alberta Teachers' Association.

MITCHELL, S. (1971) *A Woman's Profession — A Man's Research*, Edmonton, Alberta: Alberta Association of Registered Nurses.

MORRISON, F., PAWLEY, C., BONYN, R. and UNITT, J. (1986) *Aspects of French Immersion at the Primary and Secondary Levels*, Twelfth Annual Report to the Minister of Education. Toronto: Queen's Printer.

NATIONAL COMMISSION ON EXCELLENCE IN EDUCATION (1983) *A Nation at Risk: The Imperative of Educational Reform*, Washington, DC: US Government Printing Office.

NODDINGS, N. (1987) 'Fidelity in teaching, teacher education and research in teaching', in OKAZOWA-REY, M., ANDERSON, J. and TRAVERS, R. (Eds) *Teaching, Teachers and Teacher Education*, Cambridge: Harvard University Press.

Samuel Mitchell

OLSON, L.P. (1987) 'Who computes?' in LIVINGSTONE, D. (Ed.) *Critical Pedagogy and Cultural Power*, Toronto: Garamond Press.
PEDERSON, E., FAUCHER, T.A. and EATON, W. (1978) 'A new perspective on the effects of first-grade teachers on children's subsequent adult status', *Harvard Educational Review*, 48, pp. 1–31.
PETERS, T. and WATERMAN, R. (1982) *In Search of Excellence*, New York: Warner Books.
PRESSEISEN, B. (1985) *Unlearned Lessons*, London: The Falmer Press.
RYAN, K., NEWMAN, K., MAGER, G., APPLEGATE, J., LASLEY, T., FLORA, R. and JOHNSTON, J. (1980) *Biting the Apple*, New York: Longman.
SARASON, S. (1982) *The Culture of the School and the Problem of Change*, (2nd Edn), New York: Allyn and Bacon.
SARASON, S. and DORIS, J. (1979) *Educational Handicap, Public Policy and Social History*, New York: The Free Press.
SERGIOVANNI, T. (1984) 'Leadership and excellence in schooling', *Educational Leadership*, 41, pp. 5–13.
SHIMAHARA, N. (1988) 'The college entrance examination and policy issues in Japan', *International Journal of Qualitative Studies in Education*, 1, pp. 39–50.
SHOR, I. (1986) *Cultural Wars*, London: Routledge and Kegan Paul.
SINGER, J. and BUTLER, J. (1987) 'The Education for All Handicapped Children Act: Schools as agents of social reform', *Harvard Educational Review*, 57, pp. 125–52.
SMITH, L., KLEIN, P., PRUNTY, J. and DWEYER, D. (1966) *Educational Innovators*, New York: The Falmer Press.
SPEIER, M. (1976) 'The child as conversationalist: Some culture contact features of conversational interactions', in HAMMERSLY, M. and WOODS, P. (Eds) *The Process of Schooling*, London: Routledge and Kegan Paul.
STEWART, D. (1987) 'Cutting to the core: Curriculum mishaps in Saskatchewan', in COCHRANE, D. (Ed.) *So Much for the Mind*, Toronto: Kagan and Woo.
STINCHCOMBE, A.L. (1964) *Rebellion in a High School,*. Chicago: Quadrangle.
SUSSMAN, L. (1977) *Tales Out of School*, Philadelphia: Temple University.
TIMAR, T.B. and KIRP, D.L. (1988) *Managing Educational Excellence*, London: The Falmer Press.
TOMLINSON, T.M. and WALBERG, H.J. (1986) *Academic Work and Educational Excellence*, Berkeley: McCutchan.
TOURAINE, A., DUBET, F., WIEVIORKA, M. and STRZELECKI, J. (1980) *Solidarity, The Analysis of a Social Movement: Poland 1980–82*, Cambridge: Cambridge University Press.
WALLER, W. (1967) *The Sociology of Teaching*, New York: John Wiley.
WAX, M., WAX, R. and DUMON, T.V. (1964) 'Formal education in an American Indian community', *Journal of Social Problems*, 11, pp. 1–126.
WEILER, K. (1988) *Women Teaching for Change*, South Hadley, MA: Bergin and Garvey.
WILLIS, P. (1978) *Learning to Labour*, Westmead, England: Saxon House.

18   The Unfinished System of Education

Samuel Mitchell

Introduction

An educational system, consisting of schools at various levels, appears closely
structured and complete. Nonetheless, in reality, the schools and levels
within it are by themselves incomplete, open and, to some degree, independent. These characteristics make schools interesting to some commentators
(Tyler, 1988). They enable parts of the educational system to adapt gradually
to change in society in their own ways (Weick, 1978). If the system were more
unified and organically linked, it would lend to control by the stronger forces
of business and government in society. Under such control, it can appear
efficient and rational, but it is likely to overact to all social changes as if they
all were major ones. Schools may actually use their separate operations and
functions as an instrument in their quest for autonomy. Different types and
levels of schools can develop a degree of autonomy from society. However, if
autonomy is carried too far, problems arise. Autonomy for the benefit of
educators alone can be the equivalent of corruption in society (Waller, 1967).
Autonomous teachers who do not want students will find administrators who
want neither teachers nor students. Yet autonomy is important for educators.
Their attempt to secure autonomy is the problem explored in this chapter.
Within the emerging educational system, the concerns of administrators,
teachers and clients are each to be considered independently and then
together.

The Administrator's Invention: The System

Educators in the Nineteenth Century were able to link the stages of education
so that elementary and secondary levels were connected and the first two
levels were tied, in turn, to higher education. Previously, individuals received
their education in unrelated parts. Home tutoring substituted for the first two
levels of schooling for those who could afford it. Private academies competed

with high schools. Universities often ran preparatory programs (Tyack, 1974). Earlier competition and overlap appear to have yielded to the present system.

At any given time, the current system can appear to be a final and balanced structure. However, the recent evolution of the system reveals how incomplete the institutional structure has actually been. In the last two decades large additions to the system have been made through adding early childhood education and by wedging junior colleges between universities and high schools (Joffre, 1977; Clark, 1960). Adult education remains largely outside the system and, significantly, roles within it are based upon work and community status rather than internal class or school activities (Davis, 1961).

Those within the current system are aware of how open-ended their roles are; they must write the play as well as play their roles within the play (Tyler, 1988). Those who have had their roles added to the system usually reveal the extent to which these roles are transitional. Early childhood education has been shown to function as a 'boot camp' in training students in the routines for the elementary school (Gracey, 1972). Junior colleges have been described as engaged in a process of cooling students' ambitions so that they will aim less for academic programs and more for the less inspiring vocational programs through the actions of guidance counsellors (Clark, 1960).

Programs that have evolved close to the public school system, such as community schools, have been shown to involve administrators more than anyone else. Students have been affected very little by such schools (Harvey, 1986); teachers show some limited involvement in these schools, but they are more affected by closer, more additive innovations such as vocational schools or socio-economic programs. In contrast, administrators get involved in promoting extension of the basic educational system by introducing both community schools and vocational innovations (House, 1974). The wider contacts of administrators compared with those of teachers are one important reason why they are likely to push beyond classrooms to system changes (Daft and Becker, 1978). Administrators often involve themselves with classrooms only to collect school information for use in obtaining support from outside bodies (Tyler, 1988, pp. 92–3).

The evolution of the public system has been from separate schools with moral concerns and monitorial methods to bureaucracies with whole class teaching and grading of classes based upon technical rationality (Tyler, 1988). From the eighteenth century to the twentieth century, the administrative function became relatively more important than the teaching and learning relationship. Because the administrators have become record writers and gate keepers, it is surprising that top level administrators in particular often seem to be undone by that same system. Many such administrators are either unable to see beyond their system (Lind, 1974) or are reduced to using word magic in an attempt to prevent their schools from being tossed about by the forces of society (Blumberg, 1985). The exceptional superintendent seeks conflict resolution or new issues in education. Just below the superintendent, the central office staff play games to maintain their autonomy by such farcical procedures as pretending to conduct an open search for new candidates when the person they want has already been picked (McGivney and Haught, 1972). Central office staff often act to protect themselves from the influence of those that they see watching them in the fish bowl which they see education to be. Neither superintendents nor central office staff appear to have been empowered by the system!

More hidden from view of outside provocateurs, principals seek to maintain their autonomy while working with their sponsors among higher administrators (Wolcott, 1973). Principals can maintain their precarious position within schools by delivering resources for their staff (Cross and Herridt, 1965); they can also arrange schedules for teachers in exchange for teacher support for school public relations functions (Cusick, 1983, pp. 92–8). Principals and teachers together can be entrepreneurs who raise funds from parents and obtain financial support from outside the school; the former control this process, however. Principals may be isolated within their own schools unless they can influence their staff. It is between top administration and teaching professionals that principals find themselves squeezed as the person in the middle.

The Incapacity of Professionals to Work with the System

Teachers as well as other professionals follow a narrow and winding road in attempting to maintain their own autonomy. Teachers, guidance counselors and social workers are among the better known specialists who increasingly work with schools (Sarason, 1982). Each of these groups, as well as many lesser known ones such as speech specialists, is separated from each other by the walls of professional autonomy. Teachers' concern for the general abstractions of academic learning highlights the difference between them and social workers who are much more concerned with the particular context of family and neighborhood (Tyler, 1988, p. 219). Guidance counselors have been shown scouring the halls looking for students with personal problems; teachers, in contrast, are shown resentful of this invasion (Cicourel and Kitsuse, 1963).

On a more general basis, the difficulty of integrating different professional groups within the administrative structure is revealed by problems coordinating the views of teachers at different levels of the system. Almost all teachers accept the existence of a hierarchy among the levels and talk of moving up in the system if and when they are promoted. Still, there is tension between the levels, which is revealed by the procedures used in passing student records and recommendations from one level in the system to another. Elementary teachers labor long and diligently in preparing reports on students; these reports are regularly ignored by junior high school teachers who want to form their own independent judgments (Sarason, 1982). Similarly, the reports of junior high school teachers appear to be ignored by high school teachers. Each group wants to make its own evaluation, using their own standards; but the higher levels resist any influence by lower levels, or anyone else, for that matter. The administrative hierarchy has added to these professional differences without providing for direct communication between professionals who might, otherwise, correct the problem.

Similarly, the division between special education and regular classes is reinforced by the administrative hierarchy. The professional separation of faculties of education and departments of psychology further divides the two fields. As a result of their professional training and administrative divisions, regular and special education teachers develop disturbing stereotypes about each other (Sarason, 1982). Special education teachers see regular program teachers as dumping their students into special education with little awareness that there can never be enough specialists to resolve human problems. Regular teachers think of special education teachers as having small teaching loads. They believe that special education teachers and other specialists are certainly capable of taking on more problem students if the procedures for moving the students out of special classes and returning them to regular ones is simplified.

Regular and special education teachers reflect different perspectives. Regular teachers are more independent of their students. Special education teachers are so related to their students that they seem to share the problems which their students are thought to possess. Special education teachers are so linked to those they teach that advocacy of the students' rights has become a role extension for them (Grant and Steeter, 1986). The problems of the two teachers' groups trying to implement an innovation like mainstreaming have been described in Chapter 17. Here, it is important to realize that any division between professions, or professional division within education, creates indirect lines of communication. Such indirect communication as well as the rituals that keep people apart, is the reason that bureaucracy has been described as a form of organization that cannot correct its own mistakes (Crozier, 1964).

Other divisions in teaching are related to different types of knowledge even more than they are linked to different organizational structures. Early childhood educators, for example, have been seen as having a developmental bias that separates them from educators oriented toward knowledge of science or serious academic preparation (King, 1978). Every level in the educational system has had a kind of knowledge-focus based on its connections with some disciplinary sources. Yet, no level in the system can be easily integrated into one system. The practical orientation toward basic skills expected of the elementary school is hardly the same as the general education function of colleges (Dworkin, 1959, pp. 71–3). Similarly, the moral function of the kindergarten differs from the utility function of advanced technical schools. However, the hierarchy of education means that the knowledge criteria of the higher level can be used to criticize the lower level by those who want to play the critic's role.

The administrative subordination of one level to another creates more problems when it goes beyond the gamesmanship of the playing critic. When early childhood education was integrated into the public system, trained elementary school teachers replaced childhood education teachers because seniority was the criterion used when budget cuts occurred (Joffre, 1977).

The hierarchy of professional groups is frequently used to divide the thinkers and the doers. Liberal arts faculties see themselves as the thinkers and those in fields like education as the doers (Sarason, 1982). Students and faculty in vocational schools are seen as less able to do general thinking than those in academic positions. When elementary teachers and university professors were involved in an experiment in which they reversed roles, the elementary teachers were noticeably wanting to do anything — cut, paste or knit — so they could avoid the abstract discussion with university professors (Lanier, 1983). Hierarchies polarize particular, concrete views from universal, abstract perspectives.

The World of People Like Us

Though elementary teachers and special education teachers are seen to represent the world of particular situations, they are still removed from that personal world emphasizing unique events. Only students, parents and community members are not caught by the net of administrative and professional talk. Only they can see the educational other as a member of a primary, personal group (Waller, 1967). The professionals and administrators in a reverse way may be kept out of that world by the primary groups who want to be more than an audience. Thus, students, as they move into adolescent stage, attract attention by provoking conflict between the abstract world of educational authorities and their own situational world. By junior high school, if not by late elementary school, students become preoccupied with their own status system. In such a system, status is built upon one's standing in a dating and rating complex. The system is very much a context in which the abstract approach of education becomes foreign. In the traditional small town of the past, the students' world was very localized and teachers presented a general culture (Waller, 1967). In the urban and modern world, students bring evanescent music and fads into their social relationships. A high ranking group of male students, the jocks, talk their way out of trouble by joking with the principal; they believe that if 'he threw us out, the school would fall apart' (Cusick, 1973, p. 119). Teachers claim that they are independent of students' social relationships, but teachers' use of group dynamics, such as role playing, or subjective approaches, such as diaries, often brings the students' world into the classroom (*ibid.*, pp. 182–4). Students' non-academic, extra-curricular activities also distort academic evaluation. Whether they are aware of it or not, teachers award increasingly higher marks to students as they become more involved in extra-curricular activities through their years of high school (Gordon, 1957).

Figure 1   The pupils' point of view

1   Though not related to the measurement of learning, student evaluations of schooling are revealing.
2   Elementary students report that they enjoy schooling far more than secondary students.
3   Secondary students not only view schools very negatively but they often talk about schools as if they were 'prisons'.
4   Secondary students see other students much as a problem as they do teachers; their sense of being excluded from important student groups can be intense.
5   All students are concerned about the status and recognition they are given in schools.
6   Students often make recommendations about changing schools so that the schools become more stimulating environments or that they are provided with a territory of their own in schools.
7   Students are not able to consider technical aspects of schooling such as teacher questions and teaching aids in a valid and reliable manner.
8   Students have a consistent view of the qualities of teachers as persons and of the actions of these teachers in classrooms that they find objectionable. For example, nasty and strict teachers who explain their subject well will be accepted.
9   Pupils are able to recognize most of the processes occurring within schools and record their reactions to these processes. Students, for example, see the labeling of students and classes even when they are not personally affected.
10 Only a small minority of students with higher status ever participate in classes or make suggestions for improving education. Students alone are not able to change the size of the contributing groups because of the sensitivities of students to each other. Teachers may, in contrast, work with the quiet students, including practising questions they will be asked in advance, to change the relative numbers of contributing students.
   Source: (Meighen, 1981, pp. 29–37; and Fullan, 1982, pp. 147–51)

Whatever impact student culture has on educational authorities, they certainly bring with them a world of their own. The language and thought of adolescence is an example of what is called a localized culture rather than a cosmopolitan one, even though the localized culture is now a part of change. In this culture, ideas are closely intertwined with specific context. In contrast, academic knowledge held by educators, is based upon an understanding that is deliberately removed from its context. In the localized culture, knowledge is appreciating or understanding; in the cosmopolitan culture, knowledge is causally explaining (Merton, 1957). The conflict between students and impersonal schools has increased because students have been reared in a participatory culture in which relationships are accentuated (Friedenberg, 1965).

Student reports of being humiliated by teachers who make them aware of their insignificance is the most immediate cause of the students' culture conflicting with the professional knowledge of teachers. Figure 1 records this conflict (Fullan, 1982; Meighen, 1981). It is unquestionably true that students become more critical of parents and other institutions just as they become more negative about teachers. The students' ability to criticize a knowledge code separate from what they possess is probably much more limited than Figure 1 suggests. Students are unable to evaluate teachers in so-called technical issues. One technical issue includes teachers' ability to ask questions. This ability to ask questions can be seen at the very heart of the educational process which students are unable fully to understand. In any case, the summary in Figure 1 reveals the alienation that students are shown to experience. The alienation leads them to feel more separated and lonely while with each other than they are with teachers; surprisingly, the students stress that other students are less likely to understand their point of view than their teachers do (Fullan, 1982). Moreover, the status system of students causes the splits and alienation among them. The top status students are chosen for all student functions even when they are not the best performers on those occasions (Cusick, 1973). Ironically the subordinated students do not realize that the top students decide very few questions within the school (Everhart, 1983). The hierarchical school structure, as was true concerning divisions among teachers, cannot integrate groups of students. Medium ability students, particularly girls, may be ignored in the current stratified system.

A Creation Myth of Focusing on Students in Research

Alternatives to existing structures can arise from a different perspective. Creative work is based upon changing thought patterns. The creation of human beings by God has usually been seen as the extension of an already existing form. Creation can, however, be thought about as an action of a dominant power which so constrains itself as to allow the development of a new independent agent, say, the student. This creation myth which includes contraction and critical extension of power has been used as a guide for developing the leadership of administrators (Simon, 1982). The original source is Isaac Luria, a mystical rabbi. The myth could be even more significant for teachers who need to develop independence among students since the human meaning which is suggested by myths is closer to the students' world than it is to that of the system makers. A myth about the iron cage of bureaucracy where people are captured by their beliefs about what is required to be king/queen would seem more appropriate for administrators.

Students' involvement and development through traditional roles or through more modern forms of power-sharing are frequently mentioned in the literature written for administrators on how to relate with students (Rutter, 1983). However, these approaches to students are through extensions of the already existing professional structure. In the literature on administrative and organizational factors affecting students, more creative conceptions need to be added. Concerning small and large classes, what options are available to students in small classes that are different from their alternatives in large classes? Very small classes have been shown to benefit very young and disabled students rather than the older and healthy ones who might be expected to work in a more independent manner (*ibid.*). In large classes students may successfully avoid being smothered by teachers as they try to exercise their initiative, but they may not have received the grounding that they still need. Teachers have been shown more interested in personalizing classes by relating to students than they are in individualizing instruction and curricula for them (Tyler, 1988, p. 114). Do teachers use small classes to relate more to students and diagnose their weaknesses? Or, do they teach in the same mechanical way as they have previously done in large classes?

We need to reconceptualize available findings on bureaucracy and community size. In both these areas curvilinear findings have been reported concerning organizational size and community numbers (Tyler, 1988, pp. 48–52). We know that greater freedom is experienced under some structure governed by rules than under the arbitrary discretion of administrators (Moeller and Charters, 1966). We know that highly bureaucratic schools limit the likelihood of schools developing innovations (Anderson, 1968). We also know that student examination results in schools in communities of less than a million are higher than those in schools in either small towns or large cities (Tyler, 1988). We do not know why this is so. Students may have both the order and freedom they need in structured schools in middle-sized communities.

The interesting findings concerning peer group balance might, perhaps, have the closest relevance to the creation myth. The findings show that the presence of large numbers of able students in a school raises the performance of individual students more than many things a school does directly (Rutter, 1983). Neither higher occupational background of students' families nor the students' racial origin is nearly as powerful as the context of intellectual ability in its effect on the work of individual students. Furthermore, the comparative ability context is unrelated to either school or teacher approaches, though more effective schools show that the peer effect is greater than with lower-rated ones (Rutter, Maughan, Mortimore, Ouston and Smith, 1979). Since intelligence scores are generally known by students and incorporated into their own thinking, it is reasonable that the peer effect is part of the invidious comparisons that students themselves make (Werthman, 1963). While a positive peer context for students in one school can mean that they avoid being alienated from one another and thus perform, students in schools with negative peer context could be in comparative disadvantage.

Student Tutoring and the Innovation Process

Perhaps the best way of using the creation myth to understand comparative peer effects in school findings is demonstrated by studies that reverse the usual social hierarchy among students. When retarded students are trained to tutor regular students, both student groups benefit in their learning of skills (Top and Osguthorpe, 1987). Similarly, when white children are taught Indian language, the self-respect and cultural integrity of Indian children benefit enormously as does the white children's understanding of their Indian peers (Mitchell, 1989). In both of these reversals, the position of the subordinated group is expanded. Thus, exceptional programs promoting role reversals may provide children an opportunity to transcend self-fulfilling prophecies with new and higher expectations.

Unfortunately, there is very little evidence that peer tutoring or similar school innovations have expanded the horizons of most students. Peer tutoring is often practised by distinguishing between tutors and tutees. Single skills are taught, first, to one group, and then, to another. The teaching of the tutors follows the language of sports and is called a *huddle* (Heward, Heron and Cooke, 1982). A particularly explicit report on this return to a form of the monitorial system states: '... every child in a class can receive 10 minutes of direct practice time on key instructional skill, whether it is math, spelling, vocabulary, oral reading or comprehension' (Delquadri, Greenwood, Whorton, Carta and Hall, 1986, p. 536).

Peer tutoring is easily compatible with teachers being the primary definers of learning. Administrators can accept peer tutoring because it is both cheap and easily fitted into most traditional schools in the system (Jenkins and Jenkins, 1987). Outside of formal peer tutoring systems, students sometimes compare learning strategies and develop open discussions (Chen, 1985, p. 54). However, for either formal peer tutoring or similar schemes, creative thinking by students is a result that can only happen in spite of the system. When administrators think of the contributions that students can make, they repeatedly have focused upon improving attendance, avoiding vandalism or making the physical facilities more attractive (Rutter, 1983; Lieberman and Miller, 1984; Cusick, 1973). Not too surprisingly, students who are enjoying their adolescent status and who are pursuing the dating and rating game are not too interested in responding positively (Cusick, 1973).

When not specifying caretaker roles for students, the planners of innovations have tended to ignore students entirely. In one classic study, experts, administrators, teachers and parents are shown to form a hierarchy for the innovation process; students are not even put on the pyramid diagram (Seeley, Sim and Loosley, 1956). An early influential definition of innovation provides no suggestion of discovering how students were using any innovation or what their thoughts about the innovation were. Any innovation is said to be:

> ... the (1) acceptance, (2) over time, (3) of some specific item — an idea or practice, (4) by individuals, groups or other adopting units linked to (5) specific channels of communication, (6) to a social structure, and (7) to a given system of values or culture. (Katz, Levin and Hamilton, 1963)

Later approaches, such as stage theories, have not significantly changed the emphasis on innovation as an in-house approach that is brought to students without the controllers reducing their powers (Fullan, 1982). More open views of innovation have largely remained managerial approaches (Baldridge and Deal, 1983). A leading Canadian researcher who has studied students' reactions to innovation can only see the students as subjects for change decisions made by others (Fullan, 1982).

The reason that students are ignored is that managers and planners of change are constantly trying to bring the system of education together through their reforms. To be sure, they do not want to threaten more dominant powers in society and bring about any revolutionary changes. Innovations that are technological, such as computers, can be more closely controlled by managers (Baldridge, 1975). Innovations that are transferable between classes and schools will go beyond the narrow visions of teachers and widen the influence of administrators. Innovations are generally not intended to present administrators with an articulate opposition from teachers (Wolcott, 1977). Except for lacking a polished technological facade, peer tutoring meets most of these expected conditions for expanding the influence of administrators in the school. Its lack of a technological component can be an advantage in securing teacher acceptance.

Status Barriers and Streaming

Attempts by any one of the key players in school to widen his or her influence are usually curbed by the status order in the school. The attempt to bring about most changes can increase status differences, particularly the subordinate's perception of the status barriers (Metz, 1978; Everhart, 1983). Students can become unconcerned about the system that neither supports nor nourishes them. Teachers can become resentful toward any innovation that the Americans have tried and found to fail (Mitchell, 1984). Subordinates can become more questioning of the motivation and commitment of their superiors, particularly when failure of, or political opposition to, innovation is encountered (Sproul, Weiner and Wolf, 1978).

At every level in the system, status limits the tendency of subordinates to act independently of superiors in spite of the occasional questioning of the latter's motivations. Teachers, for example, act like students in raising their hands to speak in faculty meetings, but they assert themselves by often expressing desires to keep administrators out of their classrooms (Sarason, 1982). Teachers, who have been constantly reported to do the overwhelming amount of talking, have been said to do so in an attempt to keep their teachers' agenda dominant and the students' world out of the classroom. The informal world of students becomes so separated from the formal structure of the school that students are observed never to mention teachers or school innovations in their casual talk (Cusick, 1973).

Even when determined attempts are made to encourage more student participation, few students actually become involved. In a typical class, less than a fifth of its members participate (Fullan, 1982). The normal pattern of student participation is strongly affected by the tendency of the elite group of students to show their superiority to subordinate students by talking more

(Cusick, 1973). If isolated students speak or attempt to participate in classes or extra-curricular activities, they are ignored, put down or humiliated. The division among student groups is part of a pattern in which they become separated from each other and, ultimately, from themselves. Students learn loneliness together while laughing at teachers and schools (Everhart, 1983).

Teachers are the only direct link to mobilize students for innovations. Students can support innovation movements when they identify with teachers (Whiteside, 1978). More typically, students distance themselves from innovations by desensitizing themselves to teachers. Among the typical junior high students, there is nothing worse than being a 'dog' in terms of looks and clothes. Students believe you can prove you are in the higher student group by putting someone else down. Furthermore, they try to be the reverse of what they think teachers want in well behaved students. Teachers are particularly rejected if their dress and mannerisms can be treated as a joke (Everhart, 1983, pp. 70–6). If you can go even further and trick the teacher into believing that you are the teacher's pet when you are actually making fun of him or her, you have achieved virtually the peak of student power.

There are, of course, significant exceptions to this characterization of students turning the system and themselves upside down. Students who are headed towards professional and managerial positions can see themselves as future experts. The future experts may find a program for the gifted, which allows them to develop a monopoly on specialized knowledge. Students who link with teachers pursuing their own careers can make very positive suggestions for improving education and innovations.

In contrast to students linked with teachers through reciprocal careers are students who reject the teachers and like 'skinheads'. Teachers can expect, at most, to achieve a truce with such openly defiant students (Tyler, 1988). Such contrary students will brag about how little writing they have done in school (Willis, 1978). The tough lads expect masculine and working-class jobs in the future, to which schooling will make no serious contribution. The students most alienated from schooling openly will demonstrate their opposition to schooling; they can be held down but seldom eliminated.

The differences between tough students and the cooperative ones are often structured by the streaming that is practised in schools. Pro-school students and anti-school ones are splintered and defined in opposite stereotypes. Subordinate, anti-school students see the academic ones as the 'country club' or 'preppies' while the academics see the anti-school cliques as the 'zoo' or 'dumbbells' (Rosenbaum, 1976). The students, even more than the phrases suggest, accept labels among themselves and devastate the opposite groups with the accepted stereotypes. Tracking makes things out of people (Lind, 1974). Unfortunately, removing tracking does not empower students. Rather, students are likely to take advantage of the missed classes by getting away with more misbehavior and lowered achievements when they see the bars are down (Tyler, 1988, p. 112). Mixed ability classes can lead to lower expectations by adolescents.

Tracking is associated with the larger bureaucratic forms of organization that have replaced more unique and particularistic structures. The Renaissance schools, such as the *lycee* in France or the boarding school in England, provide times for misbehavior and role reversals. Such schools provide not only specific areas for different kinds of behavior, but also a clear structure that one could reject (Tyler, 1988, p. 148). The more unique schools have processes similar to puberty rites in primitive society. They serve as processes by which independence could be secured and the stamp of society affixed at the same time (Ong, 1963). More uniform and bureaucratic schools count all violations of norms the same way, offer few opportunities for role reversals, and provide no possibility for rejecting the system. They are so tightly linked through careers to adult roles that separation must be more like a revolution.

The Principal and the Intercom

Principals have relied upon technical or structural solutions in trying to fix systems or programs. The principal is often directly responsible for establishing the tracking system or new super programs such as the international baccalaureate (Boocock, 1972). The principals are, nevertheless, limited by their procedures as much as, if not more than, anyone else. They often try to form their own union when they are caught between the teachers' union and the administration. Principals see their discretion being limited by the development of bureaucracy. Questions of professionalism and leadership seem to have a cutting edge for principals who, perhaps, are only too aware that they may be practicing neither professionalism nor leadership.

Principals are as limited by the division of status groups within schools as students are; unlike students, they have, however, matured. A typical principal, who does all the talking with teachers in a staff room, does very little talking when meeting with other principals and administrators. (Wolcott, 1973). The behavior of principals, similar to the participation of students in classes, is clearly related to the status that they have within their particular caste. Within industry those with higher status have been shown more likely to work without interruptions. Those with lower status can be interrupted very frequently (Brown, 1965). Principals seem to follow the same rule when they use the intercommunications systems to interrupt teachers with announcements. The intercom is part of a change whereby schools have become more impersonal; speaking to people has replaced talking with them. Communication through a shared ritual, such as opening day ceremonies, once characterized schools; speeches and use of the intercom have replaced these rituals (Waller, 1967).

Among existing schools, the links between principals, teachers and students are greater in relatively small elementary schools than in the larger, more bureaucratic high school. Through the National Principals Study in the United States, it was possible to see the links among all the key players in the school drama at the elementary level (Gross and Herriott, 1965). The complexities of schools made it impossible to see such links at higher levels. At one level, there was still evidence of the ways in which the school system was open and unfinished. Measurement of the leadership of all administrators in the system found that one intermediate level in the hierarchy, between a dynamic superintendent and a challenging principal, was enough to eliminate any influence of the former upon the latter's leadership over teachers. It was also found that the principal's training in educational administration was unrelated to his leadership as rated by teachers and as measured by the number of courses taken; the number of educational administration courses was, however, negatively related to reported leadership. The more such courses were taken, the lower the leadership was rated by teachers. The quality of education as measured by the principal being an honors graduate was, however, positively related to leadership.

For the teachers in the same study, there were clear signs that connections with the school were far from complete. Teacher professional competence could *not* be explained by either the principal's leadership or the tendency of teachers to work together. Teacher professional competence may be ascribed to those who do more than the minimum role requirement in the school. For example, it is possible to argue that teachers who teach out of the textbook get 'it' across to students, but it is very difficult to reason that textbook teaching takes a great deal of skill. Teaching that goes beyond textbook teaching is something that teachers bring with them to schools and may be an indicator of professional competence. Professional teacher performance probably comes from quality education and enlightening experiences, but this one study does not show its correlators. Teacher professional performance may not derive from teacher morale either. However, the methodology of the study does not allow drawing such a conclusion decisively.

As the diagram of the best solution on Figure 2 shows, teacher behavior is a part of a system with principals and students. When the two aspects of teacher behavior, namely teacher morale and teacher performance, are taken into account, principals have no direct effect on pupil performance; the original correlation of .25 drops to a partial correlation with controls of .05. Principals, even if they think otherwise, do not directly influence pupil performances; rather they affect teacher morale and teacher performance, whereas teacher professional performance directly affects pupil performance. It may seem unfair to include two aspects of teacher behavior and only one set of factors for the principals, namely, the executive professional leadership. However, when the managerial behavior of principals was included, only extreme considerations, such as failing to order supplies, affected the system at all.

Most importantly, this study showed that all school effects could be unraveled only when an environmental measure, family income, was taken into account first. In the measurement of direct school effects on student learning, teacher morale with a partial correlation of .21, and teacher per-

Samuel Mitchell

Figure 2   The principal leadership in elementary schools

A   TERMS: Pupil Performance   percentage of students more than a grade behind in
                                                                   reading ability as well as general measures of
                                                                   interest in subject and performance to grade level.

                Executive Professional   shows interest in upgrading teacher performance
                Leadership   including making teaching meetings into an
                                                                    educational activity and providing materials and
                                                                    support to teachers in a professional manner.

                Teacher Morale   working together while accepting the judgment of
                                                                    administrators and the philosophy of the school.

                Teacher Professional   by a process of elimination, professional
                Performance   competence cannot occur when most teachers only
                                                                    do textbook teaching, teach all students the same
                                                                    or do not go beyond minimum demands upon
                                                                    students.

B   *BEST SOLUTION TO SEEING THE RELATIONSHIP*

Source: Gross and Herriott (1965).

formance with correlation of .39, are still less than the initial effects of family
income (r = .61). School effects are not swamped by family influences. Recent
research has shown that the more the measure is related to the work actually
done in schools, the higher the school effect is in comparison to environmental ones (Rutter, 1983).

Though showing school effects higher than the findings in a more publicized research work (Coleman, Campbell, Hobson, McPartland, Mood,
Weinfield and York, 1966), this social system study still reveals some substantial contradictions in the principal's role. Principals were far more encouraged
by higher administration to improve teaching methods than they were encouraged to experiment with educational ideas (79 per cent versus 44 per
cent) (Gross and Herriott, 1965, p. 118). As reported by teachers, neither
innovation was uniformly and consistently related to the leadership of the
principal. Later work has shown the principal as being caught in a dilemma
between controlling the school and exerting leadership (Wolcott, 1973; Sarason, 1982). Improving teaching methods involved fewer risks of losing control
of the school than did encouraging experimental ideas. Moderate risks with
innovation are more related to administrative promotion than are larger
efforts (Huberman and Miles, 1982). Principals are expected to work within
the larger system while they assert some efforts to improve their schools.

The principal's dilemma is conditioned by one's experiences with the
teacher role. As a former teacher, a principal would have dealt with the

dilemma of maintaining order and teaching within one's classroom; for the new position one must learn when to get on one's high horse and when to get off it. It was long ago observed that the new principals often treated teachers the same way they treated students (Waller, 1967). Furthermore, the principal knows that a teacher cherishes autonomy within the classroom. Now, as a principal, the former teacher hesitates to enter the classroom scene (Sarason, 1982). The principal is likely to deal with problems with either teachers or students in the privacy of his/her office rather than in the social scene of the classroom.

The larger system creates an emphasis on budget, physical facilities and planning, which can move the principal away from staff and even further away from students. The emphasis on the external trappings of one's office is a likely reason why teachers judge principals in terms of the resources delivered to the school from administration. The opening of the school is an important event for the new principal; on this occasion, all the school's physical facilities and resources are on display. The emphasis on student attendance and tidiness is also a likely result of concern with external appearances rather than with educational motivation (Sarason, 1982). These external considerations are apparent, particularly in high schools, where principals are competing with each other and where invidious comparisons between them are likely to be emphasized. The principal who wants to have a high profile may emphasize the holding power of the school or may stress academic excellence. The net effect may be to make the school quite competitive. Fortunately, there are principals who do not develop a body-count view of education and thus are likely to see through the system. Such principals are likely to be aware of the autonomy they have from central administration (Sarason, 1982). The principals who are more open may practise the very innovations that their counterparts caught in the system believe are illegal or impossible. The principals who gamble are likely to have allies; they are likely to have a greater sense of power within school.

The principal's success in implementing a more open leadership is dependent upon having followers who want to relate to the principal and who can do so. For many teachers the best administrator is one who does not create problems for them. For other teachers, a good administrator is one who backs them up before complaining parents or students. Few teachers are provided with direct incentives for joining with the principal unless they want support in obtaining administrative positions themselves (House, 1974). Once teachers have obtained tenure, principals can, at worst, transfer them to the school in local Siberia; principals have few rewards and only rare punishments to offer experienced teachers.

Principals can, however, influence teachers substantially if they understand the latter's ambiguities within teaching. They can praise teachers or suggest certain directions to follow when they are uncertain about the consequences of their work (Waller, 1967). Teachers and principals can develop a common language for viewing teaching and detailed records in discussing a variety of teaching occasions (McLaughlin and Pfeifer, 1986). They can also reverse roles so that teachers can evaluate a principal when teaching so that their focus is on the activity rather than on judging the person (Hart and Ripley, with Poulin and Maguire, 1989). Until shared problem solving emerges between teachers and principals, the evaluation conference can be expected to be little more than a limited ritual of subordination.

The principal playing a problem-solving role can benefit both teachers and students immeasurably. The case is nowhere clearer than at the junior high school level (Dreeben and Gross, 1965). At the elementary school, older teachers are the significant source of leadership. At the high school level, leadership must often emerge from specialized structures of departments or coordinating committees. But, at the junior high level, the difficulties result from the ambiguity in the demands made by the transitional school on teachers as the discussion of the creation myth would suggest. All participants at this level — whether teachers or students — need structure and opportunity to develop their own autonomy. Junior high teachers often speak of it being time to move to another school. Junior high students talk about there being more to school than academics (Everhart, 1983). Contradictions within this middle level of education seem more striking than anywhere else in the system. In this context, the principal's problem-solving role is vital.

The Feudal Structure of the Teachers' Kingdom

At every school level, teaching is filled with contradictions that are only partly resolved. Teachers want to be recognized as a profession yet stress their personalities and experiences rather than their knowledge (Tyler, 1988). They want a more autonomous professional role for themselves but do not allow autonomy for their students. In their preoccupation with the explainer role to get students excited about learning, they develop the monotone that neutralizes any possibility of excitement (Waller, 1967). Teachers' concern with explaining gives rise to use of classroom control which rules valuable resources from the students' social world out of the classroom (Cusick, 1973). Teachers exert efforts to lead students yet are limited by their increasingly frantic efforts to escape the net of an institutionalized role cast over themselves.

However, it is in their relationship to school administrators that teachers' anxieties are most often aroused. Elementary teachers are so subordinated and insecure that, as one survey report put it, a significant minority of them wanted the principal to check on them (Lortie, 1975). The studies of teachers' evaluation suggest that all teachers would rather be evaluated than ignored (McLaughlin and March, 1986). Teachers will actually worry when a principal refuses to check to see if they are supervising the playground, for example (McPherson, 1972). Clearly, administrators can develop the allegiances of their teachers by supporting them in their hour of need. Principals can also gain the teachers' support by granting them classroom autonomy and providing reinforcement in times of conflicts.

Though principals are expected to uphold the rights and dignity of teachers, it is largely teachers themselves who are expected to uphold the teachers' side even when there is very little overt cooperation among them. However, young teachers are more likely to see themselves as friends of students, not as defenders of their colleagues or of teacher norms (Waller, 1967; Hannam, Smyth and Stephenson, 1976). The probationers in teaching will have become teachers when they start to think and act like a teacher. When they no longer see themselves as outsiders and make the 's' sound to control students, the roles of the teacher have been assumed (McPherson, 1972). When they worry about being considered an easy mark in grading, associate primarily with teacher friends, and are first to sit down at a party, then, they have become established teachers (Waller, 1967). Also, they will have become defenders of their colleagues and teacher norms.

In siding with teachers, new teachers are little different from other professionals in experiencing alienation from their clients. In all professions, future members learn to be students first and members of the profession later (Becker, Greer, Hughes and Strauss, 1961; Bucher and Telling, 1977). Members of professions seem to experience a cultural shock as they enter the actual professions and discover the way things actually are in contrast with what they have been told the professions are supposed to be. This shock is exacerbated by the realization that the profession they have entered is distrusted by the public.

Indeed, the public disillusionment with educational achievements as well as public distrust of the educational establishment is disturbing for old and new teachers alike. It has undermined teacher autonomy following increased implementation of tests and evaluations (Shor, 1987). The excellence movement, which is responsible for the increased number of tests, evaluations and career stages, has placed non-teacher 'heroes' on commissions. Such commissions, rather than teachers in their classrooms, are seen as the answer to educational problems. Naturally, this is problematic. Teachers need public confidence if they are to be autonomous. Unfortunately, the reform movement, intending to transform all aspects of schooling into an educative experience, is both a result of decline in confidence and a factor in hastening the decline. Teachers' autonomy remains suspect.

Effective Schools: The False Dream

Some educators embrace the conservative trend in education as a solution even before knowing what the problem is. The supporters of effective schools believe that they have shown that schools do make a difference. They also believe that schools can make more of a difference if they develop a common culture with higher expectations and provide an ordered process of growth for children. Still, the excellence movement has been uncertain about whether or not it accepts the effective school idea (Tomlinson and Walberg, 1986). The effective school group has been quite certain that it supports the excellence movement (Sergiovanni, 1984). Yet, the excellence movement has demanded more attention to curriculum which the effective school advocates have largely omitted (Murphy, Hollinger and Mesa, 1985, p. 622).

Aside from its partial overlap with the excellence movement, the effective schools movement is representative of a long series of attempts to reform the schools through centralized planning. The efficiency movement tried to get more value in teacher ratios and distributions in the 1920s. In the 1960s and 1970s advocates of sensitivity training and organizational development tried to work with the whole school in developing people (Tyler, 1988, pp. 85–6). Now the idea of effective schools has returned as the central factor in developing plans for a common culture in the school. School improvement is seen to be the prime task for school administrators in the effective school idea.

The effective school approach involves whole school planning. However, there are many differences between groups of students and teachers that would require less than a whole school approach. Also the effective school movement actually shows no convincing evidence to support institutional acceptance of the effective school idea (Levine and Leibert, 1987). Inconsistent findings (involving the influence of informal, supportive principals) that might even challenge the entire school planning concept have never been followed up (Brookover and Lezotte, 1979).

Rather than examining their assumptions, supporters of effective schools have presented long and inconsistent lists of requirements. The major divisions in Figure 3 between productivity and satisfaction can be seen to represent traditional and progressive elements (Calgary Board of Education, 1982). It is seldom clear how a teacher can automatically achieve both the development of better skills among students and the students' realization of greater personal worth. In the list of individual components, it is not very clear how teachers are to use reward and praise with students when the latter are asked to participate as an active body in the operation of the classroom and school. Are students expected to be their own patrons? For teachers the items on the list also contain apparent contradictions: They are expected to be models of behavior by understanding students, but they are also expected to excel in preparing lessons and in punctuality. What if they can help students only by talking to them outside the school and thus start their classes late? Principals are similarly placed in a dilemma by the list. They are expected to provide support and display empathy yet they have to maintain school-wide standards to be applied impersonally.

The scope of the effective school idea is constantly widened and lists have become much longer (Rosenholtz, 1985; Purkey and Smith, 1985; Murphy, Weil, Hallinger and Mitman, 1985). However, it is often impossible to do more than circle the key words in a list which mixes traditional and progres-

Figure 3   Effective school program in Calgary: traditional and progressive elements

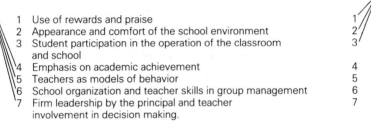

P R O D U C T I V I T Y

ACHIEVING BASIC SKILLS
DEVELOPING CONSTRUCTIVE ATTITUDES
DEVELOPING AND EXPANDING AN ADEQUATE KNOWLEDGE BASE
CLARIFYING VALUES AND PURPOSES
UTILIZING INQUIRY AND PROBLEM-SOLVING PROCESSES

S A T I S F A C T I O N

GAINING A SENSE OF PERSONAL WORTH
ENJOYING SCHOOL AS A PLEASANT PLACE TO LIVE AND WORK
GAINING REWARDS FROM PARTICIPATION IN WORTHWHILE ACTIVITIES

EFFECTIVE SCHOOLS

1	Use of rewards and praise	1
2	Appearance and comfort of the school environment	2
3	Student participation in the operation of the classroom and school	3
4	Emphasis on academic achievement	4
5	Teachers as models of behavior	5
6	School organization and teacher skills in group management	6
7	Firm leadership by the principal and teacher involvement in decision making.	7

sive concepts together. For the progressive view, the catch words are *demo-cratic decision making, parental involvement, sense of community* and *collaborative planning.* For the traditional view, the key words are *safe, orderly environment, clear academic mission, direct instruction* and *tightly coupled curriculum.*

The most significant work on effective schools has produced some recon-ciliation of the ideological contradictions in terms of external influences like social class and concentration of governmental programs (Hallinger and Mur-phy, 1986; Fuller and Izu, 1986). For example, lower social class schools are associated with tighter organizational control over the curriculum and a basic skills approach while higher class schools are associated with looser coupling of the school organization and a broader academic emphasis. Ironically, the control and structure of schools make best sense when social conditions are considered. However, since the original target of the effective school move-ment was the direct school situation that administrators could control, it is understandable that some theorists want to return to the basics. This allows a focus on a set of factors that can be controlled (Purkey and Smith, 1985).

The Loosely Linked System: A Contrast to our Conclusions

The liberal interpreters of the effective schools, who have shown the links between such schools and the environment, have also introduced modifica-tions on the idea that school and classroom teaching are linked (Hallinger and

Murphy, 1986). Particularly with respect to the curriculum, they have explored how classroom teaching could be linked to schools for different social classes. In middle-class schools, testing and teaching are more tightly linked whereas, in working-class schools, some of the negative findings of tests are ignored so that teachers can concentrate on teaching a few crucial skills. In fact, instead of considering social class, the original paper on loosely linked schools showed that task and authority in an organization could be separated as could action and motivation (Weick, 1978). The interpretation of loosely linked behavior was related to professional groups acting independently of administrators in schools; this approach has probably been followed more than any other in the literature. However, the idea of the loosely linked system uses other approaches. One approach, for example, links structural changes with integrated codes of knowledge and suggests subtle forms of controls to direct tight discipline (Tyler, 1988).

With different approaches and focus, it appears that the loosely linked system is like division by zero; the concept means both everything and nothing. In the original study, fifteen different meanings of the loosely linked system were given, The only curricular view in that study pertained to courses having prerequisites (Weick, 1978). Clearly, consideration of course prerequisites is a long way from issues related to teaching strategies to be used with working-class students, to changes in the hidden knowledge codes, and to seeing government proclamations of educational policy as a consensus ceremony in symbolic politics — issues now addressed by loosely linked system theorists.

It is certainly understandable that the loosely linked systems concept could emerge as a rationalization for educators who do not want tight controls placed upon them by legislators. However, the idea is, at best, a reaction against an emphasis on formal and rational organizations. As is true of other similar approaches, there are key problems in the loosely linked system.

First, the lines between school groups can be so sharply drawn that possibility of meaningful relationship between them is eliminated. Thus, such demarcation can be drawn between student groups in schools. The process of innovation, gradual or dramatic, can sharpen divisions between these and other groups (Cusick, 1973). The focus of the system theorists on administrative and professional relationships has blinded them to the possible emergence of status and caste divisions.

Second, the system's theory ignores the competition within the hierarchy that characterizes the segmented divisions in education. Administrators, teachers and students forming the hierarchy are not only in conflict; also they are all further divided into competing groups that battle for their relative positions. High school principals and central office staff develop frustrations that their positions within the formal organization do not begin to suggest. Regular and special education teachers are stereotyped just like racial groups. Other divisions between teachers, as well as related professionals, have been found to be substantial. However, it is among student groups that conflict is most acute. They become alienated not only from the school and teachers, but also from one another.

The creation myth has attempted to suggest how students can develop so that they have both social ties and independence. They need social support and links that would tie them closer to schools while developing their autonomy. In this way, they could avoid the twin dangers of being overcontrolled and undercontrolled. Similar development for administrators is needed. The administrative segment of schools is, perhaps, too controlled. Compared with administrators and students, however, teachers and similar professionals constitute a more complicated case. They have some degree of autonomy from the administration, but they do not want to be ignored by their superiors. They lack power to deal with administrators, parents and students; they have also tied themselves down in a feudal pattern of subordination. Teachers are often impervious to major social changes. They need the vision of a social movement that can provide them with allies and empower them as professionals. Moreover, they need, as student advocates, ideas on how to enable students to learn the exercise of rightfully earned freedom or autonomy. But, most significantly, they have to earn their own autonomy. Despite what has been said about loosely linked systems, for teachers to be loosely linked can mean that they are more than free of experts who would reconstruct their music. Teachers could come to play their own music from their own internal sources.

Bibliography

ANDERSON, J. (1968) *Bureaucracy in Education*, Baltimore: John Hopkins University Press.

BALDRIDGE, J.V. and DEAL, T.E. (Eds) (1983) *The Dynamics of Organizational Change in Education*, Berkeley: McCutchan.

BALDRIDGE, J.V. (1975) 'Organizational innovation: Individual, structural and environmental impacts', in BALDRIDGE, J.V., and DEAL, T.E. (Eds) *Managing Change in Educational Organizations*, Berkeley: McCutchan.

BECKER, H.S., GREER, B., HUGHES, E.C. and STRAUSS, A.L. (1961) *Boys in White*, Chicago: The University of Chicago Press.

BOOCOCK, S. (1972) *An Introduction to the Sociology of Learning*, Boston: Houghton, Miflin.

BROOKOVER, W.B. and LEZOTTE, L.W. (1979) *Changes in School Characteristics Coincident with Changes in Student Achievement (Executive summary)*, East Lansing, Michigan: The Institute for Research on Teaching, Michigan State University.

BROWN, W. (1965) *Exploration in Management*, Harmondsworth, Middlesex: Penguin.

BUCHER, R. and STRAUSS, A. (1961) 'Professions in process', *American Journal of Sociology, 66*, pp. 325–34.

CHEN, M. (1985) 'A macro-focus on microcomputers: Eight utilization and effect issues', in CHEN, M. and PAISLEY, W. (Eds) *Children and Microcomputers*, Beverly Hills: Sage.

CICOUREL, A. and KITSUSE, J. (1963) *The Educational Decision Makers*, New York: Bobbs Merrill.

CLARK, B. (1960) *The Open Door College*, New York: McGraw-Hill.

COHEN, L. and MANION, L. (1981) *Perspectives on Classrooms and Schools*, London: Holt, Rinehart and Winston.

COLEMAN, J., CAMPBELL, E., HOBSON, C., McPARTLAND, J., MOOD A., WEINFIELD, E. and YORK, R. (1966) *Equality of Educational Opportunity*, Washington: US Office of Education.

CROZIER, M. (1964) *The Bureaucratic Phenomenon*, Chicago: the University of Chicago Press.

CUSICK, P.A. (1973) *Inside High School*, New York: Holt, Rinehart and Winston.

CUSICK, P. (1983) *The Equalitarian Ideal and the American High School*, New York: Longman.

DAFT, R. and BECKER, S. (1978) *The Innovative Organization*, New York: Elsevier.

DAVIS, J.A. (1961) *Great Books and Small Groups*, Glencoe Illinois: The Free Press.

DELQUADRI, J., GREENWOOD, C.R., WHORTON, D., CARTA, J. and HALL, R.V. (1986) 'Classroom peer tutoring', *Exceptional Children*, 52, pp. 535–42.

DREEBEN, R. and GROSS, N. (1965) The role behavior of school principals. Unpublished manuscript. Graduate School of Education, Harvard University.

DWORKIN, M. (1959) *Dewey on Education*, New York: Teachers College, Columbia University.

FRIEDENBERG, E.Z. (1965) *Coming of Age in America*, New York: Random House.

FULLAN, M. (1982) *The Meaning of Educational Change*, Toronto: Ontario Institute of Studies in Education.

FULLER, B. and IZU, J. (1986) 'Explaining social cohesion: What sharpens the organizational beliefs of teachers?' *American Journal of Education*, 94, pp. 501–35.

GORDON, C. (1957) *The Social System of the High School*, Glencoe: The Free Press.

GRACEY, A. (1972) *Curriculum or Craftmanship*, Chicago: The University of Chicago.

GRANT, C. and STEETER, C. (1986) *After the School Bell Rings*, London: The Falmer Press.

GRANT, G. (1988) *The World We Created at Hamilton High*, Cambridge: Harvard University Press.

GROSS, N. and HERRIOTT, R.E. (1965) *Staff Leadership in Public Schools*, New York: John Wiley.

HALLINGER, P. and MURPHY, J.F. (1986) 'The social context of effective schools', *American Journal of Education*, 94, pp. 328–55.

HANNAM, C., SMYTH, P. and STEPHENSON, N. (1976) *The First Year of Teaching*, Harmondsworth: Penguin.

HART, C., RIPLEY, D. with POULIN, L. and MAGUIRE, N. (1989) 'Improving teachers in their evaluation', *The ATA Magazine*, 69, pp. 4–7.

HARVEY RESEARCH LTD. (1986) *Evaluation of Community Schools*, Edmonton: Alberta Education.

HEWARD, W.L., HERON, T.E. and COOKE, N.L. (1982) 'Tutor huddle: Key element in a classwide peer tutoring system', *Elementary School Journal*, 83, pp. 115–23.

HEWTON, E. (1982) *Rethinking Educational Change*, Guildford, Sussex: Society for Research into Higher Education.

HOUSE, E. (1974) *The Politics of Educational Innovation*, Berkeley: McCutchan.

HUBERMAN, A.M. and MILES, M.B. (1982) *Innovation Up Close*, Andover, Mass: The Network.

JENKINS, J.R. and JENKINS, L.M. (1987) 'Making peer tutoring work', *Educational Leadership*, 44, pp. 64–8.

JOFFRE, C.E. (1977) *Friendly Intruders*, Berkeley: University of California Press.

KANTER, R. (1977) *Men and Women of the Corporation*, New York: Basic Books.

KATZ, E., LEVIN, M.L. and HAMILTON, H. (1963) 'Traditions of research on the diffusion of innovations', *American Sociological Review*, 28, pp. 237–52.

KING, A.R. (1967) *The School at Mopass*, New York: Holt, Rinehart and Winston.

KING, R. (1978) *All Things Bright and Beautiful?* Chichester: Wiley.

LANIER, J. (1983) 'Tensions in teaching teachers the skills of pedagogy', In GRIFFITH, G. (Ed.) *Staff Development*, Chicago: The University of Chicago.

LEVINE, D.U. and LEIBERT, R.E. (1987) 'Improving school improvement plans', *Elementary School Journal*, 87, pp. 397–412.

LIEBERMAN, A. and MILLER, L. (1984). *Teachers, Their World, Their Work*, Alexandria, VA: Association for Supervision and Curriculum Development.

LIND, L.J. (1974) *The Learning Machine*, Toronto: Anansi Press.

LORTIE, D. (1975) *School Teacher*, Chicago: the University of Chicago Press.

McGIVNEY, J.H. and HAUGHT, J.M. (1972) 'The politics of education: A view from the perspective of the central office staff', *Educational Administration Quarterly*, 8, pp. 18–38.

McLAUGHLIN, M.W. and PFEIFER, R.S. (1986) *Teacher Evaluation: Learning for Improvement and Accountability — Case Studies*, Stanford: School of Education, Stanford University.

McPHERSON, G. (1972) *Small Town Teacher*, Cambridge: Harvard University Press.

MEIGHEN, R. (1981) *A Sociology of Education*, London: Holt, Rinehart and Winston.

MERTON, R. (1957) *Social Theory and Social Structure*, Glencoe, Illinois: The Free Press.

METZ, M.H. (1978) *Classrooms and Corridors*, Berkeley: University of California Press.

MEYER, J. and ROWAN, B. (1978) 'Institutionalized Organizations: Formal structure as myth and ceremony', in MARSHALL, W. (Ed.) *Environments and Organizations*, San Francisco: Jossey Boss.

MITCHELL, S. (1984) 'The Canadian imperial view of educational change: An essay on a problem in the sociology of knowledge posed in "The Meaning of Educational Change"' *Canadian and International Education*, 13, pp. 73–87.

MITCHELL, S. (1989) Innovation and reform: Conflicts within educational change. Unpublished manuscript, The University of Calgary, Alberta.

MOELLER, G. and CHARTERS, W. (1966) 'Relations of bureaucratization to sense of power', *Administrative Science Quarterly*, 10, pp. 444–55.

MURPHY, J., WEIL, M., HALLINGER, P. and MITMAN, A. (1985) 'School effectiveness: A conceptual framework', *The Educational Forum*, 49, pp. 361–74.

MURPHY, J., HALLINGER, P. and MESA, R.P. (1985) 'School effectiveness: Checking progress and assumptions and developing a role for state and federal government', *Teachers College Record*, 86, pp. 615–42.

ONG, W. (1963) 'Latin language study as a Renaissance puberty rite', in SPINDLER, G. (Ed.) *Education and Culture*, New York: Holt, Rinehart and Winston.

PURKEY, S. and SMITH, M. (1985) 'School Reform: The district policy implications of the effective school literature', *Elementary School Journal*, 85, pp. 353–89.

ROSENBAUM, J.E. (1976) *Making Inequality*, New York: John Wiley.

ROSENHOLTZ, L.J. (1985) 'Effective schools: Interpreting the evidence', *American Journal of Education*, 93, pp. 352–88.

RUTTER, M., MAUGHAN B., MORTIMORE, P., OUSTON, J. with SMITH, A. (1979) *Fifteen Thousand Hours: Secondary Schools and their Effects on Children*, Cambridge: Harvard University Press.

RUTTER, M. (1983) 'School effects on pupil progress', *Child Development*, 54, pp. 1–29.

SARASON, S. (1982) *The Culture of the School and the Problem of Change* (2nd Edn), New York: Allyn and Bacon.

SEELEY, J.R., SIM, R.A. and LOOSLEY, E.W. (1956) *Crestwood Heights*, Toronto: University of Toronto Press.

SERGIOVANNI, T. (1984) 'Leadership and excellence in schooling', *Educational Leadership, 41*, pp. 5–13.

SHOR, I. (1987) *Culture Wars*, London: Routledge and Kegan Paul.

SIMON, R. (1982) 'Mysticism, management and Marx', in GRAY, H. (Ed.) *The Management of Educational Institutions*, London: The Falmer Press.

SPROULL, L., WEINER, S. and WOLF, D. (1978) *Organizing an Anarchy*, Chicago: The University of Chicago Press.

TOMLINSON T. and WALBERG, H. (1986) *Academic Work and Educational Excellence*, Berkeley: McCutchan.

TOP, B. and OSGUTHORPE, R. (1987) 'Reverse-role tutoring: The effects of handicapped students tutoring regular class students', *Elementary School Journal, 87*, pp. 413–27.

TYACK, D. (1974) *The One Best System*, Cambridge: Harvard University Press.

TYLER, W. (1988) *School Organization*, London: Croom Helm.

WALLER, W. (1967) *The Sociology of Teaching*, New York: John Wiley.

WERTHMAN, C. (1963) 'Delinquents in school: A test for the legitimacy of authority', *Berkeley Journal of Sociology, 8*, pp. 39–60.

WHITESIDE, T. (1978) *The Sociology of Educational Innovation*, London: Methuen.

WIECK, K. (1978) 'Educational organizations as loosely coupled systems', *Administrative Science Quarterly, 23*, pp. 541–52.

WILLIS, P. (1978) *Learning to Labour*, Westmead, England: Saxon House.

WOLCOTT, H. (1973) *The Man in the Principal's Office*, New York:

WOLCOTT, H. (1977) *Teachers vs. Technocrats*, Eugene: University of Oregon Center for Educational Policy and Management.

VII
Teachers and the Teaching Profession

INTRODUCTION

The persistent and defiant questioning of authority, which marked the 1960s, has continued unabated and has changed people's attitudes toward leaders and experts in society. The traditional deference to political and governmental figures and to experts in different professions has given way to detectable skepticism and, sometimes, even contempt. The area of education has not escaped the impact of this development. Increasingly, policies and administrative decisions on school curricula, structures, closures, and the like are being challenged not only through political action but also through litigation.

Teachers, who occupy the educational frontlines, are naturally more subject to challenge than others within school systems. Pressures come partly from parents who have justified or unjustified criticisms of the processes and content in schooling such as teachers' giving homework to their pupils and the inclusion of sex education in the curriculum. More frequently, the challenge to authority comes from pupils who, for one reason or another, resist compliance with teachers' demands and requirements.

Rod Clifton and Lance Roberts explore, using the sociological perspective, why teachers' exercise of authority is problematic and how the legitimate exercise of such authority may be facilitated. Their sociological analysis reveals that teacher authority over pupils is, on one hand, more restricted and differentiated than parental authority and more difficult to exercise, on the other hand, than the authority wielded by their professional counterparts in other public institutions. Schooling, as we know it, exhibits certain distinctive characteristics which frustrate the unhampered exercise of teacher authority. Other means of securing compliance, such are coercion or persuasion, are objectionable and unprofessional. How, then, can the use of authority be an effective tool for teachers in educating the young?

Clifton and Roberts' analysis suggests that student compliance may be fostered through the judicious use of institutional legal-rational authority together with the teachers' expertise and emphatic conduct in treating students. To restore teacher authority, there is no substitute for teachers' scholarship, competence in different aspects of the teaching-learning process, knowledge of the social organization of classrooms and schools, and empathy toward students.

However, securing student compliance is one thing; determining the boundaries of the teacher authority to require compliance is another matter. In recent decades, concern about extensive teacher discretion in the treatment of their students has arisen. And for that matter, concern about administrative discretion in dealing with teachers has surfaced. These concerns have been discussed — and adjudicated — as rights issues in education.

In his article, Douglas Ray seeks awareness of teachers' rights and obligations in our increasingly litigious society. He defines *rights* as claims, whether to certain benefits or to certain freedoms, which are enforceable through the law. Noting that rights draw from several sources, and distinguishing between individual and group rights, he surveys the entitlements of several disadvantaged groups in society. However, he focuses mainly on teachers — their rights vis-à-vis their administrators and the community, and their obligations corresponding to the rights of their students. Though documents, such as federal and provincial legislation and the Charter of Rights and Freedoms, provide the bases for ensuring the rights of students and teachers, hesitation in implementing such documents in education is evident. Ingrained ways may account for part of this. In any case, Ray believes that their implementation will bring definite gains to the educational process.

19 The Authority of Teachers: A Sociological Perspective

Rodney A. Clifton and Lance W. Roberts

Introduction

Recent evidence suggests that schools are in trouble. Specifically, a growing body of research illustrates that in Canada, the United States and many Western European countries the curriculum content is deteriorating, students are increasingly disengaged from the learning process, the quality of learning is low, and student violence is increasing (see Adelson, 1983; Adler, 1982; Goodlad, 1984; Hurn, 1978 and 1985; Husen, 1979, pp. 9–19; McNeil, 1986; Sedlak, Wheeler, Pullin and Cusick, 1986, pp. 1–10). Both Hurn (1978, pp. 1–16) and Husen (1979, pp. 9–19) identify these as symptoms of an educational crisis particularly in relation to the authority of teachers. In this regard, Adelson (1983, p. 46) notes: 'Anyone who spends any time at all in the schools soon realizes that a great many of those persons nominally in authority have a sense of having lost it'.

Like many other issues in education, the difficulty teachers experience in maintaining authority in classrooms has typically been studied from a psychological perspective (see Geer, 1968; Hurn, 1985; Johnson, 1978; Spady, 1977). Yet, research and social policy derived from a psychological perspective is often limited because it fails to consider the social dynamics of classrooms and schools (Boocock, 1978; Tyler, 1985). In an attempt to overcome this limitation, this chapter analyzes teachers' authority from a sociological perspective by focusing upon both institutional and individual characteristics of authority.

For the purpose of this chapter, the terms *classrooms*, *students* and *teachers* will be used without distinguishing between elementary, junior high and senior high school grades, and without distinguishing between students and teachers in parochial, private and public schools. We realize that the

We thank Sharon Bailin, Gunther Baureiss, Edward D. Boldt, Michael J.B. Jackson, and Jonathan Young for their comments and suggestions on previous drafts.

authority of teachers is, to some degree, dependent upon these institutional characteristics, but to develop a general conception of the authority of teachers, these distinctions need not be taken into account. Nevertheless, it is not our intention to neglect all differences in school organization or teachers' attributes. Throughout the chapter we stress that, in schools, teaching is a social process which takes place between persons occupying the statuses of student and teacher. The teaching role is circumscribed by rights and responsibilities derived, in large measure, from both the institutional characteristics of classrooms and schools and the individual characteristics of teachers. Our central point is that teachers need authority derived from both the institution and their own competencies in order to provide high quality instruction and to ensure that students engage in productive work (LeCompte, 1978).

Moreover, we need to state explicitly that our objective is to analyze the existing school system and propose some policies which may help improve this system. We agree with many critics who argue that the present educational system has serious flaws, and like many of these critics, we have considered and (in other articles) proposed radically different, and more humanistic, ways of educating students. Nevertheless, we also recognize that the existing educational system has inertia and, in the short term, radical changes are unlikely. For these reasons we have confined our analyses and our suggestions to ways of improving the existing system. In our view, the proposals we advance seem feasible within the present cultural and social context.

The following section examines the authority of teachers by comparing the institutional characteristics of schools, which delimit the authority of teachers, with the institutional characteristics of families and workplaces, which, respectively, delimit the authority of parents and employers. It is argued that teachers have fewer resources for obtaining and maintaining the compliance of students than parents and employers have for obtaining and maintaining the compliance of children and employees. Following this, we focus upon the legitimate means teachers have for obtaining and maintaining the compliance of students. Specifically, we argue that the acquiescence of students is dependent upon teachers using institutional resources, such as the tradition of the school and the legal rights which have been granted to them by school administrators, and individual attributes, such as their expertise and empathy. The chapter concludes with some policy recommendations which are derived from this analysis.

The Institutional Characteristics of Schools

Several sociologists have characterized schools as the critical link between the family and childhood responsibilities on the one hand, and the world of work and adult responsibilities on the other. In this respect, schools are mediating institutions between the 'private world' of the home and the 'public world' of the workplace. Early in the twentieth century, Emile Durkheim (1922) pointed out the importance of the school in initiating the child into the moral life of the society. Durkheim noted that schools reflect the normative priorities of the society, and, therefore, they are institutions through which established members of a society recreate values in their new recruits. This theme is reiterated in the cultural literacy movement which emphasizes the importance of the public education system in transmitting a common medium of discourse to all students (Hirsch, 1988).

As mediating institutions, schools are expected to advance the socialization process which begins in families (see Lubeck, 1984). This is a difficult task. In Western societies, families are generally characterized by primary group relationships and are small units held together by strong emotional bonds, frequent and close personal attachment, dependency and expectations of mutual support in diffuse situations (Dreeben, 1971, p. 110; Peters, 1973, p. 36). In families of this type, children develop a heightened sense of personal dignity, importance and respect for freedom. Moreover, since these types of families are structured for the enhancement of identity and meaning, children experience authority as diffuse and personal (Berger, 1977). This initial experience sets the stage for potential problems relating to the exercise of authority in schools. In the family, parental authority is experienced by children as an undifferentiated mixture of personal power, specific competencies, persuasion based upon affection, and dependency, which are all exercised over a broad range of situations (Bredemeier, 1978, pp. 441–2; Dreeben, 1971, p. 113). That is, parents commonly use a mixture of rational and emotional strategies in obtaining and maintaining compliance from their children.[1]

Schools also have close linkages with the adult world. The adult public world is generally characterized by secondary group relationships and does not generally operate on the bases of undifferentiated mixtures of personal power, persuasion based upon affection, and dependency exercised over a broad range of situations. As Max Weber (1923) pointed out, bureaucratic organizations are the typical means for organizing the adult world in modern industrialized societies. According to Weber, a bureaucracy is an organization with an administrative hierarchy designed to reduce emotional interaction between people and to facilitate impersonal interaction in order to increase the efficiency of achieving well-established objectives. In bureaucracies, the authority ascribed to statuses is allocated to those who are experts, qualifications for these positions are specified, and codified rules define the authority of the personnel who occupy the various statuses. In this respect, statuses and the rewards of these positions, such as promotion and remuneration, are obtained on the basis of merit rather than on the basis of criteria such as emotional relationships, wealth or other extraneous factors.

In part, the bureaucratic nature of the adult world is first exemplified to children when they begin school and find that all children are students, virtually all adults are teachers, and teachers, who are usually strangers, demand their compliance. Upon entering school, children soon learn that relationships between students and teachers are specific and impersonal, rather than diffuse and personal, as they are in families. As such, in elementary school the emotional content of the relationship between students and teachers is considerably less than in families, and in secondary school the emotional content of the relationship between students and teachers is practically nonexistent (Bidwell, 1973, p. 414). In other words, schools are more like other bureaucracies than they are like families (Etzioni, 1975, pp. xii–xiii). The bureaucratic nature of schools increases with grade levels so that secondary schools are more bureaucratic than elementary schools, and post-secondary schools are even more bureaucratic than secondary schools.

Schools have four distinguishing characteristics which are typical of many other bureaucratic organizations (Hurn, 1978, pp. 218–20; Scott, 1981, pp. 286–9; Tyler, 1985, pp. 53–6). First, schools are like other bureaucracies in that they are directed toward achieving, in an efficient manner, formally established objectives (Parsons, 1960, p. 17). In schools, these objectives are usually identified by teachers, principals, departments of education, school boards and parents.[2]

Second, schools are composed of a number of integrated statuses with regulated patterns of authority and communication. According to Weber (1923), the primary feature of all bureaucratic organizations is the presence of a hierarchy of authority. In the typical case, official positions are arranged in a pyramid of ascending authority, each lower position being under the supervision of a higher one. A delimited amount of authority is distributed and institutionalized in the various positions. This means that a person occupying an official position takes on the authority vested in that office. The interaction patterns that develop, through the various lines of authority, help to create and maintain role behavior and the achievement of the objectives of the organization.

Third, the activities of the various personnel are coordinated to be both effective and efficient in achieving the objectives within the constraints imposed by the available resources. Part of this coordination involves an administrative hierarchy with duties specified through formal rules and procedures, as well as rationally distributed responsibilities and resources.

Finally, because the bureaucracy is organized to achieve the objectives of the organization and not the particular interests of the personnel, there is a need to motivate members to work within the formal structure and to comply with the demands of those who are in superior positions. That is, bureaucracies are characterized by a need to channel the conduct of personnel so that the objectives of the organization are met.

Even though schools share these four characteristics with other bureaucracies, this does not imply that schools are typical bureaucratic organizations. In comparison with other organizations of this type, schools seem to have seven distinctive characteristics. A first distinctive characteristic of schools is that the objectives are either controversial or uncertain, and, consequently, it is difficult to determine when, and if, they have been achieved.[3] Parents, politicians, school board members, students and teachers have a variety of agendas which ensure that schools operate with objectives which are complex, shifting and frequently disputed both from within their own membership and by outside interest groups (Bredemeier and Bredemeier, 1978, p. 325; Cusick, 1983; Denscombe, 1985, p. 58; Lortie, 1975, pp. 135–6).

A second distinctive characteristic of schools, in comparison with other bureaucracies, is that the coordination of personnel is more difficult. Schools have been described as 'loosely coupled institutions' characterized by little definitive demarcation of the legitimate rights and responsibilities of the personnel occupying various statuses (Tyler, 1985, pp. 58–62). Teachers find it especially difficult to coordinate the activities of students to meet organizational objectives since, for the most part, students have not participated in establishing the objectives, have little commitment to their identity as students, and have had little experience working in other bureaucratic organizations. It is typically assumed that students are inadequately socialized for full participation in both the school and society, and, as a result, they are not qualified to participate in establishing the objectives of either system (Bredemeier and Bredemeier, 1978, p. 103). It follows that students are not as likely to commit themselves to the objectives of either the school or the society as are teachers, administrators, school board members and parents.

A third distinctive characteristic of schools is the age homogeneity of the twenty-five to thirty-five students in the typical class. This characteristic makes schools quite different from other bureaucracies where statuses are not generally distinguished by age homogeneity. As Dreeben (1968) notes, age homogeneity is functional in that it provides the teachers with a reference standard for evaluating performances, and it helps unify students by organizing them on the basis of at least one common characteristic.[4] The consequences of this arrangement, however, are not all functional. For reasons outlined earlier, there is likely to be considerable misalignment between the objectives of the school and the interests of at least some of the students. To the extent that this misalignment results in the disaffection of students, the solidarity encouraged by age homogeneity may be dysfunctional. In reacting to organizational constraints, students can more easily obtain the support of other students because they are similar in age, and, as a consequence, they can often generate more effective resistance. In short, age homogeneous classes creates problems for the teacher in obtaining and maintaining the cooperation of students. As noted previously, such problems are not usually found in other bureaucracies where statuses are not usually distinguished by age homogeneity.

A fourth distinctive characteristic of schools is the interaction between students and teachers. Specifically, the twenty-five to thirty-five students in a typical classroom have a right to demand the teacher's attention and energy at virtually any time (Bredemeier and Bredemeier, 1978, p. 104; Dreeben, 1970, pp. 52–3). Specifically, the teacher must be attentive to the demands of inquiring students, while keeping track of the activities of all the other students in the class, some of whom may be attempting to avoid surveillance. As Jackson (1968, p. 149) notes, it is extremely difficult to manage the activities of a large group of students for four or five hours a day, 200 days a year. Jackson estimates that during every school day teachers engage in approximately 1500 interactions with students, involving decisions and activities which take place in rapid succession. Maintaining authority and working toward organizational objectives under these extraordinary circumstances is not typical of other bureaucratic organizations.

A fifth distinctive characteristic is that schools have difficulties motivating students.[5] On this account, there are three aspects of motivation that must be considered. First, there are differences between students and teachers in their volunteerism. Students are conscripted while teachers are hired (Bidwell, 1970, pp. 43–4; Bredemeier and Bredemeier, 1978, p. 102; Dreeben, 1973; Lortie, 1975, p. 137). Public schools must admit, attempt to retain and try to educate virtually all children. Thus, some students are not going to be interested in, or motivated toward, attaining the objectives which have been established for them (Sedlak *et al.*, 1986, p. 157; Wegmann, 1976, pp. 76–9). Second, there are differences between students and teachers in their degree of activism. The 'good student' role is synonymous with docility and patience rather than initiative and responsibility (Hurn, 1978, p. 227; McNeil, 1986, p. 67; Sedlak *et al.*, 1986, p. 183; Wegmann, 1976). As a result, students who want to be actively involved in their lives may not be motivated to be docile participants in school. Third, students and teachers differ in their reward structures (Dreeben, 1970, pp. 54–7; Hurn, 1978, p. 224). Teachers receive financial remuneration and have opportunities to advance up the bureaucratic hierarchy as compensation for competent performances.[6] From the students' perspective, especially that of older students, rewards for competent performances are not as immediate nor are they as valuable as pay cheques. Moreover, students can hardly ever move beyond their particular status irrespective of the quality of their role performance. In this respect, schools are more like mental hospitals, prisons and welfare agencies than they are like typical bureaucratic organizations in the adult world, which operate on the principle that people who are successful in performing their role in one status can move to higher statuses on the basis of their ability, interest and motivation. In essence, because students are involuntary participants and because schools rely upon rewards which are atypical of bureaucratic organizations, teachers have problems motivating students.

A sixth distinctive characteristic of schools is illustrated by recent research which suggests that the increasing heterogeneity of student competencies and performances is adding to the difficulties that teachers are experiencing in motivating students (McNeil, 1986, p. 179). The increased heterogeneity increases the chances that teachers will make mistakes, and when they do, their mistakes are witnessed by a large audience of students. Other professionals typically interact with clients sequentially rather than simultaneously and, therefore, their mistakes are usually not observed by an audience of clients (Dreeben, 1970, p. 77; Wilson, 1962, p. 28). As such, the demands and responsibilities of teachers are much greater than those of professionals in other bureaucratic organizations who maintain their authority in environments where they have much more control.

A final distinctive characteristic of schools is in the recent trend concerning the development of the identity of students. As a number of sociologists (see Berger, 1970 and 1973; Turner, 1976) have observed, the anchoring point young people are using for their identities has shifted from institutional to individual frames of reference. In other words, the perceptions of young people have shifted, to some degree, from identities derived from their social roles (e.g., friend, sister and student) toward identities expressing their individuality (e.g., authenticity, dignity, myself). Bredemeier and Bredemeier (1978, pp. 314–15) label this shift from institutional to individual definitions of identity as 'the cult of spontaneity', with its implication that one's primary orientation is to oneself.

This shift has important consequences for the achievement of the objectives of schools because it suggests that students are less engaged with, and committed to, their role as student. Partly to accommodate this shift in the commitments of students, schools have expanded their objectives from instrumental ones, such as instructing students in academic and practical subjects, to more expressive objectives, such as 'values clarification' (Hurn, 1978, pp. 7–11; Peters, 1973, pp. 81–107). Following such changes, the responsibilities of teachers have expanded to cover a diversity of issues and concerns intended to assist students in discovering their 'authentic selves'. In reporting on research which touches on this issue, Sedlak *et al.* (1986, p. 115) note that the 'unintended by-product of the life-adjustment movement — the devaluation of school and teacher knowledge — eroded the profession's status'. In other words, as the educational agenda became more diffuse, expanding from instrumental to more expressive objectives, the expertise of teachers eroded, with a subsequent loss in their legitimacy and status (Bredemeier, 1978, p. 431; Dreeben, 1970, p. 26).[7]

In summary, we have noted that schools are mediating institutions between the organizational spheres of the family and the workplace. The authority teachers have over students is characterized as being more restricted than the authority parents have over children, largely because parental authority is undifferentiated. In fact, the bureaucratic nature of schools ensures that the authority of teachers is more differentiated than the authority of parents and, in this way, it is similar to the authority of professionals working in other bureaucratic organizations. Nevertheless, the similarity between teachers and other professionals is far from identical. At least seven characteristics of schools complicate the ability of teachers to use their authority in obtaining compliance from students. These characteristics include the existence of ambiguous and controversial organizational objectives, the loose definition of rights and obligations governing role performances, the homogeneity of the ages of students in classrooms, the complexity and observability of the role performances of teachers, the difficulties of motivating students, the heterogeneity of student competences and performances, and the shift in the identities of students from institutional to individual frames of reference. These organizational characteristics ensure that the use of authority in schools is more complicated than it is in other public institutions. With this in mind, the next section examines classrooms in terms of teachers' authority.

The Construction of Classroom Order

Clearly, students and teachers are in very different positions within the classroom, and, even though they may share certain interests, the most distinctive feature of their interaction is that they often operate with opposing objectives. Students and teachers are often depicted as protagonists locked into an ongoing negotiation to impose their expectations upon each other. Waller (1932, p. 196) highlights this point in his classic portrayal of teaching:

> Teacher and pupil confront each other with attitudes from which the underlying hostility can never be altogether removed. Pupils are the material in which teachers are supposed to produce results. Pupils are human beings striving to realize themselves in their own spontaneous manner, striving to produce their own results in their own way. Each of these hostile parties stands in the way of the other; insofar as the aims of either are realized, it is the sacrifice of the aims of the other.

As Waller (1932) went on to point out, conflicting objectives of students and teachers need not result in persistent battles. Nevertheless, the order which persists in classrooms is often relatively unstable. Students are autonomous human beings with their own needs and desires to optimize their own objectives. Although teachers are representatives of the educational system, they do not have the institutional support found in other bureaucratic organizations. The relative autonomy that teachers have in their classrooms means that they are left to create a social order in which objectives are established through interaction and negotiation with students. Teachers do not work in an institutional structure that permits them to impose order on students; rather, they are left to negotiate orderly agreements with students. In situations where the objectives of students and teachers are similar, little negotiation is required, but in situations where the objectives are misaligned, considerable negotiation is necessary.

In short, given the institutional character of schools, the classroom setting is characterized by negotiation on the part of both students and teachers as they attempt to create a social organization where their own objectives are salient and as they adapt to the expectations of each other.[8] That is, in a loosely structured classroom environment, characterized by both teacher and

Figure 1   Types of classroom order

Source of Compliance	Coercion	Persuasion	Authority
Legitimacy of Teacher's Requests	Illegitimate	Negotiated Legitimacy	Accepted Legitimacy
Alignment of Student and Teacher Objectives	Conflict	Coordination	Identity

student autonomy, the authority of the teacher is precarious, and classroom order is at constant risk of degenerating into chaos. Consequently, the teachers' sense of accomplishment and satisfaction is dependent upon students' cooperation (Goodlad, 1984; Lortie, 1975; McNeil, 1986; Sedlak *et al.*, 1986). Teachers must take account of what students desire to know, their definition of knowledge, their role in the classroom and their interaction with other students and teachers. The underlying issue is the principle of legitimacy through which students are willing to acknowledge the rights of teachers to direct their conduct (Dreeben, 1971, p. 113).

We may have a better understanding of this point if we imagine a teacher asking a student to comply with a particular demand and the student responding with 'Why should I?' There are three responses that teachers can give to this hypothetical question. These responses are coercion, persuasion and authority, which vary with the degree of legitimacy attributed to the teachers' requests and with the extent of alignment between the objectives of the students and objectives of the teachers. Compliance is illegitimate when coercion is used, has negotiated legitimacy when persuasion is used, and has accepted legitimacy when authority is employed. Students identify with their teachers when authority is used, they have to coordinate their activities with their teachers' expectations when persuasion is used, and they are in conflict with their teachers' objectives when coercion is used. Most teachers, of course, use a mixture of coercion, persuasion and authority in obtaining the compliance of their students. But, an understanding of these ideal ways of obtaining compliance may help us appreciate the importance of authority in relation to coercion and persuasion. Figure 1 represents these three ways of obtaining compliance in terms of the legitimacy of the demands of teachers and the alignment between the objectives of students and teachers.

The first answer to the hypothetical question 'Why should I?' is embodied in the notion of coercion. According to Weber (1923, p. 152), coercion is 'The probability that one actor ... will be in a position to carry out his or her own will despite resistance'. Here, the teacher answers the hypothetical question by saying something like: 'If you do not comply with my request, I will force you to comply'. The assumption behind this approach is that

Rodney A. Clifton and Lance W. Roberts

teachers are capable of controlling critical resources in such a way that students cannot sustain their present state of affairs without enduring some intolerable losses. When coercion is used, compliance is achieved by threat or force. In this case, classroom order is based on power.

The use of threat or force is, in the words of Bredemeier (1978, p. 439), 'the rock-bottom way' of obtaining compliance. Coercion is an effective means for obtaining a certain amount of compliance, but it breeds resentment and alienation (Etzioni, 1975, pp. 12–13, 47–8). Thus, coercion does not engender stable and positive affective relationships between students and teachers that are necessary for teaching and learning (Bredemeier, 1978, p. 444; Metz, 1978, p. 27; Spady, 1977, p. 363).

In fact, coercing students is most likely to generate what sociologists call 'role distance' and 'behavioral conformity'. These terms describe student conduct that minimally meets role expectations but lacks seriousness and enthusiasm. Such conduct is governed by attention to external consequences and is misaligned with the personal objectives of students. For these reasons, coercion may be an effective way of forcing a student to leave a room, but it is not an effective way of helping a student learn French. Moreover, coercion is also incongruent with the professional role that teachers have assumed in Western societies. Coercion is reserved for people to whom the state has delegated the right to use force. As such, it is a mode of compliance that may be more acceptable in prisons, where guards are not professionals, than in schools, where teachers are professionals.

A second answer to the hypothetical question 'Why should I?' is embodied in the notion of persuasion. Persuasion operates on the basis of bargaining. In this response, the assumption is that there is some degree of misalignment between the objectives of teachers and the objectives of students, and that through negotiation a coordination of these objectives may be established. Students and teachers may, for example, negotiate over learning objectives and discipline (see Clifton, 1979; Clifton and Rambaran, 1987). In terms of the hypothetical question, the teacher's response is something like the following: 'If you comply with my request, I will give you something that you value more than you value what I am asking you to sacrifice'.

Persuasion is an improvement over coercion as a strategy for teachers to use in obtaining compliance from students. Persuasion does not involve the use of threat or force, and although students select among available alternatives, the choices are based on the teacher's ability to convince them of the inherent advantages of selecting certain alternatives (Spady, 1977, p. 363). In this way, persuasion facilitates more positive relations between students and teachers, and it eliminates some of the negative aspects of coercion.

Nevertheless, persuasion can create the conditions for endless negotiation on virtually all aspects of classroom life. This can occur because the objectives of the school are controversial, students are conscripted and they are not necessarily committed to the objectives. When persuasion becomes the central mode of obtaining compliance from students, teachers risk having to negotiate and justify, to each student, every activity that takes place in the classroom.

Recent research illustrates that in many Western societies teachers spend considerable time and effort bargaining with students in order to maintain reasonable decorum within classrooms (Sedlak *et al.*, 1986, pp. 99–103). Even though persuasion is compatible with a democratic, market-oriented society, and consistent with a humanistic educational system, it places enormous role strain on teachers as they try to negotiate with twenty-five to thirty-five students for four or five hours a day, 200 days a year. For this reason, persuasion is not an efficient method of attempting to achieve the objectives of the school. Moreover, while persuasion may be acceptable for used-car salesmen to bargain with their customers, it is not generally perceived as being acceptable for professional teachers to negotiate with students.

Even though coercion and persuasion have substantial disadvantages as ways of obtaining and maintaining the compliance of students, there is considerable evidence which suggests that teachers, particularly substitute teachers and student teachers, attempt to use these techniques (Clifton, 1979; Clifton and Rambaran, 1987; Denscombe, 1985; LeCompte, 1978; Martin, 1975; McNeil, 1986; Wegmann, 1976). Moreover, there are considerable differences in the use of coercion and persuasion in schools between different countries. For example, White (1984, p. 96) reports that American teachers spend approximately 60 per cent of their classroom time in persuading students to comply with their demands, whereas Japanese teachers spend approximately 10 per cent of their classroom time in such activities.

The third answer to the hypothetical question 'Why should I?' is found in the exercise of authority. In classrooms based upon authority, students perceive the teachers' requests as being legitimate, where legitimacy 'refers to the normative right to make a decision that is accepted as morally binding on all members of the organization' (Corwin, 1978, p. 66). According to Weber (1923), authority means that people comply voluntarily. Voluntary compliance is rooted in a shared set of objectives and mutual acceptance of the existing social structure. That is, students and teachers value both the institutional structure and the objectives of the institution. In classrooms that are based upon authority, the hypothetical question is answered by teachers in words, such as 'We both agree that the educational system gives me the right to make these legitimate requests of you, and it assigns to you the obligation to comply with my legitimate requests'.[9]

One distinct advantage of classrooms based on authority is that extensive resources are not consumed in bargaining with students as is the case in classrooms based on persuasion. Moreover, compared with classrooms based on coercion, classrooms based on authority need not continuously devote resources to overcoming the resistance of students. In short, classroom order which is based on authority is more efficient, and therefore more desirable, than classroom order which is based on either coercion or persuasion, This results because in classrooms based upon authority minimum resources are devoted to organizational problems; this optimizes the resources available for the pursuit of the objectives of the school, specifically learning and teaching. Given the desirability of authority, it deserves a closer examination as a basis of organizing classrooms.

As Weber (1923) noted, there are three types of authority: traditional authority, charismatic authority and rational-legal authority. Traditional authority is based upon the perceived sanctity of heritage and on the belief that the guardians of the traditions have a legitimate right to make demands of others in order to preserve their heritage. In other words, the social organization of group life is legitimate because it is rooted in customs. Those in superordinate positions take it as their right to make demands on their subordinates who, in turn, feel obligated to comply. In appealing to tradition, the teacher responds to the hypothetical question 'Why should I?' by saying something like: 'It is my right to tell you, and it is your duty to comply because traditionally people in your status have always complied with such demands from people in my status'.

In contrast with tradition, charismatic authority is legitimated by the respect that people have for the attributes and performances of a specific individual (Gerth and Mills, 1946, p. 295). These gifts are often associated with a sense of mission intended to fulfill specific needs of subordinates (Spady, 1977, pp. 364–5).[10] Thus, the language used to describe charismatic authority is filled with the connotations of altruism, care and love. This type of authority is more diffuse, intense and personalized than traditional authority (Etzioni, 1975, p. 305). In appealing to charisma, a teacher may respond to the hypothetical question 'Why should I?' by saying something similar to: 'It is my right to ask you to comply, because you recognize that I value your welfare and you will be better off if you follow my advice'.

The third type of authority Weber identified, rational-legal authority, contains two dimensions: official (legal) and expert (rational) authority (Olsen, 1968; Spady, 1977). Official authority is inherent within an organizational position. That is, a person is given the legal or official right to demand compliance from subordinates by virtue of the office that he or she holds. Expert authority is based upon access to technical knowledge and experience which, in turn, makes it sensible for a subordinate to comply within the boundaries defined by the individual's expertise and experience. Thus, teachers may appeal to their official status and expertise in legitimating the demands they make on students by saying something like: 'It is my right to ask for compliance and it is your duty to comply because due process (official) and rational considerations (expertise) have been properly used to define our obligations to each other in terms of the objectives of the school'.

The essence of rational-legal authority in schools centers on students and teachers sharing educational objectives, teachers being defined as possessing the expertise and experience necessary for attaining these objectives, and students and teachers working within an institution which grants them legal statuses.[11] Under these conditions, students and teachers can legitimately expect each other to comply with reasonable demands directed at achieving the objectives of the educational system.

In this section we have noted that classroom order is not something teachers can necessarily take for granted, but it is something that they must manage through interaction with students. Thus, we argue that teachers can employ a limited set of ways to constrain the conduct of students and to bring order to the classroom. The basic means teachers have for creating classroom order include the use of coercion, persuasion and authority. In our analysis, we have noted that while teachers probably employ both coercion and persuasion, these ways of obtaining and maintaining compliance from students have serious limitations. In contrast, the use of authority in classrooms seems to hold more potential for obtaining and maintaining compliance from students. In the final section of this chapter, we examine teachers' authority in greater detail, and we suggest some policies which may assist teachers to be more effective and efficient in their use of authority.

Policy Implications of Institutional and Professional Authority

Following the argument presented in the previous section, and given our objective of suggesting how the existing system may be improved, teachers have four dimensions of authority at their disposal. Two of these, legal and traditional, are derived from the educational institution, and the other two, charismatic and expertise, are derived from the individual attributes of teachers, In this analysis, we assume that these four dimensions of authority have mutual and reciprocal effects upon each other, The relationships between the four dimensions of authority are presented in Figure 2. Each dimension of authority may vary along a continuum, but for reasons of parsimony each is presented as being either high or low. That is, at the institutional level there may be either high or low legal and traditional authority, and at the individual level there may be either high or low charismatic and expert authority. The numbers in the upper right corner of each cell indicate the number of high scores that would be represented in a classroom of a specific type. For example, the cell in the upper right-hand corner of the figure contains a 2. This implies that this type of classroom has high scores on two dimensions of authority, charisma and expertise.

In examining the numbers in the cells in this figure, it is clear that the authority of teachers in classrooms generally increases as we move from the cell in the lower right-hand corner to the cell in the upper left-hand corner. The cell in the upper left-hand corner represents functional schools because they are high on both legal and traditional authority, and functional teachers because they are high on both charisma and expertise. These schools and teachers are functional because they have greater likelihood of effectively and efficiently achieving their objectives. In contrast, the cell in the lower right-hand corner represents dysfunctional schools, because they are low on both

Figure 2   Institutional and individual dimensions of authority

INSTITUTIONAL AUTHORITY

		High Legal Authority		Low Legal Authority	
		High Traditional Authority	Low Traditional Authority	High Traditional Authority	Low Traditional Authority
High Charisma	High Expertise	Best Schools & Best Teachers 4	3	3	2
High Charisma	Low Expertise	3	2	2	1
Low Charisma	High Expertise	3	2	2	1
Low Charisma	Low Expertise	2	1	1	Worst Schools & Worst Teachers 0

(Left axis label: PROFESSIONAL AUTHORITY)

legal and traditional authority, and dysfunctional teachers, because they are low on both charisma and expertise. These schools and teachers are dysfunctional because they are likely to be ineffective and inefficient in achieving their objectives.

To date, there are no large surveys examining the distribution of these four dimensions of authority among teachers and across schools. Nevertheless, a few small studies suggest that a number of schools are low on both legal and traditional authority, and contain teachers who are low on both charismatic and expert authority (Sedlak *et al.*, 1986, pp. 117–23). Also, some research suggests that private and parochial schools, in comparison with public schools, are more likely to be high on legal and traditional authority, and the teachers, in comparison with teachers in public schools, are more likely to be high on charismatic and expert authority (see Coleman, Hoffer and Kilgore, 1982; Morgan, 1983; Salganik and Karweit, 1982).

Whatever future investigations of the distribution of authority discover, this typology assists us in conceptualizing authority and thinking about ways of improving the authority of teachers within classrooms and schools. Overall, this figure suggests that the ability of teachers to obtain and maintain the compliance of students may be enhanced by increasing the authority which is vested in the institution and the authority which is vested in the individual teacher.

The initial basis for establishing authority in classrooms is often derived from the institution. Generally, when students first enter a new classroom, they encounter a teacher whose professional dispositions are unknown. Thus, the teacher must initially rely upon institutional authority which has been established by the school. As routines are established, the individual authority of a teacher may begin to play a more prominent role in obtaining and maintaining the compliance of students. For this reason, we begin by discussing four policy implications related to the exercise of institutional authority, and then we discuss four policy implications related to the exercise of individual authority.

Enhancing Institutional Authority

In order to improve institutional authority in schools, we must appreciate that students and teachers are part of a formal organization. Like all formal organizations, the school is composed of statuses and normative expectations which govern the conduct of students and teachers. These statuses and the concomitant expectations are integrated with other parts of society. In fact, the statuses and the expectations obtain their legitimacy because they are designed to achieve particular objectives which are valued and supported by society. Without having valued objectives, and without being integrated with other parts of society, an organization risks becoming an arbitrary set of social arrangements to which people are not willing to commit themselves.

Accordingly, our first policy recommendation stresses the necessity of schools establishing a restricted set of clearly articulated objectives. It may seem surprising that schools do not already have objectives which are clearly defined, but as Goodlad (1984, p. 29) notes, 'Schools appear not to be acutely self-conscious about what they are trying to do'. In other words, the objectives of schools are often unstated and may be as diverse as baby-sitting, offering wholesome meals, development of the authentic self of students, intellectual development, job preparation and sex education (see Spady, 1977, pp. 359–62; Wilson, 1962, p. 19). Schools cannot reasonably be expected to be directed toward achieving such a diverse, and often unstated, set of objectives without a dilution of their institutional authority. Better articulated and less diverse objectives, specifically directed toward cognitive development, would probably improve the authority of the institution (Adler, 1982; Hirsch, 1988; Toby, 1989). Toward this end, it would be helpful if departments of education, parent-teacher associations, school boards and teachers' associations took the initiative in emphasizing how problematic it is for schools even to attempt fulfilling the diverse agendas which have been imposed upon them by various interest groups (Goodlad, 1984, pp. 59, 275).

Second, in order to obtain clearly articulated and defined objectives, the organization of schools must be decentralized, to some extent, so that parents, students and teachers have greater input in defining the objectives of 'their' school (Goodlad, 1984, pp. 272–6; Lubeck, 1984). Generally, organizational objectives which are externally imposed engender less commitment than those which students, teachers and parents have had a role in establishing. This principle underlies the notion of mediating institutions, which stand 'between the individual in his private life and the larger institutions of public life' (Berger and Neuhaus, 1977, p. 2). Some critics have noted that the decreased sense of community in schools has resulted in an increase in disruptive behavior on the part of students (Hurn, 1985, pp. 38–9). It seems plausible that if parents, students and teachers had greater input into articulating the objectives of the school, they may also have greater commitment to achieving the objectives.[12]

Third, it is important to define carefully and precisely the rights and duties of students, teachers, department heads, principals, superintendents and school boards, as well as define clearly the authority structure of the school (Bredemeier and Bredemeier, 1978, p. 324; Werthman, 1963). In order for institutional authority to be credible, it must be clear, when people join an organization such as a school, that they are being assigned to a status which defines their rights and duties, and that they are expected to comply with the legitimate demands from those in superordinate statuses.

Finally, the institutional authority in schools would be improved by establishing systematic methods of determining the success of the institution in achieving the objectives. Moreover, it is necessary to have methods of determining whether or not the various role players have followed the legitimate demands from those in superordinate positions. There is little use in setting objectives and specifying authority relationships without examining how well the system is operating and, where necessary, taking corrective action. Such a system of surveillance would help ensure that school administrators, teachers, school board members and parents would support the legitimate teacher authority (Bredemeier and Bredemeier, 1978, p. 110). It would also mean that if students, or teachers, are wilfully defying the legitimate expectations of the school, principals would have the authority to expel them (Cusick, 1983; Denscombe, 1985, p. 52; McNeil, 1986, p. 78; Sedlak *et al.*, 1986, p. 117; Toby, 1989). In formal organizations, recalcitrance on the part of role players cannot be tolerated because it signals a lack of seriousness about the organizational structure which, in turn, diminishes credibility in the objectives which have been established.

Enhancing Individual Authority

To this point, the policy recommendations have been directed towards improving the institutional authority of schools, That is, each of these four recommendations has been directed towards enhancing the tradition of educational institutions and strengthening the legal rights and duties of teachers. These recommendations are designed to develop the legitimacy of the school as an institution, and, as a result, to enhance the authority of teachers. Following improvements in institutional authority, the individual authority of teachers in classrooms may be improved. The following four policy recommendations are aimed at enhancing the charisma and expertise of teachers.

Our first policy recommendation is that teachers must work towards becoming members of the intellectual elite of a society so that they see themselves, and are perceived by others, as being members of this elite. The idea here is that the individual authority of teachers is enhanced by their identity as exemplary students. On this account, Adler (1982, pp. 58–9) notes that an important indicator of intellectual stature is the interest teachers have in their own education, as illustrated by their motivation to continue studying and learning while teaching. Early this century, Durkheim (1922) pointed out that it is impossible for teachers to initiate children into the moral life of a society without possessing a good understanding of the ideas upon which this life is based. Thus, teachers must be educated in the arts, mathematics, philosophy and the natural and social sciences. In Hirsch's (1988) terms, teachers must be 'culturally literate'. In addition, teachers must be well educated in the subject areas they teach. A teacher of mathematics, for example, must be well educated in algebra, calculus and geometry, just as a teacher of social studies must be well educated in history, philosophy and sociology.[13] In other words, teachers must be well-educated professionals who can speak with clarity and exactness as well as write lucidly. Deficiencies in this regard can only detract from their individual authority as teachers, despite whatever institutional authority the school provides.

Second, teachers must be well educated in pedagogy, human development, theories of learning, moral development and measurement of achievement. These competencies are necessary for teachers to understand the aptitudes and capabilities of students at various ages. These competencies are also essential for the development of lessons and programs of study which are compatible with the emotional, intellectual and social development of students. In other words, teachers must have both an expert understanding of the disciplines necessary for establishing and defending the objectives that have been set for students, as well as expertise in the disciplines and the methods relevant to evaluating student achievement. Teachers charged with the care, development and assessment of students will not be treated with the seriousness and legitimacy required to do their work well if they lack these competencies.

Third, teachers must be knowledgeable about the social organization of classrooms and schools. Both teaching and the control of disorderly behavior are fundamentally social activities, and an understanding of these activities must be embedded in a sociological framework (see Clifton, 1979; Clifton and Rambaran, 1987). Knowledge of this type is particularly relevant as modern classrooms shift from more traditional, tightly structured organizations to more loosely structured organizations. With looser structures in schools, classroom order and legitimacy becomes increasingly dependent upon negotiations with students where a variety of possible social arrangements may emerge. Thus, an understanding of the social processes and outcomes associated with a more loosely structured organization is necessary if teachers are effectively and efficiently to achieve the objectives of the school.

Finally, in order to enhance their individual authority, teachers must show a great deal of affection and empathy towards students. As Spady (1977, p. 365) notes, affection and empathy are inherent aspects of charisma. Affectionate and empathetic conduct is fundamental to the preservation of students' self-respect during the learning process. Wilson (1962, p. 25) argues that affection is the first language which people understand, and it becomes the conduit by which all other content, especially self-respect, is learned. Self-respect is so fundamental that Rawls' (1971, p. 63) conception of justice identifies it as a primary good that all people, including both students and teachers, continually strive to maintain. Self-respect consists of three components (Bredemeier and Bredemeier, 1978, p. 59). First, self-respect implies that students have a sense that their role performance is important. In other words, the performance of students must be appreciated and valued by other people, particularly by their significant others — parents, other students and teachers — whose opinions are important. Second, students must sense that their role is challenging; they must appreciate that performing the student role requires abilities, effort, self-discipline and skills that are not easily obtained. Third, students must sense that they are competently performing their role. In terms of this conception, a central task of teachers is to develop a student's abilities competently to perform tasks which are difficult and valued by society.

Given the importance of self-respect, teachers are imprudent if they routinely tell students that their behavior is inferior, even if it is the case, because students are likely to withdraw, devote their resources to preserving their self-respect, and show a reluctance to comply with future demands made by the teacher. When this occurs, a teacher's individual authority over the students is diminished. In general, teachers' legitimacy declines if students are told that they are incompetent, if their behavior is not valued, or if their assigned tasks are so easy that their dignity is insulted (Bredemeier and Bredemeier, 1978, p. 296). In line with this reasoning, professional teachers are distinguished by their routine attempts to be empathetic towards students and help them maintain their self-respect, even if the students do not reciprocate in helping the teacher maintain his or her self-respect (see Werthman, 1963).[14]

In sum, we argue that the individual authority of teachers is grounded in the charisma and expertise they display towards students. We suggest that a particular kind of liberal education and an understanding of the sociology of classrooms are aspects of expert knowledge, which enhance a teacher's individual authority. In addition, we note that preserving the self-respect of students is important. This suggests that teachers who are empathetic towards students will increase their individual authority.

Summary

This chapter began by noting that recent research illustrates that schools are having increasing difficulties which seem to be related to students depreciating and being irreverent toward the authority of teachers. We argue that an examination of the authority of teachers may provide both a better understanding of the problems schools face and some recommendations for improving the situation. Initially, we examined the authority of teachers by comparing the characteristics of schools with the characteristics of families and workplaces. We argued that teachers have fewer resources for obtaining and maintaining the compliance of students than parents have with respect to their children or employers have with respect to their employees. Following this, we examined the legitimate means that teachers may use in obtaining and maintaining compliance from students. Specifically, we argued that teachers must rely upon both institutional authority, derived from the tradition of the school and their legal rights, and individual authority, based upon their expertise and empathy.

A typology was developed to suggest that the congruence of both institutional and individual authority probably characterizes functional schools and teachers. If the strength of one or both of these sources of authority decreases, the credibility of teachers and the compliance of students probably become much more tenuous. As authority recedes, teachers are likely to rely increasingly upon coercion or persuasion — each of which is a less effective and less efficient means for pursuing the objectives of the school. The chapter concluded with some recommendations for enhancing the institutional authority of schools and the individual authority of teachers. Our major theme has been that schools that achieve their objectives in an effective and efficient manner require teachers who have authority and who are in control. Typically, administrators and teachers fail to appreciate the complexity and difficulty of this prerequisite for effective education.

Notes

1   *Compliance* is used throughout this chapter to identify the relationship between superordinates and subordinates. As Etzioni (1975, pp. 3–4) points out, compliance is a universal phenomenon which exists in all social organizations. We do not assume that superordinates have total power to enforce compliance while subordinates have no power. Rather, we note that in schools students may have considerable power, and, in some circumstances, they may be able to force teachers to comply with their wishes.
2   In a broad sense, these objectives usually have the support of members of society

because they are determined by representatives of society, and members of society pay a substantial cost in providing education. In Canada, approximately 7 per cent of the gross national product is used to support education (Martin and Macdonell, 1982, p. 146).

3 In this respect, Spady (1977, pp. 359–62) summarizes the diverse objectives of schools as being custody-control, evaluation-certification, selection, instruction and socialization.

4 In this chapter, *functional* refers to individual characteristics and institutional structures which help facilitate compliance to institutional norms, and *dysfunctional* refers to individual characteristics and institutional structures which hinder compliance to institutional norms (see Etzioni, 1975, pp. 312–28).

5 Etzioni (1975, p. 16) notes that often people holding subordinate statuses in organizations are less motivated to achieve the objectives of the organization than people holding superordinate statuses. He argues that this results, in part, because they are often not as committed to both the organization and the objectives as the people holding superordinate statuses.

6 It has been noted that teachers have fewer opportunities for mobility than people in other bureaucracies. That is, teachers have relatively few opportunities to become heads of departments, vice-principals or principals. In this respect, Lortie (1975, p. 84) calls teaching 'a relatively unstaged career'.

7 An examination of public perceptions of elementary and secondary school teachers illustrates how attention to expressive objectives is associated with the prestige of teachers. In Canada and the United States, for example, many people seem to think that elementary school teachers deal with less complex knowledge, and consequently have and deserve less authority, respect and status than secondary school teachers, even though they may have the same amount of education, years of experience and salary.

8 The process of negotiating between students and teachers involves numerous activities which can be classified into a parsimonious set of four processes: obtaining things, disposing of things, avoiding things and retaining things (Bredemeier and Bredemeier 1978, p. 26). For example, teachers may spend considerable energy and time attempting to have students obtain knowledge, dispose of disorderly behavior, avoid open conflict and retain their self-respect. Sociological research illustrates that extensive differences exist among students and between students and teachers regarding the kinds and amounts of things they seek to obtain, dispose of, retain and avoid (see Wegmann, 1976).

9 Complying with requests may not necessarily have beneficial consequences for individuals. Individuals may be asked to go to war, for example, which may not benefit them even though it may benefit the society.

10 Weber (1923; Gerth and Mills, 1946, pp. 52–3) distinguishes between pure and routinized charisma. Pure charisma is exhibited by a natural leader, unencumbered by a bureaucratic office, while routinized charisma is exhibited by a leader who holds a bureaucratic office. We restrict our use of charisma to the pure form. We think that official authority is a better way to reference the authority a person has as a result of his or her official position in a bureaucracy. In this respect, routinized charisma is very closely related to official authority, while pure charisma is different from official authority because it is a characteristic of the individual rather than a characteristic of the institution (Etzioni, 1975, pp. 308–9). More specific to this argument, Etzioni (1975, p. 311) notes that 'professionals draw their ascribed [routinized] charisma from their special knowledge or skill and from their organizational rank'.

11 In most Western societies this expectation is underwritten by the fact that teachers receive differential pay on the basis of both their expertise, which is determined by their level of education, and their teaching experience.

12 This type of policy has recently been implemented in England where the new Education Reform Act permits parents to decide whether their school will continue under the jurisdiction of the local government or become an independent school. Similarly, parent and school committees are used in Quebec to ensure that the perspectives of the parents are reflected in local schools, A similar trend also appears to be emerging in the United States.

13 A number of researchers report that students continually test their teachers' intellectual competencies (Metz, 1978). King and Ripton (1970, pp. 46–7), for example, report that a number of the teachers they interviewed were frustrated because they were not as intellectually prepared as they should have been. In this respect, one teacher asked: 'How often can you tell a class that you don't know something? Not too often. From my own experience at high school, we found that if a teacher can't answer a question on a certain subject, invariably a lot of students would ask questions in that particular subject area to stump the teachers'.

14 A number of studies report that many students, particularly in junior and senior high school, exhibit a great deal of disrespect towards the authority of schools and the authority of teachers. This results in intense frustration on the part of many teachers (Wilson, 1962, p. 24). The literature also suggests that in order to control students, teachers often make school work easy (McNeil, 1986, p. 179; Sedlak *et al.*, 1986, p. 123; Werthman, 1963). In this way, teachers denigrate one of the three conditions which facilitate the self-respect of both themselves and the students.

Bibliography

ADELSON, J. (July, 1983) 'How the schools were ruined', *Commentary*, pp. 45–54.

ADLER, M. (1982) *The Paideia Proposal: An Educational Manifesto*, New York: Macmillan.

BERGER, P. (1970) 'On the obsolescence of the concept of honor', *European Journal of Sociology, 11*, pp. 339–47.

BERGER, P. (1973) '"Sincerity" and "authenticity" in modern society', *The Public Interest, 31*, pp. 81–90.

BERGER, P. (1977) *Facing up to Modernity*, New York: Basic Books.

BERGER, P. and NEUHAUS, R. (1977) *To Empower People: The Role of Mediating Structures in Public Policy*, Washington, DC: American Enterprise Institute.

BIDWELL, C.E. (1970) 'Students and schools: Some observations on client trust in client-serving organizations', in ROSENGREN, W.R. and LEFTON, M. (Eds) *Organizations and Clients: Essays in the Sociology of Service*, Columbus, OH: Charles E. Merrill, pp. 37–69.

BIDWELL, C.E. (1973) 'The social psychology of teaching', in TRAVERS, R. (Ed.) *Second Handbook of Research on Teaching*, Chicago: Rand McNally, pp. 413–49.

BOOCOCK, S.S. (1978) 'The social organization of the classroom', *Annual Review of Sociology, 4*, pp. 1–28.

BREDEMEIER, H.C. (1978) 'Exchange theory', in BOTTOMORE, T. and NISBET, R. (Eds) *A History of Sociological Analysis*, New York: Basic Books, pp. 418–56.

BREDEMEIER, M.E. and BREDEMEIER, H.C. (1978) *Social Forces in Education*, Sherman Oaks, CA: Alfred Publishing Co.

CLIFTON, R.A. (1979) 'Practice teaching: Survival in a marginal situation', *Canadian Journal of Education, 4*, pp. 60–74.

CLIFTON, R.A. and RAMBARAN, R. (1987) 'Substitute teaching: Survival in a marginal situtation', *Urban Education, 22*, pp. 310–27.

COLEMAN, J.S., HOFFER, T. and KILGORE, S. (1982) *High School Achievement: Public, Catholic and Other Private Schools Compared*, New York: Basic Books.

CORWIN, R.G. (1978) 'Power', in SAGARIN, E. (Ed.) *Sociology: Basic Concepts*, New York: Holt, Rinehart and Winston, pp. 65–85.

CUSICK, P.A. (1983) *The Egalitarian Ideal and the American High School: Studies of Three Schools*, New York: Longman.

DENSCOMBE, M. (1985) *Classroom Control: A Sociological Perspective*, London: George Allen and Unwin.

DREEBEN, R. (1968) *On What is Learned in School*, Reading, MA: Addison-Wesley.

DREEBEN, R. (1970) *The Nature of Teaching: Schools and the Work of Teachers*, Glenview, IL: Scott Foresman.

DREEBEN, R. (1971) 'American Schooling: Patterns and processes of stability and change', in BARBER, B. and INKELES, A. (Eds) *Stability and Social Change*, Boston, MA: Little, Brown, pp. 82–119.

DREEBEN, R. (1973) 'The school as a workplace', in TRAVERS, R. (Ed.) *Second Handbook of Research on Teaching*, Chicago: Rand McNally, pp. 450–73.

DURKHEIM, E. (1956) *Education and Sociology* (S.D. Fox, Trans.), New York: Free Press. (Original work published 1922.)

ETZIONI, A. (1975) *A Comparative Analysis of Complex Organizations: On Power, Involvement and their Correlates* (2nd Edn), New York: The Free Press.

GEER, B. (1968) 'Teaching', in SILLS, D.L. (Ed.) *International Encyclopedia of the Social Sciences* (vol. 15), New York: The Free Press, pp. 560–5.

GERTH, H.H. and MILLS, C.W. (1946) *From Max Weber: Essays in Sociology*, New York: Oxford University Press.

GOODLAD, J. (1984) *A Place called School: Prospects for the Future*, New York: McGraw-Hill.

HIRSCH, E.D. JR. (1988) *Cultural Literacy: What Every American Needs to Know*, New York: Random House.

HURN, C.J. (1978) *The Limits and Possibilities of Schooling*, Boston: Allyn and Bacon.

HURN, C.J. (1985) 'Changes in authority relationships in schools: 1960–1980', *Research in Sociology of Education and Socialization*, 5, pp. 31–57.

HUSEN, T. (1979) *The School in Question: A Comparative Study of School and its Future in Western Societies*, Oxford: Oxford University Press.

JACKSON, P.W. (1968) *Life in Classrooms*, New York: Holt, Rinehart and Winston.

JOHNSON, D.W. (1978) 'Conflict management in the school and classroom', in BAR-TAL, D. and SAXE, L. (Eds) *Social Psychology of Education: Theory and Research*, New York: John Wiley, pp. 299–326.

KING, A.J.C. and RIPTON, R.A. (1970) 'Teachers and students: A preliminary analysis of collective reciprocity', *Canadian Review of Sociology and Anthropology*, 7, pp. 35–48.

LeCOMPTE, M.D. (1978) 'Establishing a workplace: Teacher control in the classroom', *Education and Urban Society*, 11, pp. 87–105.

LORTIE, D.C. (1975) *Schoolteacher: A Sociological Study*, Chicago: University of Chicago.

LUBECK, S. (1984) 'Kinship and classrooms: An ethnographic perspective on education as cultural transmission', *Sociology of Education*, 57, pp. 219–32.

MARTIN, W.B.W. (1975) 'Teacher-pupil interactions: A negotiation perspective', *Canadian Review of Sociology and Anthropology*, 12, pp. 529–40.

MARTIN, W.B.W. and MACDONELL, A.J. (1982) *Canadian Education: A Sociological Analysis*, Scarborough, ON: Prentice-Hall.

McNEIL, L.M. (1986) *Contradictions of Control: School Structure and School Knowledge*, New York: Routledge and Kegan Paul.

METZ, M.H. (1978) 'Clashes in the classroom: The importance of norms for authority', *Education and Urban Society*, 11, pp. 13–47.

MORGAN, W.R. (1983) 'Learning and student life quality of public and private school youth', *Sociology of Education, 56*, pp. 187–202.

OLSEN, M.E. (1968) *The Process of Social Organization*, New York: Holt, Rinehart and Winston.

PARSONS, T. (1960) *Structure and Process in Modern Societies*, Glencoe, IL: The Free Press.

PETERS, R.S. (1973) *Authority and Responsibility in Education*, London: George Allen and Unwin.

RAWLS, J. (1971) *A Theory of Justice*, Cambridge, MA: Harvard University.

SALGANIK, L.H. and KARWEIT, N. (1982) 'Voluntarism and governance in education', *Sociology of Education, 55*, pp. 152–61.

SCOTT, W.R. (1981) *Organizations: Rational, Natural, and Open Systems*, Englewood Cliffs, NJ: Prentice-Hall.

SEDLAK, M.W., WHEELER, C.W., PULLIN, D.C. and CUSICK, P.A. (1986) *Selling Students Short: Classroom Bargains and Academic Reform in the American High School*, New York: Teachers College.

SPADY, W.G. (1977) 'Power, authority and empathy in schooling', in CARLTON, R.A., COLLEY, L.A. and MACKINNON, N.J. (Eds) *Education, Change and Society: A Sociology of Canadian Education*, Toronto: Gage, pp. 359–75.

TINTO, V. (1978) 'Reflections on classroom authority', *Education and Urban Society, 11*, pp. 107–18.

TOBY, J. (1989) 'Of dropouts and stay-ins: The Gershwin approach', *The Public Interest, 95*, pp. 3–14.

TURNER, R.H. (1976) 'The real self: From institution to impulse', *American Journal of Sociology, 81*, pp. 989–1016.

TYLER, W.B. (1985) 'The organizational structure of the school', *Annual Review of Sociology, 22*, pp. 49–73.

WALLER, W. (1932) *The Sociology of Teaching*, New York: Wiley.

WEBER, M. (1947) *The Theory of Social and Economic Organization* (A.M. HENDERSON and T. PARSONS, Trans.), New York: Free Press. (Original work published 1923).

WEGMANN, R.G. (1976) 'Classroom discipline: An exercise in the maintenance of social reality', *Sociology of Education, 49*, pp. 71–9.

WERTHMAN, C. (1963) 'Delinquents in schools: A test for legitimacy of authority', *Berkeley Journal of Sociology, 8*, pp. 39–60.

WHITE, M.E. (1984) 'Japanese education: How do they do it?' *The Public Interest, 76*, pp. 87–101.

WILSON, B.R. (1962) 'The teacher's role — A sociological analysis', *British Journal of Sociology, 13*, pp. 15–31.

20   Rights and Obligations of Teachers

Douglas Ray

Rights: Definition, Sources and Constraints

The currency of talk about rights reflects its significance in society. Teachers, in particular, are testing the boundaries of their rights in educational systems, whether in the United States (Fischer and Schimmel, 1982) or in Canada (Dickinson and MacKay, 1989). Unfortunately, the definition of the word *rights* in popular usage is unduly flexible so some conceptual precision needs to be introduced to render its discussion meaningful. There is also a need for identifying the areas where claimed rights are employed to challenge present educational structures and arrangements. Such challenges, if successful, will affect the rights and obligations of teachers, namely, those held by teachers as private persons and citizens, those of significance to pedagogy, and those associated with teachers' role in the care of children.

Rights are claims that have the backing of law. They are enforceable. 'Every child has the right to be brought up in a loving household' becomes more than a wish when there is a legal means of removing children from abusive situations. Consequently, rights exist whenever some persons or group can legally claim a benefit, but not where such benefits may be conferred or withdrawn at the discretion of an authority with the legal power to withhold them. In that case, we may speak of privileges. Also, rights exist only where the benefits attached to them can be made available. Thus, students' rights to fair treatment is negated by the absence not only of educators' specialized knowledge required to treat students fairly but also of requisite guidelines or regulations to implement fair treatment. Rights are not the result of knowledge exclusively, but also of practices. Eventually, they may be reflected in widespread attitudes — for example, the tolerance of differences. In the final analysis, however, the existence of rights depends on more or less explicit statement of entitlements and legal prohibitions of discrimination in their exercise and enjoyment (Tarnopolsky, 1982).

Necessarily, rights are limited, not absolute. For example, most Canadian employees have the legal right to strike. However, it may be exercised only under lawful conditions. Wildcat strikes — sudden and unofficial — are punishable by law and are not legal entitlements of workers.

The essential relationships among the terms and conditions may be summarized. First, rights are not privileges conferred by authorities upon only some persons, but are claims accessible to all whose entitlements are recognized by law. They are normally enforceable at law for cases under a given category of rights-holders. However, rights may legally be withheld if their exercise fails to meet the test of reasonable conditions. Rights imply obligations, including the obligations by other persons in the same category. Thus, all teachers, including dissenters, are expected to respect majority opinion after a properly conducted strike vote. Rights also oblige all persons, of a different category, who occupy certain functional relationships with the rights-holder. For example, teachers and principals are obliged to ensure that a particular student or group of students receive fair treatment not only from students but also from themselves.

Rights derive from a number of sources. The broadest source is perhaps the various statements on human rights. The usual reference for this source is the *Universal Declaration of Human Rights*, which was adopted without dissent by the United Nations on December 10, 1948.[1] For Canadians, the listing of rights usually begins with constitutional documents, of which *The Canadian Charter of Rights and Freedoms (1982)* and *The Constitution Act (1867)* are paramount because they set conditions upon both the federal and provincial governments, and because they cannot be modified without complex procedures. The second source consists of provincial constitutions which are also very significant legally for they are similarly protected against easy changes that might erode whatever safeguards they contain.[2] The third source is in the form of specific human rights legislation (charter, code or act) for each province or the federal government, in which specified grounds for discrimination are prohibited.[3] However, any of these human rights codes can be (and have been) set aside by governments unwilling to enforce the protection that they promise.

These sources of rights are available to all, including teachers. However, the latter are affected by legal documents not only granting rights but also imposing some disabilities. Thus, teachers are affected by laws with direct impact upon their profession (The Education or School Act, The Teaching Profession Act, etc.), by all the Ministry regulations and directives that are made under these Acts, and by all the school board and teaching profession decisions.[4] There is also some important general legislation, either federal (such as the Young Offenders Act and the Criminal Code of Canada) or provincial (for example, the Family and Child Services legislation).

Finally, there are thousands of legal judgments that influence teaching by ruling on the lawfulness of a particular action. Some of them establish benchmark procedures and terminology by which similar cases are subsequently conducted and in that way help to define human rights. The 'Careful Parent', 'The Kind, Loving and Judicious Parent', and 'attentions which were known or ought to have been known to be unwelcome' are phrases that frequently lack precise meaning in statutes or legislation but they are the tests by which supervision and punishment are measured in court. Some of these judgments may have been made by tribunals that are quasi-judicial in nature, but are not strictly those of the courts.[5]

Many of the rights discussed in this section were identified long before the documents mentioned above came into existence. They were exercised effectively to the extent that all the population were in agreement with the principles. A good example is *The Ten Commandments* which has served as a general guide for society, despite some disagreement among Canadians concerning their interpretation (for example, on possible exceptions to 'Thou Shalt not Kill'). Today, there would be some difficulty in enforcing claims to rights based exclusively on a particular religion because Canada has become a highly diversified society. This confusion of heritage with current situations is reflected in the apparent contrast between the theocratic assumption of the preamble to the Canadian Charter of Rights and Freedoms (1982) and the religious non-discrimination clause included in its Section 15.[6]

Important Legal Foundations of Human Rights in Education

Human rights may be divided into *individual* and *group* rights, the first primarily concerned with the provision of political and legal services to individuals regardless of any affiliations that they may have with groups, and the second primarily concerned with the economic, social or cultural services to groups sharing important aspects of their identity (Bernstein-Tarrow, 1987, pp. 3–16). Several important examples of group rights in different areas in Canadian education will be examined first.

Religious Education

The oldest constitutional document that still directs educational rights concerning religion in Canada is *The Constitution Act (1867)* — formerly called the British North America Act (1867). Article 93(1) indicates that provinces may not infringe rights to religious control of schools that were entrenched at the time of Confederation. This provision providing for religious protection for the four original provinces has counterpart provisions in the legislation that created subsequent provinces. Thus, minority religious schools in Ontario or Quebec are protected by the 1867 Act, but those in Alberta or Saskatchewan are secured by their 1905 Constitutions, and those in Newfoundland and Labrador by its 1949 Constitution. As a Supreme Court of Canada decision indicated (Reference Re An Act to Amend the Education Act (Ontario) (1987), 77 N.R. 241), the rights of minority religions can be extended by the provinces. However, they cannot be diminished without very special procedures, so a small minority will usually be able to defend its rights against the majority of a province.

Several clauses of *The Canadian Charter of Rights and Freedoms* help to define educational rights in religion. Section 29 indicates that protection of religious schools (Constitution Act, 1867, article 93) is not undermined by the Charter. Section 15 prohibits discrimination on the basis of religion (and many other things) unless it 'has as its object the amelioration of conditions of disadvantaged individuals or groups' — i.e., affirmative action (section 15,2). This protection allows for separate and dissentient schools which collectively provide for the rights of certain minority groups of parents to obtain denominational education for their children. Freedom of expression is also guaranteed in section 2. Protection of such freedom was established in Canada even before the Charter. Thus, it was under this protection that the infamous Padlock law[7] (which impacted most severely upon certain religious minorities) was struck down by the Supreme Court a generation before the Charter (Berger, 1981, Chapter 6).

There are several special letters and legislation outlining the conditions under which certain religious minorities were admitted to Canada (Epp, 1974). These have a moral power, but their legal status has not recently been tested rigorously. One example of these pertains to the Mennonites who were promised that the immigrants and their descendants would not have to bear arms. This has not always been observed by Canadian governments.

The challenge of the future may come from religions of the East, for many Canadian laws were framed in the knowledge that the majority of the population was Christian. The non-Western religious minorities are growing in numbers, diversity and influence within the total population. Although there is very little legislation to help any of them, a recent Ontario Court of Appeal decision (*Zylberberg et al. v. The Director of Education of the Sudbury Board of Education*, 1988) has safeguarded them from domination by majority religious views. In addition, the right to serve their members through private schooling is established in law, both through legislation and the use of the court interpretation of common law (*R. v. Wiebe*, 1978). The Charter of Rights and Freedoms has not yet been a factor in defence of private schools.

Language Education

The first Canadian legal documents to promise language rights were the 1763 Treaty of Paris and the 1774 Quebec Act, both of which affirmed or extended existing French rights. The Quebecois and governments of Quebec still regard these as bedrock protection of their language rights, deplore those occasions when the promises came close to be broken (as in the case of Lord Durham), and believe that the *Constitution Act (1867)* should be regarded as adding to this protection rather than eliminating it. In most reviewers' eyes, the 1867 constitution gave scant protection for French rights (formally the right to use French or English in the legislatures or courts of Canada or Quebec), and various challenges have demonstrated the need for more protection, particularly from abuses of the French occurring in other provinces.[8]

Language and religion are intricately intertwined in the typical French Quebecer's sense of historical identity (Moniere, 1981), but the widespread existence of anglophone Catholics and numerous French non-Catholics challenges this linkage. Not all French Canadians share the Quebec perspective in detail, but most of them believe passionately in their right to education in French and, where possible, to control of their schools in order to ensure this right. Magnet (1982) identified education as the most explosive issue dividing French and English Canadians. So intense is this feeling that the Quebecois have a provincial psyche safeguarding these group rights — if necessary, at a cost to the rights of individuals or other groups. This identification of a French *nation* with its heart in Quebec gives rise to the 'separate identity' claim that pervades Canadian history (Laurin, 1978). The current prohibition of English signs on the outside of shops owned by Anglophones responds to the widely felt need to create an environment that proclaims French to be the official language of the province.

The shabby past treatment of the Francophone population (even in Quebec)[9] justifies this collective feeling, although a new perspective may develop among youth because they did not actually experience the personal slights, economic disadvantages, political neglect and betrayal, and educational constraints that dogged the adults who sought relief through the Quiet Revolution and the Parti Quebecois. The legislation that responded to these disadvantages includes the Official Languages Act (1969) and various amendments to provincial laws, including the education acts. However, legal decisions were an important means for the French minority to obtain their educational and political rights in most provinces (Dickinson and Mackay, 1989). The revolution is still in process.

Native Rights and Responsibilities

It is difficult to define what aboriginal rights in education are, or to identify what they should be (National Indian Brotherhood, 1988). Recent federal-provincial constitutional conferences dedicated to this matter (also attended by leaders of several native groups) failed to reach an agreement. There is no consensus in international law about what aboriginal education should be, although Canadian practices violate some widely-held ideas.

In law, certain native rights are protected under treaties signed at various times in the past, but these rights are difficult to interpret after years or even centuries of change. The Indian Act is a federal statute, and it is periodically revised and reinterpreted, unfortunately without meeting the minimum claims of most Native leaders. Most provincial laws (including those affecting education) do not specify programs for Indians but theoretically provide for all, and every Human Rights Code or Charter or Act prohibits discrimination on the basis of race. The use of the courts to defend aboriginal rights has sometimes been effective and, in the last decade, Native groups have tried to identify issues where legal remedies would be easier to achieve than political or economic measures. This has not been very successful.

Education — even schooling — is instrumental to achieving most aboriginal rights. There are two aspects of education to be considered: the promotion of identity (whether distinctive or shared) through such processes as teaching Indian languages, traditions, religions, aspirations of their leaders, and similar measures; and the provision of good education to every child in every part of Canada. It is quite clear that neither equal nor good education has been typically available to Indian and Inuit children, so Native leaders are either seeking Band control or buying into provincial systems. Individual families are not making the fundamental decisions, so pursuit of group rights is clearly a primary concern (National Indian Brotherhood, 1988).

The Protection of Racially Distinguishable Groups

Increasingly, Canadians are aware that racial differences among the population are broader and more divisive than has been assumed (Ontario, 1987). Racism is a factor in Canadian society and in schooling. Although it has usually been subliminal (despite the Cole Harbor incident of 1988 in Nova Scotia) most provinces are seeking a race relations policy that will improve the prospects for the future. Typically, this approach goes beyond the 'non-discrimination' protection of Human Right Codes by advising school boards to develop plans for dealing directly and clearly with racial issues. These policies prevent incidents from being regarded as harmless pranks or exercise of freedom of expression. The object is to ensure that their policies are perceived to be fair *to* and accepted *by* the minority community.

The usual problems of racism in schooling include streaming of persons from certain groups into vocational or terminal programmes (Samuda, 1984) and hiring or promoting to major responsibility only token numbers of the minority professionals. Consequently, some school boards have an explosive situation that must be dealt with soon and adroitly. It may be inappropriate to rely upon the modest protections of human rights (anti-discrimination) codes.

Protection Against Sexual Exploitation

Sexual exploitation is widespread in Canadian society, in the workplace, the family and in most institutions. It occurs even in schools, although it is perhaps less prominent there because of severe criminal sanction attached to it. Sexual exploitation of children is a criminal offence, and teachers are advised that 'touching in a way calculated to arouse' is an assault. Assault may include not only actual contact but also the threat of it. In addition, comments, leering and similar unwanted attention, which is either known or ought to be known to be unwelcome, are sexually offensive and may result in professional reprimands. Almost all the recorded offenses are by men, but laws regarding sexual offenses are not gender specific.

Teachers' Rights and Obligations

Three classes of rights and obligations for teachers are discussed in this section; those available to ordinary Canadians to live their lives free from public or political intrusion; those necessary for teaching the curriculum; and those necessary for the management of the school.

Teachers and Their Personal Lives

Teachers are no longer drawn from an exclusive community. They need not be native born, and may not even need to be Canadian citizens. They are not required to live in the community that employs them. In principle, they are no longer required to be unmarried, male, religious, abstainers or heterosexual. After a long struggle, they are no longer the bullied community servants who once accepted isolated working conditions, low wages, interference with their private lives, and career uncertainty (Chalmers, 1968). Now teachers are better trained, are protected by professional organizations, work in larger and much richer school boards, and are more secure under comprehensive and compassionate legislation, such as the revised federal *Criminal Code of Canada* and the *Narcotics Control Act*, and provincial regulations.

Now generally well educated and prosperous, teachers are respected in their communities. They are therefore eagerly courted for political offices, welcomed into various community projects, and regarded as 'off the job' role models for children. In many regions they are advantaged economically, with security and opportunities that are envied by their neighbours. Teachers are also protected in many ways against discrimination — at least partly through the efforts of their professional organizations. For example, the teaching profession does not bar membership on the basis of race, gender or physical disadvantage, and it provides nearly equal opportunity and equal pay for these widely disadvantaged groups.

Because teachers provide important role models during the most malleable period of every child's life, professional selection, preparation and supervision are among the most demanding in society. The academic requirements (which have effectively become a Bachelor's degree or equivalent) may in fact be achieved more easily than some other requirements which are rigorously specified in codes of conduct, statutory provisions and collective agreements invigilated by various authorities. These demands are usually accepted as reasonable limitations. Professional leaders accept the need for preserving their collective reputation and try to ensure that all teachers uphold the expected standards. For example, teachers who violate laws against possession of various drugs, drink excessively, use profane language in the classroom, leer at attractive students, or otherwise breach a relatively conservative standard, are likely to face disciplinary action, possible dismissal or even decertification.

The professional association determinedly protects its members against intrusion into their private lives, so that political advocacy or private personal lifestyle are rarely grounds for disciplinary action. It is partly for this reason that a teacher who writes pornography or political tracts that would be unacceptable in the classroom is generally not subjected to disciplinary measures. Also under the protection of freedom of expression section of the charter, teachers can advocate for adults what they cannot teach children.[10] Personal lifestyle is strongly supported, but once lifestyle becomes public knowledge, it significantly affects teachers' role modelling and may cause trouble.[11] For example, homosexual teachers might live together without attracting much attention, but publicizing their relationship with a form of marriage would likely result in great difficulties for them.

Pedagogical Rights and Obligations of Teachers

The role of teaching includes choosing methods and content for teaching, assisting in the selection of students for various programs, and evaluating the performance of students. Some of the activities associated with these roles are influenced by the wishes of the community insofar as general agreement has been reached concerning reasonable limitations on teacher behavior. For example, no school teacher is likely to teach figure drawing with nude models, to advocate sexual promiscuity among teenagers, to encourage dishonesty in business, to ridicule the elected leaders of Canada or the provinces, to teach hatred of any cultural or religious group, or otherwise to violate accepted community standards.

But to encourage children to think, be more critical of emerging social concerns, explore alternatives, experience compassion for disadvantaged persons, and promote awareness of the interests of other peoples, teachers may decide that it is appropriate to introduce controversial ideas through the arts or social studies. To introduce such ideas is not necessarily to advocate them. This stimulation of children's critical awareness and creativity is a professional obligation, typically outlined in the ministry of education guidelines for teaching in these areas. In fact, most educators consider that boring the students or failing to challenge their emerging ideals may be a greater shortcoming than proposing something controversial.

Examples from the selection of literature for high schools illustrate the problem. Should *The Diviners* be studied in senior literature? Is *Romeo and Juliet* pornographic?[12] Is *Huckleberry Finn* racist? The social sciences raise slightly different questions: Which political views are considered fit for analysis in high school? Should visiting speakers or selection by students for projects, and the like, be vetted by a morality group? Are the Ku Klux Klan, apartheid or the Nazi party to be studied or not? Which particular events from the past or the present should be taught with particular attention rather than silently buried? How does one justify the Holocaust or the use of the atomic bomb for compulsory analysis of horrible events? How can respect for religion be distinguished from inculcation of a particular creed? How can reverence be achieved while respecting the rights of non-religious persons? How should accomplishments associated with a past that is no longer well understood be honored by the community — those associated with the Canadian Legion, for example? How do we deal with current advocates who have a message to convey to the youth as well as to adults? Can we admit to our classrooms the Chamber of Commerce but not the unions? Although other subjects have their equivalent questions (including which field trips are most worthwhile), they are more technical and less controversial. In deciding what issues to raise, the personal views of individual teachers may be distinguished from the consensus of experts in the field. Although the influence of experts is important, it is not absolute. The teachers decide in most cases.

Political decisions have occasionally been imposed by provincial or local authorities. More frequently, community pressure groups advocate censorship of particular authors or books, propose or condemn one side of controversial topics (such as family planning or even particular alternatives to it like abortion), try to control substance abuse, introduce creationism as an alternative to evolution, and/or avert racial confrontations. Community interests and activities are an important part of a democratic society where free speech and the opportunity to demonstrate are considered to be important. Yet teachers, who must assess competing community interests, have the responsibility for the formation of well conceived personal opinions and life styles which reflect them. For example, the curriculum identifies differences in values and practices between generations and transmits views — even opposing ideas found within certain communities (McGowan, 1983) — based on scholarship and the law. In this respect, the teachers' major responsibility is to encourage respect for different value systems and to develop critical awareness. Shapiro (1985, pp. 41–2) proposes that pupils acquire some knowledge of diversity in both the Canadian and international contexts.

One of the newly emerging notions in human rights in Canada is that children are entitled to 'informed participation' in decisions that affect their lives.[13] Freedom of expression and freedom of investigation for the pupils are best fostered when the teacher has the professional freedom to encourage or to set reasonable limits on the children's activities and when, within the classroom, the children are encouraged to develop codes of behavior for their own members.[14]

The typical education act and regulations of a province make it clear that an education ministry's curriculum shall be the normal basis for classroom activities, that the local school board may provide further guidelines, and that the teachers may select activities and materials within these broad guidelines. If a teacher breached professional standards, disciplinary action (such as cautioning against the use of the particular source or material) might follow. However, dismissal is rare.

Sometimes there is unwarranted harassment from persons who have no legal stake in the community — from persons who are not community residents, not parents of the children involved, and not entrusted by educational authorities to advise on the matters in question. Principals and boards have the power and obligation to deal with such intrusions, and may not succumb to their pressure. A few vigilantes continually prowl for weak-kneed boards where their influence may sway a by-law. Sometimes the intruders develop a political following that influences board elections, but rarely is teacher tenure much threatened. The more likely casualties are the programmes and the children's education.

Some individuals hold that the guideline for the choice of subject matter is not human knowledge but divine law and, accordingly, lobby for their desired curriculum content. The teacher is justified in resisting such narrow-minded, though well-intentioned, efforts. A typical example is in the field of science, where some parents believe that evolution is blasphemy and try to prevent it from being taught as science (McGowan, 1983). Another recent example is children's instruction about AIDS, a tabooed subject for certain groups. Given that such instruction promotes protection of not only their health but also their lives, its inclusion in the curriculum can be argued even if it necessarily includes sex education. Teachers will therefore have a degree of protection from an education ministry with which to teach even against community standards. Perhaps *responsibility*, rather than rights, is the explanation for most of their decisions in such matters.

The interplay of teacher right and responsibility is tested most after the classroom door is closed. Teachers interpret the curriculum and even the events of the world in their typical teaching activities. This right carries a corresponding responsibility so that the child may develop a balanced and responsible idea of society.[15] Teachers are not restricted to a narrow interpretation of the curriculum, nor are they encouraged to 'follow the text' without applying its relationships to the real world. They have the *right* of professionals to innovate. Yet, teachers are required to teach the subjects assigned and to teach them effectively. They cannot choose to teach a different subject because of their training or preference, for the staff is obliged to provide for the full range of subjects that students have a right to choose in a particular school. Problems result occasionally. For example, when a teacher of chemistry is not available, the principal and board may decide to ask a teacher with stale or limited qualifications to teach that subject, recognizing that the students will suffer to some degree. When this type of solution places the students at risk, it is possible that the principal or the board will be found partially liable for any injuries that result in the classes of the under-qualified teacher.[16]

Lawsuits are not typically entertained by the Canadian courts for failures of the educational process, such as a child not learning to read (MacKay, 1984, p. 159). Nor are lawsuits or criminal charges likely when a teacher fails to teach the subject as outlined in the curriculum, for example by bringing extraneous material into the class. However, there may be disciplinary action — as the Keegstra case demonstrated.

Because satisfactory teaching is required in order to fulfill the teachers' obligations, boards periodically monitor the performance of their employees, using visits to the classroom and external examinations as data. Ineffective teachers are usually spotted during the initial weeks of their employment and dismissed at an early opportunity. Long-serving (tenured) employees are usually cautioned, given a chance to improve their performance, then closely monitored before a decision to fire is entertained. Although the public mistakenly believes that ineffective but senior teachers cannot be fired, tenure protects only against abusive reasons for dismissal. Because the first obligation of the school system is to the students, that may mean firing a popular and well-meaning but unsatisfactory teacher. When the root of the problem is substance abuse, ill-health or overwork, the board will often seek a medical or sabbatical leave to permit some chance of recovery.

Disciplinary Rights and Obligations of Teachers

Educational or school legislation in Canadian provinces gives teachers the authority to maintain proper order and discipline in carrying out their duties. Thus, their decisions and actions done in respect of their teaching responsibility have basis in law. Their *lawful power* neither requires nor assumes that all their decisions will be wise and prudent, but it gives teachers the necessary authority to assume responsibility for directing a child or a crowd of children. In the rare event that their ad hoc decisions (for example concerning the behavior or appearance of a child or group of children) are later repudiated by the board, ministry, courts or the profession, there is unlikely to be sole personal liability for actions taken in their apparent line of duty. Instead, any repudiations become part of the information upon which future decisions will be made by other members of the profession.[17]

The two areas where teachers most need official affirmation of their rights concerning the control of the children in their care are those of *discipline* and *negligence*. Teachers must care for children who are sometimes unruly and lack judgment. They are required by law to maintain order, and that includes providing reasonable protection for other students. *The Criminal Code of Canada* provides teachers with the requisite authority to defend themselves and school children if necessary by the use of reasonable force, and it provides legal protection for the teacher who administers corporal punishment by way of correction and in a suitable manner considering the age, physical condition and sex of the child. Some parents and a few teachers believe that discipline depends upon corporal punishment being available, even if rarely used. Current efforts are to discourage or even to eliminate cruel and unusual punishment, and to ensure that there is *no punishment without fair treatment of the alleged offender.* Typically this implies that the teacher should not act as prosecution attorney, witness for the prosecution, judge and executioner. There should be some opportunity for the alleged offender to provide a statement of explanation or excuse. So far, teachers have not been dealt with severely when they abused their powers to discipline. However, the practices of the past are no longer tolerated in courts dealing with parental abuse, and the same legal tendency is likely to curtail violence by teachers.[18]

The Criminal Code of Canada still allows for corporal punishment *provided that it is reasonable and administered by way of correction.* Some provinces and many school boards and schools have withdrawn permission for corporal punishment, and it may soon be deleted from *The Criminal Code.* The teacher who may legally use corporal punishment is obliged to ensure that it is justified, not applied beyond the endurance of the child, and does not cause any injury or permanent marks. However, the legal protection given to teachers by the Criminal Code may disappear in its next amendment due to widespread opposition to this method of discipline. In any event, in some provinces, many school boards and schools have regulations that make corporal punishment increasingly rare. They have developed an array of alternative means of maintaining discipline, which have been found to be equally effective and more appropriate to developing a sense of self-worth among the children.[19]

When it seems appropriate for police to investigate activities within the school, it is important that the teachers and more particularly the principal assume a special responsibility for the student, that of acting in the place of the parents. They should ensure that the child is presumed to be innocent, is not asked to provide information that is legally a confession, and has access to legal counsel. In some cases, the police have been called to the school because of initial investigations by the school staff. In these cases, information gathered when the child was not informed of the legal right to remain silent and to have legal counsel cannot be entered as evidence.

A teacher has a right to reasonable protection against liability. Liability arises when the teacher (1) had a legal duty of care for the student and (2) failed to maintain this care at a standard required of professionals, and when (3) an injury resulted and (4) the child (actually the family or guardian of the child) sues for damages. The teacher has a legal duty of care when employed as a teacher,[20] and this duty may extend beyond the walls of the school and the hours of operation. This duty of care varies with the circumstances but, in general, the more inherent the danger and the less qualified the pupil to assume personal responsibility for coping with it, the higher the standard of care required to defend against a suit of negligence. However, in those situations where the teacher takes all reasonable precautions to prevent injuries but one occurs, anyway, it is ruled an accident and there is no liability.

Where the injury results in a lawsuit, the teacher is normally sued jointly with the principal and the school board under the doctrine of *vicarious liability*.[21] If the suit is successful and if the teacher was conducting school business, the insurance company of the board will have to pay. In the event that the activity was personally undertaken (for example, taking children somewhere that was not clearly connected with schooling, probably in the car of the teacher) the board might not be bound. Teachers should be aware that liability awards may run to millions of dollars.

Teachers are required to be good role models for their pupils. The phrasing differs among different jurisdictions and is sometimes archaic,[22] but it survives in an era when most occupations are protected by human rights legislation. Typically teachers must deal with several constraints on their behavior, and these are justified at law as reasonable limitations in a free and democratic society. In theory, any teacher could be disciplined at any time, for the obligation is cast so wide that undoubtedly many teachers fail to meet its expectations. In practice, the teachers disciplined are those employed by the separate or other denominational schools and have violated their employing church regulations concerning marriage and divorce (*Stuart v. Caldwell*, 1984). Some teachers are dismissed for marriage to persons who are not eligible to marry according to the laws of the church, or for living with persons to whom they are not married. Failure to maintain an acceptable relationship with the church employer is likely not only to cost an offer of a job but also to lead to a dismissal. These actions by religious schools have been found repeatedly to be lawful under the Constitution Act (1867) and Canadian Charter of Rights and Freedoms (1982). Any potential remedies lie in political action rather than the courts.

Teachers have been disciplined for violations of the exemplary citizen clauses in public schools, too. One case involved a teacher who submitted a photo of his nude wife (also a teacher) to a magazine for publication. The picture was published and the small community rocked. The case was not helped by the fact that the Criminal Code of Canada defines obscenity as 'any publication a dominant characteristic of which is the undue exploitation of sex'. Both teachers were dismissed, but, after litigation the penalty was reduced to four weeks without pay. This reinforces the idea that the public schools are still expected to ensure that their teachers act as role models in their community (*Abbotsford v. Shewan*, 1986). A difficult matter that may face principals and boards is whether a teacher who is accused of a minor felony should be dismissed on that account alone. In general, if children are not placed at risk, the teacher continues the discharge of professional duties. However, if there is any possible danger to them, the accused will be reassigned to non-classroom activities. Following the trial, if convicted, most boards would dismiss. In the case of serious offenses such as assault of children, they would likely also be decertified. Teachers' professional associations generally support these decisions but ensure that the teacher has legal and professional advice for the inquiry.

Conclusion

Human rights are important aspects of many other chapters of this book, and are integral to many other decisions in education. Teachers find that human rights complicate some of their work but, in various ways, it serves them well. Of course, the other participants in the educational process — pupils, parents, community groups and others, also experience these benefits and burdens. On balance, there will be difficulties in the application of human rights legislation to the school system, the school and the classroom. However, once human rights provisions are incorporated and implemented in school policies (on race relations, for example), arrangements and new curricula, the gains to education should be evident.

Notes

1   There are two problems with the list of rights in *The Universal Declaration*. First, an international document, even one that is accorded great respect, is not Canadian law so it is not used directly in the courts. Second, teachers may not always be able to claim the rights apparently identified, for their work necessarily limits their freedom of personal decision because of their special responsibilities to students, parents, minority groups, professional organizations and the like.

2   Examples, of recent interest to the Prairie Provinces, are the limited but ultimately enforceable protection of French as an official language in the Manitoba Act (1870), The Saskatchewan Act (1905) and the Alberta Act (1905).

3   In the case of the Quebec Charter, the protection extends much beyond typical anti-discrimination legislation.

4   For purposes of this chapter, school board regulations and school policies will not be called human rights, although many of them are worthy objectives.

5   For example, following a tribunal's hearing, Young was dismissed for participating in a political demonstration, despite a denial of her request to participate on the grounds that her classes were to be taught on that day. The tribunal found freedom of expression to be subject to the reasonable limitation that the class had to be conducted. See *The Huron County Board of Education and the Ontario Secondary School Teachers' Federation* (1984).

6   Thus, the preamble of the Charter explicitly refers to God, as follows: 'Whereas Canada is founded upon principles that recognize the supremacy of God and the rule of law ...'

7   A 1937 Quebec legislation was so-called because it allowed the police to lock up any premises used to distribute information on communism. This legislation was also used against the Jehovah's Witnesses. See Greene (1989, p. 22) and Berger (1981, p. 170).

8   An important analysis of this relationship between cultural identity and its religious manifestation is contained in Thomas R. Berger (1981). Fragile freedoms:

Freedom and dissent in Canada are *Reference Re Language Rights under the Manitoba Act, 1870* (1985) and *Reference Re Education Act of Ontario and Minority Language Education Rights* (1984).

9 The Royal Commission on Bilingualism and Biculturalism (1967) documents the different treatments on the basis of language, for both the private and public sector. It recommended changes in federal policies to be implemented at once, and identified desirable changes for provinces and the private sector. See Volume 1 for the general situation, Volume 2 for education, and Volume 3 for the employment situation.

10 The Civil Liberties Association must frequently champion the right of free expression without endorsing the views expressed by its client, and the courts will usually agree.

11 Recent cases relevant to this discussion are *Abbotsford School District v. Shewan and Shewan* (1986) and *Casagrande v. Hinton* (1987).

12 A Federal draft legislation defining pornography tries to distinguish between art (Romeo and Juliet) and smut. The same concern affects the choice of literature to be taught to particular grades.

13 The International Convention on the Rights of the Child is being finalized as this is written, and may be approved by the United Nations in due course. If this happens, there would likely be a debate within Canada to decide whether children here should be given all the rights proposed. Most parents would agree with the majority of clauses, but their authority to guide the child's moral and spiritual development would be subject to the tests of fairness to other groups and of acceptance by the child.

14 Sample codes have been developed and published by The Canadian Human Rights Foundation, with individual schools or classrooms devising the local versions that affect children's personal values.

15 The famous example of James Keegstra, in which the teacher took substantial liberties with his interpretation of the Holocaust, showed that the board and the supervisory officers would have specifically to instruct the teacher to avoid certain activities, following which persistent digression would be grounds for dismissal. Keegstra misused the right to interpret in such an aberrant and repugnant manner that he was not only reprimanded but also dismissed and decertified. These two steps in professional censure are made by the profession and are not criminal offenses. Although Keegstra was also tried for the criminal charge of inciting hatred against a defined group (Jews in this case), the conviction was not sustained on appeal. See *R.V. Keegstra* (1985) and Bercuson and Wertheimer (1985).

16 For a good discussion on malpractice, see Foster (1987).

17 One example concerns the legal right of the teacher, principal or board to direct the pupils to dress in a particular way. When a particular board banned blue jeans, for example, the parents objected to the usurpation of their responsibilities and the court did not agree that the board's arguments were convincing. But they were legal. Of course, political action followed. See *Devereaux, Colbran and Coloran v. Lambton County RC Separate School Board* (1988).

18 Haberstock was charged with assault of a student for punishment that took place three days after the alleged offence. He apparently caused some injury to the face, which is not a region of the body where corporal punishment is usually administered. The injury was inflicted with the hand rather than a strap. Although he was convicted, the conviction was quashed on appeal (*R. v Haberstock*, 1970).

19 It has been found that many of those responsible for beating other members of their family learned that behavior through being beaten in their childhood. Violence is a learned response.

20 A special case arises where the teacher may be required to use force in defence of

herself or other persons. This is not assault, and failure to try to defend others would probably be negligence.

21 In some cases, the responsibility arose from an unqualified or overburdened teacher being pressed by the administration to accept an additional assignment.

22 The Ontario Education Act (1986) proclaims the duties of teachers 'to inculcate by precept and example respect for religion and the principles of Judaeo-Christian morality and the highest regard for truth, justice, loyalty, love of country, humanity, benevolence, sobriety, industry, frugality, purity, temperance and all other virtues' (235 (1) (c)). The Ontario Human Rights Code (1981) indicates that 'This act does not apply to affect the application of the Education Act with respect to the duties of teachers (18(2)).

Bibliography

Abbotsford School District v. Shewan and Shewan (1986) 70 BCLR 40 (SC).

BERGER, T.R. (1981) *Fragile Freedoms: Human Rights and Dissent in Canada*, Toronto: Clarke, Irwin and Company.

BERCUSON, D. and WERTHEIMER, D. (1985) *A Trust Betrayed. The Keegstra Affair*, Toronto: Doubleday Canada.

BERNSTEIN-TARROW, N. (Ed.) (1987) *Human Rights and Education*, London: Pergamon.

CALDWELL V. STUART (1984) 15 DLR (4th) (SCC).

CASAGRANDE V. HINTON *et al.* (1987) 51 ALR (2nd) 349.

CHALMERS, J.W. (1968) *Teachers of the Foothills Province*, Toronto: University of Toronto Press.

DEVEREAUX, COLBRAN and COLBRAN V. LAMBTON COUNTY RC Separate School Board. Decision of the Ontario Divisional Court, 1988.

DICKINSON, G.M. and MACKAY, A.W. (1989) *Rights, Freedoms and the Education System in Canada*, Toronto: Edmond Montgomery.

EPP, F.H. (1974) *Mennonites in Canada, 1786–1920: The History of a Separate People*, Toronto: Macmillan of Canada.

FISCHER, L. and SCHIMMEL, D. (1982) *The Rights of Students and Teachers*, New York: Harper and Row.

FOSTER, W. (1987) 'Educational malpractice: Educate or litigate', *Canadian Journal of Education, 11*, pp. 122–51.

GREENE, I. (1989) *The Charter of Rights*, Toronto: James Lorimer and Co.

HURON COUNTY BOARD OF EDUCATION AND THE ONTARIO SECONDARY SCHOOL TEACHERS' FEDERATION. Arbitration decision given in October 1984, in London, Ontario.

LAURIN, C. (1978) 'Emerging ethnic boundaries', *Canadian Ethnic Studies, X*, (1), pp. 5–11.

MAGNET, J. (1982) 'Minority language educational rights', *Supreme Court Law Review, 4*, pp. 195–200.

MCGOWAN, C. (1983) *In the Beginning: A Scientist Shows Why the Creationists are Wrong*, Toronto: Macmillan of Canada.

MCKAY, A.W. (1984) *Education Law in Canada*, Toronto: Edmond Montgomery.

MONIERE, D. (1981) *Ideologies in Quebec: The Historical Development*, Toronto: University of Toronto Press.

NATIONAL INDIAN BROTHERHOOD (1988) *Towards a Vision of our Future* (3 Volumes), Ottawa: Assembly of First Nations.

ONTARIO. Education Act, 1986.

ONTARIO. Human Rights Code, 1981.

ONTARIO GOVERNMENT (1987) *The Development of a Policy on Race and Ethnocultural Equity*, Toronto: Ministry of Education.

R. v. HABERSTOCK (1970), 1 CCC (2d) 433 (Sask. CA).

R. v. KEEGSTRA (1988), 60 ALR (2d) 1.

R. v. WIEBE (1978), 3 WWR 36.

ROYAL COMMISSION ON BILINGUALISM AND BICULTURALISM (1967 et seq.) *Report of the Royal Commission on Bilingualism and Biculturalism in Canada.*

Vol. I General Introduction, The Official Languages.

Vol. II Education.

Vol. III The Work World.

Vol. IV The Cultural Contributions of the Other Ethnic Groups.

OTTAWA: Queen's Printer.

SAMUDA, R.J. (1984) 'Assessing the abilities of minority students within a multiethnic milieu', in SAMUDA, R.J., BERRY, J.W. and LAFERRIERE, M. *et al. Multiculturalism in Canada: Social and Educational Perspectives* (pp. 353–67), Toronto: Allyn and Bacon.

SHAPIRO, B.J. (1985) *The Report of the Commission on Private Schools in Ontario*, Toronto: Ministry of Education.

TARNOPOLSKY, W.S. (1982) *Discrimination and the Law in Canada*, Toronto: Richard de Boo.

RE ZYLBERBERG AND DIRECTOR OF EDUCATION OF THE SUDBURY BOARD OF EDUCATION, Ont. C.A. No. 567186, September 23, 1988.

Notes on Contributors

Ishmael J. Baksh is Professor in the Faculty of Education at Memorial University of Newfoundland, in St. John's, Canada. His articles have appeared in such journals as *Canadian and International Education, Social and Economic Studies, Interchange, Caribbean Journal of Education* and *Catalyst*. Co-author of eight monographs published by his Faculty, he is also author of a novel, *Black Light* (1988). His current research focuses on attitudes, expectations and perceptions of high school students in Trinidad and Tobago, as well as (with Dr W.B.W. Martin) on student perspectives on schools and schooling.

Joyce E. Bellous is a sessional lecturer in the Department of Educational Policy and Administrative Studies, Faculty of Education, The University of Calgary. She teaches courses on sociology of education (e.g., Language, Culture and Canadian Consciousness), multicultural education, philosophy of moral development, introduction to teaching theory, and English as a Second Language. She is currently Associate Editor for the *Proceedings*, Far Western Philosophy of Education Society. Her current research is in the area of multicultural education, particularly on the problem of diversity and the relationship between pluralism and moral theory.

Rodney A. Clifton is Professor in the Department of Educational Administration and Foundations, Faculty of Education, The University of Manitoba, where he specializes in the sociology of education. He is also a Fellow in St. John's College. A recipient of several research and writing awards, Professor Clifton has published extensively on the topics of teacher education and teacher expectations, as well as on issues concerning Native education. He has conducted research and written on the quality of university student life and is working on a study of the acquisition of professional teacher identity. He is presently President of the Canadian Association of Foundations of Education.

Jerrold Coombs, Professor, The University of British Columbia, is well known for his various publications in *Educational Theory, Studies in Philosophy* *and Education* and other prestigious educational journals. He has edited and contributed to the *Proceedings* of the Philosophy of Education Society (USA) and is author of numerous chapters in edited anthologies, such as *Development of Moral Reasoning* (1980).

Leroi Daniels, Professor, The University of British Columbia, is widely published in various journals in Canada, the United States and England. He has contributed numerous chapters in published books, such as *Philosophy of Education: Canadian Perspectives*. Among his research interests are moral philosophy, moral education, curriculum and educational policy.

Harold Entwistle is Professor in the Department of Education, Sir George Williams Campus, Concordia University, in Montreal. His several books and chapters in edited collections center on political education; education and socialism; education, work and leisure; social class, culture and education; philosophy of adult education; and the relationship between theory and practice. His articles have appeared in Canadian, American and British journals. His current research interests focus on the meaning and criticism of liberal education, education and conceptions of citizenship, and the Machiavellian conception of political education.

William Hare is Professor of Education and Philosophy at Dalhousie University where he has taught since 1970. His publications include *Open-mindedness and Education* (1979), *In Defence of Open-mindedness* (1985) and *Controversies in Teaching* (with P. O'Leary, 1985). More recent publications include *Philosophy of Education: Introductory Readings* (co-edited with J. Portelli, 1988) and *Reason in Teaching and Education* (1989). He was President of the Canadian Philosophy of Education Society.

John C. Long is Associate Professor in the Department of Educational Administration and Foundations, Faculty of Education, The University of Manitoba. He has specialized in educational policy issues and has written monographs and articles related to the professionalization of teachers, politics in education and educational policy-making. He co-authored, with J.G.T. Kelsey, the chapter on educational administration in *Education Studies: Foundations of Policy*. He is presently investigating legal issues in education, particularly with respect to the rights of students, teachers and religious groups.

Romulo F. Magsino is Professor and Head, Department of Educational Administration and Foundations, Faculty of Education, The University of Manitoba. He has authored, co-authored or co-edited a number of monographs; has contributed chapters in books; and has published in such journals as *Canadian Journal of Education, Interchange and Educational Theory*. He has also published in, and served as member of the Editorial Board of, *Education and Law Journal*. He is presently President of the Canadian Philosophy of Education Society (1988–1990).

Wilfred B.W. Martin is Professor of Sociology of Education in the Faculty of Education at Memorial University of Newfoundland. Author of three books, *The Negotiated Order of the School* (1976), *Canadian Education: A Sociological Analysis* (with A. McDonnell, 1978, rev. 1982), and *Voices from the Classroom* (1985), he is also author of more than fifty articles. Some of them appeared in *The Canadian Review of Sociology and Anthropology*, *Sociology of Education*, *American Journal of Sociology*, *Contemporary Sociology*, *Journal of Learning Disabilities* and *The International Journal of the Sociology of the Family*. In 1977, he received the University of New Brunswick Excellence in Teaching Award. He is currently conducting research, with I. Baksh, on student perspectives on schools and schooling.

Daniel McDougall is Professor of Educational Psychology at the University of Calgary. Aside from his many other works, he co-authored, with A. Bowd and C. Yewchuk, the book *Educational Psychology: A Canadian Perspective*, the first Canadian introductory textbook in educational psychology. He was President of the Alberta Association for Multicultural Education, 1985–1986. In 1981, he received the Superior Teacher Award from the Student Union of the University of Calgary. His current research addresses the reduction of prejudice and discrimination through education.

Norma Mickelson is Professor in the Faculty of Education, the University of Victoria, British Columbia. Author of numerous articles, book chapters and monographs, she is a founding member of the University of Victoria Center for Whole Language and is founder and Director of the University of Victoria Whole Language Summer Institute. She is listed in *Who's Who in Canada*, *Who's Who in British Columbia*, *Who's Who in the Commonwealth* and the *International Directory of Distinguished Leadership*. When not busy with her research on language, reading and teacher education, she attends to her hobbies — bridge and Japanese floral arrangement.

Samuel Mitchell is Associate Professor in the Department of Educational Policy and Administrative Studies in the University of Calgary. He teaches courses on change and innovations, sociology of education and adult education, and has taught occupational and industrial sociology. His research studies on women and the professions are widely publicized; among them is *A Woman's Profession, A Man's Research* (1971). His articles have appeared in *Industrial and Labor Relations Review*, *Labor Studies Journal*, *Case Analysis*, *Canadian Journal of Education* and *Canadian and International Education*. His forthcoming book focuses on the professions and social change.

Paul T. O'Leary is Associate Professor of Philosophy of Education in the Division of Educational Policy Studies, The University of Western Ontario. *He is co-editor (with W. Hare) of Controversies in Teaching* (1985). His articles have appeared in various journals, such as *Educational Theory, Canadian Journal of Education, Cambridge Journal of Education* and the *Transactions of the Charles S. Peirce Society.* He is the current Editor-in-Chief of *Paedeusis,* journal of the Canadian Philosophy of Education Society. He has also served as Review Editor of the *Journal of Moral Education, Interchange* and the *Canadian Journal of Education.* His current interests include the education of desire, the role of virtues in moral education, and teaching and ethics of belief.

Evelina Orteza y Miranda is Professor in the Department of Educational Policy and Administrative Studies, The University of Calgary, and teaches graduate and undergraduate courses in the philosophy of education. Her publications have appeared in various journals, including *Educational Theory, Canadian and International Education, Journal of Christian Education, Journal of Research and Development in Education, Journal of Educational Thought* and *Perspectives on Science and Christian Faith.* She is currently Editor of the *Proceedings* of the Far Western Philosophy of Education Society, and serves on the Editorial Board of *Educational Theory, Educational Foundations, Perspectives on Science and Christian Faith* and *Journal of Christian Education.* With Dr Rosa Bruno-Jofre, she is completing an edited collection of articles on Latin American women in higher education. Her current research includes the study of the foundations and post-modernity, religion and education, self and nationalism in the Philippines.

Douglas Ray is Professor in the Department of Educational Policy Studies at the University of Western Ontario. He is co-editor of *Social Change and Education in Canada* (1987), *Values, Lifelong Education and the Aging Canadian Population* (1983) and *Human Rights in Canadian Education* (1983). His most recent book is *Peace Education: Canadian and International Perspectives* (1988). His many articles have been published in Canadian, American and British journals. Some of his research studies, which focus on human rights, have been funded by the Secretary of State, CIDA, the Ontario Ministry of Education, the UNESCO and The University of Western Ontario.

Lance W. Roberts is Associate Professor of Sociology, a Fellow at St. John's College, and Associate Head in the Department of Sociology, The University of Manitoba. His research interests lie in the areas of social psychology, applied sociology and sociology of education. He has published extensively in a wide range of books and academic journals. He is presently collaborating with R. Clifton in the study of the acquisition of the professional identity of teachers in teacher training institutions.

R.L. Schnell is Professor in the Department of Educational Policy and Administrative Studies, The University of Calgary. He is co-author of *Foundation Disciplines and the Study of Education* (1968), *Discarding the Asylum* (1983), *No Bleeding Heart* (1987), and co-editor of *Studies in Childhood History* (1982) and *Education Studies* (1983). His articles have appeared in the *Canadian Review of American Studies, Paedagogica Historica, British Journal of Education Studies, Journal of Psychohistory, International Review of History and Political Science* and *American Review of Canadian Studies*, among others. He was a scholar-in-residence at the Bellagio Study Centre, Rome, as a recipient of a Rockefeller Foundations Award and was a Killam Resident Fellow at the University of Calgary. His research interests include the child welfare activities of the League of Nations, 1919–1946, and of the International Organization and the promotion of child life, 1880–1950.

J. Douglas Stewart is Professor of Education at the University of Regina, Saskatchewan, where he teaches philosophy of education and moral education. His publications and reviews have appeared in Canadian, American and British journals. His current research centers on moral theory and education and on the nature of knowledge and the curriculum. He is Associate Editor of *Paedeusis*, journal of the Canadian Philosophy of Education Society.

John Walsh received his PhD degree in 1987, and is currently Assistant Professor in the Faculty of Education at Simon Fraser University in Burnaby, British Columbia. Dr Walsh's primary area of specialization is instructional psychology. His current research interests are focused on learner cognition and instruction, with particular emphasis on the interplay between students' self-perceptions and motivation.

J. Donald Wilson is Professor in the Department of Social and Educational Studies, the University of British Columbia. He is co-author or co-editor of nine books, the most recent of which is *Quality in Canadian Public Education: A Critical Assessment* (1988). He is a recipient of book awards for *Aspects of 19th Century Ontario* (1974), *Schooling and Society in 20th Century British Columbia* (1980) and *Schools in the West* (1986). His articles and reviews have been published in *Histoire sociale\Social History, Labour\Le travail, Canadian Historical Review, Canadian Ethnic Studies, History of Education Review* and *Scandinavian-Canadian Studies*. He is an Executive Member of the Association for the Advancement of Scandinavian Studies in Canada, 1989–1992. His current research includes history of education in British Columbia, immigration and ethnic history and history of rural schools and teachers.

Philip H. Winne received his PhD degree in 1976 from Stanford University. Presently, he is Professor of Education and Psychology at Simon Fraser

University in Burnaby, British Columbia. His main research interests focus on students' cognition and instructional settings, and on using advanced computer technologies as tools for teaching and for doing research in instructional psychology. He has published more than fifty journal articles and book chapters in these areas. Dr Winne is President of the Canadian Association for Educational Psychology and Past President of the Canadian Educational Researchers' Association. He also has been elected Fellow of the American Psychological Association and the Canadian Psychological Association. In the winter of 1985–1986, he was a Distinguished Visiting Professor at the Max Planck Institute for Psychological Research in Munich, West Germany.

Author Index

Subject Index

432